D1156786

# LAND USE LAW

---
## Fourth Edition
---

## Daniel R. Mandelker

*Stamper Professor of Law*
*Washington University in St. Louis*

LEXIS® LAW PUBLISHING
CHARLOTTESVILLE, VIRGINIA

6458411

This book is dedicated to the late Donald Hagman
scholar, teacher, friend.

# Preface and Acknowledgments

This fourth edition of my treatise is a thorough revision that includes discussion of the Supreme Court's *Dolan* decision on exactions, the Court's *Suitum* decision on ripeness, and the Court's *City of Ladue* case on the application of the free speech clause to sign regulation. Discussion of the taking clause is revised to include the effect of *Dolan* and other recent Supreme Court cases, and new sections are added on the whole parcel rule, delay as a taking, and state takings legislation. I have paid special attention to the sections on exactions. Discussion of other federal law topics, such as due process and equal protection, ripeness, the Fair Housing Act amendments that apply to group homes for the handicapped, and Section 1983 actions, is expanded and revised. I have also revised and expanded discussion of state law topics as necessary, including judicial review and variances.

This edition includes citations from the third edition, citations from its supplements and cases decided since these supplements were published. The citations include cases current in the advance sheets through July 1, 1997. Statutory citations are illustrative, not exhaustive, and were current at the time the book went to press. Supplements will be published periodically.

My research assistants, Bryan Hebert, Douglas Nieder, and Kimberly Reed, provided helpful assistance in the preparation of this edition, and I would like to thank the many students who, over the years, have been indispensable in the preparation and development of this book. Stuart Meck and Rodney Cobb at the American Planning Association also assisted greatly with this edition.

I must again thank the many colleagues who, over the years, have shaped my ideas and thinking on land use law. The late Roger Cunningham, who co-authored our land use casebook, was especially helpful, as were Brian Blaesser at Robinson & Cole, Richard Lazarus at Georgetown University, Dean Tom Sullivan at the University of Minnesota, and my colleague, Jules Gerard. There are many others too numerous to mention.

The fourth edition is again dedicated to the late Donald Hagman. His influence on us all is not forgotten.

*Daniel R. Mandelker*

*St. Louis, Missouri*
*July 8, 1997*

# Summary Table of Contents

# Table of Contents

# TABLE OF CONTENTS

# Chapter 1

## CONTROLLING LAND USE: AN OVERVIEW

## § 1.01. Providing a Focus.

Public control of land use has a long history. The Roman Twelve Tables adopted in the fourth century B.C.E. included building site restrictions. Six centuries of English and American legislation enacted a variety of land use regulations, including restrictions on the growth of London adopted during the reign of Elizabeth I. Early legislation in the United States often dealt with specific regulatory problems such as building and height regulation, but the precedent for more extensive land use control is clear.

Modern land use regulation began with the first comprehensive zoning ordinance, adopted by New York City in 1916. Earlier municipal laws prohibited noxious uses in residential neighborhoods, but New York was the first to adopt a comprehensive zoning ordinance assigning land uses to zoning districts throughout the city. Comprehensive zoning has since spread throughout the country.

All states have legislation authorizing municipal zoning, and all major cities except Houston have zoning ordinances. Practically all states authorize zoning by counties. In some states, local governments may adopt and administer zoning and other land use controls under their constitutional home rule powers.

Legislation in all states authorizes local governments to do comprehensive planning and adopt comprehensive plans. Some states make the adoption of comprehensive plans mandatory. Comprehensive plans include land use policies that guide land use controls. Although the courts did not initially impose this requirement, some state legislation now requires zoning to be consistent with the comprehensive plan.

State planning and zoning legislation is based on separate Standard Acts for planning and zoning drafted by the U.S. Department of Commerce in the 1920s. Every state adopted the Standard Zoning Act, either as published or with minor variations. The Standard Planning Act was not as widely adopted, but state planning legislation generally follows its format.

This book covers local planning and land use controls. It includes zoning and the regulation of residential development through subdivision controls. It also includes newer forms of land use regulation, such as growth management, aesthetic, historic preservation and environmental controls.

Federal and state constitutions impose limitations on land use controls, which local governments adopt under what is known as the "police power." The taking clause is one of the most important. Courts must determine whether a land use regulation "goes so far" that it "takes" property without the just compensation required by the Constitution. If a court holds that a land use regulation violates the taking clause, the U.S. Supreme Court requires compensation for a temporary taking for the period of time the regulation was in effect.

Land use controls must also satisfy the substantive and procedural limitations of the due process clause. Courts hold that a land use regulation satisfies substantive due process if it advances a legitimate governmental purpose. Courts also apply procedural due process requirements to land use controls to ensure that the procedures used in land use regulation are fair.

Courts apply the equal protection clause to the regulatory classifications included in land use controls. They apply a deferential standard of equal protection review when land use controls and their administration affect economic interests in land. Courts apply a more rigorous standard of judicial review when a land use control is suspect. A racially discriminatory classification is an example of a suspect classification.

This common statutory and constitutional base for land use controls provides a unifying structure for land use law. Extensive state adoption of model legislation provides a common statutory base that makes case law transferable from one state to another. Taking, equal protection, and due process clauses are included in the federal as well as state constitutions and provide a common constitutional base for land use jurisprudence.

### § 1.02. Substantive Differences in Federal and State Constitutional Law.

State courts for many years decided the vast majority of land use cases, but the federal courts are now more active especially as the Supreme Court continues to decide taking and other land use cases. Similar constitutional provisions provide the basis for litigation in federal and state courts, and plaintiffs may sue on the federal constitution in state courts, but whether a litigant sues in federal or state court can make a difference.

State courts usually apply federal court interpretations of the free speech clause in land use cases, such as sign regulation cases, perhaps because federal courts developed the law of free speech as applied to land use regulation. The U.S. Supreme Court has decided several important land use taking cases, and state courts usually apply these cases to taking claims.

Due process and equal protection cases are more complicated. The U.S. Supreme Court has held that most land use controls advance legitimate governmental purposes, including zoning that separates incompatible uses and historic preservation, open space, and aesthetic controls. State courts agree, but may be more aggressive in applying substantive due process to invalidate exclusionary zoning and other restrictive controls, such as controls on group homes.

Both federal and state courts apply procedural due process to administrative land use decisions. Federal courts apply procedural due process requirements only when a land use agency is required to make an administrative decision that approves an applicant's proposal. Supreme Court cases provide a doctrinal framework for procedural due process claims. State courts also insist that administrative agencies follow fundamental rules of fairness, but the constitutional basis for these rules is not always clear and courts differ in how to apply them.

Equal protection claims are usually unsuccessful in federal court absent a racial discrimination claim, because courts apply deferential judicial review when regulations affect only economic interests. Equal protection law under the state constitutions is not always as clear. An equal protection claim is implicit in the ambiguous, but common, state court rule that a zoning restriction is invalid as applied to a tract of land if it is "arbitrary and capricious."

## § 1.03. The Land Use Control System.

This section reviews the regulatory goals and purposes of land use controls. It provides illustrations of typical constitutional issues likely to arise under land use control programs and indicates how courts respond to these constitutional claims.

## § 1.04. Zoning for Land Use and Density.

Zoning ordinances comprehensively assign compatible land uses to zoning districts throughout the community. The zoning ordinance contains a text and a map. The map designates the location of zoning districts. The text contains use, density, and site development regulations for the land uses permitted in each district. It also contains administrative and enforcement provisions.

Zoning is an elaboration of nuisance doctrines the courts developed in the days before zoning became common. Land use nuisance cases usually arose when a commercial or industrial use planned to locate in a residential neighborhood, where it would be detrimental to residential land uses. Courts recognized the importance of preserving established residential areas by prohibiting the location of these invading uses in residential neighborhoods. The comprehensive zoning ordinance ratifies this land use structure. It divides the municipality into a number of zoning districts that separate residential, commercial, and industrial uses.

Within residential zoning districts, the zoning ordinance makes distinctions among permitted residential uses based on their density. One clear distinction is between single-family and multi-family residential development. The ordinance usually creates a number of single-family and multi-family zoning districts. They permit increasingly higher residential densities as they progress from the most restrictive single-family to the least restrictive multi-family use. Commercial and industrial districts also distinguish between different intensities of land use. For example, the ordinance may contain different commercial districts permitting neighborhood, community, and regional commercial uses. Zoning ordinances were originally cumulative. They permitted "higher" less intensive uses in the "lower" zones that permitted more intensive uses. Most modern zoning ordinances are not cumulative. Each zoning district is exclusive and allows only the uses permitted in that zone.

Much land use litigation arises from the way in which the zoning text and ordinance classify land into zoning districts. This litigation can raise a variety of constitutional questions. A landowner can argue that a zoning classification as applied to his land is a taking of property because it does not allow him a reasonable use of his land. Courts determine whether a zoning ordinance is a taking of property "as applied" by comparing the uses allowed by the ordinance on the restricted property with the zoning and land uses in the surrounding area. This method of analysis reflects the nuisance origins of zoning. In the nuisance cases, the courts evaluate the impact of an invading land use on its immediate neighborhood. Adjacent land uses also provide the benchmark for evaluating the impact of a land use regulation on a tract of land under the taking clause. Equal protection problems can also arise. Neighbors may object if the municipality amends the zoning map to allow a commercial use in the middle of a residential neighborhood. They can argue this is "spot" zoning that violates the equal protection clause by unfairly benefiting a single landowner.

### § 1.05. Historic District Zoning.

Historic district zoning enacts regulations to preserve the character of historic buildings in historic areas. Historic district regulations are usually adopted in a separate ordinance. The historic district ordinance prohibits any development and any change in the exterior of an historic building that is incompatible with the historic buildings in the district. Unlike traditional zoning, historic district zoning implements aesthetic purposes because it preserves the aesthetic character of historic areas.

This distinction requires qualification because traditional zoning also implements aesthetic purposes. Traditional zoning prohibits nonresidential uses in residential areas, for example, because they can be aesthetically displeasing in a residential environment. Perhaps the aesthetic characterization of historic district zoning reflects its novelty. Traditional zoning is based on nuisance law, which historically protected residential areas from incompatible nonresidential uses. The courts did not extend nuisance law to protect the character of historic buildings in historic areas.

The aesthetic purposes of historic districts raise a substantive due process problem. Courts must decide whether aesthetic land use controls advance a legitimate governmental purpose under the due process clause. A majority of courts now hold that aesthetic purposes alone are a legitimate basis for land use regulation.

### § 1.06. Environmental Land Use Regulation and Historic Landmark Preservation.

Two important types of land use controls are not based on the maintenance of compatible uses within zoning districts but seek to preserve the character of individual historic buildings or environmental areas. Historic landmark preservation ordinances authorize the designation of historic landmarks and prohibit their demolition or exterior modification without governmental approval. Environmental land use regulations preserve the natural character of areas such as wetlands and floodplains by prohibiting or restricting any development in them. Agricultural zoning allows only agricultural uses or limited residential development in agricultural areas.

These land use controls advance a variety of governmental purposes. Like historic district zoning, historic landmark ordinances advance the aesthetic interest in historic preservation. Wetlands ordinances preserve the natural character of these areas. Floodplain zoning implements public health and safety objectives by preventing development in areas where flooding would cause damage to life and property. The courts have held these governmental objectives constitutional under the substantive due process clause.

Historic landmark and environmental land use regulations raise taking problems. Traditional zoning separates incompatible uses that otherwise might locate next to each other. The benefits conferred and burdens imposed by the ordinance are spatially confined. Historic landmark and resource protection ordinances are different. The regulatory burdens they impose are concentrated, but the benefits they confer are widely dispersed among the general public. All residents of a community benefit from the protection of historic landmarks and the preservation of natural resource areas. The regulatory burden is concentrated on owners of historic landmarks and natural resource areas.

It was once held that land use regulations were a taking of property if their purpose was to confer a benefit on the general public. The U.S. Supreme Court has now disapproved of this rule, but it is possible an environmental land use or historic landmark regulation could be a per se taking if it prohibited all economically beneficial uses of a property.

### § 1.07. Aesthetic Regulation.

Sign regulation, which preceded comprehensive zoning, is an example of an aesthetic regulation. Municipalities initially regulated the size and height of signs, and the courts upheld these regulations. Municipalities now regulate the location of signs and may exclude them from residential areas or prohibit them anywhere. Municipalities also regulate on-premise signs.

The exclusion of billboard signs from residential areas serves legitimate governmental purposes by prohibiting a disruptive use in residential surroundings. An ordinance prohibiting billboards throughout a community presents more difficult constitutional problems because billboards could be appropriate in a community's nonresidential areas. Most courts hold that a community's interest in its aesthetic appearance justifies a total billboard exclusion. The courts also uphold the aesthetic purposes of on-premise sign regulations. Sign regulation also raises free speech problems under the First Amendment of the Constitution.

Many municipalities have architectural design review boards that review the design of signs, residential dwellings and other new developments. The review of major planned developments can also incorporate a design review. The cases have upheld architectural design review as an appropriate aesthetic control.

### § 1.08. Growth Management.

Many communities throughout the country have adopted growth management programs. They are aware that rapid growth can overwhelm community facilities and services and create heavy fiscal burdens. Growth management programs may regulate the timing and phasing of new development and may impose quotas on the amount of new development allowed. They may also regulate new development to avoid damage to environmental areas. A community may impose a moratorium on new development until it can adopt a growth management program. Several states have now passed statutes authorizing local governments to adopt growth management programs.

Growth management programs present a number of constitutional problems. Courts must determine whether they serve a legitimate governmental purpose. Equal protection problems arise because some landowners may not be able to develop their land when they wish. This equal protection problem has a time dimension, because growth management programs delay development in some areas of the community for substantial periods of time by phasing new development or by imposing a development moratorium. Taking issues may arise, as a court could hold that a delay in development is a temporary taking of the landowner's property.

The courts have upheld development phasing under growth management programs and they uphold development moratoria when they are reasonably limited in time. Development quotas have not fared as well in court.

A number of states authorize local governments to adopt land use controls to reserve land for development until it is acquired for highways, parks, and other public facilities. These controls present a taking problem because they usually prohibit any development on the reserved land until it is acquired by a public agency for its intended use.

### § 1.09. Subdivision Controls and Planned Development.

Controls over residential subdivisions preceded comprehensive zoning. Nineteenth century state legislation authorized the platting of raw land into lots and blocks to facilitate conveyancing. Some states later amended their legislation to add controls over streets. The model planning legislation proposed in the 1920s incorporated an expanded statutory authority for controls over new subdivisions.

Legislation in all states now authorizes local governments to impose a number of requirements on new subdivisions when they are platted and approved. Subdivision control ordinances require the appropriate design of lots and blocks, subdivision access, and such necessary internal improvements as internal streets and drainage, and water and sewer facilities. Developers may also have to provide land without compensation for external streets, public schools, or parks, or pay a development fee the community can use for these purposes. Requirements of this type are known as subdivision exactions. Some state legislation prohibits subdivisions in floodplain or natural hazard areas.

Courts usually uphold the constitutionality of subdivision control requirements for subdivision design and necessary internal improvements. Other subdivision exactions, such as land dedications for streets and parks, present a more difficult taking problem. Courts will uphold these exactions if there is a nexus between the exaction and a need created by the subdivision, but recent U.S. Supreme Court cases, which state courts must follow, have adopted a more demanding nexus test than what state courts had previously applied.

An impact fee is another type of exaction on new development. It is usually levied when building permits are issued and not in the subdivision control process. Impact fees are usually used for off-site facilities, such as water and sewage treatment plants. The nexus test also applies to impact fees.

Many local governments have regulations for the approval of planned residential developments, usually as part of the zoning ordinance. Planned development regulations combine requirements found in zoning and subdivision controls. Although most state legislation does not expressly authorize planned development regulations, the courts have held that they are authorized by implication.

### § 1.10. The Exclusion Problem.

If land use controls are too restrictive they will exclude lower income groups from the community. Exclusionary land use controls are primarily a suburban zoning problem. Suburban municipalities may adopt large-lot residential zoning or prohibit multi-family housing in order to exclude lower-income groups and racial minorities.

Exclusionary zoning raises a number of constitutional problems. It violates the equal protection clause if it discriminates against racial minorities and lower-income groups. It violates the substantive due process clause if a court decides that a municipality must provide for its share of the affordable housing, which is required in the region in which it is located. Courts can also interpret state zoning legislation, which requires land use regulation to serve the general welfare, to include a similar obligation.

### § 1.11. How the Book Is Organized.

This book is an introduction to the major principles of land use law and concentrates on case law in the federal and state courts. The text is primarily a descriptive summary of judicial doctrine and discusses leading and representative cases to illustrate textual principles. The footnotes cite additional representative cases. They also contain citations to annotations in the American Law Reports that collect cases on land use topics. Selected citations to books and articles are included at the end of each chapter. Periodic supplements will update the statutory, case, and reference material.

The book also discusses the land use practice problems raised by different types of land use regulations. It reviews applicable Standard Planning Act and Standard Zoning Act provisions and examples of modifications in the Standard Acts the states have adopted. Statutes cited are current as of the date the text was prepared.

The plan of the book is straightforward. Chapter 2 provides an outline of basic constitutional doctrines. Chapter 3 discusses the comprehensive plan and its role in land use controls. Chapter 4 discusses the nuisance origins of zoning and the basic statutory and governmental structure of the zoning system. Chapter 5 discusses zoning for land use, density, and site development. Chapter 6 discusses the zoning process. The remaining chapters discuss exclusionary zoning, land use litigation and remedies, subdivision control, and the newer land use controls such as growth management, historic preservation, and environmental and sign controls.

A word on terminology is in order. Land use controls are adopted by a variety of local governments, including cities, villages, and counties. To simplify the textual presentation, these local governments are referred to as "municipalities." This term includes all local governments that have the authority to adopt and administer land use regulations.

## § 1.12.  Standard Judicial Attitudes.

Land use regulation enjoys the usual presumption of constitutionality accorded regulation that affects economic interests in property. The presumption has important consequences. It means that the party attacking a land use regulation in court has the burden to prove it unconstitutional, and that a court will hold a land use regulation constitutional if the governmental purposes it serves are fairly debatable. As the courts sometimes state, they do not sit as super-zoning agencies.[1]

Courts apply the presumption when they consider substantive due process objections to land use regulations. They also apply the presumption to equal protection objections when only economic interests are affected.

Courts reverse the presumption in equal protection cases when a land use classification is suspect or when a regulation affects a fundamental constitutional interest. The courts also reverse the presumption of constitutionality in other types of land use cases. They review regulatory classifications and governmental purposes more rigorously when a land use regulation affects free speech. This more rigorous judicial review is the equivalent of a presumption reversal. Some state courts reverse the presumption of constitutionality when they review exclusionary zoning and ordinances that exclude group homes or unrelated families from single-family zoning districts. The courts have reversed the presumption of constitutionality in so many types of land use cases that it is difficult to claim that the presumption usually applies in land use litigation. This shift in judicial attitude is one of the most important recent trends in land use law.[2]

Another presumption that influences land use cases, although it appears out of place in modern legal jurisprudence, is the rule that a court must construe a zoning ordinance strictly because it is in derogation of property rights.[3] The rule

---

**1.** *See* Robinson v. City of Bloomfield Hills, 86 N.W.2d 166 (Mich. 1957), discussed in § 2.34.

**2.** For discussion, see Mandelker & Tralock, "Shifting the Presumption of Constitutionality in Land Use Law," 24 Urb. Law. 1 (1992).

**3.** For typical cases, see Whistler v. Burlington N.R.R., 741 P.2d 422 (Mont. 1987); Knappett v. Locke, 600 P.2d 1257 (Wash. 1979). *But see* City of Portland v. Carriage Inn, 676 P.2d 943 (Or.

survives, but its impact is more limited than its statement suggests. Courts usually apply the strict construction rule only when they interpret definitions and restrictions in zoning ordinances.

A strict construction rule also applies when courts interpret the statutory authority delegated to local governments by legislation authorizing land use controls. This rule is not limited to land use law but reflects the strict construction rule many courts apply to a statutory delegation of authority to local governments. The courts vary in their application of the strict construction rule to statutory delegations of land use control authority.[4] They apply the rule more rigorously to subdivision regulations than they do to zoning ordinances.

## § 1.13. Judicial Perspectives in the Federal Courts.

Trial courts in the federal system are called District Courts. A party to a case can take an appeal as of right from these courts to intermediate appellate courts, known as Courts of Appeals. The Supreme Court decides in its discretion whether to take a case from a Court of Appeals, and it can also decide to take cases from state courts. The Supreme Court takes very few cases that are presented to it.

Decisions by the Supreme Court are binding on the lower federal courts, but they often exercise considerable judgment in deciding how to apply Supreme Court land use cases. One reason is that Supreme Court cases often provide only general guidelines for the land use questions they consider. Another is that the Supreme Court may not have decided an issue that the lower federal courts are asked to decide. Lower federal courts may disagree on how to decide a land use question when the Supreme Court has not considered it or has given incomplete guidance.

## § 1.14. Judicial Perspectives in the State Courts.

Land use law varies significantly among the states, even though the Standard Zoning and Planning Acts provide a common denominator for land use law. This section concentrates on zoning law, which makes up the vast majority of the decided land use cases. State judicial attitudes on subdivision and other controls such as growth management are more difficult to characterize.

---

App. 1984) (casting doubt on rule and stating that primary function of courts is to determine legislative intent).

**4.** *See* Rotter v. Coconino Cty., 818 P.2d 704 (Ariz. 1991) (strict construction rule not applied to ordinance restricting nonconforming uses because policy favoring their termination should be encouraged).

## § 1.15. Variations in the States.

One important feature of zoning law is its concentration in a limited number of states that have produced the clear majority of the important decisions. California and New Jersey stand in the forefront. New York and Pennsylvania have also produced a number of major zoning decisions, although the importance of these states has diminished because their highest appellate courts have been deciding fewer zoning cases. States with smaller populations that have produced important zoning cases include Maryland, Massachusetts, and Connecticut. The volume of zoning decisions is comparatively large in some states, such as Michigan, Illinois, and Texas, but cases from these states are not always influential.

The influence of the state courts on zoning law varies with appellate court attitudes toward the zoning function and the style and content of court decisions. States divide, under one classification, depending on whether they are favorable or unfavorable toward the exercise of the zoning power. California, New Jersey, Maryland, and Massachusetts historically are comparatively strong pro-zoning states, although changes in these courts may produce more conservative zoning decisions. Illinois and Rhode Island are more often pro-developer. Other states, such as Texas, Michigan, and Ohio, are either erratic or difficult to characterize. Some states have not produced enough zoning law to be classified.

This summary of state judicial attitudes is somewhat misleading. It assumes a court is pro-zoning if it usually upholds a municipality against constitutional attacks by developers on zoning ordinances. It does not include judicial attitudes on zoning changes that favor developers and are opposed by neighbors. Neither does it include judicial attitudes on land use controls that raise social problems, such as exclusionary zoning. New Jersey is usually considered a pro-zoning state but has invalidated exclusionary zoning. Some critics argue a strong position against exclusionary zoning is a positive judicial attitude even though it is not pro-zoning in the traditional sense.

The style and content of zoning opinions also determines the character of state zoning decisions. Some courts, such as the California and New Jersey courts, often consider policy issues in their decisions, a tendency that increases their influence. Other states are less policy-oriented. Illinois decisions, especially in the intermediate appellate courts, usually contain lengthy factual discussions and may be conceptually narrow. Massachusetts decisions often turn on an interpretation of the state's enabling legislation, which differs somewhat from the Standard Zoning Act. Judicial attitudes on zoning also are influenced by the type of zoning controversy that reaches the appellate courts. Some states have a large volume of zoning decisions, such as Texas and Illinois, but the cases deal with routine controversies. Smaller states, such as the Rocky Mountain states, may not produce many zoning decisions but their courts sometimes decide important zoning questions.

## § 1.16. State Appellate Court Structure.

A state's appellate court structure has an important influence on the prece-
dential value of its land use decisions. Most states have intermediate appellate,
as well as supreme, courts. A supreme court may have a discretionary jurisdiction, and it may refuse most appeals from intermediate appellate courts in land
use cases. In these states, intermediate appellate courts decide the vast bulk of
land use cases, leaving many issues undecided if the supreme court decides relatively few land use cases. The precedent problem is even more complicated
when the intermediate appellate court is divided into geographic districts because doctrinal differences can occur among them. Some state supreme courts
have also indicated that they will not consider cases where there is an attack on a
land use regulation as applied to a particular property.[5]

Trial court decisions are reported in a few states. Decisions by the New York
Supreme Courts, which are trial courts, appear in the New York Supplement.
Selected decisions by the New Jersey trial courts appear in the Atlantic Reporter.
New York trial court opinions are usually brief and of limited interest, but some
New Jersey trial court opinions are significant. Trial court decisions in these
states are sometimes affirmed on appeal without a written opinion.

The refusal of many state supreme courts to decide many land use cases
makes the intermediate appellate court decisions the most important body of
land use law, and the depth of analysis and content in these cases varies. The
California intermediate courts of appeal, which are divided into geographic districts, produce thoughtful and important land use decisions. So do intermediate
appellate courts in other states, such as Arizona, New Jersey, and Wisconsin.

Pennsylvania has an intermediate Commonwealth Court that hears cases
arising in governmental programs, including land use regulation. Commonwealth Court opinions are usually brief and may be short on detailed analysis.
Illinois intermediate appellate courts are divided into geographic districts. Their
decisions contain extensive factual detail and often deal with the constitutionality of land use restrictions as applied to an individual property. So do
decisions of the Texas intermediate appellate courts, which also are divided into
geographic districts.

Decisions by the intermediate New York Appellate Divisions, also divided
into geographic districts, are usually well-done. Summary affirmance of Appellate Division decisions by the Court of Appeals, the highest appellate court in
the state, gives some of these decisions additional value as precedent. Other Appellate Division and even Supreme Court decisions are occasionally recognized
by the Court of Appeals as authoritative, even though it has not taken them on
appeal.

---

**5.** Tidewater Oil Co. v. Mayor & Council, 209 A.2d 105 (N.J. 1965), discussed in § 2.49.

This book cites and discusses decisions by the highest state courts whenever possible. It includes decisions by intermediate appellate courts only when they establish important doctrine or contain thoughtful discussions of land use law problems.

### § 1.17. The Stages of Land Use Law.

Commentators frequently refer to the different stages through which land use law has moved. This kind of commentary must carefully distinguish between stages of development in the state as compared with the federal courts. A series of distinct stages is more marked in the state courts. The "stages" analysis also applies primarily to zoning, which has produced the vast majority of the decisions.

In the state courts, an early period in which they were hostile to zoning ended after the U.S. Supreme Court upheld comprehensive zoning in the *Euclid* case.[6] In the period following *Euclid* and lasting to the present time in most states, state courts adopted a pro-zoning attitude and looked favorably on the exercise of the zoning power. The standard judicial attitudes[7] are typical of this stage and still prevail in most states for most land use questions.

The second stage is marked by a two-tiered approach to land use questions. Courts usually uphold or are receptive to most zoning regulations. They may review the validity of zoning as applied to individual properties more carefully. The presumption of constitutionality protects zoning from a successful attack in as-applied cases, but the courts may disregard the presumption if they wish and hold against the local government. Some states are more likely to hold a zoning restriction unconstitutional as applied to a landowner's property than others.

The beginning of a new and more judicially assertive stage in land use law is difficult to identify. This stage probably began with cases in the mid-1960s that held large-lot and other suburban land use restrictions invalid as a form of exclusionary zoning. *National Land & Inv. Co. v. Kohn*[8] is a major landmark case of this type. This new stage in zoning law is marked by a concern with social issues in land use regulation. The exclusionary zoning cases are an example. Concern about social issues has spilled over into a number of related areas, such as zoning for group homes.[9] Some state courts invalidate socially unacceptable zoning by breathing new life into traditional due process and equal protection limitations. A few have relied on other constitutional limitations, such as a guarantee of a right to privacy.

---

**6.** Village of Euclid v. Ambler Realty Co., 272 U.S. 365 (1926), discussed in § 2.12.

**7.** § 1.12.

**8.** 215 A.2d 597 (Pa. 1965) (holding large-lot zoning invalid), discussed in § 5.27.

**9.** §§ 5.05-5.08.

Courts also gain greater control on zoning in some states by holding that zoning must be consistent with the comprehensive plan.[10] Some state zoning legislation has a consistency requirement. The consistency requirement is a judicial reaction against arbitrary decision making in the zoning process and is not hostile to zoning. A requirement that zoning be consistent with previously adopted planning policies helps to prevent arbitrary decision making.

Some state courts restrict arbitrary decision making in the zoning process by characterizing zoning by the local governing body as quasi-judicial rather than legislative. This characterization imposes minimum requirements of fair procedure on the zoning process. States that adopt the quasi-judicial characterization may also secure more control over zoning by reversing the presumption of constitutionality.

A new stage in land use law in the federal courts began in the mid-1980s, when the U.S. Supreme Court decided a large number of land use cases. The Court adopted a more rigorous taking clause doctrine, held that successful plaintiffs in taking cases may secure compensation for a temporary taking, and applied the equal protection clause to strike down a special permit denial for a group home for the mentally retarded.

The Court also granted constitutional free-speech protections to some land use regulations and applied the federal antitrust act to local land use regulation.[11] The Court has now somewhat curtailed the application of the free speech clause to land use regulation and has almost entirely eliminated municipal liability under the antitrust act.

---

**10.** §§ 6.32-6.34.

**11.** *See generally* D. Mandelker, J. Gerard & T. Sullivan, Federal Land Use Law (updated annually).

# REFERENCES

**Books and Monographs**

R. Babcock, The Zoning Game (1966).
R. Babcock & C. Siemon, The Zoning Game Revisited (1985).
Wipeouts and Their Mitigation (J. DiMento ed. 1990).

**Articles**

Developments in the Law Zoning, 91 Harv. L. Rev. 1427 (1978).
Karkkainen, Zoning: A Reply to the Critics, 10 J. Land Use & Envtl. L. 45 (1994).
Krasnowiecki, The Fallacy of the End-State System of Land Use Control, Land Use L. & Zoning Dig., Vol. 38, No. 4, at 3 (1986).
Libby, The Great Zoning Debate — More Heat Than Light, Land Use L. & Zoning Dig., Vol. 38, No. 11, at 3 (1986).
Rose, New Models for Local Land Use Decision, 79 Nw. L. Rev. 1155 (1985).
Williams, Three Systems of Land Use Control, 25 Rutgers L. Rev. 80 (1970).
Wyckoff, Zoning Critics: Proposed Reforms Over the Past 20 Years, Land Use L. & Zoning Dig., Vol. 38, No. 11, at 5 (1986).

# Chapter 2

# THE CONSTITUTIONAL FRAMEWORK

## A. THE TAKING ISSUE.

## § 2.01. The Taking Problem.

The Fifth Amendment to the U.S. Constitution provides that "private property shall not be taken for public use, without just compensation." Most state constitutions also contain taking clauses, and the Fourteenth Amendment makes the federal taking clause applicable to the states. The taking clause raises the all-important taking issue in land use regulation. Local governments enact land use regulations under their police power, which does not require the payment of compensation. When a land use regulation excessively restricts the use of land without compensation, the restricted landowner can argue that a taking of his land without compensation has occurred.

A strict reading of the taking clause suggests that it does not apply to land use regulation but only when a government entity takes or physically occupies land for a public use. Judicial doctrine through the latter part of the nineteenth century supported this view. In a leading case, *Mugler v. Kansas*,[1] the U.S. Supreme Court held a taking had not occurred when a state prohibition law forced the closing of a brewery without compensation. The Court distinguished the power of eminent domain and the police power. "A prohibition simply upon the use of property" for purposes legislatively declared to be injurious to the health or safety of the community "cannot … be deemed a taking … of property for the public benefit."

This early interpretation of the taking clause gave way to a more expansive view. This view sees a governmental restriction of land use through regulation as a "taking" of rights incidental to property ownership. Under this view, a regula-

---

1. 123 U.S. 623 (1887).

tory restriction on land use is as much a taking as a physical taking of land by a government entity. From this expanded view of the taking clause grew the extensive body of law under which courts can hold land use regulation unconstitutional as a taking of property.

Some important distinctions are necessary at this point. The text of a land use regulation may be so restrictive that no application of its requirements can avoid a taking. An example is an open space regulation that does not allow substantial development of any kind. In this type of case the land use regulation may be a "facial" taking of property, and landowners can bring a facial challenge to its restrictions based on the taking clause.

Other land use regulations may not be a facial taking but may possibly be a taking "as applied" to a particular property. An example is a zoning ordinance dividing a community into land use districts. The ordinance may not be a taking as applied to some property but may be a taking as applied to other property it covers. This distinction between facial unconstitutionality and unconstitutionality as applied is also applicable to the equal protection clause and the due process clause.

If a court holds that a land use regulation is a taking of property it will invalidate the regulation. The U.S. Supreme Court requires the payment of compensation for the temporary period during which the regulation was in effect. Some state courts also provide a compensation remedy.[2]

## § 2.02. Taking Clause Rules.

This section examines the rules courts and commentators have adopted for applying the taking clause to land use regulation. Rules applied by the state courts and by the U.S. Supreme Court have differed historically, even though Supreme Court taking rules adopted under the federal taking clause are enforceable in state courts. Federal and state court taking doctrine is now beginning to converge. Beginning with its taking trilogy in 1987, the Supreme Court has decided a number of land use taking cases, and state courts are applying these cases in land use litigation.

## § 2.03. A Taxonomy of Supreme Court Taking Rules: When Is a Taking Per Se?

The Supreme Court has adopted defined categories of taking rules that determine the outcome of a taking case in federal courts. The categories turn on whether a land use regulation is a physical or regulatory taking of land, and on whether the taking is per se or subject to review under a multi-factor balancing test. A physical taking of land is a per se taking, and a physical taking occurs

---

2. For a discussion of remedies for a taking of property, *see* §§ 8.23-8.25.

when a government regulation authorizes the permanent physical occupation of land. A regulation that only regulates the use of land, such as a zoning ordinance, may or may not be a taking per se. It is a taking per se if it denies an owner all economically beneficial use of his land, and if the harm regulated would not have been a nuisance at common law. The regulation is reviewed under a balancing test adopted by the Court if it does not deny an owner all economically beneficial use of his land.

### § 2.04. Purpose-Based Rules.

One set of taking rules turns on the purposes served by the regulation. Some of these rules have been proposed by academic commentators on the taking clause.

Professor Joseph Sax proposed a theory of the taking clause that distinguishes between activities carried out by government in its enterprise capacity and regulation carried out in its capacity as arbitrator.[3] A taking occurs "when economic loss is incurred as a result of government enhancement of its resource position in its enterprise capacity." A taking does not occur when economic losses are "incurred as a consequence of government acting merely in its arbitral capacity."[4] A regulation severely restricting land use in the vicinity of an airport would presumably fall within the enterprise category. A comprehensive zoning regulation would presumably fall within the arbitration category.

A classic text on the police power proposed a harm-benefit rule at the turn of the century.[5] This rule would uphold a land use regulation that prevents a harm to private landowners and invalidate a regulation that confers a public benefit. A land use regulation prohibiting industrial uses in residential districts prevents a harm because it prevents industrial uses from harming the residential neighborhood. A land use regulation requiring the preservation of historic landmarks confers a public benefit under this theory. It imposes an economic burden on the landmark owner to secure the benefit of landmark protection for the general public. Although this rule played a role in some state taking cases, the Supreme Court has now rejected it.[6]

Supreme Court cases now require that a regulation must "substantially advance legitimate state interests" to satisfy the taking clause.[7] This rule brings into taking law the evaluation of governmental purpose that courts undertake when

---

3. Sax, "Takings and the Police Power," 74 Yale L.J. 36 (1964). *But see* Maryland Port Admin. v. J C Corp., 528 A.2d 529 (Md. 1987); Thompson v. City of Red Wing, 455 N.W.2d 512 (Minn. App. 1990) (applying theory to hold rezoning not in enterprise category).

4. *Sax, supra,* at 63.

5. E. Freund, The Police Power 546-47 (1904). *See also* Durham, "A Legal and Economic Basis for City Planning." 58 Colum. L. Rev. 650 (1958).

6. § 2.17.

7. § 2.15.

they apply the substantive due process clause to government regulation. The rule determines whether the purposes of a regulation are facially acceptable and whether the purposes of the regulation are acceptable as applied.

## § 2.05. Economic Loss Rules.

As the U.S. Supreme Court has indicated, an important factor in land use taking cases is whether a land use regulation denies a landowner the "economically viable" use of his land.[8] The Supreme Court[9] and a clear majority of the state courts hold that a landowner is not denied an economically viable use unless the land use regulation does not allow him to make any reasonable use of his land.[10] Courts adopting the majority view sometimes state that a landowner's property is "confiscated" if he is not allowed a reasonable use of his land. An example is a case in which a court hold a zoning ordinance, as applied, does not allow a landowner an economically viable use of her land.

The Supreme Court holds that a denial of an economically viable use is not only a factor courts should consider but requires a holding that a taking has occurred per se.[11] This rule makes economic loss a critical threshold factor in the application of the taking clause to land use regulation.

Some state courts hold that a mere diminution in the value of the land is enough to find a taking, but it is not enough under the majority view. The diminution in value rule has a number of problems. One is that the courts never specify precisely how much loss is necessary when they apply the diminution of value rule. Neither is it clear whether the loss must be absolute or relative. A land use regulation imposing a $1,000 loss on land worth $2,000 may be a taking. A land use regulation reducing the value of a five million dollar property by $500,000 may not be a taking.

Another problem with economic loss theories generally is that the decline in value claimed by the landowner is self-serving. Assume the zoning ordinance restricts his property to a residential use. He now claims his land should be zoned for commercial development and that the difference in value between the commercial and residential use is a taking. What prevents him from demanding more and claiming that the appropriate land use is industrial? His economic loss will then be much greater.

Courts usually resolve the economic loss problem by looking at land uses in the area surrounding the restricted property. If a zoning ordinance restricts property to residential use in an industrial area, for example, the owner of the restricted land will have to take a heavily depreciated price for his property. The

---

**8.** Keystone Bituminous Coal Ass'n v. DeBenedictus, 480 U.S. 470 (1987).
**9.** Penn Cent. Transp. Co. v. New York City, 438 U.S. 104 (1978).
**10.** § 2.34.
**11.** § 2.18.

difference in the value of the property for the restricted residential use, and its value if it were available for industrial use, is probably so great that a taking has occurred under either economic loss theory. This type of case is known as a "zoning island" case.

An economic loss does not occur when a land use regulation confers an "average reciprocity of advantage," a phrase adopted by Justice Holmes.[12] The U.S. Supreme Court has confirmed its application to land use regulation.[13] Residential zoning is a land use regulation that confers an average reciprocity of advantage. All the land within a residential district is burdened by the residential land use restriction, but all the land is also benefited. Property owners within the district suffer from the burden but gain from the benefit because all of the land is equally restricted. Benefits cancel burdens. There is no taking.

Economic expectations also figure in a rule adopted by the Supreme Court[14] that a taking may occur if a land use regulation denies a landowner her reasonable "investment-backed expectations." The courts apply this rule, but it has not developed an understandable meaning. It is clear that the mere purchase of property with an intent to develop it is not enough to create an investment-backed expectation that is protected under the taking clause.

### § 2.06. Balancing Tests vs. Decision Rules.

The Supreme Court has not clarified whether taking cases are to be decided under decision rules or under a multi-factor balancing test. The Court has adopted a decision rule that a taking occurs per se if a landowner is denied all economically beneficial use of his land.[15] Another of its taking cases states a taking occurs if a regulation does not advance a legitimate government interest or denies a landowner all economically viable use of his property.[16] The Court did not hold that a taking in these circumstances would be per se.

The Supreme Court had earlier adopted a three-part balancing test to decide land use taking cases. Courts are to use their judgment in deciding how these factors apply. The factors are the character of the government action, the economic impact of the action and whether the regulation interferes with distinct "investment-backed expectations." Courts continue to apply these factors in regulatory taking cases if a land use regulation does not deny a landowner all economically beneficial use of his land.

Some state courts apply a balancing test to land use regulation that balances the harm suffered by the property owner from the land use regulation against the

---

**12.** Pennsylvania Coal Co. v. Mahon, 260 U.S. 393, 415 (1922).

**13.** Keystone Bituminous Coal Ass'n v. DeBenedictus, 480 U.S. 470 (1987).

**14.** § 2.13.

**15.** § 2.18.

**16.** § 2.15.

Some state courts apply a balancing test to land use regulation that balances the harm suffered by the property owner from the land use regulation against the public purposes it serves. This balancing test reflects to some extent the classic three-part substantive due process test first stated in *Lawton v. Steele*.[17] That test requires a holding that the public interest must justify the interference with land use, that the means adopted are reasonably necessary to accomplish that purpose, and that the means selected are not unduly oppressive on the property owner.

### § 2.07. A Summary and Perspective.

The sections that follow describe taking theories adopted by the Supreme Court and the state courts in land use cases. The Supreme Court's more active role in land use takings cases has blurred the line between federal and state taking doctrine, because state courts now apply Supreme Court taking doctrine more frequently. State court taking doctrine still has a distinctive character but may not track Supreme Court taking law that may include elegant taking theory. The discussion is purposely general at this point. The more detailed application of the taking clause to different categories of land use regulation is reserved for later chapters.

### § 2.08. U.S. Supreme Court Taking Doctrine.

Supreme Court taking doctrine is affected by the failure of the Court to give extensive consideration to mainstream land use problems. Many of the important Supreme Court cases considered nontraditional land use regulations, such as historic landmark preservation, restrictions on coal mining, and unusual land use exations. The limited scope of Supreme Court taking doctrine makes it difficult to generalize Supreme Court decisions as a coherent body of taking law. Each case turns, to some extent, on its regulatory setting. This review of the Court's taking doctrines accepts this limitation by addressing the Court's principal taking cases individually. The cases are presented for the most part in chronological order so that the development of the Court's taking doctrines can be understood.

### § 2.09. The Bundle of Property Rights Cases.

In one group of cases, the Supreme Court considered claims that the destruction of one of the rights in a landowner's bundle of property was a taking. Although they were not land use taking cases, they have influenced the taking cases that considered land use regulations. These cases indicate that the destruction of a "strand" in the property rights bundle can be a taking, but do not clearly indicate what "strands" are protected by the taking clause.

---

**17.** 152 U.S. 133 (1894).

In *Andrus v. Allard*,[18] regulations adopted under federal legislation prohibited the sale of Indian artifacts made from the feathers of certain birds. The Court held the regulations were not a taking. Even though they prohibited the most profitable use of the artifacts, their owners could possess, transport, donate, or devise them. The destruction of one "strand" in the bundle of property rights is not a taking "because the aggregate must be viewed in its entirety." A loss of future profits, when there is no "physical property restriction," is a "slender reed" on which to rest a taking claim.

In *Kaiser Aetna v. United States*,[19] a private developer improved a coastal pond and dredged a channel to provide private access to the ocean. The U.S. Army Corps of Engineers sued the developer to prevent it from denying public access to the pond through the channel. The Court held the government's attempt to create a public access was a taking. It held the property owner's "right to exclude" was a property right "that the Government cannot take without compensation." It also held that the improved pond and channel was not navigable water subject to the federal government's navigational servitude. The Court also relied on the Corps' failure to require permits for the improvements to the pond and channel. Although this failure did not estop the government, it created a number of expectancies that are embodied in property that the taking clause protects.

In *PruneYard Shopping Center v. Robins*,[20] a shopping center owner brought suit to exclude students who were distributing political literature. The Court held that a taking of the "right to exclude" had not occurred. Political solicitation in the shopping center would not "unreasonably impair the value or use" of the property, and the shopping center owner could adopt regulations that would minimize any interference with retailing. The Court distinguished *Kaiser Aetna* because the developer had a substantial investment in the pond and channel, the navigational servitude did not justify public access, and the federal government did not have the "residual authority" to define property rights. In *PruneYard,* the right to exclude was not "essential to the use or economic value" of the property.[21]

---

**18.** 444 U.S. 51 (1979). *But see* Hodel v. Irving, 481 U.S. 704 (1987) (invalidating statute providing for automatic escheat of small Indian holdings).

**19.** 444 U.S. 164 (1979).

**20.** 447 U.S. 74 (1980).

**21.** *See also* Nollan v. California Coastal Comm'n, 483 U.S. 825, 838 n.1 (1987) (noting that owner in *PruneYard* had opened shopping center to public and that permanent access was not required).

## § 2.10.  The Noxious Use Cases.

In its first set of land use taking cases, the Supreme Court upheld land use regulations applied retroactively to terminate noxious uses in residential neighborhoods. The regulations upheld in the noxious use cases were not comprehensive zoning ordinances. They were "police power" ordinances that terminated noxious uses in neighborhoods where they were out of place. The present vitality of the noxious use cases is uncertain. Courts continue to uphold ordinances that terminate nuisances. The Court's *Lucas* decision[22] casts doubt on these decisions. The Court characterized them as an "early attempt" to explain the limitations of the taking clause now replaced with a "contemporary understanding of the broad realm within which government may regulate without compensation."

*Hadacheck v. Sebastian*[23] is one of the earliest and best known noxious use cases. A landowner constructed a brick manufacturing facility on land containing clay worth $800,000 for brick making but only $60,000 for other purposes. The land was isolated at that time and not surrounded by residential development. Residences were built later in the surrounding area, which remained sparsely settled. The city then adopted an ordinance that retroactively prohibited brick works in designated areas of the city, including the area where this brick works was located.

The equities of the case lay strongly with the brick works owner. The residential homeowners had "come to the nuisance" because the brick works was there first. The homeowners might well have lost had they sued to prohibit the brick works as a nuisance. Some courts deny relief in nuisance cases to landowners who come to a nuisance. Los Angeles bypassed this problem by using its regulatory police power to adopt an ordinance requiring the retroactive termination of the brick-making facility. This retroactive application of the ordinance to eliminate a profitable land use raised a taking issue.

The Supreme Court upheld the ordinance in an opinion remarkably unsympathetic to the owner's economic plight. The Court held that the ordinance prohibited only brick making, not clay removal. If he wished, the brick works owner could remove the clay for brick making to another location, although he argued that this alternative was not practicable. The Court did not balance the public gain from the prohibition against the owner's economic loss. It also disregarded the owner's claim that the prohibition was invalid because his use was first in time.

In an enigmatic passage, the Court held that the brick works owner could not assert vested interests against the ordinance because of conditions previously existing in the area:

---

22. § 2.20.
23. 239 U.S. 394 (1915).

To so hold would preclude development and fix a city forever in its primitive conditions. There must be progress, and if in its march private interests are in the way they must yield to the good of the community.[24]

In *Goldblatt v. Town of Hempstead*[25] the Court, in a confusing opinion, upheld an ordinance that prohibited additional mining below the water table in a mining pit and the refilling of any excavation below this level. The ordinance prevented any further use of the property for mining. The Court has since discredited the taking clause analysis in *Goldblatt*.[26]

## § 2.11. *Pennsylvania Coal*: A Landmark Case.

*Pennsylvania Coal Co. v. Mahon*,[27] a landmark decision, was the first Supreme Court case to hold a land use regulation unconstitutional under the taking clause. This opaque and brief opinion by Justice Holmes still provides the starting point for judicial analysis of the taking clause in land use cases, even though a later Supreme Court decision qualified it.[28]

The coal company conveyed the surface rights to a tract of land but reserved the right to remove subsurface coal. The state later adopted a statute that prohibited the mining of coal that would cause the subsidence of any dwelling unit. The owners of the land brought an action to prohibit the mining of coal that would cause their residence to subside, and the coal company contended that the statute was unconstitutional.

Holmes found that the statute accomplished a taking of the coal company's reserved mining rights. He decided the case largely with aphorisms that still remain the most quotable taking maxims in any court decision:

Government could hardly go on if to some extent values incident to property could not be diminished without paying for every such change in the general law. . . . But . . . the implied limitation must have its limits . . . .

---

**24.** *Id.* at 410, *citing* Reinman v. Little Rock, 237 U.S. 171 (1915) (upholding ordinance prohibiting livery stables in designated areas).

**25.** 369 U.S. 590 (1962). *Compare* Sucesion Suarez v. Gelabert, 541 F. Supp. 1253 (D.P.R. 1982) (restriction on sand and gravel mining not a taking), *aff'd*, 701 F.2d 231 (1st Cir. 1983), *with* Silva v. Township of Ada, 330 N.W.2d 663 (Mich. 1982) (holding invalid a prohibition on gravel excavation on agriculturally zoned land).

**26.** Nollan v. California Coastal Comm'n, 483 U.S. 825, 836 n.3 (1987) (rejecting assumption in *Goldblatt* that judicial inquiry under taking clause is same as under due process and equal protection clauses). *See* § 2.16.

**27.** 260 U.S. 393 (1922).

**28.** Keystone Bituminous Coal Ass'n v. DeBenedictis, 480 U.S. 470 (1987), discussed in § 2.15.

When it reaches a certain magnitude, in most if not all cases there must be an exercise of eminent domain and compensation.[29]

Justice Holmes provided very little additional guidance on when a regulation is a taking because it goes "too far," but some commentators believe he adopted a balancing test to decide this question. At one point in the opinion, Holmes stated that the statute applied to a "single house." He did not consider the widespread incidence of subsidence throughout mining areas in the state. Holmes concluded that damage to a single house was not a public nuisance, that the public interest was limited, and that any personal safety problems caused by coal mining could be handled by a statute requiring notice to property owners. "On the other hand the extent of the taking" was great, and abolished an interest in land.

Because the statute destroyed a property right reserved to the coal company under this analysis, Holmes could have held that the statute unconstitutionally transferred an interest in land to a private owner without compensation. The statute effectively destroyed the subsurface mining rights the company reserved and transferred them to residential property owners. A title transfer of this kind requires compensation, as Holmes noted.

Holmes failed to recognize that the statute did not expressly prohibit the mining of subsurface coal. It simply prohibited any mining that caused subsidence, a consequence the coal company could have avoided by leaving pillars of coal underground. Holmes failed to indicate how much coal could be extracted had the underground pillars been provided. Brandeis explicitly made this point in his dissent. A later Supreme Court opinion upheld a similar statute by holding that the amount of coal required for supporting pillars was insignificant.[30]

### § 2.12. *Euclid*: Comprehensive Zoning.

The Supreme Court established the basis for modern land use controls when it considered and upheld a comprehensive zoning ordinance in *Village of Euclid v. Ambler Realty Co.*[31] This case came four years after *Pennsylvania Coal*. In *Euclid*, a zoning ordinance that restricted the plaintiff's land to residential use imposed a fourfold loss on the value of its property, which it wanted to put to an industrial use. The complaint relied on this fact to allege that the zoning ordinance confiscated and destroyed a "great part" of the value of the land, but the landowner did not pursue this claim. Its major complaint was that the zoning ordinance was unconstitutional because it prohibited nonresidential uses in residential zoning districts. For this reason, *Euclid* is a substantive due process and

---

**29.** 260 U.S. at 413.

**30.** *See case* cited *supra* note 33.

**31.** 272 U.S. 365 (1926).

equal protection rather than a taking case.[32] The Court specifically noted that the action was brought against the "threatened enforcement" of the zoning ordinance. It reserved for another day a decision on the constitutionality of the ordinance as applied to any particular property.

Some commentators claim *Euclid* holds that a zoning ordinance causing a severe diminution in the value of land is constitutional. This interpretation may be correct. The complaint alleged a taking had occurred and the Court specifically referred to the drastic reduction in property value. But this interpretation is undercut by the Court's treatment of the case as a facial attack on a zoning ordinance rather than an attack on the constitutionality of the ordinance as applied to the landowner's property.

### § 2.13. *Penn Central*: Multi-Factor Balancing.

More than fifty years passed before the Supreme Court again considered a taking question in a land use case. In *Penn Central Transp. Co. v. New York City*,[33] the Court upheld an historic landmark designation applied to prevent the construction of a high-rise office tower over Grand Central Station. Unlike comprehensive zoning, historic landmark designation falls within the public benefit category of land use regulations. The designation imposes a severe restriction on the use of the landmark site to confer the benefits of historic landmark preservation on the general public.

The special circumstances of the *Penn Central* decision weaken, to some extent, its value as a holding on the taking issue. Unlike many historic preservation cases, the decision attacked by the property owner in *Penn Central* did not prohibit the demolition of the landmark and the use of the residual landmark site for a more intensive use. *Penn Central* conceded it could earn a reasonable return on the terminal. It argued only that the restriction on its use of the air rights over the terminal required compensation. Curiously, the Court did not address the compensation claim.

The Court's decision vacillated between equal protection, due process, and taking issues and defies generalization. Justice Brennan's opinion for the majority opened with a review of Supreme Court taking doctrine and noted that the Court had never adopted a "set formula" for the taking clause. He adopted a multi-factor balancing test by identifying several factors the Court had considered when it made these "ad hoc, factual inquiries." These factors include the "character of the governmental action." Justice Brennan noted that a taking is more easily found when government physically invades property than when it adjusts "the benefits and burdens of economic life to promote the public good." The second category clearly includes land use regulation.

---

32. *See* § 2.34, 2.42.
33. 438 U.S. 104 (1978).

The taking factors also include the economic impact of the regulation, and particularly whether the regulation interferes with "distinct investment backed expectations." Justice Brennan did not define this phrase, although he noted that Penn Central had not established a taking "simply by showing that they have been denied the ability to exploit a property interest that they heretofore had believed was available for development."[34]

Brennan's discussion of taking doctrine also included a long analysis of the noxious use cases, such as *Hadacheck*. He stated in a footnote that these cases did not rest on the nuisance qualities of the uses prohibited. He explained the Court upheld single-use zoning in the *Hadacheck* line of cases because this zoning implemented a policy intended to produce a widespread public benefit. Historic landmark protection, he believed, accomplishes the same purpose.

Justice Brennan also rejected "Penn Central's related contention that a 'taking' must be found to have occurred whenever a land use restriction may be characterized as imposing a 'servitude' on the claimant's property." This statement is difficult to square with *Kaiser Aetna,* which found a taking in the deprivation of private access rights.

Justice Brennan next considered what he termed a "broad" constitutional attack on the landmark program. He noted that Penn Central did not claim that historic landmark preservation was an inappropriate governmental purpose. He rejected an argument that a taking occurred because the restriction on development deprived the property owner of a valuable property interest in air space. Taking jurisprudence, he observed, "does not divide a single parcel into discrete segments and attempt to determine whether rights in a particular segment have been entirely abrogated." Brennan added in a footnote that the full use of air rights is not so bound up with investment-backed expectations that a deprivation of their use constitutes a taking, rejecting any implication of such a rule from *Pennsylvania Coal.*

Without recognizing his shift in position, Brennan next considered a number of equal protection problems raised by the ordinance and the landmark designation. He considered an objection that the landmark designation was reverse "spot zoning" because it arbitrarily singled out the terminal for restrictions not imposed on its neighbors. Brennan answered that the city's "comprehensive plan" to preserve landmark structures foreclosed this objection. Brennan's reliance on the city's comprehensive plan is questionable. New York may have had a landmark designation ordinance that applied comprehensively throughout the city, but it did not base its ordinance on a true comprehensive plan.

Penn Central also argued the landmark ordinance was "inherently incapable of producing the fair and equitable distribution of benefits and burdens ... characteristic of zoning." This argument appears to invoke the average reciprocity of

---

**34.** *See also* § 2.20.

advantage rule as a reason for striking down the ordinance. Brennan answered that "more severe" impacts on some landowners do not constitute a taking, again relying on the *Hadacheck* line of cases.

Brennan next turned to Penn Central's argument that it was solely burdened but not benefited by the landmark designation. He answered that the landmark law "benefits all New York citizens" in economic terms and by improving "the quality of life of the city as a whole." This holding substantially undercuts the harm-benefit rule. The rule that a land use restriction is a taking when it confers public benefits loses force if these public benefits avoid a taking because they offset the burdens of the restriction on the landowner. The Court rejected this rule in a later case.[35] Brennan also held that the landmark designation did not fall within the enterprise category of land use regulation because it did not arise "from any entrepreneurial operations of the city."

Brennan easily dismissed arguments that the landmark law was a taking as applied to the terminal. The law neither interfered with the present use of the property nor precluded the possibility of a less intrusive structure in the terminal's airspace. The city's zoning ordinance allowed the transfer of development rights from the terminal to nearby property owned by Penn Central. Brennan held the development rights transfer option could mitigate a taking claim.

This puzzling mixture of taking and other constitutional doctrines leaves much to be desired. The Court's holding on the taking issue is also limited by its statement that the terminal owners could reapply for approval of a smaller building. This statement suggests that the taking claim was not ripe for decision.

### § 2.14. *Loretto* and *Yee*: Physical Occupation.

In its next taking case, *Loretto v. Teleprompter Manhattan CATV Corp.*,[36] the Court adopted a per se taking rule for permanent physical invasions of property. A New York statute authorized cable TV companies to install equipment on apartment buildings upon payment of reasonable compensation as determined by the state cable regulatory commission. The commission ruled that a nominal one dollar payment was sufficient compensation unless a landowner could show that he suffered greater damages.

An apartment owner brought an action claiming a taking had occurred when a cable company installed cable lines and boxes containing roof cables on the roof of its building. The Court held that a taking occurs when there is "a permanent physical occupation authorized by government . . . without regard to the public interest it may serve," even though the physical interference is minimal. In this case, the government did not take merely a single "strand" from the bundle of property rights but sliced through the bundle and took every "strand." The taking

---

**35.** § 2.17.
**36.** 458 U.S. 419 (1982).

destroyed the property owner's right to exclude, denied her the right to make a nonpossessory use of the property, and emptied the right to sell the property of any value.[37]

The Court held the per se taking rule did not apply to temporary physical invasions, cases where action outside the owner's property caused consequential damage, "and a regulation that merely restricts the use of property." The Court characterized the taking test it applies in cases where a physical invasion is not permanent as a "balancing test" or a "multifactor balancing test."

The dissent criticized the majority for having adopted a rigid per se taking rule based on formalistic quibble. The dissent also criticized the taking distinctions made by the majority. It argued, for example, that the statute was not a taking even if it affected the property owner's right to exclude because taking law does not prohibit a legislative redefinition of property rights.

The Supreme Court limited its *Loretto* holding in *Yee v. City of Escondido*.[38] Plaintiffs were mobile home park owners who rented pads of land to owners of mobile homes. Under state law, a park owner may not require the removal of a mobile home when it is sold or disapprove a purchaser who is able to pay rent. A city ordinance rolled back rents to an earlier level and prohibited rent increases without city approval. The Court held a taking by physical occupation had not occurred, and that a claim of regulatory taking was not properly before the Court.

The Court rejected an argument that the rent control ordinance authorized a physical taking because, together with the state law's restrictions, it increased the value of a mobile home by giving the owner the right to occupy the pad indefinitely at a sub-market rent. A physical taking occurs only when a law requires an owner to submit to a physical occupation of his land, and here the mobile home park owners voluntarily rented their land to mobile home owners and were not required to do so by either state or local law. These laws merely regulated the landlord-tenant relationship, and a transfer of wealth to mobile home owners does not convert regulation into a physical taking.

### § 2.15. *Keystone* and *Agins*: A Two-Part Taking Rule.

The Court has also adopted a two-part taking rule that contrasts with the multi-factor balancing test adopted in *Penn Central*. The Court first adopted this rule in *Agins v. City of Tiburon*.[39] The city placed five acres of undeveloped land in a Residential Planned Development and Open Space Zone to implement an open space element the state law requires in comprehensive plans. The Court

---

37. *See* Ferguson v. City of Mill City, 852 P.2d 205 (Or. App. 1983) (ordinance requiring easement for sewer lines held a taking). *See* § 2.09.

38. 503 U.S. 519 (1992).

39. 447 U.S. 55 (1980).

dismissed a facial taking attack on the ordinance in which plaintiffs sought compensation for the zoning restriction.

The Court held a taking had not occurred. It adopted a two-part taking rule for land use cases that differs from the multi-factor test the Court adopted in *Penn Central*:

> The application of a general zoning law to particular property effects a taking if the ordinance does not substantially advance legitimate state interests, . . . or denies an owner economically viable use of his land, . . . [T]he question necessarily requires a weighing of private and public interests.[40]

The Court held the open space zoning ordinance advanced legitimate state goals because it protected the residents of the city from the "ill effects of urbanization." Neither did the ordinance prevent the "best use" of the land nor extinguish a "fundamental attribute of ownership." The landowners would "share with other owners the benefits and burdens of the city's exercise of the police power." The Court decided three important taking cases in 1987, in what has come to be known as the "1987 trilogy." The Court confirmed *Agins'* two-part taking rule in *Keystone Bituminous Coal Ass'n v. DeBenedictus*,[41] in which it upheld a Pennsylvania statute that prohibited subsidence from coal mining that was similar to the statute invalidated in *Pennsylvania Coal*.[42] The subsidence act upheld in *Keystone* prohibited mining that causes subsidence to public buildings, dwellings used for human habitation, and cemeteries. Plaintiffs, an association of coal mine operators, sued in federal court to enjoin the enforcement of the act and its regulations and claimed the act was a facial taking.

In a 5-4 decision written by Justice Stevens, the Court concluded that Justice Holmes had invalidated the subsidence act in *Pennsylvania Coal* because it served only private interests and made it "commercially impracticable" to mine coal:

> The two factors that the Court [in *Pennsylvania Coal*] considered relevant have become integral parts of our takings analysis. We have held that land use regulation can effect a taking if it "does not substantially advance legitimate state interests . . . or denies an owner economically viable use of his land."[43]

The Court adopted this two-part taking in *Agins*, and the Court applied it to distinguish *Pennsylvania Coal*. Unlike the statute invalidated there, the new subsidence act advanced legitimate state interests because it protected the public

---

40. *Id.* at 260-61.
41. 480 U.S. 470 (1987).
42. § 2.16.
43. 480 U.S. at 484, quoting Agins v. City of Tiburon, 447 U.S. 255, 260 (1980).

interest in health, the environment, and the fiscal integrity of the area. The Court noted its "hesitancy" to find a taking "when the State merely restrains uses of property that are tantamount to public nuisances," and added that this

> is consistent with the notion of "reciprocity of advantage." . . . While each of us is burdened somewhat by such restrictions, we, in turn, benefit greatly from the restrictions that are placed on others. . . . These restrictions are properly treated as part of the burden of common citizenship.[44]

This holding is an application of *Penn Central's* interpretation of the harm-benefit rule.[45]

Because their taking attack was facial, the Court held the plaintiffs faced an "uphill battle" to show that the subsidence act denied them the economically viable use of their land. They did not claim the act made mining unprofitable, but only that the act denied them the economically viable use of the two percent of the coal left in place to prevent subsidence. The Court applied the "whole property" rule adopted in *Penn Central*; and held it would not treat this coal as a separate segment of property for taking clause purposes. The duty to retain this "small percentage" of coal, when viewed against any "reasonable unit" of the plaintiff's coal mining operations, did not deny plaintiffs the economically viable use of their property or affect their reasonable investment-backed expectations.

The Court rejected a claim that the subsidence act took the plaintiff's legal interest in their support estates, an estate in land recognized only in Pennsylvania. This estate was only part of the bundle of rights owned by the coal operators. They could mine virtually all of the coal in their mineral estates even though the act prohibited the subsidence of surface structures. This claim failed, in any event, because the plaintiffs did not show what percentage of their support estates was affected by the act.

*Keystone* marks an important change in taking clause doctrine. The Court referred to *Penn Central's* list of taking clause factors in a footnote[46] and applied the investment-backed expectations factor, but the two-part taking test it adopted from *Agins* is a distinctly different "set" taking formula. This test protects land use regulation from taking attacks by injecting an emphasis on governmental purpose that is also required by substantive due process doctrine. The Court's adoption of the average reciprocity of advantage rule from *Pennsylvania Coal*, and its application of *Penn Central's* "whole parcel" rule, also protect land use regulations from taking clause attacks.

---

**44.** *Id.* at 491, quoting Kimball Laundry Co. v. United States, 338 U.S. 1, 5 (1949).

**45.** *But see* § 2.26 (later case rejecting harm-benefit rule).

**46.** *Id.* at 490, n.18. *But see* Hodel v. Irving, 481 U.S. 704 (1987) (applying *Penn Central* taking factors to hold federal statute consolidating Indian lands was a taking).

## § 2.16.  *Nollan*: The Nexus Test.

In *Nollan v. California Coastal Comm'n,*[47] another 1987 decision, the Court held that a condition attached to a permit for a beachfront house that required the dedication of a public easement to cross the beach was a taking of property. This condition is similar to the exactions required from subdividers under subdivision control ordinances.[48] Justice Scalia, who dissented in *Keystone,* wrote the opinion for a 5-4 majority.

The Nollans planned to replace a small bungalow on their beachfront lot with a larger house. A concrete seawall approximately eight feet high separates the beach portion of their property from the rest of the lot. The Commission agreed to grant a permit for the house subject to a condition that they allow the public a lateral easement to cross that part of their property bounded by the high tide line and the seawall.

The Commission required the access dedication because the new house would contribute to a wall of residential structures that prevented the public from realizing "psychologically" that they had a right to enjoy the coastline. The house would also increase private use of the beachfront and, with other development in the area, burden the public's ability to pass along the beach. The Commission imposed similar conditions on all but 17 of the 60 development permits it granted in the same tract.

The Court held a taking clearly would have occurred if the Commission had required an easement across the Nollans' property and had not imposed an access requirement as a permit condition. The question was whether requiring access as a condition to a land use permit "alters the outcome." To answer this question, the Court reaffirmed the two-part taking test adopted in *Keystone* but elaborated the standard for determining when a regulation "substantially advances" a "legitimate state interest":

> [O]ur opinions do not establish that these standards are the same as those applied to due process or equal-protection claims. To the contrary, our verbal formulations in the takings field have generally been quite different. We have required that the regulation "substantially advance" the "legitimate state interest" sought to be achieved, . . . not that "the State *'could rationally have decided'* the measure adopted might achieve the State's objective."[49]

This holding could modify taking doctrine if it means the Court will apply a heightened standard of judicial review when it considers whether governmental

---

**47.** 483 U.S. 85 (1987).

**48.** §§ 9.11-9.19.

**49.** 483 U.S. at 836 n.3, quoting Agins v. City of Tiburon, 447 U.S. 255, 260 (1980) and Minnesota v. Clover Leaf Creamery Co., 449 U.S. 456, 466 (1981) (emphasis in original).

interests are advanced by a land use regulation. However, the footnote has had little influence on takings cases.[50]

The Court next reviewed the justifications advanced by the Commission for the permit condition. It held a permit condition is not a taking if it serves the same legitimate governmental purpose that a refusal to issue the permit would serve. As an example, the Court pointed out that the Commission could impose a height limitation on a house to preserve the view of the beach if, as the Court only assumed, it could prohibit the construction of the house to preserve the view. This condition would be valid even if it required a "permanent grant of continuous access" so that the public could view the beach from a viewpoint on the property.

A different problem arises, the Court held, if "the condition substituted for the prohibition utterly fails to further the end advanced as the justification for the prohibition." In this case, the "essential nexus is omitted."[51] The Court found that none of the reasons given by the Commission for the Nollan access condition provided a "nexus" with the original purpose of the building restriction. The Court noted that its holding was consistent with exaction decisions on the nexus requirement in every state except California and cited a long list of these decisions.[52]

The Court next considered a Commission justification for the access condition "unrelated to land use regulation." The Commission found that the condition was part of a comprehensive program to provide continuous access along the beach. Although this was a "good idea," the Commission would have to pay compensation if it wanted the Nollans to provide an access easement across their property.

### § 2.17. *Dolan*: More on Nexus.

In 1994 the Supreme Court decided another exaction case, *Dolan v. City of Tigard*.[53] The city adopted a comprehensive plan noting that flooding had occurred along a creek near plaintiffs' property. The plan suggested a number of improvements to the creek basin, and recommended that the floodplain be kept free of structures and preserved as a greenway to minimize flood damage. A plan for the downtown area proposed a pedestrian/bicycle pathway to encourage alternatives to automobile transportation for short trips in the business district.

Plaintiffs planned to double the size of their store in the city's central business district, pave a 39-space parking lot, and build an additional structure on the property for a complementary business. To implement its plans and land devel-

---

**50.** *See* Builders Service Corp. v. Planning & Zoning Comm'n., 545 A.2d 530, (Conn. 1988) (rejecting footnote).

**51.** *See* §§ 9.11-9.16 (state courts apply similar test in exaction cases).

**52.** 483 U.S. at 838-40, citing a long list of exaction cases.

**53.** 512 U.S. 374 (1994).

opment code, the city conditioned plaintiffs' building permit with a requirement that they dedicate roughly ten percent of their property to the city. The dedication included land within the floodplain for the improvement of a storm drainage system along the creek and a 15-foot adjacent strip for a pedestrian-bicycle pathway. To justify the dedication the city found that the pathway would offset traffic demand and relieve congestion on nearby streets, and that the floodplain dedication mitigated the increase in stormwater runoff from plaintiffs' property.

The Court held a "nexus" existed, as required by the *Nollan* case, between a legitimate government purpose and the permit condition on plaintiffs' property. It was "obvious" that a nexus existed between preventing flooding along the creek and limiting development in the creek's floodplain. A nexus also existed between the city's attempt to reduce traffic congestion by providing for alternative means of communication and the pedestrian/bicycle pathway requirement. But the Court found a taking because "the degree of the exactions demanded by the city's permit conditions [did not] bear the required relationship to the projected impact of [plaintiffs'] proposed development."

The Court reviewed the tests state courts adopted to decide this question and rejected all of them. It held that the "reasonable relationship" test adopted by a majority of state courts was closest to "the federal constitutional norm," but rejected it because it is "confusingly similar" to the minimal level of scrutiny courts require under the equal protection clause.

Instead, the Court adopted a "rough proportionality" test to determine whether a taking has occurred under the Federal Constitution. "No precise mathematical calculation is required, but the city must make some sort of individualized determination that the required dedication is related both in nature and extent to the impact of the proposed development." In a footnote, the Court added that the city had made an "adjudicative decision" to condition plaintiffs' building permit, and that "in this situation" the burden of proof lies with the city.

*Dolan* is important because its "rough proportionality" test elevates the level of scrutiny courts must give to exactions. This test suggests that something closer to "strict scrutiny" review is required rather than the more relaxed judicial review most state courts apply under the "reasonable relationship" test.

The Court's holding that the burden of proof shifted to the city because the exaction was imposed through adjudication as a condition also is important. An adjudication and a shift in the burden of proof also should occur when a dedication is imposed as a condition to other land use approvals, such as subdivision and planned unit development approvals.

### § 2.18. *Lucas*: A Per Se Rule for Regulatory Takings.

In a 1992 case, *Lucas v. South Carolina Coastal Council*,[54] the Court adopted a new "categorical" rule for cases of total deprivation of all economically viable use that adds yet more mysteries to the jurisprudence of the taking clause. Lucas bought two lots on a barrier island on which he intended to build homes similar to those on immediately adjacent parcels. At the time of purchase, these lots were not subject to the state's coastal building permit requirement, but a Beachfront Management Act adopted in 1988 prohibited any permanent structures on the property. Lucas brought suit, claiming the prohibition was a taking because the prohibition deprived him of all economically viable use of his property, and the state trial court agreed. The state supreme court reversed, holding that a taking does not occur when a regulation restricting the use of property is intended to prevent a "serious public harm." The Supreme Court, in an opinion by Justice Scalia, reversed.

After briefing and oral argument in the state court, but before its decision, the beachfront law was amended to authorize the Council to grant a special permit for a dwelling on Lucas' lots. This change raised a ripeness problem because the Court requires landowners to apply for any available land use approval before bringing a taking claim.[55] Scalia decided the ripeness rules did not apply. The state court had decided the case on the merits, not on ripeness grounds. Justice Scalia believed this disposition prevented Lucas from litigating in state court his claim for a temporary taking for the period during which construction on his lots was absolutely prohibited under the state law. This claim was now ripe.

Justice Scalia next reviewed the Court's taking law, and concluded there were "at least two discrete categories" of regulation that were compensable "without case-specific inquiry into the public interest advanced in support of the restraint." One was physical invasion of property, and the other was regulation that "denies all economically beneficial or productive use of land." A total denial of all use is a taking even if the purpose of the regulation is to prevent a harm rather than confer a public benefit.

Early Supreme Court cases holding that regulations prohibiting harmful uses were not takings were simply a transition "to our contemporary understanding of the broad realm within which government may regulate without compensation." In addition, the distinction between a regulation that prevents a harm and one that confers a public benefit is difficult, if not impossible, to make. Any regulation can be viewed as serving either purpose, and "noxious-use" logic cannot be the basis for distinguishing regulations that are not takings from those that are. The state legislature's recitation, in its legislative findings, "of a noxious-use

---

**54.** 505 U.S. 1003 (1992).

**55.** *See* § 2.23, *supra.*

justification cannot be the basis for departing from our categorical rule that total regulatory takings must be compensated."

Justice Scalia next qualified his "categorical" rule by indicating there are limited circumstances in which a regulation that effects a total taking can be upheld. A regulation that is "so severe" that it prohibits all economically viable use of land must "do no more than duplicate the result that could have been achieved in the courts under the State's law of private nuisance, or by the State under its complementary power to abate nuisances that affect the public generally, or otherwise."[56] An example is the owner of a lake bed who is denied a permit for landfilling that would flood the land of others. The case was remanded to the state court for a new trial under the nuisance exception, but the state court decided a taking had occurred and remanded to the trial court to determine compensation.[57]

Justice Blackmun dissented. He believed it was a mistake to create a new categorical rule that would find a per se taking whenever a regulation totally prohibits all use of land. Justice Blackmun believed "the State has full power to prohibit an owner's use of property if it is harmful to the public." He also pointed out that the nuisance principles the Court adopted as an exception to its categorical rule were based on the same harm-benefit distinction the Court rejected in its decision as impossible to apply. Justice Stevens' dissent was similar.

Justice Scalia has avoided the complexities of taking law by carving out yet another category of regulation held to be a per se taking. This may be a creative strategy, but the new category is likely to be limited. Most land use regulations allow some use of land.[58] When they don't, as in floodplain regulation, the harm prevented is usually apparent and will justify the restriction.

### § 2.19.  *Lucas* Applied.

*Lucas* has created some confusion about the way in which courts should apply its takings rules. The courts divide on whether it is enough to show a lack of legitimate purpose if a denial of all economically viable use is not shown.[59] When courts have applied *Lucas* they have not usually found a taking because the land

---

**56.** *See* Erb v. Maryland Dep't of the Env't., 676 A.2d 1017 (Md. App. 1996) (applies nuisance exception).

**57.** 424 S.E.2d 484 (S.C. 1992).

**58.** Community Concerned Citizens, Inc. v. Union Twp. Bd. of Zoning Appeals, 613 N.E.2d 580 (Ohio 1993) (conditional use requirement not a total denial of all use). *But see* Concrete Pipe & Prods., Inc. v. Construction Laborers Pension Trust, 508 U.S. 602 (1993) (pension taking case applying balancing test after *Lucas*).

**59.** *Compare* City of Pompano Beach v. Yardarm Restaurant, 641 So. 2d 1377 (Fla. App. 1994) (enough to show improper purpose), *cert. denied,* 115 S. Ct. 2583 (1995), *with* Estate & Heirs of Sanchez v. County of Bernalillo, 902 P.2d 550 (N.M. 1995) (contra); Gerijo, Inc. v. City of Fairfield, 638 N.E.2d 533 (Ohio 1994) (same), *cert. denied,* 115 S. Ct. 1101 (1995).

use regulation attacked did not deny the landowner all economically viable use.[60] Only a few cases found a denial of all use sufficient for a per se taking. An example is a case where the municipality denied a landowner the right to build a house on an undersized lot.[61]

### § 2.20. More on Investment-Backed Expectations.

The Supreme Court has not clarified the investment-backed expectations taking factor introduced into taking law by *Penn Central*,[62] and state and lower federal courts do not agree on how they should apply it. The courts have properly recognized an owner's investment-backed expectations when he substantially proceeds in good faith after government approval of his development.[63] Another group of cases protects landowner expectations at the time of purchase.[64] These cases are consistent with the holding in *Penn Central* that courts should protect "primary" expectations concerning the use of land.[65] Expectations arising after purchase are not protected.[66]

*Penn Central* also held that unilateral expectations are not protected under the taking clause. In a later non-land use case, the Court held a property owner does not have protected investment-backed expectations when he is on notice of a regulation that may affect the value of his property.[67] A number of courts applied the notice rule to uphold land use regulations, including wetlands and open space regulations, against taking claims.[68] In some of these cases, the courts held that

---

**60.** Cannone v. Noey, 867 P.2d 797 (Alaska 1994) (subdivision denial); Ramona Convent of the Holy Name v. City of Alhambra, 26 Cal. Rptr. 2d 140 (Cal. App. 1993) (no taking where only diminution in value); Tim Thompson, Inc. v. Village of Hinsdale, 617 N.E.2d 1227 (Ill. App. 1993) (same); Iowa Coal Mining Co. v. Monroe City, 494 N.W.2d 664 (Iowa 1993) (zoning change partly blocking proposed land use); Taub v. City of Deer Park, 882 S.W.2d 824 (Tex. 1994) (rezoning denial), *cert. denied,* 115 S. Ct. 904 (1995); Jones v. King County, 874 P.2d 853 (Wash. App. 1994) (downzoning).

**61.** Moroney v. Mayor & City Council, 633 A.2d 1045 (N.J. App. Div. 1993). *See also* § 12.05 (denial of wetlands permits held a taking).

**62.** § 2.13.

**63.** Resolution Trust Corp. v. Town of Highland Beach, 18 F.3d 536 (11th Cir. 1994); County of Kauai v. Pacific Standard Life Ins. Co., 653 P.2d 766 (Haw. 1982). *See* §§ 6.12-6.23 (discussing vested rights).

**64.** Gil v. Inland Wetlands & Watercourses Agency, 593 A.2d 1368 (Conn. 1991).

**65.** *See* MacLeod v. County of Santa Clara, 749 F.2d 541 (9th Cir. 1984) (expectation not primary), *cert. denied,* 472 U.S. 1009 (1985); Long Beach Equities, Inc. v. Superior Court of Ventura County, 282 Cal. Rptr. 877 (Cal. App. 1991) (right to exploit not protected).

**66.** Indiana Dep't of Natural Resources v. Indiana Coal Council, Inc., 542 N.E.2d 1000 (Ind. 1989), *cert. denied,* 493 U.S. 1078 (1990); Iowa Coal Mining Co., Inc. v. Monroe County, 494 N.W.2d 664 (Iowa), *cert. denied,* 508 U.S. 940 (1993).

**67.** Ruckelshaus v. Monsanto Co., 467 U.S. 986 (1984).

**68.** Sucesion Suarez v. Gelabert, 541 F. Supp. 1253 (D.P.R. 1982), *aff'd,* 701 F.2d 231 (1st Cir. 1983); Furey v. City of Sacramento, 592 F. Supp. 463 (E.D. Cal. 1984), *aff'd on other grounds,*

the mere purchase of property did not create an investment-backed expectation. A footnote in *Nollan* casts doubt on these cases.[69] It held the "right to build on one's own property" is not a unilateral expectation, even though it is subject to government regulation. It also held the purchase of property after a government begins the implementation of a regulatory program does not defeat a taking claim. Despite *Nollan*,[70] some courts continue to hold that landowners do not have investment-backed expectations in the development of their land if they knew[71] or should have known[72] that their land would be restricted by land use regulations.[73]

## § 2.21. Ripeness and Finality.

### § 2.22. Early Supreme Court Cases.

Beginning with *Agins v. City of Tiburon*,[74] the Supreme Court restricted access to the federal courts in taking cases through an application of ripeness and finality rules it applied to taking litigation. The Court held the cases were not

---

780 F.2d 1448 (9th Cir. 1986); Graham v. Estuary Props., Inc., 399 So. 2d 1374 (Fla.), *cert. denied*, 454 U.S. 1083 (1981); Claridge v. New Hampshire Wetlands Bd., 485 A.2d 287 (N.H. 1984). *But see* Kirby Forest Indus. v. United States, 467 U.S. 1 (1984) (dictum; expectations protected when regulatory burden unforeseeable).

**69.** Nollan v. California Coastal Comm'n, 483 U.S. 815, 833 n.2 (1987).

**70.** *See* Kim v. City of New York, 681 N.E.2d 312 (N.Y. 1997) (denying compensation for fill placed on property and rejecting *Nollan* footnote).

**71.** National Advertising Co. v. Village of Downers Grove, 561 N.E.2d 1300 (Ill. App. 1990) (sign regulations), *cert. denied*, 501 U.S. 1261 (1991); Parranto Bros,, Inc. v. City of New Brighton, 425 N.W.2d 585 (Minn. App. 1988) (downzoning); Kelly v. Tahoe Regional Planning Agency, 855 P.2d 1027 (Nev. 1993) (denial of development plans); Gazza v. New York State Dept. of Envtl. Conservation, 679 N.E.2d 1035 (N.Y. 1997) (wetlands); Finch v. City of Durham, 384 S.E.2d 8 (N.C. 1989) (downzoning); Board of Supervisors v. Omni Homes, Inc., 481 S.E.2d 460 (Va. 1997) (risk of acquiring access).

**72.** Naegele Outdoor Advertising, Inc. v. City of Durham, 803 F. Supp. 1068 (M.D.N.C. 1992) (sign regulation), *aff'd without opinion*, 19 F.3d 11 (4th Cir. 1994), Elias v. Town of Brookhaven, 783 F. Supp. 758 (E.D.N.Y. 1992) (downzoning); McNulty v. Town of Indialantic, 727 F. Supp. 604 (M.D. Fla. 1989) (coastal setback); FIC Homes of Blackstone, Inc. v. Conservation Comm'n, 673 N.E.2d 61 (Mass. App. 1996) (wetlands); Parranto Bros., Inc. v. City of New Brighton, 425 N.W.2d 585 (Minn. App. 1988) (downzoning); White v. City of Brentwood, 799 S.W.2d 890 (Mo. App. 1990) (zoning). *Contra* Carpenter v. Tahoe Regional Planning Agency, 804 F. Supp. 1316 (D. Nev. 1992); Ciampitti v. United States, 22 Cl. Ct. 310 (1991).

**73.** *But see* Cottonwood Farms v. Board of County Comm'rs, 763 P.2d 551 (Colo. 1988) (landowner may bring taking claim though he purchased land subject to regulation attacked); Lopes v. City of Peabody, 629 N.E.2d 1312 (Mass. 1994) (same).

**74.** § 2.15. *See* 111 A.L.R. Fed. 83 (1993).

ripe for decision or that the lower court had not entered a final judgment.[75] In *Agins*, the ordinance permitted one to five single-family residences on plaintiffs' land and required developers to submit a development plan so that the city could determine how many residences it would allow within this range. The Supreme Court remanded the case because the plaintiffs had not submitted the development plan required by the ordinance. The Court did not use the term "ripeness," but the case clearly means that a taking case is not ripe for decision unless the plaintiff has submitted a development plan for approval when an ordinance requires one. Other development approval requirements in zoning ordinances, such as site plan review, also trigger the *Agins* rule.[76]

*San Diego Gas & Elec. Co. v. City of San Diego*[77] applied the final judgment rule. The city adopted an open space zoning ordinance to implement an open space plan. The landowner brought an inverse condemnation action and the trial court awarded compensation. The California appellate courts dismissed on the authority of *Agins,* and the landowner appealed to the Supreme Court. The Court held that the state court judgment was not a final judgment subject to review because the state courts had not finally determined whether a taking had occurred. The Court remanded to give the landowner an opportunity to resolve disputed facts that would determine whether a taking had occurred.

### § 2.23.  *Hamilton Bank.*

The Court extended the ripeness rule in *Williamson County Regional Planning Comm'n v. Hamilton Bank.*[78] The commission granted preliminary subdivision approval for a residential development. The plat indicated that 736 dwelling units were allowable but drew lines for only 436 units. The developer then spent 3.5 million dollars on water and sewer facilities and a golf course to serve the entire development. The commission later gave final approval for 212 dwelling units.

The commission refused preliminary approval of a revised subdivision plat for the remaining sections of the development. By that time, the zoning ordinance had been amended to reduce the number of dwelling units permitted. The commission noted a number of problems with the revised plat, including an excessive number of dwelling units, the placement of dwelling units on slopes where development was prohibited and problems with roads and grading.

---

**75.** *See also* Penn Cent. Transp. Co. v. New York City, 438 U.S. 104 (1978) (plaintiff did not seek approval for a smaller structure than the high rise building they proposed over Grand Central Terminal).

**76.** *See also* Hodel v. Virginia Surface Mining & Reclamation Ass'n, 452 U.S. 264 (1981) (court dismissed taking attack on federal surface mining act because plaintiff had not presented concrete controversy or sought variance or waiver from act's provisions).

**77.** 450 U.S. 621 (1981).

**78.** 473 U.S. 172 (1985).

The court of appeals affirmed a compensation award for a temporary taking, but the Supreme Court reversed and remanded. Although the developer had submitted a development plan as required by *Agins,* it had not sought variances from the zoning and subdivision ordinances that would have overcome the commission's objections to its plat. The Court could not evaluate the taking claim until the administrative agency had arrived at a "final, definitive position" that applied the regulations to the developer's land. The Court added that the developer was not required to file a declaratory judgment to review the commission's decision or to appeal the variance decision in a state court. It held that an appeal to the board of adjustment was not necessary because the board did not participate in the commission's decision.

The case also was not ripe for decision because the developer had not utilized a state statute that authorized compensation awards in inverse condemnation actions in land use taking cases. The Court held that the availability of post-taking state compensatory procedures was an adequate remedy because the Federal Constitution does not require the payment of compensation in advance of a taking.

### § 2.24. *Yolo County.*

In the next ripeness case, *McDonald, Sommer & Frates v. Yolo County,*[79] the county board refused to approve a residential subdivision that would help alleviate a severe regional housing shortage. It stated that the property could be used only for agricultural purposes, despite its finding that the property was "agriculturally impaired" by insect infestation, the removal of topsoil, and the proximity of residential development. The county's refusal to approve the subdivision was induced by the city, which advised the county that the residential use of the subdivision conflicted with the city's designation of the property as an agricultural reserve in its general plan. The city also advised the county that it would not annex the property, permit extension of a city street into the subdivision, or provide city services.

The plaintiff brought suit for compensation and claimed the county had appropriated the "entire economic use" of its property. The plaintiff also claimed that any application for a zoning change, variance, or other relief was futile. The state trial court sustained a demurrer to the complaint and held that the rejection of plaintiff's development did not preclude "less intensive, but still valuable development." The state appellate court affirmed.

The Supreme Court noted that this case was different from its earlier ripeness cases because the plaintiff obtained a ruling on "one" subdivision proposal. It had still failed to obtain a final, dispositive position on the application of the regulations to its land because the state court holding left open "the possibility

---

**79.** 477 U.S. 340 (1986).

that some development will be permitted." The Court indicated in a footnote that it did not require repeated "futile" development applications.[80]

### § 2.25. Later Supreme Court Cases.

Later Supreme Court cases have dismissed ripeness claims to taking cases by finding the ripeness rules did not apply. The Court held a compensation remedy is available to landowners for a taking of property by holding that only the compensation remedy, not the taking issue, was before the court.[81] The Court decided a taking case that arguably was not ripe by holding that the state supreme court had precluded the landowner from litigating the taking issue in the state courts.[82]

In *Suitum v. Tahoe Regional Planning Agency*,[83] plaintiff applied to the agency to build a home on her lot. The agency refused permission because the lot was located in an area, classified as a Stream Environment Zone, that carried runoff into the lake's watershed. Plaintiff appealed to the agency's governing board, which affirmed the agency's decision. To ease the impact of its development restrictions, the agency had a transfer of development rights (TDR) program.[84] It granted transferable development rights a landowner could sell to owners of other parcels, subject to the agency's approval based on the eligibility of the receiving parcel for development.

Plaintiff sued for a taking without applying for permission to the agency to sell her development rights. The Court held the plaintiff satisfied the finality requirement of the ripeness rules. The agency had finally determined her land was in a zone in which it did not permit development. Neither was action by the agency allowing plaintiff to transfer her development rights the type of final action required by the ripeness rules. The parties agreed on the TDRs to which the plaintiff was entitled, and discretionary action by the agency was not necessary for her to obtain them or offer them for sale. *Suitum* has a limited effect on taking claims in land use cases because most land use decisions require an exercise of discretion by government agencies.

---

80. *Id.* at 353 n.8. *See also* First English Evangelical Lutheran Church v. County of Los Angeles, 482 U.S. 304 (1987) (taking claim for compensation ripe for decision because state courts decided case only on remedial issue).

81. First English Evangelical Lutheran Church v. County of Los Angeles, 482 U.S. 304 (1987). *See* § 8.25.

82. Lucas v. South Carolina Coastal Council, 505 U.S. 1003 (1992). *See* § 2.15.

83. 117 S. Ct. 1659 (1997).

84. *See* §§ 11.34, 12.15.

## § 2.26. Lower Federal Court Cases.

The lower federal courts have vigorously applied the Supreme Court's ripeness doctrines to refuse jurisdiction in as-applied taking cases.[85] Most lower federal courts, relying on an expansive dictum in *Yolo County*,[86] have also applied the ripeness rules to equal protection and due process claims.[87]

## § 2.27. Final Decision Rule.

A case is not ripe unless an application is made,[88] and the agency has made a final decision.[89] It is not necessary for an agency to make a formal outright denial of an application. A court can find an agency has made a final decision rejecting an application when an agency's decision is the functional equivalent of a denial.[90] Rejection of a proposed development is not enough because application for an alternative development must be made if this opportunity exists under the ordinance.

A plaintiff must apply for administrative relief, such as a variance, to make her case ripe. The courts are divided on whether an application for a legislative rezoning also is required.[91] Lower federal courts also have dismissed taking claims because they did not satisfy the holding in *Yolo County*, that a taking claim is not ripe simply because a municipality has rejected a developer's grandiose plans.[92]

---

**85.** *See also* § 8.08 (federal ripeness rules applied in state courts).

**86.** 477 U.S. 340, 351 (1986) (suggesting ripeness rules apply to all constitutional claims).

**87.** Herrington v. County of Sonoma, 857 F.2d 567 (9th Cir. 1988) (substantive due process and equal protection), *cert. denied,* 489 U.S. 1090 (1990); Unity Ventures v. County of Lake, 841 F.2d 770 (7th Cir.) (procedural due process), *cert. denied,* 488 U.S. 891 (1988). *Contra,* Harris v. County of Riverside, 904 F.2d 497 (9th Cir. 1990). *See also* Eide v. Sarasota Cty., 895 F.2d 1326 (11th Cir. 1990) (reapplication requirement does not apply to substantive due process claims).

**88.** Suitum v. Tahoe Regional Planning Agency, 80 F.3d 359 (9th Cir. 1996) (must apply for transfer of development rights; *cert. granted*); Kawaoka v. City of Arroyo Grande, 17 F.3d 1227 (9th Cir. 1994) (failure to submit development plan).

**89.** Covington Court, Ltd. v. Village of Oak Brook, 77 F.3d 177 (7th Cir. 1996) (no decision made).

**90.** A.A. Profiles, Inc. v. City of Ft. Lauderdale, 850 F.2d 1483 (11th Cir. 1988) (city suspended project approval and downzoned property), *cert. denied,* 490 U.S. 1020 (1989).

**91.** *Compare* Southern Pacific Transp. Co. v. City of Los Angeles, 922 F.2d 4988 (9th Cir. 1990), *with* Tahoe-Sierra Preservation Council, Inc. v. Tahoe Regional Plan. Agency (II), 938 F.2d 153 (9th Cir. 1991).

**92.** Pace Resources, Inc. v. Shrewsbury Twp., 808 F.2d 1023 (3d Cir.), *cert. denied,* 482 U.S. 906 (1987). *But see* Del Monte Dunes Ltd. v. City of Monterey, 920 F.2d 1496 (9th Cir. 1990) (final decision rule satisfied when city unfairly protracted application process). *See also* Resolution Trust Corp. v. Town of Highland Beach, 18 F.3d 1536 (11th Cir. 1994) (decision not to extend zoning is final decision).

The Supreme Court had suggested there is a futility exception to the final decision rule. *Kinzli v. City of Santa Cruz*[93] is the leading case applying this exception. The court rejected the case-specific analysis of futility claims that had been undertaken in previous Ninth Circuit cases. It held that compliance with the final decision rule was not futile simply because a land use regulation prohibits any beneficial use of the land or inhibits its marketability. This inquiry would require the same sort of speculation that the ripeness doctrine prohibits. The court held that a plaintiff could not make a futility claim unless he had made at least one "meaningful" application or had requested a variance. Ninth Circuit cases since *Kinzli* have not been consistent,[94] and the ripeness doctrine in that circuit remains confused. Other courts have adopted the *Kinzli* interpretation of the futility rule.[95]

### § 2.28. Compensation Requirement.

The courts have applied the rule that a plaintiff must seek compensation in state court if a state compensation remedy is available.[96] Many of these cases find a taking case unripe only if they conclude from an examination of state law that the compensation remedy is available. Other cases hold that the state compensation remedy must be used unless the state court has clearly held that the remedy is unavailable.[97] These cases misapply *Hamilton Bank*. The holding of some courts,[98] that the state compensation remedy requirement is satisfied by the availability of a federal compensation remedy in state courts, may also be a misapplication of the federalism underpinnings of the ripeness rules.

---

**93.** 818 F.2d 1449, *amended,* 830 F.2d 968 (9th Cir. 1987), *cert. denied,* 484 U.S. 1042 (1988).

**94.** *See* Hoehne v. County of San Benito, 870 F.2d 529 (9th Cir. 1989) (finding additional applications futile), and Herrington v. County of Sonoma, 857 F.2d 567 (9th Cir. 1988) (need not apply for variance that would not be granted), *cert. denied,* 489 U.S. 1090 (1990).

**95.** Strickland v. Alderman, 74 F.3d 260 (11th Cir. 1996) (futility claim rejected); Landmark Land Co. v. Buchanan, 874 F.2d 717 (10th Cir. 1989); Amwest Investments, Ltd. v. City of Aurora, 701 F. Supp. 1508 (D. Colo. 1988). *But see* A.A. Profiles, Inc. v. City of Ft. Lauderdale, 850 F.2d 1483 (11th Cir. 1988) (case ripe because downzoning not appealable to local board).

**96.** *E.g.,* Gamble v. Eau Claire County, 5 F.3d 285 (7th Cir. 1993) (unripe; failure to pursue state condemnation claim), *cert. denied,* 510 U.S. 1129 (1994); Executive 100, Inc. v. Martin Cty., 922 F.2d 1536 (11th Cir. 1991); Bateson v. Geisse, 857 F.2d 1300 (9th Cir. 1988). *Cf.* Samaad v. City of Dallas, 940 F.2d 925 (5th Cir. 1991).

**97.** *E.g.,* Villager Pond, Inc. v. Town of Darien, 56 F.3d 375 (2d Cir. 1995), *cert. denied,* 117 S. Ct. 50 (1996); Estate of Himelstein v. City of Fort Wayne, 898 F.2d 573 (7th Cir. 1990); Austin v. City & Cty. of Honolulu, 840 F.2d 678 (9th Cir.), *cert. denied,* 488 U.S. 852 (1988).

**98.** *E.g.,* Christensen v. Yolo County Bd. of Supvrs., 995 F.2d 161 (9th Cir. 1993); Barima Inv. Co. v. United States, 771 F. Supp. 1187 (S. D. Fla. 1991), *aff'd mem.,* 959 F.2d 972 (11th Cir. 1992). *Contra* Dodd v. Hood River County, 59 F.3d 852 (9th Cir. 1995).

## § 2.29. State Court Taking Doctrine.

State court taking cases provide a more substantial body of law than the U.S. Supreme Court cases. The state courts regularly decide taking cases as part of the normal flow of land use decisions. They have not usually adopted a "set" taking formula, and taking doctrine varies from court to court. As-applied taking cases are the rule rather than the exception at the state level. States have also decided cases in the enterprise category of taking law[99] and that has received limited attention in the federal courts.

## § 2.30. The Enterprise Cases.

*Hager v. Louisville & Jefferson County Planning & Zoning Comm'n*[100] is an example of an enterprise category case. The commission amended its comprehensive plan to designate ponding areas as temporary storage basins in connection with a flood protection project. The court held that the designation transferred "rights in property" to the public agency that it should have acquired by purchase or eminent domain. Courts may also require the payment of compensation when a land use regulation prohibits the development of land in order to convert it to a public use.[101]

## § 2.31. Airport Zoning.

State court decisions on the constitutionality of height and similar restrictive land use regulations adjacent to airports are divided.[102] A court may find a taking under the enterprise theory when a municipality adopts height limitations or restricts land use adjacent to airports to provide clear zones for overflights. *McShane v. City of Faribault*[103] is an example. The city created two zones in the area near the airport runways. It prohibited above-ground structural uses in the zone next to the runways. In the adjacent zone it limited population density to

---

**99.** § 2.04.

**100.** 261 S.W.2d 619 (Ky. 1953).

**101.** Kraft v. Malone, 313 N.W.2d 758 (N.D. 1981) (drainage ditch).

**102.** Held unconstitutional: Sneed v. County of Riverside, 32 Cal. Rptr. 318 (Cal. App. 1962); Roark v. City of Caldwell, 394 P.2d 641 (Idaho 1964); Indiana Toll Rd. Comm'n v. Jankovich, 193 N.E.2d 237 (Ind. 1963), *cert. denied,* 379 U.S. 487 (1965); Yara Eng'r Corp. v. City of Newark, 40 A.2d 559 (N.J. 1945); State v. City of Columbus, 209 N.E.2d 405 (Ohio 1965). Held constitutional: Land Assocs. v. Metropolitan Airport Auth., 547 F. Supp. 1128 (M.D. Tenn. 1982) (refusal to upzone), *aff'd per curiam,* 712 F.2d 248 (6th Cir. 1983); Baggett v. City of Montgomery, 160 So. 2d 6 (Ala. 1963); LaSalle Nat'l Bank v. County of Cook, 340 N.E.2d 79 (Ill. 1975); Kimberlin v. City of Topeka, 710 P.2d 682 (Kan. 1985); Greenberg v. State, 502 A.2d 522 (Md. App. 1986); Davis v. City of Princeton, 401 N.W.2d 391 (Minn. App. 1987); Patzau v. New Jersey Dep't of Transp., 638 A.2d 866 (N.J. App. Div. 1994) (state airport zoning act held not facial taking). Rogers v. City of Cheyenne, 747 P.2d 1137 (Wyo. 1987), *cert. denied,* 485 U.S. 1017 (1988).

**103.** 292 N.W.2d 253 (Minn. 1980).

fifteen persons per acre and required three-acre lots. The court found a taking and relied on the enterprise theory. It distinguished traditional zoning where "there is believed to be a reciprocal benefit and burden accruing to all landowners from the planned and orderly development of land use." The court gave the city the option of repealing the ordinance or paying compensation.

Another court[104] reached a different result when a city prohibited residential development in areas adjacent to airports, where it was undesirable because of airport noise, but permitted agricultural use. The court did not find a taking because it viewed the ordinance as a comprehensive attempt to zone for the city and because the permitted agricultural uses were reasonable. If a restrictive zoning ordinance or height restriction left a landowner with no economically beneficial use of his property, a court could find a taking per se based on the Supreme Court's *Lucas* decision.[105]

### § 2.32. Planning and Zoning with Acquisitory Intent.

In another type of case falling in the enterprise category, a taking can occur if a municipality improperly uses the planning and zoning power in conjunction with the power to condemn land. Mere planning is not enough. It is well-established that mere planning for a public facility, such as the designation of a highway route on a comprehensive plan, is not a taking.[106] Yet courts will find a de facto taking if a municipality prohibits the development of land it or another agency intends to acquire in order to depress its market value prior to condemnation. Courts are especially likely to find a taking if there is an unreasonable delay in acquiring land following its designation for acquisition or an announcement that a taking will occur.

In *People ex rel. Dep't of Transp. v. Diversified Props. Co. III,*[107] a city cooperated with the state to refuse to approve the development plans on property the state intended to acquire for a freeway. The court held that the delay due to these unreasonable precondemnation activities amount to a de facto taking. It found that the state knew the city's development restriction had made the property virtually unmarketable, that the city's restrictions were imposed because the property was located in a freeway route, and that the state had no intention of condemning the property for many years. Courts have found that a de facto taking occurred under similar facts.[108] Courts have not found a taking in these cases

---

104. Eck v. City of Bismarck (II), 302 N.W.2d 739 (N.D. 1981).

105. *But see* Fitzgerald v. City of Iowa City, 492 N.W.2d 659 (Iowa 1992) (no taking post-*Lucas* when height restriction left landowner with economically viable use of property).

106. § 3.21. *See also* § 10.12 (official maps).

107. 17 Cal. Rptr. 2d 676 (Cal. App. 1993).

108. Peacock v. County of Sacramento, 77 Cal. Rptr. 391 (Cal. App. 1969); City of Plainfield v. Borough of Middlesex, 173 A.2d 785 (N.J.L. Div. 1961) (rezoning to park and playground use).

when the precondemnation delay was not unreasonable. In one such case,[109] the city delayed for one year a decision for a building permit on land designated for possible acquisition as a park in its comprehensive plan. The city then decided not to acquire the land and amended its plan to allow development of the land.

### § 2.33. Zoning to Depress Market Value.

In a variant of the acquisitory intent cases, a municipality adopts a restrictive zoning classification to depress the value of land it intends to acquire but does not announce or begin condemnation. In most of these cases, the municipality adopted a land use classification that was incompatible with surrounding land uses. An example is a restrictive residential zoning classification applied to a tract in an industrial area. The courts hold that these zoning restrictions do not serve a proper zoning purpose if they were adopted to depress the value of property in advance of acquisition.[110]

Courts will also find a taking if a municipality denies a building permit or other land use approval in order to hold down the cost of land prior to its acquisition. In *San Antonio River Auth. v. Garrett Bros.,*[111] the city's legal department advised its planning officials that they could not deny approval of subdivision to hold down the cost of acquisition. The planning director then advised other agencies to deny additional permits that were necessary to complete the project. The court found a taking had occurred.

---

*See also* Benenson v. United States, 548 F.2d 939 (Ct. Cl. 1977); Martino v. Santa Clara Valley Water Dist., 703 F.2d 1141 (9th Cir.), *cert. denied,* 464 U.S. 847 (1983).

**109.** Guinnane v. City & County of San Francisco, 241 Cal. Rptr. 787 (Cal. App. 1987), *cert. denied,* 488 U.S. 823 (1988). *Accord* Toso v. City of Santa Barbara, 162 Cal. Rptr. 210 (Cal. App.), *cert. denied,* 449 U.S. 801 (1980); Sproul Homes v. State Dep't of Highways, 611 P.2d 620 (Nev. 1980).

**110.** City of Conway v. Housing Auth., 584 S.W.2d 10 (Ark. 1979); Kissinger v. City of Los Angeles, 327 P.2d 10 (1958); Hermanson v. Board of County Comm'rs, 595 P.2d 694 (Colo. App. 1979); Carl M. Freeman Assocs. v. State Roads Comm'n, 250 A.2d 250 (Md. 1969); Riggs v. Township of Long Beach, 538 A.2d 808 (N.J. 1988). *See* 76 A.L.R.3d 751, 761-78 (1971). *Compare* Mira Dev. Co. v. City of San Diego, 252 Cal. Rptr. 825 (Cal. App. 1988) (rezoning denial not done to depress property values); Carl Bolander & Sons v. City of Minneapolis, 378 N.W.2d 826 (Minn. App. 1985) (moratorium on development not adopted to depress property values); Department of Transp. v. Lundberg, 825 P.2d 641 (Or.) (sidewalk dedication requirement did not depress value of property), *cert. denied,* 506 U.S. 975 (1992); Howell Plaza, Inc. v. State Hwy. Comm'n, 284 N.W.2d 887 (Wis. 1979) (adopts rule but taking not found).

**111.** 528 S.W.2d 266 (Tex. Civ. App. 1975). *Accord* State ex rel. Senior Estates v. Clarke, 530 S.W.2d 30 (Mo. App. 1975); Winepol v. Town of Hempstead, 300 N.Y.S.2d 197 (Sup. Ct. 1969). *But see* City of Walnut Creek v. Leadership Hous. Sys., Inc., 140 Cal. Rptr. 690 (Cal. App. 1977) (taking not found when city refused to approve development permit for land shown on open space plan and filed action to condemn it).

### § 2.34. "As-applied" Cases Claiming "Confiscation" or a Diminution in Value.

State courts regularly decide cases in which a landowner claims a zoning restriction has "confiscated" her land or caused a diminution in value. These cases have a distinct litigation setting. The municipality zoned the property for a restrictive use and the landowner wishes to put her land to a more intensive use. She claims that the restrictive zoning as applied to her land is a taking. The courts in these cases do not always apply taking theory. If they hold that a land use restriction is unconstitutional as applied, they may strike it down as "arbitrary and capricious." Because landowners in these cases attack the zoning "line," courts sometimes call them "line-drawing" cases.

Judicial taking analysis in these "as-applied" cases is accompanied by a number of well-established rules that favor the constitutionality of the land use restriction. These rules reflect standard judicial attitudes described earlier[112] that are typical of most state courts. One rule the courts usually apply places the burden on the property owner to prove that the zoning restriction is unconstitutional.[113] The restriction is not a taking just because the property owner wishes to put her property to a more profitable use. *Robinson v. City of Bloomfield Hills*[114] is a leading case adopting a highly deferential judicial review standard in a line-drawing case:

> But many of the cases coming to us involve merely the legislative judgment. They are the peripheral problems (should the line be drawn here, or there?) and the allegations of more advantageous use, with its corollary of "confiscation" (the property is worth more if devoted to some other use). Save in the most extreme instances, involving clearly whimsical action, we will not disturb the legislative judgment.[115]

Although a substantial diminution in value is a factor the courts may consider,[116] a majority of state courts find a taking only if the landowner cannot make any economically viable use of her land under the zoning restriction.[117]

---

**112.** § 1.13. *See* Tilles v. Town of Huntington, 547 N.E.2d 90 (N.Y. 1989) (landowner attacking residential zoning failed to rebut presumption of constitutionality).

**113.** City of Phoenix v. Beall, 524 P.2d 1314 (Ariz. App. 1974); Northern Westchester Professional Park Assocs. v. Town of Bedford, 458 N.E.2d 809 (N.Y. 1983); Lakewood Dev. Co. v. Oklahoma City, 534 P.2d 23 (Okla. App. 1975); Tillo v. City of Sioux Falls, 147 N.W.2d 128 (S.D. 1966).

**114.** 86 N.W.2d 166 (Mich. 1957).

**115.** *Id.* at 172.

**116.** Galt v. Cook County, 91 N.E.2d 395 (Ill. 1950); Alsensas v. Brecksville, 281 N.E.2d 21 (Ohio App. 1972).

**117.** Maider v. Town of Dover, 306 N.E.2d 274 (Mass. App. 1974); Krause v. City of Royal Oak, 160 N.W.2d 769 (Mich. App. 1968); Megin Realty Corp. v. Baron, 387 N.E.2d 618 (N.Y.

State courts usually decide whether an economically viable use of the land is possible by determining whether the use allowed by the zoning ordinance is reasonable in the area in which it is located. A court may characterize the zoning restriction as "confiscatory" if it holds that an economically viable use of the land is not possible. The U.S. Supreme Court will find a per se taking in this situation.[118]

*Stevens v. Town of Huntington*[119] illustrates the state court approach in these cases. The municipality downzoned to residential use a tract of land in an area of mixed uses. The tract was surrounded on three sides by extensive commercial development, including a shopping center, and on one side by a residentially zoned area. This area contained only one residential dwelling. The rest of this area was to be used for storing electronic equipment, a permitted use in the residential zone. As the court put it, the restricted tract was "immersed in a well-travelled, highly commercial shopping area."

The municipality defended the downzoning as necessary to maintain the character of the adjacent residentially zoned area and to avoid traffic congestion, but the court held the downzoning unconstitutional. "These aims, admirable as they may be, have the effect of depriving a property owner of making any reasonable use of his property."[120] The presence of adjacent commercial uses made the land unsuitable for residential development.

The dissent saw the matter differently:

> Although the court is acting upon words having heavy implications of invalidity, such as "confiscatory," . . . the issue in actuality amounts to a routine controversy turning on a difference of opinion between local zoning officials and property owners on zoning classifications. The merits are arguable either way, but it takes more than that to invalidate a zoning restriction.[121]

*Stevens* illustrates a typical "line-drawing" case in which the area surrounding the restrictively zoned property is mixed. Courts in these cases must determine the dominant character of the surrounding area in order to decide whether the ordinance is a taking as applied to the restricted land. As the opinions in *Stevens*

---

1979). As-applied attack on zoning restriction rejected: Terminals Equip. Co. v. City & Cty. of San Francisco, 270 Cal. Rptr. 329 (Cal. App. 1990); Gerchen v. City of Ladue, 784 S.W.2d 232 (Mo. App. 1989); Buskey v. Town of Hanover, 577 A.2d 406 (N.H. 1990); Columbia Oldsmobile, Inc. v. City of Montgomery, 564 N.E.2d 455 (Ohio 1990), *cert. denied,* 501 U.S. 1231 (1991). *But see* Reuschenberg v. Town of Huntington, 532 N.Y.S.2d 148 (App. Div. 1988) (need not show deprivation of all use if restriction invalid as discriminatory).

**118.** § 2.17.

**119.** 229 N.E.2d 591 (N.Y. 1967).

**120.** *Id.* at 593.

**121.** *Id.* at 595. *See* Grimpel Assocs. v. Cohalan, 361 N.E.2d 1022 (N.Y. 1977) (zoning island case). *Compare* McGowan v. Cohalan, 361 N.E.2d 1025 (N.Y. 1977).

indicate, this determination is not always easy. The majority viewed the residentially restricted property as a "zoning island" and struck down the ordinance. The dissent believed the case raised a debatable line-drawing issue and would have applied the presumption of validity to uphold the zoning restriction.

The Supreme Court's decision in *Lucas* raises some concern about state court takings rules because the Court ruled a per se taking occurs when a landowner is denied all use of his property. State courts, however, have held their takings rules that find a taking in this situation are the equivalent of the Supreme Court's per se rule.[122]

### § 2.35. Balancing and Multi-Factor Tests.

Some state courts apply a balancing test in taking cases in which they weigh the diminution in value of the property against the benefit of the zoning restriction to the community.[123] Balancing often is implicit rather than explicit. The court explicitly applied the balancing test in *State v. Pacesetter Constr. Co.*[124] It rejected taking objections to a state statute restricting the height of buildings in coastal areas to prevent a loss of view. The court applied the balancing test even though it recognized criticisms that the test only considers legislative purpose and disregards the economic impact of the regulation. Other state courts applied the balancing test to uphold environmentally protective land use regulation.[125]

The Illinois Supreme Court adopted a multi-factor test for as-applied cases in *LaSalle Nat'l Bank v. County of Cook.*[126] The six *LaSalle* factors are: (1) the existing uses and zoning of nearby property; (2) the extent to which property values are diminished by the particular zoning restriction; (3) the extent to which the destruction of property value promotes health, safety, morals, or general welfare purposes; (4) the relative gain to the public as compared to the hardship of the individual property owner; (5) the suitability of the property for the zoned use; and (6) the length of time the property has been vacant as zoned. Note the mixture of diminution in value, substantive due process, and balancing criteria. The *LaSalle* factors are a call for active judicial intervention. The Illinois courts

---

122. Bauer v. Waste Management, 662 A.2d 1179 (Conn. 1995); Security Mgt. Corp. v. Baltimore County, 655 A.2d 1326 (Md. App. 1995), *cert. denied,* 116 S. Ct. 917 (1996); Zealy v. City of Waukesha, 548 N.W.2d 528 (Wis. 1996).

123. § 2.35. *See* White v. City of Brentwood, 799 S.W.2d 890 (Mo. App. 1990) (applying balancing test).

124. 571 P.2d 196 (Wash. 1977). *See* Orion Corp. v. State (II), 747 P.2d 1062 (Wash. 1987).

125. Pope v. City of Atlanta, 249 S.E.2d 16 (Ga. 1978); Krahl v. Nine Mile Creek Watershed Dist., 283 N.W.2d 538 (Minn. 1979). *But see* Northern Westchester Professional Park Assocs. v. Town of Bedford, 458 N.E.2d 809 (N.Y. 1983).

126. 145 N.E.2d 65 (Ill. 1957).

often find for landowners when they attack zoning restrictions as an as-applied taking. A few other states have adopted the *LaSalle* factors.[127]

## § 2.36. The "Whole Parcel" Rule.

An important issue in land use taking law is the application of the "whole parcel" rule to taking claims. The rule originated with *Penn Central*,[128] which held that courts must decide taking claims by considering the impact of a land use restriction on an entire parcel. Later Supreme Court cases affirmed this rule.[129] The "whole parcel" rule took on more importance after the Supreme Court's decision in *Lucas*.[130] Because the Court held a denial of all economically viable use is a taking, determining the parcel that is the basis for a taking claim is critical.

Determining the geographic extent of a parcel is the most difficult "whole parcel" problem. The courts have not been consistent in making this determination, but an important factor is whether the property was purchased at one time and is under single ownership. In taking cases of this type that challenge zoning ordinances, the courts tend to treat the entire property as the whole parcel, even though different parts of the property are zoned differently.[131]

When more than one parcel is involved, courts tend to take a more flexible approach. Although the factors considered vary, the underlying principle is one of fairness. In one wetlands case, for example, the court held it would consider factors such as the degree of contiguity, dates of acquisition, the extent to which the parcel was treated as a single parcel, and the extent to which the regulated lands enhance the value of the remaining lands. The court added that "no doubt many others would enter into the calculus."[132] Courts may also apply these fac-

---

**127.** Guhl v. Holcomb Bridge Road Corp., 232 S.E.2d 830 (Ga. 1977); Landau v. City Council, 767 P.2d 1290 (Kan. 1989) (court adopts deferential review standards and holds Golden factors only suggestive); Par Mar v. City of Parkersburg, 398 S.E.2d 532 (W.Va. 1990) (applies La Salle factors to as-applied taking attack).

**128.** § 2.13.

**129.** § 2.16 (discussing *Keystone* decision).

**130.** § 2.17.

**131.** Ramona Convent of the Holy Name v. City of Alhambra, 26 Cal. Rptr. 2d 140 (Cal. App. 1993) (same zoning on entire parcel), *cert. denied,* 115 S. Ct. 315 (1994); FIC Homes of Blackstone, Inc. v. Conservation Comm'n, 673 N.E.2d 61 (Mass. App. 1996) (wetlands; 38 parcels purchased at one time); Bevan v. Brandon Township, 475 N.W.2d 37 (Mich. 1991) (same), *cert. denied,* 502 U.S. 1060 (1992); Quirk v. Town of New Boston, 663 A.2d 1328 (N.H. 1995) (part of property zoned as buffer); Zealy v. City of Waukesha, 548 N.W.2d 528 (Wis. 1996) (two zones on property). *Contra* Twain Harte Assocs. v. County of Tuolumne, 265 Cal. Rptr. 737 (Cal. App. 1990) (two zones on property).

**132.** Ciampitti v. United States, 22 Cl. Ct. 310 (1991) (lots held not separate when lots treated as single parcel for purpose of purchase and financing).

tors to single parcels in one ownership. These factors have led courts to broad[133] or narrow[134] definitions of the "whole parcel" affected by the taking claim. Narrowing the parcel, of course, increases the possibility that a taking claim will be successful.

## § 2.37. Delay as a Taking.

As *First English* indicated, unreasonable delay during the land use decision-making process may be a temporary taking. As the Supreme Court has also stated, mere fluctuations in the value of property during the government's decision-making process, absent extraordinary delay, are incidents of ownership and do not give rise to a taking.[135] In most of the cases, courts have held that prolonged governmental decision making that temporarily deprives a landowner of the use of his property is not an "extraordinary delay" giving rise to a taking of property.[136]

The key factor in evaluating the reasonableness of a delay in decision making is whether it is extraordinary.[137] No set standard exists to identify an extraordinary delay. Courts evaluate the lengths of delay on an ad hoc basis. In *Dufau v. United States*,[138] for example, the court held a sixteen-month delay was not long enough under the circumstances to constitute a temporary taking of the plaintiff's 70 acres of wetlands.

Courts give extreme deference to the actions of government officials in temporary taking cases.[139] They presume government officials carry out their duties

---

**133.** Broadwater Farms Joint Venture v. United States, 35 Fed. Cl. 232 (1996) (wetlands; single parcel); Tabb Lakes, Ltd. v. United States, 10 F.3d 796 (Fed. Cir. 1993) (same); Deltona Corp. v. United States, 657 F.2d 1184 (Ct. Cl. 1981) (same), *cert. denied*, 455 U.S. 1017 (1982); Volkema v. Department of Natural Resources, 542 N.W.2d 282 (Mich. App. 1995) (same).

**134.** Loveladies Harbor, Inc. v. United States, 28 F.3d 1171 (Fed. Cir. 1994) (wetlands permit denial); Florida Rock Indus. v. United States, 18 F.3d 1560 (Fed. Cir. 1994) (same); K & K Constr., Inc. v. Department of Natural Resources, 551 N.W.2d 413 (Mich. App. 1996) (wetlands). *See also* American Savings and Loan Association v. County of Marin, 653 F.2d 364 (9th Cir. 1980) (zoning; case remanded).

**135.** Agins v. City of Tiburon, 477 U.S. 255, 286 n.9 (1980).

**136.** Tabb Lakes, Ltd. v. United States, 10 F.3d 796 (Fed. Cir. 1993); Guinanne v. San Francisco, 241 Cal. Rptr. 787 (Cal. App. 1988); McCutchan Estates v. Evansville-Vanderburgh County Airport, 580 N.E.2d 339 (Ind. App. 1991).

**137.** Lachney v. United States, 22 Env't Rep. Cas. (BNA) 2031 (Fed. Cir. 1985) (two-year delay not extraordinary); 1902 Atlantic Ltd. v. United States, 26 Cl. Ct. 575 (Cl. Ct. 1992) (five-year delay held cost of doing business in regulated society); Philric Assocs. v. South Portland, 595 A.2d 1061 (Me. 1991) (two years deemed adequate to consider subdivision application); Hutchinson v. City of Huntington, 479 S.E.2d 649 (W. Va, 1996) (four months not unreasonable).

**138.** Dufau v. United States, 22 Cl. Ct. 156 (Cl. Ct. 1990).

**139.** Bello v. Walker, 840 F.2d 1124 (3d Cir. 1988) (seven-month delay did not constitute taking); 1902 Atlantic Ltd. v. United States, 26 Cl. Ct. 575 (Cl. Ct. 1992).

in good faith, and it requires a "well-nigh irrefragable proof" to overcome this presumption.[140] Despite unreasonable, lengthy, and even unlawful delays, courts attribute the actions of zoning administrators to the normal workings of governmental legal processes.[141] Courts also require plaintiffs to show that government delay denied them substantially all economically viable uses of their property.[142]

### § 2.38. State Takings Legislation.

A number of states have been active in considering and enacting takings legislation, and at least 20 states have adopted takings legislation so far. Some of this legislation is based on a takings Executive Order issued by President Reagan in 1988 that requires a "takings impact analysis" by federal agencies on actions that might generate a takings claim.[143] Most of these laws apply only to state agencies and require a takings assessment, or in some states an impact statement, on agency rules and regulations.[144] The agency carries out the assessment in most states, but in a few, the attorney general conducts the review. Some statutes contain a list of factors to be included in a checklist, which becomes the basis for the takings assessment. A few laws require takings assessments by local governments, but the state guidelines are only advisory. Most of the statutes do not specify any legal consequences if a takings assessment is not done.

A few state takings acts go beyond takings impact analysis and require compensation for takings. Florida legislation requires compensation when a regulation places an "inordinate burden" on property. An inordinate burden exists if a property owner is unable to attain the reasonable investment-backed expectations to an existing or vested use of the property or, in the alternative, if the owner must permanently bear "a disproportionate share of a burden imposed for the good of the public, which in fairness should be borne by the public at large."[145]

---

**140.** Dufau v. United States, 22 Cl. Ct. 156, 164 (Cl. Ct. 1990).

**141.** Philric Assocs. v. South Portland, 595 A.2d 1061 (Me. 1991); First Peoples Bank v. Medford, 599 A.2d 1248 (N.J. 1991); Old Tuckaway Assocs. Ltd. Partnership v. City of Greenfield, 509 N.W.2d 323 (Wis. App. 1993).

**142.** Tabb Lakes v. United States, 10 F.3d 796 (D.C. Cir. 1993).

**143.** Executive Order 12630, 53 Fed. Reg. 8859 (1988).

**144.** *E.g.,* Idaho Code §§ 67-8001 to 67-8004; Ind. Code Ann. § 4-22-32; Mont. Code Ann. §§ 2-20-104, 2-10-105; Tenn. Code Ann. §§ 12-1-203 to 12-1-206; Utah Code Ann. §§ 63-90-1 to 63-90-4; W. Va. Code §§ 22-1A-1 to 22-1A-6.

**145.** Fla. Stat. Ann. § 70.001. *See also* Tex. Gov't Code § 2007.001 et seq. (compensation for 25% reduction in value).

## B. SUBSTANTIVE DUE PROCESS.

### § 2.39. The Substantive Due Process Problem.

Land use controls must satisfy the substantive limitations imposed on land use regulation by the due process clause. Courts interpret this clause to mean that land use controls must advance legitimate governmental interests that serve the public health, safety, morals, and general welfare. State zoning legislation restates these purposes as the guiding objectives in land use regulation. The general welfare predominates in this litany of police power nouns. Whether land use regulation serves the general welfare is the major substantive due process question.

Substantive due process overlaps other constitutional limitations on land use regulations. In taking cases, for example, the U.S. Supreme Court requires a similar showing that a land use regulation must advance a legitimate governmental interest. Equal protection doctrine demands that an appropriate public purpose must justify zoning and other land use classifications. The overlap with substantive due process is clear.

Substantive due process objections to the purposes of land use regulations do not usually succeed. The Supreme Court has approved the governmental purposes advanced by most land use regulations, including landmark preservation, and open space and residential zoning.[146] State courts have also been receptive. For example, a majority approve aesthetic zoning, which once presented serious substantive due process problems.[147] However, federal and state courts can also use substantive due process to strike down abusive land use regulations and practices.

Substantive due process problems in federal and state courts, as they arise in land use regulation cases, are discussed throughout this book. This Part provides an overview of substantive due process doctrine in the federal courts. It first discusses Supreme Court cases that upheld the constitutionality of comprehensive zoning and zoning regulations that define the type of family permitted in single-family residential districts. It then discusses lower federal court cases that apply substantive due process cases to land use cases. As the discussion will show, some federal courts are reluctant to apply substantive due process to land use regulations.

---

146. Nollan v. California Coastal Comm'n, 483 U.S. 825, 834 (1987).
147. § 11.02.

## § 2.40.  Supreme Court Decisions.

### § 2.41.  *Euclid.*

*Village of Euclid v. Ambler Realty Co.*[148] is a major landmark Supreme Court case, decided in 1926, that upheld a residential district in a comprehensive zoning ordinance that excluded nonresidential and multi-family uses. These exclusions raised equal protection and substantive due process problems.

*Euclid* upheld these exclusions by looking to nuisance law as "a fairly helpful clew" in zoning cases. It applied the rule from nuisance cases that the acceptability of a land use designation depends on "the circumstances and the locality." "A nuisance may be merely a right thing in the wrong place — like a pig in the parlor instead of the barnyard."[149] The Court held that the exclusion of nonresidential uses presented "no difficulty" because it increased the safety and security of home life and reduced street accidents. The apartment exclusion was more difficult, probably because the nuisance cases had not considered the exclusion of apartment houses from residential districts. To justify the apartment house exclusion, the Court adopted a "parasite" theory to describe the effect of apartment houses on residential areas. Apartment houses, the court held, destroyed areas devoted to single-family use, interfered with light and air, and attracted large numbers of automobiles that block public streets.

The Supreme Court clearly had a model of apartment development in mind when it wrote these words. Apartments in that day were built on single lots, towered over adjacent homes and did not provide off-street parking. Modern apartment developments in the typical "garden apartment" complex avoid all of these problems. Some courts still accept[150] but some reject the *Euclid* characterization of apartment development.[151]

Although the Court's decision upholding the exclusion of multi-family dwellings is clear, the basis on which municipalities can make this exclusion is not clear. *Euclid* relied primarily on density, height, and parking problems presented by multi-family dwellings to uphold their exclusion from residential districts. This analysis suggests that the differences between apartments and other residential dwellings is a density and bulk problem, but the state courts treat this separation as a problem in use classification. This characterization is questionable, now that apartment development no longer fits the *Euclid* model. The exclusion of multi-family dwellings from residential districts remains an important and troublesome land use issue.

---

148. 272 U.S. 365 (1926). *See* § 2.12.

149. *Id.* at 388.

150. Krause v. City of Royal Oak, 160 N.W.2d 769 (Mich. App. 1968).

151. Allred v. City of Raleigh, 173 S.E.2d 533 (N.C. App. 1970), *rev'd on other grounds,* 178 S.E.2d 432 (N.C. 1971).

### § 2.42. *Belle Terre* and *Moore*.

The Supreme Court did not consider a residential zoning case for almost fifty years until it handed down its decision in *Village of Belle Terre v. Boraas*.[152] A zoning ordinance in a small suburban residential community near New York City defined a "family" as no more than two unrelated individuals. Plaintiffs, who rented their home to six unrelated college students, challenged this definition on several constitutional grounds, some of which suggested a substantive due process violation. They claimed, for example, that the definition was unconstitutional because "social homogeneity is not a legitimate interest of government."

The Court upheld the ordinance in an opinion by Justice Douglas. He did not separate the due process and equal protection problems, but he clearly held that the definition did not violate substantive due process:

> The regimes of boarding houses, fraternity houses and the like present urban problems. More people occupy a given space; more cars continuously pass by; more cars are parked; noise travels with crowds. A quiet place where yards are wide, people few, and motor vehicles restricted are legitimate guidelines in a land use project addressed to family needs.

> This goal is a permissible one within *Berman v. Parker*. . . . The police power . . . is ample to lay out zones where family values, youth values, and the blessings of quiet seclusion, and clean air make the area a sanctuary for people.[153]

*Berman v. Parker*[154] was an urban renewal decision written by Justice Douglas. It contains a much-quoted dictum that defines the "public welfare" to include spiritual and aesthetic as well as physical values.

*Belle Terre* does not provide a satisfactory link between the limitation in the zoning ordinance on the number of unrelated individuals who can live together and the broad social objectives Justice Douglas endorsed. One interpretation of the decision is that the due process clause justifies zoning ordinances that distinguish between different types of families, a holding some state courts reject.[155]

The Supreme Court qualified *Belle Terre* in *Moore v. City of East Cleveland*.[156] *Moore* struck down a local housing code that restricted the number of related individuals who could live together, but the decision also applies to zoning ordinances. The Court distinguished *Belle Terre* but could not produce a

---

**152.** 416 U.S. 1 (1974).
**153.** *Id.* at 9.
**154.** 348 U.S. 26 (1954).
**155.** § 5.03.
**156.** 431 U.S. 494 (1977).

majority opinion. The plurality opinion made the point that the restriction in *Belle Terre* applied only to unrelated rather than related individuals.

The Court clearly viewed *Moore* as a substantive due process case, but the opinions were troubled by this latter-day attempt to invoke the substantive due process clause. Not for some time had the Supreme Court struck down a police power regulation as a violation of substantive due process. The plurality noted, quite properly, that the restriction on related individuals living together did little to meet legitimate community objectives, such as the prevention of overcrowding and traffic congestion. Yet it viewed substantive due process as a "treacherous field" and struck down the ordinance because it interfered with the sanctity of the family.

### § 2.43. In the Lower Federal Courts.

Whether the substantive due process clause is still a viable basis for challenging land use regulations and decisions in federal court has become somewhat uncertain. The Seventh Circuit has especially taken a negative view on the application of substantive due process in land use cases.[157] The Supreme Court has held that substantive due process claims may not be made if another more specific constitutional claim is available, such as the Fourth Amendment.[158] In zoning cases, this decision means a plaintiff cannot make a substantive due process claim when another constitutional claim is available, such as a taking claim. Some circuits have rejected this rule in zoning cases,[159] but others have not agreed.[160] The Eleventh Circuit does not apply substantive due process to claims to executive denials of a state-created property right, such as the denial of a license for a legal nonconforming use.[161]

The lower federal courts also disagree on whether a plaintiff must have an entitlement before she can bring a substantive due process claim in a land use case. The entitlement rule means that, as in procedural due process cases,[162] a plaintiff must show it is entitled to a land use or land use approval because the land use agency does not have the discretion to deny the use. Cases requiring an

---

**157.** Coniston Corp. v. Village of Hoffman Estates, 844 F.2d 461 (7th Cir. 1988).

**158.** Graham v. Connor, 490 U.S. 386 (1990) (Fourth Amendment claim). *See also* Collins v. City of Harker Heights, 503 U.S. 115 (1992) (suggesting substantive due process clause has limited application in constitutional adjudication).

**159.** Tri County Indus., Inc. v. District of Columbia, 104 F.3d 455 (D.C. Cir. 1997); Pearson v. City of Grand Blanc, 961 F.2d 1211 (6th Cir. 1992).

**160.** Sinclair Oil Corp. v. County of Santa Barbara, 96 F.3d 401 (9th Cir. 1996). *See also* Bickerstaff Clay Prods. Co. v. Harris County, 89 F.3d 1481 (11th Cir. 1996) (substantive due process police power limitation subsumed within taking clause). *Accord* Miller v. Campbell County, 945 F.2d 348 (10th Cir. 1991) (non-zoning case), *cert. denied,* 502 U.S. 1096 (1992).

**161.** DeKalb Stone, Inc. v. County of DeKalb, 106 F.3d 956 (11th Cir. 1997).

**162.** § 2.45.

entitlement refuse to find one when the land use agency has the discretion to disapprove a land use proposal.[163] Other cases do not require an entitlement,[164] or either assume an entitlement exists or do not discuss this issue.[165]

There also is considerable disagreement in the lower federal courts over the substantive due process standard to be applied in zoning cases. The question is whether the traditional rational relationship standard applies, or whether there must be a stronger showing, such as whether a municipality's conduct "shocked the conscience" of the court.[166]

Plaintiffs frequently claim a denial of a permit or some other land use approval violated substantive due process. Some circuits apply the relaxed standard of substantive due process review to uphold these denials.[167] Other lower federal courts have found substantive due process violations when municipalities have arbitrarily withheld a building permit or other approval or have refused approval for political or other improper reasons.[168]

## C. PROCEDURAL DUE PROCESS.

### § 2.44. The Procedural Due Process Problem.

Administrative decision making in the land use control process must meet procedural due process requirements. The due process clause of the federal con-

---

**163.** Triomphe Investors v. City of Northwood, 49 F.3d 198 (6th Cir.) (city had discretion to deny special use permit), *cert. denied,* 116 S. Ct. 70 (1995); Sylvia Dev. Co. v. Calvert County, 48 F.3d 810 (4th Cir. 1995) (approval of transfer zone); Gardner v. City of Baltimore, 969 F.2d 63 (4th Cir. 1992); MacKenzie v. City of Rockledge, 920 F.2d 1554 (11th Cir. 1991); Spence v. Zimmerman, 873 F.2d 256 (11th Cir. 1989); R.R.I. Realty Corp. v. Village of Southampton, 870 F.2d 911 (2d Cir.), *cert. denied,* 493 U.S. 893 (1989). *See also* Kelley Prop. Dev. Co. v. Town of Lebanon, 627 A.2d 909 (Conn. 1993) (adopts entitlement rule).

**164.** De Blasio v. Board of Zoning Adjustment, 53 F.2d 592 (3d Cir. 1995); Coniston Corp. v. Village of Hoffman Homes, 844 F.2d 461 (7th Cir. 1988).

**165.** Jacobs, Visconsi & Jacobs v. City of Lawrence, 927 F.2d 1111 (10th Cir. 1991) (rezoning); G.M. Eng'rs & Assocs., Inc. v. West Bloomfield Township, 922 F.2d 328 (6th Cir. 1990) (lot split); Scott v. Greenville County, 716 F.2d 1409 (4th Cir. 1983) (vested right).

**166.** *See* Pearson v. City of Grand Blanc, 961 F.2d 1211 (6th Cir. 1992) (reviewing standards applied in the federal circuits). *See also* Kawaoka v. City of Arroyo Grande, 17 F.3d 1227 (9th Cir. 1994); Chesterfield Dev. Corp. v. City of Chesterfield, 963 F.2d 1102 (8th Cir. 1992).

**167.** Anderson v. Douglas County, 4 F.3d 574 (8th Cir. 1993) (conditional use permit), *cert. denied,* 510 U.S. 1113 (1994); Corn v. City of Lauderdale Lakes, 997 F.2d 1369 (11th Cir. 1993) (denial of shopping center development), *cert. denied,* 114 S. Ct. 1400 (1994); Neston Colon Medina & Sucesores, Inc. v. Custodio, 964 F.2d 32 (1st Cir. 1992) (landfill and tourist complex).

**168.** Resolution Trust Corp. v. Town of Highland Beach, 18 F.3d 1536 (11th Cir. 1994) (denial of vested right to develop); Marks v. City of Chesapeake, 883 F.2d 308 (4th Cir. 1989) (neighborhood opposition); Bateson v. Geisse, 857 F.2d 1300 (9th Cir. 1988) (municipality refused to issue building permit when all requirements met); Brady v. Town of Colchester, 863 F.2d 205 (2d Cir. 1988) (refusal to issue site plan or certificate of occupancy).

stitution includes a procedural as well as a substantive requirement and requires constitutionally acceptable procedures in administrative decision making. State zoning legislation requires minimum procedures, such as a notice and hearing. State courts impose additional procedural requirements, such as findings of fact on variance decisions, but they do not usually base these requirements on the constitution.

### § 2.45. In the Federal Courts.

Procedural due process protections apply if a land use decision is administrative or quasi-judicial rather than legislative. The federal courts treat zonings and rezonings as legislative. In *Rogin v. Bensalem Township*,[169] the court held a downzoning was legislative and said:

> The act of legislating necessarily entails political trading, compromise, and ad hoc decision making which, in the aggregate, produce policies that at least approximate a fair and equitable distribution of social resources and obligations.[170]

The court indicated it would hold a land use decision administrative only if it "inherently treats a particular class of persons inequitably." Although a general plan amendment is usually held legislative, the Ninth Circuit held a plan amendment adjudicative because it reclassified a single parcel of land to a more restrictive use and was directed solely to that landowner.[171]

Even if a land use decision is administrative, procedural due process requirements apply in the federal courts only if a landowner has an entitlement to a property interest protected by state law rather than a mere expectancy. This problem arises when a landowner claims a procedural due process violation occurred when a land use agency or official denied his application for a land use permit or approval. Whether a landowner has an expectancy rather than an entitlement depends on whether the decision on his application requires an exercise of discretion by the agency or official. The courts have held that variances, exceptions, and subdivision and similar approvals are discretionary.[172]

---

**169.** 616 F.2d 580 (3d Cir. 1980), *cert. denied,* 450 U.S. 1029 (1981). *Accord* Pro-Eco, Inc. v. Board of Comm'rs, 57 F.3d 305 (7th Cir.), *cert. denied,* 116 S. Ct. 672 (1995); Jackson Court Condominiums, Inc. v. City of New Orleans, 874 F.2d 1070 (5th Cir. 1989).

**170.** 616 F.2d at 693.

**171.** Harris v. County of Riverside, 904 F.2d 497 (9th Cir. 1990). *Accord,* Naierowski Bros. Inv. Co. v. City of Sterling Heights, 949 F.2d 890 (6th Cir. 1992).

**172.** Sylvia Dev. Co. v. Calvert County, 48 F.3d 810 (4th Cir. 1995) (rezoning); Jacobs, Visconsi & Jacobs v. City of Lawrence, 927 F.2d 1111 (10th Cir. 1991) (rezoning; federal court not bound by state determination of what is legislative); Bateson v. Geisse, 857 F.2d 1300 (9th Cir. 1988) (approval of plat); Yale Auto Parts, Inc. v. Jackson, 758 F.2d 54 (2d Cir. 1985) (junkyard permit).

The Supreme Court has adopted a three-part test to determine which procedural due process limitations apply when a landowner has an entitlement.[173] The courts have held that procedural due process is violated if a decision maker was biased.[174] They usually do not hold that decision making procedures violate procedural due process, but there are exceptions when procedures are clearly inadequate.[175]

### § 2.46. In the State Courts.

Procedural due process requirements in the state courts apply to administrative zoning decisions, such as decisions on variances.[176] They do not apply to zoning map amendments by local governing bodies in most states because the courts hold that these decisions are legislative. This characterization can lead to abuses in the zoning process. Members of governing bodies can make ex parte contacts outside the hearing, and participants in the hearing cannot challenge the information obtained through these contacts or cross-examine witnesses. The governing body can inhibit judicial review by making generalized findings of fact or by failing to make any findings at all.

*Fasano v. Board of County Comm'rs*,[177] a case challenging a mobile home rezoning, was the first case that attempted to correct these abuses by holding a rezoning quasi-judicial. The court held that ordinances laying down legislative policies were entitled to the usual constitutional presumptions. Ordinances applying these policies to individual properties were "an exercise of judicial

---

**173.** Mathews v. Eldridge, 424 U.S. 319, 335 (1976) (private interest affected; risk of erroneous deprivation of such interest and probable value of additional procedural safeguards; and government's interest, including fiscal and administrative burdens of additional safeguards).

**174.** Leverett v. Town of Limon, 567 F. Supp. 471 (D. Colo. 1983). *See* Withrow v. Larkin, 421 U.S. 35 (1976) (as found in licensing procedures).

**175.** Violation not found: First Assembly of God v. Collier County, 20 F.3d 419 (11th Cir. 1994) (deficiencies in notice of hearing); Anderson v. Douglas County, 4 F.3d 574 (8th Cir. 1993) (plaintiff failed to take advantage of available procedures), *cert. denied,* 510 U.S. 1113 (1994); Landmark Land Co. v. Buchanan, 874 F.2d 717 (10th Cir. 1989) (ex parte contacts); Chongris v. Board of Appeals, 811 F.2d 36 (1st Cir.) (notice and opportunity to be heard; no right of cross-examination), *cert. denied,* 483 U.S. 1021 (1987).
Violation found: Resolution Trust Corp. v. Town of Highland Beach, 18 F.3d 1536 (11th Cir. 1994) (notice inadequate); Harris v. County of Riverside, 904 F.2d 497 (9th Cir. 1990) (same); Herrington v. County of Sonoma, 857 F.2d 567 (9th Cir. 1988) (notice and hearing inadequate), *cert. denied,* 489 U.S. 1090 (1988).

**176.** §§ 6.40-6.52.

**177.** 507 P.2d 23 (Or. 1973). *See* Cherry Hills Resort Dev. Co. v. Cherry Hills Village, 757 P.2d 622 (Colo. 1988) (explaining nature of quasi-judicial actions in zoning and holding approval of PUD quasi-judicial); Snyder v. Board of Cty. Comm'rs, 627 So. 2d 469 (Fla. 1993) (adopts *Fasano* view).

authority" and subject to different tests. The mobile home rezoning fell in the second category.

*Fasano* has attracted a following in some states.[178] The most important recent case holding the zoning process quasi-judicial is *Snyder v. Board of County Comm'rs*.[179] The court held a denial of a rezoning quasi-judicial. The court held that "comprehensive rezonings affecting a large portion of the public are legislative." It concluded that rezonings are quasi-judicial when they affect a limited number of persons or property owners and identifiable parties and interests, when the decision is based on facts arrived at from distinct alternatives presented at a hearing, and when the decision can be functionally viewed as policy application. A holding that zoning decisions are quasi-judicial has important effects on judicial review, as review is on the record and the court may shift the burden of proof to the municipality to defend its zoning decision.

## D. EQUAL PROTECTION.

### § 2.47. The Equal Protection Problem.

Zoning and other land use regulations raise an equal protection problem because they classify land uses. Landowners can make two types of equal protection objections to zoning ordinances. They can object to classifications between land uses in the zoning ordinance text. They can also accept the textual classifications but object to the land use classifications made by the zoning map.

The first equal protection claim is a facial attack on the ordinance. The second is an attack on the zoning ordinance as applied. In a typical as-applied case, a landowner agrees that the zoning ordinance properly distinguishes between residential and commercial uses but claims that these classifications as applied by the zoning map violate equal protection. He may argue, for example, that the zoning map has improperly placed his land in a residential district because commercial zoning for his land is more appropriate. This is a typical "line-drawing" zoning case, discussed earlier as a taking problem. Often a court does not indicate whether it is considering a taking or an equal protection claim in cases of this kind.

Equal protection, as noted earlier, overlaps with substantive due process. The judicial review standard applied to legislative classifications affecting economic interests, such as zoning classifications, requires a rational relationship between the classification and a legitimate governmental objective. Courts apply a similar standard when land use regulations are challenged under the due process clause.

---

178. § 6.26.
179. 627 So. 2d 469 (Fla. 1996).

## § 2.48. Judicial Standards for Equal Protection Review.

The judicial review standard courts apply to equal protection claims differs depending on the interest affected by the legislative classification. The majority and dissenting opinions in *Village of Belle Terre v. Boraas*,[180] illustrate the different standards courts use in equal protection cases. In this case, the Court upheld a zoning ordinance that allowed no more than two unrelated persons to qualify as a "family" in a single-family zoning district. The majority opinion applied the relaxed rational relationship standard. Under this standard, a court will uphold a legislative classification if it finds any rational basis for its justification. State courts are more aggressive than the federal courts in their application of the rational relationship standard to zoning classifications.

The Supreme Court's *Euclid*[181] decision illustrates the application of the rational relationship standard to uphold the usual zoning district classifications in zoning ordinances. The Court upheld the exclusion of industrial and multi-family uses from single family residential districts. It held that any legislation needs "inclusion of a reasonable margin to insure effective enforcement," and that, in some fields, "the bad fades into the good by ... insensible degrees." The Court added that the exclusion of nonresidential uses from residential districts "bears a rational relation to the health and safety of the community."

The Supreme Court also applies a strict scrutiny standard in equal protection cases. To apply this standard, a court must find that the classification is suspect or that it burdens a fundamental interest. Racially discriminatory classifications are an example of suspect classifications subject to strict scrutiny review. In *Village of Arlington Heights v. Metropolitan Hous. Dev. Corp.*,[182] the Court held that a suburban refusal to adopt a rezoning to allow construction of a federally subsidized multi-family housing project was not racially discriminatory. The Court held that the equal protection clause requires proof of discriminatory racial intent rather than discriminatory racial effect as the basis for an equal protection zoning violation. The Court's discriminatory intent requirement makes it very difficult to find racial discrimination in zoning except in extreme cases.

Justice Marshall's dissenting opinion in *Belle Terre* illustrates the application of the more rigorous strict scrutiny standard when fundamental interests are affected. Justice Marshall believed that the exclusion of unrelated families with more than two members burdened a fundamental interest in privacy and association.

The strict scrutiny standard requires a compelling governmental interest to justify the classification, but the courts hardly ever find a governmental interest compelling. In *Belle Terre,* for example, Justice Marshall did not find a compel-

---

**180.** 416 U.S. 1 (1974). *See* § 2.37.
**181.** § 2.41.
**182.** 429 U.S. 252 (1977). *See* § 7.03.

ling governmental interest for the restriction on unrelated families. It did not achieve its goal of protecting residential neighborhoods because it did not prohibit large related families from living together. It prohibited large unrelated families from living together even though they did not impair residential quiet.

Justice Marshall's attempt to find fundamental interests in the zoning process has not borne fruit in the Supreme Court. Although the Court under Justice Warren created a number of fundamental interests entitled to strict scrutiny review, such as the right to vote, it has not extended these categories. The Court might have laid a foundation for strict scrutiny review in zoning cases had it found that the right to housing was a fundamental right. This holding would have applied strict scrutiny review to any zoning ordinance that restricted the right to housing opportunity. The Supreme Court dashed any hope that it might adopt this position in *Lindsey v. Normet*.[183] A state landlord-tenant law did not allow tenants to defend an eviction action by showing that their dwelling was uninhabitable. A tenant claimed this law violated equal protection because defenses in other civil actions were not subject to this restriction. The Court held that the federal constitution did not guarantee a right to housing and rejected this claim under the rational relationship standard.

The Supreme Court has adopted a middle-tier judicial review standard in equal protection cases when classifications are quasi-suspect. The middle-tier standard requires a legislative classification to bear a substantial rather than a necessary relationship to an important rather than a compelling governmental interest. The Court refused to apply this standard in a group home zoning case,[184] but one state court held that it applies to the judicial review of all zoning ordinances.[185]

### § 2.49. Applying the Rational Relationship Standard: The State Courts.

Since *Euclid*, the traditional zoning classifications have usually been safe from an equal protection attack in the state courts. They occasionally strike down underinclusive commercial zoning,[186] and several courts have invalidated exclusions of lower income housing, mobile homes, unrelated families, and group homes from residential districts.[187] These decisions do not always turn on the equal protection clause. The lower federal courts usually hold that most land use regulations and decisions do not violate the equal protection clause in the

---

183. 405 U.S. 56 (1972).
184. § 2.51.
185. Town of Chesterfield v. Brooks, 489 A.2d 600 (N.H. 1985).
186. § 5.32.
187. §§ 5.02-5.08, 7.07-7.25.

usual case where no suspect classification is claimed, or there is no claimed violation of a fundamental right.[188] The rational relationship standard applies.

Restrictive land use classifications adopted by zoning maps raise equal protection problems similar to the line-drawing problems considered in as-applied taking cases.[189] As in the taking cases, a court may defer to the municipality under the presumption of constitutionality and approve the zoning classification. A court can also take a more aggressive view and invalidate the zoning classification adopted by the zoning map even though the presumption applies.

A court's reaction to a zoning map classification may depend on whether the municipality adopted the classification as part of a comprehensive zoning ordinance. Assume a municipality wishes to distinguish between "heavy" and "light" commercial uses. It creates "limited" and "general" commercial use districts as part of a comprehensive rezoning. Automobile service stations are allowed in the general but not in the limited district. At a street intersection where the two districts meet, a service station is located on the southeast corner in a general commercial district. The southwest corner across the street is in the limited commercial district. Can the owner of the southwest corner, who wishes to construct a service station, claim that the ordinance violates equal protection? In *State ex rel. American Oil Co. v. Bessent,*[190] the court sustained a mapped zoning classification of this type. Although it was troubled by the distinction between the two districts, it was influenced by the adoption and mapping of the districts in a comprehensive zoning ordinance, which "rests upon the interdependency of adjoining parcels of land in a community."

A court may be less generous when the mapping is not comprehensive. In *City of Tulsa v. Swanson,*[191] the court struck down on the "physical facts" a one-lot zone for professional office uses that served as a buffer between commercial and residential development. The limited professional office zone was on a corner, and the court was skeptical of the use of streets as dividing lines.

Equal protection problems also arise from a municipality's administration of a zoning ordinance. Assume a municipality grants a number of multi-family rezonings on street corners adjacent to commercial development. A landowner then applies for a similar rezoning and is refused. May she claim an equal protection violation? Most courts do not find an equal protection violation in this

---

**188.** Sylvia Dev. Co. v. Calvert County, 48 F.3d 810 (4th Cir. 1995) (rezoning denial); Zahra v. Town of Southold, 48 F.3d 674 (2d Cir. 1995) (arbitrary enforcement); Anderson v. Douglas County, 4 F.3d 574 (8th Cir. 1993) (denial of conditional use permit), *cert. denied,* 510 U.S. 1113 (1994).

**189.** § 2.34.

**190.** 135 N.W.2d 317 (Wis. 1965).

**191.** 366 P.2d 629 (Okla. 1961). *Compare* Perron v. Village of New Brighton, 145 N.W.2d 425 (Minn. 1966); Carlson v. City of Bellevue, 435 P.2d 957 (Wash. 1968).

type of case. They hold that each zoning case depends on its own facts and refuse to bind the municipality by its earlier rezoning decisions.[192]

A few cases hold that as-applied attacks on zoning classifications are not appealable to the state's supreme court as-of-right as matters arising under the state constitution, even though the appeal is based on the equal protection clause. These cases treat the zoning classification problem as statutory rather than constitutional. As one case noted,[193] zoning legislation contains a clause that requires uniform regulations within zoning districts, and that an arbitrary classification in a zoning map violates this statutory requirement. It then held that "[w]hile these statutory prerequisites have loose constitutional connotations, the fundamental question here resolves itself into a matter of application of statutory standards to a particular fact situation under long established principles."

### § 2.50. Applying the Rational Relationship Standard: The Federal Courts.

The lower federal courts have usually applied the rational relationship standard to hold that land use regulations and decisions to not violate equal protection. In one group of cases, for example, the courts do not find an equal protection violation when a landowner is denied a zoning, site plan, subdivision or similar land use approval.[194] The federal courts have also rejected equal protection claims when a municipality prohibited a land use or restricted the area where a land use could be located,[195] and when claims were made that a land use ordinance was arbitrarily implemented or enforced.[196]

---

**192.** *See* Houston v. Board of City Comm'rs, 543 P.2d 1010 (Kan. 1975); Krause v. City of Royal Oak, 160 N.W.2d 769 (Mich. App. 1968); Ranken v. Lavine, 363 N.E.2d 343 (N.Y. 1977); State ex rel. Miller v. Cain, 242 P.2d 505 (Wash. 1952). *Compare* Aspen Hill Venture v. Montgomery County Council, 289 A.2d 303 (Md. App. 1972); Wilson v. Borough of Mountainside, 201 A.2d 540 (N.J. 1964). *But see* City of Birmingham v. Morris, 396 So. 2d 53 (Ala. 1981).

**193.** Tidewater Oil Co. v. Mayor and Council of Carteret, 209 A.2d 105, 108 (N.J. 1965). *Accord,* First Nat'l Bank & Trust Co. v. City of Evanston, 197 N.E.2d 705 (Ill. 1964).

**194.** Anderson v. Douglas County, 4 F.3d 574 (8th Cir. 1993), *cert. denied,* 114 S. Ct. 1059) (conditional use permit); Conti v. City of Fremont, 919 F.2d 1385 (9th Cir. 1990) (refusal to amend zoning permit); New Burnham Prairie Homes, Inc. v. Village of Burnham, 910 F.2d 2474 (7th Cir. 1990) (building permit); Studen v. Beebe, 588 F.2d 560 (6th Cir. 1978) (extension of nonconforming use).

**195.** Hayes v. City of Miami, 52 F.3d 918 (11th Cir. 1995); Howard v. City of Garland, 917 F.2d 898 (5th Cir. 1990); Greene v. Town of Blooming Grove, 879 F.2d 1061 (2d Cir. 1989); City of Highland Park v. Train, 519 F.2d 861 (7th Cir. 1977).

**196.** Crowley v. Courville, 76 F.3d 47 (2d Cir. 1996); Strickland v. Alderman, 74 F.3d 260 (11th Cir. 1996); Muckway v. Craft, 789 F.2d 517 (7th Cir. 1986); Kuzinich v. County of Santa Clara, 689 F.2d 1345 (9th Cir. 1982); Cook v. City of Price, 566 F.2d 699 (10th Cir. 1977).

## § 2.51. *Cleburne*: Reviving the Rational Relationship Standard.

In *City of Cleburne v. Cleburne Living Center,*[197] the Supreme Court reviewed a denial of a special use permit for a group home for the mentally retarded. The group home planned to locate in an "apartment house" district where the zoning ordinance required a special use permit for homes for the "insane or feeble-minded" and for alcoholics and drug addicts. It did not require a special use permit in this district for hospitals, sanatariums, nursing homes, or homes for convalescents or the aged.

The Court held the mentally retarded were not a quasi-suspect class that required middle-tier equal protection review.[198] It found there were legitimate reasons to distinguish the mentally retarded from other groups. It was difficult to claim they should all be treated alike because the mentally retarded, as a class, were very different from each other. Neither was there a principled basis for distinguishing other groups, such as the aged and mentally ill, who could also claim they were a quasi-suspect class because they were subject to public prejudice.

The Court also noted that federal and state legislation protected the mentally retarded, and that this legislation indicated they were not politically powerless. The Court pointed out that legislatures might not adopt protective legislation for the mentally retarded if courts subjected this legislation to stringent judicial review.

Although the Court did not invalidate the special permit requirement for the group home, it held the permit denial unconstitutional under the rational relationship standard. It pointed out that the zoning ordinance did not require a permit for similar uses in the district, but that the differences between these uses and a home for the mentally retarded were largely irrelevant to the city's legitimate zoning interests. Neither were the reasons for denying the permit acceptable. The city denied the permit because of neighborhood fears, but "mere negative attitudes" are not a sufficient reason. Nor were fears that nearby junior high school students might harass the group home residents. Objections that the group home would be overcrowded and located in a floodplain were not acceptable because the same objections applied to similar group homes the ordinance allowed without a permit.

*Cleburne* indicates that the Supreme Court will not apply the middle-tier standard of equal protection review to zoning ordinance classifications even though they disadvantage a vulnerable social group. Yet the reasons for holding legislative classifications quasi-suspect clearly influenced the Court's holding that the permit denial was unconstitutional under the rational relationship standard. Some lower federal courts have applied *Cleburne* to invalidate zoning re-

---

197. 473 U.S. 432 (1985).
198. § 2.48.

quirements for group homes and other uses that are vulnerable to discrimination in the zoning process.[199]

## E. FREE SPEECH.

### § 2.52. Application of the Free Speech Clause to Land Use Regulation.

The free speech clause has always covered land use regulations that affect noncommercial speech. An example is a sign ordinance that regulates signs with political or noncommercial messages. The Supreme Court extended the application of the free speech clause to land use regulation when it held in the mid-1970's that the free speech clause protects commercial speech.[200] A zoning ordinance that regulates adult book stores and movie theaters is an example of a land use ordinance that affects commercial speech. Another example is a sign ordinance that regulates signs with commercial messages. This section outlines the doctrines the Supreme Court applies to laws, such as land use regulations, that affect free speech. Later sections discuss the application of the free speech clause to land uses that raise free speech problems.[201]

Most land use ordinances that implicate the free speech clause regulate commercial speech. The Supreme Court reviews the constitutionality of these ordinances under a multi-part test, as modified in later cases, that it adopted in *Central Hudson Gas & Elec. Co. v. Public Serv. Comm'n.*[202] Under this test, the Court will uphold a land use regulation against free speech objections if (1) the governmental interest is substantial; (2) the regulation directly advances that governmental interest; and (3) The regulation is not more extensive than necessary to serve that interest. The *Central Hudson* tests are similar to the tests the courts impose under the substantive due process clause but are more rigorous. The *Central Hudson* tests effectively reverse the presumption of constitutionality

---

**199.** Bannum, Inc. v. City of Louisville, 958 F.2d 1354 (6th Cir. 1992) (conditional use permit for group homes); Cornerstone Bible Church v. City of Hastings, 948 F.2d 464 (8th Cir. 1991) (remanding claim that exclusion of church from central business district violated equal protection); Burstyn v. City of Miami Beach, 663 F. Supp. 528 (S.D. Fla. 1987) (zoning restrictions on housing for elderly); Kirsch v. Prince George's County, 626 A.2d 372 (Md.) (occupancy restrictions on student housing), *cert. denied,* 510 U.S. 1011 (1993). *Contra* Bannum, Inc. v. City of St. Charles, 2 F.3d 267 (8th Cir. 1993) (halfway house for convicted criminals); Freedom Ranch, Inc. v. Board of Adjustment, 878 P.2d 380 (Okla. App.) (denial of special exception for home for convicts nearing release), *cert. denied,* 115 S. Ct. 636 (1994).

**200.** Virginia State Bd. of Pharmacy v. Virginia Citizens Consumer Council, 425 U.S. 748 (1976); Bigelow v. Virginia, 421 U.S. 809 (1975).

**201.** §§ 5.53-5.58 (adult uses); § 6.59 (conditional uses); §§ 11.12-11.21 (signs).

**202.** 447 U.S. 557 (1980).

the courts usually apply to land use regulations.[203] There is some indication the Court may revise and make even more rigorous the tests it applies to regulations that affect commercial speech such as messages on signs.[204]

The Supreme Court applies the *Central Hudson* tests to what it calls time, place and manner regulations. A time, place, and manner regulation protects governmental interests other than the content of speech. The Supreme Court has adopted tests for time, place, and manner regulations that are similar to the tests it adopted for commercial speech in *Central Hudson*.[205] Land use regulations affecting commercial speech are often in this category, although they are usually hybrids. An example is a zoning ordinance that requires the spacing of adult movie theaters. The ordinance is a time, place, and manner regulation because it prevents the neighborhood deterioration that would result from the overconcentration of adult businesses in one neighborhood. The ordinance also regulates the content of speech because the content of the movies shown determines whether a movie theater is adult. The Supreme Court has upheld carefully tailored land use regulations that affect commercial speech by treating them as time, place, and manner regulations, despite their hybrid character.

Another important distinction the Supreme Court makes under the free speech clause is the distinction between a law affecting speech that is content-neutral and a law affecting speech that is viewpoint-neutral. A regulation is not viewpoint-neutral if it prohibits a point of view. An example is a sign ordinance prohibiting messages on signs that oppose nuclear power. A regulation is not content-neutral if it regulates the content of speech. An example is a sign ordinance that prohibits signs with any messages on nuclear power, no matter what point of view they take.[206]

The tests the Supreme Court applies to laws that are not content-neutral are more rigorous than the *Central Hudson* tests and more rigorous than the tests it applies to laws that are not viewpoint-neutral. If a law is not content-neutral, the

---

**203.** *But see* Board of Trustees v. Fox, 492 U.S. 469 (1989) (*Central Hudson* rules do not include "less restrictive alternative" test; Court requires only "reasonable fit" between legislative ends and means).

**204.** 44 Liquormart, Inc. v. State of Rhode Island, 116 S. Ct. 1495 (1996) (plurality opinion; indicating commercial speech doctrine does not apply when regulation prohibits "truthful, non-misleading commercial messages for reasons unrelated to the preservation of a fair bargaining process").

**205.** United States v. O'Brien, 391 U.S. 367 (1968).

**206.** Ward v. Rock Against Racism, 491 U.S. 781, 791 (1989) (principal inquiry in determining content neutrality in speech and time, place, or manner cases is whether government has adopted regulation of speech because of disagreement with message it conveys; government's purpose is the controlling consideration).

Court requires government to justify its effect on free speech by a "compelling" rather than a "substantial" governmental interest.[207]

## F. THE CONTRACT CLAUSE.

### § 2.53. General Principles.

The Constitution provides: "No State shall pass any . . . Law impairing the Obligation of Contracts. . . ."[208] Although the contract clause is not often a factor in land use cases, a claim under the clause can sometimes be made. One example is the case of a developer who obtains an option on a property on which he plans a development that is permitted by the zoning ordinance. A contract clause claim may arise if the municipality downzones the property to impose a more restrictive classification.

The contract clause remained dormant for many years, but in *United States Trust Co. v. New Jersey*,[209] the Supreme Court held invalid a legislative repeal of a statutory covenant that prohibited the use of port authority revenues for mass transit subsidies. The contract clause is not an absolute bar to a land use regulation that impairs a contract. A court must first find that an impairment of a contract has occurred, but even an impairment is valid if it is justified by a legitimate governmental purpose. Judicial scrutiny of contract impairment under the contract clause is heightened when the state or local government is party to a contract.[210]

### § 2.54. In Land Use Cases.

The Supreme Court considered a contract clause objection in a land use case, *Keystone Bituminous Coal Ass'n v. Benedictus*,[211] that also decided important taking issues. Property owners in land conveyances from mining companies had contractually waived any liability for surface damage from mining. The companies claimed a state statute prohibiting subsidence from mining violated the contract clause by not allowing the company to hold the property owners to the waivers.

---

**207.** City of Ladue v. Gilleo, 114 S. Ct. 2038 (1994) (invalidating sign regulation; concurring opinion of O'Connor, J.).

**208.** U.S. Const. art. I, § 10.

**209.** 431 U.S. 1 (1977).

**210.** *See generally* Energy Reserves Group, Inc. v. Kansas Power & Light Co., 459 U.S. 400 (1983); Allied Structural Steel Co. v. Spannaus, 438 U.S. 234 (1978). *See* Board of Cty. Comm'rs v. East Prince Frederick Corp., 559 A.2d 822 (Md. App. 1989) (no contract clause violation when county imposed two-year limit on use of sewer and water service allocation unless developer paid user fee; impairment not severe and justified by need to allocate limited capacity).

**211.** 480 U.S. 470 (1987). *See* § 2.24.

The Court held the statute was a substantial impairment of a contractual relationship, and the critical inquiry was whether the impairment was justified.[212] The Court held the state had a "strong public interest" in preventing harm from subsidence, and the environmental effect of the harm transcended any private contractual agreements. The Court then noted that a significant and legitimate public purpose is not enough to justify a contract impairment. The legislative adjustment of contractual rights must also be based on reasonable conditions and must be appropriate to the public purpose that justified the legislation.

The Court then held it must defer to the legislative judgment on this issue unless the state was a contracting party, and concluded that the environmental purposes of the subsidence act "clearly survived" its standards for evaluating contract impairment. The few additional land use cases that have considered contract clause claims have also dismissed them.[213]

---

**212.** *Compare* Northwestern Nat'l Life Ins. Co. v. Tahoe Reg'l Planning Agency, 632 F.2d 104 (9th Cir. 1980) (adoption of restrictive zoning ordinance not a contract impairment solely because it made collection of assessment for payment of improvement bonds more difficult).

**213.** Pitts v. Pilkerton, 714 F. Supp. 285 (M.D. Tenn. 1989) (ordinance prohibiting display of portable signs that affected existing leases for the display of these signs); Beasley v. Potter, 493 F. Supp. 1059 (W.D. Mich. 1980) (denial of special use permit that caused loan default).

# REFERENCES

## Books and Monographs

Takings: Land-Development Conditions and Regulatory Takings After *Lucas* and *Dollan* (D. Callies ed. 1996).

F. Bosselman, D. Callies, & J. Banta, The Taking Issue (1973).

S. Eagle, Regulatory Takings (1996).

D. Mandelker, J. Gerard & T. Sullivan, Federal Land Use Law (updated annually).

Land Use and The Constitution: Principles for Planning Practice (B. Blaesser & A. Weinstein eds., 1989).

## Articles

Blaesser, Closing the Federal Courthouse Door on Property Owners: The Ripeness and Abstention Doctrines in Section 1983 Land Use Cases, 2 Hofstra Prop. L.J. 73 (1989).

Blais, Takings, Statutes, and the Common Law: Considering Inherent Limitations on Title, 70 S. Cal. L. Rev. 1 (1996).

Bley & Axelrad, The Search for Constitutionally Protected "Property" in Land-Use Law, 29 Urb. Law. 251 (1997).

Brauneis, "The Foundation of our 'Regulatory Takings' Jurisprudence": The Myth and Meaning of Justice Holmes' Opinon in *Pennsylvania Coal Co. v. Mahon,* 106 Yale L.J. 613 (1996).

Brownstein, Illicit Legislative Motive in the Municipal Land Use Regulation Process, 57 U. Cin. L. Rev. 1 (1988).

Burton, Predatory Municipal Zoning Practices: Changing the Presumption of Constitutionality in the Wake of the Takings Trilogy, 44 Ark. L. Rev. 65 (1991).

Coletta, Reciprocity of Advantage and Regulatory Takings: Toward a New Theory of Takings Jurisprudence, 40 Am. U.L. Rev. 297 (1990).

Connors, Back to the Future: The "Nuisance Exception" to the Just Compensation Clause, 19 Cap. U.L. Rev. 139 (1989).

Coursen, Property Rights Legislation: A Survey of Federal and State Assessment and Compensation Measures, 29 Envtl. L. Rptr. 10239 (1996).

Delaney, What Does It Take to Make a Take? A Post-*Dolan* Look at the Evolution of Regulatory Takings Jurisprudence in the Supreme Court, 27 Urb. Law. 55 (1995).

DiMento, Mining the Archives of *Pennsylvania Coal:* Heaps of Constitutional Mischief, 11 J. Legal Hist. 349 (1990).

Ellis, Neighborhood Opposition and the Permissible Purposes of Zoning, 7 Land Use & Envt'l L. Rev. 275 (1992).

Halper, Why the Nuisance Knot Can't Undo the Takings Muddle, 28 Ind. L. Rev. 329 (1995).

Kassouni, The Ripeness Doctrine and the Judicial Relegation of Constitutionally Protected Property Rights, 29 Cal. W. L. Rev. 1 (1993).

Kmiec, Disentangling Substantive Due Process and Taking Claims, 13 Zoning & Plan. L. Rep. 57 (1990).

Kmiec, Inserting the Last Remaining Pieces into the Takings Puzzle, 38 Wm. & Mary L. Rev. 995 (1997).

Lisker, Regulatory Takings and the Denominator Problem, 27 Rutgers L.J. 663 (1996).

Lyman, Finality Ripeness in Federal Land Use Cases From *Hamilton Bank* to *Lucas,* 9 J. Land Use & Envtl. L. 101 (1994).

Mandelker, Investment-Backed Expectations in Taking Law, 27 Urb. Law. 215 (1995).

Mandelker & Tarlock, Shifting the Presumption of Constitutionality in Land Use Law, 24 Urb. Law. 1 (1992).

Martinez, Statutes Enacting Takings Law: Flying in the Face of Uncertainty, 26 Urb. Law. 327 (1994).

Overstreet, The Ripeness Doctrine of the Taking Clause: A Survey of Decisions Showing Just How Far Federal Courts Will Go to Avoid Adjudicating Land Use Cases, 10 J. Land Use & Envtl. L. 91 (1994).

Roberts, Ripeness and Forum Selection in Fifth Amendment Takings Litigation, 11 J. Land Use & Envtl. L. 37 (1995).

Roberts, Mining With Justice Holmes, 39 Vand. L. Rev. 287 (1986).

Rose, Mahon Reconstructed: Why the Takings Issue Is Still a Muddle, 57 S. Cal. L. Rev. 561 (1984).

Symposium: Perspectives on Regulatory Takings, 6 Fordham Envtl. L.J. 405 (1995).

Thomas, The Illusory Restraints and Empty Promises of New Property Protection Laws, 28 Urb. Law. 223 (1996).

Washburn, "Reasonable Investment-Backed Expectations" As a Factor in Defining Property Interest, 49 J. Urb. & Contemp. L. 63 (1996).

Ziegler, Partial Taking Claims and Horizontal Equity: Making Sense of Fundamental Fairness and Development Restrictions, 19 Zon. & Plan. L. Rep. 53 (1996).

**Student Work**

Note, Florida's Takings Law: A Bark Worse Than Its Bite, 16 Va. Envtl. L.J. 313 (1997).

Note, Have They Gone "Too Far"? An Evaluation and Comparison of 1995 State Takings Legis-lation, 30 Ga. L. Rev. 1061 (1996).

Note, The Origins and Original Significance of the Just Compensation Clause of the Fifth Amendment, 94 Yale L.J. 694 (1985).

Note, *Penn Central Transportation Company v. New York City:* Easy Taking-Clause Cases Make Uncertain Law, 1980 Utah L. Rev. 369.

Note, Takings 1992: Scalia's Jurisprudence and a Fifth Amendment Doctrine to Avoid *Lochner Redivivus*, 28 Val. U. L. Rev. 743 (1994).

Comment, Texas Private Real Property Rights Preservation Act: A Political Solution to the Regulatory Takings Problem, 27 St. Mary's L.J. 557 (1996).

Comment, Unearthing the Denominator in Regulatory Taking Cases, 61 U. Chi. L. Rev. 1535 (1994).

Recent Development, The Supreme Court, 1987 Term: Equal Protection and Rational Basis Analysis, 12 Harv. J.L. & Pub. Pol'y 235 (1989).

Casenote, *Dolan v. City of Tigard:* Individual Property Rights v. Land Management Systems, 17 U. Haw. L. Rev. 193 (1995).

## SELECTION OF ARTICLES ON THE SUPREME COURT'S 1987 TAKING TRILOGY

Berger, Happy Birthday, Constitution: The Supreme Court Establishes New Ground Rules for Land-Use Planning, 20 Urb. Law. 735 (1988).

Berger, The Year of the Taking Issue, 1 B.Y.U.J. Pub. L. 262 (1987).

Callies, Property Rights: Are There Any Left?, 20 Urb. Law. 597 (1988).

Epstein, Takings: Descent and Resurrection, 1987 Sup. Ct. Rev. 1 (1987).

Freilich & Morgan, Municipal Strategies for Imposing Valid Development Exactions: Responding to *Nollan*, 10 Zoning & Plan. L. Rep. 169 (1987).

Large, The Supreme Court and the Takings Clause: The Search for a Better Rule, 18 Envtl. L. 3 (1987).

Lawrence, Means, Motives, and Takings: the Nexus Test of Nollan v. California Coastal Commission, 12 Harv. Envtl. L.J. 231 (1988).

Lawrence, Regulatory Takings: Beyond the Balancing Test, 20 Urb. Law. 389 (1988).

Mandelker, Waiving the Taking Clause: Mixed Signals from the Supreme Court, Land Use L. & Zoning Dig., Vol. 40, No. 11, at 3 (1988).

Martinez, A Critical Analysis of the 1987 Takings Trilogy: The *Keystone, Nollan and First English* Cases, 1 Hofstra Prop. L.J. 39 (1988).

Myers, Some Observations on the Analysis of Regulatory Takings in the Rehnquist Court, 23 Val. U.L. Rev. 527 (1989).

Peterson, The Takings Clause: In Search of Underlying Principles Part I — A Critique of Current Takings Clause Doctrine, 77 Calif. L. Rev. 1299 (1989).

Peterson, The Takings Clause: In Search of Underlying Principles Part II — Takings as Intentional Deprivations of Property Without Moral Justification, 78 Calif. L. Rev. 53 (1990).

Salsich, *Keystone Bituminous Coal, First English* and *Nollan:* A Framework for Accommodation?, 34 Wash. U.J. Urb. & Contemp. L. 173 (1988).

Sax, Property Rights in the U.S. Supreme Court: A Status Report, 7 UCLA J. Envtl. L. & Pol'y 139 (1988).

Siemon, Who Owns Cross Creek? 5 J. Land Use & Envtl. L. 323 (1990).

Siemon & Larson, The Taking Issue Trilogy: The Beginning of the End, 33 Wash. U.J. Urb. & Contemp. L. 169 (1988).

Williams & Ernst, And Now We Are Here on a Darkling Plain, 13 Vt. L. Rev. 635 (1989).

## SELECTED ARTICLES ON THE SUPREME COURT'S *LUCAS* DECISION

Berlin, Just Compensation Doctrine and the Workings of Government: The Threat From the Supreme Court and Possible Responses, 17 Harv. Envtl. L. Rev. 97 (1993).

Brown, Takings: Who Says it Needs to be So Confusing?, 22 Stetson L. Rev. 379 (1993).

Delaney, Advancing Private Property Rights: The Lessons of *Lucas,* 22 Stetson L. Rev. 395.

Hartman, *Lucas v. South Carolina Coastal Council*: The Takings Test Turns a Corner, 23 Envt'l L. Rep. 10003 (1993).

Humbach, Evolving Threshold of Nuisance and the Taking Clause, 18 Colum. J. Envtl. L. 1 (1993).

Lazarus, Putting the Correct "Spin" on *Lucas*, 45 Stan. L. Rev. 1411 (1993).

*Lucas v. South Carolina Coastal Council,* Colloquium, 10 Pace Envt'l L. Rev. 1 (1992).

Mandelker, Of Mice and Missiles: A True Account of *Lucas v. South Carolina Coastal Council,* 8 J. Land Use & Envt'l L. __ (1993).

Morgan, Takings Law: Strategies for Dealing with *Lucas,* Land Use L. & Zoning Dig., Vol. 45, No. 1, at 3 (1993).

Pershkow & Houseman, In the Wake of *Lucas v. South Carolina Coastal Council:* A Critical Look at Six Questions Practitioners Should be Asking, 23 Envt'l. L. Rep. 10008 (1993).

Sax, Property Rights and the Economy of Nature: Understanding *Lucas v. South Carolina Coastal Council,* 45 Stan. L. Rev. 1433 (1993).

Washburn, Land Use Control, the Individual, and Society: *Lucas v. South Carolina Coastal Council,* 52 Md. L. Rev. 162 (1993).

# Chapter 3

# THE COMPREHENSIVE PLAN

## A. ROLE OF THE COMPREHENSIVE PLAN.

### § 3.01. Planning and Land Use Regulation.

As any planner can tell you, comprehensive plans come first. Municipalities adopt and administer land use controls, such as zoning, in order to implement comprehensive plans. As any land use lawyer can tell you, the courts were slow to recognize this relationship. For the first fifty years or so of zoning, the courts did not require a comprehensive plan as the basis for the adoption and administration of zoning ordinances. Several state legislatures have rejected this rule by mandating the adoption of local comprehensive plans and consistency between plans and zoning. A few courts have also required consistency between zoning and plans. This chapter reviews the role of planning in the land use control process.

Comprehensive plans, sometimes known as "general" or "master" plans, have a number of standard characteristics. They plan for the physical development of the community. They are future-oriented and project the development of a community to a future point in time or a future point in the community's growth. Comprehensive plans are geographically and functionally comprehensive. They cover all of the geographic area of the community and include all of the physical elements that determine future community development. Land use, public facilities, and transportation elements are common to all plans. The zoning ordinance is based on and implements the development policies contained in the land use element of the comprehensive plan.

Comprehensive plans usually contain both textual policies and maps. For the land use element the text states the land use policies adopted by the plan. The land use map indicates where development proposed by land use policies should occur. Some comprehensive plans contain highly generalized maps or may dispense with maps altogether and rely on the text to state the community's planning policies. The zoning ordinance implements the land use policies in the comprehensive plan through textual zoning regulations that create land use districts and specify the land uses permitted in these districts. A zoning map classifies all land within the community into one of these zoning districts.

### § 3.02. The Planning Process and the Plan.

Planners prepare comprehensive plans for community adoption in a "rational" planning process. The rational planning process is well-established in planning practice. It requires a series of steps leading up to the preparation and adoption of the comprehensive plan.

The rational planning process begins with a survey and analysis of the data that provide the basis for the plan's policies. Projections are then made for the future development of the community. These projections cover population, the economy, public services and facilities, and private land use. The planning staff then develops a set of goals for the future growth of the community that take these projections into account. Planning goals are highly generalized. They provide the rationale for more detailed planning policies for land development and the other elements in the comprehensive plan. Some plans have three levels of textual statement, although the names given to these levels may vary. In one type of textual hierarchy, planning objectives provide the basis for planning goals, which in turn provide the basis for the more detailed planning policies.

Multi-family housing illustrates how a plan with two levels of textual statement is organized. The plan's housing goal may state that a balanced housing supply is one of the goals the plan seeks to implement. This goal contemplates multi-family development. A detailed planning policy on multi-family housing would then indicate the conditions under which this kind of development can occur. The policy may state, for example, that multi-family housing should occur at highway interchanges near nonresidential development to minimize journeys to work.

Problems can arise in translating the land use map into mapped zoning districts when a comprehensive plan contains a land use map. Land use categories in the plan's land use map are usually more generalized than the land use districts in the zoning ordinance. The zoning map must translate these generalized land use categories into more detailed land use districts in a manner that implements the policies of the comprehensive plan.

Planners usually develop more than one set of planning goals and policies for the comprehensive plan. They test these goals and policies for feasibility and acceptability, usually through public hearings and other forms of public participation. The goals and policies selected form the basis for the preparation of the final comprehensive plan.

### § 3.03. Criticisms of Planning.

Critics raise several objections to rational planning. They claim the political process is unable to specify planning goals and policies with sufficient precision. They claim that land use policies for future development are subject to error because the planner cannot control all of the factors that influence new development. He cannot control changes in economic conditions, for example, which may depress housing construction or require industrial developers to modify development plans.

Critics also claim planning ignores the nonphysical consequences of community development. One criticism is that planners ignore the social impact of their plans, which is difficult to measure and quantify. Until recently, comprehensive plans also paid little or no attention to the environmental impact of new development. These omissions lead to what some call "partial planning" — the inability to integrate all of the necessary variables affected by community development in a comprehensive plan.

A final criticism of comprehensive planning concentrates on the limitations of a process that assembles complex data to make conditional predictions. Professor Lindblom articulated these criticisms in a leading article.[1] He argued that limited intellectual capacity and resources, the interdependence between fact and value judgments, inadequate analytic systems, and the diversity of forms in which problems actually arise prevent successful comprehensive planning. Lindblom suggested an alternative planning process known as "incremental" planning.

Problems are not "solved" through incremental planning but are marginally and repeatedly attacked. Ends and means are chosen simultaneously and are continually explored. Policy analysis and policy making are incomplete at any one point. They are remedial because they move away from perceived problems

---

1. "The Science of Muddling Through," 19 Pub. Admin. Rev. 79 (1959). *See also* Lindblom, "Still Muddling, Not Yet Through," 39 Pub. Admin. Rev. 517 (1979).

rather than toward fixed objectives. The political process ensures that issues ignored at one stage in the planning process receive attention at a later stage. Incrementalists claim that incremental planning can avoid the errors that may occur in a comprehensive planning process.

### § 3.04. Planning Today.

Planning practice today has overcome many of these criticisms. The criticism that planning is not sufficiently comprehensive or politically connected is blunted by new consensus-building approaches through citizen participation. Although citizen participation is not without its critics, it can provide a source of information and innovative approaches, secure feedback for planners, and help define the public interest in the planning process more accurately. Statutes have also made plans more comprehensive by including additional elements, such as housing and environmental elements, that were lacking historically.

A related change in comprehensive planning ties the planning process more closely with the political process. As originally conceived, planning was policy-neutral. Planners served an independent and politically removed planning commission and did not always seek political input into the planning process. Most planning directors are now appointed by the chief executive and work directly with the executive branch. Planners produce alternative goals and policies for political decision makers to consider and adopt in the political process. This view of planning sees the political decision maker as responsible for the adoption of planning policy. Planners assist by presenting and clarifying policy alternatives.

Planners can avoid the difficulties of plans that project long-range development policies in favor of plans that cover a shorter time frame. This approach helps avoid planning errors arising from inaccurate projections. These so-called "middle-range" plans are now common, and some statutes require them. Planning error is also avoidable through periodic revision of the plan, often at yearly intervals. As an alternative, the community can adopt short-range periodic plans to implement the policies of the long-range comprehensive plan.

Communities can also achieve more flexibility in planning by adopting a geographic hierarchy of land use plans. They supplement a comprehensive plan for the entire community with more detailed plans for subareas and even local neighborhoods. This planning technique allows planners to implement the plan in sequence and over time as development trends become clearer and projections are revised.

New computer-based systems have moderated criticisms that planning cannot assemble complex data to make conditional predictions. These systems include electronic spreadsheets and geographic information systems that make it much easier to test out development scenarios and impacts and react to proposed changes quickly.

Land use plans today fall into four prototypes, although many communities combine them into hybrids.[2] The traditional land use design plan proposes a future and long-range urban form that consists of designated land uses and a circulation system. The land use classification plan is a more proactive general map of growth policy areas that indicates where growth will occur. The policy plan uses verbal policy statements to project land use futures and de-emphasizes mapping. The development management plan proposes specific policy actions to guide development, such as a public investment program, and assumes the public sector will influence growth management.

## B. PLANNING LEGISLATION.

### § 3.05. The Standard Planning Act.

Model acts proposed by the U.S. Department of Commerce in the 1920s still dominate state legislation for planning and zoning. One model act provided legislative authority for planning and the other authorized zoning. The model planning legislation also authorized controls over subdivisions. Although the planning act should have come first, the strong political demand for legislation authorizing zoning led to the publication of the zoning act first. This inverted publication sequence contributed to the early failure to integrate zoning with the planning process. The model planning act was entitled A Standard City Planning Enabling Act and will be called the Standard Planning Act or Standard Act. Much modern planning legislation still shows the influence of the Standard Act, even though this Act was not as popular as its sister zoning act and was not adopted by as many states.

Several policy decisions made in the Standard Planning Act continue to influence land use planning today. In one of its most important decisions, the Act made planning optional rather than mandatory and most states followed this model. This decision had important consequences for land use regulation, because the Standard Planning Act did not prevent a municipality from zoning without having adopted a comprehensive plan. Language in the zoning act might have compelled a different result, but the courts did not initially read that statute this way. The absence of planning in some communities may have led courts to hold that the adoption and implementation of zoning ordinances did not depend on the adoption of a comprehensive plan.

The Standard Planning Act was process-oriented. It provided the authority for planning and specified the role local agencies were to play in that process. It also

---

**2.** This paragraph is based on Kaiser & Godschalk, Twentieth Century Land Use Planning: A Stalwart Family Tree, 61 J. Am. Plan. Ass'n 365 (1995).

specified the issues and elements that local comprehensive plans were required to address. The Standard Act did not include substantive planning policies but left the development of these policies to the local planning process. This decision was probably wise, because the variety of settings in which planning occurs may make the inclusion of substantive planning policies in state planning legislation undesirable. There are some exceptions, such as planning policies for lower-income housing. Some critics also claim the process-oriented requirements in the Standard Planning Act led to an elevation of process over substance. They argue that the Act's process orientation allows communities to adopt regressive social policies. Exclusionary land use policies are an example. The American Planning Association is developing statutory proposals for planning that will provide alternative models for carrying out the planning process.

### § 3.06.  The Planning Commission.

The Standard Planning Act delegated the development of planning policy to a planning commission appointed by the local chief executive. This choice was deliberate. Reformist local government theory at the time held that independent local commissions responsible for policy development should be independent of local politics. In the case of planning, this independence was considered a strength. Many communities reinforce this political independence by making planning staff responsible to the planning commission.

The Standard Act contemplated a lay planning commission. In an important footnote to the Act, its drafters pointedly stated that the Act provided no professional qualifications for commission members. "Capacity for leadership in city planning . . . constitutes the best qualification." The planning commission was expected to promote the advantages of city planning to the community and to the political decision makers. Many modern-day reformers criticize the political isolation of the planning process and even propose abolition of the planning commission.

The independent planning commission is partly responsible for the fragmented decision making that is typical in planning and land use regulation. The commission is an additional control point in the adoption and amendment of plans and zoning ordinances. Early reformers may have considered fragmentation desirable, but it dilutes political responsibility in a decision-making process in which political responsibility for policy decisions is essential.

### § 3.07.  The Elements of the Plan.

The Standard Planning Act provided a "shopping list" of public capital facilities and private and public utility facilities for which the plan was required to provide policies. The Standard Act did not detail the contents of plan elements, establish planning priorities, require the integration of planning policies, or demand internal consistency. Modern state planning legislation follows the Standard Act model but groups the facilities for which policies are required into several planning "elements," including a capital facilities and a transportation element. The Standard Planning Act did not require the municipality to follow the plan when making capital facility decisions. Section 9 provided that the "location, character and extent thereof" of any public capital improvement covered by an adopted plan, as well as any private utility improvement, must be submitted to the planning commission for approval. If the planning commission disapproved, the legislative body could override it but only by a two-thirds vote. Much modern planning legislation retains this provision.

The Standard Act did not require a land use element. It did require a zoning plan to control the "height, area, bulk, location, and use of buildings and premises." The zoning plan element created much confusion, and the drafters did not provide a satisfactory explanation for its inclusion. A comprehensive plan is future-oriented and general, while the zoning "plan" contemplated standards regulating the detailed use of property. Perhaps the zoning plan requirement reflected the decision to publish the planning act before the zoning act. Modern planning legislation does not usually require a zoning plan but does require a land use element.

### § 3.08. Plan Adoption.

Section 6 of the Standard Planning Act authorized adoption of the plan by the planning commission rather than the council. The drafters made this decision intentionally. They pointed out in a footnote that the plan covered a period of years longer than the term of any one council, that the council dealt only with "pressing and immediate" needs, and that a hostile council could reject a plan adopted by an earlier council. The decision to require adoption of the plan by the planning commission reflected the related decision to insulate the planning process from local politics.

The American Law Institute's (ALI) Model Land Development Code took the contrary view and requires plan adoption by the local legislative body.[3] Commentary on the Code noted that legislative adoption is necessary to achieve consideration and implementation of the plan by a representative body.

### § 3.09. State Planning Legislation.

State legislation that authorizes comprehensive planning shows the influence of the Standard Planning Act in many states. Statutory authority for the compre-

---

**3.** Model Land Development Code § 3-106(2) (1976). *See* Alameda County Land Use Ass'n v. City of Hayward, 45 Cal. Rptr. 2d 752 (Cal. App. 1995) (giving other jurisdictions veto on plan is improper delegation of legislative authority).

hensive plan may still track the language of the Standard Act and provides a comparable shopping list of elements the plan must contain.[4] A number of states have modernized their planning legislation by revising and adding to the required and optional planning elements, by providing substantive planning policies for lower-income housing, and by mandating planning.

### § 3.10. Required and Optional Planning Elements.

Most modern planning legislation requires a set of mandatory and optional planning elements that define what the comprehensive plan should contain.[5] Like the Standard Act, most state statutes do not specify the content of plan elements in detail. All states have transportation elements, practically all have land use elements, about two-third have environmental elements and half have housing elements. Pennsylvania is typical.[6] The plan is to include maps, charts and textual matter and is to include "a statement of objectives of the municipality concerning its future development." Elements in the plan are to address land use, housing needs, the "movement of people and goods," and community facilities. The plan also is to include "a discussion of short- and long-range plan implementation strategies."

Florida legislation contains detailed guidelines for the land use element of the comprehensive plan and also specifies more detailed guidance for the comprehensive plan through administrative regulations.[7] It is to show the "proposed future distribution, location, and extent" of land uses, and must have "standards" for the control and distribution of population and building densities. In addition, "the proposed distribution, location, and extent of the various categories of land use shall be shown" on a land use map. This degree of detail provides necessary guidance in determining whether zoning is consistent with a plan, which Florida requires. The Florida statute also encourages innovative planning and development strategies to accommodate growth in an environmentally acceptable manner, such as clustering, urban villages, and mixed-use development.[8]

Planning statutes may also require additional required and optional planning elements.[9] Optional elements may include environmental,[10] recreational, housing and community design elements, though in some states some or all of these elements may be mandatory.

---

4. Ohio Rev. Code § 713.02; Wis. Stat. Ann. § 62.23.

5. *E.g.,* Del. Code Ann. tit. 9, § 2656; Fla. Stat. Ann. § 163.3177; Md. Ann. Code art. 66B, § 3.05; S.C. Code Ann. § 6-29-510; Va. Code § 15.1-446.1.

6. Pa. Stat. Ann. tit. 53, § 10301.

7. Fla. Stat. Ann. § 163.3177(6)(a).

8. Fla. Stat. Ann. § 161.3177(b).

9. *E.g.,* Cal. Gov't Code § 65303; Fla. Stat. Ann. § 163.3177; Utah Code Ann. § 17-27-301 (wildlife habitat and economic stability); Wash. Rev. Code Ann. §§ 36.70.340-350.

10. *E.g.,* Md. Ann. Code art. 66B, § 3.05(1)(viii); N.Y. Town Law § 272-a(d).

One of the problems with the Standard Act was that it did not require integration and internal consistency among plan elements. To remedy this problem California provides in its statement of legislative intent that the comprehensive plan and its elements must be "an integrated internally consistent and compatible statement."[11]

## § 3.11. Planning Policies for Lower-Income Housing.

A significant number of states require a housing element in their planning legislation, and the statute usually requires the adoption of policies for lower-income housing.[12] The California legislation is a good example. It states:

> The housing element shall consist of an identification and analysis of existing and projected housing needs and a statement of goals, policies, quantified objectives, financial resources, and scheduled programs for the preservation, improvement, and development of housing. The housing element shall identify adequate sites for housing, including rental housing, factory-built housing, and mobile homes, and shall make adequate provision for the existing and projected needs of all economic segments of the community.[13]

The legislation requires an inventory and analysis of housing needs and a five-year schedule of actions to be implemented, in part, through "the administration of land use and development controls."

Florida has similar legislation that requires "a housing element consisting of standards, plans, and principles to be followed in" meeting housing needs including "the provision of housing for all current and anticipated future residents of the jurisdiction."[14] The housing element must also designate "adequate sites" for needed housing. Oregon legislation includes a comparable lower-income housing policy for its state land use planning program.[15] Local plans and land use regulations must comply with this policy. The Oregon legislation also states that "any approval standards, special conditions and the procedures for approval adopted by a local government shall be clear and objective and shall not have the effect, either in themselves or cumulatively, of discouraging needed housing through unreasonable cost or delay."[16]

---

11. Cal. Gov't Code § 65300.5, *applied in* Hernandez v City of Encinitas, 33 Cal Rptr. 2d 875 (Cal. App. 1994). *See also* Wash. Rev. Code Ann. § 36.70A.070.

12. *E.g.,* Ariz. Rev. Stat. Ann. § 9-461.05(D)(6) (municipalities); Conn. Gen. Stat. § 8-23; N.Y. Town Law § 277-a(3)(h); R.I. Gen. Laws § 45-22.2-6(C); Vt. Stat. Ann. tit. 24, § 4302(C)(11).

13. Cal. Gov't Code § 65583. *See also* § 65584. For additional discussion of the California legislation, see § 7.28.

14. Fla. Stat. Ann. § 163.3177(6)(f)1.d.

15. Or. Rev. Stat. §§ 197.303, 197.307.

16. Or. Rev. Stat. § 107.307(6).

### § 3.12. Mandatory Planning.

Legislation in at least 15 states makes planning mandatory for all or some units of local government.[17] These states require the adoption of comprehensive plans, but they may or may not require consistency between land use controls and the plan.[18] About half the states make planning conditionally mandatory by requiring the adoption of a plan, at least by the planning commission, if a municipality decides to create one.

## C. THE COMPREHENSIVE PLAN AND LAND USE CONTROLS.

### § 3.13. Zoning "in Accordance with" a Comprehensive Plan.

Whether or not a comprehensive plan is mandatory, the courts must determine whether zoning must be consistent with the comprehensive plan. The Standard Zoning Enabling Act states in § 3 that zoning must be "in accordance with a comprehensive plan." A majority of states include this language in their zoning legislation. At first glance, this language means what it says and supports a judicial interpretation that zoning must be "in accordance" with a comprehensive plan if one exists.

Commentary to the Standard Zoning Act suggests a different view and indicates that the draftsmen meant only that zoning be done comprehensively and not in a piecemeal manner.[19] This interpretation indicates that courts can find the "comprehensive plan" contemplated by the Act in the provisions of the zoning ordinance and that a comprehensive plan as a separate document is not necessary.[20] This interpretation, which a majority of the courts have adopted, is discussed in the next section.

### § 3.14. The Majority Judicial View: A Plan Is Not Required.

Most courts that have considered the question hold that the "in accordance" requirement does not mandate the adoption of a comprehensive plan as a condition to the exercise of the zoning power.[21] The leading case is *Kozesnik v. Town-*

---

17. *E.g.*, Cal. Gov't Code § 65103; Fla. Stat. Ann. § 163.3167; Ky. Rev. Stat. § 100.183; Nev. Rev. Stat. § 278.150; Or. Rev. Stat. § 197.175(2)(a); R.I. Gen. Laws § 45-22.2-5; Wash. Rev. Code Ann. § 36.70A.040.

18. § 3.16.

19. The Standard Zoning Act § 3, n. 22.

20. Ford v. Board of County Commr's, 924 P.2d 91 (Wyo. 1996), explains the difference between a comprehensive plan and a zoning ordinance.

21. Theobald v. Board of County Comm'rs, 644 P.2d 942 (Colo. 1982); Furtney v. Simsbury Zoning Comm'n, 271 A.2d 319 (Conn. 1970); Dawson Enters., Inc. v. Blaine County, 567 P.2d 1257 (Idaho 1977); Iowa Coal Mining Co. Inc. v. Monroe County, 494 N.W.2d 664 (Iowa 1993); Nottingham Village, Inc. v. Baltimore County, 292 A.2d 680 (Md. 1972); State ex rel. Chiavola v.

*ship of Montgomery.*[22] New Jersey had incorporated the "in accordance" language in its zoning legislation. The plaintiff argued that a zoning amendment was ultra vires because the municipality had violated this statutory requirement by not adopting a comprehensive plan. The court disagreed and relied on the history of the state's planning and zoning legislation to hold that it did not require a comprehensive plan. The court noted that New Jersey, following the model act sequence, adopted its zoning legislation before its planning legislation.

Although it held that the "in accordance" requirement did not require a comprehensive plan, the court held that this requirement imposed a fairness and reasonableness test on zoning. It relied on early zoning cases to hold that the intent of the "in accordance" requirement was to prevent a "capricious exercise" of the zoning power. Although it did not supply a definition of "in accordance," the court held that the term plan "connotes an integrated product of a rational process and 'comprehensive' requires something beyond a piecemeal approach, both to be revealed by the ordinance considered in relation to the physical facts and the [statutory] purposes." Later New Jersey legislation modified this holding.[23]

Other courts adopted a weak limitation on zoning, which is based on the "in accordance" requirement. As the Rhode Island court put it, this requirement means only that "the zoning regulation reflect the necessary relation between … the zoning power and the grounds upon which the police power of the state may properly be exercised."[24] This decision means that the "in accordance" requirement only restates substantive due process police power limitations, which require zoning to implement the health, safety, morals, and general welfare.

New York follows the majority view but also imposes a reasonableness requirement as an interpretation of the "in accordance" language. In *Udell v. Haas,*[25] in response to local pressure, the municipality quickly downzoned a property from commercial to residential in an area that the community's zoning policy had long identified as appropriate for commercial development. These circumstances led the court to hold that the downzoning was not "in accordance" with the comprehensive plan. More than "mock" obedience to this statutory requirement is necessary. Communities must show that a zoning change does not

---

Village of Oakwood, 886 S.W.2d 74 (Mo. App. 1994); Udell v. Haas, 235 N.E.2d 897 (N.Y. 1968); Cleaver v. Board of Adjustment, 200 A.2d 408 (Pa. 1964); Hadley v. Harold Realty Co., 198 A.2d 149 (R.I. 1964); West Hall Citizens for Controlled Dev. Density v. King County Council, 627 P.2d 1002 (Wash. App. 1981); Bell v. City of Elkhorn, 364 N.W.2d 144 (Wis. 1985) (quoting this treatise). *See also* Colo. Rev. Stat. §§ 30-28-106(3)(F), 31-23-206(3) (master plan advisory).

**22.** 131 A.2d 1 (N.J. 1957).

**23.** *See* § 3.17, n. 41.

**24.** Hadley v. Harold Realty Co., 198 A.2d 149, 153 (R.I. 1964).

**25.** 235 N.E.2d 897 (N.Y. 1968).

conflict with its basic land use policies. In states where a statute or judicial decision requires consistency with an adopted land use plan, courts apply a plan "consistency" requirement to reach similar results.[26]

## § 3.15. The Minority Judicial View: Consistency Is Required.

*Fasano v. Board of County Comm'rs*,[27] an Oregon case, adopted a consistency requirement in the absence of legislation imposing one. The court invalidated a zoning map amendment because it was not consistent with the local plan. *Fasano* was not an interpretation of the "in accordance" requirement, and Oregon legislation now mandates the adoption of comprehensive plans and requires local land use actions to be consistent with them.

*Fasano* placed two limitations on the consistency requirement. The proponent of a zoning change must prove the public need for the change and show that no other alternative available property serves that need better. A later case, *Neuberger v. City of Portland*,[28] relied on the enactment of a comprehensive state planning program to delete this part of the consistency requirement. The court held that proponents of a zoning change are no longer required to prove public need or the lack of available alternative sites. The court concluded that the requirement that local comprehensive plans must comply with state planning policies made these qualifications on the consistency requirement unnecessary.

*Fasano* applied only to a rezoning. A later decision, *Baker v. City of Milwaukie*,[29] required the land use restrictions in a zoning ordinance to be consistent with a comprehensive plan. Neighbors challenged a zoning ordinance allowing a residential density more intensive than a subsequently adopted comprehensive plan permitted. The court required revision of the zoning ordinance to comply with the plan. "Upon passage of a comprehensive plan a city assumes a responsibility to effectuate that plan and conform prior conflicting zoning ordinances to it."[30] *Baker* implies that the converse of its holding also is true: The local government must amend a zoning restriction less intensive than the plan to conform it to planning policy. An Oregon intermediate court of appeals case rejected this interpretation and limited *Baker* to its facts.[31]

---

26. § 3.16.

27. 507 P.2d 23 (Or. 1973). *But see* Green v. County Council, 508 A.2d 882 (Del. Ch. 1986) (interpreting statute to require plan as basis for zoning).

28. 603 P.2d 771 (Or. 1979).

29. 533 P.2d 772 (Or. 1975).

30. *Id.* at 779.

31. Marracci v. City of Scappoose, 552 P.2d 552 (Or. App. 1976). *Accord,* Bone v. City of Lewiston, 693 P.2d 1046 (Idaho 1984). *See also* Boyds Civic Ass'n v. Montgomery County Council, 526 A.2d 598 (Md. 1987).

Although no other court has adopted the *Fasano* and *Baker* consistency requirements, an Illinois appellate court adopted a weak variant.[32] The court held it would not give zoning the usual presumption of constitutionality if a municipality does not have a comprehensive plan. The court shifted the burden to the municipality to justify its land use regulations in this situation.[33] A Pennsylvania Supreme Court decision, which appeared to require the adoption of a comprehensive plan as the basis for land use regulation, is no longer good law in that state.[34] Courts in other states will examine a zoning ordinance or decision to determine whether it is consistent with a plan if the municipality has adopted one, even though the zoning statute does not require the adoption of a plan.[35]

### § 3.16. Statutory Consistency Requirements.

Legislation in several states requires zoning to be consistent with a comprehensive plan,[36] but most of this legislation does not define consistency. The California legislation provides a definition. Its mandatory planning legislation provides that consistency requires:

> The various land uses authorized by the [zoning] ordinance are [to be] compatible with the objectives, policies, general land uses, and programs specified in . . . [the] plan.[37]

The Florida legislation provides a more comprehensive definition:

> A development approved or undertaken by a local government shall be consistent with the comprehensive plan if the land uses, densities, or intensities, capacity or size, timing, and other aspects of the development are compatible with and further the objectives, policies, land uses, and densi-

---

**32.** Forestview Homeowners' Ass'n v. County of Cook, 309 N.E.2d 763 (Ill. App. 1974).

**33.** *Accord,* Raabe v. City of Walker, 174 N.W.2d 789 (Mich. 1970); Board of County Comm'rs v. City of Las Vegas, 622 P.2d 695 (N.M. 1980). *Contra,* First Nat'l Bank of Highland Park v. Village of Vernon Hills, 371 N.E.2d 659 (Ill. App. 1977).

**34.** Eves v. Zoning Bd. of Adjustment, 164 A.2d 7 (Pa. 1960). *See* Russell v. Penn Twp. Planning Comm'n, 348 A.2d 499 (Pa. Commw. 1975).

**35.** Palatine Nat'l Bank v. Village of Barrington, 532 N.E.2d 955 (Ill. App. 1988) (plan to be given weight in zoning decisions); Nova Horizon, Inc. v. City Council, 769 P.2d 721 (Nev. 1989) (plan commands deference and presumption of validity in zoning decisions); Mayhew v. Town of Sunnyvale, 774 S.W.2d 284 (Tex. App. 1989), *cert. denied,* 498 U.S. 1087 (1991).

**36.** *E.g.,* Ariz. Rev. Stat. Ann. § 9-462.01(F) (municipalities); Cal. Gov't Code § 65860; Fla. Stat. Ann. § 163.3194; Ky. Rev. Stat. § 100.213 (unless findings made on whether zoning appropriate or changes have occurred); Me. Rev. Stat. Ann. tit. 30, § 4352(2); N.J. Stat. Ann. § 40:55D-62 (governing body may waive); Or. Rev. Stat. § 197.010(3). *See also* N.J. Rev. Stat. § 40:55D-89.1 (land use regulations lose presumption if plan not updated regularly). *See* Olson v. City of Deadwood, 480 N.W.2d 170 (S.D. 1992) (ordinance that allows use-on-review procedure is consistent with mandatory planning statute).

**37.** Cal. Gov't Code § 65860(a)(ii).

ties or intensities in the comprehensive plan and if it meets all other criteria enumerated by the local government.[38]

When the statute does not define consistency the courts have developed their own rules to determine when zoning is consistent with a comprehensive plan.[39]

### § 3.17. Staging and Growth Management.

Staging is an important consistency issue. A comprehensive plan indicates future development patterns for the community and may specify the stages in which growth should take place. Courts must decide whether to uphold zoning denials based on a plan's staging policy.

In *Philippi v. City of Sublimity*[40] the city denied a subdivision permit for residential development on agricultural land in an area zoned for residential use. The land was designated in the comprehensive plan as an agricultural retention area. In this area, the plan favored the preservation of productive farm land until it was needed for urban development. The court held that the plan was not inconsistent with the zoning, which did not necessarily give the landowner "an automatic license" to develop his property for a permitted use. The city could rely on the plan's agricultural preservation policy to delay development until a parcel cannot be realistically or productively farmed or there is a need for additional residential lots.

The court took a different view of somewhat different facts in *Board of Supvrs. v. Allman*.[41] A county in the Washington, D.C., metropolitan area refused to upzone a 303-acre tract of land to allow a planned residential development. The upzoning was consistent with the density policies in the comprehensive plan and public facilities were adequate. The court overruled the county, even though the comprehensive plan is only advisory in Virginia. It noted that the development complied with the plan and that the county denied it primarily because it was premature. The court also held that the refusal to rezone was discriminatory. Although the county wanted to delay development in the area until a new town

---

**38.** Fla. Stat. Ann. § 163.3194(3)(b). *See also id,* § 163.3194(3)(a) (similar provision for development orders and land development regulation); *Id.* § 163.3194(4)(a) (court in reviewing local government action on land development regulations to consider reasonableness of plan and relationship of plan to action).

**39.** Little v. Board of County Comm'rs, 631 P.2d 1282 (Mont. 1981) (statutes require substantial compliance with comprehensive plan in zoning).

**40.** 662 P.2d 325 (Or. 1983). *See also* Building Indus. Ass'n v. City of Oceanside, 33 Cal. Rptr. 2d 137 (Cal. App. 1994) (numerical growth control initiative inconsistent with plan); Dade County v. Inversiones Rafamar, S.A., 360 So. 2d 1130 (Fla. App. 1978); City of Jacksonville Beach v. Grubbs, 461 So. 2d 160 (Fla. App. 1984); Clinkscales v. City of Lake Oswego, 615 P.2d 1164 (Or. App. 1980); Marracci v. City of Scappoose, 552 P.2d 552 (Or. App. 1976).

**41.** 211 S.E.2d 48 (Va. 1975).

nearby was fully completed, it had approved similar upzonings for other property in the area outside the new town.

### § 3.18. Land Use Conflicts.

As might be expected, courts apply a "rule of reason" when they determine whether land use classifications in the zoning ordinance conflict with land use designations in the comprehensive plan.[42] This problem arises because land uses permitted by the zoning ordinance may be different from the land uses designated by the plan. The court must then decide whether the zoning ordinance is consistent with the plan.

This question arose in an Oregon case, *Gillis v. City of Springfield*.[43] A comprehensive plan and a more detailed community plan designated an area of the municipality for medium density residential use. To implement the plan, the city adopted a zoning district that allowed office and certain service uses as of right but required a conditional use permit for residential uses.

Noting that the comprehensive plan stated only "broad" criteria for use, the court held that it did not prohibit nonresidential uses. But the court held that the plan's residential designation "requires at least that the area be zoned so that residential uses predominate." The court held the city's zoning district lacked "this essential feature." Although the intensity of use in the zoning district was comparable to intensity of use in a residential district, this did not transform this predominantly commercial district into one possessing a residential character. The case indicates that type of use, rather than intensity, is the key factor in determining consistency with a plan.

In another Oregon case, *Alluis v. Marion County*,[44] the county rejected a partition of land into lots of less than 1.5 acres. The ordinance authorized a one-acre minimum, but the county decided it conflicted with the comprehensive plan because the plan required a 1.5-acre minimum. The court disagreed. It read a reference in the plan to a 1.5-acre minimum as establishing only a "general" maximum density, an "optimum lot size," and an "overall" density minimum. *Allius* indicates how ambiguous plans give the courts an opportunity to establish plan-

---

42. Flavell v. City of Albany, 25 Cal. Rptr. 2d 21 (Cal. App. 1993) (no nexus between zoning ordinance increasing residential parking spaces and housing element of plan); Manalapan Realty, L.P. v. Township Comm., 658 A.2d 1230 (N.J. 1995) (zoning exclusion of unenclosed uses from shopping centers consistent with shopping center element of plan). *See also* Lesher Communications, Inc. v. City of Walnut Creek, 802 P.2d 317 (Cal. 1990) (initiative measure enacting zoning ordinance that conflicts with comprehensive plan is invalid). *See* §§ 6.32-6.34 for a discussion of when rezoning and refusals to zone are consistent with comprehensive plans.

43. 611 P.2d 355 (Or. App. 1980).

44. 668 P.2d 1242 (Or. App. 1983).

ning policy through interpretation when they apply the consistency requirement.[45]

## § 3.19. Plans and the Taking Issue.

### § 3.20. The Plan as a Defense to a Taking.

Although a comprehensive plan does not provide an absolute defense to a
taking claim, some courts give weight to comprehensive plans when they consider taking problems. They are impressed by the municipality's efforts in the
plan and planning process to comprehensively balance land use opportunities
throughout the community.

*Norbeck Village Joint Venture v. Montgomery County Council*[46] is a leading
case. The county comprehensively downzoned twenty square miles to low-
density residential use. The downzoning implemented an area plan adopted by
the county to provide a greenbelt around a suburban community designated as a
growth center. The area plan implemented a county general plan, which in turn
implemented a regional growth management plan for the Washington, D.C.,
metropolitan area.

The court held the downzoning constitutional and relied heavily on the policies of the county plans. It noted that the plaintiffs disputed the validity of the
concept underlying the plan and its legality but "did not suggest that it was not
conceived and adopted in the utmost good faith." They did not overcome the
strong presumption that the plan was valid legislative action.

Another leading case relying on a comprehensive plan to reject a taking claim
is *Golden v. Planning Bd. of Town of Ramapo*.[47] The Town of Ramapo adopted a
growth management program deferring development in the community for as
much as eighteen years. It implemented the program through a residential development permit system under which it allowed new development only if adequate
public services and facilities were available. The plaintiff objected that the plan
as implemented through the permit system was a taking because development
could be deferred in some areas for the eighteen-year growth management period. The court rejected this claim and partly based this holding on the community's adoption of the comprehensive plan as the basis for its growth management program. "The restrictions [in the growth management program] conform
to the community's considered land use policies as expressed in its comprehen-

---

**45.** Miller v. Council of City of Grants Pass, 592 P.2d 1088 (Or. App. 1979) (county incorrect
in interpreting plan to require maximum density); Board of Supvrs. v. Jackson, 269 S.E.2d 381
(Va. 1980) (upheld county's interpretation of ambiguous residential infill policy in comprehensive
plan).

**46.** 254 A.2d 700 (Md. 1969).

**47.** 285 N.E.2d 291 (N.Y.), *appeal dismissed,* 409 U.S. 1003 (1972).

sive plan and represent a bona fide effort to maximize population density consistent with orderly growth."[48]

### § 3.21. The Plan as a Taking of Property.

A comprehensive plan indicates proposals for future land use, and these proposals inevitably affect property values. A California court forcefully made this point.[49] Nevertheless, the prevailing rule is that the designation of a land use in a comprehensive plan is not a taking of property. The rule applies if a municipality designates property on a plan for future acquisition to a public facility, such as a highway.[50] *Selby Realty Co. v. City of San Buenaventura*[51] is a leading case. A joint city and county area plan showed an extension of a public street over plaintiff's property. The city refused to issue a necessary building permit when the plaintiff refused to dedicate the land required for the street extension. The court rejected a taking claim because the only action taken by the county that affected plaintiff's property was the adoption of the plan. It held that "[t]he plan is by its very nature merely tentative and subject to change," and that whether any part of plaintiff's property would be taken "depends on unpredictable future events." Plaintiff could seek relief if the plan was implemented at some future time in a manner that affected the "free use" of its property.

A court may reach a different result in states with mandatory planning statutes. Oregon cases have held the designation of a public facility in a plan can be a taking if it precludes all economically feasible use prior to acquisition, or if the designation results in a governmental intrusion that does irreversible damage.[52]

Only a few cases have considered whether the designation of a private land use in a plan is a taking. An early New Jersey case held a residential property owner had not suffered a taking when a plan designated adjacent land for an expansion of a parking area for a commercial building.[53] The court noted the plan at that time was simply a declaration of policy and did not have to be implemented by ordinance. It also noted there was no injury to plaintiff's property because a buffer zone would separate it from the parking lot, and held the plain-

---

48. *Id.* at 302. *See also* § 10.03.

49. O'Loane v. O'Rourke, 42 Cal. Rptr. 283 (Cal. App. 1965) (plan held subject to referendum).

50. Lone Star Indus., Inc. v. Department of Transp., 671 P.2d 511 (Kan. 1983); Arnold v. Prince George's County, 311 A.2d 223 (Md. 1973); Marvin E. Neiberg Real Estate Co. v. St. Louis County, 488 S.W.2d 626 (Mo. 1973); 37 A.L.R.3d 127 (1971); § 2.33.

51. 514 P.2d 111 (Cal. 1973).

52. Suess Bldrs. Co. v. City of Beaverton, 656 P.2d 306 (Or. 1982) (plan designating property for public acquisition could be taking if landowner induced to abandon all development), *on remand,* 714 P.2d 229 (Or. App. 1986) (upholding directed verdict for city); Fifth Ave. Corp. v. Washington County, 581 P.2d 50 (Or. 1978).

53. Cochran v. Planning Bd., 210 A.2d 99 (N.J.L. Div. 1965).

tiff could not claim a taking until his property was actually destroyed or damaged. In Florida, where planning is mandatory, a court held a facial taking did not occur when a village amended its plan to change the land use designation on a landowner's property from commercial to conservation and open space.[54] The court noted the plan was not a "complete ban" development, and that the residual uses did not deprive the property owner of all economically viable use.

### § 3.22. Judicial Review of Comprehensive Plans.

Courts have reviewed the content of comprehensive plans to determine whether they satisfy statutory requirements. The California courts have decided most of these cases. The California statute authorizes judicial review of comprehensive plans and authorizes the court to suspend local authority to grant building permits and zoning changes until the local government adopts a plan that complies with the statute.[55] The statutes provide that the adoption and amendment of a comprehensive plan is a legislative act,[56] and courts elsewhere have also held that plan amendments are legislative acts.[57]

The California courts require "actual compliance" with the statute but hold a plan inadequate only if the local government has acted arbitrarily, capriciously, or without evidentiary basis.[58] They have invalidated comprehensive plans when plan elements required by the statute were missing[59] and when the plan was so grossly inadequate that it did not comply with the statute.[60] They have upheld plan amendments that were consistent with the plan.[61]

The California courts have reviewed comprehensive plans to determine whether they comply with the statutory requirements for plan elements and with its internal consistency requirement. In *Twain Harte Homeowners Ass'n v.*

---

**54.** Taylor v. Village of North Palm Beach, 659 So. 2d 1167 (Fla. App. 1995).

**55.** Cal. Gov't Code §§ 65754, 65755 (residential development excepted in certain cases).

**56.** § 65301.5.

**57.** Martin County v. Yusem, 690 So.2d 1288 (Fla. 1997); Westside Hilltop Survival Comm. v. King County, 634 P.2d 862 (1981). *See also* Kindred Homes, Inc. v. Dean, 605 S.W.2d 15 (Ky. App. 1979).

**58.** Buena Vista Gardens Apt. Ass'n v. City of San Diego Planning Dep't, 220 Cal. Rptr. 732 (Cal. App. 1985).

Plans held adequate: Garat v. City of Riverside, 3 Cal. Rptr. 2d 504 (Cal. App. 1991); Kings Cty. Farm Bur. v. City of Hanford, 270 Cal. Rptr. 650 (Cal. App. 1990). *See also* Environmental Coalition of Florida, Inc. v. Broward Cty., 586 So. 2d 1212 (Fla. App. 1991) (plan map); Treisman v. Town of Bedford, 563 A.2d 786 (N.H. 1989).

**59.** Save El Toro Ass'n v. Days, 141 Cal. Rptr. 282 (Cal. App. 1977).

**60.** Camp v. Mendocino County Bd. of Supvrs., 176 Cal. Rptr. 620 (Cal. App. 1981).

**61.** Hernandez v. City of Encinitas, 33 Cal. Rptr. 2d 875 (Cal. App. 1994) (housing element); Environmental Council of Sacramento v. Board of Supvrs., 185 Cal. Rptr. 363 (Cal. App. 1982) (land designation changed from agricultural to agricultural-residential when plan called for agricultural preservation).

*County of Tuolumne*,[62] the court held that the residential density limitations in a plan were not properly stated and that the transportation element was not sufficiently correlated with the land use element. The courts have been especially strict in requiring compliance with the detailed requirements for the housing element.[63]

A court may decide to review the policies of a comprehensive plan to determine whether they are adequate. In *Holmes v. Planning Bd. of Town of New Castle*,[64] a detailed plan for a neighborhood commercial area attempted to relieve traffic congestion by requiring the dedication of common access driveways to interior parking lots. A landowner challenged a condition attached to a site plan that implemented the neighborhood plan by requiring the dedication of an easement for a common driveway. The court set aside the condition, partly because it found the plan so vague and amorphous in its impact on individual properties that it could raise taking problems. The court held that the board must prepare an "implementation strategy" that would "identify potential conflicts and assemble strategies that will achieve results."

---

**62.** 188 Cal. Rptr. 233 (Cal. App. 1982) (housing element and implementation measures held adequate). *See* § 3.10. *See also* Concerned Citizens of Calaveras County v. Calaveras County Bd. of Supvrs., 212 Cal. Rptr. 273 (Cal. App. 1985) (plan held internally inconsistent).

**63.** Black Prop. Owners Ass'n v. City of Berkeley, 28 Cal. Rptr. 2d 305 (Cal. App. 1994) (housing element held adequate); Buena Vista Gardens Apt. Ass'n v. City of San Diego Planning Dep't, 220 Cal. Rptr. 732 (Cal. App. 1985). *See* § 7.25.

**64.** 433 N.Y.S.2d 587 (App. Div. 1980). *See also* Christine Bldg. Co. v. City of Troy, 116 N.W.2d 816 (Mich. 1962) (court struck down large-lot zoning partly because it did not accept the plan's population limitation).

# REFERENCES

## Books and Monographs

J. DiMento, The Consistency Doctrine and the Limits of Planning (1980).

R. Fishman ed., Housing for All Under Law ch. 5 (1978).

E. Netter & J. Vranicar, Linking Plans and Regulations: Local Responses to Consistency Laws in California and Florida (American Planning Ass'n, Planning Advisory Serv. Rep. No. 363, 1981).

J. DeNeufville ed., The Land Use Policy Debate in the United States (1981).

F. So & J. Getzels, The Practice of Local Government Planning (2d ed. 1988).

## Articles

Brooks, Law of Plan Implementation in the United States, 16 Urb. L. Ann. 225 (1979).

Cobb, Mandatory Planning: An Overview, American Planning Ass'n, PAS Memo, Feb. 1994.

Day, Citizen Participation in the Planning Process: An Essentially Contested Concept?, 11 J. Plan. Lit. 421 (1997).

DeGrove & Stroud, New Developments and Future Trends in Local Government Comprehensive Planning, 17 Stetson L. Rev. 573 (1988).

Glenn & Apgar, Concurrency and Growth Management: A Lawyer's Primer, 7 Fla. St. Land Use & Envtl. L. Rev. 1 (1991).

Haar, In Accordance with a Comprehensive Plan, 68 Harv. L. Rev. 1154 (1955).

Haar, The Master Plan: An Impermanent Constitution, 20 Law & Contemp. Probs. 353 (1955).

Mandelker, The Role of the Local Comprehensive Plan in Land Use

Regulation, 74 Mich. L. Rev. 899 (1976).

Stach, Zoning — To Plan or to Protect?, 2 J. Plan. Literature 472 (1987).

Tarlock, Consistency with Adopted Land Use Plans as a Standard of Judicial Review: The Case Against, 9 Urb. L. Ann. 69 (1975).

Weitz, Toward a Model Statutory Plan Element: Transportation, Land Use L. & Zoning Dig., Vol.49, No. 2, at 3 (1997).

# Chapter 4

# THE ZONING SYSTEM

§ 4.40. Home Rule Problems.
§ 4.41. Legislative Solutions.

### § 4.01. An Introductory Note.

This chapter examines the zoning system. It opens with a review of cases in which the courts applied nuisance law to resolve conflicts between land uses. The courts in the nuisance cases established a judicial basis for resolving land use conflicts that provided a model for zoning legislation and the zoning ordinance. Next, the chapter reviews statutory and constitutional authority for the enactment of zoning ordinances. It examines the Standard Zoning Enabling Act, which provided the model for all state zoning legislation, and the adoption of land use controls under constitutional home rule powers. It then considers legislation that confers extraterritorial zoning powers on local governments. It concludes with a discussion of zoning for government and government-regulated land development.

### A. JUDICIAL ZONING THROUGH NUISANCE ACTIONS.

### § 4.02. The Private Nuisance Action.

Anglo-American courts have recognized the action for nuisance ever since the Elizabethan English decision in Aldred's Case.[1] Nuisance actions are an extension of the private tort of trespass to land. In the trespass action, the landowner sues for a physical invasion of her property by another. No physical invasion occurs in nuisance cases. The plaintiff landowner complains that the use of adjacent land detrimentally affects her land, and that a court can enjoin this use and award damages for any injury suffered. This chapter considers only private nuisances. It does not consider public nuisances, which are usually defined as a criminal violation that interferes with the rights of the community at large.[2] Some states have codified the judicial law of nuisance.[3]

The Supreme Court's taking decision in *Lucas v. South Carolina Coastal Council*[4] has given nuisance law an important place in land use law. The Court held that a land use regulation that denied a landowner all economically beneficial use of his land was a taking per se unless the use could have been prohibited under the state's law of nuisance. Courts must now look to state nuisance law to determine whether an exception exists to the *Lucas* per se taking rule.

The tort origins of nuisance law make its conceptual underpinnings unclear to this day. Whether success in a nuisance action requires proof of negligence on

---

**1.** [1611] 9 Coke R.D.F. 57b.
**2.** W. Prosser & W. Keeton, The Law of Torts 618 (5th ed. 1984).
**3.** *E.g.*, Ky. Rev. Stat. §§ 411.500 — 411.570.
**4.** 505 U.S. 1003 (1992). *See* § 2.18.

the part of the offending user, for example, continues to be a problem for some courts.[5] These conceptual difficulties tend to disappear in the land use nuisance cases. They reflect the Latin maxim that a landowner may make any use of his land if he does not unreasonably interfere with the use of land by others.

Courts determine the reasonableness of a use claimed to be a nuisance by determining whether it is compatible with land uses in the surrounding area. This evaluation requires a judicial "line-drawing" that is the same as the "line-drawing" municipalities make when they adopt zoning maps. The difference is that the courts make line-drawing decisions in land use nuisance cases. These cases are called "judicial zoning" for this reason. Earlier chapters explained how the *Euclid* case[6] relied on this element in nuisance law to construct a constitutional justification for zoning. Courts award either damages or an injunction in land use nuisance cases.

Although nuisance law does not require a physical invasion, courts more easily find a nuisance when a defendant's land use has a physical impact on plaintiff's land. The polluting industry in the residential neighborhood is the clearest example. Proof of physical impact is not always necessary in nuisance law because some courts enjoin aesthetic nuisances in residential areas, such as funeral homes.

A helpful way to look at nuisance law in land use cases is to construct an invader-defender model of nuisance litigation. The defendant who proposes a use in an area is the invader. The plaintiff who resists the establishment of the defendant's use is a defender of the area the defendant seeks to enter. The land use claimed to be a nuisance is usually adjacent or close to the plaintiff's property. Land use nuisances are either a nuisance *per se* or a nuisance *per accidens*. A nuisance *per se* is a nuisance wherever it locates. A nuisance *per accidens* is a nuisance only in areas in which its location is detrimental to surrounding uses. Hardly any land uses are in the *per se* category. In the usual land use nuisance case, the plaintiff claims a land use is a nuisance *per accidens*.[7] The courts have adopted an implicit land use hierarchy they apply in the *per accidens* cases. Residential land uses are at the top of the hierarchy, and courts hold that nonresidential uses that seek to enter residential neighborhoods are nuisances *per accidens*.

Nuisance actions have declined in importance as a method for resolving land use conflicts because most municipalities have adopted zoning ordinances. A nuisance action may still have advantages that enforcement of the zoning ordinances does not have. If a plaintiff is successful in securing an injunction, a

---

5. Copart Indus. v. Consolidated Edison Co., 362 N.E.2d 968 (N.Y. 1977).

6. § 2.41.

7. State v. Feezell, 400 S.W.2d 716 (Tenn. 1966).

court can order the removal of the nuisance without compensation. A plaintiff can also secure damages in a nuisance action.

## § 4.03. Anticipatory Nuisances.

Because most land use nuisances are in the *per accidens* category, the judicial reluctance to grant injunctions against anticipatory nuisances is not surprising. The rule is that a court will not grant an injunction against an anticipatory nuisance unless the plaintiff can show with certainty that the use will be a nuisance in the area in which it plans to locate.[8] The funeral parlor cases illustrate this exception.

The judicial reluctance to enjoin anticipatory nuisances reflects the judicial tendency to require the compatibility of an invading use with the surrounding area. Many anticipatory nuisance cases arise in open undeveloped areas, where compatibility is not a problem because the character of the area is not yet determined. Judicial reluctance to enjoin anticipatory nuisances also reflects the usual judicial reluctance to enjoin a nuisance because of the fears and apprehensions of the plaintiff.

The judicial reluctance to enjoin anticipatory nuisances has important consequences for future residents of the surrounding area. New arrivals who build residences in the area will find themselves in the position of "coming to the nuisance." Should they later sue to enjoin the nuisance because it is incompatible with the area as subsequently developed, a court may decide not to grant the injunction because the nuisance enjoys priority in occupation.

One court has noted the relationship between anticipatory nuisance actions and the failure to enact comprehensive zoning to protect undeveloped areas. In *Henn v. Universal Atlas Cement Co.*,[9] plaintiffs sued to enjoin the operation of a quarry as an anticipatory nuisance after a referendum on a zoning ordinance lost at the polls. A second referendum was pending. The court noted that the granting of an injunction would determine future land use in the area and would lend the weight of the court to one of the factions in the "zoning battle." It held that "[t]he benefits of zoning must be won at the polls, not in the courtroom."

## § 4.04. Priority of Occupation.

Priority of occupation is a factor some courts consider in nuisance cases. If the defendant's use is in existence when a plaintiff establishes his use, a court may apply the priority of occupation rule and deny relief to the plaintiff because he "came" to the nuisance. The priority of occupation rule derives from princi-

---

**8.** Green v. Castle Concrete Co., 509 P.2d 588 (Colo. 1973); Connecticut Bank & Trust Co. v. Mularcik, 174 A.2d 128 (Conn. 1961); Camp v. Warrington, 182 S.E.2d 419 (Ga. 1971); Conner v. Smith, 433 S.W.2d 911 (Tex. Civ. App. 1968); 55 A.L.R. 880 (1928).

**9.** 144 N.E.2d 917 (Ohio C.P. 1957). *See also* Menger v. Pass, 80 A.2d 702 (Pa. 1951).

ples of equity that require plaintiffs to come into court with "clean hands." Because the plaintiff came into the area knowing that the nuisance existed, he does not have "clean hands." Courts do not regard priority of occupation as an absolute defense available to a defendant whose use came first. They treat priority of occupation as one factor and weigh it in the balance when they decide whether to grant relief to a plaintiff. The courts are less likely to grant an injunction when the plaintiff seeking the injunction "came" to the nuisance.[10]

Courts may especially be willing to deny relief to a plaintiff who "comes to a nuisance" by building a residence in an industrial area if the area is clearly incompatible with residential uses.[11] A court may also deny relief when a plaintiff builds a home in an area that later becomes industrial if the area was likely to be developed for industrial purposes when the plaintiff built his home. In *Bove v. Donner-Hanna Coke Corp.*,[12] a plaintiff sued to enjoin coke works constructed after she had built her home. The court held for the coke works because the plaintiff "should have known" that the area would eventually be developed industrially because "in a growing community, changes are inevitable."

The rule denying relief to a plaintiff who "comes" to the nuisance is questionable. If a court applies this rule to deny relief against a nuisance, an accidental priority in time will determine the future development of the area. The arrival of the nuisance "first in time" will impose a "negative servitude" on the surrounding area that allows it to remain even though it is incompatible with the way in which the area develops. Cases like *Bove* reject the "negative servitude" doctrine implicit in the priority of occupation rule.

### § 4.05. Nuisances in Residential Neighborhoods.

Courts recognize the land use hierarchy implicit in nuisance cases by granting relief to plaintiffs who sue to prohibit noxious nonresidential uses in residential neighborhoods. Nuisance suits against industrial uses seldom present difficulties. In *Schlotfelt v. Vinton Farmers' Supply Co.*,[13] for example, the court enjoined a feed grinding and mixing business in a residential neighborhood. No case was

---

10. Kriener v. Turkey Valley Community School Dist., 212 N.W.2d 526 (Iowa 1973); Schlotfelt v. Vinton Farmers' Supply Co., 109 N.W.2d 695 (Iowa 1961); Williams v. Oeder, 659 N.E.2d 379 (Ohio App. 1995); Weida v. Ferry, 493 A.2d 824 (R.I. 1985); Kellogg v. Village of Viola, 227 N.W.2d 55 (Wis. 1975); Abdella v. Smith, 149 N.W.2d 537 (Wis.1967); 42 A.L.R.3d 344 (1972). *But see* Jerry Harmon Motors, Inc. v. Farmers Union Grain Term. Ass'n, 337 N.W.2d 427 (N.D. 1983) (plaintiff coming to nuisance has "heavy burden to establish liability").

11. Powell v. Superior Portland Cement, 129 P.2d 536 (Wash. 1942).

12. 258 N.Y.S. 229 (App. Div. 1932).

13. 109 N.W.2d 695 (Iowa 1961). *See also* Wilson v. Interlake Steel Co., 649 P.2d 922 (Cal. 1982); Padillo v. Lawrence, 685 P.2d 964 (N.M. App. 1984). *Compare* Rose v. Chaiken, 453 A.2d 1378 (N.J. Ch. Div. 1982) (noise from windmill held a nuisance in a residential neighborhood).

found in which a plaintiff attempted to prohibit a different type of residential dwelling, such as multi-family apartments, in residential neighborhoods.[14]

### § 4.06. Commercial Uses.

The physical basis for nuisance actions leads to mixed results when plaintiffs attempt to prohibit commercial uses in residential neighborhoods. A commercial use is not usually physically noxious. Homeowners in residential neighborhoods must rely on some other physically intrusive aspect of commercial uses if they seek to prohibit them as nuisances.

A pair of Pennsylvania cases indicates the mixed judicial view toward commercial uses in residential areas. In *Essick v. Shillam,*[15] residential homeowners asked for an injunction to prohibit the construction of a supermarket in a residential area. They claimed a nuisance would be created by the traffic congestion caused by the store's parking lot and patrons who would shop in the store. They also claimed that bright lights that would illuminate the store would be a nuisance. The court denied an injunction, noting in part that the expected disturbance from the store was anticipatory.[16]

In *Diehl v. Lockard,*[17] the court granted an injunction against construction of a drive-in restaurant in a residential area. It upheld findings by the lower court that traffic, smells, lights, and other disturbances would constitute a nuisance.[18] Judicial holdings on filling stations as nuisances in residential areas are also mixed.[19]

### § 4.07. Funeral Parlors.

Funeral parlors are usually located in well-kept residences or buildings, do not attract substantial amounts of traffic on a regular basis, are pleasant and attractive in appearance, and certainly do not create noise or disturbances. Despite these characteristics, the majority of courts enjoin a funeral parlor in residential areas as an anticipatory nuisance.

The funeral parlor cases usually point out that funeral parlors are different from similar commercial uses as nuisances, such as stores and restaurants that are not drive-ins. They invade the integrity of residential neighborhoods and disturb the seclusion to which residents of these neighborhoods are entitled. Re-

---

**14.** *But cf.* Scoville v. Ronalter, 291 A.2d 222 (Conn. 1971) (suggesting that apartments are not nuisances in single-family neighborhoods).

**15.** 32 A.2d 416 (Pa. 1943).

**16.** *Accord* Winget v. Winn-Dixie Stores, Inc., 130 S.E.2d 363 (S.C. 1963); 146 A.L.R. 1407 (1943).

**17.** 385 A.2d 550 (Pa. Super. 1978).

**18.** *Accord* Wade v. Fuller, 365 P.2d 802 (Utah 1961). *See* Reid v. Brodsky, 156 A.2d 334 (Pa. 1959); 91 A.L.R.2d 572 (1963).

**19.** Bortz v. Troth, 59 A.2d 93 (Pa. 1948); 124 A.L.R. 383 (1940).

minders of death, and the coming and going of caskets and mourners, are depressing. When the neighborhood is clearly residential, the majority of courts enjoin the establishment of funeral parlors for these reasons.[20]

### § 4.08. People as Nuisances.

In a few cases, the courts considered actions to prohibit as nuisances the establishment of half-way houses and other group homes in residential areas. Like funeral parlors, these uses are located in residential dwellings and do not have the physically noxious characteristics that lead courts to enjoin a use as a nuisance.

*Nicholson v. Connecticut Half-Way House, Inc.*[21] is a leading case refusing to enjoin the establishment of a home for prison parolees in a dwelling in a residential neighborhood. The court's opinion is consistent with other cases refusing injunctions against anticipatory nuisances. It held it would not grant an injunction based solely on the fears and apprehensions of neighborhood residents. The court left for another day the question whether it would grant an injunction if problems arose in the operation of the home.

Other courts granted injunctions against similar group homes after they began operation and after disturbing incidents occurred,[22] although some "incidents," such as a conversation with a resident who acted "silly," hardly justified an injunction. One case that granted an injunction was based on the fears and apprehensions rejected in the *Nicholson* opinion.[23]

### § 4.09. Aesthetic Nuisances.

The decisions on aesthetic nuisances are also divided. The automobile junkyard cases illustrate the aesthetic nuisance problem. Junkyards are visually offensive but physically passive. In *Parkersburg Bldrs. Material Co. v. Barrack,*[24] an early and leading junkyard case, the court reversed a trial judge who refused an injunction and explicitly addressed the aesthetics issue. It noted that "a thing visually offensive may seriously affect the residents of a community in the reasonable enjoyment of their homes, and may produce a decided reduction in

---

**20.** Potter v. Bryan Funeral Home, 817 S.W.2d 882 (Ark. 1991) (not enjoinable; area not residential); Powell v. Taylor, 263 S.W.2d 906 (Ark. 1954); Dawson v. Laufersweiler, 43 N.W.2d 726 (Iowa 1950); Travis v. Moore, 377 So. 2d 609 (Miss. 1979); 8 A.L.R.4th 324 (1981).

**21.** 218 A.2d 383 (Conn. 1966). *Accord* Deep East Texas Regional Mental Health & Mental Retardation Servs. v. Kinnear, 877 S.W.2d 550 (Tex. App. 1994).

**22.** Smith v. Gill, 310 So. 2d 214 (Ala. 1975). *Compare* Everett v. Paschall, 111 P. 879 (Wash. 1910) (injunction granted against tuberculosis sanitarium).

**23.** Arkansas Release Guidance Found. v. Needler, 477 S.W.2d 821 (Ark. 1972) (home for parolees). *See also* Armory Park Neighborhood Ass'n v. Episcopal Community Serv., 712 P.2d 914 (Ariz. 1985) (indigent food distribution center held a public nuisance).

**24** 191 S.E. 368, 192 S.E. 291 (W. Va. 1937).

property values." It added that a court should act "only when there is presented a situation which is offensive to the view of the average persons in the community." Other cases have agreed[25] or disagreed[26] with this decision in junkyard as well as other cases brought against uses as diverse as a used-car lot and the raising of livestock. The cases rejecting *Parkersburg* are questionable as most courts now recognize aesthetic purposes in zoning. Two recent cases have also held that the deprivation of light and air is a nuisance, a rejection of the majority view on this question.[27] Some of the land uses that raise aesthetic nuisance problems are now regulated under statutory programs. All states, for example, regulate junkyards under requirements imposed by the federal Highway Beautification Act.[28]

### § 4.10. Legalizing Nuisances Through Zoning.

A zoning ordinance allowing a use claimed to be a nuisance creates a problem in nuisance law. Courts enjoin nuisances because they are unreasonable uses in the areas in which they are present, but the zoning ordinance is a legislative declaration that the use is compatible with the surrounding area. Some courts give the zoning ordinance at least some weight when they decide whether to enjoin a nuisance,[29] and this may be the majority view.

The majority view is that a zoning ordinance allowing a use is not an absolute bar to an injunction against a nuisance,[30] but a minority of courts adopt the contrary view.[31] Cases following the majority rule are short on analysis but usually hold that a municipality may not legalize a use that could be a nuisance in the area in which it is located.

---

**25.** Allison v. Smith, 695 P.2d 791 (Colo. App. 1984); Ward v. Scott, 93 A.2d 385 (N.J. 1952).

**26.** B & W Mgt., Inc. v. Tasea Inv. Co., 451 A.2d 879 (D.C. App. 1982); Green v. Castle Concrete Co., 509 P.2d 588 (Colo. 1973); Noakes v. Gaiser, 315 P.2d 183 (Colo. 1957); Robie v. Lillis, 299 A.2d 155 (N.H. 1972); Crabtree v. City Auto Salvage Co., 340 S.W.2d 940 (Tenn. App. 1960). *Cf.* Carroll v. Hurst, 431 N.E.2d 1344 (Ill. App. 1982).

**27.** Tenn v. 889 Assocs., 500 A.2d 366 (N.H. 1985); Prah v. Moretti, 321 N.W.2d 182 (Wis. 1982).

**28.** 23 U.S.C. § 136.

**29.** Harrison v. Indiana Auto Shredders Co., 528 F.2d 1107 (7th Cir. 1976); Weltshe v. Graf, 82 N.E.2d 795 (Mass. 1948); Rockenbach v. Apostle, 47 N.W.2d 636 (Mich. 1951).

**30.** Armory Park Neighborhood Ass'n v. Episcopal Community Serv., 712 P.2d 914 (Ariz. 1985); Sierra Screw Prods. v. Azusa Greens, Inc., 151 Cal. Rptr. 799 (Cal. App. 1979); Allison v. Smith, 695 P.2d 791 (Colo. App. 1984); Ferreira v. D'Asaro, 152 So. 2d 736 (Fla. App. 1963); Valley Poultry Farms, Inc. v. Preece, 406 S.W.2d 413 (Ky. 1966); Weltshe v. Graf, 82 N.E.2d 795 (Mass. 1948); Rockenbach v. Apostle, 47 N.W.2d 636 (Mich. 1951); Kozesnsik v. Township of Montgomery, 131 A.2d 1 (N.J. 1957); Dunaway v. City of Austin, 290 S.W.2d 703 (Tex. App. 1956).

**31.** Kirk v. Mabis, 246 N.W. 759 (Iowa 1933); Winget v. Winn-Dixie Stores, Inc., 130 S.E.2d 363 (S.C. 1963).

This conclusion requires some qualification. The decisions on the effect of zoning on a nuisance action are best explained by the effect the court gives to the zoning ordinance. The decisions indicate that the enactment of a zoning ordinance authorizing a use precludes only a holding that the use is a nuisance *per se*.[32] A zoning ordinance cannot preclude a court from holding the use a nuisance *per accidens*.[33] This distinction may explain what courts mean when they hold that a zoning ordinance may not legalize the creation of a nuisance. Some statutes cover the zoning question.[34]

### § 4.11. The Injunction Remedy.

### § 4.12. Balancing the Equities.

The uncertain state of land use nuisance law is explained in part by the injunction remedy plaintiffs usually seek in these cases. Under standard equity principles, a court will not grant an injunction as a matter of right. It balances the equities to determine whether an injunction is appropriate. In many nuisance cases, the balancing test works to the disadvantage of the plaintiff. He may be a single homeowner who seeks to prohibit a use, such as a manufacturing plant, that provides substantial economic benefit to the community. A court may conclude that the benefits to the plaintiff as balanced against the costs to the defendant do not warrant an injunction under the facts of the case.

The rule that courts will balance the equities in nuisance cases is well-established in most jurisdictions.[35] Courts consider a number of factors when applying the balancing test in land use cases. As in equity cases generally, the availability of damages as an adequate legal remedy is one factor.[36] The economic impact on the defendant and the economic importance of the defendant's use are other factors courts consider.[37]

The balancing test takes on a somewhat different coloration in land use nuisance cases. Because the appropriateness of a use at its location is so decisive in these cases, the nature of the area in which the nuisance use is located may help

---

**32.** Weaver v. Bishop, 52 P.2d 853 (Okla. 1935).

**33.** *Cf.* City of St. Louis v. Golden Gate Corp., 421 S.W.2d 4 (Mo. 1967) (city may not confer jurisdiction on court).

**34.** Cal. Civ. Proc. Code § 731(a) (manufacturing, commercial, or airport uses authorized by zoning enjoinable if employ unnecessary and injurious methods of operation, and nuisance can be eliminated at reasonable cost). *See* Sierra Screw Prods. v. Azusa Greens, Inc., 151 Cal. Rptr. 799 (Cal. App. 1979); Venuto v. Owens-Corning Fiberglas Corp., 99 Cal. Rptr. 350 (Cal. App. 1971).

**35.** Helmkamp v. Clark Ready Mix Co., 214 N.W.2d 126 (Iowa 1974); Storey v. Central Hide & Rendering Co., 226 S.W.2d 615 (Tex. 1950); 40 A.L.R.2d 601 (1971).

**36.** Daigle v. Continental Oil Co., 277 F. Supp. 875 (1967); McCarty v. Macy & Co., 334 P.2d 156 (Cal. App. 1959); Haack v. Lindsay Light & Chem. Co., 66 N.E.2d 391 (Ill. 1946).

**37.** Riter v. Keokuk Electro-Metals Co., 82 N.W.2d 151 (Iowa 1957); York v. Stallings, 341 P.2d 529 (Or. 1959).

decide the injunction issue. If the court characterizes the area as mixed residential and industrial, for example, it may decide that the equities do not require an injunction.[38] The decision on whether the offending use is a nuisance merges with the decision on the remedy.

A court is in a quandary if it believes the offending use is a nuisance but that it cannot modify its operations to avoid damage to adjacent homeowners. A decision to grant an injunction may impose substantial costs on the defendant. Damages may be an adequate legal remedy in this situation but do not give the plaintiff the relief he seeks from continuing disturbance. A damages remedy also leaves the residential neighborhood permanently impaired.

Some courts resolve this quandary by favoring the plaintiff, even though the economic loss to the defendant is substantial. In *Schlotfelt v. Vinton Farmers' Supply Co.*,[39] the court held that a feed grinding, feed mixing, and fertilizer sales business was a nuisance in a residential neighborhood. The disturbance to the plaintiff was partly physical, consisting of vibrations from defendant's machinery, as well as dust and noxious odors from the grinding and mixing.

Although the trial court decree would have allowed the defendant to continue its operations if it could remedy the physical disturbances to the plaintiff, the defendant claimed it could not meet this requirement. Closing the business was the only alternative. The court weighed the equities and granted an injunction even though the plant might have to close, partly because priority of occupation favored the plaintiff. The plaintiff had found its "clean and quiet" residential neighborhood invaded by this noxious use. Other courts reached similar results.[40]

### § 4.13. No Injunction Allowed.

In a leading case, *Boomer v. Atlantic Cement Co.*,[41] the plaintiff sought an injunction against a cement plant because of vibrations and air pollution caused by the plant's operation. The court rejected the previously accepted rule in New York that courts will grant an injunction in a nuisance case if the damage to the plaintiff is substantial. It held that payment of compensation to the plaintiff for permanent injury was the proper remedy.

The facts of the case clearly influenced the court. It noted the disparity between the damage suffered by the plaintiff and the loss to the community should the defendant's plant close. It observed that the defendant could abate the nui-

---

**38.** McCarty v. Macy & Co., 334 P.2d 156 (Cal. App. 1959); Roy v. Chevrolet Motor Car Co., 247 N.W. 774 (Mich. 1933); York v. Stallings, 341 P.2d 529 (Or. 1959).

**39.** 109 N.W.2d 695 (Iowa 1961).

**40.** Pendoley v. Ferreira, 187 N.E.2d 142 (Mass. 1963); Mahoney v. Walter, 205 S.E.2d 692 (W. Va. 1974). *But see* Hartford Penn-Cann Serv. v. Zymblosky, 549 A.2d 554 (Pa. Super. 1988) (court should have ordered alternative to remedy dust problem rather than issuing order that closed business).

**41.** 257 N.E.2d 870 (N.Y. 1970).

sance by making technological improvements in its operations, but that its ability to achieve the technological advances necessary for these improvements was not certain. Nor should the defendant be burdened with the research necessary to develop a new technology, a need common to the entire industry. The court held that damages would adequately redress the harm to the plaintiff and spur the research necessary to produce the required technological improvements. The dissent viewed the majority opinion as a judicially mandated private inverse condemnation not supported by judicial precedent. *Boomer* could apply to many land use nuisance cases in which physical disturbance by the defendant is an issue, but may not apply when a nuisance use is incompatible with the area in which it is located and technological modification is not an issue.[42]

### § 4.14. Compensation to Defendant.

A modification of the injunction remedy can avoid the imposition of excessive costs on a defendant. This alternative, which some scholars recommend, allows the court to grant an injunction if the plaintiff pays damages to the defendant to meet its relocation costs. Advocates of this remedy claim it is more efficient. Plaintiffs will not provide compensation for relocation unless the benefits of the defendant's relocation exceed the relocation costs they must shoulder. Only one case approved this remedy. In *Spur Indus. v. Del E. Webb Dev. Co.*,[43] a plaintiff that developed a new residential community in an agricultural area sued to enjoin the operation of an adjacent feedlot. The developer had "come" to the feedlot by expanding its development. The court recognized that this fact justified a denial of an injunction only if the plaintiff had alleged a private nuisance. Plaintiff also alleged a public nuisance based on an injury to all homeowners in the surrounding area. The court granted an injunction because the defendant's nuisance was public as well as private. It required the plaintiff to compensate the defendant for its relocation costs as a condition to injunctive relief because the defendant enjoyed priority of occupation.

Whether this remedy is practicable in many situations is problematic. In *Spur,* the plaintiff was a developer of a large residential community and could afford the compensation costs. It also was the only landowner in the area. A court would not likely place all of the costs of relocation on an individual plaintiff who sues for an injunction. Overcoming the "freeloader" problem by requiring other adjacent homeowners to participate in the compensation burden may stretch judicial competence.

---

**42.** *Compare* Little Joseph Realty, Inc. v. Town of Babylon, 363 N.E.2d 1163 (N.Y. 1977) (asphalt plant enjoined as violation of zoning ordinance).

**43.** 494 P.2d 700 (Ariz. 1972).

## B. STATUTORY AUTHORITY.

### § 4.15. The Standard Zoning Act.

All state zoning legislation is based on a Standard Zoning Enabling Act proposed by the U.S. Department of Commerce in the mid-1920s that preceded by a few years the publication of a Standard Planning Act.[44] Although many states have modified the Standard Zoning Act, some substantially, these changes do not alter the basic statutory framework of this legislative model. The Standard Zoning Act provides a common statutory basis for zoning that makes court decisions on zoning applicable nationwide.

The drafters of the Standard Zoning Act built carefully on the nuisance concept as applied in land use conflict cases. They noted that courts draw lines to determine the established residential districts that are protected from invading offensive uses. The Zoning Act adopted this concept as the basis for the zoning ordinance. The Act authorized municipalities to designate zoning districts in which only compatible uses are allowed and incompatible uses are excluded. As implemented at the local level, the zoning ordinance establishes a land use hierarchy with residential districts at the top of the land use pyramid.

Careful inspection of the Standard Zoning Act also indicates that the drafters contemplated a static zoning system in which the zoning districts would indicate land uses permitted "as of right" throughout the community. This legislative intent is apparent from the limited opportunities the Standard Act provided for administrative relief. The Act created a board of adjustment with limited powers to grant hardship variances and special exceptions specifically enumerated in the zoning ordinance. The drafters borrowed the variance idea from the local building code and indicated that the variance was an experiment subject to statutory modification as localities gained experience with zoning. The zoning variance has become standard practice, but major modification has not occurred.

Although the drafters contemplated a zoning system in which uses would be permitted as of right and modifications few, everyone knows that municipalities do not manage the zoning process in this manner. In urban areas with little land available for development, the zoning ordinance is comparatively stable. Incremental modifications through variances and exceptions are the rule. In suburban areas, localities usually adopt low-density residential zones that do not permit intensive land development. This practice allows localities to adopt a "wait and see" zoning system in which developers must secure a major zoning change before they can develop their land. Because almost all development requires a zoning change, the "wait and see" approach allows local zoning agencies to exercise considerable control over the land development process.

---

44. § 3.05.

The Standard Act contains an anachronism no longer common in local zoning practice. It authorized a "zoning commission" with the authority to recommend the adoption of zoning districts and regulations. The Act stated that "[w]here a city plan commission already exists, it may be appointed as the zoning commission." The drafters authorized a zoning commission because the Standard Zoning Act preceded the Standard Planning Act. Although some state legislation still authorizes a zoning commission, the planning commission carries out the functions of the zoning commission in almost all communities.

### § 4.16. Zoning Purposes.

Section 1 of the Standard Zoning Act provides the basic "Grant of Power." It authorizes the local legislative body

> to regulate and restrict the height, number of stories, and size of buildings and other structures, the percentage of lot that may be occupied, the size of yards, courts, and other open spaces, the density of population, the location and use of buildings, structures, and land for trade, industry, residence, or other purposes.[45]

This section provides the statutory authority for density, site development, bulk, and use restrictions. Note that the Act contemplates regulation of the "use" of land for the three major land use categories. The reference to "land for trade" is intended to cover commercial development.

Section 3, which states the "purposes" of local zoning regulation, further elaborates the scope of zoning:

> Sec. 3. Purposes in View. Such regulations shall be made in accordance with a comprehensive plan and designed to lessen congestion in the streets; to secure safety from fire, panic, and other dangers; to promote health and the general welfare; to provide adequate light and air; to prevent the overcrowding of land; to avoid undue concentration of population; to facilitate the adequate provision of transportation, water, sewerage, schools, parks, and other public requirements. Such regulations shall be made with reasonable consideration, among other things, to the character of the district and its peculiar suitability for particular uses, and with a view to conserving the value of buildings and encouraging the most appropriate use of land throughout such municipality.[46]

---

**45.** *See* Bittinger v. Corporation of Bolivar, 395 S.E.2d 554 (W.Va. 1990) (explaining distinction between planning and zoning).

**46.** *See* Board of Township Trustees v. Funtime, Inc., 563 N.E.2d 717 (Ohio 1990) (act does not authorize control of hours of operation).

This section is critical. Its quaint language indicates the origins of zoning in New York City and a concern with zoning problems specific to Manhattan. The concern over "safety from fire" and "adequate light and air" reflects the drafters' concern with the height and siting of the tall skyscrapers that, even then, were common to that city.

Sections 1 and 3 provide the statutory authority for zoning ordinances. They have not proved especially troublesome for courts asked to consider the statutory basis for a zoning regulation, although some modern forms of land use regulation are not included. Aesthetic regulation is one example. Nor have all of the statutory authorizations received extensive judicial consideration. The statutory direction to conserve "the value of buildings" is an example. Some courts rely on this delegation of authority to uphold architectural design review ordinances that protect the aesthetic integrity of residential areas.[47]

### § 4.17. The District Concept.

Section 2 of the Standard Zoning Act provides the necessary authority to divide the community

> into districts of such number, shape, and area as may be deemed best suited to carry out the purposes of this act; and within such districts ... [to] regulate and restrict the erection, construction, reconstruction, alteration, repair, or use of buildings, structures, or land.

The Act appears to provide authority to regulate building construction as well as land use, but that was not the intent. The statute was intended to authorize land use regulations in zoning ordinances that municipalities apply when buildings are erected, constructed, reconstructed, altered, or repaired. A final sentence in this section requires uniformity of regulations within districts but allows regulations in the various zoning districts to differ from each other.

### § 4.18. Adoption and Amendment.

Sections 4 and 5 of the Standard Act authorize the local legislative body to adopt and amend zoning "regulations and restrictions and ... [district] boundaries." The Act does not provide statutory standards to guide the adoption and amendment process, which the drafters apparently treated as a legislative function. The Act also requires notice by publication and a hearing for all zoning ordinance adoptions and amendments. A three-fourths vote by the legislative body is required to adopt a zoning amendment if twenty percent of the affected property owners or twenty percent of adjacent or opposite property owners protest its

---

47. § 11.03.

adoption. The cases indicate that this provision does not apply to a comprehensive revision of a zoning ordinance.[48]

### § 4.19. Board of Adjustment.

The Standard Act confers the administrative powers to be exercised under the zoning ordinance on a board of adjustment, which is called a board of zoning adjustment in some state legislation and some zoning ordinances. The board has three powers. It may hear appeals from interpretations of the zoning ordinance. It may "hear and decide special exceptions to the terms of the ordinance upon which such board is required to pass under such ordinance." The board may also authorize variances from the zoning ordinance not "contrary to the public interest, where, owing to special conditions, a literal enforcement of the provisions of the ordinance will result in unnecessary hardship, and so that the spirit of the ordinance shall be observed and substantial justice done."

In practice, and in the court decisions, the distinction between special exceptions and variances is confused. The conventional understanding is that a special exception is a use in a zoning district that is authorized by the zoning ordinance and requires permission from the board. Zoning ordinances may use the term "conditional use" as an alternative. Conditional uses do not require proof of unnecessary hardship.

### § 4.20. Enforcement.

Section 8 of the Standard Act provides that any violation of the Act or a zoning ordinance is a misdemeanor, punishable by fine, imprisonment, or civil penalties. The municipality may also bring "appropriate" proceedings against any violation of the Act or a zoning ordinance.

### § 4.21. Modern Zoning Legislation.

California, New Jersey, and Pennsylvania are among the states that have enacted comprehensive revisions of their zoning legislation that modify the Standard Act. Some of these modifications, such as statutory authority for the approval of planned unit developments, are discussed in later chapters in this book. The innovations adopted in these states do not change the basic structure of the Standard Act. They retain the zoning district concept and do not usually modify the role of the legislative body or the board of adjustment. A number of states

---

**48.** Wanamaker v. City Council, 19 Cal. Rptr. 554 (Cal. App. 1962); Benesh v. Township of Frenchtown, 228 N.W.2d 459 (Mich. App. 1975).

have adopted comprehensive revisions of their zoning enabling legislation in recent years.[49]

California zoning legislation illustrates changes in the Standard Act that expand its regulatory authority and change the distribution of administrative responsibilities. This legislation specifically authorizes regulations for site development, such as off-street parking, setbacks and land use intensity; signs and billboards and sexually-oriented businesses.[50] It strengthens the role of the planning commission by making the commission's recommendation against a zoning map change final unless "otherwise provided by ordinance" or unless an "interested party" requests a hearing before the legislative body.[51]

California authorizes the creation of a board of zoning adjustment, the office of zoning administrator, or both.[52] The zoning administrator may grant variances and the zoning ordnance may authorize him to grant conditional uses or other permits, and he may grant variances.[53] A local government may establish a board of appeals to hear appeals from the board of zoning adjustment or the zoning administrator.[54] A municipality may also authorize the planning commission to exercise the functions of the board of adjustment or zoning administrator.[55]

## § 4.22. Extraterritorial Zoning.

Land development beyond municipal borders presents a difficult regulatory problem. Areas adjacent to a municipality may develop without the benefit of planning or zoning or may develop under county zoning regulations which are inconsistent with the municipality's planning and zoning policies.

Municipalities can acquire some control over adjacent areas by prezoning adjacent land. This technique requires statutory authority.[56] The California legislation, for example, authorizes the municipalities to prezone adjacent areas to predetermine the zoning that will take effect upon annexation.[57]

State legislation authorizing extraterritorial zoning usually limits this power. Illinois legislation states that municipal extraterritorial zoning "shall be reasonable with respect to the area outside the corporate limits so that future develop-

---

**49.** *E.g.,* R.I. Gen. Laws § 45-22.2-1 et seq.; Utah Code Ann. § 10-9-101 et seq., § 17-27-101 et seq.

**50.** Cal. Gov't Code § 65850.

**51.** *Id.* § 65856.

**52.** *Id .* § 65900.

**53.** *Id.* § 65901.

**54.** *Id.* § 65903.

**55.** *Id.* § 65902.

**56.** *Cf.* City of Carlsbad v. Caviness, 346 P.2d 310 (N.M. 1959). *See also* Smeltzer v. Messer, 225 S.W.2d 96 (Ky. 1949) (extraterritorial zoning statute did not authorize zoning in another county).

**57.** Cal. Gov't Code § 65859.

ment will not be hindered or impaired."[58] Nor may a municipality exercise extraterritorial zoning powers if a county has adopted a zoning ordinance. North Carolina has a similar prohibition and, municipalities must define their extraterritorial zoning area by ordinance, "based upon existing or projected urban development and areas of critical concern to the city."[59] Florida requires an agreement between the city and the county on the boundaries of the extraterritorial zoning area, and on joint procedures in the preparation and adoption of comprehensive plans and the administration of land development regulations.[60]

## § 4.23. Constitutional Problems.

The state legislation that authorizes municipalities to adopt extraterritorial zoning does not give residents in the extraterritorial area the right to vote on the zoning ordinance. This omission may raise problems under the U.S. Supreme Court's right-to-vote cases. In *Holt Civic Club v. City of Tuscaloosa*[61] the court upheld a statute that extended the city's licensing, police, sanitary, and criminal court jurisdiction to a three-mile extraterritorial area against right-to-vote objections.

The Court held a right-to-vote problem arises only when a city denies the vote to individuals physically resident within its limits. Any other rule, it held, would be difficult to apply. Nonresidents could argue that many municipal actions taken within municipal limits require voting by nonresidents because they affect their interests. The Court also held a state legislature has a legitimate interest in the exercise of necessary governmental powers in developed but unincorporated areas adjacent to cities. Extraterritorial legislation reasonably advances this interest.

*Holt* may not apply to extraterritorial zoning because the Court pointed out in a footnote that the statute upheld did not include the power to zone, levy property taxes, and use eminent domain, which it characterized as "vital and traditional authorities." However, a state court has applied *Holt* to uphold extraterritorial zoning against right-to-vote objections.[62]

State courts have also upheld statutes conferring extraterritorial zoning powers. In *Schlientz v. City of North Platte*[63] nonresidents objected, as in *Holt,* that state legislation denied them the right to vote on zoning ordinances applicable to extraterritorial areas. The court curtly dismissed this objection, noting that nonresidents "have neither a constitutional nor inherent right to local self-

---

**58.** § 65 Ill. Comp. Stat. Ann. 5/11-13-1.
**59.** N.C. Gen. Stat. § 160A-360.
**60.** Fla. Stat. Ann. § 163.3171(1).
**61.** 439 U.S. 60 (1978).
**62.** Town of Northville v. Village of Sheridan, 655 N.E.2d 22 (Ill. App. 1995).
**63.** 110 N.W.2d 58 (Neb. 1961).

government." *Schlientz* was decided before the U.S. Supreme Court's voting rights cases, but it states the majority rule on the inherent right doctrine.[64]

## C. HOME RULE.

### § 4.24. Constitutional Home Rule Authority.

A majority of state constitutions authorize municipal home rule, and some state constitutions authorize home rule for counties. Local governments in home rule states may be able to exercise land use control powers under their constitutional home rule authority.[65] The exercise of land use controls under constitutional home rule provisions has several advantages. Local governments could modify the administrative structure provided by the Standard Act for the zoning process, reassigning zoning responsibilities and even substituting alternative agencies and officers for the agencies specified in the Act. One possibility is the substitution of an administrative hearings officer for the board of adjustment, an option the California legislation authorizes. Local governments could also exercise substantive land use control powers under their constitutional home rule authority that the Standard Zoning Act does not expressly confer. Aesthetic controls are an example.

Whether land use controls are authorized by constitutional home rule depends to some extent on the type of home rule provision the constitution contains.[66] Under the traditional form of home rule the constitution specifies an area of concern in which local governments can legislate without statutory authority. A traditional home rule provision may authorize local governments to legislate concerning their "municipal" or "corporate" affairs. Traditional home rule provisions do not usually elaborate the powers that are of local concern, a function the courts have assumed.

Courts usually classify areas of regulatory concern under traditional home rule as belonging exclusively to the state, exclusively local, or of concern both to the state and its local governments. If the area of concern is both state and local, the local government may regulate but state legislation may preempt. If the area of concern is exclusively local, a local government has the authority to regulate and state legislation may not preempt. If the area of concern belongs to the state,

---

**64.** Upholding extraterritorial zoning as reasonable exercise of police power: Board of Comm'rs v. Kokomo City Plan. Comm'n, 310 N.E.2d 877 (Ind. App. 1974), *rev'd on other grounds,* 330 N.E.2d 92 (Ind. 1975); City of Raleigh v. Morand, 100 S.E.2d 870 (N.C. 1957); Walworth Co. v. City of Elkhorn, 133 N.W.2d 257 (Wis. 1965).

**65.** *See also* N.J. Const. art. IV, § 6, ¶ 2 (authorizes state legislature to adopt zoning legislation); Ga. Const. art. 9, § 2, ¶ 4 (counties and municipalities may exercise zoning power subject to general laws establishing procedures).

**66.** D. Mandelker, D. Netsch, P. Salsich & J. Wegner, State and Local Government in a Federal System 128-62 (4th ed. 1996).

a local government may not regulate in that area at all. Home rule cases considering land use powers in states adopting the traditional form of home rule appear to treat land use powers as falling in the shared state-local category.

A number of states have adopted a newer form of constitutional home rule, which is called legislative home rule.[67] Under this type of home rule, local governments may exercise all powers the state legislature is capable of delegating to them even though the legislature has not delegated the power. Legislative home rule clearly confers land use control powers. It also allows the state legislature to deny a home rule power a local government might otherwise exercise, and some state courts allow legislative denial by implication. These courts could construe state zoning legislation as an implied denial of local zoning powers.

Local governments usually implement their constitutional home rule powers by adopting a charter that specifies their home rule authority. Most state courts hold that local governments have only those home rule powers granted by their charters. A few state courts hold that local charters only limit home rule powers granted by the constitution.

## § 4.25. Home Rule Land Use Powers.

Although a few courts hold that zoning is not included in a home rule grant under traditional home rule,[68] most courts hold to the contrary. In some of these states, zoning is a matter of shared state and local concern and the exercise of zoning powers by home rule municipalities is subject to controlling provisions in the state zoning enabling act.[69]

Other states hold that zoning is a matter only of local concern and that the state statutes do not control. In *Service Oil Co. v. Rhodus*,[70] a city adopted a zoning ordinance requiring the termination of an abandoned nonconforming use. The state zoning statute did not authorize this provision. The court held that

---

**67.** *See, e.g.,* National Municipal League Alternative Home Rule Model § 8.02.

**68.** City of Livonia v. Department of Social Servs., 378 N.W.2d 402 (Mich. 1985); Asian Americans for Equality v. Koch, 514 N.Y.S.2d 939 (App. Div. 1987). *See also* City of Moore v. Atchison, Topeka & Santa Fe Ry. Co., 699 F.2d 507 (10th Cir. 1983) (zoning based on statute if not authorized by charter).

**69.** Gumprecht v. City of Coeur D'Alene, 661 P.2d 1214 (Idaho 1983); Scadron v. City of Des Plaines, 606 N.E.2d 1154 (Ill. 1992) (signs); Adams Outdoor Advertising v. East Lansing, 483 N.W.2d 38 (Mich. 1992) (sign ordinance authorized by home rule act); A.C.E. Equip. Co. v. Erickson, 152 N.W.2d 739 (Minn. 1967); Rispo Realty & Dev. Co. v. City of Parma, 564 N.E.2d 425 (Ohio 1990) (procedures in zoning ordinance conflicted with state law); State ex rel. Ekern v. City of Milwaukee, 209 N.W. 860 (Wis. 1926). *Compare* Nelson v. City of Seattle, 395 P.2d 82 (Wash. 1965) (city may reject statutory authority and zone under home rule powers).

**70.** 500 P.2d 807 (Colo. 1972). *See also* Board of County Comm'rs v. City of Thornton, 629 P.2d 605 (Colo. 1981) (home rule city has standing to object to zoning in adjacent county); Moore v. City of Boulder, 484 P.2d 134 (Colo. App. 1971) (zoning for low-income housing a local concern).

zoning was a matter of purely local concern and that the legislature could not limit the local zoning power. Some courts also hold that the procedures employed in local zoning and other land use controls are a matter of local concern and are governed by local charters or ordinances despite conflicting statutory provisions.[71]

A municipality in some traditional home rule states may exercise home rule powers, including land use powers, unless a statutory or other limitation prohibits the exercise of the power. In *Ayres v. City Council*,[72] the court held that a city could require land dedications from a residential developer even though the state subdivision control legislation, the city's charter, and the city's subdivision ordinance did not authorize these dedications. California is a "limitation" home rule state. The court found no limitation on the dedication requirement in the statute, the charter, or the ordinance.[73]

*White v. City of Dallas*[74] is a similar case. A home rule zoning ordinance gave the board of adjustment an original jurisdiction to hear and decide cases on the continuance of nonconforming uses. The court upheld the ordinance against a contention that it was inconsistent with the state zoning statute, which gave the board the authority only to hear and decide appeals.

Land use controls are clearly a delegated home rule power in the legislative home rule states because the constitution delegates all powers the legislature could exercise.[75] The issue in these states is whether a statute has denied a home rule municipality the power to adopt a land use ordinance. The answer to this question turns on the legislative intent.[76]

---

**71.** Thompson v. Cook County Zoning Bd. of Appeals, 421 N.E.2d 285 (Ill. 1981); Vito v. City of Garfield Heights, 200 N.E.2d 501 (Ohio App. 1962); Bartle v. Zoning Bd. of Adjustment, 137 A.2d 239 (Pa. 1958).

**72.** 207 P.2d 1 (Cal. 1949). *Compare* City of Los Angeles v. State, 187 Cal. Rptr. 893 (Cal. App. 1982) (home rule cities subject to requirement that zoning be consistent with plan).

**73.** *See also* Brougher v. Board of Pub. Works, 271 P. 487 (Cal. 1928) (statutory procedures for adoption of zoning ordinance do not apply to home rule city); Boulder Bldrs. Group v. City of Boulder, 759 P.2d 752 (Colo. 1988) (growth control ordinance limiting development held authorized under home rule powers); School Dist. of Philadelphia v. Zoning Bd. of Adjustment, 207 A.2d 864 (Pa. 1965). *See also* Sherman v. Frazier, 446 N.Y.S.2d 372 (App. Div. 1982) (zoning authority of towns).

**74.** 517 S.W.2d 344 (Tex. Civ. App. 1974). *See also* City of College Station v. Turtle Rock Corp., 680 S.W.2d 802 (Tex. 1984); Hollingsworth v. City of Dallas, 931 S.W.2d 699 (Tex. App. 1996).

**75.** Hollywood, Inc. v. Broward County, 431 So. 2d 606 (Fla. App. 1983) (subdivision exactions). *See* City of Boca Raton v. State, 595 So. 2d 25 (Fla. 1992) (home rule city may levy special assessment; reviews development of home rule powers).

**76.** Tisei v. Town of Ogunquit, 491 A.2d 564 (Me. 1985) (sewage usage ordinance held not in conflict with state law); Board of Appeals of Hanover v. Housing Appeals Comm., 294 N.E.2d 393 (Mass. 1973) (local zoning subject to state "snob zoning" law); City of Springfield v. Goff, 918 S.W.2d 786 (Mo. 1996) (city may not modify zoning protest provision in state statute).

## D. ZONING FOR GOVERNMENT AND GOVERNMENT-REGULATED LAND DEVELOPMENT.

### § 4.26. The Governmental Immunity Problem.

The Standard Zoning Act does not limit the application of zoning ordinances to private land uses. Nothing in the Act prevents a local government from applying its zoning ordinance to governmental facilities. The courts take a different view. They have adopted a number of rules to determine when zoning applies to the capital facilities of public agencies. Earlier cases found an absolute immunity based on sovereign immunity principles. The leading case adopting the sovereign immunity rule for state facilities is *Kentucky Institute for Educ. of the Blind v. City of Louisville*.[77] Some of the more recent cases have adopted a more flexible "balancing test" that views sovereign immunity as only one factor to consider in intergovernmental land use conflict cases.

A variant of the intergovernmental land use conflict problem arises when a municipality applies its zoning ordinance to a public or private facility licensed or approved by a state agency. Examples are a local waste disposal facility licensed under a state environmental protection law, a private utility power transmission line approved by a state public utility commission, and a group home for mentally retarded children licensed by a state welfare agency. State regulation may confer immunity from local zoning.

In the intergovernmental land use conflict cases considered here, the zoning ordinance prohibits the facility claiming immunity. A court may not confer immunity if the zoning ordinance applies only off-street parking or similar restrictions on site development.[78] Nor may a court confer immunity for a use accessory to a public facility even if the local zoning ordinance is prohibitory.[79]

Although a few states have legislation expressly addressing the intergovernmental conflict problem,[80] in most states the planning and zoning legislation does not explicitly address this issue. The Standard Planning Act requires a three-fourths approval of the local governing body to override a planning commission determination that a proposed capital facility is not consistent with the local comprehensive plan. This provision does not address the zoning problem. Section 9 of the Standard Zoning Act also provides that "higher standards" contained in the zoning ordinance prevail over standards imposed under other legislation. This provision does not explicitly address the intergovernmental conflict problem, although a few courts have relied on it to accord priority to a zoning regulation applicable to a public facility.

---

77. 97 S.W. 402 (Ky. 1906). *See also* Montgomery v. Town of Sherburne, 514 A.2d 702 (Vt. 1986) (federal immunity).

**78.** School Dist. of Philadelphia v. Zoning Bd. of Adjustment, 207 A.2d 864 (Pa. 1965).

**79.** Shell Oil Co. v. Board of Adjustment, 185 A.2d 201 (N.J. 1962).

**80.** § 4.41.

The absence of explicit legislative direction on the intergovernmental conflict problem sometimes leads courts to consider legislative intent when resolving intergovernmental conflicts in land use cases. Courts determine legislative intent even though the absence of published legislative histories in most states makes it difficult to make this determination. The rule applied by some courts that priority goes to the agency exercising the superior governmental power is an application of the legislative intent rule. The courts determine whether the legislature intended the local zoning power or the public agency's power to undertake capital facility projects to be the superior power. This view gives the courts considerable discretion. A court will usually observe that both powers come from the state legislature and that both are presumptively entitled to equal stature. The court then applies its own analysis of legislative intent to determine which power is superior.

Although a court may apply the same rule, such as the legislative interpretation rule, to a variety of intergovernmental conflict problems, the cases tend to divide depending on the status of the government seeking zoning immunity. Cases in which a state agency claims immunity, for example, may take a different view than cases in which one local government claims immunity from the zoning ordinance of another local government. The sections that follow divide the cases along these lines.

## § 4.27. State Agencies.

The primary sovereign status of the state initially led courts to give the capital projects of state agencies an absolute immunity from local zoning ordinances. Many of these cases simply follow *Kentucky Institute* and hold that the sovereign status of the state confers an absolute immunity on state agencies from local zoning.[81] Some of these cases limit state immunity to governmental as distinguished from proprietary functions. A judicial rule conferring absolute immunity on state agencies is questionable. It exalts sovereignty over substance, disregarding the impact a state facility can have on local zoning policies.[82]

---

**81.** Board of Regents v. City of Tempe, 356 P.2d 399 (Ariz. 1960); Regents of Univ. of Cal. v. City of Santa Monica, 143 Cal. Rptr. 276 (Cal. App. 1978); City of New Orleans v. State, 364 So. 2d 1020 (La. 1978); Morse v. Vermont Div. of State Bldgs., 388 A.2d 371 (Vt. 1978). *But see* Varnado v. Southern Univ. at New Orleans, 621 So. 2d 176 (La. App. 1993) (university not agent of state when its parking lots violated zoning ordinance); Senders v. Town of Columbia Falls, 647 A.2d 93 (Me. 1994) (lessee from state agency immune from zoning); City of Detroit v. Volunteers of America, 426 N.W.2d 743 (Mich. App. 1988) (independent contractor operating group home does not have state immunity); 84 A.L.R.3d 1187 (1978).

**82.** *But see* Snohomish County v. State, 648 P.2d 430 (Wash. 1982) (legislature expressly provided exemption for state prison).

A few courts have adopted a balancing test for state agency immunity that takes local zoning policies into account. The leading case is *Rutgers v. Piluso.*[83] The university was unable to build a dormitory for married students because it violated a local zoning ordinance limiting the number of dormitories for married, but not unmarried, students. The court held that the university was immune from the ordinance and that the "true test" of immunity in these cases was to determine the legislative intent by considering a number of "obvious and common" factors, including

> the nature and scope of the instrumentality seeking immunity, the kind of function or land use involved, the extent of the public interest to be served thereby, the effect local land use regulation would have upon the enterprise concerned and the impact of legitimate local interests.[84]

The court indicated that this list of factors was not all-inclusive.

The court emphasized that state agency immunity was not unbridled, and that a state agency must not assert immunity in an unreasonable and arbitrary manner. It held that the local zoning restriction did not serve a legitimate interest in this case. The municipality's interest in avoiding the cost of educating children living in university housing was not a legitimate zoning concern. Other courts have adopted the *Rutgers* balancing test and have applied it to some or all state agencies.[85]

In *Commonwealth, Dep't of Gen. Servs. v. Ogontz Area Neighbors Ass'n,*[86] the municipality refused to issue permits for a state workshop and development center for mentally handicapped persons that did not comply with the zoning ordinance. The court overruled an earlier case adopting the balancing test and held that courts should resolve state and local land use conflicts by determining the legislative intent. Because legislative intent was difficult to determine from the applicable statutes, the court applied the rule of construction that determines legislative intent by considering the consequences of a particular interpretation. The court concluded that giving priority to the zoning ordinance would give effect to the legislative mandates of both government entities. Allowing the state agency to override local zoning would frustrate local zoning powers, and a state agency prohibited from using one location could always find another.

---

**83.** 286 A.2d 697 (N.J. 1972). *See* Mayor & Council v. Clark, 516 A.2d 1126 (N.J. App. Div. 1986) (citing cases applying *Rutgers*).

**84.** 286 A.2d at 702.

**85.** Hayward v. Gaston, 542 A.2d 760 (Del. 1988); City of Newark v. University of Del., 304 A.2d 347 (Del. Ch. 1973); Kunimoto v. Kawakami, 545 P.2d 684 (Haw. 1976); Herrmann v. Board of Cty. Comm'rs, 785 P.2d 1003 (Kan. 1990); Brown v. Kansas Forestry, Fish & Game Comm'n, 576 P.2d 230 (Kan. App. 1978); Brownfield v. State, 407 N.E.2d 1365 (Ohio 1980).

**86.** 483 A.2d 448 (Pa. 1984). *See also* Olon v. Commonwealth, 626 A.2d 533 (Pa. 1993) (finding legislative intent to override local zoning ordinance), *cert. denied,* 510 U.S. 1044 (1994).

Although *Ogontz* rejected the balancing test, its legislative intent rule is similar to the multifactor "balancing" rule adopted in *Rutgers* that also emphasizes legislative intent. These decisions illustrate a growing line of cases that refuse to give absolute immunity to state agencies under a superior sovereignty theory.[87]

## § 4.28. Local Governments Exercising State Functions.

State-transferred immunity can bar local zoning in a category of cases in which local governments exercise state functions. Counties and school districts are in this category. Courts view these local government units as state "agencies" in the loose sense that they carry out state-delegated functions at the local level. County authority for the administration of justice is an example. Courts classify these governmental units as "quasi-local governments" to distinguish them from local governments exercising comprehensive local government powers.

A number of cases transfer the absolute immunity of the state to quasi-local governments exercising state functions.[88] These cases rely on the role of these governmental units in carrying out responsibilities for the state, such as the administration of justice, within their territorial areas. These cases are a strained interpretation of the state immunity rule. All local governments exercise powers delegated by the state. To separate so-called "quasi-local government" entities, such as counties and school districts, from general-function municipalities is improper. Decisions granting them immunity from local zoning are another example of exalting sovereignty over substance.

School districts present a special problem. Most courts exempt school districts from local zoning because the state retains extensive control over the education function. They may also rely on the statutory authority delegated to school districts to determine locations for school facilities.[89] These cases conclude that the grant of statutory authority to determine "location" overrides the authority of a local government to make the same decision under its zoning ordinance. Off-

---

87. *See also* Dearden v. City of Detroit, 245 N.W.2d 700 (Mich. App. 1976); City of Hattiesburg v. Region XII Comm'n on Mental Health & Retardation, 654 So. 2d 516 (Miss. 1995) (regional mental health facility subject to local zoning).

88. Vagim v. Board of Supvrs., 40 Cal. Rptr. 760 (Cal. App. 1964); County of Los Angeles v. City of Los Angeles, 28 Cal. Rptr. 32 (Cal. App. 1963); Lake Charles Harbor & Term. Dist. v. Calcasieu Parish Police Jury, 613 So. 2d 1031 (La. App. 1993); Glascock v. Baltimore Cty., 581 A.2d 822 (Md. 1990); County Comm'rs v. Conservation Comm'n of Dartmouth, 405 N.E.2d 637 (Mass. 1980).

89. Town of Atherton v. Superior Court, 324 P.2d 328 (Cal. App. 1958); Board of Coop. Educ. Serv. v. Gaynor, 303 N.Y.S.2d 183 (Sup. Ct. 1969); Appeal of Radnor Twp. School Auth., 252 A.2d 597 (Pa. 1969); Austin Indep. School Dist. v. City of Sunset Valley, 502 S.W.2d 670 (Tex. 1973); 71 A.L.R.3d 136 (1976). *See also* § 5.22 (zoning for private schools).

street parking requirements are an exception,[90] but they do not force school districts to select another site for a school.

Many states have constitutional provisions requiring the establishment of a system of public education. Some courts view state enabling legislation for school districts as a statutory implementation of this constitutional requirement. This constitutional authority for establishing a system of public education is another reason courts give for exempting school districts from local zoning.

The school cases stand apart. Provision of an adequate educational system requires the location of schools close to or within the neighborhoods they serve. Municipalities may attempt to exclude schools from these locations because residential neighbors consider schools an intrusive land use. The courts believe that educational necessity overrides local zoning powers often used to exclude schools at locations the school district considers appropriate.

### § 4.29.  State-Regulated Facilities and Businesses.

State legislation commonly provides for the licensing and regulation of a number of public and private facilities and private businesses. This legislation may authorize a state agency to permit the operation of a business or the construction of a facility at a designated location if the regulatory standards in the legislation are satisfied. An example is a permit for the operation of a private airport issued by the state aeronautics agency. Conflicts arise when a zoning ordinance prohibits the facility or business at the location the state agency designates. The state legislation may indicate whether the state agency can override the local zoning ordinance. If the legislation does not resolve the state-local conflict, the courts must determine whether the state agency can override local zoning.

The cases that have considered conflicts between state regulation and licensing and local zoning do not usually turn on the superior sovereignty of the state. Most courts examine the legislative intent to determine whether the state legislation preempts the local zoning ordinance, either expressly or by implication. To decide this question courts look at a number of factors, including the purpose of the statute, whether the subject matter requires a uniform system of state regulation, and whether the local regulation conflicts with or frustrates the purposes and objectives of the state law.

### § 4.30.  State Environmental Programs.

Many states, prodded by federal environmental legislation, have adopted statutes that require permits for environmental facilities. Legislation requiring per-

---

**90.** Robinson v. Indianola Mun. Separate School Dist., 467 So. 2d 911 (Miss. 1985); School Dist. of Philadelphia v. Zoning Bd. of Adjustment, 207 A.2d 864 (Pa. 1965).

mits for hazardous waste disposal facilities is an important example. A statute may make an environmental permit subject to local zoning regulations.[91] A number of states also have adopted statutes stating that a local government may not require permits for state-permitted hazardous waste facilities.[92] In the absence of an express provision covering local zoning, the courts must decide whether the legislature intended, by implication, that the state legislation overrides local zoning powers.

Courts are split on the issue of implied preemption. Although some courts hold to the contrary,[93] other courts hold a state statute preempts local zoning even without an express preemption provision.[94] Often when a court decides a state law does not preempt local zoning the reason is that the state law has a different purpose,[95] that the legislature did not intend to cover the entire regulatory field[96] or that the state statute included only minimum standards, which the local ordinance could exceed.[97] The home rule status of the zoning municipality may affect the resolution of this question.[98]

*Welsh v. City of Orono*[99] illustrates the cases finding preemption. The Minnesota Supreme Court held a municipality did not have the authority to require a conditional use permit for dredging and filling. The court held the legislature had clearly delegated water resource conservation, particularly jurisdiction over dredging and filling, to the state resources agency.[100]

---

91. Conn. Gen. Stat. § 22a-124; § 415 Ill. Comp. Stat. Ann. 5/39; La Stat. Ann. § 30:2180(C); Minn. Stat. Ann. § 115.28; N.C. Gen. Stat. § 13-215-108(f).

92. Ind. Code Ann. § 13-7-8.6-13(a); N.C. Gen. Stat. § 130A-293; Pa. Stat. Ann. tit. 52, § 681.20c.

93. Water Dist. No. 1 of Johnson County v. City Council of Kansas City, 871 P.2d 1256 (Kan. 1994) (state monofill law does not preempt); IT Corp. v. Solano County Bd. of Supvrs., 820 P.2d 1023 (Cal. 1991) (same; hazardous waste disposal); Council of Middletown Twp. v. Benhjam, 523 A.2d 311 (Pa. 1987) (same); Resource Conservation Mgt., Inc. v. Board of Supvrs., 380 S.E.2d 879 (Va. 1989) (same; landfills).

94. Holmes v. Maryland Reclamation Assocs., 600 A.2d 864 (Md. 1992) (solid waste management law); Applied Chem. Tech., Inc. v. Town of Merrimack, 490 A.2d 1348 (N.H. 1985) (hazardous waste); Little Falls Twp. v. Bardin, 414 A.2d 559 (N.J. 1979) (landfills).

95. Palermo Land Co. v. Planning Comm'n, 561 So. 2d 482 (La. 1990).

96. Resource Conservation Mgt., Inc. v. Board of Supvrs., 380 S.E.2d 879 (Va. 1989). *See also* Town of Beacon Falls v. Posick, 549 A.2d 656 (Conn. App. 1988) (statute interpreted to deny immunity).

97. IT Corp. v. Solano County Bd. of Supvrs., 820 P.2d 1023 (Cal. 1991).

98. *See* § 4.39.

99. 355 N.W.2d 117 (Minn. 1984).

100. Arthur Whitcomb, Inc. v. Town of Carroll, 686 A.2d 743 (N.H. 1996) (comprehensive state legislation on commercial excavation preempts local zoning); River Springs Ltd. Liability Co. v. Board of County Comm'rs, 899 P.2d 1329 (Wyo. 1995) (state agency has pervasive control over mining). *See also* 67 A.L.R.4th 822 (1988).

*Ad+ Soil, Inc. v. County Commissioners*[101] held the state sewage management legislation did not preempt local zoning. The court found the state legislation intended to foster local control under state supervision, and that its purpose was to coordinate and supplement local zoning through the enactment of a statewide regulatory program.

### § 4.31. State Permits for Other Private Activities.

State legislation often requires a location permit for a number of private activities that also can be regulated by zoning ordinances. Examples are motor vehicle storage,[102] airports or heliports,[103] agricultural and forestry activities,[104] oil and gas well drilling and petroleum storage,[105] and gambling.[106] Courts again will look at the usual factors they apply in preemption cases to determine whether the local zoning ordinance is preempted. For example, in *Big Creek Lumber Co. v. County of San Mateo*,[107] the county zoning ordinance prohibited timber harvesting in designated rural areas within 1,000 feet of any dwelling. The court held the state Forest Practice Act did not preempt the county zoning ordinance. The Act regulated how timber operations should be conducted, while the county zoning ordinance regulated where they can take place.

### § 4.32. Private Utilities.

State utility regulation authorizes comprehensive regulations of an entire industry by the state utility agency. As part of its regulatory authority the state agency must approve the location of utility facilities, such as transmission lines and power stations. Municipalities may object to these facilities and exclude them through zoning or impose financially burdensome requirements, such as requiring the undergrounding of utility lines.

---

101. 513 A.2d 893 (Md. 1986).

102. Board of County Comm'rs v. Martin, 856 P.2d 62 (Colo. App. 1993) (zoning preempted); Joe Horisk's Salvage Pool Systems of Ohio v. City of Strongsville, 631 N.E.2d 1097 (Ohio App. 1993) (contra).

103. Helicopter Assocs. v. City of Stamford, 519 A.2d 49 (Conn. 1986) (zoning not preempted); Garden State Farms, Inc. v. Bay, II, 390 A.2d 1177 (N.J. 1978) (same); County of DuPage v. Harris, 231 N.E.2d 195 (Ill. App. 1967) (same).

104. Big Creek Lumber Co. v. County of San Mateo, 37 Cal. Rptr. 2d 159 (Cal. App. 1995) (timber harvesting; zoning ordinance not preempted).

105. Newbury Twp. Bd. of Twp. Trustees v. Lomak Petroleum (Ohio), Inc. 583 N.E.2d 302 (Ohio 1992) (oil and gas well drilling; zoning preempted); Northeastern Gas Co. v. Foster Twp. Zoning Hearing Bd., 613 A.2d 606 (Pa. 1992) (gasoline storage; zoning not preempted).

106. St. Charles Gaming Co. v. Riverboat Gaming Comm'n, 648 So. 2d 1310 (La. 1995) (zoning not preempted).

107. 37 Cal. Rptr. 2d 159 (Cal. App. 1995).

Exclusion of a utility's facility from a municipality may compel it to select a more expensive location. Rerouting of a power transmission line, for example, may be more expensive because the new route may be less direct. Most utilities also serve an area wider than the municipality that excludes or burdens its operations. State agency resolution of conflicts with local governments may be necessary to take the needs of the wider service area into account.

Many of the utility cases do not present a zoning problem. The overhead power line cases are an example. A municipality may simply adopt a "police power" ordinance that requires the utility to place power lines underground. Most courts hold that the state utility commission's approval of the overhead line under state legislation comprehensively regulating the utility industry confers immunity from this ordinance.[108]

Most courts reach the same result in the zoning cases for the same reason and grant immunity from zoning ordinances prohibiting a utility company facility.[109] The few zoning cases reaching a contrary result have not always considered the effect of comprehensive utility regulation on local zoning.[110] The cases that give priority to the state utility agency's decision effectively decide the land use controversy these cases present. The state utility agency is primarily concerned with the economic health and efficiency of the utility industry and is not likely to uphold a prohibitory local zoning ordinance. Some state legislation expressly authorizes the state utility agency to preempt local zoning.[111] The court decisions tend to uphold the state utility agency under this legislation when it sets aside a local zoning decision.[112] Legislation in other states requires utilities that receive state permits to comply with local zoning.[113]

Some states have adopted legislation dealing expressly with the siting of electric power stations and transmission lines. This legislation authorizes the

---

**108.** Union Elec. Co. v. City of Crestwood, 499 S.W.2d 480 (Mo. 1973); Cohen v. Ford, 339 A.2d 175 (Pa. Commw. 1975).

**109.** For zoning cases, see Harbor Carriers, Inc. v. City of Sausalito, 121 Cal. Rptr. 577 (Cal. App. 1975); Graham Farms, Inc. v. Indianapolis Power & Light Co., 233 N.E.2d 656 (Ind. 1968); Howard Cty. v. Potomac Elec. Power Co., 573 A.2d 821 (Md. 1990); Consolidated Edison Co. of N.Y. v. Village of Briarcliff Manor, 144 N.Y.S.2d 379 (Sup. Ct. 1955); Duquesne Light Co. v. Upper St. Clair Twp., 105 A.2d 287 (Pa. 1954); Commonwealth v. Delaware & Hudson Ry. Co., 339 A.2d 155 (Pa. Commw. 1975).

**110.** Wolf v. Village of Mt. Prospect, 40 N.E.2d 778 (Ill. App. 1942); Porter v. Southwestern Pub. Serv. Co., 489 S.W.2d 361 (Tex. 1972); City of Richmond v. Southern Ry., 123 S.E.2d 641 (Va. 1962).

**111.** *E.g.,* Md. Nat. Res. Code Ann. § 3-306.1; Mass. Gen. L. ch. 40A, § 3; N.Y. Pub. Serv. Law § 126. *See also* Ohio Rev. Code Ann. § 4905.65(B).

**112.** New England LNG Co. v. City of Fall River, 331 N.E.2d 536 (Mass. 1975); Public Serv. Co. v. Town of Hampton, 411 A.2d 164 (N.H. 1980); In re Monmouth Consol. Water Co. v. Board of Pub. Util. Comm'rs, 220 A.2d 189 (N.J. 1966).

**113.** *E.g.,* Ky. Rev. Stat. Ann. § 278.040(2); Nev. Rev. Stat. § 704.890(2)(d).

governor or a specially created state siting agency to make the siting decision. Like the utility agency legislation, this legislation may expressly preempt local zoning.[114] Court decisions under these laws have upheld decisions by state agencies authorizing utility facilities not permitted by local zoning even though the state legislation does not authorize preemption. They rely on the legislative intent to provide a comprehensive state-wide solution to the siting problem that considers land use as well as industry problems.[115]

### § 4.33. Group Homes.

In a number of cases, the courts considered local zoning ordinances that prohibited group homes for the care of abandoned or mentally disturbed or retarded children and other disadvantaged groups. The group homes operated under state supervision and received state funding and approval. State approval included the authority to operate the home at a designated location but did not consider its land use impacts. In the typical case, the group home planned to use a residence located in a single-family residential district. The definition of "family" in the zoning ordinance precluded this use, usually by limiting the number of unrelated persons living together who may constitute a "family."

Most courts exempt group homes operating under state approval from zoning restrictions.[116] They hold that the state legislation authorizing group homes implies that local zoning restrictions may not frustrate the treatment policy of the state law by restricting their location. The courts have also struck down zoning ordinances that restrict the location of group homes.[117]

### § 4.34. Liquor Licensees.

State liquor control legislation raises a zoning preemption problem. In addition to determining the fitness of the applicant for a liquor license, the state liq-

---

**114.** *Compare* Conn. Gen. Stat. § 16-50x(d) (preserves local zoning power) *with* Or. Rev. Stat. § 469.401 (contra) *and* Wash. Rev. Code Ann. § 80.50.110(2) (same).

**115.** Detroit Edison Co. v. Township of Richmond, 388 N.W.2d 296 (Mich. App. 1986); Vermont Elec. Power Co. v. Bandel, 375 A.2d 975 (Vt. 1977); Petition of Vermont Elec. Power Co., 306 A.2d 687 (Vt. 1973).

**116.** City of Temple Terrace v. Hillsborough Ass'n for Retarded Citizens, 322 So. 2d 571 (Fla. App. 1975), *aff'd,* 332 So. 2d 610 (Fla. 1976); Berger v. State, 364 A.2d 993 (N.J. 1976); Town of Southern Pines v. Mohr, 226 S.E.2d 865 (N.C. 1976); Region 10 Client Mgt., Inc. v. Town of Hampstead, 424 A.2d 207 (N.H. 1980); Abbott House v. Tarrytown, 312 N.Y.S.2d 841 (App. Div. 1970) (neglected children). *Contra* Macon Ass'n for Retarded Citzens v. Macon-Bibb County Planning & Zoning Comm'n, *314 S.E.2d 218 (Ga.), appeal dismissed,* 469 U.S. 802 (1984); Board of Child Care v. Harker, 561 A.2d 219 (Md. 1989); Village of Nyack v. Daytop Village, Inc., 583 N.E.2d 928 (N.Y. 1991) (drug treatment facility). *See also* §§ 5.09-5.11 (discrimination against group homes under the federal Fair Housing Act).

**117.** § 5.06.

uor control agency also grants a license for the sale of liquor at a designated location. The question that arises is whether the state liquor control law preempts a zoning restriction that prohibits the sale of liquor at the location designated in a state license.

Some state liquor licensing statutes expressly provide that a liquor licensee must comply with local zoning.[118] The courts divide on whether the state liquor control law preempts local zoning in the absence of such a provision.[119] Courts that find preemption usually base their holding on the comprehensive scope of the state liquor control law. Even when this legislation is not comprehensive, a court may conclude that local zoning is preempted by holding that the zoning ordinance attempted to "veto" or set aside the state license. Courts that hold to the contrary find that the state liquor control legislation does not provide the authority to resolve land use conflicts. They hold that this authority is conferred on the municipality under state zoning legislation.

## § 4.35. Local Governments.

Intergovernmental land use conflicts arise when a local government plans to build a facility that a zoning ordinance prohibits. The courts apply a variety of rules to determine whether a local government not enjoying state immunity is subject to the zoning ordinance of another municipality. The sections that follow discuss these rules. Local governments must comply with their own zoning ordinance unless exempted by the ordinance or protected by one of these judicially adopted immunity rules.[120]

## § 4.36. Governmental-Proprietary Rule.

Most courts originally applied a governmental-proprietary rule to local government land use conflicts. This rule exempts a local government facility from

---

118. *E.g.,* Cal. Bus. & Prof. Code § 23790; Conn. Gen. Stat. § 30-44; Tex. Alco. Bev. Code Ann. § 109.32 (authorizing regulation of sale of beer).

119. Preempted: Application of Melkonian, 355 S.E.2d 503 (N.C. App. 1987); 7-Eleven, Inc. v. McClain, 422 P.2d 455 (Okla. 1967); Salt Lake County v. Liquor Control Comm'n, 357 P.2d 488 (Utah 1960). Not preempted: Korean American Legal Advocacy Found. v. City of Los Angeles, 28 Cal. Rptr. 2d 530 (Cal. App. 1994); O'Banion v. State ex rel. Shively, 253 N.E.2d 739 (Ind. App. 1969); Town of Hilton Head Island v. Fine Liquors, Ltd., 397 S.E.2d 662 (S.C. 1990); City of Clute v. Linscomb, 446 S.W.2d 377 (Tex. Civ. App. 1969); City of Norfolk v. Tiny House, Inc., 281 S.E.2d 836 (Va. 1981); Longwell v. Hodge, 297 S.E.2d 820 (W. Va. 1982) (reviewing cases). *See* 9 A.L.R.2d 877 (1950).

120. Clark v. Town of Estes Park, 686 P.2d 777 (Colo. 1984) (rejecting governmental-proprietary rule); Sinn v. Board of Selectmen of Acton, 259 N.E.2d 557 (Mass. 1970); Hagfeldt v. City of Bozeman, 757 P.2d 753 (Mont. 1988) (applies legislative intent test); Scotch Plains Twp. v. Town of Westfield, 199 A.2d 673 (N.J.L. Div. 1964); Davidson County v. City of High Point, 354 S.E.2d 280 (N.C. App. 1987) (legislative intent rule); Nunes v. Town of Bristol, 232 A.2d 775 (R.I. 1967). *Compare* City of Lubbock v. Austin, 628 S.W.2d 49 (Tex. 1982).

the zoning ordinance of another municipality if the facility is to be used to carry out a governmental as distinguished from a proprietary function.[121] Courts borrowed the governmental-proprietary rule from local government tort law. Local governments historically were immune from tort liability when exercising governmental functions but were liable for torts committed in the exercise of proprietary functions.

Almost all courts have abandoned the governmental-proprietary rule in local government tort liability cases. They concluded that the rule is irrelevant to the solution of local government tort liability problems. Many critics also argue that this rule is irrelevant to the solution of intergovernmental land use conflicts, and some courts have rejected this rule as a test for resolving these conflicts.

### § 4.37. Eminent Domain Rule.

The eminent domain rule is another well-established rule courts use to resolve local government land use conflicts. Under this rule, courts exempt the local government that plans to construct a public facility from compliance with the zoning ordinance of another municipality if it has the authority to exercise the power of eminent domain.[122] These courts believe that the eminent domain power is superior to the zoning power. They reason that the exercise of the power of eminent domain is an attribute of state sovereignty limited only by the constitution.

The eminent domain rule also is questionable. It is irrelevant to the land use conflict problem and favors the local government that plans to build the facility because this government usually has the power of eminent domain.

### § 4.38. Superior Power Rule.

Some courts decide intergovernmental land use conflicts by determining which local government has the superior power. The court must choose between the zoning power and the power under which a local government plans to con-

---

121. Lauderdale County Bd. of Educ. v. Alexander, 110 So. 2d 911 (Ala. 1959); City of Scottsdale v. Municipal Court of Tempe, 368 P.2d 637 (Ariz. 1962); AIA Mobile Home Park v. Brevard County, 246 So. 2d 126 (Fla. App. 1971); Macon-Bibb County Hospital Auth. v. Madison, 420 S.E.2d 586 (Ga. App. 1992); Baltis v. Village of Westchester, 121 N.E.2d 495 (Ill. 1954); Taber v. City of Benton Harbor, 274 N.W. 324 (Mich. 1937); City of Vinita Park v. Girls Sheltercare, Inc., 664 S.W.2d 256 (Mo. App. 1984) (court also applied superior power rule); 61 A.L.R.2d 970 (1958).

122. Mayor of Savannah v. Collins, 84 S.E.2d 454 (Ga. 1954); City of Des Plaines v. Metropolitan San. Dist., 268 N.E.2d 428 (Ill. 1971); City of Washington v. Warren County, 899 S.W.2d 863 (Mo. 1995); Seward County Bd. of Comm'rs v. City of Seward, 242 N.W.2d 849 (Neb. 1976); State ex rel. Helsel v. Board of County Comm'rs, 78 N.E.2d 694 (Ohio App.), *appeal dismissed,* 79 N.E.2d 911 (Ohio 1948); South Hill Sewer Dist. v. Pierce County, 591 P.2d 877 (Wash. App. 1979); 61 A.L.R.2d 970 (1958).

struct a public facility. The superior power rule may require the courts to examine the legislative intent to determine which power is superior.

*Wilkinsburg-Penn Joint Water Auth. v. Borough of Churchill*[123] illustrates the superior power rule. A water authority planned to construct an elevated water tower at a site where a zoning ordinance did not permit it. The court held that the authority was subject to the zoning ordinance. It noted that the state zoning act, like the Standard Act, required zoning to be in accordance with a comprehensive plan and to implement a number of statutory objectives, including the adequate provision of water. These provisions indicated "that the objectives of zoning regulation are more comprehensive than and, in fact, include the objectives of the water authority." Some courts take the contrary position. They hold that the legislation authorizing the construction of a public facility is superior to the zoning legislation.[124]

Courts may accord a special status to historic preservation. In *Mayor of Annapolis v. Anne Arundel County*[125] the court upheld a decision by the city's Historic District Commission that prohibited the demolition of a church owned by the county in an historic district. The court held that historic preservation ordinances were entitled to more judicial protection than conventional zoning because they regulate the preservation of building exteriors rather than land use. Historic preservation also imposes more rigorous procedural requirements. Governmental noncompliance would frustrate the goals of historic zoning because "a valuable building is just as much lost by destruction by a public body as it would by a private owner."

### § 4.39. Balancing Test.

A number of courts have adopted a balancing test to resolve land use conflicts between local governments. These cases reject the traditional tests, such as the governmental-proprietary rule, because they believe they are not appropriate for resolving local government land use conflicts. As some courts note, the traditional tests are acceptable when a local government seeks exemption from its own zoning ordinance. They should not apply when a local government seeks exemption from another local government's zoning ordinance.[126] New Jersey

---

**123.** 207 A.2d 905 (Pa. 1965). *Accord* Jefferson County v. City of Birmingham, 55 So. 2d 196 (Ala. 1951); Wilmette Park Dist. v. Village of Wilmette, 490 N.E.2d 1282 (Ill. 1986) (but holding that zoning decision is judicially reviewable); County of Venango v. Borough of Sugarcreek Zoning Hearing Bd., 626 A.2d 489 (Pa. 1993) (county's zoning power superior under court's legislative intent rule; see § 4.28); City of Richmond v. Board of Supvrs., 101 S.E.2d 641 (Va. 1958).

**124.** Village of Swansea v. County of St. Clair, 359 N.E.2d 866 (Ill. App. 1977). *Cf.* City of Kirkwood v. City of Sunset Hills, 589 S.W.2d 31 (Mo. App. 1979).

**125.** 316 A.2d 807 (Md. 1974). *Accord* City of Ithaca v. County of Tompkins, 355 N.Y.S.2d 275 (Sup. Ct. 1974). *Contra* State v. City of Seattle, 615 P.2d 461 (Wash. 1980).

**126.** Orange County v. City of Apopka, 299 So. 2d 652 (Fla. App. 1974).

adopted a balancing test for state-local land use conflicts in *Rutgers v. Piluso*.[127] The New Jersey courts have applied the *Rutgers* balancing test to local government land use conflicts, and other courts have adopted it for land use conflicts between local governments.[128]

Some courts adopted a different version of the balancing test. *In City of Temple Terrace v. Hillsborough Ass'n for Retarded Citizens*,[129] a home for the mentally retarded, which operated under a contract with a state agency, planned to locate in an area where a local zoning ordinance did not allow it. Although the case was not a land use dispute between two local governments, the court held that it would apply a balancing test to local government land use conflicts.

Unlike *Rutgers, Temple Terrace* did not investigate legislative intent to resolve the land use conflict. It held that legislation granting an exemption from a zoning restriction must be explicit and added that:

> When the state legislature is silent on the subject, the governmental unit seeking to use land contrary to local zoning regulations should have the burden of proving that the public interests favoring the proposed use outweigh those mitigating against a use not sanctioned by the zoning regulations of the local government.[130]

The court also held that, "under normal circumstances," a local government should attempt to secure the approvals required by a zoning ordinance before raising the exemption issue.

*Temple Terrace* favors the local zoning ordinance over the public facility. Its holding that a local government carries the burden to justify a violation of a zoning ordinance is contrary to *Rutgers,* which appears to put the burden on the opposing municipality to justify its zoning.

*Lincoln County v. Johnson*[131] also adopted a different version of the balancing test. A city planned to locate a waste disposal facility outside its limits, but within the county, at a site where the county zoning ordinance did not permit it. The city made no attempt to obtain a zoning change. The state agency issued a permit for the facility but declined to decide the zoning issue.

This case also favored the zoning power. It held that a local government should apply for a zoning change when it plans to build a facility on a site where the zoning ordinance does not allow it. If it is not satisfied with the zoning deci-

---

127. 286 A.2d 697 (N.J. 1972), discussed in § 4.27.

128. City of St. Louis v. City of Bridgeton, 705 S.W.2d 524 (Mo. App. 1985); Hagfeldt v. City of Bozeman, 757 P.2d 753 (Mont. 1988); Matter of Cty. of Monroe, 530 N.E.2d 202 (N.Y. 1988) (overruling case adopting governmental-proprietary test); Independent School Dist. No. 89 v. City of Oklahoma City, 722 P.2d 1212 (Okla. 1986).

129. 322 So. 2d 571 (Fla. App. 1975), *aff'd,* 332 So. 2d 610 (Fla. 1976).

130. *Id.* at 579.

131. 257 N.W.2d 453 (S.D. 1977) (also adopting burden of proof rule of *Temple Terrace*).

sion, the local government can appeal to a trial court. The court should then consider the "zoning factors," the local government's legislative authority, the public need for the facility, and alternative locations and methods for carrying out the project. Other courts have adopted modified versions of the balancing test for local government land use conflicts.[132]

Proponents of the balancing test favor it because the traditional tests often give priority to the local government facility and do not allow courts to consider local zoning policies. Balancing test proponents view the traditional tests as bad land use law. This argument overlooks the difficulties the balancing test presents. It allows courts to displace local zoning policies with their own policy for resolving local government land use conflicts, a form of judicial zoning that may be unwise. The case-by-case adjudication required by the balancing test also makes the application of zoning restrictions to the public facilities of other local governments dependent on the uncertainties of judicial review. Some courts have rejected the balancing test for some or all of these reasons.[133]

As an alternative to the balancing test, a court could hold that the local zoning power is superior because zoning, especially if it implements a comprehensive plan, can comprehensively resolve local government land use conflicts. A court should set aside the zoning ordinance only if it improperly excludes a needed governmental facility that cannot find a feasible alternative location. This test contemplates judicial policy-making, but the court's role is more limited and better focused.

Courts should also be sensitive to the status of the public agency whose facility violates the local zoning ordinance. The superior state sovereignty view has merit when a state agency administers a state program that requires a comprehensive resolution of intergovernmental land use conflicts. State waste disposal programs are an example. Local governments and private entities that have state agency approval in these programs are entitled to immunity from zoning restrictions. Status counts least when one local government invades the territory of another. Judicial resolution of these intergovernmental land use disputes is necessary and probably inevitable.

## § 4.40. Home Rule Problems.

Under the traditional grant of constitutional home rule powers to local governments, the legislature can preempt local home rule authority, including zon-

---

132. City of Ames v. Story County, 392 N.W.2d 145 (Iowa 1986); City of Fargo v. Harwood Twp., 256 N.W.2d 694 (N.D. 1977).

133. City of New Orleans v. State, 364 So. 2d 1020 (La. 1978); Dearden v. City of Detroit, 269 N.W.2d 139 (Mich. 1978); Everett v. Snohomish Cty., 772 P.2d 992 (Wash. 1989) (adopting legislative intent test). *See also* Commonwealth, Dep't of Gen. Servs. v. Ogontz Area Neighbors Ass'n, 483 A.2d 448 (Pa. 1984) (rejecting balancing test for state agencies; see § 4.27).

ing authority, through general legislation. A court could find a home rule zoning ordinance preempted under this rule by a statute that authorizes the construction of a public facility to implement a state legislative policy. A school built by a school district is an example.[134]

Constitutional home rule powers can favor the zoning ordinance in the resolution of intergovernmental land use conflicts. If a municipality adopts its zoning ordinance under its home rule powers, a court may rely on the constitutional grant of home rule authority to give priority to the zoning ordinance.[135] *Temple Terrace*[136] took a different view. In a case in which a state-supervised group home violated a local zoning ordinance, the court held that home rule authority for the zoning ordinance "weakened" the immunity of the state-regulated agency.

Home rule status may sometimes protect an invading local government. In one case, a city exercising home rule powers to construct a campsite outside its limits was exempted from compliance with a county zoning ordinance.[137]

## § 4.41. Legislative Solutions.

The usual failure of state legislation to provide more guidance on intergovernmental land use conflicts is surprising in view of the conflicting court decisions. A few statutes resolve this problem for specific facilities,[138] and an occasional statute enacts a more general rule. An Oregon statute,[139] provides that local zoning ordinances are applicable to publicly owned property.

---

**134.** Board of Educ. v. Houghton, 233 N.W. 834 (Minn. 1930). *See also* Town of Atherton v. Superior Court, 324 P.2d 328 (Cal. App. 1958).

**135.** City of Plano v. City of Allen, 395 S.W.2d 927 (Tex. App. 1965).

**136.** 322 So. 2d 571 (Fla. App. 1975), *aff'd,* 332 So. 2d 610 (Fla. 1976). *See* § 4.39. *See also* City of New Orleans v. Board of Comm'rs, 640 So. 2d 237 (La. 1994) (home rule authority is basis for applying zoning ordinance to state agency).

**137.** McDonald v. City of Columbus, 231 N.E.2d 319 (Ohio App. 1967).

**138.** Bielunski v. Tousignant, 149 N.E.2d 801 (Ill. App. 1958); Zubli v. Community Mainstreaming Assocs., 423 N.Y.S.2d 982 (1979); Town of Westborough v. Department of Pub. Utils., 267 N.E.2d 110 (Mass. 1971); Vermont Div. of State Bldgs. v. Town of Castleton Bd. of Adjustment, 415 A.2d 188 (Vt. 1980).

**139.** Or. Rev. Stat. § 227.286. *See also* Cal. Gov't Code §§ 53,090, 53091; City of Lafayette v. East Bay Mun. Utility Dist., 20 Cal. Rptr. 2d 658 (Cal. App. 1993); Lawler v. City of Redding, 9 Cal. Rptr. 2d 392 (Cal. App. 1992).

# REFERENCES

## Books

M. Brough, A Unified Development Ordinance (1987).
J. Hand & J. Smith, Neighboring Property Owners (1988).
W. Prosser & W. Keeton, The Law of Torts (5th ed. 1984).
B. Siegan, Land Use Without Zoning (1972).
R. Wakeford, American Development Control (1990).

## Articles

Beuscher & Morrison, Judicial Zoning Through Recent Nuisance Cases, 1955 Wis. L. Rev. 440.

Chapman, Land Use Regulatory Jurisdiction of Local Governments Over State Agencies and Other Local Governments, 25 Gonz. L. Rev. 65 (1989-90).

Ellickson, Alternatives to Zoning: Covenants, Nuisance Rules, and Fines as Land Use Controls, 40 U. Chi. L. Rev. 681 (1973).

Forrest, An Alternative for Illinois Land Use Legislation, 12 N. Ill. L. Rev. 741 (1992).

Kosman, Toward an Exclusionary Jurisprudence: A Reconceptualization of Zoning, 54 Cath. U. L. Rev. 59 (1993)

Knack, Meck & Stollman, The Real Story Behind the Standard Planning and Zoning Acts of the 1920s, Land Use L. & Zoning Dig., Vol. 48, No. 2, at 3 (1996).

Levi, Gehring & Groethe, Application of Municipal Ordinances to Special Purpose Districts and Regulated Industries: A Home Rule Approach, 12 Urb. L. Ann. 77 (1976).

Lewin, Comparative Nuisance, 50 U. Pitt. L. Rev. 1009 (1989).

Liebman, The Modernization of Zoning: Enabling Act Revision as a Means to Reform, 23 Urb. Law. 1 (1991).

Madigan, State Liquor Control Boards v. Local Government: Who Should Control the Location of Liquor Establishments?, 26 Duq. L. Rev. 851 (1988).

Rabin, Nuisance Law: Rethinking Fundamental Assumptions, 63 Va. L. Rev. 1299 (1977).

Rasso, Exempting Government From Zoning: Court Tests, Land Use L. & Zoning Dig., Vol. 38, No. 10, at 3 (1986).

Riseberg, Exhuming the Funeral Home Cases: Proposing a Private Nuisance Action Based on the Mental Anguish Caused by Pollution, 21 B.C. Envtl. L. Rev. 557 (1994).

Reynolds, The Judicial Role in Intergovernmental Land Use Disputes: The Case Against Balancing, 71 Minn. L. Rev. 611 (1987).

Reynolds, Of Time and Feedlots: The Effect of *Spur Industries* on Nuisance Law, 40 Wash. U.J. Urb. & Contemp. L. 75 (1992).

Smith & Fernandez, The Price of Beauty: An Economic Approach to Aesthetic Nuisance, 15 Harv. Envtl. L. Rev. 53 (1991).

Sterk, Neighbors in American Land Law, 87 Colum. L. Rev. 55 (1987).

Travalio, Pay Up or Shut Down: Some Cautionary Remarks on the Use of Conditional Entitlements in Private Nuisance Cases, 38 U. Fla. L. Rev. 209 (1986).

Van Gorder, Alternative Solutions to the Judicial Doctrine of Strict Compliance With Statutory Procedures for the Adoption of Local Land Use Regulations, 29 Wash. U.J. Urb. & Contemp. L. 133 (1985).

Ziegler, Governmental Immunity From Zoning: Balancing of Interests and Legislative Intent, 14 Zoning & Plan. L. Rep. 105 (1991).

Ziegler, Zoning Regulation Based On Identity of Land User, or Form of Ownership, 11 Zoning & Plan. L. Rep. 73 (1988).

**Student Work**

Note, Governmental Immunity From Zoning, 22 B.C.L. Rev. 783 (1981).

Note, Transmission Line Siting: Local Concerns Versus State Energy Interests, 19 Urb. L. Ann. 183 (1980).

Comment, Limited Local Zoning Regulation of Electric Utilities: A Balanced Approach in the Public Interest, 23 U. Balt. L. Rev. 563 (1994).

Comment, An Ounce of Prevention: Rehabilitating the Anticipatory Nuisance Doctrine, 15 B.C. Envtl. Aff. L. Rev. 627 (1988).

# Chapter 5

# ZONING FOR LAND USE, DENSITY AND DEVELOPMENT

## § 5.01. An Introductory Note.

Land use, density, and site development regulations are the heart of the zoning ordinance. The standard zoning format contains the three basic residential, commercial, and industrial use categories and subdivides each category into a number of zoning districts. The textual regulations for each zoning district specify permitted use and density limitations. The ordinance usually regulates densities through minimum lot size requirements or by limiting the number of dwelling units that are allowed on an acre of land.

Zoning ordinances also contain site development regulations for each zoning district that include minimum front, rear, and side yard requirements. They may also include a minimum street frontage requirement and a limit on the percentage of a lot a building can occupy. The ordinance also limits the height of buildings. Height, setback, and other site development requirements control density indirectly. The table that follows illustrates a simplified standard zoning format for a typical zoning ordinance.

### A Standard, Simplified Zoning Format

| | |
|---|---|
| SF-1, Single-Family Large Lot | One-Acre Lots |
| SF-2, Single-Family Medium | Half-Acre Lots |
| SF-3, Single-Family Standard | 6,000 Sq. Ft. Lot Minimum |
| MF-1, Multi-family Low Density | 18-26 Units/Acre |
| MF-2, Multi-family Medium Density | 27-36 Units/Acre |
| MF-3, Multi-family High Density | 37-44 Units/Acre |
| GO, General Office | Offices and Limited Uses Serving Community and City-Wide Needs |
| NC, Neighborhood Commercial | Neighborhood Retail and Office Facilities |
| CC, Community Commercial | Shopping Centers Providing Sub-Regional and Regional Retail and Office Facilities |
| SC, Service Commercial | Commercial Service Facilities Incompatible with Retail and Office Development |
| CBD, Central Business District | Office and Commercial Facilities in Central Business Area |
| LI, Limited Industrial | Light Manufacturing |
| HI, Heavy Industrial | Heavy Manufacturing |

The constitutionality of comprehensive zoning is well-established since *Euclid.* Problems arise when courts must decide whether a zoning restriction is constitutional as applied to a particular property or whether a zoning ordinance advances suspect governmental purposes, such as the exclusion of group homes.

This chapter reviews the case law that applies to the standard trio of zoning controls: use, density, and site development regulations. It highlights cases in which the courts invalidated zoning restrictions they considered suspect. This judicial assertiveness illustrates the new and emerging stage of land use law. The chapter also reviews the application of the federal antitrust law and the free speech clause of the federal constitution to land use regulation.

## A. RESIDENTIAL DISTRICTS.

### § 5.02. The Definition of "Family."

A threshold problem in residential zoning is the definition of the "family" entitled to reside in single-family dwellings. Zoning ordinances do not limit the number of related family members who can live together but often limit the number of unrelated persons who can live together as a family. The numerical limitation on unrelated families probably was an attempt to prohibit boarding-house living in single-family neighborhoods.[1]

In *Village of Belle Terre v. Boraas*,[2] the U.S. Supreme Court upheld a zoning ordinance that limited the number of unrelated persons who could live together as a family.[3] The *Belle Terre* dissent would have applied strict scrutiny, equal protection review, and invalidated the ordinance because it infringed fundamental rights of privacy and association. Some state courts have followed the *Belle Terre* dissent and have applied strict scrutiny judicial review to strike down zoning ordinances that limited the size of unrelated families or that excluded group homes from residential districts.

### § 5.03. Unrelated Families.

A number of states have followed *Belle Terre* and have upheld zoning ordinances limiting the size of unrelated families.[4] Several states have also held them

---

1. *Compare* Borough of Glassboro v. Vallorisi, 568 A.2d 888 (N.J. 1990) (group of college students living together held to be family) *and* Appeal of Miller, 515 A.2d 904 (Pa. 1986) (boarders held to be housekeeping unit) *with* Appeal of Summers, 551 A.2d 1134 (Pa. Commw. 1988) (temporary care of mentally retarded held not a family) *and* Commonwealth v. Jaffe, 494 N.E.2d 1342 (Mass. 1986) (boarders held to be unrelated tenants).

2. 416 U.S. 1 (1974). *See* § 2.35.

3. *See also* City of Ladue v. Horn, 720 S.W.2d 745 (Mo. App. 1986) (upholding ordinance allowing only married couples to live together).

4. Zavala v. City & Cty. of Denver, 759 P.2d 664 (Colo. 1988); Dinan v. Board of Zoning Appeals, 595 A.2d 864 (Conn. 1991); State v. Champoux, 555 N.W.2d 69 (Neb. App. 1996); Town of Durham v. White Enters., Inc., 348 A.2d 706 (N.H. 1975); Farley v. Zoning Hearing Bd., 636 A.2d 1232 (Pa. Commw. 1994) (student housing); City of Brookings v. Winker, 554 N.W.2d 827 (S.D. 1996).

invalid,[5] although these cases may allow municipalities to limit the use of single-family dwellings to "functional" families.[6]

City of Santa Barbara v. Adamson[7] is a leading case that invalidated a restriction on the size of unrelated families on state constitutional grounds. A zoning ordinance allowed no more than five unrelated persons to live together as a family unit. The court relied on a right of privacy guaranteed by the state constitution's declaration of rights to strike down this "rule of five." Applying an "ends and means" analysis similar to strict scrutiny equal protection review, the court demanded a "compelling public need" to justify the restriction. It found none. The restriction did not enhance the maintenance of a residential environment because the "rule of five" was irrelevant to noise, parking, or other conditions that might affect residential areas. Neither was the ordinance justified by a belief that unrelated families create an immoral environment for families with children. The court applied the "least restrictive alternative" rule and held that other regulations, such as population density and parking restrictions, could accomplish the purposes the "rule of five" attempted to serve. Zoning ordinances, the court noted, are much less suspect when they focus on uses rather than the users.

Strict scrutiny judicial review was a key factor in many of the cases invalidating limitations on the size of unrelated families. It was based either on an equal protection clause or a state constitutional provision that recognized a fundamental interest, such as the right of privacy. Cases that apply strict scrutiny judicial review reverse the presumption of constitutionality and require a compelling governmental interest to justify the restriction, which they find lacking. Some state courts have also held that restrictions on the size of unrelated families are unauthorized by the zoning legislation.[8]

---

**5.** Kirsch v. Prince George's County, 626 A.2d 372 (Md.) (occupancy limitation on student housing violates equal protection), cert. denied, 510 U.S. 1011 (1993); Charter Twp. of Delta v. Dinolfo, 351 N.W.2d 831 (Mich. 1984); Borough of Glassboro v. Vallorisi, 529 A.2d 1028 (N.J. Ch. Div. 1987); Ocean Cty. Bd. of Realtors v. Township of Long Beach, 599 A.2d 1309 (N.J.L. 1991); State v. Baker, 405 A.2d 368 (N.J. 1979); Baer v. Town of Brookhaven, 537 N.E.2d 619 (N.Y. 1989); McMinn v. Town of Oyster Bay, 488 N.E.2d 1240 (N.Y. 1985). See also City of Chula Vista v. Pagard, 171 Cal. Rptr. 738 (Cal. App. 1981). See 71 A.L.R.3d 693 (1976); 12 A.L.R.4th 238 (1982).

**6.** Stegeman v. City of Ann Arbor, 540 N.W.2d 724 (Mich. App. 1995).

**7.** 610 P.2d 436 (Cal. 1980). See also College Area Renters & Landlord Ass'n v. City of San Diego, 50 Cal. Rptr. 2d 515 (Cal. App. 1996) (occupancy requirements cannot distinguish between tenant-occupied and owner-occupied dwellings).

**8.** City of Des Plaines v. Trottner, 216 N.E.2d 116 (Ill. 1966), rev'd by § 65 Ill. Comp. Ann. Stat. 5/11-13-1(9).

### § 5.04. Discrimination Against Families with Children Under the Fair Housing Act.

In 1988, Congress added discrimination against "familial status" as another type of discrimination covered by the Fair Housing Act.[9] Congress adopted this amendment to prohibit discrimination against families with children in the sale and rental of housing, but the amendment may invalidate zoning that restricts residences in single family zoning districts to older persons. The effect of this zoning is to prohibit families with children from occupying residences in these districts. The amendment may also invalidate zoning ordinances that prohibit occupancy by families in group homes.[10]

The Act exempts "housing for older persons" from the prohibition against familial status discrimination.[11] This exemption was clearly intended to apply to private owners of such housing, not age-restricted zoning.[12]

### § 5.05. Group Homes.

### § 5.06. As a Permitted "Family" Use.

The definition of "family" contained in zoning ordinances also comes under attack if it is applied to exclude group homes from residential districts. State legislation that regulates group homes may exempt them from zoning restrictions.[13] The courts have also held that the group that plans to live in a group home is a "family" as defined by the zoning ordinance or that the application of a "family" definition to exclude a group home is unconstitutional.[14]

Other state courts followed *Belle Terre* and held that the application of a family definition to exclude a group home from a residential district was constitutional.[15] The U.S. Supreme Court approved one of these cases as a correct inter-

---

**9.** 42 U.S.C. § 3602(k).

**10.** Doe v. City of Butler, 892 F.2d 315 (3d Cir. 1989) (remanding for trial claim that Act violated by limitation on occupancy in group home for abused women because limitation would prevent abused mothers from bringing children into home).

**11.** 42 U.S.C. § 3607(b)(1).

**12.** H.R. Rep. No. 711, 100th Cong., 2d Sess. 31-32 (1988). *See* 24 C.F.R. § 100.304.

**13.** § 4.33.

**14.** Cherry Hill Township v. Oxford House, Inc., 621 A.2d 952 (N.J. App. Div. 1993).

**15.** Behavioral Health Agency of Cent. Ariz. (BHACA) v. City of Casa Grande, 708 P.2d 1317 (Ariz. App. 1985); Hayward v. Gaston, 542 A.2d 760 (Del. 1988); Penobscot Area Hous. Dev. Corp. v. City of Brewer, 434 A.2d 14 (Me. 1981). *See also* Browndale Int'l, Ltd. v. Board of Adjustment, 208 N.W.2d 121 (Wis. 1973), *cert. denied,* 416 U.S. 936 (1974) (can allow foster homes but exclude therapeutic home).

pretation of the *Belle Terre* decision.[16] In *Doe v. City of Butler*,[17] the Third Circuit relied on *Belle Terre* to uphold, as applied to a medium density residential district, a zoning ordinance that allowed group homes as conditional uses in all residential districts. The ordinance limited to six and a supervisor the number of persons who could live in these homes. The court remanded for trial the question whether the numerical limitation was valid in higher-density residential districts, where apartments and other high-density uses were permitted.

A number of cases interpreted the family definition or the definition of an accessory use in a zoning ordinance to include group homes.[18] Some of these cases contain constitutional overtones and suggest that constitutional problems would arise if the ordinance excluded group homes. They may stress, for example, that the zoning ordinance may regulate only uses, not the users, implying that a regulation based on users would violate substantive due process.[19] Some of these cases require the group home to be the functional equivalent of a family,[20] but other cases do not adopt this requirement.[21]

*City of White Plains v. Ferraioli*[22] is a leading case that adopted the functional equivalency rule. The court held that a foster home headed by a married couple and including two of their own natural children was a family as defined by the zoning ordinance. The court distinguished *Belle Terre,* and noted that the foster home in this case was a "relatively normal, stable, and permanent family unit." Because the group home "bears the generic character of a family unit" and was not a place for transients, it was consistent with the purposes of single-family zoning.

---

**16.** City of Cleburne v. Cleburne Living Center, 473 U.S. 432 (1985), approving Macon Ass'n for Retarded Citizens v. Macon-Bibb County Planning & Zoning Comm'n, 314 S.E.2d 218 (Ga.), *appeal dismissed,* 469 U.S. 802 (1984). *See* § 2.51.

**17.** 892 F.2d 315 (3d Cir. 1989).

**18.** White v. Board of Zoning Appeals, 451 N.E.2d 756 (Ohio 1983) (held accessory use); Saunders v. Clark County Zoning Dep't, 421 N.E.2d 152 (Ohio 1981) (delinquent boys); Collins v. City of El Campo, 684 S.W.2d 756 (Tex. App. 1984); Citizens for a Safe Neighborhood v. City of Seattle, 836 P.2d 235 (Wash. App. 1992).

**19.** Linn County v. City of Hiawatha, 311 N.W.2d 95 (Iowa 1981); City of West Monroe v. Ouachita Ass'n for Retarded Children, Inc., 402 So. 2d 259 (La. App. 1981); Hopkins v. Zoning Hearing Bd., 423 A.2d 1082 (Pa. Commw. 1980); State ex rel. Catholic Family & Children's Servs. v. City of Bellingham, 605 P.2d 788 (Wash. App. 1979).

**20.** City of Vinita Park v. Girls Sheltercare, Inc., 664 S.W.2d 256 (Mo. App. 1984); Unification Theological Seminary v. City of Poughkeepsie, 607 N.Y.S.2d 383 (App. Div. 1994) (upholds ordinance limiting number of unrelated people unless functional equivalent of a family); Eichlin v. Zoning Hearing Bd., 671 A.2d 1173 (Pa. Commw. 1996) (group home met functional family requirements of ordinance).

**21.** Hessling v. City of Broomfield, 563 P.2d 12 (Colo. 1977); Oliver v. Zoning Comm'n, 326 A.2d 841 (Conn. C.P. 1974); Y.W.C.A. v. Board of Adjustment, 341 A.2d 356 (N.J. 1975).

**22.** 313 N.E.2d 756 (N.Y. 1974). *See also* Group House of Port Wash., Inc. v. Board of Zoning & Appeals, 380 N.E.2d 207 (N.Y. 1978).

Several cases applied the functional equivalency rule or interpreted the family definition to hold that the zoning ordinance excluded group homes.[23] These cases usually relied on *Belle Terre* and sometimes emphasized that the group home was supervised by resident staff rather than a resident married couple.[24]

### § 5.07. As a Conditional Use.

A zoning ordinance may authorize the approval of a group home as a conditional use. The state cases apply the usual rules governing conditional uses[25] when they decide whether to uphold or reverse a denial of a conditional use for a group home.[26] In *City of Cleburne v. Cleburne Living Center,*[27] the U.S. Supreme Court invalidated the denial of a conditional use permit for a group home for the mentally retarded under the rational relationship standard of equal protection review. The Court held that fears of neighbors were not a sufficient reason for denying the permit, and that the city could not reject the group home for reasons that applied to group homes the ordinance allowed without a permit. *Cleburne* may encourage state courts to review the denial of conditional uses for group homes more stringently. The cases since *Cleburne* have divided on whether a municipality can constitutionally require a conditional use permit for a group home.[28]

---

**23.** Civitans Care, Inc. v. Board of Adjustment, 437 So. 2d 540 (Ala. 1983); Behavioral Health Agency of Cent. Ariz. (BHACA) v. City of Casa Grande, 708 P.2d 1317 (Ariz. App. 1985); Planning & Zoning Comm'n v. Synanon Found., Inc., 216 A.2d 442 (Conn. 1966); City of Kenner v. Normal Life of La., Inc., 483 So. 2d 903 (La. 1986); Metropolitan Dev. Comm'n v. Villages, Inc., 464 N.E.2d 367 (Ind. App. 1984); Northern Maine Gen. Hosp. v. Ricker, 572 A.2d 479 (Me. 1990); Open Door Alcoholism Program, Inc. v. Board of Adjustment, 491 A.2d 17 (N.J. App. Div. 1985).

**24.** Wengert v. Zoning Hearing Bd., 414 A.2d 148 (Pa. Commw. 1980); Culp v. City of Seattle, 590 P.2d 1288 (Wash. App. 1979); 100 A.L.R.3d 876 (1980).

**25.** §§ 6.56-6.58.

**26.** *Compare* Gaslight Villa, Inc. v. Governing Body, City of Lansing, 518 P.2d 410 (Kan. 1974) (upholding denial), *and* Normal Life of La., Inc. v. Jefferson Parish Dep't of Inspection & Code Enforcement, 483 So. 2d 1123 (La. App. 1986) (same), *with* City Planning Comm'n of Greensburg v. Threshold, Inc., 315 A.2d 311 (Pa. Commw. 1974) (contra).

**27.** 473 U.S. 432 (1985). *See* § 2.51.

**28.** *Compare* Bannum, Inc. v. City of Louisville, 958 F.2d 1354 (6th Cir. 1992) (invalidating requirement), *with* Bannum, Inc. v. City of St. Charles, 2 F.3d 267 (8th Cir. 1993) (contra); Freedom Ranch, Inc. v. Board of Adjustment, 878 P.2d 380 (Okla. App. 1994), *cert. denied,* 115 S. Ct. 636 (1994) (same).

## § 5.08. State Legislative Regulation.

Legislation in a number of states has addressed the group home zoning problem, although some statutes apply only to one type of group home, such as a group home for the mentally disabled.[29]

Some statutes require municipalities to allow small group homes as a permitted use in residential districts. Other statutes allow municipalities to approve group homes as a conditional use in residential districts. The statute usually requires state licensing and may require the dispersal of group homes throughout residential areas to avoid excessive concentration through spacing or other requirements. Model legislation proposed by the American Bar Association's Commission on the Mentally Disabled includes similar protective provisions but does not authorize conditional use permits.[30]

Most courts have upheld statutes that regulate zoning for group homes. They find that these statutes bear a substantial relation to a legitimate governmental purpose and reject arguments that they infringe on land use controls adopted under home rule charters.[31] Zoning ordinances requiring a minimum spacing between group homes have been upheld as not in violation of these laws.[32]

---

**29.** *E.g.,* Ariz. Rev. Stat. Ann. §§ 36-581, 36-582; Cal. Welf. & Inst. Code §§ 5115-5116; Ind. Code Ann. § 16-13-21-12; Kan. Stat. Ann. § 12-736; Mich. Comp. Laws Ann. § 125.216g; N.J. Stat. Ann. § 30:4C-26(d); Or. Rev. Stat. § 97.665. *See* Campbell v. City Council, 616 N.E.2d 445 (Mass. 1993) (group home protected by state educational use law); Trible v. Bland, 458 S.E.2d 297 (Va. 1995) (statute allows municipality to be more permissive in definition of group home).

**30.** *See* Hopperton, "A State Legislative Strategy for Ending Exclusionary Zoning of Community Homes," 19 Urb. L. Ann. 47, 77 (1980).

**31.** Los Angeles v. State Dep't of Health, 133 Cal. Rptr. 771 (Cal. App. 1976); Glennon Heights, Inc. v. Central Bank & Trust, 658 P.2d 872 (Colo. 1983); Hayward v. Gaston, 542 A.2d 760 (Del. 1988) (statutory zoning exemption may distinguish between different types of group homes); City of Livonia v. Department of Social Servs., 333 N.W.2d 151 (Mich. App. 1983); Zubli v. Community Mainstreaming Assocs., 423 N.Y.S.2d 982 (Sup. Ct. 1979); Nichols v. Tullahoma Open Door, Inc., 640 S.W.2d 13 (Tenn. App. 1982). *Contra* Garcia v. Siffrin Residential Ass'n, 407 N.E.2d 1369 (Ohio 1980) (held to violate local home rule powers). *See also* City of Torrance v. Transitional Living Centers for Los Angeles, Inc., 638 P.2d 1304 (Cal. 1982) (interpreting state statute); Northwest Residence, Inc. v. City of Brooklyn Center, 352 N.W.2d 764 (Minn. App. 1984) (group home law generally preemptive of local zoning).

**32.** Verland C.L.A., Inc. v. Zoning Hearing Bd., 556 A.2d 4 (Pa. Commw. 1989) (one mile); Shannon & Riordan v. Board of Zoning Appeals, 451 N.W.2d 479 (Wis. App. 1989) (2500 feet).

## § 5.09.  Discrimination Against Group Homes for the Handicapped Under the Fair Housing Act.

### § 5.10.  Statutory Prohibitions.

Amendments to the Fair Housing Act in 1988 make the Act applicable to discrimination against handicapped persons.[33] The definition of "handicap" incorporates the definition used in section 504 of the Rehabilitation Act of 1973.[34] This definition is broad. It includes, for example, persons with AIDS.

Although the amendments do not expressly apply to zoning, the legislative history makes it clear that the Act applies to zoning practices, such as restrictions on group homes, that discriminate against housing for handicapped persons. The House Judiciary Committee's report states:

> The Act is intended to prohibit the application of special requirements through land-use regulations, . . . and conditional or special use permits that have the effect of limiting the ability of such individuals to live in the residence of their choice in the community.[35]

This language means that a zoning restriction or requirement is invalid if it singles out housing for the handicapped for discriminatory treatment. This inference is supported by a footnote at this point in the committee report that cites *City of Cleburne v. Cleburne Living Center*.[36] The legislative history also indicates that the courts are to apply a discriminatory effect test to discrimination against the handicapped in zoning ordinances.

The legislative history indicates that the courts should apply to zoning that discriminates against group homes the prima facie case test that they apply to racially discriminatory zoning. This test shifts to the defendant municipality the burden to show that a zoning restriction is justified by a legitimate reason not related to discrimination against the handicapped.[37]

The statute also requires that "reasonable accommodation" be made for group homes protected under the Act.[38] The courts have applied this requirement to zoning ordinances. Unfortunately, there is considerable disagreement in the cases on what constitutes a violation of these statutory provisions.

---

**33.** 42 U.S.C. § 8604(f).

**34.** 29 U.S.C. § 794. *See* 54 Fed. Reg. 3232, 3245 (1989).

**35.** H.R. Rep. No. 711, 100th Cong., 2d Sess. 24 (1988).

**36.** 473 U.S. 435 (1985); § 2.51. *But see* 54 Fed. Reg. 3232, 3246 (1989) (HUD regulations do not discuss application of Act to zoning).

**37.** *See* Children's Alliance v. City of Bellevue, 950 F. Supp. 1491 (W.D. Wash. 1997).

**38.** 42 U.S.C. § 3604(f)(3)(B).

## § 5.11. Exceptions, Variances and Other Zoning Practices.

Many municipalities treat group homes for the handicapped as special exceptions and conditional uses, and group home owners may also apply for zoning variances. The courts have invalidated denials of special use permits and variances for group homes for the handicapped when they found a discriminatory intent or a discriminatory impact on these homes,[39] although legitimate zoning reasons may support a denial of a special use.[40] However, a court of appeals held the reasonable accommodation requirement did not exempt a group home from applying for and receiving a special use permit.[41] The court held that any burdens that residents of the group home might suffer from going through the special use procedure did not outweigh the municipality's interest in applying this requirement to all applicants for special use approval. In another important case, a court of appeals held a city must make reasonable accommodation through its zoning ordinance for a group home, but held the district court did not have the power to compel an amendment to the ordinance to enforce this requirement.[42]

Courts have held a definition of "family" in zoning ordinances that excludes group homes for the handicapped from single family residential districts violates the Act.[43] Whether occupancy restrictions violate the Act is less clear. The statute contains an exemption for "reasonable . . . restriction[s] regarding the maximum number of occupants permitted to occupy a dwelling."[44] The exemption as it is written applies to discrimination against group homes. In *City of Edmonds v. Oxford House, Inc.*,[45] the city claimed the exemption covered a restriction on the number of unrelated persons who could live together, which blocked a group home. However, the Court interpreted the legislative history to limit the exemption to claims of discrimination based on familial status, another prohibition added by the 1988 amendments. The purpose of the exemption, the Court said, is to allow restrictions on the number of persons who may live in a dwelling, which

---

**39.** Special use: Association of Relatives & Friends of AIDS Patients v. Regulation & Permits Admin., 740 F. Supp. 95 (D.P.R. 1990); Baxter v. City of Belleville, 720 F. Supp. 720 (S.D. Ill. 1989). Variance: Hovson's, Inc. v. Township of Brick, 89 F.3d 1096 (3d Cir. 1996).

**40.** Erdman v. City of Fort Atkinson, 84 F.3d 960 (7th Cir. 1996); Gamble v. City of Escondido, 104 F.3d 300 (9th Cir. 1997). *See also* Elderhaven, Inc. v. City of Lubbock, 98 F.3d 175 (5th Cir. 1996).

**41.** United States v. Village of Palatine, 37 F.3d 1230 (7th Cir. 1994).

**42.** Smith & Lee Assocs. v. City of Taylor (II), 102 F.3d 781 (6th Cir. 1996). *See also* "K" Care, Inc. v. Town of Lac du Flambeau, 510 N.W.2d 697 (Wis. App. 1993) (invalidating refusal to rezone).

**43.** Support Ministries for Persons With AIDS, Inc. v. Village of Waterford, 808 F. Supp. 120 (N.D.N.Y. 1992); Oxford House v. Township of Cherry Hill, 799 F. Supp. 450 (D.N.J. 1992). *See also* Easter Seal Soc'y of New Jersey, Inc. v. Township of North Bergen, 798 F. Supp. 228 (D.N.J. 1992) (classifying group home as non-family use held discriminatory).

**44.** 42 U.S.C. § 3607(b)(1).

**45.** 514 U.S. 725 (1995) (quoting this treatise).

are usually contained in housing codes, so that the prohibition on discrimination against families would not lead to overcrowding.

The court left open the question of whether a limitation on the number of persons who can live together is valid under the federal act. Some courts have held that a limit on the number of unrelated persons who can live together does not violate the federal Act, even though the effect of the restriction is to prohibit the location of the group home at its intended location.[46]

## § 5.12. Density and Spacing Requirements.

Provisions regulating the density of group homes for the handicapped by regulating the spacing between them are common in zoning ordinances and in statutes providing zoning protection for these homes. Although the Eighth Circuit held that a spacing requirement in a zoning ordinance did not violate the Act,[47] this decision is clearly wrong. The Sixth Circuit invalidated a similar requirement in a state statute.[48] The court rejected arguments that the spacing requirement was valid because it integrated the disabled into the community and prevented "ghettoization." Integration is not a justification for maintaining quotas, the court held, and any clustering that occurs is caused by the free choice of the disabled.

## § 5.13. Single-Family Use.

Ever since the U.S. Supreme Court's landmark *Euclid* decision, the separation of residential uses by building type has been a well-established practice in zoning. Most zoning ordinances contain a set of single-family zoning districts in which single-family dwellings are the exclusive use. The ordinance permits multi-family residential uses in a separate set of residential districts.

Judicial acceptance of single-family zoning leads many municipalities to rely on it as the key element in a "wait and see" development timing strategy. They effectively preclude development by zoning more land for single-family use than the market requires, often at low densities. No development is likely to occur until the municipality adopts a zoning change to authorize either nonresidential development or residential development at a higher density. Courts have allowed municipalities to maintain the character of single-family residential districts by

---

**46.** Oxford House-C v. City of St. Louis, 77 F.3d 249 (8th Cir. 1996), *cert. denied*, 117 S. Ct. 65 (1996); City of St. Joseph v. Preferred Family Healthcare, Inc., 859 S.W.2d 723 (Mo. App. 1993).

**47.** Familystyle of St. Paul, Inc. v. City of St. Paul, 923 F.2d 91 (8th Cir. 1991). *Accord* Plymouth Charter Twp. v. Department of Soc. Servs., 501 N.W.2d 186 (Mich. App. 1993).

**48.** Larkin v. State of Michigan Dep't of Soc. Servs., 89 F.3d 295 (6th Cir. 1996). *Accord* Horizon House Develpmt'l Servs., Inc. v. Township of Upper Southampton, 804 F. Supp. 683 (E.D. Pa. 1992), *aff'd without opinion*, 995 F.2d 217 (3d Cir. 1993).

prohibiting transient rentals,[49] denying the construction of an accessory unit,[50] prohibiting more than one kitchen in a dwelling unit,[51] and zoning a townhouse buffer between a residential area and commercial development.[52]

Although zoning for single-family use is clearly a constitutional exercise of the zoning power, the court in *Arverne Bay Constr. Co. v. Thatcher*,[53] an early New York case, struck down an exclusive single-family zoning restriction on a major boulevard in Brooklyn because it was premature. The case was brought by a plaintiff, who wished to construct an automobile service station. The court noted that the area was undeveloped, that single-family development probably would not occur for some time, and that conditions near the site, including an incinerator and garbage disposal plant and a dumping ground, made the area unsuitable for single-family use.

An implication from *Arverne Bay*, that municipalities may not use single-family zoning to hold undeveloped areas for future residential development is qualified by a later New York decision.[54] *Arverne Bay* does reflect the assumption, carried into zoning from the nuisance land use cases, that residential zoning should normally be used to protect established residential areas from incompatible uses.[55]

A suburban municipality may attempt to preserve the quality of its residential environment by zoning its entire area for single-family use. This type of zoning raises obvious exclusionary problems. A few decisions upheld single-family zoning for an entire community against objections by developers who planned to build either commercial or industrial facilities. They emphasized the availability of adequate facilities of this type in adjacent communities but did not consider the exclusionary zoning problem.[56]

---

**49.** Cope v. City of Cannon Beach, 855 P.2d 1083 (Or. 1993).

**50.** Desmond v. City of Contra Costa, 25 Cal. Rptr. 2d 842 (Cal. App. 1993).

**51.** Zarrinnia v. Zoning Hearing Bd., 639 A.2d 1276 (Pa. Commw. 1994).

**52.** Central Motors Corp. v. City of Pepper Pike, 653 N.E.2d 639 (Ohio 1995).

**53.** 15 N.E.2d 587 (N.Y. 1938).

**54.** § 10.03.

**55.** *But see* Petersen v. City of Decorah, 259 N.W.2d 553 (Iowa App. 1977) (may not use agricultural use district to reserve land for future industrial development). *Compare* Rodo Land, Inc. v. Board of County Comm'rs, 517 P.2d 873 (Colo. App. 1974) (upholding single-family zoning in rural area).

**56.** Valley View Village, Inc. v. Proffett, 221 F.2d 412 (6th Cir. 1955); Barolomeo v. Town of Paradise Valley, 631 P.2d 564 (Ariz. App. 1981); Cadoux v. Planning & Zoning Comm'n, 294 A.2d 582 (Conn.), *cert. denied,* 408 U.S. 924 (1972); Blank v. Town of Lake Clarke Shores, 161 So. 2d 683 (Fla. 1964). *See also* Folsom Rd. Civic Ass'n v. Parish of St. Tammany, 407 So. 2d 1219 (La. 1981).

## § 5.14. Apartments.

Although *Euclid* held that the exclusion of apartments from residential districts does not violate due process or equal protection, it did not tell municipalities how they should map zoning districts that separate apartments from other residential uses. This problem frequently arises when a landowner attacks the constitutionality of a single-family zoning restriction on property he would like to develop for apartment use. The state courts have decided practically all of these cases. Although they clearly raise an as-applied taking problem, a state court may not consider the taking issue but simply hold that a zoning restriction is "arbitrary and capricious" if they invalidate it.[57]

Courts usually examine the zoning and existing development in the area surrounding land restricted to single-family use to determine whether the restriction is a taking or is arbitrary and capricious. If the surrounding area is zoned and developed for single-family use, a court will uphold the single-family restriction because single-family development is a reasonable use of the restricted property.

More difficult problems arise when the area surrounding property restricted to single-family use contains a mixture of single-family and multi-family development. *Krause v. City of Royal Oak*[58] is a typical case. Plaintiff owned a 3.5-acre tract that formed an imperfect right triangle at an intersection of two roads. A railroad ran along the hypotenuse of the triangle. Northeast of the railroad the land was zoned and partially developed for single-family use. The area south of the triangle was developed with apartments. A golf course was located across the road to the west. A row of single-family dwellings was located on the western fringe of plaintiff's property, across from the golf course. The governing body refused to rezone plaintiff's tract for multi-family use.

The plaintiff, who wished to build apartments on his property, claimed that the single-family zoning was a taking. The court disagreed. It held that the neighborhood affected by the plaintiff's proposed apartments was the single-family area lying to the northeast. The court quoted *Euclid* for the proposition that apartments are "parasites" in single-family neighborhoods and held that noise and congestion from the plaintiff's apartment development would detrimentally affect this single-family area. It then held that the disparity between the value of plaintiff's property for multi- as compared with single-family use was not enough to "subvert the interests of the public" in the single-family zoning of plaintiff's land.

In an interesting holding on the use of apartments to buffer single-family residences from more intensive uses, the court dismissed the presence of the railroad tracks as a significant factor. As the court noted, more people live in apartments

---

57. § 2.30. *See* Ewing v. City of Carmel-by-the-Sea, 286 Cal. Rptr. 382 (Cal. App. 1991) (ordinance prohibiting temporary occupancy held not a taking).

**58.** 160 N.W.2d 769 (Mich. App. 1968).

than in single-family housing. To place apartments next to the railroad tracks would subject even more people to the noise and inconvenience of railroad traffic. The court also believed that the plaintiff's case was weakened because he did not challenge a previous downzoning of his property but asked instead for an upzoning to allow a more profitable use of his property. This point of view is unusual in as-applied taking cases.

The dissenting opinion would have held the single-family zoning "confiscatory" because it prevented any reasonable use of plaintiff's property, whether or not it had some "exchange value" under the single-family zoning. In the dissent's view, the railroad tracks made the plaintiff's property unsuitable for residential development. This holding would have made the restriction a per se taking under the Supreme Court's *Lucas* decision.[59]

Although unusual in its treatment of the upzoning and buffer issues, the *Krause* majority illustrates a typical as-applied taking opinion on single-family zoning. The disagreement between the majority and dissenting opinions indicates how courts can go either way in cases where a mixed-use area surrounds the property whose owner brings a taking challenge. Most courts review the facts in as-applied taking attacks on single-family zoning without so clearly specifying the criteria that govern their decision.[60]

A total exclusion of apartments is another matter. A few early cases invalidated zoning ordinances that totally excluded apartments from suburban communities but did not provide a comprehensive review of exclusionary zoning problems. *Appeal of Girsh*[61] is the leading case. The court held that a suburban zoning ordinance that excluded apartments was an improper limitation on suburban growth. It refused to accept the community's justification that apartment development would fiscally burden municipal services. "[I]f . . . [this suburb] is a logical place for development to take place, it should not be heard to say that it will not bear its rightful part of the burden."[62] Later cases have elaborated the tests the Pennsylvania court applies to exclusionary zoning.[63]

The supply of rental housing is also reduced by the conversion of rental apartments to condominium ownership. Some municipalities attempt to regulate condominium conversions through the zoning ordinance by requiring a conditional use permit or by limiting conversions to certain areas of the community. The courts have invalidated these restrictions by holding that condominium con-

---

59. *See* § 2.18.

60. Davis v. Sails, 318 So. 2d 214 (Fla. App. 1975); Wheeler v. City of Berkeley, 485 S.W.2d 707 (Mo. App. 1972). *See* 2 N. Williams, *American Land Planning Law*, ch. 53 (1974).

61. 263 A.2d 395 (Pa. 1970).

62. *Id.* at 398-99. *See also* Dowsey v. Village of Kensington, 177 N.E. 427 (N.Y. App. 1937) (accord); Zelvin v. Zoning Bd. of Appeals, 306 A.2d 151 (Conn. C.P. 1973) (contra).

63. §§ 7.18-7.21.

versions are a change in ownership, not a change in use the zoning ordinance can regulate.[64]

## § 5.15. Accessory Uses.

Accessory uses are secondary activities that are necessary and convenient to the principal use of the property. Zoning ordinances usually allow accessory uses that are related, subordinate, and customarily incidental to the principal use. They also require the location of accessory uses on the same lot as the principal use and may prohibit them if they alter the character of the surrounding area.[65] The cases apply these criteria to determine whether a particular use is allowable as an accessory use under the ordinance.[66]

Zoning ordinances often allow accessory uses or buildings that are "customarily incidental" to a residential use, and courts impose a similar requirement if the ordinance does not contain one. The test is whether the accessory use is normally incidental to a residential use.[67] It is not necessary to show that a majority or even a substantial number of homes in a neighborhood have a particular accessory use, such as a tennis court.[68]

A zoning ordinance may permit homeowners to rent rooms in single-family dwellings and will often limit the number of rooms the homeowner can rent and their total floor area. Some courts hold that this practice is an impermissible business activity if the zoning ordinance does not permit it,[69] but other courts approve the occasional renting of a small number of rooms.[70] The ordinance may

---

**64.** Griffin Dev. Co. v. City of Oxnard, 199 Cal. Rptr. 739 (Cal. App. 1984); McHenry State Bank v. City of McHenry, 46 N.E.2d 521 (Ill. App. 1983) (may not restrict conversion to condominium zones); Graham Court Assocs. v. Town Council, 281 S.E.2d 418 (N.C. App. 1981); Backer v. Town of Sullivan's Island, 310 S.E.2d 433 (S.C. 1983).

**65.** Redfearn v. Creppel, 455 So. 2d 1356 (La. 1984).

**66.** Perron v. City of Concord, 150 A.2d 403 (N.H. 1959) (use of large part of house by roofing contractor held not incidental); Charlie Brown of Chatham, Inc. v. Board of Adjustment, 495 A.2d 119 (N.J. App. Div. 1985) (sleeping accommodation in restaurant held not accessory); Presnell v. Leslie, 144 N.E.2d 381 (N.Y. 1959) (tall amateur radio transmitting tower not appropriate in small compact neighborhood); Boreth v. Philadelphia Zoning Bd. of Adjustment, 151 A.2d 474 (Pa. 1959) (home beauty shop not incidental); Pearson v. Evans, 320 P.2d 300 (Wash. 1958) (boathouse held incidental to house one-quarter its size); 60 A.L.R.4th 901 (1988); 54 A.L.R.4th 1034 (1987).

**67.** Dettmar v. County Bd. of Zoning Appeals, 273 N.E.2d 921 (Ohio Misc. 1971); Pratt v. Building Inspector, 113 N.E.2d 816 (Mass. 1953); Town of Alta v. Ben Hame Corp., 836 P.2d 797 (Utah 1992) (overnight rental as lodging facility not customarily incidental).

**68.** Klien v. Township of Lower Macungie, 395 A.2d 609 (Pa. 1978).

**69.** Kewseling v. City of Baltimore, 151 A.2d 726 (Md. 1959); Township of Berlin v. Christiansen, 215 A.2d 593 (N.J.L. Div. 1965).

**70.** Brady v. Superior Court, 19 Cal. Rptr. 242 (Cal. App. 1962); Baddour v. City of Long Beach, 18 N.E.2d 18 (N.Y. 1938).

prohibit separate residential apartments located in accessory structures or within the primary dwelling.[71] The courts have allowed accessory apartments for friends, relatives, or domestic servants if the ordinance does not prohibit them.[72]

An accessory structure is a building located on the same lot as the principal building that either houses or serves as an accessory use. Accessory structures must comply with special height, size, and location requirements that keep them away from lot lines and prevent inappropriate placement. Placement in the front yard is usually prohibited. The courts hold that additions to principal buildings are not accessory structures.[73]

The courts have usually held that the parking of commercial or recreational vehicles is neither accessory nor incidental to residential uses.[74] They hold that commercial vehicles create excessive noise and that their overnight parking or permanent storage adversely affects the character of residential neighborhoods.[75]

## § 5.16. Home Occupations.

Home occupations are income-producing activities that take place within dwellings or accessory structures in residential districts. Most zoning ordinances define home occupations in general terms, but some list home occupations that are prohibited or permitted. They may also limit the amount of floor space home occupations can use, prohibit equipment not normally used for domestic purposes, and prohibit or limit the number of nonresident employees. Zoning ordinances may also confine home occupations to indoor activity, regulate exterior

---

**71.** Sanders v. Board of Adjustment, 445 So. 2d 909 (Ala. App. 1983) (accessory structure); City of Peru v. Nienaber, 424 N.E.2d 85 (Ill. App. 1981) (within dwelling).

**72.** Trent v. City of Pittsburg, 619 P.2d 1171 (Kan. 1980); Township of Randolph v. Lamprecht, 542 A.2d 36 (N.J. App. Div. 1988) (separate dwelling unit for servant held accessory use); Farr v. Board of Adjustment, 326 S.E.2d 382 (N.C. App. 1985).

**73.** Olson v. Zoning Bd. of Appeal, 84 N.E.2d 544 (Mass. 1949) (garage and connecting breezeway); City of Cleveland v. Young, 111 So. 2d 29 (Miss. 1959) (carport).

**74.** Sechrist v. Municipal Court, 134 Cal. Rptr. 733 (Cal. App. 1976) (motor vehicles and junk); Becker v. Town of Hampton Falls, 374 A.2d 653 (N.H. 1977) (road grader); Galliford v. Commonwealth, 430 A.2d 1222 (Pa. Commw. 1981) (large truck).

**75.** People v. Tolman, 168 Cal. Rptr. 328 (Cal. App. 1980); Recreational Vehicle United Citizens Ass'n v. City of Sterling Heights, 418 N.W.2d 702 (Mich. App. 1987) (setback restrictions on motor vehicle parking upheld); Township of Livingston v. Marchev, 205 A.2d 65 (N.J. App. Div. 1964).

signage, and prohibit structural alterations.[76] The courts have rejected substantive due process and equal protection objections to these restrictions.[77]

Courts approve home occupations that are incidental and subordinate to the principal use if the ordinance does not list permitted home occupations. Some courts compare the scale of the home occupation with the scale of the principal use.[78] They usually approve professional offices for the practice of law, medicine, dentistry, and architecture and the use of the home to give music and dance lessons.[79] The cases divide on whether the sale of real estate is an acceptable home occupation.[80] They usually allow minor commercial services in large apartment buildings.[81]

## § 5.17. Mobile Homes.

Mobile homes are a residential building type that zoning ordinances often exclude from the community or restrict to undesirable areas or mobile home parks. A mobile home is a dwelling that is manufactured off-site and shipped fully assembled to a building site. It is then placed on a foundation or on supports and is seldom moved again. Some legislation now refers to this type of housing as "manufactured" housing. This term also applies to housing that is assembled on site from manufactured modular components.

Municipalities object to mobile homes for a number of reasons, such as their transient use, their unpleasant appearance, their unsafe construction, and the inadequate tax revenues that are produced by their taxation as personal rather than

---

**76.** State v. Baudier, 334 So. 2d 197 (La. 1976) (limited floor space to 15% of dwelling unit); Holsheimer v. Columbia County, 890 P.2d 447 (Or. App. 1995) (commercial business requiring daily movement of vehicles and equipment not allowed under statute); City of Aberdeen v. Herrmann, 301 N.W.2d 674 (S.D. 1981) (limiting nonresident employees).

**77.** Farrell v. City of Miami, 587 F. Supp. 413 (S.D. Fla. 1984); Levinson v. Montgomery County, 620 A.2d 961 (Md. App. 1993); City of Manassas v. Rosson, 294 S.E.2d 799 (Va.), *appeal dismissed,* 459 U.S. 1166 (1982); City of Florence v. Turbeville, 121 S.E.2d 437 (S.C. 1961).

**78.** Metropolitan Dev. Comm'n v. Mullin, 399 N.E.2d 751 (Ind. App. 1979); Franchi v. Zoning Hearing Bd., 543 A.2d 239 (Pa. Commw. 1988).

**79.** Eisner v. Farrington, 209 N.Y.S.2d 673 (App. Div. 1961) (veterinarian's office); Osborne v. Planning Bd., 536 N.Y.S.2d 244 (Sup. Ct. 1989) (social worker); Stewart v. Humpheries, 132 N.E.2d 758 (Ohio 1955) (dance studio); Parks v. Board of Adjustment, 566 S.W.2d 365 (Tex. Civ. App. 1978) (music school with 110 students). *But see* County of Butte v. Bach, 218 Cal. Rptr. 613 (Cal. App. 1985) (law office not permitted when lawyer did not reside in residence); Schweitzer v. Board of Zoning Appeals, 167 N.Y.S.2d 767 (Misc. 1957) (ceramics class not permitted).

**80.** *Compare* People v. Cully Realty, Inc., 442 N.Y.S.2d 847 (Misc. 1981) (not permitted) *with* Vislisel v. Board of Adjustment, 372 N.W.2d 316 (Iowa App. 1985) (contra). *See also* Board of Adjustment v. Levinson, 244 S.W.2d 281 (Tex. Civ. App. 1951) (beauty shop not a home occupation).

**81.** City of Neward v. Daley, 214 A.2d 410 (N.J. 1965) (vending machine); 140 Riverside Drive v. Murdock, 95 N.Y.S.2d 860 (App. Div. 1950) (newsstand).

real property. Many of these objections are no longer valid. New developments in mobile home construction can make them comparable to conventional construction. Legislation can remedy taxation problems, and federal, state and local legislation now imposes safety requirements. Mobile home residents are no longer transient rather than permanent occupants.

The discussion that follows reviews a number of common zoning restrictions on mobile homes, including total or partial exclusion and zoning that limits mobile homes to mobile home parks. A municipality may also place other burdensome restrictions on mobile homes, such as a conditional use requirement, appearance requirements, or a limitation on the number of mobile homes permitted in the municipality. Judicial reaction to these prohibitions is mixed.[82]

### § 5.18. As a Dwelling.

Single-family zoning restricts single-family uses to residential "dwellings," a building type classification. A mobile home owner may claim that her mobile home is permitted as a "dwelling" in a single-family district. The court must then decide whether the mobile home qualifies under the definition of a dwelling in the zoning ordinance. *Town of Manchester v. Phillips*,[83] an early leading case, held that the exclusion of mobile homes from a definition of a "dwelling" in a zoning ordinance applied to a mobile home placed on a foundation. The court was hostile to mobile homes and held that the town could limit them to areas where they would not injure the investment in conventional houses, "hurt taxable values, and impede town development."

Other cases, perhaps easier because the ordinance did not expressly exclude mobile homes, held that the definition of a "dwelling" included mobile homes.[84] These cases usually turned on an analysis of legislative intent. Their refusal to distinguish mobile homes from conventional dwelling units implies a rejection of the older mobile home image.

---

**82.** Campbell v. Monroe County, 426 So. 2d 1158 (Fla. App. 1983) (ordinance requiring masonry construction held to violate state statute prohibiting differential treatment of mobile homes); Jensen's, Inc. v. City of Dover, 547 A.2d 277 (N.H. 1988) (upholding conditional use requirement because of density increase). *Compare* Riverview Park, Inc. v. Town of Hinsdale, 313 A.2d 733 (N.H. 1973) (upholds numerical limit) *with* Begin v. Inhabitants of Town of Sabattus, 409 A.2d 1269 (Me. 1979) (contra), *and* Town of Glocester v. Olivo's Mobile Home Court, Inc., 300 A.2d 465 (R.I. 1973) (same); 42 A.L.R.3d 598 (1972).

**83.** 180 N.E.2d 333 (Mass. 1962).

**84.** Fedorich v. Zoning Bd. of Appeals, 424 A.2d 289 (Conn. 1979); Village of Moscow v. Skeene, 585 N.E.2d 493 (Ohio App. 1989) (after mobile home placed on foundation); In re Willey, 140 A.2d 11 (Vt. 1958); State v. Work, 449 P.2d 806 (Wash. 1969). *See also* Bourgeois v. Parish of St. Tammany, 628 F. Supp. 159 (E.D. La. 1986) (invalidating ordinance excluding mobile homes but not modular homes from residential district); Geiger v. Zoning Hearing Bd., 507 A.2d 361 (Pa. 1986) (invalidating ordinance allowing two-section but prohibiting one-section homes delivered to the site). *Contra* Warren v. Municipal Officers, 431 A.2d 624 (Me. 1981).

## § 5.19. Partial Exclusion.

A zoning ordinance may exclude mobile homes from designated zoning districts. Some courts uphold their exclusion from residential districts,[85] and some even uphold their exclusion from industrial and commercial districts and from rural and agricultural areas.[86] A partial exclusion problem also arises when a municipality allows mobile homes only in mobile home parks and excludes them from its residential districts. A majority of the cases upheld ordinances that contained these restrictions.[87] Some of these cases pointed out that the isolation of mobile homes in parks makes adequate public supervision easier. This holding implies that mobile homes create special regulatory problems.

A landmark Michigan case, *Robinson Twp. v. Knoll*,[88] held a *per se* prohibition on the location of mobile homes outside mobile home parks unconstitutional. The court reviewed the usual objections to mobile homes but noted that changes in mobile home construction made them as attractive as conventional single-family dwellings. Aesthetic objections to mobile homes were no longer justified, and the investment required for a modern mobile home precluded any objections based on transient occupancy. More appropriate regulations, such as local plumbing codes and a regulation requiring attachment to a solid founda-

---

**85.** Jensen's, Inc. v. Town of Plainville, 150 A.2d 297 (Conn. 1959); City of Lewiston v. Knieriem, 685 P.2d 821 (Idaho 1984) (excluded from farm zone but allowed in residential districts); Mack T. Anderson Ins. Agency, Inc. v. City of Belgrade, 803 P.2d 648 (Mont. 1990) (although modular homes allowed); Village Bd. of Trustees v. Zoning Bd. of Appeals, 562 N.Y.S.2d 973 (App. Div. 1990); Duggins v. Town of Walnut Grove, 306 S.E.2d 186 (N.C. App. 1981); Corning v. Town of Ontario, 121 N.Y.S.2d 288 (Sup. Ct. 1953); Duckworth v. City of Bonney Lake, 586 P.2d 860 (Wash. 1978).

**86.** Camboni's, Inc. v. County of Du Page, 187 N.E.2d 212 (Ill. 1962) (upholds exclusion from industrial zone); Lakeland Bluff v. County of Will, 252 N.E.2d 765 (Ill. App. 1969) (contra, rural area); 42 A.L.R.3d 598 (1972). *But see* Town of Chesterfield v. Brooks, 489 A.2d 600 (N.H. 1985) (may not confine to areas with unpaved roads).

**87.** Cooper v. Sinclair, 66 So. 2d 702 (Fla.), *cert. denied,* 346 U.S. 867 (1953); People of Village of Cahokia v. Wright, 311 N.E.2d 153 (Ill. 1974); City of Saco v. Tweedie, 314 A.2d 135 (Me. 1974); Town of Granby v. Landry, 170 N.E.2d 364 (Mass. 1960); State v. Larson, 195 N.W.2d 180 (Minn. 1972); Mobile Home Owners Protective Assoc. v. Town of Chatham, 305 N.Y.S.2d 334 (App. Div. 1969); Town of Scranton v. Willoughby, 412 S.E.2d 424 (S.C. 1991); Mobile Home City of Chattanooga v. Hamilton County, 552 S.W.2d 86 (Tenn. App. 1976); City of Brookside Village v. Comeau, 633 S.W.2d 790 (Tex.), *cert. denied,* 459 U.S. 1087 (1982); Town of Stonewood v. Bell, 270 S.E.2d 787 (W. Va. 1980); 17 A.L.R.4th 106 (1982).

**88.** 302 N.W.2d 146 (Mich. 1981). *See also* Cannon v. Coweta Cty., 389 S.E.2d 329 (Ga. 1990) (exclusion held unconstitutional); Gackler Land Co. v. Yankee Springs Twp., 359 N.W.2d 226 (Mich. App. 1984) (upholding restrictions promoting compatibility and relative uniformity of site-built and mobile home housing); Luczynski v. Temple, 497 A.2d 211 (N.J. Ch. Div. 1985) (following *Robinson*). *Contra* Barre Mobile Home Park v. Town of Petersham, 592 F. Supp. 633 (D. Mass. 1984).

tion, could handle health and safety problems. A municipality could also prohibit the exposure of the wheels and chassis.

Although limited to a mobile home park restriction, *Robinson Township* has much broader implications for mobile home zoning. The court rejected a *per se* restriction on the location of mobile homes and adopted the less restrictive alternative test to demand the regulation of mobile home problems outside the zoning ordinance. The case suggests that any restrictive zoning of mobile homes is suspect.

### § 5.20. Total Exclusion.

Although no longer good law in New Jersey, *Vickers v. Township Comm.*[89] is a leading case that illustrates the reasons why courts upheld the exclusion of mobile homes from an entire community. *Vickers* justified the mobile home exclusion by holding that mobile homes have a negative impact on single-family development, and that the exclusion implemented a municipal policy to plan for a quality residential environment.

Some of the exclusionary zoning cases invalidated total mobile home exclusions as one of several restrictions they found unacceptable in an exclusionary zoning ordinance.[90] Other courts have invalidated total exclusions that were not part of an exclusionary ordinance.[91]

Municipalities often authorize mobile homes as a special exception in designated zoning districts. Although a municipality may provide reasonable opportunities for mobile homes through special exceptions, it may also draft or administer a special exception provision so that it is exclusionary. Some courts are sensitive to these possibilities and strike down vaguely drafted special exception provisions, such as a provision requiring proof of "necessity" as the basis for allowing a mobile home use.[92]

### § 5.21. State and Federal Regulation.

The courts do not imply a preemption of local zoning from legislation that merely authorizes the state licensing of mobile homes.[93] A few states have

---

**89.** 181 A.2d 129 (N.J. 1962), *cert. denied,* 371 U.S. 233 (1963).

**90.** §§ 7.08-7.23. *But see* Town of Pompey v. Parker, 377 N.E.2d 741 (N.Y. 1978) (validity of mobile home exclusion reserved).

**91.** Oak Forest Mobile Home Park v. City of Oak Forest, 326 N.E.2d 473 (Ill. App. 1975) (holding mobile home is legitimate use and noting need for affordable housing).

**92.** Pioneer Trust & Sav. Bank v. County of McHenry, 241 N.E.2d 454 (Ill. 1968) (necessity requirement invalidated); Lakewood Estates, Inc. v. Deerfield Twp. Zoning Bd. of Appeals, 194 N.W.2d 511 (Mich. App. 1977) (vague standards); Walworth Leasing Corp. v. Sterni, 316 N.Y.S.2d 851 (Sup. Ct. 1970) (denial as special use reversed); 42 A.L.R.3d 598 (1972).

**93.** Adams v. Cowart, 160 S.E.2d 805 (Ga. 1968); County of Winnebago v. Hartman, 242 N.E.2d 916 (Ill. App. 1968).

adopted legislation that explicitly prohibits the discriminatory treatment of mobile homes in zoning ordinances.[94] The language enacting this type of prohibition varies, with mixed results in the courts.[95] A number of states have also adopted legislation authorizing the state certification of mobile homes that meet state construction standards. This legislation preempts local regulation of mobile homes under building codes, and some of these laws preempt local zoning.[96]

Federal legislation requires mobile home manufacturers to comply with federal construction and safety standards.[97] This legislation does not preempt local zoning,[98] but some states have adopted legislation that prohibits municipalities from adopting restrictive zoning for manufactured housing certified under the federal law.[99] The Eleventh Circuit invalidated an ordinance that allowed mobile homes certified under federal law in residential areas only if they met additional safety requirements.[100] The court held the city could not do land use planning through a safety provision that is preempted by federal law.

## § 5.22. Private Schools.

Private nonsectarian schools present special regulatory problems in residential districts. Public schools are often not subject to zoning regulations because they are state-supervised.[101] Attempts are still made to prohibit private schools from residential zones, or to require a conditional use permit for them. Although arguments can be made that private schools present special zoning problems, the majority rule is that attempts to prohibit private nonsectarian schools while al-

---

94. Cal. Gov't Code § 65852.3 (if certified under federal law); N.H. Rev. Stat. § 674:32; Vt. Stat. Ann. tit. 24, § 4406(4)(A). *See* Pope v. Town of Hinsdale, 624 A.2d 1360 (N.H. 1993) (existing nonconforming manufactured housing park not covered by statute). *See also* Idaho Code § 67-6509A (imposes minimum size and design requirements); Neb. Rev. Stat. § 14-402(2)(a) (same).

95. Paladac v. City of Rockland, 558 A.2d 372 (Me. 1989) (invalidating setback requirement; statute required municipalities to find locations for mobile homes); Ettinger v. City of Lansing, 546 N.W.2d 652 (Mich. App. 1996) (ordinance allowing mobile home parks in residential districts on special permit did not "generally" exclude them); Jensen's, Inc. v. City of Dover, 547 A.2d 277 (N.H. 1988) (statute requiring reasonable opportunities for mobile homes did not invalidate ordinance limiting mobile homes to rural zones).

96. Warren v. Municipal Officers, 431 A.2d 624 (Me. 1981).

97. 42 U.S.C. § 5415.

98. Gackler Land Co. v. Yankee Springs Twp., 398 N.W.2d 393 (Mich. 1986); City of Brookside Village v. Comeau, 633 S.W.2d 790 (Tex.), *cert. denied,* 459 U.S. 1087 (1982); Washington Manufactured Housing Ass'n v. Public Util. Dist. No. 3, 878 P.2d 1213 (Wash. 1994) (federal law does not preempt public utility district's new facility charge for connecting electricity).

99. Iowa Code Ann. § 414.28; Me. Rev. Stat. Ann. tit. 30(A), § 4358(2).

100. Scurlock v. City of Lynn Haven, 858 F.2d 1521 (11th Cir. 1988) (provision also held invalid under state law).

101. *See* § 4.28.

lowing other schools in residential zones are invalid.[102] The courts have upheld special use permit requirements for private schools because they are less onerous than total prohibition.[103] Religious schools receive different judicial treatment because of the protection accorded religious uses under federal and state constitutions.[104] Statutes may also protect private schools.[105]

## B. LARGE LOTS AND MINIMUM HOUSE SIZE.

### § 5.23.  The Zoning Problem.

Municipalities often control residential densities and amenities through large-lot zoning and minimum house size restrictions. These restrictions are exclusionary if they are excessive, but the earlier decisions often upheld them because they implemented a legitimate zoning purpose by ensuring a quality residential environment. Many later decisions are more hostile.

### § 5.24.  Minimum House Size.

Proponents of minimum house size restrictions advance a number of justifications. They claim they serve an aesthetic purpose, but why the size of a house is related to its aesthetic qualities is not clear. They also claim that minimum house size restrictions advance the health objective of zoning by preventing overcrowding. Housing codes provide a less restrictive alternative that can accomplish the same objective. These codes commonly require a minimum floor area for each habitable room.[106] Proponents of minimum house size restrictions also argue that they implement the statutory purposes of zoning by conserving property values.

---

**102.** Roman Catholic Welfare Corporation of San Francisco v. City of Pledmont, 289 P.2d 438 (Cal. 1955) (invalidating ordinance permitting public schools but not private or parochial schools); Catholic Bishop of Chicago v. Kingery, 20 N.E.2d 583 (Ill. 1939) (same; ordinance permitting public schools but not parochial schools); City of Miami Beach v. State ex rel. Lear, 175 So. 537 (Fla. 1937) (same; public schools allowed but private schools prohibited in multi-family zone); State v. Northwestern Preparatory School, 37 N.W.2d 370 (Minn. 1949) (same; public and religious schools permitted but private schools prohibited). *Contra* Wisconsin Lutheran High School Conference v. Sinar, 65 N.W.2d 43 (Wis. 1954). *Compare* Yanow v. Seven Oaks Park, 94 A.2d 482 (N.J. 1953) (upholding ordinance that allowed public and parochial schools but disallowed schools of higher learning and specialty schools).

**103.** Creative Country Day School, Inc. v. Montgomery County Board of Appeals, 219 A.2d 789 (Md. 1966).

**104.** *See* §§ 5.59-5.60 (zoning for religious uses); § 6.59 (conditional use permits).

**105.** Trustees of Tufts College v. City of Medford, 616 N.E.2d 433 (Mass. 1993) (statute prohibiting zoning of educational institutions except for reasonable regulations.)

**106.** Nolden v. East Cleveland City Comm'n, 232 N.E.2d 421 (Ohio C.P. 1966).

Early decisions that considered substantive due process attacks on minimum house size restrictions were divided.[107] They usually turned on the willingness of the court to recognize aesthetic objectives and the conservation of property values as a legitimate zoning purpose. A pair of New Jersey cases indicates how judicial views have changed since these early decisions. An early, leading, and much-debated decision, *Lionshead Lake, Inc. v. Wayne Twp.*,[108] upheld a minimum house size restriction adopted by a suburban community that was not substantially developed. The court viewed the restriction as far-sighted planning intended to protect the quality of the community's environment, its health and its property values.

The New Jersey Supreme Court overruled *Lionshead* in *Home Bldrs. League of S. Jersey, Inc. v. Township of Berlin*.[109] It held that the minimum house size restriction raised overlapping constitutional and statutory "general welfare" issues. The court noted that minimum house size restrictions may serve the general welfare but may be exclusionary because they are clearly cost-related. The court held a minimum house size provision unrelated to any other factor would be presumed enacted for improper purposes. The municipality then has the burden to establish a valid basis for the provision, and the court must then weigh and balance its "exclusionary and salutary effects."

The court held that the municipality had not justified the minimum house size restriction. Its impact on health and safety was indirect, and housing code occupancy requirements could better serve this purpose. The court noted that minimum house size restrictions varied by zoning district, even though minimum health and safety needs were "unquestionably the same" throughout the municipality.[110]

The court also rejected a property conservation justification, and noted that the minimum house size requirement would not maintain the aesthetic quality of the municipality's residential environment because beauty is not related to size.

## § 5.25. Large-Lot Zoning.

Suburban municipalities often adopt zoning ordinances that require large lots of one acre or more for single family residential development. Large-lot zoning can serve a number of zoning purposes. A municipality may limit large-lot zon-

---

107. Valid: Flower Hill Bldg. Corp. v. Village of Flower Hill, 100 N.Y.S.2d 903 (Sup. Ct. 1950); Thompson v. City of Carrollton, 211 S.W.2d 970 (Tex. App. 1948). Invalid: Northwood Props. Co. v. Perkins, 39 N.W.2d 25 (Mich. 1949); Elizabeth Lake Estates v. Waterford Twp., 26 N.W.2d 788 (Mich. 1947); Senefsky v. Lawler, 12 N.W.2d 387 (Mich. 1943). *See* 87 A.L.R.4th 294 (1991) 76 A.L.R.2d 1409 (1964).

108. 89 A.2d 693 (N.J. 1952), appeal dismissed, 344 U.S. 919 (1953).

109. 405 A.2d 381 (N.J. 1979).

110. *See also* Appeal of Medinger, 104 A.2d 118 (Pa. 1954) (invalidating variable minimum house size requirements).

ing to areas where the market for upper-income housing can absorb the large lots that are available. It may also zone more land for large lots than the market can absorb. Zoning of this type can have two objectives. A municipality may adopt large-lot zoning to keep land off the market as a permanent open space or "green belt" preserve. It may also adopt large-lot zoning to create a temporary holding zone and rezone for higher residential densities or nonresidential use when developers apply for a zoning change. The large-lot holding zone is one way to implement a "wait and see" zoning policy.

Large-lot zoning is exclusionary if it increases the cost of land for housing, but a price increase is not inevitable. A builder can build only one dwelling on a lot, no matter what its size, so that increasing the size of the lot does not necessarily increase its price. The price of land per square foot may decrease sufficiently to offset the increased size of the lot. Whether this price effect occurs is not clear. Some of the more convincing studies indicate that increasing the size of a lot increases its price.[111]

If a large-lot requirement increases the price of a lot it will increase the cost of housing because builders usually maintain a constant ratio between the price of a lot and the price of the dwelling that is built on it. Assume that the constant ratio between lot price and house price is 1:4. If this ratio applies, the price of a house will increase by $4.00 for each $1.00 increase in the price of a lot. The ratio amplifies the exclusionary effect of large-lot zoning if this zoning increases lot prices.

In some states, notably New Jersey, New York, and Pennsylvania, the courts invalidated large-lot zoning that was included in exclusionary zoning ordinances the courts held unconstitutional. The case law is mixed in other states. Many of the early cases upheld large-lot zoning when suburban municipalities adopted it to preserve low-density residential areas. Later cases invalidated large-lot zoning as an impediment to suburban growth. All of these cases treated large-lot zoning as a permanent density limitation rather than a temporary "holding zone" intended to prohibit new development.[112]

## § 5.26. Held Valid.

*Simon v. Needham*[113] is a leading case that upheld large-lot zoning as a density control. A comparatively small and primarily residential suburb, twelve miles from the center of Boston, placed nearly all of its southern area in a one-

---

**111.** W. McEachern, "Large-Lot Zoning in Connecticut: Incentives and Effects," U. Conn. Center for Real Est. & Urb. Econ. Studies (1979); Nat'l Comm'n on Urban Problems, Building the American City 213-15 (1968).

**112.** *But see* Rodo Land, Inc. v. Board of County Comm'rs, 517 P.2d 873 (Colo. App. 1974). *See also* 2 A.L.R.5th 553 (1992); 1 A.L.R.5th 622 (1992).

**113.** 42 N.E.2d 516 (Mass. 1942).

acre residential zone. The planning board disapproved a residential development that did not comply with the one-acre zoning, and the developer then challenged the large-lot zoning ordinance. The court held that language in the state zoning act that authorized the regulation of "the size and width of lots" authorized large-lot zoning. The Standard Zoning Act contains different but equally sufficient language that authorizes the municipality to regulate "the size of yards . . . and other open spaces."

The court next held that the one-acre zoning implemented legitimate zoning purposes. They included the establishment of residential neighborhoods of high quality that "would tend to improve and beautify the town and would harmonize with the natural characteristics of the locality." One-acre lots would also provide more residential amenities. They ensured more freedom from noise, less danger from fire, and a better opportunity for rest and relaxation. The court held that the benefits of large-lot zoning made its constitutionality fairly debatable and upheld the ordinance under standard substantive due process doctrine.

The court dismissed a taking objection because the ordinance only diminished the value of the developer's land. Most of the decisions apply this rule to reject taking objections to large-lot zoning. It does not prohibit residential development but only makes it less profitable by limiting the number of dwellings allowed.

*Simon* also addressed the exclusionary potential of large-lot zoning. The planning board reported that large-lot zoning would reduce municipal costs by prohibiting "low cost houses" that would require more service. Assuming, but not deciding, that municipalities could not use zoning for fiscal purposes, the court stated that it would not tolerate an ordinance that was used to exclude.[114] The court also decided that large-lot zoning served the public interest because communities also had large-lot zoning. Later, more sophisticated, exclusionary zoning cases recognize that large-lot zoning can have exclusionary effects if applied extensively in metropolitan areas.

The residential amenity justifications for large-lot zoning adopted in *Simon* are dubious. Why is it easier to relax on a large lot than a small lot? The court was sensitive to this issue because it reserved decision on whether it would uphold larger minimum lot sizes. Some of the cases that invalidated large-lot zoning picked up on this suggestion.

The argument that large-lot zoning will provide a high-quality, low-density environment is more acceptable because this zoning reinforces existing low residential densities in partly developed communities. This use of large-lot zoning is a more sophisticated application of the compatibility rationale for the nuisance

---

**114.** *See also* Senior v. Zoning Comm'n of New Canaan, 153 A.2d 415 (Conn. 1959), *appeal dismissed,* 363 U.S. 143 (1960); De Bruler Homes, Inc. v. County of Lake, 222 N.E.2d 689 (Ill. App. 1967); Gignoux v. Village of Kings Point, 99 N.Y.S.2d 280 (Sup. Ct. 1950).

cases. Large-lot zoning ensures that residential development will take place on compatible, low-density residential lots. If the community is undeveloped, large-lot zoning "plans" for a low-density residential environment by requiring development at low-density levels. Some of the favorable large-lot zoning cases accepted this justification to uphold large-lot zoning adopted by developing communities.[115] A Maryland court upheld large lot zoning intended to limit development in a watershed, and rejected an argument it denied the landowner all economically viable use of the property under the *Lucas* test.[116]

Large lots are necessary under some soil conditions to provide sufficient drainage that will avoid water pollution if the developer intends to use on-site facilities to provide water and dispose of sewage. Some courts relied on this necessity to uphold large-lot zoning, even though its use to accomplish these health and safety objectives is questionable. The health code or the subdivision control ordinance provides more appropriate opportunities for this kind of regulation.

*Salamar Bldrs. Corp. v. Tuttle*[117] is a leading case that accepted health and safety justification for large-lot zoning. Topography and soil conditions prevented the installation of public water and sewer systems and required wells and septic tanks on individual lots. The court upheld two-acre large-lot zoning because it would prevent pollution to individual wells and a reservoir by reducing the number of septic tanks and increasing lot area.[118] The court rejected a claim that the large-lot zoning was a taking because it reduced the profitability of residential development. The developer argued that the more expensive houses it would have to build on two-acre lots could not be sold in the local land market.

---

**115.** Senior v. Zoning Comm'n of New Canaan, 153 A.2d 415 (Conn. 1959), *appeal dismissed,* 363 U.S. 143 (1960); Flora Realty & Inv. Co. v. City of Ladue, 246 S.W.2d 771 (Mo.), *appeal dismissed,* 344 U.S. 802 (1952); Levitt v. Incorporated Village of Sands Point, 160 N.E.2d 501 (N.Y. 1959); 95 A.L.R.2d 716 (1964). For cases on large-lot zoning in rural areas, see Steel Hill Dev., Inc. v. Town of Sanbornton, 469 F.2d 956 (1st Cir. 1972); County Comm'rs of Queen Anne's County v. Miles, 228 A.2d 450 (Md. 1967).

**116.** Security Mgt. Corp. v. Baltimore County, 655 A.2d 1326 (Md. App. 1995), *cert. denied,* 116 S. Ct. 917 (1996).

**117.** 275 N.E.2d 585 (N.Y. 1971).

**118.** *See also* Wermager v. Comorant Twp. Bd., 716 F.2d 1211 (8th Cir. 1983) (five-acre zoning for lots more than 300 feet from lake high water mark); Zygmont v. Planning & Zoning Comm'n, 210 A.2d 172 (Conn. 1965); De Mars v. Zoning Comm'n, 115 A.2d 653 (Conn. 1955); Honeck v. County of Cook, 146 N.E.2d 35 (Ill. 1957) (poor topography as justification); Norbeck Village Joint Venture v. Montgomery County Council, 254 A.2d 700 (Md. 1969); Wilson v. Town of Sherborn, 326 N.E.2d 922 (Mass. App. 1975); Serpa v. County of Washoe, 901 P.2d 690 (Nev. 1995); Sanderson v. Town of Greenland, 453 A.2d 1285 (N.H. 1982); Albano v. Mayor & Twp. Comm., 476 A.2d 852 (N.J. App. Div. 1984); Ketchel v. Bainbridge Twp., 557 N.E.2d 779 (Ohio 1990) (three acres upheld where purpose was to protect groundwater supplies); State v. Kiefaber, 181 N.E.2d 905 (Ohio App.), *aff'd on other grounds,* 170 N.E.2d 848 (Ohio 1960); Reimer v. Board of Supervisors, 615 A.2d 938 (Pa. Commw. 1992); Kelly v. Zoning Hearing Bd., 487 A.2d 1043 (Pa. Commw. 1985).

## § 5.27. Held Invalid.

Several decisions have held large-lot zoning invalid when it would make residential development economically infeasible.[119] Some of these were as-applied cases in which the courts held that the large-lot zoning was inconsistent with residential densities in the surrounding area.[120] In another case, in which the municipality may have been too candid, the Massachusetts court held that a large-lot zoning ordinance improperly substituted the police power for the use of eminent domain. In *Aronson v. Town of Sharon*,[121] a suburban community twenty-one miles southwest of Boston zoned one-third of its area for two-and-one-half-acre lots. The large-lot ordinance implemented a comprehensive plan that included a land acquisition program for conservation purposes. The court seized on this point to hold that the municipality improperly used the large-lot ordinance as a substitute for eminent domain. It distinguished *Simon,* which upheld one-acre zoning. A "law of diminishing returns" sets in, the court held, and a two-acre lot did not improve on the environmental amenities provided by one-acre lots.

Other courts held that large-lot zoning was exclusionary. *Board of County Supvrs. v. Carper*[122] struck down two-acre large-lot zoning that covered two-thirds of a developing county near Washington, D.C. It held that the large-lot zoning excluded low-income people who wished to live in the county.

The most important cases invalidating large-lot zoning come from Pennsylvania. In the first case, *National Land & Inv. Co. v. Kohn*,[123] a small suburban municipality in the path of development in the Philadelphia area adopted a four-acre lot size minimum that applied to thirty percent of its area. A developer challenged the four-acre requirement and claimed it reduced the value of its land. The court noted that the land zoned for four acres had no "readily available market." It applied a balancing test, weighed the purposes of the four-acre zoning against the loss in value suffered by the landowner, and held the four-acre zoning unconstitutional.

The court rejected a number of justifications advanced for the four-acre zoning. It found testimony on drainage and sewage problems unconvincing and held that the municipality could adopt sanitary regulations to handle these problems. It held further that four-acre zoning was neither "a necessary nor a reasonable

---

**119.** Zeltig Land Dev. Corp. v. Bainbridge Township Bd. of Trustees, 599 N.E.2d 383 (Ohio App. 1991) (bedrock made public sewers necessary but development then not economically feasible at required five-acre lot size).

**120.** Hamer v. Town of Ross, 382 P.2d 375 (Cal. 1963); LaSalle Nat'l Bank v. City of Highland Park, 189 N.E.2d 302 (Ill. 1963); Du Page County v. Halkier, 115 N.E.2d 635 (Ill. 1953); Guy v. Brandon Twp., 450 N.W.2d 279 (Mich. App. 1989) (2½ acres; taking found).

**121.** 195 N.E.2d 341 (Mass. 1965).

**122.** 107 S.E.2d 390 (Va. 1959).

**123.** 215 A.2d 597 (Pa. 1965).

method" to protect the community from pollution. The municipality argued that fire and road services were inadequate, but the court held that zoning "may not be used . . . to avoid the increased responsibilities and economic burdens which time and natural growth inevitably bring."

The municipality also argued that the four-acre zoning created a green belt that was necessary to preserve the "character" of the community. This argument, the court held, supported its conclusion that the zoning was unconstitutional. The four-acre zoning would create a green belt only if four-acre lots were unmarketable, but in that event the zoning would be confiscatory. Alternative measures were available to achieve open space preservation, including condemnation and cluster zoning, which reduces lot sizes in return for common open space.

In the second case, *Concord Twp. Appeal (Kit-Mar)*,[124] the court struck down two- and three-acre zoning adopted by a suburban municipality and required "extraordinary justification" for lots of this size. The court also held that the size of a lot was irrelevant to sewage disposal. *National Land and Kit-Mar* are important turning points in zoning jurisprudence. They began a new generation of cases in which courts struck down exclusionary suburban zoning.

## C. COMMERCIAL AND INDUSTRIAL DISTRICTS.

### § 5.28. The Zoning Problem.

Commercial and industrial uses present a number of zoning problems. Municipalities must decide how to classify and map these uses in zoning districts. They may face constitutional objections if they exclude these uses entirely or place them in noncumulative zoning districts. Restrictive commercial zoning may also violate the rule that control of competition is not a proper zoning purpose and raises a problem under federal antitrust laws. Free speech problems arise if a municipality adopts zoning restrictions on the location of adult businesses, such as adult movie theaters.

### § 5.29. Commercial Uses.

### § 5.30. The Mapping Problem.

One common mapping problem arises when a municipality maps small, scattered zoning districts for neighborhood retail uses. Courts usually hold that the need to provide convenience neighborhood shopping overcomes objections that this type of mapping is discriminatory.[125]

---

124. 268 A.2d 765 (Pa. 1970). *See also* Hock v. Board of Supvrs., 622 A.2d 431 (Pa. Commw. 1993); Berman v. Board of Comm'rs, 608 A.2d 585 (Pa. Commw. 1992).

125. *See* Marshall v. Salt Lake City, 141 P.2d 704 (Utah 1943).

Mapping problems also arise when a property owner proposes a commercial use for a tract of land that the zoning ordinance restricts to residential use. In this situation, the property owner may bring an as-applied taking attack on the residential land use restriction. The typical case is brought by an owner of a residentially zoned lot that is located on a street or highway. The owner argues that she could make a more profitable use of the land if it were zoned commercial. As usual, courts decide these cases by examining the zoning and land use in the surrounding area. They uphold the residential classification if the residential development of the land is reasonable in the area in which it is located. Location on a busy thoroughfare and a claim that the land is more valuable for commercial use are not enough to overturn the residential zoning under the standard presumption of constitutionality and the fairly debatable rule.[126]

The landowner will probably succeed if the residentially restricted property is an "island" surrounded by commercial uses. The court will not apply the presumption of constitutionality in this type of case and will hold that the residential land use classification is not fairly debatable. The court must determine which use is dominant if the surrounding area is mixed. Although municipalities are not bound by their prior zoning actions, a court may hold that a residential zoning restriction is invalid as applied if the municipality changed the character of the area by approving a large number of commercial uses.[127]

## § 5.31. Commercial Use Classifications.

Zoning ordinances classify commercial uses into a number of commercial zoning districts. Incompatible commercial uses are excluded from each district. The exclusion of filling stations from retail commercial districts is a common example. Courts uphold these use classifications if they are reasonable.[128] Municipalities may also impose site development standards on commercial development. The Georgia court held a requirement for minimum barrier curbs and

---

126. For typical cases, see City of Birmingham v. Morris, 396 So. 2d 53 (Ala. 1981); Kelber v. City of St. Louis Park, 185 N.W.2d 526 (Minn. 1971); Tealin Co. v. City of Ladue, 541 S.W.2d 544 (Mo. 1976); Leslie v. City of Toledo, 423 N.E.2d 123 (Ohio 1981); Lakewood Dev. Co. v. Oklahoma City, 534 P.2d 23 (Okla. App. 1975).

127. City of Birmingham v. Morris, 396 So. 2d 53 (Ala. 1981).

128. Caldwell v. Pima County, 837 P.2d 154 (Ariz. 1992) (requirement that business be conducted within enclosed buildings); Manalapan Realty, L.P. v. Township Comm., 658 A.2d 1230 (N.J. 1995) (ordinance excluding unenclosed uses from shopping center); Mahony v. Township of Hampton, 651 A.2d 525 (Pa. 1994) (ordinance prohibiting private operation of gas wells but allowing public operation); State ex rel. American Oil Co. v. Bessent, 135 N.W.2d 317 (Wis. 1965).

landscaping areas equal to at least ten percent of a lot was not a physical taking.[129]

A court may strike down a commercial use exclusion if it finds no basis for the classification. In *Board of Supvrs. v. Rowe*,[130] the court struck down a number of exclusions from a commercial use district. The commercial district included hotels but excluded banks and included restaurants but excluded drive-in restaurants. The court found equal protection and substantive due process violations. It noted that the district excluded a large number of "legitimate retail uses" from a retail business district, even though the excluded uses were no more detrimental than the uses included.

*Rowe* applies the compatibility principle that underlies zoning. It suggests that this principle requires commercial zoning categories that allow an adequate range of commercial uses.[131] Most zoning ordinances take this approach, often by including long lists of permitted uses within each commercial district. This practice creates problems when a landowner requests a commercial rezoning. His neighbors may not find his proposed development objectionable, but they may oppose the rezoning if it allows other commercial uses that they consider undesirable. This concern has prompted the use of "conditional" zoning, under which the landowner voluntarily restricts his property to the intended use through a contract or a recorded covenant. Flexible zoning techniques, such as conditional uses and the floating zone, are another answer to this problem. These techniques allow the municipality to restrict its approval to the use the landowner proposes.

A commercial rezoning for a single use is another alternative. The American Law Institute's Model Land Development Code authorizes a procedure for special amendments limited to a single use.[132] Another alternative is an overlay Neighborhood Conservation or similar district that includes environmental and

---

**129.** Parking Ass'n of Ga. v. City of Atlanta, 450 S.E.2d 200 (Ga. 1994), *cert. denied*, 115 S. Ct. 2268 (1995) (with dissent from denial of certiorari claiming recent Supreme Court cases should apply).

**130.** 216 S.E.2d 199 (Va. 1975).

**131.** *Compare* Reedy v. City of Wheaton, 430 N.E.2d 273 (Ill. App. 1981) (upholding exclusion of gasoline filling stations from local business district) *with* Gas 'N Shop, Inc. v. City of Kearney, 539 N.W.2d 423 (Neb. 1995) (cannot require off-premises liquor retailer to sell liquor from separate premises), *and* Layne v. Zoning Bd. of Adjustment, 460 A.2d 1088 (Pa. Commw. 1983) (boarding houses cannot be excluded from residential districts where rooming houses are permitted).

**132.** § 2-312. *But see* Pierson Trapp Co. v. Peak, 340 S.W.2d 456 (Ky. 1960) (holding invalid a rezoning to a single commercial use).

urban design criteria that limit commercial uses to those that are compatible with the surrounding neighborhood.[133]

## § 5.32. Total Exclusion.

A total commercial exclusion problem arises when small residential suburban communities zone their entire area for residential use. A few cases upheld this type of zoning, usually because adequate commercial facilities were available nearby in the surrounding area.[134]

Courts will review the total exclusion of one type of commercial use from a community to determine, on a case-by-case basis, whether the exclusion advances legitimate zoning purposes.[135] *Town of Los Altos Hills v. Adobe Creek Props., Inc.*[136] illustrates these cases. The court upheld an ordinance that excluded almost all commercial uses from a suburban community. It noted that the town had a rural-residential character, that it had a small population, and that it was in close proximity to urban areas.

Pennsylvania has long taken the singular position that a zoning ordinance that totally excludes a land use type is unconstitutional and has applied this rule to apartments as well as nonresidential uses.[137] The court invalidated a total exclusion of gasoline filling stations in *Beaver Gasoline Co. v. Zoning Hearing Bd.*[138] The court held that the usual presumption of constitutionality does not apply when a municipality excludes "an otherwise legitimate business activity," and that the burden shifts to the municipality to justify the exclusion. The exclusion of a "particularly objectionable" business would be prima facie reasonable. Other states have not followed *Beaver,* and Florida has explicitly rejected it.[139]

In a variant of the exclusion case, a landowner who plans a commercial development may attack a residential zoning restriction on her site because her development will serve commercial needs in the area outside the community. In

---

133. Bell v. City of Waco, 835 S.W.2d 211 (Tex. App. 1992) (upholding neighborhood conservation district); Franchise Devs., Inc. v. City of Cincinnati, 505 N.E.2d 966 (Ohio 1987) (same: environmental quality overlay district).

134. § 5.13.

135. Town of Beacon Falls v. Posick, 563 A.2d 285 (Conn. 1989) (upholding exclusion of landfill); Ottowa County Farms, Inc. v. Township of Polkton, 345 N.W.2d 672 (Mich. App. 1983) (invalidating exclusion of landfill); McNeil v. Township of Plumstaed, 522 A.2d 469 (N.J. App. Div. 1987) (remanding for determination whether prohibition on soil removal was reasonable).

136. 108 Cal. Rptr. 271 (Cal. App. 1973). *See also* City of Alameda v. Van Horn, 219 Cal. Rptr. 764 (Cal. App. 1985) (massage parlor).

137. § 5.13.

138. 285 A.2d 501 (Pa. 1971).

139. Lambros, Inc. v. Town of Ocean Ridge, 392 So. 2d 993 (Fla. 1981). *Compare* Suburban Ready Mix Corp. v. Village of Wheeling, 185 N.E.2d 665 (Ill. 1962) (cannot exclude ready-mix concrete plant).

*Wrigley Props., Inc. v. City of Ladue*,[140] a suburb in a metropolitan area zoned a tract of land on a highway intersection at its city limits for residential use. The court held that the need to provide land for commercial development to satisfy regional shopping demand did not make the residential zoning unconstitutional. It added that commercial development on the site would have a negative impact on an adjacent residential neighborhood. The court also noted that land across the highway in another municipality was zoned for commercial use.

### § 5.33. Ribbon Development.

Ribbon commercial development along major streets and highways is a major zoning problem. Once a community allows some commercial development along these thoroughfares, the pressure to zone additional frontage for commercial use is overwhelming. The unattractive commercial ribbon development typical of American cities indicates that these pressures are difficult to resist. Some communities attempt to halt the spread of commercial ribbon development by inserting a buffer zone covering one or two lots between residential and commercial segments on a street or highway. The community may limit the buffer zone to a nonintensive commercial use, such as a small office building, to provide a transition between residential and commercial development. This strategy is not always successful. A commercial developer can successfully attack a buffer zone if he can convince the court that commercial uses dominate the surrounding area or that land uses in the area are irreversibly mixed.[141]

A community can also prevent ribbon development by limiting intensive commercial uses to intersections and by zoning thoroughfares between intersections for residential use. The Arizona court upheld this practice in *City of Phoenix v. Fehlner*.[142] The zoning ordinance applied the least restrictive residential zone, which allowed some of the less intensive commercial uses, to land adjacent to thoroughfares. An owner of land that was included in this residential zone challenged its constitutionality. The land was an "island" in the middle of a commercially zoned strip 6,400 feet in length. The court did not consider the "island" problem but upheld the ordinance under the fairly debatable rule.[143]

---

**140.** 369 S.W.2d 397 (Mo. 1963).

**141.** Spaid v. Board of County Comm'rs, 269 A.2d 797 (Md. 1970); City of Tulsa v. Swanson, 366 P.2d 629 (Okla. 1961). *See also* Jefferson County v. O'Rorke, 394 So. 2d 937 (Ala. 1981). *But see* State v. Gallop Bldg., 247 A.2d 350 (N.J. App. Div. 1968) (upholding landscaped buffer requirement).

**142.** 363 P.2d 607 (Ariz. 1961).

**143.** *See also* City of Tempe v. Rasor, 536 P.2d 239 (Ariz. App. 1975); Primerica v. Planning & Zoning Comm'n, 558 A.2d 646 (Conn. 1989) (upholding ordinance limiting office building occupancy to one occupant as valid method of controlling traffic and not confiscatory).

## § 5.34. Industrial Uses.

The courts uphold industrial zoning classifications if they are reasonable[144] and not a taking of property.[145] An interesting New York case upheld density restrictions adopted in an industrial zoning ordinance. In *Marcus v. Town of Huntington*,[146] the zoning ordinance limited each building or "premises" to no more than three industrial uses. It also required each industrial use to occupy no less than 20,000 square feet of a building's gross floor area. The court rejected a substantive due process objection and noted that density regulation was a legitimate purpose in industrial as well as residential zoning. It upheld the town's density regulation because it was intended to preserve the industrial character of the community. Existing industrial development met the density requirements.

## § 5.35. Industrial Performance Standards.

Industrial performance standards are a zoning technique that attempts to control industrial use incompatibilities more effectively than traditional zoning. Industrial use classifications in zoning ordinances cannot control industrial use incompatibilities effectively because uses allowed in the same district may have different impacts on the surrounding area. Performance standards attempt to remedy this problem by imposing specific requirements for noise, vibrations, smoke, odors, and the emission of air pollutants. Many of the problems covered by industrial performance standards are also covered by federal and state environmental legislation, but there are gaps in this legislation that need to be addressed by local standards.

Although theoretically an excellent technique for regulating the nuisance qualities of industrial uses, industrial performance standards have significant limitations. Administration is expensive and difficult, and most communities are unlikely to impose drastic remedies on noncomplying industries. Performance standards are also imprecise, and may not effectively protect neighbors against adverse effects from industrial uses.

Because they deal with health and nuisance problems, the courts have had no difficulty upholding industrial performance standards against constitutional attacks. For example, in *DeCoals, Inc. v. Board of Zoning Appeals*[147] an industrial

---

144. Tidewater Oil Co. v. Mayor & Council, 209 A.2d 105 (N.J. 1965).

145. Bernardsville Quarry v. Borough of Bernardsville, 608 A.2d 1377 (N.J. 1992) (holding ordinance limiting depth below which property could not be quarried not a taking).

146. 382 N.E.2d 1323 (N.Y. 1978).

147. 284 S.E.2d 856 (W. Va. 1981). *See also* City of Rochester v. Superior Plastics, Inc., 480 N.W.2d 620 (Mich. App. 1992) (standard requiring control of noise held authorized by zoning law); Terino v. Town of Hartford Zoning Bd. of Adj., 538 A.2d 160 (Vt. 1987) (town properly applied performance standard to deny industrial use; consideration of offsite problems held authorized by statute).

use was denied a building permit because it was unable to comply with industrial dust, noise, and sound performance standards. The dust standard was absolute and prohibited dust "of any kind." The court held that industrial performance standards were clearly an appropriate exercise of the police power. It would not interfere with the legislative judgment that a "no-dust" standard was appropriate. Citing air pollution control cases, the court held that "[a]lleged technical infeasibility or economic hardship need not be considered" and noted that the courts had upheld "technology-forcing" air pollution regulations. The court added that a different question might arise if a no-dust standard precluded "development of any industry in an industrial zone." The courts have also considered claims that industrial performance standards are unconstitutional because they are too vague, with mixed results.[148]

## § 5.36. Total Exclusion.

The leading case upholding a zoning ordinance that excluded all industrial uses is *Duffcon Concrete Prods., Inc. v. Borough of Cresskill*.[149] The court took a regional view of municipal zoning obligations and upheld the exclusion because sites for industrial development were available in the surrounding area.[150] The Pennsylvania cases have also struck down total exclusions of industrial uses in an application of their rule that a zoning ordinance is invalid if it totally excludes a particular use.[151]

## § 5.37. Noncumulative Zoning: Exclusive Nonresidential Zones.

Early zoning ordinances were cumulative. They allowed "higher" uses in the "lower" zoning districts. Under this system a residential use can locate in a commercial or industrial zone, and commercial uses can locate in industrial zones. Cumulative zoning is undesirable. It prevents municipalities from adopting industrial and commercial zones in which only industrial and commercial development is permitted. Cumulative zoning also creates development expectations the community may not have intended. A landowner in an industrial zone can use his land for residential and commercial uses. This development expecta-

---

148. *See also* State v. Zack, 674 P.2d 329 (Ariz. App. 1983) (performance standard prohibiting "offensive vibration" held not vague); Stephen Renedy Mem. Fund v. Town of Old Saybrook, 492 A.2d 533 (Conn. App. 1985) (same; lighting standard). *But see* Lithonia Asphalt Co. v. Hall Cty. Planning Comm'n, 364 S.E.2d 860 (Ga. 1988) (performance zoning standard held vague). *See also* § 6.05.
149. 64 A.2d 347 (N.J. 1949).
150. *See* Oregon City v. Hartke, 400 P.2d 255 (Or. 1965) (upholding junkyard exclusion on aesthetic grounds).
151. Exton Quarries, Inc. v. Zoning Bd. of Adjustment, 228 A.2d 169 (Pa. 1967); General Battery Corporation v. The Zoning Hearing Board of Alsace Township, 371 A.2d 1030 (Pa. Commw. 1977).

tion may increase land values and make local attempts to zone away these expectations politically difficult.

Modern zoning ordinances are noncumulative. The land use permitted in each district is the exclusive and only use allowed. The Supreme Court upheld exclusive residential zoning in *Euclid* because it protected residential uses from incompatible nonresidential development. This could imply that exclusive nonresidential zoning is unconstitutional because "lower" commercial and industrial uses do not require protection from "higher" residential uses.

The courts have not accepted this line of reasoning. In *People ex rel. Skokie Town House Bldrs., Inc. v. Village of Morton Grove*,[152] a builder who planned to build townhouses in an exclusive industrial district attacked the exclusive industrial zoning. He claimed that "such an ordinance conflicts sharply with the generally acknowledged principle that zoning is intended to preserve rather than to restrict dwellings."

The court disagreed, and held that the compatibility principle cuts both ways. A legislative body could assume that the exclusion of residences from industrial and commercial areas "would tend in the long run to insure a better and more economical use of municipal services." It noted that industrial or commercial development would be impossible or prohibitively expensive if a few lots were sold for residential use "at important points in a district."[153]

Exclusive industrial zoning can raise a taking problem if the demand for industrial development is not sufficient to absorb exclusively zoned industrial land in a reasonable period of time. Exclusive commercial zoning raises the same problem. The *Skokie* case indicated that excessive mapping for exclusive industrial use might be unconstitutional. Another case held an exclusive industrial zoning ordinance unconstitutional partly for this reason.[154] Excessive mapping of exclusive nonresidential districts can also be exclusionary. In the *Mt. Laurel* exclusionary zoning case, the New Jersey Supreme Court held that zoning for exclusive industrial use far in excess of expected demand was a major element in the community's exclusionary residential zoning strategy and effectively excluded lower-income housing.[155]

The use of exclusive industrial zoning for fiscal purposes is constitutional if it does not exclude lower-income housing. "[A] zoning scheme seeking balanced land use to obtain a sound municipal economy by encouraging industry on which

---

**152.** 157 N.E.2d 33 (Ill. 1959).

**153.** *Id.* at 36. *Accord* Roney v. Board of Supvrs., 292 P.2d 529 (Cal. App. 1956); Lamb v. City of Monroe, 99 N.W.2d 566 (Mich. 1959); Kozesnik v. Township of Montgomery, 131 A.2d 1 (N.J. 1957). *Compare* Grubel v. MacLaughlin, 286 F. Supp. 24 (D.C.V.I. 1968) (upholding exclusive commercial district); Katobimar Realty Co. v. Webster, 118 A.2d 824 (N.J. 1955) (invalidating exclusion of retail business from light industrial district).

**154.** Corthouts v. Town of Newington, 99 A.2d 112 (Conn. 1953).

**155.** § 7.09.

taxes may be levied to help meet the deficit in the cost of municipal services to home owners is a proper exercise of the zoning power, subject always to the reasonableness of the classification and regulations. . . ."[156]

## § 5.38. Control of Competition.

The use of zoning to control market demand creates a special set of commercial zoning problems. A hypothetical case illustrates the problem. Assume a municipality does a market study showing that market demand will support only two regional shopping centers in the community. It then designates two sites in its comprehensive plan for regional shopping centers. A developer applies for a rezoning for a regional shopping center at a site not designated on the comprehensive plan and the municipality denies it. The shopping center developer then brings suit claiming that the municipality has improperly used the zoning power to control competition. This problem also arises when a municipality rezones land for a shopping center. If the owner of another shopping center brings an action to challenge the rezoning, the municipality may ask the court to dismiss the suit because its purpose is to protect the plaintiff's competitive position.

A court may decide for the developer who was denied a rezoning in the problem by applying the well-established maxim that zoning may not be used to control competition. The maxim is not absolute. Some courts recognize that zoning always affects competitive opportunities in the use of land. They uphold zoning that affect competition if control of competition is not its primary purpose and if it implements other legitimate zoning objectives.

## § 5.39. As a Zoning Purpose.

## § 5.40. Disapproved.

A large number of cases hold, apparently without qualification, that the control of competition is not a proper purpose in zoning.[157] A close examination of these cases indicates that they do not support so broad a rule. In some of them, a competitor opposed or attempted to prevent commercial rezoning in order to maintain a competitive advantage. Courts adopt the rule that control of competition is not a proper purpose in zoning when a competitor attempts to use zoning solely to shield its competitive position.

---

**156.** Newark Milk & Cream Co. v. Parsippany-Troy Hills Twp., 135 A.2d 682, 695 (N.J.L. 1957). *Accord* Gruber v. Raritan Twp., 186 A.2d 489 (N.J. 1962).

**157.** Benson v. Zoning Bd. of Appeals, 27 A.2d 389 (Conn. 1942); Chicago Title & Trust Co. v. Village of Lombard, 166 N.E.2d 41 (Ill. 1960); Pearce v. Village of Edina, 118 N.W.2d 659 (Minn. 1962); Herman Glick Realty Co. v. St. Louis County, 545 S.W.2d 320 (Mo. App. 1977); Schneiderman v. Shenkenberg, 281 N.Y.S.2d 459 (Sup. Ct. 1967); State v. City of East Cleveland, 153 N.E.2d 177 (Ohio App. 1958), *aff'd,* 160 N.E.2d 1 (Ohio 1959).

*Circle Lounge & Grill, Inc. v. Board of Appeal*[158] illustrates these decisions. Circle Lounge, which was in a commercial zone, brought an action challenging a zoning variance the board granted for a restaurant in a residential zone across the street. The court held that the threat of competition did not give Circle Lounge standing to challenge the variance. Nor was the action brought by the Lounge based on a proper zoning interest. Zoning, the court held, ensures the compatibility of land uses. Homeowners in a residential district could object to a variance for a commercial use in their district. The Lounge was in a commercial district and could not object to a variance in a neighboring residential district for a commercial use that was consistent with its own commercial use.[159]

Some courts invoke the rule that zoning may not be used to control competition to strike down ordinances that require a minimum distance between commercial uses, such as filling stations.[160] They may also invalidate the denial of a special exception for a commercial use if the denial is based on a finding that other businesses adequately serve the same commercial need.[161] These zoning problems are discussed more fully in the next section, which indicates that some courts take a different view.

## § 5.41. Approved.

Control of competition problems arise when a zoning ordinance authorizes the approval of a commercial use as a special exception only if there is a "need" for the use. A zoning board can find that a commercial use is not needed if existing commercial uses satisfy the market demand for that use in the community. Some courts approve zoning ordinances that authorize the approval of a conditional use only if need is shown and hold that they do not violate the control of compe-

---

**158.** 86 N.E.2d 920 (Mass. 1949).

**159.** *Accord* Earth Movers of Fairbanks, Inc. v. Fairbanks North Star Borough, 865 P.2d 741 (Alaska 1993); Westwood Meat Mkt., Inc. v. McLucas, 361 P.2d 776 (Colo. 1961); Nautilus of Exeter, Inc. v. Town of Exeter, 656 A.2d 407 (N.H. 1995); Sun-Brite Car Wash, Inc. v. Board of Zoning & Appeals, 508 N.E.2d 130 (N.Y. 1987); Cord Meyer Dev. Co. v. Bell Ray Drugs, Inc., 229 N.E.2d 44 (N.Y. 1967). *See also* Swain v. County of Winnebago, 250 N.E.2d 439 (Ill. App. 1969). *But see* Westgate Shopping Village v. City of Toledo, 639 N.E.2d 126 (Ohio App. 1994) (rival mall has standing to challenge rezoning for mall competitor when there is property injury from increased traffic).

**160.** Mobil Oil Corp. v. Board of Adjustment, 283 A.2d 837 (Del. Super. 1971); Chicago Title & Trust Co. v. Village of Lombard, 166 N.E.2d 41 (Ill. 1960); Exxon Co., U.S.A. v. Township of Livingston, 489 A.2d 1218 (N.J. App. Div. 1985); Caudill v. Village of Milford, 225 N.E.2d 302 (Ohio C.P. 1967). *See also* Fogg v. City of South Miami, 183 So. 2d 219 (Fla. App. 1966) (drive-in businesses prohibited in commercial zoning district).

**161.** Metro 500, Inc. v. City of Brooklyn Park, 211 N.W.2d 358 (Minn. 1973); Cardinal Props. v. Borough of Westwood, 547 A.2d 316 (N.J. App. Div. 1988).

tition rule.[162] *Van Sicklen v. Browne*[163] illustrates these cases. A planning commission refused to approve a special permit for a filling station. It partly based its decision on a showing that there was no demonstrated need for an additional station in the neighborhood. Although it accepted the maxim that zoning cannot be used to control competition, the court noted that planning and zoning also serve a number of legitimate public purposes. They include the maintenance of property values and neighborhood economic and social stability. The court added:

> Whether these be classified as "planning considerations" or "economic considerations," we hold that so long as the primary purpose of the zoning ordinance is not to regulate competition, but to subserve a valid objective pursuant to a city's police powers, such ordinance is not invalid even though it might have an indirect impact on economic competition.[164]

Cases like *Van Sicklen* illustrate the rule some courts adopt that control of competition may be a factor in zoning if it is not its primary purpose.[165] The gasoline filling station cases also illustrate this rule. In the typical case, a zoning board refuses to approve a filling station as a special exception because there is no community need for additional filling stations. The board may also rely on more traditional zoning reasons for the refusal, such as the traffic congestion the filling station would create. Some cases uphold the board in this type of case and avoid the control of competition issue by relying on the traditional zoning reasons for the denial.[166] Cases that uphold minimum distance requirements between filling stations also rely on noncompetitive justifications for the restriction, such as the avoidance of fire and other hazards.[167]

Ensign *Bickford Realty Corp. v. City Council*[168] indicates that commercial zoning may not be invalid as an improper control of competition if it is based on a comprehensive plan. The city's comprehensive plan designated a site for a shopping center in one of its neighborhoods. The court upheld the city when it turned down an application for another shopping center in the same neighbor-

---

162. Technical & Professional Serv. v. Board of Zoning Adjustment, 558 S.W.2d 798 (Mo. App. 1977).

163. 92 Cal. Rptr. 786 (Cal. App. 1971).

164. *Id.* at 790.

165. Appeal of Lieb, 116 A.2d 860 (Pa. 1955).

166. American Oil Co. v. Board of Appeals, 310 A.2d 796 (Md. 1973); Peterson v. Mayor & Council, 21 A.2d 777 (N.J. 1941); Application of Max Kirsch, Inc., 202 N.Y.S.2d 547 (Sup. Ct. 1960).

167. Stone v. City of Maitland, 446 F.2d 83 (5th Cir. 1971); Chicago Title & Trust Co. v. Village of Lombard, 166 N.E.2d 41 (Ill. App. 1961).

168. 137 Cal. Rptr. 304 (Cal. App. 1977). *Accord* Lucky Stores, Inc. v. Board of Montgomery County, 312 A.2d 758 (Md. 1973). *Compare* Fallon v. Baker, 455 S.W.2d 572 (Ky. 1970) (invalidating shopping center rezoning inconsistent with plan).

hood. It noted that the zoning decision was based on the city's comprehensive plan and added that "a zoning ordinance may be expected to depress the value of some land while it operates, in its total effect, to achieve an end which would benefit the whole community."

### § 5.42. Protection of Business Districts.

Rezonings for shopping malls in outlying areas threatens the existence of established downtown and main street business districts. Downtown or main street merchants may bring suit to challenge a shopping mall rezoning because it is a threat to their commercial future. Their lawsuit raises a standing problem.

In *Swain v. County of Winnebago*,[169] the court refused to grant standing to downtown city merchants who challenged a rezoning in the county for a regional shopping center located "a substantial distance" from the central business district. They claimed that the rezoning would adversely affect the value of their property as well as the use and development of public facilities. They did not claim that the rezoning would increase general tax burdens in the city. The court held that distance alone did not preclude a showing of the special damage necessary to confer standing but added that a distant plaintiff who claims standing has a more onerous pleading and proof burden.

Some municipalities have adopted zoning ordinances that protect the downtown business core by limiting retail uses outside the core to neighborhood shopping facilities. *Forte v. Borough of Tenafly*[170] is a leading case upholding a zoning ordinance of this type against a control of competition objection. The borough acted on a planning consultant's recommendation and adopted a zoning ordinance which stated that one of its purposes was to protect the economic health of the central business core. About ninety-three percent of the borough's retail businesses were located in the central core area. To implement this purpose, the ordinance established a retail use district for the area outside the central core, which was limited to neighborhood convenience retail stores. This district did not allow general retail businesses of the type located in the central core.

The plaintiffs planned to build a supermarket in the limited retail use district, where it was a prohibited use. They argued that the district was unconstitutional as an improper control of competition because the municipality adopted it "for the sole benefit of the merchants in the central business core." The court rejected this argument and held that the use of zoning to maintain and revitalize central

---

169. 250 N.E.2d 439 (Ill. App. 1969).

170. 255 A.2d 804 (N.J. App. Div. 1969). *Accord* Carty v. City of Ojai, 143 Cal. Rptr. 506 (Cal. App. 1978); Sprenger, Grubb & Assocs., Inc. v. City of Hailey, 903 P.2d 741 (Idaho 1995); E & G Enters. v. City of Mount Vernon, 373 N.W.2d 693 (Iowa App. 1985); Chevron Oil Co. v. Beaver County, 449 P.2d 989 (Utah 1969). *But cf.* Cape Ann Dev. Corp. v. City Council, 373 N.E.2d 218 (Mass. 1978); State ex rel. Diehl v. City of Helena, 593 P.2d 458 (Mont. 1979).

business districts is valid, even though "the ordinance may give the central area a virtual monopoly over retail business." It held that the limited retail district was reasonable even though there were a number of nonconforming retail uses in the vicinity of plaintiffs' property that were similar to its proposed use. The court noted that "plaintiffs may use their property for the many purposes allowed by the ordinance."

## § 5.43. Federal Antitrust Law.

Anticompetitive commercial zoning may violate the federal antitrust law. Section 1 of the Sherman Act prohibits contracts, combinations, or conspiracies that restrain trade in interstate commerce. This section could apply to a zoning ordinance or decision that restricted competition. An example is a denial of a shopping center rezoning to protect a rezoning for a shopping center for another developer.

## § 5.44. State Action Doctrine.

Municipalities can claim immunity from the federal antitrust law under a state action doctrine adopted by the Supreme Court. The Court adopted the state action doctrine in *Parker v. Brown*,[171] which held that states are absolutely immune from antitrust liability. In *City of Lafayette v. Louisiana Power & Light Co.*,[172] the Court for the first time held that the state action doctrine did not automatically protect municipalities from federal antitrust liability. A plurality of the Court held that municipalities are immune under this doctrine only if the state legislation under which the municipality acted clearly articulates and affirmatively expresses a policy to displace competition. In *California Retail Liquor Dealers Ass'n v. Midcal Aluminum Co.*,[173] an antitrust action against a state agency, the Court added as a requirement for antitrust immunity that the state must supervise the practices claimed to restrain competition.

## § 5.45. *Boulder.*

In *Community Communications Co. v. City of Boulder*.[174] the court held that a city's home rule status did not afford it immunity under the state action doctrine. The city granted a twenty-year nonexclusive license to a cable television company but later adopted a three-month moratorium on additional expansion of the company's business so it could consider granting licenses to potential competitors. The company brought an action under Section 1 of the Sherman Act to en-

---

171. 317 U.S. 341 (1943).
172. 435 U.S. 389 (1978).
173. 445 U.S. 97 (1980).
174. 455 U.S. 405 (1982).

join enforcement of the moratorium. The Court held that the city was not immune from the antitrust law.

A majority of the Court confirmed the rule adopted in *Lafayette* that municipal immunity from the antitrust law requires clearly and affirmatively expressed state policy to displace competition. The Court held that the constitutional home rule authority under which the city adopted the moratorium did not confer immunity under this test. The test is not satisfied when the state's position concerning the municipal action challenged as anticompetitive is neutral. A state does not contemplate anticompetitive action by allowing a municipality to do as it pleases under a home rule delegation of authority. The Court left open the question whether local government immunity requires active state supervision.

### § 5.46. *Town of Hallie.*

*Town of Hallie v. City of Eau Claire*[175] eased the application of the federal antitrust law to municipalities acting under statutory authority. Four adjacent unincorporated townships brought an antitrust action against the city. They claimed they were potential competitors and that the city used its monopoly power over sewage treatment to gain an unlawful monopoly in the provision of sewage collection and transportation services. The Court upheld the trial court's dismissal of the complaint.

Wisconsin statutes give cities the authority to construct sewage systems and determine the area they wish to serve. The Court held that these statutes evidenced a clearly articulated and affirmatively expressed state policy to displace competition in the municipal provision of sewage service. It is enough if the suppression of competition is the "foreseeable result" of the statutory authority. The Court also held that municipalities are entitled to state action immunity even though the state has not "compelled" the city to act. The legislature need not state explicitly that it expected the city to engage in anticompetitive conduct. Anticompetitive effects would logically result from the broad, delegated statutory authority to provide sewage services and determine the area to be served.

The Court also held that the active state supervision requirement does not apply to municipalities because there is little or no danger that a municipality will engage in private price-fixing.[176] The only real danger is that a municipality will advance parochial public interests instead of compelling state goals, but the re-

---

175. 471 U.S. 34 (1985).

176. *But see* Southern Motor Carriers Rate Conference, Inc. v. United States, 471 U.S. 48 (1985) (private parties have state action immunity if authorized by state law and if active state supervision).

quirement that a municipality must act under a clearly articulated state policy minimizes this possibility.[177]

### § 5.47. Omni.

In *City of Columbia v. Omni Outdoor Adv., Inc.*,[178] the Supreme Court held that state action immunity protected a municipality from antitrust liability claimed to arise from a billboard regulation and rejected a conspiracy exception. Because the basis for antitrust liability in *Omni* was especially strong, and because the city acted under the Standard Zoning Enabling Act,[179] the decision substantially protects municipalities from antitrust liability that could arise from land use regulation.

Columbia Outdoor Advertising controlled 95% of the local market in billboards. When Omni began erecting billboards in the city, Columbia worked with city officials, with whom it had close relationships, to adopt billboard regulations that would block Omni. A six-month moratorium on new billboards was held unconstitutional by a state court because it conferred too much discretion on the city council to authorize exceptions. The city then adopted, after comprehensive study, an ordinance restricting the size, location, and spacing of billboards. These restrictions, especially those on spacing, benefited Columbia because they already had billboards in place and severely hindered Omni.

Omni brought an antitrust action in which it claimed the city's billboard ordinances were the result of an anticompetitive conspiracy that stripped the city of antitrust immunity. Omni was awarded damages after a jury trial, but the Supreme Court held that the city was entitled to state action immunity.

The Court held that state action immunity was conferred by the city's "unquestioned zoning power over the size, location, and spacing of billboards" that was authorized by the state zoning act. The Court rejected an argument that state action immunity does not apply if a municipality acts beyond its delegated authority because its regulation is substantively or procedurally defective. This defense would undermine "the very interests of federalism" the state action doctrine was designed to protect. This holding means immunity is available even if a state court holds a zoning regulation invalid under the well-established state doctrine that the control of competition is not a proper purpose in zoning.[180]

---

177. *See also* Fisher v. City of Berkeley, 475 U.S. 260 (1986) (Court applied preemption doctrine to hold that federal antitrust law did not preempt city rent control ordinance adopted by popular initiative).

178. 499 U.S. 365 (1991). *See* The Supreme Court, 1990 Term: Leading Cases, 105 Harv. L. Rev. 177, 361 (1991). *See also* Fisichelli v. Town of Methuen, 956 F.2d 12 (1st Cir. 1992) (refusal to issue development bonds for development protected by immunity, applying *Omni*).

179. §§ 4.15-4.21.

180. § 5.35.

The Court next held the "clear articulation" rule was "amply met here" because "[t]he very purpose of zoning regulation is to displace unfettered business freedom in a manner that regularly has the effect of preventing normal acts of competition, particularly on the part of new entrants." An ordinance restricting the size, location, and spacing of billboards, which the Court characterized as "a common form of zoning," necessarily protects existing billboards from new competition. The Court's discussion of the foreseeability requirement indicates that any "common" form of zoning that limits market entry is entitled to state action immunity.

The Court in *Omni* did not overrule or even discuss its holding in *Boulder* that the delegation of constitutional home rule power to municipalities does not confer state action immunity under the antitrust act. The home rule exception may be of limited application. Home rule municipalities can also exercise land use and other powers under statutory authority, and there do not seem to be serious limitations under state law that prohibit municipalities from making this election.[181] Some states have also adopted legislation conferring state action immunity from federal antitrust laws.[182]

Early antitrust cases suggested a conspiracy exception to the state action immunity; the court of appeals in *Omni* adopted it, but the Supreme Court held that "[t]here is no such conspiracy exception." Language in *Parker v. Brown* suggesting a conspiracy exception meant only that state action immunity "does not necessarily obtain where the State acts not in a regulatory capacity but as a commercial participant in a given market." Alternatively, the Court held that application of the co-conspirator exception would be impracticable and would "swallow up" the *Parker* rule. "Since it is both inevitable and desirable that public officials often agree" with their constituency, such a definition would make "all anticompetitive regulation . . . vulnerable to a 'conspiracy' charge."

The Court also held that bribery and misconduct would not make state action immunity unavailable. The Antitrust Act condemned trade restraints, not political activity, and the Court held that this type of problem should be dealt with by statutes created specifically for this purpose.

---

**181.** *E.g.,* Nelson v. City of Seattle, 395 P.2d 82 (Wash. 1964) (reliance on zoning legislation held to be optional with home rule city). *See* Note, Land-Use Control, Externalities, and the Municipal Affairs Doctrine, 8 Loy. L.A.L. Rev. 432 (1975).

**182.** *E.g.,* N.D. Cent. Code § 40-01-22 (exempting local governments from federal antitrust liability).

## § 5.48. Land Use Cases After *Omni*.

Federal court cases decided after *Boulder* but before *Town of Hallie* held that anticompetitive zoning decisions violated the federal antitrust law.[183] Some of these cases were decided on the conspiracy theory now rejected by *Omni*.[184] Cases decided after *Hallie* held local government zoning actions immune under the state action doctrine for antitrust liability.[185] In *Racetrac Petroleum, Inc. v. Prince George's County*,[186] for example, the county denied Racetrac a special exception for a gasoline filling station because a needs analysis found there were thirty-one filling stations within a two-mile radius of the Racetrac site. The court held the state planning and zoning legislation contained a clearly articulated and affirmatively expressed policy to displace competition among owners and users of land with "local regulation by planning and zoning." This policy authorized the county to consider public need for a land use in special exception cases. *Omni* confirms the *Racetrac* holding. Cases since *Omni* have extended antitrust immunity to zoning actions claimed to violate the antitrust act.[187]

Private parties who participate in anticompetitive zoning actions, as in *Racetrac*, may still face antitrust liability. The active state supervision doctrine still

---

**183.** Parks v. Watson, 716 F.2d 646 (9th Cir. 1983) (city refused to vacate platted streets unless plaintiff dedicated land); Mason City Center Assocs. v. City of Mason City, 468 F. Supp. 737 (N.D. Iowa) (city denied commercial rezoning after entering into agreement with developers of a competing downtown shopping facility), *aff'd on immunity holding,* 671 F.2d 1146 (8th Cir. 1982).

**184.** Westborough Mall, Inc. v. City of Cape Girardeau, 693 F.2d 733 (8th Cir.), *cert. denied,* 461 U.S. 945 (1983), *remanded for new trial,* 794 F.2d 330 (8th Cir.), *reh'g denied,* 804 F.2d 108 (8th Cir. 1986), *cert. denied,* 480 U.S. 918 (1987).

**185.** Jacobs, Visconsi & Jacobs Co. v. City of Lawrence, 927 F.2d 1111 (10th Cir. 1991) (suburban shopping center zoning denied to implement plan designating downtown as primary retail area); Traweek v. City & Cty. of San Francisco, 920 F.2d 989 (9th Cir. 1990) (prohibition of condominium conversion); LaSalle Nat'l Bank v. County of DuPage, 777 F.2d 377 (7th Cir. 1985) (denial of sewage service and special use permit); Russell v. Kansas City (I), 690 F. Supp. 947 (D. Kan. 1988) (city denied office rezoning to protect renewal area development for office use; court found zoning action implemented renewal law); Pinehurst Enters. v. Town of Southern Pines, 690 F. Supp. 444 (M.D.N.C. 1988) (rezoning on condition that developer hook up to town sewage system), *aff'd without opinion,* 887 F.2d 1088 (4th Cir. 1989); Pendleton Constr. Co. v. Rockbridge County, 652 F. Supp. 312 (W.D. Va. 1987) (refusal to renew conditional use permit); Plaza Mobile & Modular Homes, Inc. v. Town of Colchester, 639 F. Supp. 140 (D. Conn. 1986) (mobile home moratorium), *aff'd mem.,* 810 F.2d 1160 (2d Cir. 1986).

**186.** 601 F. Supp. 892 (D. Md. 1985), *aff'd per curiam* post-*Hallie,* 786 F.2d 202 (4th Cir. 986).

**187.** James Emory, Inc. v. Twiggs County, 883 F. Supp. 1546 (M.D. Ga. 1995) (zoning exclusion of landfill); Phillips v. Town of Brookhaven, 628 N.Y.S.2d 723 (App. Div. 1995) (rezoning to protect established businesses by limiting competition from shopping centers). *But see* Pine Ridge Recycling, Inc. v. Butts County, 855 F. Supp. 1264 (M.D. Ga. 1994) (county's attempt to exclude private landfill would violate commerce clause so not protected by state immunity).

applies to private parties. The Supreme Court tightened this doctrine in *Federal Trade Commission v. Ticor Title*.[188] The Court held that private parties claiming state action immunity must show that the state "has played a substantial role in determining the specifics of economic policy." This is not the case with zoning actions taken at the local level.

### § 5.49. *Noerr-Pennington* Doctrine.

The *Noerr-Pennington* doctrine provides a first amendment antitrust defense for competitors who petition to influence governmental action. This doctrine protects private parties who participate in anticompetitive zoning actions. The doctrine is named after two U.S. Supreme Court decisions that exempted anticompetitive lobbying from the antitrust laws.[189] The courts have extended the *Noerr-Pennington* doctrine to administrative and judicial proceedings brought to challenge competitive commercial activity. An example in the zoning context is a lawsuit challenging a zoning amendment that allows a competitive use. Local governments are protected under *Noerr-Pennington* by legislative process immunity. This immunity covers a governmental entity that listens to "anticompetitive pleas" if "the public body acts within its legal discretion and in what it considers the public interest."[190]

*Noerr-Pennington* immunity does not protect "sham" proceedings brought by an antitrust defendant to prevent a competitor from gaining access to the courts and public agencies.[191] *Racetrac*[192] indicates how the sham exception applies in land use cases. The court held the sham exception does not apply if a defendant attempts to influence a government decision that would harm a competitor. The exception applies if a defendant attempts to bar a competitor from the decision-making process or if the defendant's motive was to corrupt the decision-making process through bribery or misrepresentation. The court held that the trade association's conduct was not disqualifying under either of these tests. Although it influenced the county to deny a competitor a special exception, the competitor initiated the conditional use proceedings and it did not show that the trade association corrupted the decision-making process.[193] The Supreme Court has now

---

**188.** 504 U.S. 621 (1992).

**189.** United Mine Workers v. Pennington, 381 U.S. 657 (1965); Eastern R.R. Presidents' Conference v. Noerr Motor Freight Co., 365 U.S. 127 (1961).

**190.** Duke & Co. v. Foerster, 521 F.2d 1277 (3d Cir. 1975). *But see* Racetrac Petroleum, Inc. v. Prince George's County, 601 F. Supp. 892 (D. Md. 1985), (*Noerr-Pennington* does not apply to local governments), *aff'd per curiam post-Hallie,* 786 F.2d 202 (4th Cir. 1986).

**191.** California Motor Transp., Inc. v. Trucking Unlimited, 404 U.S. 508 (1972).

**192.** § 5.48.

**193.** *Accord* Miracle Mile Assocs. v. City of Rochester, 617 F.2d 18 (2d Cir. 1980); Pendleton Constr. Co. v. Rockbridge County, 652 F. Supp. 312 (W.D. Va. 1987); Interstate Props., Inc. v. Pyramid Co., 586 F. Supp. 1160 (S.D.N.Y. 1984). *But see* Ernest W. Hahn, Inc. v. Codding, 615

held that the sham exception defense is based on an objective, not a subjective, evaluation of a competitor's conduct.[194]

Although some courts had applied a conspiracy exception to the *Noerr-Pennington* doctrine, the Supreme Court rejected this exception in *Omni*. The Court held that "*Parker* and *Noerr* are complementary expressions of the principle that the antitrust laws regulate business, not politics." The elimination of the conspiracy exception greatly expands the scope of *Noerr-Pennington* immunity.

### § 5.50. Basis for Liability.

The Supreme Court applies two different rules to determine whether there is a restraint on competition that violates the antitrust act. It applies a *per se* invalidity rule to conduct that is inherently anticompetitive. It evaluates conduct not inherently anticompetitive by considering the facts peculiar to the business, the history of the restraint, and the reasons why it was imposed.[195] This test is called a "rule of reason."

Chief Justice Rehnquist's dissent in *Boulder*[196] argued that courts should not apply traditional antitrust liability standards to municipalities. The *per se* standard would force municipalities to obtain legislation authorizing for anticompetitive activities, and the rule of reason would subject municipal activities to wide-ranging judicial review. Later Supreme Court decisions have not endorsed Chief Justice Rehnquist's concerns, but the Court indicated in *Town of Hallie*[197] that it might apply a more liberal antitrust liability standard to local governments. Although the Court has rejected a conspiracy exception to state action immunity, municipalities remain liable for conspiracies in restraint of trade if state action immunity does not apply. Corporations are liable for intra-enterprise conspiracies between parent corporations and partially owned subsidiaries.[198] At the municipal level, an intra-enterprise conspiracy is a unilateral governmental action, as the adoption of a zoning ordinance that restricts competitive opportunity. The Supreme Court has held that the intra-enterprise conspiracy doctrine does not apply to the unilateral adoption of a regulatory ordinance by a city council.[199]

---

F.2d 830 (9th Cir. 1980); Ross v. Bremer, 1982-2 Trade Cas. (CCH) Par. 64747 (W.D. Wash. 1982) (denying exemption for bringing zoning suit even though suit successful).

**194.** Professional Real Estate Investors, Inc. v. Columbia Pictures Industries, Inc., 508 U.S. 49 (1993).

**195.** National Soc'y of Professional Eng'rs v. United States, 435 U.S. 679 (1980).

**196.** § 5.43.

**197.** § 5.44.

**198.** Copperweld Corp. v. Independence Tube Corp., 467 U.S. 752 (1984).

**199.** Fisher v. City of Berkeley, 475 U.S. 260 (1986) (rent control ordinance). *See* Russell v. Kansas City (II), 1988 U.S. Dist. Lexis 12170 (D. Kan. 1988) (intra-enterprise conspiracy doctrine does not apply to city and its official implicated in zoning actions).

## § 5.51. Local Government Antitrust Act.

Prior to 1984, local governments faced the possibility of substantial monetary liability under the antitrust act because it authorizes the recovery of treble damages and attorney's fees. The Local Government Antitrust Act of 1984 eliminated the recovery of monetary damages and attorney's fees in cases in which a court holds that a local government is not immune from liability under the state action doctrine.[200] Plaintiffs may obtain injunctions in these cases.

Legislative history indicates that the relief from damages and attorney's fees in cases in which a local government is not immune applies to any action or inaction of a local government that could "reasonably" be construed to be within its authority.[201] This interpretation is broad enough to include home rule as well as statutory authority. Legislative history also indicates that immunity attaches only if local government officials act in good faith, which means a reasonable belief that the conduct was within a local government's authority.[202]

The relief from damages and attorney's fees provided by the Act also applies to claims against private defendants "based on any official action directed by a local government" or an official or employee acting in an official capacity.[203] Legislative history indicates that the private activity must be "expressly required." It cited a "zoning permit" requiring the building of a hotel with certain specifications on rezoned land as an example that "probably" meets this test.[204]

## § 5.52. Free Speech Problems in the Regulation of Adult Businesses.

The U.S. Supreme Court imposed a new constitutional limitation on zoning for adult commercial businesses when it extended the free speech clause to commercial speech.[205] Live entertainment in commercial establishments is one example. Adult movies are another.

Municipalities often believe that adult businesses are a detrimental influence on commercial and residential neighborhoods. To avoid this problem, a zoning ordinance may require a specified distance between adult businesses to prevent their excessive concentration. It may also require adult businesses to locate at a specified distance from residential areas. An alternative zoning strategy concentrates adult businesses in a designated area so that they will not interfere with residential and other commercial uses. Exclusion from the community is another alternative. The application of the free speech clause to adult business zoning is governed by a series of U.S. Supreme Court decisions, which are discussed in

---

200. 15 U.S.C. §§ 34, 35, 36.
201. H.R. Rep. No. 965, 98th Cong., 2d Sess. 20 (1984).
202. *Id.*
203. 15 U.S.C. § 36(a).
204. H.R. Rep. No. 965, 98th Cong., 2d Sess. 21, 22 (1984).
205. § 2.52.

the following sections.[206] A few states have statutes authorizing local regulation of adult businesses or imposing restrictions on them.[207]

### § 5.53. Mini-Theatres.

In *Young v. American Mini Theatres, Inc.*,[208] the Supreme Court upheld a deconcentration zoning strategy for adult businesses adopted by the City of Detroit. The zoning ordinance required a distance of 1,000 feet between adult businesses, and this requirement applied to a number of other businesses, such as hotels and bars. The ordinance also prohibited any of these businesses from locating within 500 feet of a residential area. Operators of two adult movie theaters brought an action challenging the constitutionality of both requirements as a free speech violation. Justice Stevens wrote a plurality opinion upholding the ordinance, in which Justice Powell concurred.

Justice Stevens noted that the free speech clause did not absolutely prohibit the deconcentration ordinance. The ordinance did not regulate free speech because of its viewpoint, and he would not give adult sexual expression the same protection under the free speech clause that he would give to political debate. He upheld the city's adoption of a spacing requirement for adult theaters because it did not suppress speech and was adopted to avoid its "secondary effects." Justice Stevens found a factual basis for concluding that the zoning ordinance would have its desired effect of preserving the character of city neighborhoods. He held that "the city's interest in attempting to preserve the quality of urban life is one that must be accorded high respect." He emphasized that the case would raise a different question if the ordinance "had the effect of suppressing, or greatly restricting access to, lawful speech."

### § 5.54. Schad.

In *Schad v. Borough of Mount Ephraim*,[209] a suburban municipality adopted a zoning ordinance that excluded all live entertainment, including nude dancing. An adult bookstore owner installed glass booths in which customers could observe nude dancers. He brought an action challenging the ordinance as a violation of free speech. The Court wrote five opinions, including a plurality opinion signed by three Justices, three concurring opinions that adopted different views

---

**206.** *See also* Deerfield Med. Center v. City of Deerfield Beach, 661 F.2d 328 (5th Cir. 1981) (invalidating prohibition on abortion clinics as interference with constitutional right of privacy).

**207.** Cal. Gov't Code § 65850 (authorizes local regulation subject to free speech guidelines); N.J. Stat. Ann. § 2C:34-7 (distance requirements and limitations on signs); Tenn. Code Ann. §§ 7-51-1401 to 7-51-1406 (hours of operation and design of premises); Tex. Local Gov't Code §§ 243.001-243.011 (authorizes local regulation).

**208.** 427 U.S. 50 (1976).

**209.** 452 U.S. 61 (1981).

of the case, and a dissenting opinion. The actual holding in the case was quite narrow. The seven Justices whose different opinions made up a majority agreed only that the ordinance was facially overbroad and that the borough had not justified it.

The plurality opinion rejected a borough claim that the ordinance was constitutional because it authorized only businesses that met the "immediate needs" of its residents. The plurality could not accept this claim because the ordinance permitted businesses such as motels and lumber yards that met more than local needs. The plurality also rejected a borough argument that it could exclude live entertainment businesses because they presented parking, trash, police, and medical protection problems. The borough did not present evidence on these problems, and it was "immediately apparent as a matter of experience" that live entertainment businesses did not present any more problems than businesses the ordinance permitted.

The plurality rejected a borough argument that the ordinance did not violate the free speech clause because it was a reasonable time, place, and manner regulation.[210] Under this exception, a regulation of a land use protected by the free speech clause is constitutional if it advances a governmental interest other than the suppression of free speech. The borough did not offer evidence that justified a prohibition on live entertainment under this exception because it did not show that live entertainment was "basically incompatible" with uses normally permitted in a commercial district. The ordinance also closed adequate channels of communication for live entertainment uses. The plurality added that *Young* "did not purport to approve the total exclusion from the city of theaters showing adult, but nonobscene, materials."

### § 5.55. *Renton.*

In *City of Renton v. Playtime Theatres, Inc.*,[211] the Court wrote a majority opinion that clarified many of the uncertainties left open by its earlier adult business zoning cases. Renton is a small city in the Seattle metropolitan area. Its zoning ordinance prohibited adult theaters within 1,000 feet of any residential zone, single-family or multi-family dwelling, church, park, or school. The plaintiffs, who planned to exhibit adult movies in two theaters, challenged the constitutionality of the ordinance.

The Court held that the Renton ordinance was a content-neutral time, place, and manner regulation because its purpose was unrelated to the suppression of speech and it did not regulate a point of view. The Court will uphold a content-neutral time, place, and manner regulation if it serves a substantial governmental

---

210. § 2.52.
211. 475 U.S. 41 (1986).

interest and allows for reasonable alternative avenues of communication. The Renton ordinance passed this test. It was entitled to "high respect" because it served the governmental interest of preserving the quality of urban life. Renton had not made independent studies of the adult business problem, but the free speech clause did not require new studies independent of studies done elsewhere. Renton relied on a state supreme court decision reviewing studies in nearby Seattle, and this was enough.

Although the ordinance dispersed rather than concentrated adult businesses, the Court held that either strategy was acceptable and that cities should be allowed to experiment with different zoning techniques. The ordinance was not overbroad, like the ordinance in *Schad,* because it was narrowly tailored to cover only theaters that would create the problem the city was trying to eliminate.

The Court held that adequate alternative channels of communication were available even though the ordinance limited adult theaters to 520 acres, which was about five percent of the city's land area. The trial court found that this area contained "ample, accessible real estate" in all stages of development and was "criss-crossed" by highways and roads. The Court dismissed an argument that much of this land was occupied and that "practically none" was for sale or lease. It held that the free speech clause is not violated just because adult businesses "must fend for themselves in the real estate market on an equal footing with other prospective purchasers and lessees." Renton need only provide a "reasonable opportunity" for adult theaters to open and operate.

### § 5.56. Post-*Renton* Cases.

The lower federal and state courts have not decided a case post-*Renton* in which a community excluded adult uses entirely. They have considered cases that raised an effective preclusion claim. The effective preclusion claim arises from the holding in *Renton* that "reasonable alternative channels of communication" be available for adult uses. In effective preclusion cases the claim is that areas for adult uses, though reasonably plentifully, are not truly available, or that they are too undesirable, too few or too small to be meaningful. Some courts have rejected effective preclusion claims.[212] Other courts found effective preclu-

---

**212.** SDJ, Inc. v. City of Houston, 636 F. Supp. 1359 (S.D. Tex. 1986), *aff'd,* 837 F.2d 1268 (5th Cir. 1988), *cert. denied,* 489 U.S. 1052 (1989); County of Cook v. Renaissance Arcade & Bookstore, 522 N.E.2d 73 (Ill.), *appeal dismissed,* 488 U.S. 882 (1993). *See also* Boos v. Barry, 485 U.S. 312 (1988) (explaining Renton as upholding ordinance aimed at manner of expression and not content of speech).

sion post-*Renton*,[213] but differed in defining the circumstances in which an effective preclusion claim would be justified.[214]

The Supreme Court cases approved distance requirements that require adult uses to be separated from each other, and courts usually uphold these requirements if they do not effectively preclude adult uses from a community.[215] The courts also usually uphold ordinances that limit adult businesses to certain districts, such as commercial districts, or exclude them from other districts, such as residential districts if they do not raise an effective preclusion problem.[216] Courts have followed *Renton's* relaxation of the requirement that municipalities must make independent studies of the adult use problem as the basis for adopting adult use ordinances.[217]

The Supreme Court in *Young* observed in a footnote that the adult business ordinance it upheld did not apply to existing uses but did not say that a grandfather clause was essential. Most courts have not required them, and have upheld provisions in zoning ordinances that require the amortization of a nonconforming adult use after a period of time.[218] A court may strike down an ordinance

---

**213.** Walnut Properties, Inc. v. City of Whittier (II), 861 F.2d 1102 (9th Cir. 1988) (would force only adult theater in district to close), *cert. denied,* 490 U.S. 1006 (1989); People Tags, Inc. v. Jackson County Legislature, 636 F. Supp. 1345 (W.D. Mo. 1986) (ordinance intended to close one business invalidated); City of Stanton v. Cox, 255 Cal. Rptr. 682 (Cal. App. 1989) (locations zoned for adult businesses severely limited).

**214.** *Compare* Woodall v. City of El Paso, 959 F.2d 1305 (5th Cir. 1992) (may consider physical or legal but not economic unsuitability of land), *followed in* Woodall v. City of El Paso, 49 F.3d 1120 (5th Cir. 1995), *with* Topanga Press, Inc. v. City of Los Angeles, 989 F.2d 1524 (9th Cir. 1993) (disagreeing and holding property not potentially available when it is unreasonable to believe it would ever become available to any commercial enterprise).

**215.** Ambassador Books & Video, Inc. v. City of Little Rock, 20 F.3d 858 (8th Cir. 1994); Lakeland Lounge of Jackson, Inc. v. City of Jackson, 973 F.2d 1255 (5th Cir. 1992); International Eateries of America, Inc. v. Broward County, 941 F.2d 1157 (11th Cir. 1991); Hart Bookstores, Inc. v. Edmisten, 612 F.2d 821 (4th Cir. 1979); City of National City v. Wiener, 838 P.2d 223 (Cal. 1992).

**216.** Holmberg v. City of Ramsey, 12 F.3d 140 (8th Cir. 1994); Lakeland Lounge of Jackson, Inc. v. City of Jackson, 973 F.2d 1255 (5th Cir. 1992), *cert. denied,* 507 U.S. 1030 (1993); U.S. Partners Financial Corp. v. Kansas City, 707 F. Supp. 1090 (W.D. Mo. 1989); Jeffrey Lauren Land Co. v. City of Livonia, 326 N.W.2d 604 (Mich. 1982); Northend Cinema, Inc. v. City of Seattle, 585 P.2d 1153 (Wash. 1978), *cert. denied,* 441 U.S. 946 (1979). *But see* CLR Corp. v. Henline, 702 F.2d 637 (6th Cir. 1983).

**217.** ILQ Investments, Inc. v. City of Rochester, 25 F.3d 1413 (8th Cir. 1994); Alexander v. City of Minneapolis, 928 F.2d 278 (8th Cir. 1991); Thames Enterprises v. City of St. Louis, 851 F.2d 199 (8th Cir. 1988); Town of Islip v. Caviglia, 540 N.E.2d 215 (N.Y. 1989). *But see* World Wide Video, Inc. v. City of Tukwila, 816 P.2d 18 (Wash. 1991) (en banc).

**218.** Ambassador Books & Video, Inc. v. City of Little Rock, 20 F.3d 585 (8th Cir. 1994); Hart Bookstores, Inc. v. Edminsten, 612 F.2d 821 (4th Cir. 1979), *cert. denied,* 447 U.S. 929 (1980); County of Cook v. Renaissance Arcade & Bookstore, 522 N.E.2d 73 (Ill.), *appeal dismissed,* 488

prohibiting advertising by adult businesses if it finds the ordinance restricts speech and is not supported by other governmental purposes, such as preventing loss of property values.[219]

## D. RELIGIOUS USES.

## § 5.57. Religious Uses.

### § 5.58. In the State Courts.

The cases are divided on whether a zoning ordinance may exclude religious uses, such as churches, from residential areas. Several courts hold that the ordinance may exclude religious uses from residential areas if they create traffic problems or have an adverse effect on property values or municipal services.[220] When the impact on residential areas is less extreme, the cases suggest that allowing religious uses as a conditional use is a more "balanced" alternative.[221]

A number of cases treat religious uses as a preferred use and hold that a zoning ordinance may not exclude them from residential neighborhoods. Some of these cases rely on state constitutions that protect the free exercise of religion, and some reverse the presumption of constitutionality the courts usually apply to

---

U.S. 882 (1988); Town of Islip v. Caviglia, 540 N.E.2d 215 (N.Y. 1989); Northend Cinema, Inc. v. City of Seattle, 585 P.2d 1153 (Wash. 1978). *But see* Ebel v. City of Corona, 767 F.2d 635 (9th Cir. 1985) (invalidating 60- to 120-day period when user had five-year lease and had made substantial investment). *See* § 5.74.

**219.** MD II Entertainment, Inc. v. City of Dallas, 28 F.3d 492 (5th Cir. 1994). *But see* Hamilton Amusement Center, Inc. v. Poritz, 689 A.2d 201 (N.J. App. Div. 1997) (upholding state statute limiting size, number and content of signs).

**220.** Seward Chapel, Inc. v. City of Seward, 655 P.2d 1293 (Alaska 1982) (exclusion of parochial school); Corporation of Presiding Bishop of Church of Jesus Christ of Latter-Day Saints v. City of Porterville, 203 P.2d 823 (Cal.), *appeal dismissed,* 338 U.S. 805 (1949); West Hartford Methodist Church v. Zoning Bd. of Appeals, 121 A.2d 640 (Conn. 1956); Lutheran High School Ass'n v. City of Farmington Hills, 381 N.W.2d 417 (Mich. App. 1986); Cornell Univ. v. Bagnardi, 503 N.E.2d 509 (N.Y. 1986); Milwaukie Company of Jehovah's Witnesses v. Mullen, 330 P.2d 5 (Or. 1958), *appeal dismissed,* 359 U.S. 436 (1959). *But see* Jehovah's Witness Assembly Halls of New Jersey, Inc. v. City of Jersey City, 597 F. Supp. 972 (D.N.J. 1984) (may not exclude from commercial area).

**221.** Cornell Univ. v. Bagnardi, 503 N.E.2d 509 (N.Y. 1986). *Contra* Love Church v. City of Evanston, 671 F. Supp. 508, 515 (N.D. Ill. 1987). *See* § 6.58.

zoning ordinances.[222] Religious uses must comply with reasonable site development regulations, such as parking requirements.[223]

### § 5.59. Federal "Free Exercise" and "Establishment" Clauses.

The federal courts have held that zoning restrictions on religious uses did not violate the "free exercise of religion" clause of the federal constitution. In *Lakewood, Ohio Congregation of Jehovah's Witnesses, Inc. v. City of Lakewood*,[224] the court upheld a restriction on churches in residential districts as applied to a congregation that planned to build a church. The court held that the right to build a church was not protected by the free exercise clause because it was not a "fundamental tenet" or "cardinal principle" of the religion's faith. The ordinance prohibited only "the secular act of building" and imposed only "an indirect financial burden and a subjective aesthetic burden." The ordinance permitted churches in nonresidential districts covering ten percent of the city. The church could build in these districts even though this would be more expensive and "less conducive to worship." The courts have found a violation when a zoning ordinance has been applied against a religious use in a discriminatory way.[225]

---

**222.** Ellsworth v. Gercke, 156 P.2d 242 (Ariz. 1945); City of Colorado Springs v. Blanche, 761 P.2d 212 (Colo. 1988) (qualifying earlier case adopting rule); Jehovah's Witnesses Assembly Hall v. Wollrich Twp., 532 A.2d 276 (N.J.L. Div. 1987) (citing cases); State ex rel. Synod of Ohio v. Joseph, 39 N.E.2d 515 (Ohio 1942); Simms v. City of Sherman, 181 S.W.2d 100 (Tex. Civ. App.), *aff'd*, 183 S.W.2d 415 (Tex. 1944); Lake Shore Drive Baptist Church v. Village of Bayside Bd. of Trustees, 108 N.W.2d 288 (Wis. 1961). *See* State v. Cameron, 498 A.2d 1217 (N.J. 1985) (ordinance excluding church held vague).

**223.** East Side Baptist Church v. Klein, 487 P.2d 549 (Colo. 1971); Board of Zoning Appeals v. Decatur, Ind. Congregation of Jehovah's Witnesses, 117 N.E.2d 115 (Ind. 1954); Wellspring Zendo, Inc. v. Trippe, 625 N.Y.S.2d 334 (App. Div. 1995) (screening buffer). *See also* Lucas Valley Homeowners Ass'n v. County of Marin, 284 Cal. Rptr. 427 (Cal. App. 1991) (permit conditions).

**224.** 699 F.2d 303 (6th Cir.), *cert. denied*, 464 U.S. 815 (1983). *Accord* First Assembly of God v. Collier County, 20 F.3d 419 (11th Cir. 1994) (upholding zoning ordinance prohibiting church shelter for homeless); Messiah Baptist Ch. v. County of Jefferson, 859 F.2d 829 (10th Cir. 1988); Grosz v. City of Miami Beach, 721 F.2d 729 (11th Cir. 1983), *cert. denied*, 469 U.S. 829 (1984); Daytona Rescue Mission, Inc. v. City of Daytona Beach, 885 F. Supp. 1554 (M.D. Fla. 1995); Congregation Beth Yitzchok of Rockland, Inc. v. Town of Ramapo, 593 F. Supp. 655 (S.D.N.Y. 1984). *See also* Church of the Lukumi Babalu Aye v. City of Hialeah, 508 U.S. 520 (1993) (invalidating local zoning and other laws targeting use of animal sacrifice for religious purposes); Bethel Evangelical Lutheran Ch. v. Village of Morton, 559 N.E.2d 533 (Ill. App. 1990) (upholding enrollment cap on church school). *See* 11 A.L.R.4th 1084 (1982).

**225.** Islamic Center of Miss., Inc. v. City of Starkville, 840 F.2d 293 (5th Cir. 1988). *See also* Cornerstone Bible Ch. v. City of Hastings, 948 F.2d 464 (8th Cir. 1991) (church excluded from central business district; court reversed summary judgment for city and remanded).

A Washington case held a landmarks law violated the free exercise clause,[226] but the Supreme Court remanded in light of its decision holding a state may deny unemployment benefits to persons discharged for religious use of a prohibited drug. In the unemployment benefits case, the Court indicated it would uphold a neutral, generally applicable law to religiously-motivated conduct. This decision, and the remand in the Washington case, suggests that zoning ordinances are to receive a less rigorous review when a violation of the Free Exercise clause is claimed. However, on remand the Washington Supreme Court adhered to its original decision that the landmarks law was a free exercise violation.[227]

In *Larkin v. Grendel's Den, Inc.*,[228] the Supreme Court invalidated a Massachusetts statute providing that a city could not issue a liquor license if a church or school located within 500 feet of the premises vetoed it. The Court held that the statutory veto violated the "establishment of religion" clause of the federal constitution. The statute could advance or inhibit religion because it did not contain standards for the exercise of the veto, which churches could use for religious purposes. The veto also "enmeshes churches in the process of government" and could create political fragmentation on religious issues. *Grendel's Den* casts doubt on the cases that give churches a preferred use status under zoning ordinances.

### § 5.60. Federal Religious Freedom Restoration Act.

Congress passed a Religious Freedom Restoration Act[229] in 1993 to restore the "compelling" governmental interest test the Supreme Court previously required to justify governmental action affecting the free exercise of religion. The Act applied to state and local governments. It did not mention zoning, but it was clear from the legislative history that Congress intended the Act to apply to zoning actions,[230] and courts applied it in zoning cases. However, the Supreme Court held the Act unconstitutional as an unauthorized exercise of congressional power because it redefined the meaning of the free exercise clause.[231]

---

**226.** First Covenant Ch. v. City of Seattle, 787 P.2d 1352 (Wash. 1990), *vacated and remanded,* 499 U.S. 901 (1991).

**227.** 840 P.2d 174 (Wash. 1992).

**228.** 459 U.S. 116 (1982).

**229.** Formerly 42 U.S.C. §§ 2000b to 2000b-4.

**230.** *See, e.g.,* H.R. Rep. No. 103-88, 103d Cong., 1st Sess. 6, n. 14 (1993) (disapproving, *e.g., Saint Bartholomew's Church* decision, discussed in § 11.35).

**231.** City of Boerne v. Flores, 117 S. Ct. 2157 (1997).

# E. SITE DEVELOPMENT REQUIREMENTS.

## § 5.61. Yards and Setbacks.

The constitutionality of yard and setback requirements has been secure since a post-*Euclid* Supreme Court case, *Gorieb v. Fox*.[232] The Court relied on *Euclid* to uphold a street setback requirement in a residential area because it separated residences from the noise of the street, improved the attractiveness of residential environments, and ensured the availability of light and air. The courts have upheld the constitutionality of setback and yard requirements since *Gorieb*.[233]

Cases occasionally invalidate setback requirements when they do not serve the zoning purposes approved in *Gorieb*. The Pennsylvania Supreme Court held that the zoning purposes that support the constitutionality of setbacks in urban areas do not apply in rural areas.[234] A court may also hold setback and yard requirements invalid as a taking of property if they excessively restrict the area available for building. In *Board of Supvrs. v. Rowe*,[235] the court invalidated front setback and perimeter open space requirements that eliminated twenty-nine percent of the buildable area of a lot.

## § 5.62. Frontage Requirements.

Courts uphold minimum street frontage requirements for the same reasons that the Supreme Court upheld street setbacks in *Gorieb*. Minimum street frontage requirements control density and the open space required around dwellings because they effectively determine the size of the lot.[236] Large-lot zoning provisions often contain frontage requirements, although the large-lot zoning cases do not usually consider the frontage requirement separately.

Frontage requirements can be exclusionary if they require excessive additional expense for streets, curbs, and sewer and water lines, as this can substantially increase housing costs. The comprehensive exclusionary zoning cases have not yet considered frontage requirements, although the zoning ordinance held exclusionary in the *Mt. Laurel* case included excessive frontage requirements as well as other exclusionary zoning measures.[237]

---

**232.** 274 U.S. 603 (1927).

**233.** City of Leadville v. Rood, 600 P.2d 62 (Colo. 1979); Quirk v. Town of New Boston, 663 A.2d 1328 (N.H. 1995) (buffer zone); Miller & Son Paving, Inc. v. Wrightstown Twp., 451 A.2d 1002 (Pa. 1982); 93 A.L.R.2d 1223 (1964); 94 A.L.R.2d 398 (1964).

**234.** Schmalz v. Buckingham Twp. Zoning Bd. of Adjustment, 132 A.2d 233 (Pa. 1957).

**235.** 216 S.E.2d 199 (Va. 1975). *See also* Giambrone v. City of Aurora, 621 N.E.2d 475 (Ohio App. 1993).

**236.** Di Salle v. Giggal, 261 P.2d 499 (Colo. 1953). *See* Emond v. Board of Appeals, 541 N.E.2d 380 (Mass. App. 1989) (upholding special permit provision that authorized frontage limitation based on neighborhood average); 96 A.L.R.2d 1367 (1964).

**237.** § 7.09.

Doubts about the zoning purposes served by frontage requirements occasionally produce an unfavorable decision. In *Metzger v. Town of Brentwood (II)*,[238] the zoning ordinance required a 200-foot frontage for single-family dwellings, but the property owner had only a 123-foot frontage on part of a road that was open to the public. The court noted that "frontage requirements can be justified on the basis that they are a method of determining lot size to prevent overcrowding" but pointed out that the size of the property owner's lot far exceeded the frontage requirement. Nor did the shorter frontage restrict access by fire trucks and other public vehicles.

## § 5.63. Site Ratios.

Site ratios regulate building bulk by specifying the maximum percentage of a lot a building may occupy. When applied along with height limitations in multi-family and office districts, the site ratio controls density by limiting the square footage allowed in apartment and office buildings. Developers can vary density somewhat by varying the size of apartment and office units, but the allowable square footage imposes an important density control.

Although obviously quite important as a zoning control, site ratio requirements have received little judicial attention. A much-cited leading case, *La Salle Nat'l Bank v. City of Chicago*,[239] upheld a site ratio requirement that applied to multi-family dwellings. The evidence in the case did not indicate that the site ratio was unreasonable, and the court upheld it under the usual presumption of constitutionality.

## § 5.64. Height Limitations.

Zoning district regulations usually contain height limitations as part of the site development controls package. Height limitations are an important density control because they limit the building bulk permitted by other site development requirements, such as the site ratio. The height limitation also ensures access to light and air.

In *Welch v. Swasey*,[240] the U.S. Supreme Court upheld a Massachusetts statute that adopted two height districts for the city of Boston. A landowner challenged the lower height requirement in the residential district. The Court upheld the statute in a traditional substantive due process decision and relied especially on the "aesthetic" considerations underlying the height limitation. The Court

---

**238.** 374 A.2d 954 (N.H. 1977). *Contra* McNeil v. Town of Avon, 435 N.E.2d 1043 (Mass. 1982). *See also* Damurjian v. Board of Adjustment, 890 A.2d 655 (N.J. App. Div. 1997) (method of calculation vague).

**239.** 125 N.E.2d 609 (Ill. 1955).

**240.** 214 U.S. 91 (1909).

also upheld the differential height requirements in the two districts. The land-owner did not make a taking objection.

Although there are few recent decisions, the courts have upheld height limita-tions contained in comprehensive zoning ordinances.[241] A few cases considered the usual mapping problems and upheld or struck down a height limitation de-pending on whether it was consistent with building heights in the surrounding area.[242]

The U.S. Supreme Court's *Penn Central* decision[243] held the property interest in airspace is not absolutely protected from regulation under the taking clause. Height limitations may be vulnerable to "as-applied" taking claims despite this holding. In *William C. Haas & Co. v. City & County of San Francisco*,[244] the city adopted a building height limitation as part of an urban design plan. A property owner on Russian Hill challenged the limitation and claimed it imposed a $1.9 million dollar loss on a $2 million dollar land investment. The court rejected the taking claim because the ordinance merely diminished the value of the property. It also held that the height limitation was not "reverse" spot-zoning because it was part of a comprehensive plan and all property owners in the area were equally affected.[245] *Haas* is an extreme case and is suspect post-*Lucas*.[246]

## § 5.65. Floor Area Ratio.

Site development regulations can create design problems when they are ap-plied to multi-family and office development. Conventional setback, yard, site ratio, and height requirements can produce a uniform building design that is mo-notonous and unattractive. The floor area ratio is a zoning technique that at-tempts to avoid these design problems. It specifies a ratio between the square footage allowable in a building and the square footage of the lot. A floor area ratio of 1:1, for example, allows one square foot of building for each square foot of the lot. A developer can use the square footage allowed by the floor area ratio in any building shape he prefers if it complies with any applicable perimeter

---

241. Landmark Land Co. v. City & County of Denver, 728 P.2d 1281 (Colo. 1986) (to protect views); Loyola Fed. Sav. & Loan Ass'n v. Buschman, 176 A.2d 355 (Md. 1961); Alexander v. Hampstead, 525 A.2d 276 (N.H. 1987); 8 A.L.R.2d 963 (1949).

242. *Compare* LaSalle Nat'l Bank v. City of Chicago, 125 N.E.2d 609 (Ill. 1955) (invalid), and Anderson v. City of Seattle, 390 P.2d 994 (Wash. 1964) (same), *with* LaSalle Nat'l Bank v. City of Evanston, 312 N.E.2d 625 (Ill. 1974) (contra).

243. § 2.13.

244. 605 F.2d 1117 (9th Cir. 1979), *cert. denied,* 445 U.S. 928 (1980).

245. *See also* City of St. Paul v. Chicago, St. Paul, Minneapolis & Omaha Ry., 413 F.2d 762 (8th Cir.) (limitation applied to single-property owner), *cert. denied,* 396 U.S. 985 (1969); State v. Pacesetter Constr. Co., 571 P.2d 196 (Wash. 1977) (residential height limitation in shoreline man-agement act).

246. *See also* § 2.31 (discussing height limitations near airports as taking of property).

open space and height requirements. If the floor area ratio is 1:1, a two-story building would occupy one-half of the lot. A three-story building would occupy one-third of the lot. Floor area ratios in the more intensive multi-family and office districts are usually higher and allow even more variation in building design.

Although no court has considered the constitutionality of floor area ratios, they do not present constitutional questions different from those raised by other site development regulations. An important California case reviewing a floor area ratio variance stressed the importance of the floor area ratio as a zoning control.[247]

## § 5.66. Bonuses and Incentives.

A number of cities have adopted an innovative zoning technique that authorizes density bonuses to office and commercial developers in return for on-site and other facilities available to the public. The city usually increases densities by increasing the floor area ratio. A street-level plaza or open space is an example of an on-site facility, although cities utilize density bonuses to secure other facilities, such as pedestrian skyways linking commercial uses in downtown areas. New York City used its density bonus program to secure the provision of commercial theaters in new office buildings.[248]

The zoning ordinance can make a density bonus available as a matter of right by specifying the density increases permitted for designated facilities. This type of density bonus, like conventional site development regulations, can produce monotonous designs. A city can avoid this problem by awarding density bonuses on a discretionary, case-by-case basis. This approach requires an even-handed administration of the density bonus option, which may be difficult to achieve. Under another alternative, the city can prepare a detailed plan for a commercial area that specifies the density bonuses available on each lot. New York City has used this approach.

The density bonus is intended to avoid the taking problem that would arise if a municipality required developers to provide a facility for public use without a density increase that offsets its cost. A different taking problem may arise if the density bonus is optional. In an optional program, a city must make the density bonus so attractive that developers will want to participate in the bonus program. A city can improve developer participation by adopting restrictive densities that make development economically unattractive. Developers will then seek the higher densities available in the bonus program.

---

247. Broadway, Laguna, Vallejo Ass'n v. Board of Permit Appeals, 427 P.2d 810 (Cal. 1967).

248. *See* N.Y. Town Law § 261-6; Village Law § 7-703 (authorizing incentive zoning and bonuses).

In *Montgomery County v. Woodward & Lothrop, Inc.*,[249] the county adopted a density bonus program for a suburban business district. A developer claimed a taking occurred because the density and other requirements established as-of-right in the business district were "superficial." Landowners would not be able to develop their land under these requirements and would have to apply for a density bonus. The court dismissed the taking challenge. It held that nothing in the record showed that the developer had to obtain a density bonus in order to make a reasonable use of its land.

### § 5.67. Off-Street Parking.

Zoning ordinances usually contain off-street parking requirements for uses permitted in zoning districts. In multi-family districts the ordinance usually requires a specified number of parking spaces, usually two or more, for each dwelling unit. In commercial districts the parking requirement depends on the type of use and the amount of traffic it will generate. Variations in off-street parking requirements by district are constitutional if they have a reasonable basis.[250]

Off-street parking requirements serve purposes similar to those served by other site development regulations. The courts have easily upheld them, although there are not many cases. In *Zilinsky v. Zoning Bd. of Adjustment*,[251] the court upheld a zoning ordinance that required every one-family dwelling to have at least two off-street parking spaces, one of which had to be in a garage. The lower courts held the ordinance unconstitutional because it did not penalize property owners who did not park a car in the garage. The state supreme court reversed. It applied the presumption of constitutionality and held that "[e]ven without mandating use, off-street parking is a rational means of advancing the legitimate municipal interest in decreasing traffic congestion."

### F. NONCONFORMING USES.

### § 5.68. The Zoning Problem.

The nonconforming use is a difficult problem in zoning administration. The mixed land use pattern that exists in built-up cities means that some uses will not conform to newly adopted or amended zoning ordinances. A zoning ordinance

---

**249.** 376 A.2d 483 (Md. 1977).

**250.** Montgomery County v. Woodward & Lothrop, Inc., 376 A.2d 483 (Md. 1977); 71 A.L.R.4th 529 (1989).

**251.** 521 A.2d 841 (N.J. 1987). *Accord* Stroud v. City of Aspen, 532 P.2d 720 (Colo. 1975); Parking Ass'n of Georgia v. City of Atlanta, 450 S.E.2d 200 (Ga. 1994) (upholding barrier curb and landscaping requirements), *cert. denied,* 115 S. Ct. 2268 (1995); Yates v. Mayor & Comm'rs, 244 So. 2d 724 (Miss. 1971); Grace Baptist Church v. City of Oxford, 358 S.E.2d 372 (N.C. 1987) (paved off-street parking).

cannot achieve its goal of separating incompatible uses in this situation unless it requires the elimination of nonconforming uses. Municipalities have long struggled with a variety of techniques to accomplish this objective, but they have usually been unsuccessful. Nonconforming uses have remained and have often become more entrenched. They are an especially serious problem in sign control programs, which must secure the removal of nonconforming signs to achieve the visual environment they seek to create.

Nonconforming "use" may not be an accurate term for zoning nonconformities. A true nonconforming use is a use of land or a building that does not conform with the use restrictions of the zoning ordinance. A zoning nonconformity also occurs when an undeveloped tract of land or a building does not conform with the site development regulations of the zoning ordinance, such as lot size and frontage requirements.

The U.S. Supreme Court held in early decisions that municipalities could adopt land use ordinances that applied retroactively to eliminate an existing use.[252] These cases suggested that municipalities could apply comprehensive zoning ordinances to eliminate nonconforming uses retroactively. The early zoning ordinances did not take advantage of this opportunity. They protected nonconforming uses from immediate termination, apparently to avoid political problems. The courts now hold that a municipality may not zone retroactively to terminate a nonconforming use.[253] Some state zoning statutes impose this limitation.[254]

Some critics believe the need to eliminate nonconforming uses is overemphasized. They argue that nonconforming uses occur in mixed areas of the city where their removal is not necessary. They would limit measures for the elimination of nonconforming uses to well-established homogenous areas where a nonconforming use is a true anomaly.[255]

Two competing philosophies influence the court decisions that consider the constitutionality of ordinances providing for the elimination of nonconforming use. One philosophy favors the gradual elimination of nonconforming uses to accomplish the zoning objective of compatible and homogenous land use envi-

---

252. § 2.10. *See* City of Dublin v. Finkes, 615 N.E.2d 690 (Ohio App. 1993) (regulations based on protection of public health or safety can be applied retroactively to nonconforming uses).

253. Jones v. City of Los Angeles, 295 P. 14 (Cal. 1930) (leading case); *See* Town of Lyons v. Bashor, 867 P.2d 159 (Colo. App. 1993) (nonconforming use runs with the land); Missouri Rock, Inc. v. Winholtz, 614 S.W.2d 734 (Mo. App. 1981).

254. Ky. Rev. Stat. § 100.253; Mass. Ann. Laws ch. 40A, § 6; Ohio Rev. Code Ann. § 713.15; R.I. Gen. Laws § 45-24-39; Utah Code Ann. § 10-9-408. *But see* Village of Valatie v. Smith, 632 N.E.2d 1264 (N.Y. 1994) (ordinance terminating nonconforming use when in ownership changes is facially constitutional).

255. The American Law Institute's Model Land Development Code adopts this recommendation. Model Land Dev. Code § 5-102.

ronments. This philosophy has its roots in an expansive view of the police power and supports zoning requirements that eliminate nonconforming uses. A competing philosophy stems from the cases that invalidate the retroactive elimination of nonconforming uses and is based on the taking clause. This philosophy places primary emphasis on protecting the "vested" rights of property owners in nonconforming uses. Courts adopting this philosophy tend to strike down zoning requirements that eliminate nonconforming uses.

Neither of these competing philosophies has triumphed in the cases. The judicial view of nonconforming use controls varies, often illogically, with the zoning technique used. Nor do the courts always address the constitutional issues implicit in the vested rights philosophy. For example, zoning provisions that prohibit the resumption of abandoned nonconforming uses raise a constitutional problem because they terminate a "vested" property right. Courts seldom address this constitutional issue but concentrate instead on how they should interpret the abandonment provision.

The courts explicitly consider the constitutional problems only in the amortization cases. Although most courts still uphold amortization, some recent decisions have struck down amortization requirements.

### § 5.69. Change and Expansion.

A nonconforming use may lose its protected status if it changes or expands. Most zoning ordinances contain provisions covering this problem. One common provision states that a nonconforming use "shall not change except to a use permitted in the district in which it is located." A zoning ordinance may also specify the type of changes allowed in nonconforming uses or may require a permit from the board of adjustment for nonconforming use changes.[256] A few zoning statutes regulate changes in nonconforming uses.[257]

The cases usually determine whether a change or expansion of a nonconforming use is permitted by considering the degree of change from the existing use and the effect of the change on the neighborhood. Many cases turn on an interpretation of the zoning ordinance. A court's view on the need to eliminate nonconforming uses may also influence its decision.

In one common case, a nonconforming use claims that an expansion in its business is protected by its nonconforming use status. Permissible expansions include an increase in business volume if there are no structural alterations that

---

256. Kopietz v. Zoning Bd. of Appeals, 535 N.W.2d 910 (Mich. App. 1995); McLaughlin v. City of Brockton, 587 N.E.2d 251 (Mass. App. 1992).

257. Ky. Rev. Stat. § 100.253; Neb. Rev. Stat. § 19-904.01 Va. Code Ann. § 15.1-492; W. Va. Code § 8-24-50. *See also* Uncle v. New Jersey Pinelands Comm'n, 645 A.2d 788 (N.J. App. Div. 1994) (upholding registration provision).

increase the size of a building.[258] Courts also allow a nonconforming use to expand to occupy an entire tract or building if the character of the use and the nature of the property indicates that use of the entire tract or building was contemplated at the time the nonconforming use was established.[259]

A change in a nonconforming business may also result in a loss of nonconforming use status.[260] For example, *Belleville v. Parrillo's, Inc.*[261] held that a change in the use of a nonconforming business from a restaurant to a renovated discotheque was impermissible. The court held that the "entire character" of the business had been altered and the effect of the change on the general welfare of the surrounding neighborhood was "demonstrably" adverse.

*Baxter v. City of Preston*[262] provides an extensive review of the case law on the change and expansion of nonconforming uses. The court adopted a flexible approach that focuses on the character of the expansion and enlargement on a

---

**258.** Change approved: State v. Szymanski, 189 A.2d 514 (Conn. Cir. Ct. App. Div. 1967) (increase in number of cars parked); Redfearn v. Creppel, 455 So.2d 1356 (La. 1984) (expansion of restaurant); Feldstein v. La Vale Zoning Bd., 227 A.2d 731 (Md. 1967) (increase in quality and height of stored junk); Powers v. Building Inspector, 296 N.E.2d 491 (Mass. 1973) (increase in business).

Change not approved: Blake v. City of Phoenix, 754 P.2d 1368 (Ariz. 1988) (plant nursery drastically expanded retail sales); SLS Partnership v. City of Apple Valley, 496 N.W.2d 429 (Minn. App. 1993) (increase in size of mobile home); Grey Rocks Land Trust v. Town of Hebron, 614 A.2d 1048 (N.H. 1992) (construction of new building); 61 A.L.R.4th 806, 902 (1988); 87 A.L.R.2d 4 (1963).

**259.** Ollinger v. Collins, 470 So. 2d 1183 (Ala. 1985) (intent to use entire property not enough); Hansen Bros. Enters. v. Board of Supervisors, 907 P.2d 1324 (Cal. 1995) (mining); Syracuse Aggregate Corp. v. Weise, 414 N.E.2d 651 (N.Y. 1980) (quarrying exception); Keller v. City of Bellingham, 600 P.2d 1276 (Wash. 1979) (manufacturing plant); 56 A.L.R.4th 769 (1987). *But see* Stuckman v. Kosciusko County Bd. of Zoning Appeals, 506 N.E.2d 1079 (Ind. 1987) (moving automobile salvage yard to adjacent lots not allowed).

**260.** Change in use approved: DiBlasi v. Zoning Bd. of Appeals, 624 A.2d 372 (Conn. 1993) (use change to probation office); Ray's Stateline Market, Inc. v. Town of Pelham, 665 A.2d 1068 (N.H. 1995) (minor change in business); Institute for Evaluation & Planning, Inc. v. Board of Adjustment, 637 A.2d 235 (N.J.L. Div. 1993) (from residential to group home); Limley v. Zoning Hearing Bd., 625 A.2d 54 (Pa. 1993) (from nonprofit private club to public restaurant and bar).

Change in use not approved: Anderson v. Board of Adjustment for Zoning Appeals, 931 P.2d 517 (Colo. App. 1996) (addition of automatic car wash to filling station); Boivin v. Town of Sanford, 588 A.2d 1197 (Me. 1991) (change from auction barn to antique business); Comforti v. City of Manchester, 677 A.2d 147 (N.H. 1996) (change from movies to live entertainment); Aboud v. Wallace, 463 N.Y.S.2d 572 (App. Div. 1983) (change from doctor's office to professional lobbying office); Knowlton v. Browning-Ferris Indus. of Va., 260 S.E.2d 232 (Va. 1979) (change from small trucking business to large trash collection business).

**261.** 416 A.2d 388 (N.J. 1980).

**262.** 768 P.2d 1340 (Idaho 1989) (citing treatise). *See also* Township of Chartiers v. William H. Martin, Inc., 542 A.2d 985 (Pa. 1988) (reviewing Pennsylvania law); 61 A.L.R.4th 912 (1988); 61 A.L.R.4th 806 (1988); 61 A.L.R.4th 724 (1988); 56 A.L.R.4th 769 (1987); 10 A.L.R.4th 1122 (1981).

case-by-case basis. It held that the nonconforming use of land for grazing live-stock could not be converted to a year-round use as a feed lot.

### § 5.70. Repair and Reconstruction.

Zoning ordinances usually contain a number of provisions that are intended to achieve the gradual elimination of nonconforming uses. One common provision permits the repair, but not the alteration or construction, of a nonconforming use. A few zoning statutes contain similar provisions.[263] The courts have upheld these restrictions against constitutional attacks,[264] but most of the cases have considered questions arising out of the interpretation of statutory and ordinance provisions.

*Granger v. Board of Adjustment*[265] is a typical case. A nonconforming manufacturer of burial vaults replaced the brick and frame walls of his building with concrete and steel. The court held that this work was a reasonable repair rather than a prohibited structural alteration, which it defined as an alteration that converts an existing building into a different one.[266]

A municipality may require the demolition of a nonconforming building under a building or housing code if it is seriously deteriorated. The question that then arises is whether the owner of the nonconforming building may reconstruct it. In *Application of O'Neal*,[267] a city ordered the demolition of a nonconforming nursing home under a state building code. The zoning ordinance did not prohibit structural alterations of nonconforming uses. The court held that the owners of the home could reconstruct a building of the same size. It pointed out that the reconstruction of the home was not a voluntary act but was necessary to meet state building code requirements. The courts have held that reconstruction is not

---

263. Cal. Gov't Code § 65852.25; Mich. Stat. Ann. §§ 5.2961(16), 5.2963(16); N.J. Stat. Ann. § 40:55D-68; Utah Code Ann. § 10-9-408. *See* Gannett Outdoor Co. v. City of Mesa, 768 P.2d 191 (Ariz. App. 1989) (replacement of multi-pole with monopole billboard not allowed); Avalon Home & Land Owners Ass'n v. Borough of Avalon, 543 A.2d 950 (N.J. 1988) (ordinance allowing demolition and total reconstruction not authorized).

264. O'Mara v. Council of City of Newark, 48 Cal. Rptr. 208 (Cal. App. 1965); Palazzola v. City of Gulfport, 52 So. 2d 611 (Miss. 1951); State ex rel. Miller v. Cain, 242 P.2d 505 (Wash. 1952).

265. 44 N.W.2d 399 (Iowa 1950); *contra* Moore v. Pettus, 71 So. 2d 814 (Ala. 1954). *See* 63 A.L.R.4th 275 (1988). *See also* Mossman v. City of Columbus, 449 N.W.2d 214 (Neb. 1989) (nonconforming mobile home may not be replaced).

266. *But see* Marris v. City of Cedarburg, 498 N.W.2d 842 (Wis. 1993) (structural repair is work that affects structural quality or contributes to longevity or permanence).

267. 92 S.E.2d 189 (N.C. 1956).

permitted when the zoning ordinance prohibits structural alterations, and when reconstruction is not required under a building or housing code.[268]

Many zoning ordinances limit the expenditure an owner is allowed to make on the restoration of a nonconforming building. These provisions apply to deteriorated buildings as well as buildings destroyed by fire or other calamity. The ordinance usually states that the owner of a nonconforming building may not restore it if the cost of restoration exceeds a maximum percentage of its value or its cost of reproduction. The maximum specified is usually at least fifty percent. The courts uphold fifty and sixty-five percent cost ratios and will uphold a municipality that applies them to prohibit restoration if the cost of restoration is substantial.[269] Some of the cases that upheld cost ratios noted that the land could be put to a conforming use once the nonconforming building was removed. Courts strike down a prohibition on restoration as confiscatory if the cost of restoration is not a substantial portion of the nonconforming building's value.

### § 5.71. Abandonment.

Zoning ordinances attempt to achieve the gradual elimination of nonconforming uses by prohibiting their resumption once they are abandoned. Most zoning ordinances have nonconforming use abandonment provisions, and a few zoning statutes authorize them.[270] Abandonment provisions present interpretive problems that have constitutional implications. A municipality could apply its abandonment provision to prevent the resumption of a nonconforming use if its owner discontinued it. A court could hold that the termination of the nonconforming use is unconstitutional because its abandonment by its owner was involuntary.[271]

Most courts avoid this constitutional problem by holding that the abandonment of a nonconforming use must be voluntary. An abandonment is voluntary if a municipality can prove an intent to abandon and an overt act of abandon-

---

**268.** Bixler v. Pierson, 188 So. 2d 681 (Fla. App. 1966); Selligman v. Von Allmen Bros., Inc., 179 S.W.2d 207 (Ky. 1944); Hanna v. Board of Adjustment, 183 A.2d 539 (Pa. 1962); State ex rel. Miller v. Cain, 242 P.2d 505 (Wash. 1952); 87 A.L.R.2d 4 (1963).

**269.** Palazzola v. City of Gulfport, 52 So. 2d 611 (Miss. 1951); Adcock v. King, 520 S.W.2d 418 (Tex. Civ. App. 1975); State v. Burt, 127 N.W.2d 270 (Wis. 1964); State v. Steinke, 96 N.W.2d 356 (Wis. 1959); 57 A.L.R.3d 419 (1974). *See* Manhattan Sepulveda, Ltd. v. City of Manhattan Beach, 27 Cal. Rptr. 2d 565 (Cal. App. 1994) (value defined as fair market value at time of fire).

**270.** Neb. Rev. Stat. § 19-904.01 (if discontinued for 12 months); Ohio Rev. Code Ann. § 713.15 (voluntary discontinuance); R.I. Gen. Laws § 45-24-39 (requires overt act). *See* Camara v. Board of Adj., 570 A.2d 1012 (N.J. App. Div. 1990).

**271.** *See* The Ansley House, Inc. v. City of Atlanta, 397 S.E.2d 419 (Ga. 1990).

ment.[272] Some courts adopt this rule even when the zoning ordinance requires only a "discontinuance" rather than an "abandonment" of a nonconforming use. They interpret "discontinuance" to mean "abandonment" and apply the intent to abandon and overt act rule.

A municipality may attempt to avoid this rule by providing in the zoning ordinance that discontinuance is proof of abandonment whatever the intent of the owner of the nonconforming use. An even more stringent provision states that a nonconforming use is abandoned if it is discontinued for a stated period of time. The time period usually is very short and may range from six months to two years.

Some courts hold that ordinances of this type creates a presumption that the nonconforming use has been abandoned.[273] Other courts go further and interpret these ordinances to mean that proof of intent to abandon is not required when a zoning ordinance provides a nonconforming use may not resume if it is discontinued, although the time period must have run if one is required. In some of these cases, the ordinance provided that proof of intent to abandon was not necessary.[274] The courts seldom consider the constitutional problems raised by this interpretation. An early New York trial court case, *Franmor Realty Corp. v. Le Boeuf*,[275] which is treated as controlling in that state, contains the most detailed discussion of the constitutional issues. The court upheld a zoning ordinance that prohibited the resumption of a nonconforming use after it had been discontinued

---

272. Magnano v. Zoning Bd. of Appeals, 449 A.2d 148 (Conn. 1982); Lewis v. City of Atlantic Beach, 467 So. 2d 751 (Fla. App. 1985); Ernst v. Johnson County, 522 N.W.2d 599 (Iowa 1994) (circumstances beyond control of parties not enough); Union Quarries, Inc. v. Board of County Comm'rs, 478 P.2d 181 (Kan. 1970); Dusdal v. City of Warren, 196 N.W.2d 778 (Mich. 1972); Forsyth County v. Shelton, 329 S.E.2d 730 (N.C. App. 1985); Boles v. City of Chattanooga, 892 S.W.2d 416 (Tenn. App. 1994); 40 A.L.R.4th 1012 (1985); 57 A.L.R.3d 279 (1974); 56 A.L.R.3d 138 (1974); 56 A.L.R.3d 14 (1974). *See also* Villari v. Zoning Bd. of Adjustment, 649 A.2d 98 (N.J. App. Div. 1994) (abandonment sustainable under either intent or objective abandonment test).

273. City of Glendale v. Aldabbagh, 928 P.2d 659 (Ariz. App. 1996); The Ansley House, Inc. v. City of Atlanta, 397 S.E.2d 419 (Ga. 1990).

274. Anderson v. City of Paragould, 695 S.W.2d 851 (Ark. App. 1985); Essex Leasing Co. v. Zoning Bd. of Appeals, 539 A.2d 101 (Conn. 1988) (contains extensive discussion of issue); Smith v. Board of Adj., 460 N.W.2d 854 (Iowa 1990); Ka-Hur Enters., Inc. v. Zoning Bd. of Appeals, 676 N.E.2d 838 (Mass. 1997); Fuller v. City of New Orleans, 311 So. 2d 466 (La. App. 1975); Canada's Tavern, Inc. v. Town of Glen Echo, 271 A.2d 664 (Md. 1970); Marchese v. Norristown Borough Zoning Bd. of Adjustment, 277 A.2d 176 (Pa. Commw. 1971); 57 A.L.R.3d 279 (1974). *See* Toys R Us v. Silva, 676 N.E.2d 862 (N.Y. 1996) (ordinance interpreted to require substantial, not complete, abandonment).

275. 104 N.Y.S.2d 247 (Sup. Ct. 1951), *aff'd*, 109 N.Y.S.2d 525 (App. Div. 1952). *See* Prudco Realty Corp. v. Palermo, 455 N.E.2d 483 (N.Y. 983). *Cf.* Lytle Co. v. Clark, 491 F.2d 834 (10th Cir. 1974); Service Oil Co. v. Rhodus, 500 P.2d 807 (Colo. 1972). *But see* A.T. & G., Inc. v. Zoning Bd. of Review, 322 A.2d 294 (R.I. 1974).

for twelve months. It relied on cases upholding the amortization of noncon-forming uses and the zoning philosophy that favors their gradual elimination.[276]

## § 5.72. Amortization.

Amortization is the most effective zoning technique for eliminating noncon-forming uses. Most amortization provisions require the removal of a noncon-forming use after a stated period of time. Other amortization provisions do not contain a fixed time period but specify the factors a municipality must apply on a case-by-case basis when it amortizes a nonconforming use, such as the original investment in the property and the extent to which it has depreciated.

The constitutional theory that supports amortization is that the amortization period allows the nonconforming user a reasonable period of time to continue his nonconforming use before it is terminated. At that point, the municipality can terminate the nonconforming use without compensation under the police power. The courts do not always require an amortization period that fully amortizes the value of the nonconforming use. Some only require an amortization period that strikes a reasonable balance between the owner's property interest in the non-conforming use and the interest of the municipality in the integrity of its zoning ordinance. Courts that hold amortization unconstitutional view it as an uncon-stitutional termination of property rights.

The success of amortization programs and the time period required for amor-tization vary with the nonconforming use that is amortized. Substantial noncon-forming buildings, such as factories, require substantial amortization periods, and amortization programs applied to them are not always successful. Munici-palities can amortize less substantial structures, such as signs, in a relatively short two- to five-year period. A study of amortization programs indicated that they were most successful when applied to billboards and land-intensive uses, such as junkyards.[277]

Some zoning statutes address the amortization problem. A few authorize the continuation of nonconforming uses and by implication preclude their amortiza-tion.[278] Some states explicitly authorize amortization.[279] In the absence of express statutory authority, some courts hold the statutory authority to zone does not confer the power to amortize nonconforming uses.[280] A statutory delegation of

---

**276.** See also Hartley v. City of Colorado Springs, 764 P.2d 1216 (Colo. 1988) ("intent to abandon" rule makes it difficult to remove nonconforming uses and intent not required in absence of express language to contrary).

**277.** R. Scott, The Effect of Nonconforming Land-Use Amortization (American Planning Ass'n, Planning Advisory Serv. Rep. No. 280, 1972).

**278.** De Mull v. City of Lowell, 118 N.W.2d 232 (Mich. 1962). See also Scottsdale v. Scottsdale Assoc. Merchants, 583 P.2d 891 (Ariz. 1978).

**279.** 65 Ill. Comp. Stat. 5/11-13-1; Utah Code Ann. § 10-9-408(2)(b).

**280.** State v. Bates, 305 N.W.2d 426 (Iowa 1981).

general welfare powers or a constitutional home rule provision may authorize the use of amortization.[281]

### § 5.73. Highway Beautification Act.

Political pressure prevented the use of amortization in the state outdoor advertising control programs authorized by the federal Highway Beautification Act. The act requires the payment of compensation by states and municipalities for the removal of nonconforming signs along federal interstate and primary highways. The compensation requirement prohibits amortization by municipalities. A state could lose ten percent of its federal highway funds if a municipality attempted to remove a nonconforming sign located on one of these highways under an amortization provision.[282] A number of states have adopted legislation that prohibits municipalities from amortizing nonconforming signs on highways covered by the federal act.[283]

### § 5.74. Constitutional.

Early U.S. Supreme Court decisions upholding retroactive single-use zoning suggested that eliminating nonconforming uses retroactively in comprehensive zoning also was constitutional. Early decisions in Louisiana also upheld short amortization periods in comprehensive zoning ordinances.[284] Despite these precedents, the courts adopted the rule that a zoning ordinance cannot apply retroactively to eliminate a nonconforming use.[285] Owners of nonconforming uses argued that amortization is unconstitutional under this rule because a nonconforming use is a vested property right that a municipality can eliminate only by paying compensation.

An early California case rejected this argument in a comprehensive opinion that fully discussed the constitutional issues. *City of Los Angeles v. Gage*[286] upheld a five-year amortization provision the city applied to remove a plumbing

---

**281.** Service Oil Co. v. Rhodus, 500 P.2d 807 (Colo. 1972) (home rule); Naegele Outdoor Adv. Co. v. Village of Minnetonka, 162 N.W.2d 206 (Minn. 1968) (general welfare clause).

**282.** 23 U.S.C. § 131(g). *But see* National Adv. Co. v. City of Ashland, 678 F.2d 106 (9th Cir. 1982) (federal act does not preempt amortization by municipalities).

**283.** City of Ft. Collins v. Root Outdoor Adv., Inc., 788 P.2d 149 (Colo. 1990); Battagliani v. Town of Red River, 669 P.2d 1082 (N.M. 1983). *See also* N.Y. Gen. Mun. Law § 74-c (compensation required for removal of nonconforming signs in industrial and commercial districts; amortization schedule imposed for nonconforming signs outside these districts).

**284.** State ex rel. Dema Realty Co. v. McDonald, 121 So. 613 (La.), *appeal dismissed,* 280 U.S. 656 (1929).

**285.** § 5.68.

**286.** 274 P.2d 34 (Cal. App. 1954). *See also* Tahoe Reg'l Planning Agency v. King, 285 Cal. Rptr. 335 (Cal. App. 1991) (*First English* and *Nollan* do not require change in rule that amortization is constitutional). *See* 8 A.L.R.5th 391 (1992).

supply business conducted in a residential dwelling. The court held that the gradual elimination of nonconforming uses was "a logical and reasonable method" for securing the integrity of residential areas. It pointed out that every zoning ordinance "effects some impairment of property rights ... [either prospectively or retroactively] because it affects property already owned by individuals at the time of its enactment." The court believed there was no distinction between amortization and other methods for eliminating nonconforming uses, such as abandonment provisions or provisions limiting the right of restoration:

> The distinction between an ordinance restricting future uses and one requiring the termination of present uses within a reasonable period of time is merely one of degree, and constitutionality depends on the relative importance to be given to the public gain and the private loss. . . . Use of a reasonable amortization scheme provides an equitable means of reconciliation of the conflicting interests in satisfaction of due process requirements.[287]

The court also noted that the loss suffered by the nonconforming user was spread over a number of years, and that the nonconforming use enjoyed a monopoly position during the amortization period. The Maryland court applied similar reasoning to uphold a five-year amortization period for a nonconforming sign in a case decided soon after *Gage*.[288]

A majority of courts upheld the constitutionality of zoning ordinances that amortized nonconforming uses prior to the Supreme Court's 1987 taking trilogy.[289] These courts did not always accept the reasoning in *Gage* that the distinction between prospective zoning and amortization is a matter of degree.

---

**287.** *Id.* at 44.

**288.** Grant v. Mayor & City Council, 129 A.2d 363 (Md. 1957).

**289.** Art Neon Co. v. City & County of Denver, 488 F.2d 118 (10th Cir. 1973), *cert. denied*, 417 U.S. 932 (1974); Donrey Communications Co. v. City of Fayetteville, 660 S.W.2d 900 (Ark. 1983), *cert. denied*, 466 U.S. 959 (1984); Metromedia, Inc. v. City of San Diego, 610 P.2d 407 (Cal. 1980), *rev'd on other grounds*, 453 U.S. 490 (1981); Mayor & Council v. Rollings Outdoor Adv., Inc., 475 A.2d 355 (Del. 1984); Lamar Adv. Assocs. of E. Fla. v. City of Daytona Beach, 450 So. 2d 1145 (Fla. App. 1984); Village of Glenview v. Velasquez, 463 N.E.2d 873 (Ill. App. 1984) (balancing test); Spurgeon v. Board of Comm'rs, 317 P.2d 798 (Kan. 1957); Naegele Outdoor Adv. Co. v. Village of Minnetonka, 162 N.W.2d 206 (Minn. 1968); University City v. Dively Auto Body Co., 417 S.W.2d 107 (Mo. 1967) (signs); Temple Baptist Church, Inc. v. City of Albuquerque, 646 P.2d 565 (N.M. 1982); Modjeska Sign Studios, Inc. v. Berle, 373 N.E.2d 255 (N.Y. 1977), *appeal dismissed*, 439 U.S. 809 (1978); Goodman Toyota, Inc. v. City of Raleigh, 306 S.E.2d 192 (N.C. App. 1983); Sullivan v. Zoning Bd. of Adjustment, 478 A.2d 912 (Pa. Commw. 1984); Collins v. City of Spartanburg, 314 S.E.2d 322 (S.C. 1984); Rives v. City of Clarksville, 618 S.W.2d 502 (Tenn. App. 1981); Lubbock Poster Co. v. City of Lubbock, 569 S.W.2d 935 (Tex. Civ. App. 1978), *cert. denied*, 444 U.S. 833 (1979); City of Seattle v. Martin, 342 P.2d 602 (Wash. 1959); 22 A.L.R.3d 1134 (1968).

Post-trilogy cases have rejected claims that amortization was a taking under either the per se taking or traditional balancing tests.[290] The courts have also upheld other techniques for removing nonconforming uses, such as a requirement that a nonconforming sign must be removed when a lot is developed.[291] Decisions in the Fourth Circuit since the taking trilogy made it more difficult to uphold the constitutionality of amortization provisions in sign ordinances. *Georgia Outdoor Adv. Co. v. City of Waynesville (II)*[292] attempts to reconcile these decisions. The court held that an amortization provision does not automatically validate or invalidate a sign ordinance but is only one fact to consider in deciding the taking issue. Summary judgment upholding the constitutionality of an amortization provision is proper only in those few cases where there are no facts to try. The court remanded for a new trial.

### § 5.75. Unconstitutional.

Some courts have held amortization unconstitutional if not used to eliminate nuisances. The Indiana Supreme Court held that amortization could not eliminate a nonconforming junkyard that was "continuing and lawful" when a municipality adopted a zoning ordinance.[293] It noted there was no claim that the junkyard was a nuisance. New Hampshire held the amortization of signs unconstitutional if based on aesthetic reasons, but indicated an ordinance that amortized nonconforming signs that are nuisances would be constitutional.[294] The Missouri Supreme Court held that amortization was unconstitutional as applied to open storage uses but held later that the amortization of billboards was constitutional.[295]

The Georgia[296] and Pennsylvania[297] courts held amortization unconstitutional. The Pennsylvania case held that its state constitution mandates the payment of compensation to owners of nonconforming uses that are required to be discon-

---

**290.** Outdoor Graphics, Inc. v. City of Burlington, 103 F.2d 690 (8th Cir. 1996) (no per se taking because plaintiff purchased nonconforming billboard); Lone v. Montgomery County, 584 A.2d 142 (Md. App. 1991) (multi-family dwellings).

**291.** Outdoor Systems, Inc. v. City of Mesa, 997 F.2d 604 (9th Cir. 1993) (held not a per se taking under *Lucas*); Circle K Corp. v. Mesa, 803 P.2d 457 (Ariz. App. 1990).

**292.** 900 F.2d 783 (4th Cir. 1990).

**293.** Ailes v. Decatur County Area Planning Comm'n, 448 N.E.2d 1057 (Ind. 1983), *cert. denied*, 465 U.S. 1100 (1984).

**294.** Loundsbury v. City of Keene, 453 A.2d 1278 (N.H. 1982). *See also* Stoner McCray Sys. v. City of Des Moines, 78 N.W.2d 783 (Iowa 1956) (indicating it would uphold amortization if period of amortization reasonable and nonconforming use endangered health, safety and welfare); Northern Ohio Sign Contractors Ass'n v. City of Lakewood, 513 N.E.2d 324 (Ohio 1987) (amortization constitutional if applied to remove public nuisance).

**295.** Hoffman v. Kinealy, 389 S.W.2d 745 (Mo. 1965). *See* § 5.70, n. 262.

**296.** Lamar Adv. of South Ga., Inc. v. City of Albany, 389 S.E.2d 216 (Ga. 1990).

**297.** Pennsylvania Nw. Distribs., Inc. v. Zoning Hearing Bd., 584 A.2d 1372 (Pa. 1990).

tinued. Amortization is not a substitute, and any requirement that a nonconforming use be terminated without compensation is per se unconstitutional.

### § 5.76. Reasonableness of Amortization Period.

Even though the constitutionality of amortization is well established in principle, constitutional problems can arise when a court is asked to determine whether amortization is constitutional as applied to remove a nonconforming use. Some amortization provisions specify amortization factors the municipality must consider when it determines the length of an amortization period. *Metromedia, Inc. v. City of San Diego*[298] upheld an amortization provision that required amortization in one to four years depending on the "adjusted market value" of a nonconforming sign. The ordinance defined this term as the sign's original cost less ten percent of the original cost for each year the sign was standing prior to the effective date of the ordinance.

Many amortization provisions do not specify amortization factors but require the removal of a nonconforming use after a designated period of years. The courts have upheld the removal of nonconforming signs under amortization periods ranging from three to seven years.[299] When a municipality removes a nonconforming use after the amortization period has expired, a court must decide whether the amortization period is constitutional as applied. In *Metromedia,* for example, the court held that the constitutionality of amortization as applied depends in part on facts peculiar to the nonconforming structure:

> Such facts include the cost of the billboard, its depreciated value, remaining useful life, the length and remaining term of the lease under which it is maintained, and the harm to the public if the structure remains standing beyond the prescribed amortization period.[300]

---

**298.** 610 P.2d 407 (Cal. 1980), *rev'd on other grounds,* 453 U.S. 490 (1981); County of Cook v. Renaissance Arcade & Bookstore, 522 N.E.2d 73 (Ill.) (adult business; one year upheld), *appeal dismissed,* 488 U.S. 882 (1988); Lone v. Montgomery Cty., 584 A.2d 142 (Md. App. 1991) (upholding ten years for multi-family use of dwellings). *See also* Art Neon Co. v. City & County of Denver, 488 F.2d 118 (10th Cir. 1973) (invalidating ordinance basing length of amortization on replacement cost), *cert. denied,* 417 U.S. 932 (1974); La Mesa v. Tweed & Gambrell Planning Mill, 304 P.2d 803 (Cal. App. 1957) (implying amortization must be based on physical life of nonconforming building); Murmur Corp. v. Board of Adjustment, 718 S.W.2d 790 (Tex. App. 1986) (ordinance required amortization based on investment cost of structures).

**299.** Major Media of the Southeast, Inc. v. City of Raleigh, 621 F. Supp. 1446 (E.D.N.C. 1985) (five and one-half years), *aff'd,* 792 F.2d 1269 (4th Cir. 1986), *cert. denied,* 107 S. Ct. 1334 (1987); Hatfield v. City of Fayetteville, 647 S.W.2d 450 (1983) (seven years); County of Cumberland v. Eastern Fed. Corp., 269 S.E.2d 672 (N.C. App. 1980) (three years).

**300.** 610 P.2d at 428. *See* note 281, *supra. See also* National Adv. Co. v. County of Monterey, 464 P.2d 33 (Cal. 1970) (upholding amortization of nonconforming signs which were fully amortized under federal income tax law).

The highest New York court approved similar amortization factors. In *Modjeska Sign Studios, Inc. v. Berle*,[301] the court held that the critical amortization factors were the length of the amortization period in relation to the investment in the nonconforming use and whether the public gain from amortization outweighed the loss suffered by the owner of the nonconforming use. The court held that the owner of the nonconforming use did not have to recover his entire investment but added that he must not suffer a substantial loss. The court held that consideration of the following factors would determine whether the loss was substantial: the owner's initial capital investment, the extent to which that investment had been realized and its life expectancy, the existence or nonexistence of lease obligations, and whether there was a contingency clause allowing the termination of a lease. Other courts approved amortization factors similar to those approved by the California and New York courts.[302]

---

**301.** 373 N.E.2d 255 (N.Y. 1977), *appeal dismissed,* 439 U.S. 809 (1978). *See also* Suffolk Outdoor Adv. Co. v. Town of Southampton, 449 N.Y.S.2d 766 (App. Div. 1982), *aff'd,* 455 N.E.2d 1245 (N.Y. 1983).

**302.** Fisher Buick, Inc. v. City of Fayetteville, 689 S.W.2d 350 (Ark. 1985); Lamar Adv. Assocs. of E. Fla. v. City of Daytona Beach, 450 So. 2d 1145 (Fla. App. 1984); Board of Adjustment v. Winkles, 832 S.W.2d 803 (Tex. App. 1992); Lubbock Poster Co. v. City of Lubbock, 569 S.W.2d 935 (Tex. Civ. App. 1978), *cert. denied,* 444 U.S. 833 (1979). *Compare* Naegele Outdoor Adv. Co. v. Village of Minnetonka, 162 N.W.2d 206 (Minn. 1968) (need not consider right to renew lease) *with* Art Neon Co. v. City & County of Denver, 488 F.2d 118 (10th Cir. 1973) (contra), *cert. denied,* 417 U.S. 932 (1974).

# REFERENCES

## Books and Monographs

R. Babcock & W. Larsen, Special Districts: The Ultimate in Neighborhood Zoning (1990).

J. Butler & J. Getzels, Home Occupation Ordinances, American Planning Ass'n, Planning Advisory Serv. Rep. No. 391 (1985).

A. Cibulskis & M. Ritzdorf, Zoning for Child Care, American Planning Ass'n, Planning Advisory Serv. Rep. No. 422 (1992).

R. Cook, Zoning for Downtown Urban Design (1980).

M. Gellen, Accessory Apartments in Single-Family Housing (1985).

J. Gerard, Local Regulation of Adult Businesses (1997).

J. Getzels & M. Jaffe, Zoning Bonuses in Central Cities, American Planning Ass'n, Planning Advisory Serv. Rep. No. 410 (1988).

P. Hare, Accessory Apartments, American Planning Ass'n, Planning Advisory Serv. Rep. No. 365 (1981).

M. Jaffe, Regulating Videogames, American Planning Ass'n, Planning Advisory Serv. Rep. No. 370 (1982).

M. Jaffe & T. Smith, Siting Group Homes for Developmentally Disabled Persons, American Planning Ass'n, Planning Advisory Serv. Rep. No. 397 (1986).

L. Kendig, New Standards for Nonresidential Uses, American Planning Ass'n, Planning Advisory Serv. Rep. No. 405 (1987).

D. Mandelker & W. Ewald, Street Graphics and the Law (1988).

D. Mandelker, J. Gerard & T. Sullivan, Federal Land Use Law (updated annually).

W. Sanders, Regulating Manufactured Housing, American Planning Ass'n, Planning Advisory Serv. Rep. No. 398 (1986).

W. Sanders, J. Getzels, E. Mosena & J. Butler, Affordable Single-Family Housing, American Planning Ass'n, Planning Advisory Serv. Rep. No. 385 (1984).

J. Schwab, Industrial Performance Standards for a New Century, American Planning Ass'n, Planning Advisory Serv. Rep. No. 444 (1993).

T. Smith, Flexible Parking Requirements, American Planning Ass'n, Planning Advisory Serv. Rep. No. 377 (1983).

C. Weaver & R. Babcock, City Zoning: The Once and Future Frontier (1980).

## Articles

Baers, Zoning Code Revisions to Permit Mixed Use Development, 7 Zoning & Plan. L. Rep. 81 (1984).

Brody, When First Amendment Principles and Local Zoning Regulations Collide, 12 N. Ill. L. Rev. 741 (1992).

Brownstein, Illicit Legislative Motive in the Municipal Land Use Regulation Process, 57 U. Cin. L. Rev. 1 (1988).

Cobb, Amortizing Nonconforming Uses, Land Use L. & Zoning Dig., Vol. 37, No. 1, at 3 (1985).

Dennison, Changing or Expanding Nonconforming Uses, Zoning News, Mar. 1997, at 1.

Dennison, Home Occupations as Accessory Uses, Zoning News, Jan. 1996, at 1.

Duerksen, Modern Industrial Performance Standards: Key Implementation and Legal Issues, 18 Zoning & Plan. L. Rep. 33 (1995).

Edmonds & Merriam, Zoning and the Elderly: Issues for the 21st Century, Land Use L. & Zoning Dig., Vol. 47, No. 3, at 3 (1995).

Gerard, New Developments in the Effective Preclusion of Adult Businesses by Zoning Ordinances, 17 Zoning & Plan. L. Rep. 26 (1994).

Gerencser, Removal of Billboards: Some Alternatives for Local Governments, 31 Stetson L. Rev. 899 (1992).

Jaffe, Performance Zoning: A Reassessment, Land Use L. & Zoning Dig., Vol. 45, No. 9, at 3 (1993).

Jaffe, Redesigning Industrial Performance Standards, Land Use L. & Zoning Dig., Vol. 47, No. 11, at 3 (1995).

Jaffe, Quantum Zoning, Land Use L. & Zoning Dig., Vol. 43, No. 10, at 3 (1991).

Jaffe & Netter, Zoning for Child Day Care Facilities, Land Use L. & Zoning Dig., Vol. 37, No. 2, at 5 (1985).

Kayden, Zoning for Dollars: New Rules For an Old Game? Comments on the *Municipal Art Society* and *Nollan* Cases, 39 Wash. U.J. Urb. & Contemp. L. 3 (1991).

Laycock, Free Exercise and the Religious Freedom Restoration Act, 62 Fordham L. Rev. 883 (1994).

Leitel & Somppi, Perspectives on Group Homes, 4 J. Plan. Literature 357 (1989).

Osborne, Zoning Private and Parochial Schools — Could Local Governments Restrict Socrates and Aquinas, 24 Urb. Law. 305 (1992).

Peterson & McCarthy, Amortization of Legal Land Use Nonconformities as Regulatory Takings: An Uncertain Future, 35 Wash. U.J. Urb. & Contemp. L. 37 (1989).

Pollak, Zoning Matters in a Kinder, Gentler Nation: Balancing Needs, Rights and Political Realities for Shared Residences for the Elderly, 10 St. Louis U. Pub. L. Rev. 501 (1991).

Reynolds, The Reasonableness of Amortization Periods for Nonconforming Uses — Balancing the Private Interest and the Public Welfare, 34 Wash. U.J. Urb. & Contemp. L. 99 (1988).

Roberts, The Regulation of Home Occupations Under Zoning Ordinances: Some Constitutional Considerations, 56 Temp. L. Rev. 49 (1983).

Saxer, When Religion Becomes a Nuisance: Balancing Land Use and Religious Freedom When Activities of Religious Institutions Bring Outsiders into the Neighborhood, 84 Ky. L.J. 507 (1995-1996).

Schoenfeld & Stein, Fighting Municipal "Tag-Team": The Federal Fair Housing Act Amendments Act and Its Use in Obtaining Access to Housing for Persons With Disabilities, 21 Fordham Urb. L.J. 299 (1994).

Sellman, Equal Treatment of Housing: A Proposed Model State Code for Manufactured Housing, 20 Urb. Law. 73 (1988).

Steinman, The Effect of Land-Use Restrictions on the Establishment of Community Residences for the Disabled: A National Study, 19 Urb. Law. 1 (1987).

Strauss & Giese, Elimination of Nonconformities: The Case of Voluntary Discontinuance, 25 Urb. Law. 159 (1993).

The Supreme Court, 1985 Term, 100 Harv. L. Rev. 1, 195 (1986) (*Renton* decision).

Weaver & Duerksen, Central Business District Planning and the Control of Outlying Shopping Centers, 14 Urb. L. Ann. 57 (1977).

Weinstein, Courts Take Close Look at Adult Use Regs, Land Use L. & Zoning Dig., Vol. 46, No. 5, at 3 (1994).

Weinstein, The *Renton* Decision: A New Standard for Adult Business Regulation, 32 Wash. U.J. Urb. & Contemp. L. 91 (1987).

White, State and Federal Planning Legislation and Manufactured Housing: New Opportunities for Affordable, Single-Family Shelter, 28 Urb. Law. 163 (1996).

Ziegler, Shaping Megalopolis: The Transformation of Euclidean Zoning by Special Zoning Districts and Site-Specific Development Review Techniques, 15 Zoning & Plan. L. Rep. 57 (1992).

## Student Work

Note, Behind the Smokescreen: Exclusionary Zoning of Mobile Homes, 25 Wash. U.J. Urb. & Contemp. L. 235 (1983).

Note, Broadway's Newest Hit: Incentive Zoning for Preserving Legitimate Theatres, 3 Cardozo Arts & Ent. L.J. 377 (1984).

Note, The Fair Housing Act Amendments of 1988: New Zoning Rules for Group Homes for the Handicapped, 37 St. Louis U. L.J. 1033 (1993).

Note, Fair Housing Laws and Fear of Adult Family Homes, 18 Seattle U.L. Rev. 425 (1995).

Note, Industrial Zoning to Exclude Higher Uses, 32 N.Y.U. L. Rev. 1261 (1957).

Note, Judicial Acquiescence in Large Lot Zoning: Is It Time to Rethink the Trend? 16 Colum. J. Envtl. L. 183 (1991).

Note, Municipal Antitrust Immunity After *City of Columbia v. Omni Outdoor Advertising, Inc.,* 67 Wash. L. Rev. 479 (1992).

Note, Religion, Zoning, and the Free Exercise Clause: The Impact of *Employment Division v. Smith,* 7 B.Y.U. J. Pub. L. 395 (1993).

Note, Rescuing Manufactured Housing from the Perils of Municipal Zoning Laws, 37 Wash. U.J. Urb. & Contemp. L. 189 (1991).

Note, Sex, Lies, and Prior Restraints: "Sexually Oriented Business" — The New Obscenity, 68 U. Det. L. Rev. 253 (1991).

Note, Zoning Away the Evils of Alcohol, 61 S. Cal. L. Rev. 1373 (1988).

Comment, Challenging Restrictive Family Definitions in Zoning Ordinances: *City of Santa Barbara v. Adamson,* 23 Wash. U.J. Urb. & Contemp. L. 235 (1983).

Comment, Looking Back: The Full-Time Baseline in Regulatory Takings Analysis, 24 B.C. Envtl. Aff. L. Rev. 199 (1996) (discusses amortization).

Comment, *Overlay Zoning, Performance Standards, and Environmental Protection After Nollan,* 16 B.C. Envtl. Aff. L. Rev. 615 (1989).

Comment, Playing the Numbers: Local Government Authority to Apply Use Quotas in Neighborhood Commercial Districts, 14 Ecology L.Q. 325 (1987).

Comment, Zoning Adult Entertainment: A Reassessment of *Renton,* 79 Calif. L. Rev. 119 (1991).

Case Comment, *City of Edmonds v. Oxford House, Inc.:* A Comment on the Continuing
Validity of Single-Family Zoning Restrictions, 71 Notre Dame L. Rev. 829 (1996).

Recent Development, Exclusionary Zoning of Abortion Facilities, 32 Wash. U.J. Urb. &
Contemp. L. 361 (1987).

# Chapter 6

# THE ZONING PROCESS

### § 6.01.  An Introductory Note.

The Standard Zoning Act clearly contemplated a limited use of the zoning process to determine the land uses permitted in a community. The Act authorized municipalities to adopt a zoning text and map designating the land uses permitted in zoning districts "as of right." The only administrative relief it authorized was the authority of the board of adjustment to grant relief from zoning restrictions through variances and special exceptions. Although the Act authorized the local governing body to amend the zoning text and map, it is doubtful that the drafters intended the zoning map amendment to play a major role in the day-to-day administration of the zoning ordinance.

Zoning does not conform to this model. Development usually occurs only when it is authorized through one of the zoning change techniques that are available in the zoning process. Governing bodies frequently adopt zoning map amendments to allow development on single lots. Many boards of adjustment grant zoning variances frequently. Zoning ordinances often contain long lists of special exceptions the board can authorize in the zoning districts where they are allowed. Municipalities have also adopted new zoning techniques to manage zoning change that the Standard Zoning Act did not authorize. They include floating zones and contract zoning.

This chapter reviews the standard and newer zoning techniques that are commonly used in the zoning process, including interim zoning and moratoria. The chapter also considers related doctrines, such as delegation of power, estoppel and vested rights that determine how the zoning process functions. A final section discusses procedural issues in the land use control process. Planned unit development controls, a zoning process in which municipalities approve large-scale residential development, are discussed in Chapter 9.

## A. DELEGATION OF POWER.

### § 6.02.  The Delegation Problem.

Although the U.S. Supreme Court has not held a statute or ordinance unconstitutional as a delegation of legislative power since the 1930s, the delegation doctrine is alive and well in the states. In the zoning cases, most state courts continue to resolve delegation problems by determining whether the standards provided in the zoning ordinance are adequate. A few courts have adopted an alternative doctrine that upholds a delegation of power if the statute or ordinance provides adequate procedural safeguards. They hold that a zoning ordinance has not improperly delegated legislative power if it imposes fact-finding or hearing requirements, or if administrative, legislative, or judicial review of a zoning decision is available.[1]

A municipality may attempt to avoid delegation of power problems by delegating the authority to grant special exceptions or other administrative permits to the legislative body. This alternative is available because the doctrine of separation of powers does not apply at the local level. A local legislative body may exercise administrative functions.

Some courts hold that a legislative body acts legislatively even when it exercises administrative functions and do not require standards for the exercise of these functions.[2] The absence of standards does not mean that administrative determinations by the legislative body are unreviewable. Courts can always review arbitrary and unreasonable decisions and impose standards similar to those they consider appropriate for inclusion in zoning ordinances.[3] The contrary view holds that the character of the function the legislative body exercises is determinative and requires standards for the exercise of administrative functions.[4] Some courts also hold that the legislative body acts quasi-judicially when it considers amendments to the zoning map for individual parcels of land.[5]

A number of communities have experimented with an administrative innovation under which discretionary zoning decisions, such as amendments, variances, and special exceptions, are heard by an appointed hearing examiner. His decision is usually appealable to the legislative body or zoning board. One case held that the use of a hearing examiner was not a delegation of power because the governing body made the "ultimate decision."[6] Statutes in a few states expressly authorize the use of hearing examiners.[7]

---

1. Economy Whsle. Co. v. Rodgers, 340 S.W.2d 583 (Ark. 1960); Ward v. Scott, 93 A.2d 385 (N.J. 1952); Katzin v. McShain, 89 A.2d 519 (Pa. 1952).

2. Kotrich v. County of DuPage, 166 N.E.2d 601 (Ill.), *appeal dismissed,* 364 U.S. 475 (1960); Green Point Sav. Bank v. Board of Zoning Appeals, 24 N.E.2d 319 (N.Y. 1939); Olp v. Town of Brighton, 19 N.Y.S.2d 546 (Sup. Ct. 1940), *aff'd,* 29 N.Y.S.2d 956 (App. Div. 1941).

3. Larkin Co. v. Schwab, 151 N.E. 637 (N.Y. 1926).

4. Wheeler v. Gregg, 203 P.2d 37 (Cal. App. 1949); Osius v. City of St. Clair Shores, 75 N.W.2d 25 (Mich. 1956); State v. Guffey, 306 S.W.2d 552 (Mo. 1957); In re Clements' Appeal, 207 N.E.2d 573 (Ohio App. 1965).

5. § 6.26.

6. West Slope Community Council v. City of Tacoma, 569 P.2d 1183 (Wash. App. 1977).

7. Or. Rev. Stat. § 227.165; Wash. Rev. Code Ann. § 36.70.970.

## § 6.03. Zoning Standards.

The Standard Zoning Act authorized the board of adjustment to grant zoning variances and special exceptions, and state zoning legislation usually includes this grant of authority. State zoning acts follow the Standard Act by authorizing the board to grant variances for "unnecessary hardship," and the courts have held that this statutory standard is adequate.[8]

The special exception, now usually called a special or conditional use, is a use of land authorized in designated zoning districts when approved by the board of adjustment. State zoning acts usually follow the Standard Act by authorizing the board to grant special exceptions "in harmony with ... [the] general purpose and intent" of the zoning ordinance. The Standard Act contemplated the adoption of standards for special exceptions in the zoning ordinance, and courts find an unconstitutional delegation of power if the ordinance does not provide them.[9]

Special exception uses are presumptively compatible with the zoning district in which they are authorized, but the board must review them so it can determine whether they are appropriate in the area in which they plan to locate. Zoning ordinances commonly implement this requirement by authorizing special exceptions when they are compatible with adjacent uses. A negative form of this standard authorizes a denial if the special exception would be a nuisance to its neighbors. A municipality can elaborate a compatibility standard by requiring consideration of the intensity of the use, its impact on traffic congestion and public facilities, and similar factors. Courts usually uphold these standards because they implement the land use compatibility principles on which zoning is based.[10]

---

**8.** Devaney v. Board of Zoning Appeals, 45 A.2d 828 (Conn. 1946); Clarke v. Morgan, 327 So. 2d 769 (Fla. 1976); Gardner v. Harahan, 504 So. 2d 1107 (La. App. 1987); Application of Arlington Village Dev. Corp., 124 N.Y.S.2d 172 (Sup. Ct. 1953), *aff'd,* 128 N.Y.S.2d 596 (App. Div. 1954); Consolidated Mgt., Inc. v. City of Cleveland, 452 N.E.2d 1287 (Ohio 1983); City of Madison v. Clarke, 288 N.W.2d 312 (S.D. 1980); 58 A.L.R.2d 1083 (1958).

**9.** City of St. Petersburg v. Schweitzer, 297 So. 2d 74 (Fla. App. 1974); State v. Waddill, 318 S.W.2d 281 (Mo. 1958); Dooling's Windy Hill v. Zoning Bd. of Adjustment, 89 A.2d 505 (Pa. 1952).

**10.** C & M Sand & Gravel v. Board of County Comm'rs, 673 P.2d 1013 (Colo. App. 1983); Alachua County v. Eagle's Nest Farms, Inc., 473 So. 2d 257 (Fla. App. 1985); Cyclone Sand & Gravel Co. v. Zoning Bd. of Adjustment, 351 N.W.2d 778 (Iowa 1984); Gorham v. Town of Cape Elizabeth, 625 A.2d 898 (Me. 1993) ("adverse effect" criterion); Certain-Teed Prods. Corp. v. Paris Twp., 88 N.W.2d 705 (Mich. 1958); Ours Properties v. Ley, 96 S.E.2d 754 (Va. 1957). *See also* Suddeth v. Forsyth Cty., 373 S.E.2d 746 (Ga. 1988) (ordinance required balancing of costs and benefits as basis for approving airports as special use); Button Gwinnett Landfill, Inc. v. Gwinnett Cty., 353 S.E.2d 328 (Ga. 1987) (delegation of conditional use authority to board of adjustment); Kopietz v. Zoning Bd. of Appeals, 535 N.W.2d 910 (Mich. App. 1995) (upholding standard authorizing change in nonconforming use if "more appropriate to the district"); Save the Pine Bush, Inc. v. City of Albany, 512 N.E.2d 526 (N.Y. 1987) (site plan review standards). *But*

Municipalities sometimes adopt generalized standards that authorize special exceptions when they are in the "public interest," when they serve the "general welfare," or when they are consistent with the "purpose or intent" of the zoning ordinance. Municipalities defend vague standards of this kind by arguing that more specific standards are difficult to draft and that zoning agencies are entitled to exercise discretion when they administer the zoning ordinance. The decisions on the constitutionality of these general standards are divided.[11] Cases that invalidate these standards emphasize the unlimited discretion they confer on zoning agencies. Cases that uphold these standards emphasize the need for flexibility in zoning administration and the difficulty of drafting more precise criteria.

## § 6.04. Delegation to Neighbors.

The Standard Zoning Act required a three-fourths vote by the legislative body to adopt a zoning amendment if it was protested by twenty percent of the owners of the affected or adjacent area.[12] Many state zoning acts and local zoning ordinances contain similar requirements. Most courts hold that this requirement is not an unconstitutional delegation of power. They note that the local legislative body retains the authority to approve or disapprove the amendment, and that amendments require closer scrutiny when landowners who are most affected indicate their objection.[13]

A related delegation to neighbors provision, which is less frequently found in zoning statutes and ordinances, is more troublesome. This provision requires the consent of neighbors for a zoning amendment, variance, or special exception. The cases on the constitutionality of zoning consent provisions are mixed. A trio of early U.S. Supreme Court cases appeared to hold that consent provisions are

---

*see* Hardin County v. Jost, 897 S.W.2d 592 (Ky. App. 1995) (holding invalid ordinance that required development approval under point system); Chandler v. Town of Pittsfield, 496 A.2d 1058 (Me. 1985) (ordinance authorizing board to "consider" or "evaluate" factors held invalid).

**11.** Valid: Burrell v. Lake County Plan Comm'n, 624 N.E.2d 526 (Ind. App. 1993); Schultz v. Board of Adjustment, 139 N.W.2d 448 (Iowa 1966); Mobil Oil Corp. v. City of Clawson, 193 N.W.2d 346 (Mich. App. 1971); Ward v. Scott, 93 A.2d 385 (N.J. 1952); Peachtree Dev. Co. v. Paul, 423 N.E.2d 1087 (Ohio 1981); Town of Richmond v. Murdock, 235 N.W.2d 497 (Wis. 1975). Invalid: Redwood City Company of Jehovah's Witnesses, Inc. v. City of Menlo Park, 335 P.2d 195 (Cal. App. 1959); Clark v. Board of Appeals, 204 N.E.2d 434 (Mass. 1965); Fitanides v. Crowley, 467 A.2d 168 (Me. 1983); Osius v. City of St. Clair Shores, 75 N.W.2d 25 (Mich. 1956); Flynn v. Zoning Bd. of Review, 73 A.2d 808 (R.I. 1950).

**12.** Standard Act, § 5.

**13.** Hope v. City of Gainesville, 355 So. 2d 1172 (Fla. 1978); Bredberg v. City of Wheaton, 182 N.E.2d 742 (Ill. 1962); Northwood Props. Co. v. Perkins, 39 N.W.2d 25 (Mich. 1949). *See also* City of Springfield v. Goff, 918 S.W.2d 786 (Mo. 1996) (home rule city may not modify state statute); Levin v. Township of Parsippany-Troy Hills, 411 A.2d 704 (N.J.1980); Board of Adjustment v. Patel, 887 S.W.2d 90 (Tex. App. 1994) (citizen right to initiate termination of nonconforming use held constitutional); Strucker v. Summit County, 870 P.2d 283 (Utah App. 1994).

valid if they waive a previously applicable zoning restriction, but are invalid if they impose a new zoning restriction.[14]

The distinction between waiver and imposition is not clear, but the state courts that have considered consent provisions have generally followed the U.S. Supreme Court holdings.[15] The state cases sometimes turn on the offensiveness of the use that is subject to the provision. A leading case, *Concordia College Inst. v. Miller*,[16] held that a consent provision is invalid when a landowner proposes an inoffensive use such as an educational building.[17]

## § 6.05. Void for Vagueness.

Legislation that contains vague or ambiguous language violates procedural due process if a court holds it is void for vagueness. The Supreme Court has adopted tests to determine when a law affecting only economic interests is facially challenged as void for vagueness.[18] The law must be vague in all its applications. A plaintiff cannot complain that a law is vague as applied to others, but only as it is applied to it.

Courts hold a land use law void for vagueness when persons of common intelligence must guess at what it requires or forbids,[19] and when a law lacks standards clear enough to prevent arbitrary or discriminatory enforcement,[20] but are

---

**14.** Washington ex rel. Seattle Title Trust Co. v. Roberge, 278 U.S. 116 (1928); Thomas Cusack Co. v. City of Chicago, 242 U.S. 526 (1917); Eubank v. City of Richmond, 226 U.S. 137 (1912). *See* Schulz v. Milne, 849 F. Supp. 708 (N.D. Cal. 1994) (claim of de facto delegation of power to neighbors stated a cause of action).

**15.** Howard Twp. Bd. of Trustees v. Waldo, 425 N.W.2d 180 (Mich. App. 1988) (approving consent requirement but disapproving ordinance because consent of 100 percent of neighbors required); Shannon v. City of Forsyth, 666 P.2d 750 (Mont. 1982); Cary v. City of Rapid City, 559 N.W.2d 891 (S.D. 1997) invalidating statute giving veto power to landowners); Davis v. Blount County Beer Bd., 621 S.W.2d 149 (Tenn. 1981); Williams v. Whitten, 451 S.W.2d 535 (Tex. App. 1970); County of Fairfax v. Fleet Indus. Park Ltd. Pt'ship, 410 S.E.2d 669 (Va. 1991) (invalidating statute giving veto power to landowners); Town of Westford v. Kilburn, 300 A.2d 523 (Vt. 1973); 21 A.L.R.2d 551 (1952). *See also* Rispo Inv. Co. v. City of Seven Hills, 629 N.E.2d 3 (Ohio App. 1993) (relying on right-to-vote cases to uphold city charters requiring approval of zoning change by voters in ward in which property located).

**16.** 93 N.E.2d 632 (N.Y. 1950).

**17.** *See also* Valkanet v. City of Chicago, 148 N.E.2d 767 (Ill. 1958) (home for aged); O'Brien v. City of Saint Paul, 173 N.W.2d 462 (Minn. 1969) (apartments); 21 A.L.R.2d 551 (1952).

**18.** Village of Hoffman Estates v. Flipside, Hoffman Estates, 455 U.S. 489 (1982).

**19.** Arizona v. Zack, 674 P.2d 329 (Ariz. App. 1983); Trice v. City of Pine Bluff, 649 S.W.2d 179 (Ark. 1983); Price v. City of Lakewood, 818 P.2d 763 (Colo. 1991); Gouge v. City of Snellville, 287 S.E.2d 539 (Ga. 1982); City of Council Bluffs v. Cain, 342 N.W.2d 810 (Iowa 1983).

**20.** Fisher v. City of Berkeley, 693 P.2d 261 (Cal. 1976); Miller v. Maloney Concrete Co., 491 A.2d 1218 (Md. App. 1985); Commonwealth v. Jaffe, 494 N.E.2d 1342 (Mass. 1986); West Bloomfield Charter Twp. v. Karchon, 530 N.W.2d 99 (Mich. App. 1995); Alexander v. Town of

generally deferential when reviewing land use laws challenged as vague. They will attempt curative constructions by relying on common meanings or dictionary definitions.[21] If standards are claimed to be imprecise, courts may try to derive precision from their narrow applicability,[22] from related[23] or in pari materia provisions,[24] or from factors enumerated to guide authorities charged with its enforcement.[25] Courts have upheld ordinances regulating signs,[26] home occupations,[27] accessory[28] and nonconforming uses;[29] defining historical significance in historical preservation districts;[30] and establishing front-yard set-back requirements.[31]

Courts engage in heightened scrutiny when a challenged law burdens a substantial amount of constitutionally protected activity[32] or imposes a prohibitory or stigmatizing civil penalty.[33] They most commonly apply heightened scrutiny when the violation of a challenged land use law is a misdemeanor. For example,

Hampstead, 525 A.2d 276 (N.H. 1987); State v. Cameron, 498 A.2d 1217 (N.J. 1985); People v. New York Trap Rock Corp., 442 N.E.2d 1222 (N.Y. 1982).

21. Sellon v. Manitou Springs, 745 P.2d 229 (Colo. 1987) (definition of plat); Life Concepts, Inc. v. Harden, 562 So. 2d 726 (Fla. App. 1990) (compatibility standard); Town of Freeport v. Brickyard Cove Assocs., 594 A.2d 556 (Me. 1991) ("timber harvesting"); Burke v. Denison, 630 N.Y.S.2d 421 (App. Div. 1995) (definition of "take-out" restaurant).

22. Lentine v. Town of St. George, 599 A.2d 76 (Me. 1991).

23. Town of Warren v. Hazardous Waste Facility Site Safety Council, 466 N.E.2d 102 (Mass. 1984); Matter of Save the Pine Bush, Inc. v. City of Albany, 512 N.E.2d 526 (N.Y. 1987).

24. Miami Dolphins, Ltd. v. Metropolitan Dade Cty., 394 So. 2d 981 (Fla. 1981).

25. Charter Township of Canton v. Department of Soc. Servs., 340 N.W.2d 306 (Mich. App. 1983) (group home licensing statute).

26. Asselin v. Town of Conway, 628 A.2d 247 (N.H. 1993) (sign illumination ordinance); J.B. Advertising Co. v. Sign Bd. of Appeals, 883 S.W.2d 443 (Tex. App. 1994) (term "premises" in sign code).

27. City of Los Altos v. Barnes, 5 Cal. Rptr.2d 77 (Cal. App. 1992).

28. City of Parma Heights v. Jaros, 591 N.E.2d 726 (Ohio App. 1990).

29. Smith v. Town of Normal, 605 N.E.2d 727 (Ill. App. 1992); City of Las Vegas v. 1017 S. Main Corp., 885 P.2d 552 (Nev. 1994) (ordinance prohibiting alteration of nonconforming use).

30. South of Second Assocs. v. Georgetown, 580 P.2d 807 (Colo. 1978) ("historical and architectural significance"); Faulkner v. Town of Chestertown, 428 A.2d 879 (Md. 1981) (visible changes to structure); In re Vermont Nat'l Bank, 597 A.2d 317 (Vt. 1991) (local "heritage").

31. Weiner v. City of Los Angeles, 441 P.2d 293 (Cal. 1968); Adams v. Brian, 212 So. 2d 128 (La. App. 1968). See also Mann v. Mack, 202 Cal. Rptr. 296 (Cal. App. 1984) (noise ordinance); Barbarino Realty & Dev. Co. v. Planning & Zoning Comm'n, 610 A.2d 1205 (Conn. 1992) (adequate facilities criteria in subdivision control ordinance); Briggs v. City of Rolling Hills Estates, 47 Cal. Rptr. 2d 29 (Cal. App. 1995) (privacy factor in neighborhood compatibility ordinance); Farley v. Zoning Hearing Bd., 636 A.2d 1232 (Pa. Commw. 1994) (definition of "student" in occupancy ordinance).

32. State v. Jones, 865 P.2d 138 (Ariz. App. 1993); State v. Cameron, 498 A.2d 1217 (N.J. 1985).

33. Village of Hoffman Estates v. Flipside, Hoffman Estates, 455 U.S. 489 (1982). See also ABN 51st Street Partners v. City of New York, 724 F. Supp. 1142 (S.D.N.Y. 1989).

although courts usually uphold zoning ordinances that permit accessory uses "incidental to the use of a premises,"[34] they have struck down such provisions when their violation constitutes a misdemeanor.[35]

A land use regulation may be found unconstitutionally vague even if it does not impose civil penalties. Examples are an ordinance so ambiguous that property owners subject to it could reasonably interpret it three different ways,[36] and design review ordinances.[37]

The vagueness challenge is not available when a party applies for a variance or special exception and fails to secure it.[38] Having made use of the provisions of the zoning ordinance, a party can no longer claim not to know what it prohibits or requires.

## B. MORATORIA AND INTERIM ZONING.

### § 6.06. Purposes and Problems.

Moratoria and interim zoning ordinances are an important part of the zoning process. Local governments often adopt interim zoning ordinances or impose development moratoria when they undertake a comprehensive revision of their zoning ordinance or comprehensive plan. An interim zoning ordinance can allow only new development that is consistent with existing zoning regulations, it can prohibit all development or certain types of intensive development, such as apartments or nonresidential uses, or it can prohibit any development unless it is approved by a local zoning agency.

A municipality may also impose a development moratorium so it can correct inadequate public facilities. The moratorium usually imposes a total or partial ban on new development until adequate facilities are provided. This kind of moratorium is common in growth management programs. Communities also impose moratoria to prevent development in transportation corridors where transportation facilities are planned for construction.[39]

---

**34.** Goode v. City of Dallas, 554 S.W.2d 753 (Tex. Ct. App. 1977).

**35.** Arizona v. Owens, 562 P.2d 738 (Ariz. App. 1977), following Wiley v. County of Hanover, 163 S.E.2d 160 (Va. 1968). *Accord* Miller v. Maloney Concrete Co., 491 A.2d 1218 (Md. App. 1985) (public nuisance prohibition); City of Independence v. Richards, 666 S.W.2d 1 (Mo. App. 1983) ("unsightly" or "annoying" accumulation of rubbish); People v. New York Trap Rock Corp., 442 N.E.2d 1222 (N.Y. 1982) (noise ordinance).

**36.** Lionshead Woods Corp. v. Kaplan Bros., 595 A.2d 568 (N.J.L. Div. 1991).

**37.** Waterfront Estates Dev., Inc., v. City of Palos Hills, 597 N.E.2d 641 (Ill. App. 1992); Anderson v. City of Issaquah, 851 P.2d 754 (Wash. App. 1993). *See also* Potomac Greens Assocs. Pt'ship v. City Council of Alexandria, 761 F. Supp. 416 (E.D. Va. 1991) (traffic management plans); U-Haul Co. v. City of St. Louis, 855 S.W.2d 424 (Mo. App. 1993) (historic preservation).

**38.** Spero v. Zoning Bd. of Appeals, 586 A.2d 590 (Conn. 1991); Bonnell, Inc. v. Board of Adj., 791 P.2d 107 (Okla. Ct. App. 1989).

**39.** *See also* § 10.10.

## § 6.07. Authority to Adopt.

The recent cases have usually implied the authority to adopt interim zoning if the statute does not authorize it.[40] In most of the decisions that did not find an implied power to adopt interim zoning the municipality did not comply with statutory procedural requirements, such as the notice and hearing requirement for the adoption of zoning ordinances.[41] Courts in some of the strong home rule states allow municipalities to adopt interim zoning ordinances under their home rule powers.[42] A growing number of statutes authorize moratoria.[43] These statutes may limit the purposes for which a moratorium may be adopted and place time limits on how long a moratorium can last.

## § 6.08. Constitutionality.

## § 6.09. Revision of Zoning Ordinance or Comprehensive Plan.

The courts have upheld interim zoning ordinances and development moratoria when they are necessary to provide time to comprehensively revise a local plan or zoning ordinance.[44] In most of these cases the municipality adopted interim land use controls for the interim period, but some cases upheld a partial prohibition on new development while the municipality was revising a zoning ordi-

---

**40.** Collura v. Town of Arlington, 329 N.E.2d 733 (Mass. 1975); Almquist v. Town of Marshan, 245 N.W.2d 819 (Minn. 1976); Brazos Land, Inc. v. Board of County Comm'rs, 848 P.2d 1095 (N.M. App. 1993); State ex rel. SCA Chem. Waste Serv. v. Konigsberg, 636 S.W.2d 430 (Tenn. 1982). *Compare* Board of Supvrs. v. Horne, 215 S.E.2d 453 (Va. 1975) (subdivision statute did not authorize moratoria), *with* Matthews v. Board of Zoning Appeals, 237 S.E.2d 128 (Va. 1977) (zoning statute; contra).

**41.** Deighton v. City Council, 902 P.2d 426 (Colo. App. 1995); City of Sanibel v. Buntrock, 409 So. 2d 1072 (Fla. App. 1981); Kline v. City of Harrisburg, 68 A.2d 182 (Pa. 1949); 30 A.L.R.2d 1196 (1970). *But see* Schrader v. Guilford Planning & Zoning Comm'n, 418 A.2d 93 (Conn. Super. 1980).

**42.** Fletcher v. Porter, 21 Cal. Rptr. 452 (Cal. App. 1962). *See* § 4.28.

**43.** Ariz. Rev. Stat. § 9-463.06 (to prevent shortage of essential public facilities in urban and urbanizable areas); Cal. Evid. Code § 669.5; Cal. Gov't Code § 65858; Minn. Stat. Ann. § 394.34 (one year for revision in comprehensive plan or ordinance); N.J. Stat. Ann. § 40:55D-90(b) (for six months when clear and imminent danger to health); Or. Rev. Stat. §§ 197.505-197.540 (facility shortage; must accommodate housing needs); Wash. Rev. Code Ann. § 36.70.790 (no time limit). *See* Bank of the Orient v. Town of Tiburon, 269 Cal. Rptr. 690 (Cal. App. 1990) (statute applies to moratorium adopted by initiative); Minster v. Town of Gray, 584 A.2d 646 (Me. 1990) (authority to adopt under statute allowing moratoria); Davis v. City of Bandon, 805 P.2d 709 (Or. App. 1991) (approving moratorium adopted under statutory authority).

**44.** Metro Realty v. County of El Dorado, 35 Cal. Rptr. 480 (Cal. App. 1963); TPW, Inc. v. City of New Hope, 388 N.W.2d 390 (Minn. App. 1986); Compana v. Clark Twp., 197 A.2d 711 (N.J. 1964); Meadowland Regional Dev. Agency v. Hackensack Meadowlands Dev. Comm'n, 293 A.2d 192 (N.J. App. Div. 1972); Walworth Co. v. City of Elkhorn, 133 N.W.2d 257 (Wis. 1965).

nance.[45] The courts view the interim control as a necessary measure to protect the municipality from development that might be inconsistent with the revised plan or ordinance.

## § 6.10. Inadequate Public Facilities.

The courts have approved development moratoria that municipalities adopted when sewer and other public facilities were inadequate because they prohibited development that could cause environmental damage.[46] *Cappture Realty Corp. v. Board of Adjustment*[47] is a leading case. To provide time to construct flood control facilities, an ordinance prohibited all development in a flood-prone area unless allowed by a special exception permit. An industrial developer who was denied a permit challenged the interim ordinance as unconstitutional. The court held that the ordinance was reasonable in time and that a taking had not occurred.[48]

The courts upheld sewer service moratoria that were in effect for a reasonable period of time to provide an opportunity to remedy inadequate facilities.[49] Environmental moratoria can raise exclusionary zoning problems. In *Associated Home Bldrs. of Greater Eastbay, Inc. v. City of Livermore*,[50] city voters adopted a ban on additional residential building permits unless adequate educational, sewage, and water supply facilities were available. The court held that the rational relationship rather than the strict scrutiny standard of judicial review ap-

---

**45.** Schafer v. City of New Orleans, 743 F.2d 1086 (5th Cir. 1984) (rejecting substantive due process and equal protection objections to moratorium on building permits for fast food restaurants in city neighborhood); Arnold Bernhard & Co. v. Planning & Zoning Comm'n, 479 A.2d 801 (Conn. 1984) (nine-month moratorium on business development in business district); Fischer v. Kellenberger, 392 N.E.2d 733 (Ill. App. 1979) (apartments); Collura v. Town of Arlington, 329 N.E.2d 733 (Mass. 1975) (same).

**46.** Tisei v. Town of Ogunquit, 491 A.2d 564 (Me. 1985); SCA Chem. Waste Serv., Inc. v. Konigsberg, 636 S.W.2d 430 (Tenn. 1982) (hazardous waste); Sun Ridge Dev., Inc. v. City of Cheyenne, 787 P.2d 583 (Wyo. 1990) (drainage).

**47.** 313 A.2d 624 (N.J.L. Div. 1973), *aff'd,* 336 A.2d 30 (N.J. App. Div. 1975).

**48.** *Compare* Westwood Forest Estates, Inc. v. Village of South Nyack, 244 N.E.2d 700 (N.Y. 1969) (invalidating ban on apartments when sewage problem not related to apartment development), *with* Belle Harbor Realty Corp. v. Kerr, 323 N.E.2d 697 (N.Y. 1974) (upholding revocation of building permit because sewers at project site inadequate).

**49.** Kaplan v. Clear Lake City Water Auth., 794 F.2d 1059 (5th Cir. 1986); Ocean Acres, Ltd. Partnership v. Dare County Bd. of Health, 707 F.2d 103 (4th Cir. 1983); Unity Ventures v. County of Lake, 631 F. Supp. 181 (N.D. Ill. 1986), *aff'd on other grounds,* 841 F.2d 770 (7th Cir.), *cert. denied,* 488 U.S. 891 (1988); Smoke Rise, Inc. v. Washington Sub. San. Comm'n, 400 F. Supp. 1369 (D. Md. 1975); Kopetzke v. County of San Mateo Bd. of Supvrs., 396 F. Supp. 1004 (N.D. Cal. 1975); Ungar v. State, 492 A.2d 1336 (Md. 1985), *cert. denied,* 475 U.S. 1066 (1986). *But see* Lockary v. Kayfetz, 917 F.2d 1150 (9th Cir. 1990) (remanding taking and other constitutional claims). *Cf.* Wincamp Partnership v. Anne Arundel County, 458 F. Supp. 1009 (D. Md. 1978).

**50.** 557 P.2d 473 (Cal. 1976).

plied. It remanded the case to determine whether the moratorium unreasonably excluded new growth and development.[51]

## § 6.11. As Applied.

In a large number of cases, landowners prevented from developing their land by interim land use controls have brought constitutional attacks on the interim regulation "as applied" to their property. The courts have held moratoria arbitrary when they did not find a necessity for them.[52] Some of these cases relied on the equities of the landowner's case to hold that the interim control did not apply.[53] Courts are especially inclined to invalidate an interim control as applied if the municipality downzoned the property to prohibit development it permitted before it adopted an interim control ordinance.[54]

Supreme Court statements and cases have an important influence on whether a moratorium is a taking of property.[55] In *First English*[56] the Court held in a moratorium case that temporary restrictions on land use are compensable takings. The Court did not decide whether the moratorium in the case was a taking, and added that the opinion did not deal with the "quite different question" of normal delays in obtaining zoning changes and similar approvals.

The Court's *Lucas*[57] decision changed the basis for reviewing taking attacks on moratoria. The Court held a land use regulation that deprives a landowner of all reasonably beneficial use is a taking per se no matter what purpose the regulation serves. The Court also rejected the rule that a land use regulation that prevents a harm is not a taking.

Most of the pre-*Lucas* cases rejected taking objections to moratoria by holding that the moratorium was adopted to prevent a harm or that the landowner was not denied all reasonable use of her land.[58] Although the harm prevention

---

**51.** *See also* Smoke Rise, Inc. v. Washington Sub. San. Comm'n, 400 F. Supp. 1369 (D. Md. 1975) (rejecting exclusionary objection to the development moratorium).

**52.** Q.C. Constr. Co. v. Gallo, 549 F. Supp. 1331 (D.R.I. 1986), *aff'd mem.* 836 F.2d 1340 (1st Cir. 1987); Pritchett v. Nathan Rodgers Constr. & Realty Corp., 379 So. 2d 545 (Ala. 1979) (case-by-case ban arbitrary); DeKalb County v. Townsend Assocs., 252 S.E.2d 498 (Ga. 1979) (no necessity for moratorium).

**53.** *Compare* Almquist v. Town of Marshan, 245 N.W.2d 819 (Minn. 1976) (valid) *with* Medical Servs., Inc. v. City of Savage, 487 N.W.2d 263 (Minn. App. 1992) (invalid), *and* Alexander v. City of Minneapolis, 125 N.W.2d 583 (Minn. 1963) (same).

**54.** Ogo Assocs. v. City of Torrance, 112 Cal. Rptr. 761 (Cal. App. 1974).

**55.** *See* Agins v. City of Tiburon, 447 U.S. 266 (1980) (mere fluctuations in value during government decision making, absent extraordinary delay, are not a taking).

**56.** § 8.25.

**57.** § 2.17.

**58.** Jackson Ct. Condominiums, Inc. v. City of New Orleans, 874 F.2d 1070 (5th Cir. 1989); Smoke Rise, Inc. v. Washington Sub. San. Comm'n, 400 F. Supp. 1369 (1975); Ungar v. State, 492 A.2d 1336 (Md. 1985), *cert. denied,* 475 U.S. 1066 (1986); Capture Realty Corp. v. Board of

defense is no longer available as a defense in a taking case, a holding that some use remains on land subject to a moratorium prevents the application of the *Lucas* per se taking rule.

The moratorium cases decided after the Supreme Court's 1987 taking trilogy held a taking had not occurred. They held either that the moratorium had not denied all reasonable use of the land, or relied on Supreme Court statements that reasonable delays in government decision making are not a taking.[59] The effect on moratoria of the *Lucas* per se taking rule that applies when all reasonably beneficial use is denied is not yet clear. A Colorado court upheld a moratorium on gaming adopted to give a city time to determine whether it could handle the growth generated by gaming facilities.[60] It held *Lucas* does not apply to land use regulations intended to be temporary. *Lucas* only requires the payment of compensation for the interim period during which a permanent land use ordinance held to be a taking was in effect.

## C. ESTOPPEL AND VESTED RIGHTS.

### § 6.12. The Problem.

Changes in zoning regulations often affect development in progress when the zoning changes are made. A developer may argue that she is entitled to proceed with her development because she has acquired a vested right in the prior zoning or because the municipality is estopped from making the zoning change. Vested rights and estoppel problems have become more serious because residential and other development projects are larger and require more time to complete.

The law of vested rights and estoppel must strike a fine balance between the competing interests of the developer and the municipality. A developer needs some protection from changes in land use requirements that prevent him from completing his project or that make completion more expensive. Municipalities need the freedom to revise their land use requirements to meet new land use

---

Adjustment, 313 A.2d 624 (N.J.L. Div. 1973), *aff'd,* 336 A.2d 30 (N.J. App. Div. 1975). *See also* Golden v. Planning Bd. of Town of Ramapo, 285 N.E.2d 291 (N.Y.), *appeal dismissed,* 409 U.S. 1003 (1972).

59. Moore v. City of Costa Mesa, 886 F.2d 260 (9th Cir. 1989) (delay in development approval did not deny all use of land), *cert. denied,* 496 U.S. 906 (1990); Zilber v. Town of Moraga, 692 F. Supp. 1195 (N.D. Cal. 1988) (rejecting facial taking claim because development not totally prohibited); S.E.W. Friel v. Triangle Oil Co., 543 A.2d 863 (Md. App. 1988); Guinanne v. City & County of San Francisco, 241 Cal. Rptr. 787 (1987), *cert. denied,* 488 U.S. 823 (1988). *But see* Lockary v. Kayfetz, 917 F.2d 1150 (9th Cir. 1990).

60. Williams v. City of Central, 907 P.2d 701 (Colo. App. 1995), following Woodbury Place Partners, Inc. v. City of Woodbury, 492 N.W.2d 258 (Minn. App. 1992) (moratorium for corridor preservation held not a taking; development prohibited only for limited period of time), *cert. denied,* 508 U.S. 960 (1993).

problems or to implement new land use policies.[61] The courts have developed an amorphous body of vested rights and estoppel law that determines when developers are protected from changes in land use regulations. A few states and some municipalities have also adopted statutes and ordinances that provide vested rights protection for developers.

### § 6.13.  The Theory.

Estoppel and vested rights doctrines provide two distinct theories for protecting landowners from changes in zoning regulations.[62] The estoppel doctrine is based in equity. It requires substantial expenditures by a landowner in good faith reliance on some act or omission of the government agency. Vested rights doctrine has a constitutional base. It confers constitutional protection on property rights a landowner has acquired in the use of his land. The factual basis for showing a vested right is the same as the factual basis for proving an estoppel, and courts may apply both theories with identical results.[63] This discussion makes no distinction between these two theories and uses the two terms interchangeably.

### § 6.14.  Governmental Act Requirement.

A landowner may not rely on the protection provided by existing zoning and may not complain when the municipality changes this zoning to his disadvantage. He is protected under the vested rights and estoppel rule only if he relies on an affirmative governmental act by the municipality. This rule arises from the implicit right of government to change its regulatory policy.[64] Some courts relax this rule in the vested rights and estoppel cases or may invalidate a downzoning that affects a landowner's development even if he cannot make an estoppel or vested rights claim.[65]

---

**61.** Carty v. City of Ojai, 143 Cal. Rptr. 506 (Cal. App. 1978); Petrosky v. Zoning Hearing Bd., 402 A.2d 1385 (Pa. 1979).

**62.** Kohn v. City of Boulder, 919 P.2d 822 (Colo. App. 1996) (estoppel claim not a tort claim); City of Key West v. R.L.J.S. Corp., 537 So. 2d 641 (Fla. App. 1989) (vested rights doctrine does not apply to tax increase or impact fees).

**63.** Allen v. City & County of Honolulu, 571 P.2d 328 (Haw. 1977). *But see* Sycamore Realty Co., Inc. v. People's Counsel, 684 A.2d 1331 (Md. 1996) (applying vested rights and rejecting estoppel doctrine).

**64.** Golden Gate Corp. v. Town of Narragansett, 359 A.2d 321 (R.I. 1976).

**65.** §§ 6.36-6.38.

## § 6.15. Building Permit Required.

Most courts hold that a building permit is necessary to provide a basis for a zoning estoppel.[66] *Avco Community Devs., Inc. v. South Coast Regional Comm'n*[67] is a leading case. The court noted that giving estoppel protection to a developer who had not been issued a building permit would impair the right of government to "control land use policy." A few jurisdictions provide absolute protection to the property owner once a building permit is issued.[68] As the *Avco* decision also held, preliminary development approvals preceding a building permit are not enough to provide a basis for a vested rights claim.[69]

## § 6.16. Building Permit Not Required.

Some courts do not require a building permit as the basis for a vested rights claim. They extend vested rights protection to a landowner who was entitled to a building permit when he applied but who was denied a permit because the municipality changed the zoning ordinance after he submitted his application. Some decisions protect the property owner who was entitled to a permit at the time of application, even though he did not substantially rely on his right to a permit by making substantial expenditures.[70] Other courts require substantial reliance.[71] Some decisions do not apply the zoning ordinance retroactively unless it was

---

66. Consaul v. City of San Diego, 8 Cal. Rptr. 2d 762 (Cal. App. 1993); City of Aspen v. Marshall, 912 P.2d 56 (Colo. 1996); Palermo Land Co. v. Planning Comm'n of Calcasieu Parish, 561 So. 2d 482 (La. 1990); Bass River Assocs. v. Mayor of Bass River Twp., 573 F. Supp. 205 (D.N.J. 1983), *aff'd*, 743 F.2d 159 (3d Cir. 1984); County Council v. District Land Corp., 337 A.2d 712 (Md. 1975); Morris v. Postma, 196 A.2d 792 (N.J. 1964); Twin Rocks Watseco Defense Comm. v. Sheets, 516 P.2d 472 (Or. App. 1973); Town of Stephens City v. Russell, 399 S.E.2d 814 (Va. 1991); State ex rel. Humble Oil & Refining Co. v. Wahner, 130 N.W.2d 304 (Wis. 1964); 26 A.L.R.5th 736 (1994). *See aksi* County of Kauai v. Pacific Stds. Life Ins. Co., 653 P.2d 766 (Haw. 1982) (no estoppel; referendum repeal before final discretionary approval given).

67. 553 P.2d 546 (Cal. 1976).

68. Clark v. International Horizons, Inc., 252 S.E.2d 488 (Ga. 1979).

69. *Accord* Zoning Comm'n v. Lescynski, 453 A.2d 1144 (Conn. 1982) (preliminary permits; unauthorized unofficial acts; certificate of occupancy); Denning v. County of Maui, 485 P.2d 1048 (Haw. 1971); Kaloo v. Zoning Bd. of Appeals, 654 N.E.2d 493 (Ill. App. 1995) (oral assurance); Gosselin v. City of Nashua, 321 A.2d 593 (N.H. 1974); Aragon & McCoy v. Albuquerque Nat'l Bank, 659 P.2d 306 (N.M. 1983) (site development plan approval).

70. Folsom Enters. v. City of Scottsdale, 620 F. Supp. 1372 (D. Ariz. 1985); WMM Props., Inc. v. Cobb County, 339 S.E.2d 252 (Ga. 1986); Pokoik v. Silsdorf, 358 N.E.2d 874 (N.Y. 1976) (municipality may not delay action on permit application); Smith v. Winhall Planning Comm'n, 436 A.2d 760 (Vt. 1981).

71. American Nat'l Bank & Trust Co. v. City of Chicago, 311 N.E.2d 325 (Ill. App. 1974) (reviewing Illinois cases); Pure Oil Div. v. City of Columbia, 173 S.E.2d 140 (S.C. 1970).

pending at the time the landowner submitted his application.[72] This rule reflects the equities of zoning estoppel and is sometimes adopted to promote stability in zoning.

Several cases found an estoppel when a municipality changed its zoning solely to frustrate a landowner who was entitled to a permit under existing regulations when he applied for one.[73] The courts find an estoppel in these cases to discipline municipalities that arbitrarily rezone to frustrate a landowner's development plans.

Another group of cases holds that an act by the municipality other than the issuance of a building permit can provide the basis for an estoppel. Some courts estop a municipality when it rezones property at the request of a landowner who relies substantially on the rezoning. A subsequent zoning change is held ineffective.[74] Other cases recognize the realities of zoning administration by holding that a municipality is estopped by informal acts on which a developer substantially relied.[75] In the typical case, the developer makes an inquiry at the zoning office and is told that his development complies with the zoning ordinance. He then relies substantially on this information. Site plan and special exception approvals may also provide the basis for an estoppel.[76] These approvals are similar to the construction approval which is provided by a building permit.

The judicial view that recognizes the right of a developer to vested rights protection prior to the issuance of a building permit is captured in *Western Land Equities, Inc. v. City of Logan.*[77] The court first noted the competing interests

---

72. Smith v. City of Clearwater, 383 So. 2d 681 (Fla. App. 1980); Casey v. Zoning Hearing Bd., 328 A.2d 464 (Pa. 1974). *See also* Ben Lomond, Inc. v. City of Idaho Falls, 448 P.2d 209 (Idaho 1968); 50 A.L.R.3d 596 (1973). *But see* Gulf Oil Corp. v. Township Bd. of Supvrs., 266 A.2d 84 (Pa. 1970) (good faith required).

73. Sunset View Cem. Ass'n v. Kraintz, 16 Cal. Rptr. 317 (Cal. App. 1961); Marmah, Inc. v. Town of Greenwich, 405 A.2d 63 (Conn. 1978); Rockville Fuel & Feed Co. v. City of Gaithersburg, 291 A.2d 672 (Md. 1972); Whitehead Oil Co. v. City of Lincoln (II), 515 N.E.2d 390 (Neb. 1994) (downzoning arbitrary and capricious); Bankoff v. Board of Adjustment, 875 P.2d 1138 (Okla. 1994); Commercial Props., Inc. v. Peternel, 211 A.2d 514 (Pa. 1965); Lake Bluff Housing Partners v. City of South Milwaukee, 525 N.W.2d 59 (Wis. App. 1994).

74. Franklin County v. Leisure Props., Ltd., 430 So. 2d 475 (Fla. App. 1983); Town of Largo v. Imperial Homes Corp., 309 So. 2d 571 (Fla. App. 1975); Benson v. City of DeSoto, 510 P.2d 1281 (Kan. 1973).

75. Nemmers v. City of Dubuque (I), 716 F.2d 1194 (8th Cir. 1983) (road improvement and receptiveness to development); Project Home, Inc. v. Town of Astatula, 373 So. 2d 710 (Fla. App. 1979); Abbeville Arms v. City of Abbeville, 257 S.E.2d 716 (S.C. 1979); 6 A.L.R.2d 960 (1949). *Contra* Colonial Inv. Co. v. City of Leawood, 646 P.2d 1149 (Kan. App. 1982) (advice from planning staff); Howard Township Bd. of Trustees v. Waldo, 425 N.W.2d 180 (Mich. App. 1988) (casual advice from township officials). *See* Healey v. Town of New Durham Zoning Bd. of Adjustment, 665 A.2d 360 (N.H. (1995).

76. Board of Supvrs. v. Medical Structures, Inc., 192 S.E.2d 799 (Va. 1972).

77. 617 P.2d 388 (Utah 1980).

that estoppel and vested rights doctrine must reconcile. Although governments should not impose economic waste on developers by halting projects without a compelling justification, "important public interests . . . may legitimately require interference with planned private development." The court then held

> that an applicant is entitled to a building permit if his proposed development meets the zoning requirements in existence at the time of his application and if he proceeds with reasonable diligence, absent a compelling, countervailing public interest.[78]

The court added that a landowner is not entitled to rely on the original zoning if he applies for a building permit after the municipality has initiated proceedings to amend the zoning ordinance.

Courts may have adopted the building permit rule because it provides a convenient and identifiable governmental act as the basis for a vested rights claim. Decisions relaxing this rule may believe that it tips the scales too heavily against the developer. A municipality can block a development simply by withholding a building permit until it has revised its zoning ordinance. The *Western Land* rule provides more equitable criteria for balancing public and private interests.

## § 6.17. Illegal Building Permit.

A different problem arises when a municipality issues a building permit that is illegal because it was issued in violation of the zoning ordinance. The equities are with the developer if she did not know that the permit was illegal, but estopping the municipality makes it responsible for the illegal acts of its official.

Most courts allow a municipality to revoke an illegally issued building permit, but their reasons differ.[79] Some allow revocation because they hold that the landowner should have known about the zoning restrictions even though the municipality issued a permit. Other courts allow revocation because they hold that a municipality may not waive its right to enforce the zoning ordinance. Some courts protect the developer if she did not know the permit was illegally issued and made expenditures in reliance on it.[80]

---

78. *Id.* at 396.

79. Smith v. County of Santa Barbara, 9 Cal. Rptr. 2d 120 (Cal. App. 1992); Miller v. Board of Adjustment, 521 A.2d 642 (Del. Super. 1986); Corey Outdoor Adv., Inc. v. Board of Zoning Adjustments, 327 S.E.2d 178 (Ga. 1985); Harris Used Car Co. v. Anne Arundel County, 263 A.2d 520 (Md. 1970); Parkview Assocs. v. City of New York, 519 N.E.2d 1372 (N.Y. 1988); Stratford Arms, Inc. v. Zoning Bd. of Adjustment, 239 A.2d 325 (Pa. 1968); Highland Park Community Club v. Zoning Bd. of Adjustment, 475 A.2d 925 (Pa. Commw. 1984); Almeida v. Zoning Bd. of Review, 606 A.2d 1318 (R.I. 1992); City of Hutchins v. Prasifka, 450 S.W.2d 829 (Tex. 1970).

80. Town of West Hartford v. Rechel, 459 A.2d 1015 (Conn. 1983); Saah v. District of Columbia Bd. of Zoning Adjustment, 433 A.2d 1114 (D.C. App. 1981); City of Peru v. Querciagrossa, 392 N.E.2d 778 (Ill. App. 1979); City of Berea v. Wren, 818 S.W.2d 274 (Ky. 1991); Petrosky v.

## § 6.18. Good Faith.

Landowners who want to claim an estoppel or a vested right must also show that they acted in good faith. The courts usually find that a property owner acted in good faith if he proceeded in reliance on his permit at a normal pace in the absence of any indication that a zoning change might occur.[81] The courts hold that a landowner acted in bad faith if he rushed to begin or complete his project with knowledge of a possible zoning change.[82]

Although the good faith rule would seem to require a subjective evaluation of a landowner's conduct, some courts have adopted an objective test of good faith. Under this test, the court asks whether a landowner's conduct was consistent with how a reasonable property owner would have acted in the same circumstances.[83]

A key issue in the bad faith cases is whether a court may infer bad faith from knowledge by the landowner that a revision of the zoning ordinance was pending. The courts are divided on this point, although the "objective" good faith courts are more likely to hold that a landowner acted in good faith in this situation.[84] The courts require some positive indication that a revision of the zoning ordinance was contemplated before they will hold that knowledge of a pending revision is bad faith. Mere knowledge of pending studies, or a landowner's expectation that political change might bring a revision of the ordinance, may not be enough.[85] A court may also require the municipality to act on a pending revision without unreasonable delay.[86]

---

Zoning Hearing Bd., 402 A.2d 1385 (Pa. 1979); Abbeville Arms v. City of Abbeville, 257 S.E.2d 716 (S.C. 1979). *See also* § 8.21.

**81.** Aries Dev. Co. v. California Coastal Zone Conservation Comm'n, 122 Cal. Rptr. 315 (Cal. App. 1975); Deshotel v. Calcasieu Parish Police Jury, 323 So. 2d 155 (La. App.), *aff'd,* 326 So. 2d 371 (La. 1976); Price v. Smith, 207 A.2d 887 (Pa. 1965); 49 A.L.R.3d 13 (1973).

**82.** Stowe v. Burke, 122 S.E.2d 374 (N.C. 1961); A.J. Aberman, Inc. v. City of New Kensington, 105 A.2d 586 (Pa. 1954).

**83.** Carty v. City of Ojai, 143 Cal. Rptr. 506 (Cal. App. 1978); Graham Corp. v. Board of Zoning Appeals, 97 A.2d 564 (Conn. 1953); Bosse v. City of Portsmouth, 226 A.2d 99 (N.H. 1967). *Contra* Miller v. Dassler, 155 N.Y.S.2d 975 (Sup. Ct. 1956).

**84.** Bad faith not found: Kasparek v. Johnson County Bd. of Health, 288 N.W.2d 511 (Iowa 1980); Yocum v. Power, 157 A.2d 368 (Pa. 1960). Bad faith found: Smith v. City of Clearwater, 383 So. 2d 681 (Fla. App. 1980); Morris v. Postma, 196 A.2d 792 (N.J. 1964); Clackamas County v. Holmes, 508 P.2d 190 (Or. 1973); Boron Oil Co. v. L.C. Kimple, 284 A.2d 744 (Pa. 1971).

**85.** Sakolsky v. City of Coral Gables, 151 So. 2d 433 (Fla. 1963); Application of Campsites Unlimited, Inc., 215 S.E.2d 73 (N.C. 1975).

**86.** Boron Oil Co. v. L.C. Kimple, 284 A.2d 744 (Pa. 1971). *See* Hill v. Zoning Hearing Bd., 626 A.2d 510 (Pa. 1993) (municipality, not neighbors, must decide whether pending ordinance applies).

The courts are also divided on the effect of an appeal by the landowner on his estoppel or vested rights claim.[87] The cases that hold against the landowner in this situation emphasize that the right to appeal would be meaningless if a landowner could assert a vested right based on activity undertaken during the appeal period.

### § 6.19. Detrimental Reliance.

Detrimental reliance is the final element necessary for proof of an estoppel claim. Most courts require substantial reliance by the developer, usually through substantial expenditures on actual construction. This is a judicial rule of convenience that requires some visible and substantial act as the basis for an estoppel. The rule has no other justification. Some courts have adopted a more flexible balancing test that does not require actual construction but turns on the equities of the developer's commitment to his project.

### § 6.20. Substantial Reliance Test.

The cases have adopted three versions of the substantial reliance test. A majority hold that the landowner must have devoted a "set quantum" of expenditures to the project.[88] The courts never indicate precisely how much expenditure is necessary to meet the "set quantum" test, and some courts avoid this dilemma by adopting a "ratio" test. This test requires that the expenditures devoted to the project must represent a substantial percentage of the total project cost.[89] A few cases reject both tests. They adopt a "balancing" test under which the expenditures made on a project are only one factor to consider. The court adopted a balancing test in a leading New Jersey case, in which it found an estoppel when a municipality revoked a building permit and changed the zoning ordinance to stop the plaintiff's development:

> The ultimate objective is fairness to both the public and the individual property owner. We think there is no profit in attempting to fix some precise concept of the nature and *quantum* of reliance which will suffice. Rather a balance must be struck between the interests of the permittee and

---

87. *Compare* Grandview Baptist Church v. Zoning Bd. of Adjustment, 301 N.W.2d 704 (Iowa 1981) (landowners barred) *with* Petty v. Barrentine, 594 S.W.2d 903 (Ky. App. 1980) (contra on facts).

88. Gackler Land Co. v. Yankee Springs Twp., 398 N.W.2d 393 (Mich. 1986); Town of Orangetown v. Magee, 665 N.E.2d 1061 (N.Y. 1996) (serious loss); 38 A.L.R.5th 737 (1996).

89. City of Rochester v. Barcomb, 169 A.2d 281 (N.H. 1961); Waterman v. Kaufman, 221 N.Y.S.2d 526 (Sup. Ct. 1961). *Contra* Clackamas County v. Holmes, 508 P.2d 190 (Or. 1973).

the right and duty of the municipality . . . [to implement planning and zoning for the general welfare].[90]

Attempts at precise formulations like the set quantum and ratio rules consider only the amount of expenditure made by the developer and do not consider the impact of the zoning change on his development. A zoning change that imposes a marginal additional cost, such as an increase in a setback, may not substantially affect the developer's return even though he has made a substantial expenditure on the project. Conversely, a developer who has made a minimal expenditure may face severe costs if the zoning change is substantial. Courts that concentrate on the amount of expenditure ignore this problem. The balancing test is preferable because it allows a court to consider the before-and-after impact of a zoning change.

### § 6.21. What Reliance Is Required.

Most courts require actual physical construction before they will find an estoppel,[91] but how much progress must be made in actual construction is not clear. Completion of a building is usually sufficient,[92] but the courts divide on whether excavation of the site is enough.[93] Developers have even less luck with less substantial commitments to their projects. The courts are likely to find that site preparation short of excavation is not sufficient.[94] They may find preliminary contractual and financial obligations sufficient but hold that other prelimi-

---

**90.** Whitehead Oil Co. v. City of Lincoln, 451 N.W.2d 702 (Neb. 1990); Tremarco Corp. v. Garzio, 161 A.2d 241, 245 (N.J. 1960) (emphasis in original). *See also* Nott v. Wolf, 163 N.E.2d 809 (Ill. 1960); Clackamas County v. Holmes, 508 P.2d 190 (Or. 1973).

**91.** Phoenix City Council v. Canyon Ford, Inc., 473 P.2d 797 (Ariz. App. 1970); County Council v. District Land Corp., 337 A.2d 712 (Md. 1975); Gruber v. Mayor & Twp. Comm., 186 A.2d 489 (N.J. 1962); Beeshos Restaurant, Inc. v. State Liquor Auth., 281 N.Y.S.2d 720 (Sup. Ct. 1967). *Contra* Town of Paradise Valley v. Gulf Leisure Corp., 557 P.2d 532 (Ariz. App. 1976) (citing cases); Town of Hillsborough v. Smith, 170 S.E.2d 904 (N.C. 1969).

**92.** Township of Pittsfield v. Malcolm, 134 N.W.2d 166 (Mich. 1965); Price v. Smith, 207 A.2d 887 (Pa. 1965). *See* Village of Palatine v. LaSalle Nat'l Bank, 445 N.E.2d 1277 (Ill. App. 1983) (completion of first phase of multi-phase project entitled developer to building permits for completion of project).

**93.** Sufficient: Boise City v. Blaser, 572 P.2d 892 (Idaho 1977); Prince George's County v. Blumberg, 407 A.2d 1151 (Md. 1979); Pemberton v. Montgomery County, 340 A.2d 240 (Md. 1975). Not sufficient: Verner v. Redman, 271 P.2d 468 (Ariz. 1954); Prince George's County v. Sunrise Dev. Ltd. Partnership, 623 A.2d 1296 (Md. 1993); Gackler Land Co. v. Yankee Springs Twp., 398 N.W.2d 393 (Mich. 1986); Kiges v. City of St. Paul, 62 N.W.2d 363 (Minn. 1953).

**94.** Not sufficient: Weiner v. City of Los Angeles, 441 P.2d 293 (Cal. 1968); Heath Twp. v. Sall, 502 N.W.2d 627 (Mich. 1993); County Council v. District Land Corp., 337 A.2d 712 (Md. 1975); County of Saunders v. Moore, 155 N.W.2d 317 (Neb. 1967); Sufficient: Griffin v. County of Marin, 321 P.2d 148 (Cal. App. 1958); Pure Oil Div. v. City of Columbia, 173 S.E.2d 140 (S.C. 1970); H.R.D.E., Inc. v. Zoning Officer, 430 S.E.2d 341 (W. Va. 1993).

nary expenditures are not enough.[95] Most courts do not usually find an estoppel when the only expenditure is the cost of purchasing the land.[96]

This summary is a fair reading of the case law, but generalization is difficult. The developer usually relies on more than one category of expenditure, the court does not always indicate how much expenditure is sufficient, and the equitable basis for an estoppel claim makes an evaluation of the decisions difficult. The judicial requirement of some tangible commitment to the project is clear. The application of this rule may be unfair when the developer makes substantial commitments sufficient to show a change in position but falls short of actual construction. An example is the developer who makes substantial expenditures on preliminary approvals, site plans, and other preliminary stages, only to find the rules of the game changed when the municipality revokes his permit and revises the zoning regulations.

### § 6.22. Statutory and Ordinance Protection.

The unsatisfactory state of estoppel and vested rights law has led some municipalities and states to adopt vested rights provisions in their zoning ordinances and statutes. A Washington statute grants vested rights to a landowner on the date he files a valid and fully complete building application for a structure permitted under the zoning or other land use control ordinances. The statute codifies existing vested rights law.[97]

A New Jersey statute protects an applicant who receives preliminary subdivision or site plan approval from any change in use requirements, and generally from any requirements applicable to layout or design, for three years.[98] Health

---

**95.** Carson v. Miller, 370 So. 2d 10 (Fla. 1979); Mattson v. City of Chicago, 411 N.E.2d 1002 (Ill. App. 1980); Stone v. City of Wilton, 331 N.W.2d 398 (Iowa 1983); Brackett v. City of Des Moines, 67 N.W.2d 542 (Iowa 1954); Robert L. Rieke Bldg. Co. v. City of Olathe, 697 P.2d 72 (Kan. App. 1985); Thomas v. Zoning Bd. of Appeals, 381 A.2d 643 (Me. 1978); Murrell v. Wolff, 408 S.W.2d 842 (Mo. 1966).

**96.** Anderson v. City Council, 40 Cal. Rptr. 41 (Cal. App. 1964); Sgro v. Howarth, 203 N.E.2d 173 (Ill. App. 1964); Union Oil Co. v. Board of County Comm'rs, 724 P.2d 341 (Or. App. 1986); Daniels v. City of Goose Creek, 431 S.E.2d 256 (S.C. App. 1993). *But see* Tremarco Corp. v. Garzio, 161 A.2d 241 (N.J. 1960) (premium paid); Gulf Oil Corp. v. Township Bd. of Supvrs., 266 A.2d 84 (Pa. 1970). *See also* Raum v. Board of Supvrs., 370 A.2d 777 (Pa. Commw. 1977) (carrying costs).

**97.** Wash. Rev. Code Ann. § 19.27.095. *See* Erickson & Assoc. v. McLerban, 872 P.2d 1090 (Wash. 1994); Valley View Indus. Park v. City of Richmond, 733 P.2d 182 (Wash. 1987). *See also* City of Portland v. Fisherman's Wharf Assocs. (II), 541 A.2d 160 (Me. 1988); FM Props. Operating Co. v. City of Austin, 93 F.3d 167 (5th Cir. 1996); Tex. Gov't Code § 481.143(a) (permit approval to be based on regulations in effect on date of application).

**98.** N.J. Stat. Ann. § 40:55D-49. *See* Board of Comm'rs v. Toll Bros., 607 A.2d 824 (Pa. Commw. 1992) (developer protected under similar statute from increase in water and sewer connection fees). *See also* Ariz. Rev. Stat. §§ 9-1202, 11-1202 (protects rights established in protected

and safety regulations are excepted. A Colorado law protects developers for three years after local approval of a site-specific plan.[99]

A Massachusetts law protects the holder of a building or special permit from a zoning change if the permit was granted before notice was given of the zoning change, if construction began within six months after the permit was issued and proceeded as continuously and expeditiously as possible.[100] Some zoning ordinances contain similar vested rights provisions.[101]

Commencement of construction and similar requirements in vested rights provisions create interpretive problems similar to those that arise under judicial vested rights doctrine, although the language of the protective provision influences the court's decision. With this qualification, the cases are again divided on whether commencement of construction or preliminary work such as excavation is sufficient to secure vested rights protection.[102] The courts require good faith diligence in the completion of construction when reasonable diligence is required by the vested rights provision or when it imposes a time period for completion.[103]

Under an alternative method of vested rights protection, the municipality provides an administrative procedure for granting exemptions when the zoning ordinance is changed. The ordinance can utilize an existing zoning technique, such as the special exception, or can create a new procedure. The ordinance should provide criteria for the vested rights determination. Possibilities include an "extraordinary hardship" or "reasonableness" standard that balances the need for landowner protection against the need to protect the integrity of newly adopted zoning requirements.

---

development right plan); N.C. Gen. Stat. § 153A-344.1 (approved site-specific development plan protected for two years).

**99.** Colo. Rev. Stat. §§ 24-68-101 to 24-68-106 (municipality must reimburse developer for expenses incurred in development if change in law makes development impossible). *See* Villa at Greely, Inc. v. Hopper, 917 P.2d 350 (Colo. App. 1996) (interpreting exception to vested rights claim).

**100.** Mass. Gen. Laws ch. 40A, § 6 (also protects approved subdivision for eight years).

**101.** *Compare* West Main Assocs. v. City of Bellevue, 720 P.2d 782 (Wash. 1986) (holding local vested rights provision unconstitutional) *with* Comparo v. Woodbridge Twp., 222 A.2d 28 (N.J. App. Div. 1966) (contra).

**102.** Must commence construction: First Nat'l Bank & Trust v. City of Rockford, 361 N.E.2d 832 (Ill. App. 1977); Murphy v. Crosby, 298 N.E.2d 885 (Mass. App. 1973); Prince George's County v. Equitable Trust Co., 408 A.2d 737 (Md. 1970). Preliminary work enough: O'Neill v. Burns, 198 So. 2d 1 (Fla. 1967); Williams v. Wofford, 140 S.E.2d 190 (Ga. 1965). *See also* Temkin v. Karagheuzoff, 313 N.E.2d 770 (N.Y. 1974); 49 A.L.R.3d 1150 (1973).

**103.** League to Save Lake Tahoe v. Crystal Enters., 490 F. Supp. 995 (D. Nev. 1980); Papalia v. Inspector of Bldgs., 217 N.E.2d 911 (Mass. 1966); City of Monett v. Buchanan, 411 S.W.2d 108 (Mo. 1967).

## § 6.23. Development Agreements.

Several states protect developers from zoning change by authorizing the execution of development agreements between a developer and a municipality. The California law is illustrative.[104] It authorizes agreements that specify permitted uses and densities and the maximum height and size of buildings. The agreement must also include provisions for the reservation or dedication of land for public purposes. The Florida law requires agreement between the parties on the responsibility for and timing of public facilities.[105]

Under the California law, the development of the property must comply with use, density, design, improvement, and construction standards applicable at the time the agreement is executed unless it provides otherwise. The agreement may authorize subsequent discretionary action by the municipality if it does not prevent development that complies with the agreed uses, densities or intensities. It may also provide that the developer must commence or complete construction within a specified period of time. The municipality must review the agreement every twelve months. It may terminate or modify the agreement if it finds that the developer has not complied with it in good faith.

Development agreements raise a number of constitutional questions. The courts have upheld agreements in which a landowner agrees to annex to a municipality in return for a municipality's promise to provide public services, especially when the agreement is authorized by a statute.[106] These cases support the constitutionality of similar provisions in development agreements. The constitutionality of development agreements that freeze existing land use restrictions is more doubtful. A court could hold that a freeze on land use restrictions is an unconstitutional bargaining away of the police power.[107]

---

**104.** Cal. Gov't Code §§ 65864-65869.5. *See also* Fla. Stat. Ann. §§ 163.3220-163.3243; Hawaii Rev. Stat. §§ 46-121 to 46-132; La. Rev. Stat. Ann. §§ 33:4781.21-33:4781.33; Nev. Rev. Stat. §§ 278.0201-278.0207; Or. Rev. Stat. § 95.504; S.C. Code Ann. §§ 6-31-10 to 6-31-160.

**105.** Fla. Stat. Ann. § 163.3227(1)(d).

**106.** Morrison Homes Corp. v. City of Pleasanton, 130 Cal. Rptr. 196 (Cal. App. 1976); Carruth v. City of Medera, 43 Cal. Rptr. 855 (Cal. App. 1965).

**107.** Delucchi v. County of Santa Cruz, 225 Cal. Rptr. 43 (Cal. App.) (zoning freeze in agricultural land preservation agreement would be invalid), *appeal dismissed and cert. denied,* 497 U.S. 803 (1986); City of Louisville v. Fiscal Court, 621 S.W.2d 219 (Ky. 1981) (annexation agreement in which city agreed to "assist and cooperate fully" in rezoning held invalid); City of New York v. 17 Vista Assocs., 642 N.E.2d 606 (N.Y. 1994) (agreement to expedite decision on development in return for payment of money to low income housing trust held invalid). *But see* Union Nat'l Bank v. Village of Glenwood, 348 N.E.2d 226 (Ill. App. 1976) (annexation agreement authorized by statute may limit land to existing zoning); Mayor & City Council v. Crane, 352 A.2d 786 (Md. 1976) (city bound by agreement providing for density increase in exchange for donation of land to city executed by developer). *See also* §§ 6.64-6.67 (contract and conditional zoning).

However, a federal court has held a city can guarantee density and retain review of design features of a development without surrendering control of its land use power.[108]

## D. ZONING MAP AMENDMENTS.

### § 6.24. The Zoning Problem.

The Standard Zoning Enabling Act authorized the local governing body to amend the zoning ordinance.[109] State zoning acts contain comparable provisions, and the typical zoning ordinance authorizes the local governing body to make zoning text and map amendments. This section discusses the zoning map amendment. A map amendment changes the zoning regulations for a tract of land by reclassifying it to a different zoning classification.

Legal remedies to challenge a refusal to rezone and a zoning map amendment are quite different. The map amendment process is legislative in most states, so a refusal to rezone cannot be appealed. An action for declaratory judgment or injunction can be brought by a landowner whose application for a map amendment is refused.[110] Neighboring landowners can bring a similar suit to challenge a rezoning map amendment.

### § 6.25. Refusals to Rezone.

A landowner's action that challenges a refusal to rezone does not challenge the refusal directly but rather the restrictive zoning that was not amended.[111] The usual attack is an as-applied attack that claims the existing restrictive zoning is a taking of property. State courts in these cases utilize the usual rules that apply to as-applied taking cases.[112] They usually require a showing that the existing zoning has left the landowner without an economically viable use of his property,[113] but some state courts apply a balancing test in as-applied taking cases.[114] Landowners who succeed in these cases usually cannot obtain a decree rezoning their land for the more intensive use they proposed.[115]

---

**108.** Stephens v. City of Vista, 994 F.2d 650 (9th Cir. 1993). *Accord* Save Elkhart Lake, Inc. v. Village of Elkhart Lake, 512 N.W.2d 202 (Wis. App. 1993) (village agreed to cooperate and extend good faith in attempting to make agreement successful).

**109.** Standard Zoning Enabling Act §§ 4, 5.

**110.** §§ 8.14, 8.15.

**111.** F.S. Plummer Co. v. Town of Cape Elizabeth, 612 A.2d 856 (Me. 1992); Copple v. City of Lincoln, 315 N.W.2d 628 (Neb. 1982).

**112.** § 2.34.

**113.** *Cf.* Iowa Coal Mining Co. Inc. v. Monroe County, 494 N.W.2d 664 (Iowa 1993).

**114.** D'Addario v. Planning & Zoning Comm'n, 593 A.2d 511 (Conn. App. 1991); § 2.35.

**115.** § 8.17.

Landowners can also bring an as-applied taking case in federal court, but these cases are not likely to succeed if the zoning restriction attacked has not deprived the landowner of all economically viable use.[116] Landowners can also bring a substantive due process challenge in federal court, but the federal courts usually apply the presumption of constitutionality to uphold refusals to rezone.[117]

## § 6.26. The Quasi-Judicial View.

The courts review zoning map amendments more rigorously if they hold that a rezoning is a quasi-judicial, rather than a legislative, act. The Oregon Supreme Court's decision in *Fasano v. Board of County Comm'rs*[118] is a leading case adopting the quasi-judicial view. The presumption of constitutionality accorded legislative actions disappears when a court holds a rezoning quasi-judicial, and the proponent of the zoning amendment has the burden of proof to justify the zoning change. The legislative body must also adopt adjudicative procedures for zoning changes and make adequate findings of fact.

The reception of *Fasano* in other states has been mixed. Several states have also held that the zoning amendment process is quasi-judicial, and they apply this characterization to rezoning denials as well as approvals.[119] The reasons for holding that the zoning amendment process is quasi-judicial vary. The Oregon court believed this rule would limit destructive piecemeal zoning changes adopted in response to pressures from developers. The Idaho Supreme Court adopted a somewhat different rationale:

> The great deference given true legislative action stems from its high visibility and widely felt impact, on the theory that appropriate remedy can be had at the polls. . . . This rationale is inapposite when applied to a local zoning body's decision as to the fate of an individual's application [to] rezone. Most voters are unaware or unconcerned that fair dealing and con-

---

116. Baytree of Inverrary Realty Partners v. City of Lauderhill, 873 F.2d 1407 (11th Cir. 1989).

117. Pearson v. City of Grand Blanc, 961 F.2d 1211 (6th Cir. 1992); Jacobs, Visconsi & Jacobs Co. v. City of Lawrence, 927 F.2d 1111 (10th Cir. 1991); South Gwinnett Venture v. Pruitt, 491 F.2d 5 (5th Cir.), *cert. denied,* 419 U.S. 837 (1974).

118. 507 P.2d 23 (Or. 1973). *See* § 2.47.

119. New Castle Cty. Council v. BC Dev. Assocs., 567 A.2d 1271 (Del. 1989); Snyder v. Board of Cty. Comm'rs, 627 So. 2d 469 (Fla. 1993) (extensive review of issues); Golden v. City of Overland Park, 584 P.2d 130 (Kan. 1978); City of Louisville v. McDonald, 470 S.W.2d 173 (Ky. 1971); Woodland Hills Conservation Ass'n v. City of Jackson, 443 So. 2d 1173 (Miss. 1983) (change-mistake and public need test make rezoning quasi-judicial); West Old Town Neighborhood Ass'n v. City of Albuquerque, 927 P.2d 529 (N.M. App. 1996); Fleming v. City of Tacoma, 502 P.2d 327 (Wash. 1972).

sistent treatment may have been sacrificed in the procedural informality which accompanies action deemed legislative.[120]

A respectable number of courts rejected the *Fasano* rule and continue to follow the majority rule that a zoning map amendment is legislative.[121] *Arnel Dev. Co. v. City of Costa Mesa*[122] is a leading California case that rejected the *Fasano* rule, although the court did not discuss it. The voters adopted a downzoning of a fifty-acre single-family and multi-family development by initiative. Because the initiative process is available only for legislative acts, the court had to determine whether downzoning a mixed-use development of this size was legislative or quasi-judicial.

The court reaffirmed the "generic" classifications it had previously adopted, which classify zoning actions depending on the nature of the zoning process. This approach classifies zoning amendments as legislative and variances and special permits as adjudicative. The court noted that any other classification, such as a classification based on the size of the parcel or the number of landowners affected, would create uncertainty because courts would have to apply it on a case-by-case basis. The court believed that the public interest in "rational and orderly land-use planning" was adequately protected by the statutory plan coexistence requirement and by a regional general welfare requirement for zoning it had previously adopted.

Courts hold a zoning action is quasi-judicial when it affects specific individuals and requires the application of previously-adopted policy to the fact situation presented to a governmental body.[123] Difficulties arise in applying this test. In *Neuberger v. City of Portland*[124] the city rezoned a 601-acre parcel of land to a more intensive single-family residential density. The court held the rezoning quasi-judicial, but not without difficulty. It noted that a land use decision is quasi-judicial "when a particular action by a local government is directed at a

---

120. Cooper v. Board of County Comm'rs, 614 P.2d 947 (Idaho 1980). *See also* American Law Institute, Model Land Development Code § 2-312.

121. South Gwinnett Venture v. Pruitt, 491 F.2d 5 (5th Cir.), *cert. denied,* 419 U.S. 837 (1974); Wait v. City of Scottsdale, 618 P.2d 601 (Ariz. 1980); Hall Paving Co. v. Hall County, 226 S.E.2d 728 (Ga. 1976); Montgomery Cty. v. Woodward & Lothrop, 376 A.2d 483 (Md. 1977), *cert. denied,* 434 U.S. 1067 (1978); State v. City of Rochester, 268 N.W.2d 885 (Minn. 1978); Quinlan v. City of Dover, 614 A.2d 1057 (N.H. 1992); Hampton v. Richland County, 357 S.E.2d 463 (S.C. 1987); Bell v. City of Elkhorn, 364 N.W.2d 144 (Wis. 1985).

122. 620 P.2d 565 (Cal. 1980).

123. Cherry Hills Resort Dev. Co. v. City of Cherry Hills Village, 757 P.2d 622 (Colo. 1988); Raynes v. Leavenworth, 821 P.2d 1204 (Wash. 1992). *See* Wash. Rev. Code Ann. § 42.36.010.

124. 603 P.2d 771 (Or. 1979). *See also* Stuart v. Board of County Comm'rs, 699 P.2d 978 (Colo. App. 1985) (comprehensive plan amendment held not quasi-judicial when development and its impact not known).

relatively small number of identifiable persons, and when that action also involves the application of existing policy to a specific factual setting."[125]

A zoning determination also is quasi-judicial if "the process is bound to result in a decision." The court held that the zoning ordinance in this case satisfied this test because it required quasi-judicial procedures. It then considered whether the rezoning was legislative because it was a "free choice among competing policies" or quasi-judicial because it was the "application of existing policy." The court concluded that both kinds of decision making were present. The rezoning required major policy determinations because it was large and would have a substantial impact on municipal services. It was quasi-judicial because it required the application of the statutory zoning criteria as well as state-wide planning goals adopted by a state agency.

*Arnel* and *Neuberger* indicate the trade-offs courts must make when they must decide how they should characterize the zoning process. A holding that the process is legislative allows the voters to adopt zoning amendments by initiative and referendum but makes judicial review more difficult. A holding that the process is quasi-judicial allows more rigorous judicial review but makes the initiative and referendum process unavailable.[126] The court in *Arnel* held that rezoning is legislative because it believed that initiatives and referenda on individual rezoning actions were unlikely.

## § 6.27. "Spot" Zoning.

### § 6.28. Definitions.

Probably no term in zoning jurisprudence is used more frequently by the courts and is less understood than "spot" zoning. Zoning statutes and ordinances authorize amendments to the zoning map without differentiating between "spot" and other types of rezonings. A "spot zoning" is a zoning map amendment that rezones a tract of land from a less intensive to a more intensive use district. Spot zoning comes under attack because objectors believe it confers a zoning "favor" on a single landowner without justification.

The courts have adopted a definition of spot zoning that they use to decide spot zoning cases. Although the definitions vary, the definition adopted by a Texas Court of Appeals is typical. It held that the term spot zoning is descriptive of the process of singling out a small parcel of land for a use classification different and inconsistent with the surrounding area, for the benefit of the owner of

---

**125.** 603 P.2d at 775.

**126.** *But see* Margolis v. District Court, 638 P.2d 297 (Colo. 1981) (rezoning subject to referendum though held quasi-judicial when judicially reviewed). *See also* §§ 6.79-6.83 (discussing initiative and referendum).

such property and to the detriment of the rights of other property owners.[127] The Texas Supreme Court adopted a similar definition and added that spot zoning "is piecemeal zoning, the antithesis of planned zoning."[128]

### § 6.29. The Standard Tests.

These definitions highlight the equal protection objection to spot zoning. They also modify the presumption of constitutionality that courts usually apply to zoning map amendments. The courts apply the presumption of constitutionality to uphold a zoning map amendment that comprehensively covers all or a substantial part of a municipality.[129] Courts are suspicious of spot zonings because of their potential for abuse and will aggressively review a spot-zoning amendment to determine whether it meets constitutional and statutory requirements.

The basis for a constitutional attack on spot zoning is unclear. Because a spot zoning is an upzoning to a more intensive use, the landowner usually is satisfied and will not bring a taking claim. An action challenging the spot zoning is usually brought by neighbors. They cannot claim a taking based on a more intensive use of neighboring property. Their objection is that the spot zoning violates equal protection because it arbitrarily favors a single landowner.[130] Courts examine the public purposes for a spot zoning to determine whether they overcome the claim of arbitrary action. Objecting neighbors can also claim that a spot zoning violates the statutory requirement that zoning must be "in accordance" with a comprehensive plan because it is arbitrary.[131]

Spot zoning definitions contain spatial and non-spatial zoning criteria that courts apply to determine whether a spot zoning is invalid. These definitions indicate that a spot zoning is invalid if it covers a small parcel of land and is inconsistent with the surrounding area. This criterion is spatial. They also indicate that a spot zoning is invalid because it confers a private benefit and injures other property owners.[132] This criterion is non-spatial.

---

**127.** Burkett v. City of Texarkana, 500 S.W.2d 242, 244 (Tex. Civ. App. 1973). *See also* Griswold v. City of Homer, 925 P.2d 1015 (Alaska 1996).

**128.** City of Pharr v. Tippitt, 616 S.W.2d 173 (Tex. 1981).

**129.** Mraz v. County Comm'rs, 433 A.2d 771 (Md. 1981); Fasano v. Board of County Comm'rs, 507 P.2d 23 (Or. 1973).

**130.** *See also* Clawson v. Harborcreek Twp. Zoning Hearing Bd., 304 A.2d 184 (Pa. Commw. 1973) (due process).

**131.** §§ 3.13-3.18.

**132.** Lee v. District of Columbia Zoning Comm'n, 411 A.2d 635 (D.C. App. 1980); Goodrich v. Town of Southampton, 355 N.E.2d 297 (N.Y. 1976); Cannon v. Murphy, 600 N.Y.S.2d 965 (App. Div. 1993); City of Rusk v. Cox, 665 S.W.2d 233 (Tex. App. 1984); Anderson v. Island County, 501 P.2d 594 (Wash. 1972); 51 A.L.R.2d 263 (1957).

Many courts elaborate these criteria by adopting a balancing test under which they weigh the benefits of a spot zoning to the public against its detriments to other landowners. A court can uphold a spot zoning under the balancing test if it finds that its benefits outweigh its detriments.[133] A court may add that a spot zoning must be "in accordance" with the comprehensive plan, as required by many zoning statutes.[134] The "in accordance" requirement means that a court must find an acceptable planning or zoning purpose for a spot zoning that overcomes the objection that it is arbitrary. This requirement does not necessarily mean that the spot zoning must be consistent with the planning policies in a comprehensive plan.

The criteria that apply to spot zoning are flexible and provide guidelines rather than rigid rules. Not all rezonings for small parcels are necessarily invalid, and not all rezonings for large parcels are necessarily valid.[135] The courts usually require consistency with surrounding land uses and zoning, but inconsistency is not necessarily fatal.[136] Recent cases have emphasized that spot zoning rules are flexible, and that "spot zoning" is merely a descriptive term. The ultimate test is the reasonableness of the zoning as determined by a number of factors such as compatibility with surrounding uses and consistency with the comprehensive plan.[137]

---

133. Woodland Estates, Inc. v. Building Inspector of Methuen, 358 N.E.2d 468 (Mass. App. 1976); Boland v. City of Great Falls, 910 P.2d 890 (Mont. 1996); Randolph v. Town of Brook-haven, 337 N.E.2d 763 (N.Y. 1975); Godfrey v. Union County Board of Comm'rs, 300 S.E.2d 273 (N.C. App. 1983); Galanes v. Town of Brattleboro, 388 A.2d 406 (Vt. 1978). *Compare* Covington v. Town of Apex, 423 S.E.2d 537 (N.C. App. 1992) (held invalid).

134. Luery v. Zoning Bd. of City of Stamford, 187 A.2d 247 (Conn. 1962); Bosse v. City of Portsmouth, 226 A.2d 99 (N.H. 1967); Palisades Props., Inc. v. Brunetti, 207 A.2d 523 (N.J. 1965).

135. Griswold v. City of Homer, 925 P.2d 1015 (Alaska 1996) (7.29 acres; held valid); Fifteen Fifty N. State Bldg. Corp. v. City of Chicago, 155 N.E.2d 97 (Ill. 1959) (single tract; held invalid); McWhorter v. City of Winnsboro, 525 S.W.2d 701 (Tex. Civ. App. 1975) (5.29 acres; held valid); Chrobuck v. Snohomish County, 480 P.2d 489 (Wash. 1971) (635 acres; held invalid).

136. Little v. Winborn, 518 N.W.2d 384 (Iowa 1994) (rezoning small parcel in agricultural zone to nonagricultural uses held spot zoning); Tennison v. Shomette, 379 A.2d 187 (Md. App. 1978) (suggesting inconsistency not always required); Sharp v. Zoning Hearing Bd., 628 A.2d 1223 (Pa. Commw. 1993) (rezoning extended preexisting institutional use in accordance with plan); Bell v. City of Elkhorn, 364 N.W.2d 144 (Wis. 1985) (upholding spot zoning consistent with adjacent uses and zoning).

137. Watson v. Town Council, 805 P.2d 641 (N.M. App. 1991); Chrismon v. Guilford Cty., 370 S.E.2d 579 (N.C. 1988) (citing this treatise); Baker v. Chartiers Tp. Zoning Hearing Bd., 677 A.2d 1274 (Pa. Commw. 1996); Smith v. Town of St. Johnsbury, 554 A.2d 233 (Vt. 1988).

### § 6.30. The Public Need and Public Purpose Tests.

Courts often rely on a public need for a land use allowed by a spot zoning to reject a claim that it arbitrarily confers a benefit on a landowner. A court can find the basis for a public need in a comprehensive plan but must base this determination on its own *ad hoc* judgment if a comprehensive plan does not exist. This judicial attitude distinguishes the spot zoning from the "as-applied" taking cases, where the public need to be served by a landowner's proposed use is not a factor in the taking decision.

The courts have upheld spot zonings in which the municipality rezoned land to a more intensive multi-family use because of a need for multi-family development in the community as indicated by a housing shortage.[138] As one court pointed out in a decision upholding a rezoning from single-family detached to single-family row house dwellings:

> [Z]oning decisions which allow the erection of apartments in districts previously classified for construction of detached residential dwellings only are not disturbed by appellate courts when a need for housing exists and injury to the land is minimal.[139]

Courts adopt a similar analysis in spot zoning cases in which a municipality rezones land from residential to commercial use in order to provide for commercial facilities. A court may consider the need for such facilities as a factor that supports the commercial rezoning.[140] It may also consider a need to broaden an area's employment base as a factor supporting the rezoning.[141]

Incompatibility with surrounding land uses may defeat a spot zoning, even if it serves a public need. A need for employment opportunities, for example, may

---

**138.** Malafronte v. Planning & Zoning Bd., 230 A.2d 606 (Conn. 1967); Miles v. Dade County Bd. of County Comm'rs, 260 So. 2d 553 (Fla. App. 1972); Decuir v. Town of Marksville, 426 So. 2d 766 (La. App. 1983) (housing shortage); State v. City of Rochester, 268 N.W.2d 885 (Minn. 1978); Fallin v. Knox County Bd. of Comm'rs, 656 S.W.2d 338 (Tenn. 1983). *See also* Ballenger v. Door County, 388 N.W.2d 624 (Wis. App. 1986) (upholding text amendment allowing ferry terminals in resort commercial district). *But see* Coughlin v. City of Topeka, 480 P.2d 91 (Kan. 1971).

**139.** Lee v. District of Columbia Zoning Comm'n, 411 A.2d 635, 642 (D.C. App. 1980).

**140.** *Compare* Griswold v. City of Homer, 925 P.2d 1015 (Alaska 1996) (held valid), *and* Bartram v. Zoning Comm'n of City of Bridgeport, 68 A.2d 308 (Conn. 1949) (same) *with* Kuehne v. Town Council, 72 A.2d 474 (Conn. 1950) (contra); 51 A.L.R.2d 263 (1957); 76 A.L.R.2d 172 (1961). *See also* Protect Hamden/North Haven From Excessive Traffic & Pollution, Inc. v. Planning & Zoning Comm'n, 600 A.2d 757 (Conn. 1991) (upholding text amendment for shopping centers).

**141.** Save Our Rural Env't v. Snohomish County, 662 P.2d 816 (Wash. 1983). *See also* Save a Neighborhood Env't v. City of Seattle, 676 P.2d 1006 (Wash. 1984) (subsidized housing).

not justify a spot zoning for an industrial use in a residential neighborhood.[142] A court may uphold a spot zoning that serves a public need if the parcel is large enough that the developer can avoid compatibility problems through a buffer and landscaping. A rezoning for a large regional shopping center is an example,[143] especially if it extends an existing commercial zone.[144]

### § 6.31. The Change-Mistake Rule.

A change-mistake rule for zoning map amendments, first adopted in Maryland and later exported to a few other states, provides more control on spot zoning than the traditional spot zoning rules. A court will uphold a zoning map amendment under the change-mistake rule only if it is based on a change in conditions in the surrounding neighborhood or a mistake in the original zoning. This rule stabilizes existing zoning by making it more difficult to secure piecemeal changes. Although the change-mistake rule does not mean that existing zoning classifications are immutable, it clearly gives objecting neighbors much greater leverage when they object to piecemeal amendments to a zoning ordinance.

In addition to Maryland,[145] a few other states have adopted the change-mistake rule.[146] Other courts rely on evidence of changed conditions when they consider a zoning amendment even though they have not adopted this rule.[147] Some courts have rejected the change-mistake rule.[148]

Unless there is a mistake in the zoning ordinance, the change-mistake rule limits zoning map amendments to cases where some change in the area surrounding the rezoned parcel has occurred. The change is usually an intensification in land use. The change-mistake rule requires the court to make a planning

---

**142.** Fritts v. City of Ashland, 348 S.W.2d 712 (Ky. 1961) (industrial rezoning). *See also* §§ 5.38-5.42 (control of competition problem).

**143.** Willott v. Village of Beachwood, 197 N.E.2d 201 (Ohio 1964).

**144.** McNaughton v. Boeing, 414 P.2d 778 (Wash. 1966).

**145.** The leading case is Wakefield v. Kraft, 96 A.2d 27 (Md. 1953). *See also* MacDonald v. Board of County Comm'rs, 210 A.2d 325 (Md. 1965). *See* Md. Ann. Code art. 66B, § 4.05(a) (codifies rule).

**146.** Zoning Comm'n v. New Canaan Bldg. Co., 148 A.2d 330 (Conn. 1959); Lewis v. City of Jackson, 184 So. 2d 384 (Miss. 1966); Miller v. City of Albuquerque, 554 P.2d 665 (N.M. 1976); Hayden v. City of Port Townsend, 613 P.2d 1164 (Wash. 1980). *See also* Ky. Rev. Stat. § 100.213(1) (must show substantial change in area involved if rezoning not consistent with plan); City of Beechwood Village v. Council of & City of St. Matthews, 574 S.W.2d 322 (Ky. 1978).

**147.** King's Mill Homeowners Ass'n v. City of Westminster, 557 P.2d 1186 (Colo. 1976); Lanner v. Board of Appeal, 202 N.E.2d 777 (Mass. 1964).

**148.** Dye v. City of Phoenix, 542 P.2d 31 (Ariz. App. 1975); Conner v. Shellburne, Inc., 281 A.2d 608 (Del. 1971); Oka v. Cole, 145 So. 2d 233 (Fla. 1962); Levitt v. Incorporated Village of Sands Point, 174 N.Y.S.2d 283 (Sup. Ct. 1958).

judgment to determine whether the changed conditions justify the rezoning. In apartment zoning cases, for example, the Maryland court has had to determine whether apartments provide an appropriate buffer zone, whether highways can properly divide different land uses, and whether improved public facilities justify the rezoning.[149]

In Maryland, a municipality may not defend a zoning map amendment by arguing that it is justified by a change in municipal land use policy. In *Chapman v. Montgomery County Council*,[150] the county rezoned a 5.8-acre parcel for a neighborhood convenience shopping center to avoid the expansion of a nearby shopping center, which the comprehensive plan did not favor. The court disapproved the amendment, even though the population in the area had grown substantially. Population growth, the court held, would justify a rezoning to higher residential densities but would not support a shopping center rezoning. States that apply the change-mistake rule may also shift the burden of proof to the proponent of an amendment.[151]

### § 6.32. Consistency with the Comprehensive Plan.

Much of the judicial concern with spot zoning arises from a belief that piecemeal rezoning undercuts the community's comprehensive planning and zoning policies. The change-mistake rule and the quasi-judicial view of zoning amendments are judicial attempts to avoid this problem by securing more judicial control over the rezoning process. A number of states take a direct approach to this problem by requiring zoning to be consistent with the comprehensive plan.[152] A court may require consistency with a comprehensive plan if the municipality has adopted one, even in states that do not have a consistency requirement.[153]

---

**149.** Palermo Land Co. v. Planning Comm'n of Calcasieu Parish, 561 So. 2d 482 (La. 1990) (citing cases rejecting rule); Brown v. Wimpress, 242 A.2d 157 (Md. 1968); Park Constr. Corp. v. Board of County Comm'rs, 227 A.2d 15 (Md. 1967). *See* D. Mandelker, The Zoning Dilemma 87-105 (1971).

**150.** 271 A.2d 156 (Md. 1970). *But see* Bjarnson v. Kitsap County, 899 P.2d 1290 (Wash. App. (1995) (change-mistake rule does not apply when rezoning implements comprehensive plan).

**151.** Pattey v. Board of County Comm'rs, 317 A.2d 142 (Md. 1974); Hughes v. Mayor & Comm'rs of City of Jackson, 296 So. 2d 689 (Miss. 1974); Parkridge v. City of Seattle 573 P.2d 359 (Wash. 1978). *Compare* West Ridge, Inc. v. McNamara, 160 A.2d 907 (Md. 1960) (contra). *See* Buckel v. Board of Cty. Comm'rs, 562 A.2d 1297 (Md. App. 1989) (reconciling change-mistake and fairly debatable rules).

**152.** §§ 3.16-3.18.

**153.** Webb v. Giltner, 468 N.W.2d 838 (Iowa App. 1991) (compliance required); Watson v. Town Council, 805 P.2d 641 (N.M. App. 1991).

## § 6.33. Zoning.

The courts apply the consistency requirement by upholding refusals to re-zone[154] and rezonings[155] that are consistent with a comprehensive plan and by invalidating rezonings and upholding refusals to rezone that are inconsistent with a comprehensive plan.[156] Judicial review to determine consistency with the plan requires judicial interpretation of planning policy, which may be inconsistent or ambiguous. Although courts often defer to a municipality's interpretation, they will review the policies in the plan and disagree with its interpretation if they decide it was incorrect.[157] There is a trend toward treating a rezoning subject to a consistency requirement as a quasi-judicial act that requires more stringent judicial review.[158]

In *Green v. Hayward*,[159] a county adopted a rezoning to allow a lumber mill to expand its operations. The court upheld the rezoning even though the county plan designated the area for agricultural uses to implement an urban containment policy. The court held that the plan indicated the "broad allocation" of land uses but did not "put a limit on the permissible uses of each and every tract within"

---

154. F.S. Plummer Co. v. Town of Cape Elizabeth, 612 A.2d 856 (Me. 1992).

155. Griswold v. City of Homer, 925 P.2d 1015 (Alaska 1996); Spenger, Grubb & Assocs. v. City of Hailey, 903 P.2d 741, (Idaho 1995); Holmgren v. City of Lincoln, 256 N.W.2d 686 (Neb. 1977); Watson v. Town Council, 805 P.2d 641 (N.M. App. 1991); Cleaver v. Board of Adjustment, 200 A.2d 408 (Pa. 1964); Bjarnson v. County of Kitsap, 899 P.2d 1290 (Wash. App. 1995) (need not be changed circumstances when rezoning consistent with plan). *See also* Greenebaum v. City of Los Angeles, 200 Cal. Rptr. 237 (Cal. App. 1984) (approval of tract map); Vella v. Town of Camden, 677 A.2d 1051 (Me. 1996) (text amendment expanding commercial uses).

156. Mira Dev. Co. v. City of San Diego, 252 Cal. Rptr. 825 (Cal. App. 1988) (rezoning held consistent with land use plan but violated adequate public facilities policy); Green v. County Council, 508 A.2d 882 (Del. Ch.) (rezoning held contrary to plan), *aff'd per curiam*, 516 A.2d 480 (Del. 1986); City of Mounds View v. Johnson, 377 N.W.2d 476 (Minn. App. 1985) (refusal to rezone consistent with plan); Gillis v. City of Springfield, 611 P.2d 355 (Or. App. 1980) (rezoning held contrary to plan); Board of Supvrs. v. Jackson, 269 S.E.2d 381 (Va. 1980) (refusal to rezone held consistent with plan); Petersen v. Dane County, 402 N.W.2d 376 (Wis. App. 1987) (same). *See also* deBottari v. Norco City Council, 217 Cal. Rptr. 790 (Cal. App. 1985) (cannot hold referendum on zoning ordinance that would be inconsistent with plan); Amcon Corp. v. City of Eagan, 348 N.W.2d 66 (Minn. 1984) (refusal to give rationale for not following plan when denying rezoning held "evidence of arbitrary action").

157. Alluis v. Marion County, 668 P.2d 1242 (Or. App. 1983); Miller v. Council of City of Grants Pass, 592 P.2d 1088 (Or. App. 1979). *See also* Bridger Canyon Property Owners' Ass'n v. Planning & Zoning Comm'n, 890 P.2d 1268 (Mont. 1995) (plan must be internally consistent).

158. Snyder v. Board of County Comm'rs, 627 So. 2d 469 (Fla. 1993); Love v. Board of City Comm'rs, 671 P.2d 471 (Idaho 1983) (council must make specific findings on consistency); Nattress v. Land Use Regulation Comm'n, 600 A.2d 391 (Me. 1991); Smith v. Town of St. Johnsbury, 554 A.2d 233 (Vt. 1988).

159. 552 P.2d 815 (Or. 1976). For similar holdings see Haines v. City of Phoenix, 727 P.2d 339 (Ariz. App. 1986); Las Virgnenes Homeowners Fed'n, Inc. v. County of Los Angeles, 223 Cal. Rptr. 18 (Cal. App. 1986); LaBonta v. City of Waterville, 528 A.2d 1262 (Me. 1987).

the area. One or a few statements in a plan should not be used "in isolation as justification for a rezoning decision."

The court next considered a set of "minimum location standards" for industrial development in areas not shown for industrial development in the plan. It upheld the rezoning even though it was not convinced that findings by the county board showed compliance with these standards. The court noted that the plant expansion would be compatible with adjacent uses and would not disrupt neighborhood continuity because it was an expansion of an existing use.

These cases indicate that requiring zoning to be consistent with a comprehensive plan may give the courts rather than municipalities the final authority to interpret planning policy. The courts may also refuse to give effect to a plan if it is outdated,[160] and may uphold a rezoning that is inconsistent with a plan if the previous restriction was arbitrary.[161]

When a plan proposes a use for a tract of land that is different from the use permitted by the zoning ordinance, a question arises whether its owner may compel a rezoning that complies with the use proposed by the plan. In *Baker v. City of Milwaukie*,[162] the comprehensive plan showed a density for a tract of land that was lower than the density permitted by the zoning ordinance. The Oregon court ordered the city to downzone the property to the density specified in the plan. Later Oregon cases refused to order upzonings to comply with a land use designation in a plan. They held that the municipality has the discretion to determine when it will approve an upzoning, at least when the plan does not contain guidelines indicating when more intensive uses in compliance with the plan should occur.[163]

### § 6.34.  Spot Planning.

A municipality can evade the consistency requirement by changing the land use designation in a plan for a tract of land so that it is consistent with a zoning map amendment it would like to adopt, a practice known as spot planning. Some courts condone "spot planning" by upholding an amendment to a comprehensive

---

160. Security Nat'l Bank v. City of Olathe, 589 P.2d 589 (Kan. 1979); Town of Bedford v. Village of Mount Kisco, 306 N.E.2d 155 (N.Y. 1973).

161. Ferguson v. Board of County Comm'rs, 718 P.2d 1223 (Idaho 1986). *See also* Holmes v. Planning Bd. of Town of New Castle, 433 N.Y.S.2d 587 (Sup. Ct. 1980) (requiring plan to include implementation program to implement complex planning policies).

162. 533 P.2d 772 (Or. 1975).

163. Clinkscales v. City of Lake Oswego, 615 P.2d 1164 (Or. App. 1980); Marracci v. City of Scappoose, 552 P.2d 552 (Or. App. 1976). *Accord* Mira Dev. Co. v. City of San Diego, 252 Cal. Rptr. 825 (Cal. App. 1988) (California consistency statute does not affect city's discretionary zoning decisions); Bone v. City of Lewiston, 693 P.2d 1046 (Idaho 1984). *But see* Nova Horizon, Inc. v. City Council, 769 P.2d 721 (Nev. 1989) (council decision refusing to rezone in accordance with plan held improper).

plan made at the same time as a zoning amendment.[164] Other courts review a plan amendment to determine whether it is consistent with other elements in the plan.[165] In some of these states, the courts hold that the amendment of a plan is a quasi-judicial act.

The Hawaii Supreme Court adopted substantive limitations on plan amendments in *Dalton v. City & County of Honolulu*.[166] The council amended its plan and zoning ordinance on the same day to allow a medium-density residential development. The court invalidated the amendments because the council did not refer them to the planning commission and planning director for advice, as its charter required.[167] The court also held the plan amendments required new studies that showed a need for additional housing and that the site selected was the "best site" available.

Some states and municipalities attempt to control spot planning by limiting the number of times a plan can be amended each year.[168] This limitation requires a municipality to consider the cumulative effect of a group of plan amendments at one time and avoid piecemeal changes that may undercut the plan. Some zoning ordinances impose similar requirements. They allow the governing body to consider zoning amendments only at stated times during the year or require frequent comprehensive rezonings on a cyclical schedule.[169]

### § 6.35. Effect on Adjacent Communities.

In some cases, a rezoned tract is located on the border of the municipality that rezones it. In this situation, some courts invalidated commercial rezonings that were inconsistent with land uses in the adjacent community. They upheld commercial rezonings that were consistent with uses in the adjacent community, even though the uses surrounding the rezoned site in the community that adopted the rezoning were residential.[170]

---

**164.** Weigel v. Planning & Zoning Comm'n, 278 A.2d 766 (Conn. 1971); Donahue v. Zoning Bd. of Adjustment, 194 A.2d 610 (Pa. 1963).

**165.** Karlson v. City of Camarillo, 161 Cal. Rptr. 260 (Cal. App. 1980); South of Sunnyside Neighborhood League v. Board of Comm'rs, 569 P.2d 1063 (Or. 1977); Marggi v. Ruecker, 533 P.2d 1372 (Or. App. 1975). *Compare* Wolff v. Dade County, 370 So. 2d 839 (Fla. App. 1979).

**166.** 462 P.2d 199 (Haw. 1969).

**167.** *See also* Colorado Leisure Prods., Inc. v. Johnson, 532 P.2d 742 (Colo. 1975); Houser v. Board of Comm'rs, 247 N.E.2d 670 (Ind. 1969); Save Our Rural Env't v. Snohomish County, 662 P.2d 816 (Wash. 1983).

**168.** Cal. Gov't Code § 65358(b).

**169.** Coppolino v. County Bd. of Appeals, 328 A.2d 55 (Md. 1974).

**170.** Liberty Nat'l Bank of Chicago v. City of Chicago, 139 N.E.2d 235 (Ill. 1957); Huttig v. City of Richmond Heights, 372 S.W.2d 833 (Mo. 1963); Borough of Cresskill v. Borough of Dumont, 104 A.2d 441 (N.J. 1954).

The Washington Supreme Court adopted a "regional general welfare" test for commercial rezonings in *Save a Valuable Env't (SAVE) v. City of Bothell*.[171] An environmental organization challenged a rezoning for a major regional shopping center in an outlying agricultural and low-density residential area of the city. The court struck down the rezoning and noted that the shopping center would have "serious detrimental effects" on areas outside the city's jurisdiction. It held the municipality must consider the "welfare of the entire affected community" if a rezoning may have serious environmental effects outside its jurisdiction. The court found the shopping center would have adverse impacts on surrounding agricultural and low-density development, create a demand for new public facilities, and cause flooding.

## § 6.36. Downzoning.

### § 6.37. The Standard Tests.

Downzoning is the reverse of upzoning and rezones land to a less intensive use. Downzoning has become more frequent as municipalities tighten zoning regulations in comprehensive zoning revisions or growth management programs that limit growth in a community. Comprehensive downzonings usually receive deferential and favorable judicial review.[172] Downzonings adopted for single tracts of land receive more rigorous judicial scrutiny. A downzoning of this type is known as a reverse "spot zoning." Some courts apply their spot zoning rules to this type of downzoning, although there are important differences.

Because a downzoning changes the land use classification to a less intensive use, a landowner can argue that the downzoning is a taking of property.[173] Courts also use the estoppel and vested rights doctrines to protect a landowner from a downzoning,[174] and will invalidate a downzoning that is adopted to depress the value of property prior to its acquisition.[175]

Although courts may apply the usual presumption of validity and fairly debatable rules to a downzoning and place the burden of proof on the landowner who challenges a downzoning,[176] they are sensitive to possibilities for abuse in the downzoning process. They may invalidate a downzoning if they believe it was

---

171. 576 P.2d 401 (Wash. 1978). *See also* Committee for Sensible Land Use v. Garfield Twp., 335 N.W.2d 216 (Mich. App. 1983) (township adequately considered regional effects of shopping center rezoning).

172. Norbeck Village Joint Venture v. Montgomery County Council, 254 A.2d 700 (Md. 1969).

173. Jafay v. Board of County Comm'rs, 848 P.2d 892 (Colo. 1993); Sprenger, Grubb & Assocs., Inc. v. City of Hailey, 903 P.2d 741 (Idaho 1995) (no taking); Tim Thompson, Inc. v. Village of Hinsdale, 617 N.E.2d 1227 (Ill. App. 1993) (same).

174. Kempf v. City of Iowa City, 402 N.W.2d 393 (Iowa 1987) (held invalid).

175. § 2.33.

176. Bird v. City of Colorado Springs, 489 P.2d 324 (Colo. 1971).

adopted to benefit adjoining landowners who preferred a less intensive use of the downzoned land,[177] just as they may invalidate an upzoning if they believe a municipality adopted it to benefit a landowner.

Compatibility with adjacent uses is an important factor in the downzoning as well as the "spot" zoning cases. Courts usually uphold a downzoning to uses that are compatible with uses in the surrounding area, even though the downzoning substantially reduces the value of the downzoned property.[178] Incompatibility with uses in the surrounding area can lead to an invalidation that may be based on a holding that a taking has occurred. The courts apply this rule to residential downzonings to a more restrictive residential zoning classification[179] and to downzonings from a nonresidential to a residential use.[180]

In *McGowan v. Cohalan*,[181] for example, the court invalidated a downzoning from business to residential use of a parcel surrounded by business uses and major thoroughfares. It noted that the downzoning reduced the value of the property by ninety-two percent. This proof, though not dispositive, "tends to establish that the property is not reasonably suited for the uses prescribed."

As in the upzoning cases, a court will uphold a downzoning if it implements a comprehensive plan[182] and will invalidate a downzoning that is inconsistent

---

177. A.A. Profiles, Inc. v. City of Ft. Lauderdale, 850 F.2d 1483 (11th Cir. 1988) (downzoning following revocation of building permit); Four States Realty Co. v. City of Baton Rouge, 309 So. 2d 659 (La. 1975); Trust Co. of Chicago v. City of Chicago, 96 N.E.2d 499 (Ill. 1951); Pace Resources, Inc. v. Shrewsbury Twp. Planning Comm'n, 492 A.2d 818 (Pa. Commw. 1985); 51 A.L.R.2d 263 (1957). *But see* Parranto Bros. v. City of New Brighton, 425 N.W.2d 585 (Minn. App. 1988).

178. Lum Yip Kee, Ltd. v. City & Cty. of Honolulu, 767 P.2d 815 (Hawaii 1989) (citing treatise); Palermo Land Co. v. Planning Comm'n of Calcasieu Parish, 561 So. 2d 482 (La. 1990); Coppolino v. County Bd. of Appeals, 328 A.2d 55 (Md. 1974); Hyland v. Mayor & Twp. Comm., 327 A.2d 675 (N.J. App. Div. 1974); Grimpel Assocs. v. Cohalan, 361 N.E.2d 1022 (N.Y. 1977); Kelly v. Zoning Bd. of Adjustment, 276 A.2d 569 (Pa. Commw. 1971).

179. City of Cherry Hills Village v. Trans-Robles Corp., 509 P.2d 797 (Colo. 1973); Aronovitz v. Metropolitan Dade County, 290 So. 2d 536 (Fla. App.), *cert. denied*, 297 So. 2d 837 (Fla. 1974); Neuzil v. Iowa City, 451 N.W.2d 159 (Iowa 1990); Odabash v. Mayor & Council of Borough of Dumont, 319 A.2d 712 (N.J. 1974).

180. Carty v. City of Ojai, 143 Cal. Rptr. 506 (Cal. App. 1978); Washington Sub. San. Comm'n v. TKU Assocs., 376 A.2d 505 (Md. 1977); National Amusements, Inc. v. City of Boston, 560 N.E.2d 138 (Mass. App. 1990); Finch v. City of Durham, 384 S.E.2d 9 (N.C. 1989) (extensive discussion of taking doctrine); Superior Uptown, Inc. v. City of Cleveland, 313 N.E.2d 820 (Ohio 1974).

181. 361 N.E.2d 1025 (N.Y. 1977). *Accord* D'Addario v. Planning & Zoning Comm'n, 593 A.2d 511 (Conn. App. 1991).

182. Carty v. City of Ojai, 143 Cal. Rptr. 506 (Cal. App. 1978); Lum Yip Kee, Ltd. v. City & Cty. of Honolulu, 767 P.2d 815 (Hawaii 1989) (citing treatise); Sprenger, Grubb & Assocs., Inc. v. City of Hailey, 903 P.2d 741 (Idaho 1995); Hibernia Nat'l Bank v. City of New Orleans, 455 So. 2d 1239 (La. App. 1984) (even though downzoning adopted because of neighbor objections);

with a plan.[183] In the absence of a comprehensive plan, a court must find an acceptable zoning purpose that justifies the downzoning. In *Mountcrest Estates, Inc. v. Mayor & Twp. Comm.*,[184] the township adopted a downzoning that increased lot sizes in one of its residential districts. The court applied the presumption of validity and upheld the ordinance even though the downzoning was inconsistent with development in much of the surrounding area. "The municipality's problems with respect to congestion, overcrowding and inability to provide public facilities due to the population explosion [will be lessened by the downzoning]."[185] Courts have also upheld downzonings to protect water supplies and environment areas and avoid health problems, even when the downzoning severely restricted the use of the downzoned land.[186]

Some courts invalidated downzonings because they found that they were exclusionary. In *Kavanewsky v. Zoning Bd. of Appeals*,[187] the court invalidated a downzoning that reduced residential densities in one of the town's zoning districts. It noted that the downzoning "'was made in demand of the people to keep Warren a rural community with open spaces and keep undesirable businesses out.'" The Iowa court upheld a downzoning from multi-family to single-family use that a municipality adopted to block a federally-subsidized multi-family housing project. The court accepted the city's claim that the multi-family zoning was inconsistent with the expected growth of the area and would create traffic and pedestrian flow problems and that public services were inadequate for multi-family development.[188]

### § 6.38. Change-Mistake Rule.

When a court holds the rezoning process is quasi-judicial it may may also require a change in circumstances to justify a downzoning. In *Parkridge v. City of*

---

Riggs v. Township of Long Beach, 514 A.2d 45 (N.J. App. Div. 1986); Horizon Adirondack Corp. v. State of New York, 388 N.Y.S.2d 235 (Ct. Cl. 1976).

**183.** Pace Resources, Inc. v. Shrewsbury Twp. Planning Comm'n, 492 A.2d 818 (Pa. Commw. 1985). *See also* Udell v. Haas, 235 N.E.2d 897 (N.Y. 1968).

**184.** 232 A.2d 674 (N.J. App. Div. 1967).

**185.** 232 A.2d at 677.

**186.** Chucta v. Planning & Zoning Comm'n, 225 A.2d 822 (Conn. 1967); Lee Cty. v. Morales, 557 So. 2d 652 (Fla. App. 1990) (barrier island); Moviematic Indus. v. Board of County Comm'rs, 349 So. 2d 667 (Fla. App. 1977); Parranto Bros. v. City of New Brighton, 425 N.W.2d 585 (Minn. App. 1988) (and because market for previously zoned use saturated); Pacific Blvd. Assocs. v. City of Long Beach, 368 N.Y.S.2d 867 (Sup. Ct. 1975). *Compare* Steel Hill Dev., Inc. v. Town of Sanbornton, 469 F.2d 956 (1st Cir. 1972).

**187.** 279 A.2d 567 (Conn. 1971).

**188.** Stone v. City of Wilton, 331 N.W.2d 398 (Iowa 1983). *But see* Ogo Assocs. v. City of Torrance, 112 Cal. Rptr. 761 (Cal. App. 1974).

*Seattle,*[189] for example, the court held there is no presumption of validity favoring the action of rezoning, that the proponents of the rezone have the burden of proof in demonstrating that conditions have substantially changed since the original zoning, and that the rezone must bear a substantial relationship to the public health, safety, morals or welfare.

The Virginia Supreme Court adopted a simlar rule in *Board of Supvrs. v. Snell Constr. Corp.*[190] Once a landowner introduces evidence showing that a piecemeal downzoning is not justified by changed circumstances, the municipality must introduce evidence of mistake, fraud, or changed circumstances sufficient to make the downzoning a reasonably debatable issue. The usual presumption of validity is weakened. Nor is a political change in the governing body a sufficient change in circumstances to justify a downzoning.

## E. VARIANCES, SPECIAL EXCEPTIONS, AND CONDITIONAL USES.

### § 6.39. Role and Function.

The drafters of the Standard Zoning Act clearly contemplated a zoning process in which the uses designated by the zoning ordinance were permitted "as of right," but they also provided for an administrative zoning function. The Standard Act delegated this function to the board of adjustment. It authorized the board to grant variances from the zoning ordinance in cases of hardship and to grant special exceptions authorized by the zoning ordinance. Many zoning ordinances use the term "special" or "conditional" use rather than "special exception."

Courts often confuse the variance with the special exception, but the distinction should be clear. The highest New York court has provided the following distinction:

> A variance is an authority to a property owner to use property in a manner forbidden by the ordinance while a special exception allows the property owner to put his property to a use expressly permitted by the ordinance.[191]

---

**189.** 573 P.2d 359 (Wash. 1978), *applied in* Englund v. King County, 839 P.2d 339 (Wash. App (1992). *Accord,* Board of Supervisers v. Snell Constr. Corp., 202 S.E.2d 889 (Va. 1974), *applied in* City of Virginia Beach v. Virginia Land Inv. Ass'n No. 1, 389 S.E.2d 312 (Va. 1990). *See also* Davis v. City of Albuquerque, 648 P.2d 777 (N.M. 1982).

**190.** 202 S.E.2d 889 (Va. 1974).

**191.** North Shore Steak House, Inc. v. Board of Appeals, 282 N.E.2d 606, 609 (N.Y. 1972). For similar definitions, see Vogelaar v. Polk County Zoning Bd. of Adjustment, 188 N.W.2d 860 (Iowa 1971); Luger v. City of Brunsville, 295 N.W.2d 609 (Minn. 1980); Verona, Inc. v. Mayor & Council of West Caldwell, 229 A.2d 651 (N.J. 1967); Nucholls v. Board of Adjustment, 560 P.2d 556 (Okla. 1977).

The court added that a variance is harder to obtain than a special exception, and that the applicant in a variance case bears a higher burden of proof. This definition is reflected in the frequently quoted judicial maxim that variances should be granted "sparingly."[192] Courts often adopt a contrary presumption for special exceptions.[193]

## § 6.40. Variances.

### § 6.41. Role and Function.

The authority to grant variances[194] is found in § 7 of the Standard Zoning Act, which most states adopted and which authorizes the board of adjustment:

> To authorize upon appeal in specific cases such variance from the terms of the ordinance as will not be contrary to the public interest, where, owing to special conditions, a literal enforcement of the provisions of the ordinance will result in unnecessary hardship, and so that the spirit of the ordinance shall be observed and substantial justice done.

This provision authorizes a hardship variance. A number of states also authorize a variance because of "practical difficulties," a standard applied principally to area variances. Some statutes and ordinances contain an additional provision that requires the board to consider the impact of the variance on the surrounding area. The language of the Standard Act that requires that the "spirit" of the ordinance be observed and "substantial justice" done does not often receive attention in the cases.[195] Statutes and ordinances may also contain a requirement that a zoning variance must not be contrary to the public interest.[196] A few states have adopted standards for variances that are more detailed than the Standard Act,[197] and New Jersey has a unique hybrid provision that authorizes a variance for "special reasons."[198]

The zoning act provides the standards that zoning boards must apply when they grant variances. Most cases hold that the zoning ordinance may not modify

---

**192.** Dolan v. Zoning Bd. of Appeals, 242 A.2d 713 (Conn. 1968); Broderick v. Board of Appeal, 280 N.E.2d 670 (Mass. 1972); Cook v. Zoning Hearing Bd., 408 A.2d 1157 (Pa. Commw. 1979).

**193.** § 6.57.

**194.** *See* Cromwell v. Ward, 651 A.2d 424 (Md. App. 1995) (discusses role of variances).

**195.** *But see* Belanger v. City of Nashua, 430 A.2d 166 (N.H. 1981); Fobe Assocs. v. Mayor & Council, 379 A.2d 31 (N.J. 1977).

**196.** Larsen v. Zoning Bd. of Adjustment, 672 A.2d 286 (Pa. 1996); State v. Winnebago County, 540 N.W.2d 6 (Wis. App. 1995).

**197.** Pa. Stat. Ann. tit. 53, § 10910.2; Va. Code Ann. § 15.1-495(2).

**198.** N.J. Stat. Ann. § 40:55D-70(d). *See* Sica v. Board of Adj., 603 A.2d 30 (N.J. 1992); Medici v. BPR Co., 526 A.2d 109 (N.J. 1987).

the statutory standards,[199] although cases in home rule states have held to the contrary.[200] A court may reverse a zoning board if its decision is not based on the statutory standards. An example is a zoning board decision that denies a variance because of neighborhood opposition.[201] A board may grant a variance to modify a definition in a zoning ordinance.[202]

The discussion that follows considers each of the standards separately but requires qualification because a court may consider all of the statutory standards together and may not indicate which standard it finds controlling. The "unnecessary hardship" standard probably receives more judicial attention than any of the others.

### § 6.42. Use and Area Variances.

Although the zoning statutes do not usually make this distinction, the courts have always distinguished use from area variances. The following judicial distinction is typical:

> A use variance is one which permits a use other than that prescribed by the zoning ordinance. . . . An area variance . . . is primarily a grant to erect, alter, or use a structure for a permitted use in a manner other than that prescribed by . . . the zoning ordinance.[203]

An area variance modifies site development requirements for permitted uses, such as lot size, yard, setback, and frontage restrictions. A landowner may also request an area variance when she seeks an increase in densities or change in type of use that arguably shifts property from one zoning district to another. An example is an area variance that substantially increases multi-family densities. The courts are divided on whether an increase in density requires a use or an area variance. Some courts hold that only an area variance is required.[204] Other

---

**199.** Nelson v. Donaldson, 50 So. 2d 244 (Ala. 1951); Celentano, Inc. v. Board of Zoning Appeals, 184 A.2d 49 (Conn. 1962); Sorg v. North Hero Zoning Bd. of Adjustment, 378 A.2d 98 (Vt. 1977).

**200.** § 4.25.

**201.** Arkules v. Board of Adjustment, 728 P.2d 657 (Ariz. App. 1986); Silverco, Inc. v. Zoning Bd. of Adjustment, 109 A.2d 147 (Pa. 1954); Appeal of Lindquist, 73 A.2d 378 (Pa. 1950); Kent v. Zoning Bd. of Review, 58 A.2d 623 (R.I. 1948). *See also* Knipple v. Geistown Borough Zoning Hearing Bd., 624 A.2d 766 (Pa. Commw. 1993) (finding conscious discrimination in denial of variance).

**202.** Cricklewood Hill Realty Assocs. v. Zoning Bd. of Adj., 558 A.2d 178 (Pa. Commw. 1989) (definition of family).

**203.** Alumni Control Bd. v. City of Lincoln, 137 N.W.2d 800, 802 (Neb. 1965). *See also* Anderson v. Board of Appeals of Chesapeake Beach, 322 A.2d 220 (Md. App. 1974); Consolidated Edison Co. of N.Y. v. Hoffman, 374 N.E.2d 105 (N.Y. 1978).

**204.** Wilcox v. Zoning Bd. of Appeals, 217 N.E.2d 633 (N.Y. 1966).

courts are not as lenient. In *O'Neill v. Zoning Bd. of Adjustment*,[205] the land-owner obtained a variance that increased the floor space permitted in a multi-family building by two and one-half times. The court held that this change had to be made by the governing body.[206]

### § 6.43. Use Variances Prohibited.

Although most cases hold that zoning statutes based on the Standard Act authorize a use variance,[207] a substantial number hold that use variances are prohibited.[208] The decisions that prohibit a use variance hold that a change in use requires an amendment to the zoning ordinance and that a use variance would usurp the amendment power. A few zoning statutes prohibit use variances.[209] Field studies that found substantial abuses in the granting of use variances lend support to decisions and statutes that prohibit them.

Some courts that do not absolutely prohibit use variances take an intermediate view and disapprove a particular use variance if they believe it constitutes an improper amendment of the zoning ordinance. The size of the parcel affected by the variance was a controlling factor in most of these cases.[210] *Township of Dover v. Board of Adjustment*[211] considered parcel size along with other related factors to determine whether the board of adjustment had engaged in "proscribed legislation" when it granted a use variance. It held that "[t]he basic inquiry in each such case must be whether the impact of the requested variance will be to substantially alter the character of the district as that character has been pre-

---

205. 254 A.2d 12 (Pa. 1969).

206. *See also* Broadway, Laguna, Vallejo Ass'n v. Board of Permit Appeals, 427 P.2d 810 (Cal. 1967); Taylor v. District of Columbia Bd. of Zoning Adjustment, 308 A.2d 230 (D.C. App. 1973); Mavrantonis v. Board of Adjustment, 258 A.2d 908 (Del. 1969); Board of Adjustment v. Willie, 511 S.W.2d 591 (Tex. Civ. App. 1974).

207. Clarke v. Morgan, 327 So. 2d 769 (Fla. 1976); Strange v. Board of Zoning Appeals, 428 N.E.2d 1328 (Ind. App. 1981); Appeal of Kennedy, 374 N.W.2d 271 (Minn. 1985); Matthew v. Smith, 707 S.W.2d 411 (Mo. 1986) (quoting treatise); Nucholls v. Board of Adjustment, 560 P.2d 556 (Okla. 1977).

208. Bradley v. Zoning Bd. of Appeals, 334 A.2d 914 (Conn. 1973); Stice v. Gribben-Allen Motors, Inc., 534 P.2d 1267 (Kan. 1975); Standard Oil Co. v. City of Warrensville Heights, 355 N.E.2d 495 (Ohio App. 1976); Banks v. City of Bethany, 541 P.2d 178 (Okla. 1975); Swain v. Board of Adjustment, 433 S.W.2d 727 (Tex. App. 1968). *Compare* Swann v. Board of Adjustment, 459 So. 2d 896 (Ala. Civ. App. 1984) (ordinance cannot prohibit use variance), *with* Zoning Bd. of Appeals v. Planning & Zoning Comm'n, 605 A.2d 885 (Conn. App. 1992) (contra).

209. Cal. Gov't Code § 65906.

210. Sinclair Pipe Line Co. v. Village of Richton Park, 167 N.E.2d 406 (Ill. 1960); Staller v. Cranston Zoning Bd. of Review, 215 A.2d 418 (R.I. 1965). *Compare* Cavanaugh v. DiFlumera, 401 N.E.2d 867 (Mass. 1980); DeSimone v. Greater Englewood Hous. Corp. No. 1, 267 A.2d 31 (N.J. 1970).

211. 386 A.2d 421 (N.J. App. Div. 1978).

scribed by the zoning ordinance."[212] The court suggested a number of factors to consider in making this determination, including the size of the parcel, its size and character in relation to the size and character of the zoning district and the municipality, and the "degree and extent of the variation from district regulations."

*Dover* also suggested an inverse relationship between a use variance and a rezoning. It suggested that a property that was too small for a rezoning might be eligible for a use variance. A large tract that is ineligible for a variance might be eligible for a rezoning.

### § 6.44. Unnecessary Hardship.

The classic statement of the unnecessary hardship test appears in a New York case, *Otto v. Steinhilber*:[213]

> Before the Board may . . . grant a variance upon the ground of unnecessary hardship, the record must show that (1) the land in question cannot yield a reasonable return if used only for a purpose allowed in that zone; (2) that the plight of the owner is due to unique circumstances and not to the general conditions of the neighborhood which may reflect the unreasonableness of the zoning ordinance itself; and (3) that the use to be authorized by the variance will not alter the essential character of the locality.[214]

A number of courts have adopted these criteria for unnecessary hardship, which reflect the restrictive judicial view toward variances.[215] Not all of these criteria apply to the unnecessary hardship determination. The second criterion reflects the limitation on variances noted earlier, that a board may not grant a variance when an amendment of the zoning ordinance is indicated. For example, a court may not grant a variance based on a hardship that does not distinguish it from other uses in the area, such as the historic character of a building. Neither may a board grant a variance because a zoning enforcement officer acted arbitrarily in applying an ordinance, or because the language of an ordinance is un-

---

212. *Id.* at 427.
213. 24 N.E.2d 851 (N.Y. 1939).
214. *Id.* at 853.
215. Deardorf v. Board of Adjustment, 118 N.W.2d 78 (Iowa 1962); Lovely v. Zoning Bd. of Appeals, 259 A.2d 666 (Me. 1969); Puritan-Greenfield Imp. Ass'n v. Leo, 153 N.W.2d 162 (Mich. App. 1967); Matthew v. Smith, 707 S.W.2d 411 (Mo. 1986). *Compare* Larsen v. Zoning Bd. of Adjustment, 672 A.2d 286 (Pa. 1996) (may not base hardship on need for additional space in dwelling); Joseph B. Simon & Co. v. Zoning Bd. of Adjustment, 168 A.2d 317 (Pa. 1961). *See* 168 A.L.R. 13 (1957).

certain.[216] New York has codified its judicially-adopted variance test, and the statutes also require proof that the applicant has been deprived of "all economic use or benefit from the property."[217]

### § 6.45. No Reasonable Return.

The requirement adopted in *Otto*,[218] that the board may grant a variance only if it finds that the landowner cannot make a reasonable return on her property, is a standard requirement in variance law.[219] This rule is similar to the rule that a landowner must show an inability to make a reasonable use of her land in order to prove an as-applied taking.[220] The "no reasonable return" rule means that the use variance is an administrative alternative to litigation that claims the zoning restriction on the land is an as-applied taking. A variance can avoid the damage that can occur to a zoning ordinance as a result of successful as-applied taking litigation.[221] Whether changes in taking doctrine adopted by the U.S. Supreme Court will result in changes in the proof of economic impairment required for a variance is not yet clear.

The "no reasonable return" rule means that a landowner does not make a case for a variance simply by showing that his property could be used for a more profitable use if the board granted the variance. The typical judicial point of view in this type of case is illustrated by *Carbonneau v. Town of Exeter*.[222] An applicant for a variance had been using the bottom floor of his home as a funeral business, which was an established nonconforming use. He applied for a variance to operate a beauty parlor on the bottom floor of a barn located on his property. The court held that a desire to make a more profitable use of the property did not justify a variance.[223]

---

216. Wnuk v. Zoning Bd. of Appeals, 626 A.2d 698 (Conn. 1993). *See* Moroney v. Mayor & Council, 633 A.2d 1045 (N.J. App. 1993) (court may award compensation for variance denial).

217. N.Y. Gen. City Law § 81-b; N.Y. Town Law § 267-b(2)(b); N.Y. Village Law § 7-712-b.

218. § 6.44.

219. Baker v. Connell, 488 A.2d 1303 (Del. 1985); Grey Rocks Land Trust v. Town of Hebron, 614 A.2d 1048 (N.H. 1992). *But see* Allegheny West Civic Council, Inc. v. Zoning Bd. of Adjustment, 689 A.2d 225 (Pa. 1997) (need not show that property has no value).

220. *See* Village Bd. v. Jarrold, 423 N.E.2d 385 (N.Y. 1981) (two rules are "much the same").

221. *See* Puritan-Greenfield Imp. Ass'n v. Leo, 153 N.W.2d 162 (Mich. App. 1967).

222. 401 A.2d 675 (N.H. 1979).

223. *Accord* Graziano v. Board of Adjustment, 323 N.W.2d 233 (Iowa 1982); State ex rel. Pitts v. Board of Zoning Adjustments, 327 So. 2d 140 (La. App. 1976); City Council of Waltham v. Vinciullo, 307 N.E.2d 316 (Mass. 1974); Lovely v. Zoning Bd. of Appeals, 259 A.2d 666 (Me. 1969); Olszak v. Town of New Hampton, 661 A.2d 768 (N.H. 1995); Enterprise Citizens Action Comm. v. Clark County Bd. of Comm'rs, 918 P.2d 305 (Nev. 1996); MacLean v. Zoning Bd. of Adjustment, 185 A.2d 533 (Pa. 1962); State v. Winnebago County, 540 N.W.2d 6 (Wis. App. 1995).

The New York court expanded the *Otto* tests by holding, in *Forrest v. Ever-shed*,[224] that the applicant must show that he made diligent efforts to sell his property without success. Although not always applied in New York, this requirement has some following elsewhere in cases that either require efforts to sell or that accept such efforts as evidence of hardship.[225] Other courts reject or are critical of the requirement that the applicant must show actual efforts to sell. They allow evidence of inability to sell to show that a reasonable return is not possible under the existing zoning restriction.[226]

This rule is preferable. The ability to sell a property may depend on factors other than the zoning ordinance, such as the state of the property market. A rule that requires diligent efforts to sell contradicts the assumption underlying the "no reasonable return" rule that variances are based on an inability to use the property under the zoning ordinance, not on circumstances personal to the user.

### § 6.46. Unique to the Owner.

The requirement adopted in *Otto*[227] that the applicant for a use variance must show a unique hardship to his property restates the rule that a variance is not proper when other forms of relief from the zoning ordinance are available. As the New York court stated in *Otto*:

> [T]he fault may lie in the fact that the particular zoning restriction is unreasonable in its application to a certain locality. . . . In . . . [this] situation, the relief is by way of direct attack upon the terms of the ordinance.[228]

Other courts allow a landowner to apply for an amendment of the zoning ordinance in this situation. Some states have codified the uniqueness requirement.[229]

The courts generally hold that a board may not grant a variance because of conditions general to the neighborhood.[230] This rule is an application of the

---

**224.** 164 N.E.2d 841 (N.Y. 1959).

**225.** Puritan-Greenfield Imp. Ass'n v. Leo, 153 N.W.2d 162 (Mich. App. 1967); Chirichello v. Zoning Bd. of Adjustment, 397 A.2d 646 (N.J. 1979).

**226.** Culinary Inst. of Am. v. Board of Zoning Appeals, 121 A.2d 637 (Conn. 1956); Valley View Civic Ass'n v. Zoning Bd. of Adjustment, 462 A.2d 637 (Pa. 1983); Guenther v. Zoning Bd. of Review, 125 A.2d 214 (R.I. 1956).

**227.** § 6.44.

**228.** 24 N.E.2d at 852. *Accord* State v. Winnebago County, 540 N.W.2d 6 (Wis. App. 1995). *See also* North v. St. Mary's County, 638 A.2d 1175 (Md. App. 1994) (discussing uniqueness requirement); Douglaston Civic Ass'n v. Klein, 416 N.E.2d 1040 (N.Y. 1980).

**229.** Cal. Gov't Code § 64906.

**230.** Smith v. Zoning Bd. of Appeals, 387 A.2d 542 (Conn. 1978); Kelly v. Zoning Bd. of Appeals, 575 A.2d 249 (Conn. App. 1990); Town of Indialantic v. Nance, 419 So. 2d 1041 (Fla. 1982); Puritan-Greenfield Imp. Ass'n v. Leo, 153 N.W.2d 162 (Mich. App. 1967); Moore v. City of Rochester, 427 A.2d 10 (N.H. 1981); Vidal v. Lisanti Foods, 679 A.2d 206 (N.J. App. 1996). *Contra,* Sherwood v. Grant County, 699 P.2d 243 (Wash. App. 1985). *Compare* Wolfman v.

uniqueness requirement. If strictly applied, it would substantially limit the power of zoning boards to grant use variances, which are often requested because of changes in the character of a neighborhood. In a typical case of this type, an owner of a single-family dwelling on the edge of a business district applies for a variance to allow a commercial use of the dwelling. He claims that the adjacent commercial uses and an increase in motor vehicle traffic in the neighborhood make a residential use of the dwelling unreasonable. A court that applies the rule that a variance cannot be based on conditions general to a neighborhood will not approve a variance in this case.

Courts will not accept policy reasons as the basis for a variance, such as a claim that a housing shortage justifies a variance for apartments in a single-family residential area.[231] Although this type of claim may indicate that the variance serves the public interest, it does not establish conditions unique to the property. Policy reasons of this kind may justify a rezoning.

### § 6.47. Impact on the Neighborhood.

The *Otto* case[232] also adopted this requirement. It noted that "the use to be authorized by the variance . . . [should] not alter the essential character of the locality." Some zoning statutes include this requirement, which courts usually refer to as the "negative" criterion.[233]

*Commons v. Westwood Zoning Bd. of Adjustment*[234] illustrates a judicial application of the negative criterion. A landowner requested a variance to build a house on an undersized lot. The court noted that "if the size and layout of the proposed house would have adversely affected the character of the neighborhood . . . a board may justly conclude that a variance should not be granted." Other courts implement the negative criterion by balancing the hardship to the property owner against detrimental impacts on the surrounding area.

---

Board of Appeals, 444 N.E.2d 942 (Mass. App. 1983) (soil conditions justified variance to avoid height increase), *with* Governor's Island Club, Inc. v. Town of Gilford, 467 A.2d 246 (N.H. 1983) (substandard lot size not a unique problem), *and* City of Burley v. McCaslin Lumber Co., 693 P.2d 1108 (Idaho App. 1984) (increasing density to make investment economically feasible not condition unique to property).

231. Zaruta v. Zoning Hearing Bd., 543 A.2d 1282 (Pa. Commw. 1988) (structure for homeless); Cass v. Board of Appeal, 317 N.E.2d 77 (Mass. 1974); Farah v. Sachs, 157 N.W.2d 9 (Mich. App. 1968); Downtown Neighborhood Ass'n v. City of Albuquerque, 783 P.2d 962 (N.M. App. 1989) (historic structure); Xanthos v. Board of Adjustment, 685 P.2d 1032 (Utah 1984) (retention of low-cost housing units). *But see* Kessler-Allisonville Civic League, Inc. v. Marion County Bd. of Zoning Appeals, 209 N.E.2d 43 (Ind. App. 1965).

232. § 6.44.

233. Jackson v. City of San Mateo, 307 P.2d 451 (Cal. App. 1957); Culinary Inst. of Am. v. Board of Zoning Appeals, 121 A.2d 637 (Conn. 1956); Amberley Swim & Country Club v. Zoning Bd. of Appeals, 191 N.E.2d 364 (Ohio App. 1963).

234. 410 A.2d 1138 (N.J. 1980).

## § 6.48. Practical Difficulties — Area Variances.

The Standard Zoning Act did not make a distinction between area and use variances and provided a single "unnecessary hardship" test for both. A number of zoning statutes and ordinances modify the Standard Act by authorizing a variance for "practical difficulties" as well as for unnecessary hardship. Many cases hold that this type of statute does not create a dual standard and apply the unnecessary hardship test and other tests for use variances to area variances.[235] *City & Borough of Juneau v. Thibodeau*[236] is a leading decision. The court pointed out that, in the cases holding that the statute adopted a separate practical difficulties test for area variances, the statute or zoning ordinance stated the two variance tests disjunctively. The court refused to adopt a separate practical difficulties test for area variances because the Juneau zoning ordinance stated the two tests conjunctively.

*Thibodeau* illustrates the application of the unnecessary hardship rule to deny an area variance. A landowner was granted a rezoning to expand a store and then applied for and received an area variance to reduce the required number of parking spaces. The court reversed. It noted that a variance must be based on "physical conditions of the land itself which distinguished it from other land in the general area." It added that if the property has substantially the same value for the permitted uses as other property within the same zoning classification, the "assertion that the ordinance merely deprives the landowner of a more profitable operation" is not sufficient.[237]

Courts have adopted a variety of tests for area variances when they do not apply the unnecessary hardship test. They have made it clear that the difference between the tests for use and area variances is a matter of degree but have also emphasized that the test for area variances is less stringent. Courts that apply the practical difficulties test have also adopted a set of factors that determine when this test justifies an area variance. These usually include the significance of the

---

**235.** Abel v. Zoning Bd. of Appeals, 374 A.2d 227 (Conn. 1977); Graziano v. Board of Adjustment, 323 N.W.2d 233 (Iowa 1982); City of Merriam v. Board of Zoning Appeals, 748 P.2d 883 (Kan. 1988); Marchi v. Town of Scarborough, 511 A.2d 1071 (Me. 1986); Matthew v. Smith, 707 S.W.2d 411 (Mo. 1986) (citing this treatise); Alumni Control Bd. v. City of Lincoln, 137 N.W.2d 800 (Neb. 1965); Ouimette v. City of Somersworth, 402 A.2d 159 (N. H.1979); Chirichello v. Zoning Bd. of Adjustment, 397 A.2d 646 (N.J. 1979); Brown v. Fraser, 467 P.2d 464 (Okla. 1970); Cummings v. City of Seattle, 935 P.2d 663 (Wash. App. 1997) (citing this treatise); Snyder v. Waukesha County Zoning Bd. of Adjustment, 247 N.W.2d 98 (Wis. 1976). *See also* Bennett v. Sullivan's Island Bd. of Adjustment, 438 S.E.2d 273 (S.C. App. 1993) ("peculiarity" requirement interpreted not to mean "unique").

**236.** 595 P.2d 626 (Alaska 1979).

**237.** *Accord* Margate Motel, Inc. v. Town of Gilford, 534 A.2d 717 (N.H. 1987). *But see* City of Olathe v. Board of Zoning Appeals, 696 P.2d 409 (Kan. App. 1986) (applying use variance criteria to approve variance for name change on sign); Marchi v. Town of Scarborough, 511 A.2d 1071 (Me. 1986) (same; setback variance).

economic injury, the magnitude of the variance sought, whether the difficulty was self-created, and whether other feasible alternatives could avoid the difficulty.[238]

Not all courts apply these criteria, and statutes or ordinances may contain different standards. For example, local ordinances or judicial decisions may modify this test by requiring "extraordinary" or "exceptional" difficulties,[239] while other courts seem to soften this test by requiring only "adverse impact" that is more than mere inconvenience.[240] Courts, or statutes and ordinances, may also impose a uniqueness requirement under the practical difficulties test.[241] New York statutes require a balancing of the benefit to the applicant against the detriment to the neighborhood or community through consideration of five statutory factors.[242] These factors are similar to factors adopted by other courts to apply the practical difficulties test.[243]

Because the tests for area variances vary so widely it is difficult to generalize the situations in which an area variance will be granted. Area variances based on the physical condition of a property are usually upheld.[244] Courts may also hold that conditions inherent in a building justify an area variance.[245]

---

**238.** Doyle v. Amster, 594 N.E.2d 911 (N.Y. 1992); Human Dev. Serv. of Porth Chester v. Zoning Bd. of Appeals, 493 N.Y.S.2d 481 (App. Div. 1985) (now modified by statute), *aff'd mem.*, 480 N.E.2d 927 (N.Y. 1986). *See also* Metropolitan Bd. of Zoning Appeals v. McDonald's Corp., 481 N.E.2d 141 (Ind. App. 1985) (statutory test); McLean v. Soley, 270 Md. 208 (Md. 1973); National Boatland, Inc. v. Farmington Hills Zoning Bd. of Appeals, 380 N.W.2d 472 (Mich. App. 1985); Duncan v. Village of Midfield, 491 N.E.2d 692 (Ohio), *cert. denied,* 497 U.S. 986 (1986).

**239.** Ivancovich v. City of Tucson, 529 P.2d 242 (Ariz. App. 1975); Board of Adjustment v. Kwik-Check Realty, Inc., 389 A.2d 1289 (Del. 1978); Palmer v. Board of Zoning Adjustment, 287 A.2d 535 (D.C. App. 1972).

**240.** Gara Realty, Inc. v. Zoning Bd. of Review, 523 A.2d 855 (R.I. 1987).

**241.** Cromwell v. Ward, 651 A.2d 424 (Md. App. 1995) (thorough review of the cases). *See also* Orinda Ass'n v. Board of Supervisors, 227 Cal. Rptr. 688 (Cal. App. 1986).

**242.** N.Y. Town Law § 267-b(3); N.Y. Village Law § 7-712-b(3). The factors are: whether there will be an undesirable change to the neighborhood or detriment to nearby properties; whether there is a feasible alternative; whether the requested variance is substantial; whether there will be an adverse physical or environmental effect on the neighborhood; and whether the variance was self-created. *Id. See also* Kaufmann v. Planning Bd., 542 A.2d 457 (N.J. 1988) (interpreting similar statute).

**243.** *But see* Sasso v. Osgood, 657 N.E.2d 254 (N.Y. 1995) (statute repeals tests previously applied to area variances).

**244.** Bressman v. Gash, 621 A.2d 476 (N.J. 1993) (setback for garage).

**245.** Wolf v. District of Columbia Bd. of Zoning Adjustment, 397 A.2d 936 (D.C. App. 1979) (reduction in lot size to allow conversion of large home to four, rather than two, dwelling units); Rowell v. Board of Adj., 446 N.W.2d 917 (Minn. App. 1989) (upholding substantial setback variance for extension of nonconforming building to conform to function and aesthetics of building); Husnander v. Town of Barnstead, 660 A.2d 477 (N.H. 1995) (zoning restrictions created unreasonable design for dwelling). *But see* Gilmartin v. District of Columbia Bd. of Adj., 579 A.2d 1164

The courts almost always approve area variances under either the unnecessary hardship or practical difficulties test for landowners who wish to build a dwelling on a substandard lot.[246] The owner of the substandard lot must show that he cannot build on the lot under the applicable zoning restrictions.

## § 6.49. Consistency with the Plan.

Most of the cases that considered the question did not require variances to be consistent with a comprehensive plan.[247] Consistency is desirable when the variance allows a major change in use, and courts could impose this requirement under consistency statutes. The New Jersey Supreme Court has interpreted its consistency statute to require variances to be consistent with the comprehensive plan.[248] A few statutes expressly apply the consistency requirement to variances.[249]

## § 6.50. Self-Created Hardship.

Courts usually hold that a board may not grant a variance when the hardship claimed by the applicant is self-created.[250] In a typical case, the landowner creates a substandard lot by conveying part of it and then seeks a variance from the lot size restrictions of the zoning ordinance.[251] This rule is correct. The purpose of a variance is to provide relief from overrestrictive zoning enacted by the municipality, not from overrestrictive zoning created by the voluntary acts of landowners.

A more complicated problem is presented when self-created hardship is claimed because the landowner purchased a lot with knowledge of the zoning restrictions. The rule that hardship is self-created in this situation stems from

---

(D.C. App. 1990) (remanding on-premise parking variance because parking inside building might be possible).

**246.** Russell v. District of Columbia Bd. of Adjustment, 402 A.2d 1231 (D.C. App. 1979); Chater v. Board of Appeals, 202 N.E.2d 805 (Mass. 1964); Lincoln v. Zoning Bd. of Review, 201 A.2d 482 (R.I. 1964). *But see* Miriam Homes, Inc. v. Board of Adjustment, 384 A.2d 147 (App. Div. 1976), *aff'd mem.*, 384 A.2d 143 (N.J. 1978) (upholding denial of variance).

**247.** Belanger v. City of Nashua, 430 A.2d 166 (N.H. 1981); C. Miller Chevrolet, Inc. v. City of Willoughby Hills, 313 N.E.2d 400 (Ohio 1974).

**248.** Medici v. BPR Co., 526 A.2d 109 (N.J. 1987).

**249.** Suess v. Vogelgesang, 281 N.E.2d 536 (Ind. App. 1972).

**250.** Chapman v. Board of Adjustment, 485 So. 2d 1161 (Ala. 1986); Farrington v. Zoning Bd. of Appeals, 413 A.2d 817 (Conn. 1979); Foxhall Community Citizens Ass'n v. District of Columbia Bd. of Zoning Adjustment, 524 A.2d 759 (D.C. App. 1987); Clarke v. Morgan, 327 So. 2d 769 (Fla. 1976); In re Schrader, 660 P.2d 135 (Okla. 1983).

**251.** Baker v. Connell, 488 A.2d 1303 (Del. 1985); Johnson v. Township of Robinson, 359 N.W.2d 526 (Mich. 1984); In re Volpe's Appeal, 121 A.2d 97 (Pa. 1956).

early New York cases[252] and is followed in some states.[253] Other courts either reject this rule[254] or hold that purchase with knowledge of the zoning restriction is only one factor to consider.[255] Pennsylvania adopted a more limited form of the rule. It holds that self-created hardship exists when the landowner pays a premium for a property that makes it unprofitable to put it to its permitted use.[256]

The present status of the New York rule is in doubt. The New York courts adopted the rule in use variance cases in which there were other reasons for denying the variance.[257] In the area variance cases they hold that self-created hardship based on purchase with knowledge of existing zoning is only one factor to consider.[258]

The cases that reject the rule that purchase with knowledge of existing zoning in self-created hardship are correct. The rule is fair in cases where a prior owner created a hardship through some action relating to the land. Purchase should not relieve a subsequent owner of this infirmity. To hold that mere purchase with knowledge of existing zoning is self-created hardship improperly makes the purchase of land a basis for denying a variance. The cases are on better ground when they deny a variance where the purchaser pays a premium for the land and uses the premium payment as the basis for claiming financial hardship.

---

**252.** Clarke v. Board of Zoning Appeals, 92 N.E.2d 903 (N.Y. 1950), *cert. denied,* 340 U.S. 933 (1951). *See* Overhill Bldg. Co. v. Delany, 271 N.E.2d 537 (N.Y. 1971).

**253.** Association for Preservation of 1700 Block of N St., N.W., & Vicinity v. District of Columbia Bd. of Zoning Adjustment, 384 A.2d 674 (D.C. App. 1978) (use variances); Josephson v. Autrey, 96 So. 2d 784 (Fla. 1957); Sanchez v. Board of Zoning Adjustments, 488 So. 2d 1277 (La. App. 1986); Marino v. City of Baltimore, 137 A.2d 198 (Md. 1957); Beaudoin v. Rye Beach Village Dist., 369 A.2d 618 (N.J. 1976); Alleghany Enters. v. Board of Zoning Appeals, 225 S.E.2d 383 (Va. 1976).

**254.** Landmark Universal, Inc. v. Pitkin County Bd. of Adjustment, 579 P.2d 1184 (Colo. App. 1978); Adolphson v. Zoning Bd. of Appeals, 535 A.2d 799 (Conn. 1988); Hehir v. Bowers, 407 N.E.2d 149 (Ill. App. 1980); Myron v. City of Plymouth, 562 N.W.2d 21 (Minn. App. 1997); Board of Adjustment v. Shanbour, 435 P.2d 569 (Okla. 1968); Hoberg v. City of Bellevue, 884 P.2d 1339 (Wash. App. 1994); Schalow v. Waupaca County, 407 N.W.2d 316 (Wis. App. 1987).

**255.** Arant v. Board of Adjustment, 126 So. 2d 100 (Ala. 1961); Twigg v. Town of Kennebunk, 662 A.2d 914 (Me. 1995); Chirichello v. Zoning Bd. of Adjustment, 397 A.2d 646 (N.J. 1979); In re Zoning Variance Application, 449 A.2d 910 (Vt. 1982) (hardship self-created when landowner purchased part of lot that violated zoning ordinance).

**256.** Appeal of Gro, 269 A.2d 876 (Pa. 1970). *See also* POA Co. v. Findlay Township Zoning Hearing Bd., 679 A.2d 1342 (Pa. Commw. 1996) (self-inflicted because applicant limited access to property).

**257.** Murphy v. Kraemer, 182 N.Y.S.2d 205 (Sup. Ct. 1958).

**258.** DeSena v. Board of Zoning Appeals, 379 N.E.2d 1144 (N.Y. 1978). *See* First Nat'l Bank v. City of Downsville, 628 N.Y.S.2d 199 (App. Div. 1995) (rule applied).

## § 6.51. Conditions.

Although the Standard Zoning Act and most state zoning acts do not expressly authorize the board of adjustment to attach conditions to variances, the power to do so is recognized everywhere as inherent in the statutory power to grant variances. As the court pointed out in *Town of Burlington v. Jencik,*[259] "[s]ince variances allow uses forbidden by the regulations, the attachment of conditions to the granting of a variance alleviates the harm which might otherwise result."[260] A few zoning statutes confer the authority to impose conditions on variances.[261]

The accepted limitation on variance conditions is that they must relate to the use of the land, not the user. Conditions that affect the development of the site, such as landscaping, paving and access conditions, are clearly acceptable.[262] Some courts void conditions that limit hours of operation[263] or that limit the variance to a period of time[264] or to the applicant[265] because they do not properly relate to the use of the land.[266]

When a use permitted by a variance will increase traffic congestion, boards of adjustment sometimes attach a condition requiring the dedication of land for a street widening. A few cases hold that the zoning board has the implied power to attach such conditions.[267] To avoid a taking problem, the dedication should be

---

**259.** 362 A.2d 1338 (Conn. 1975).

**260.** *Accord* Everson v. Zoning Bd. of Adjustment, 149 A.2d 63 (Pa. 1959); Town of Warren v. Frost, 301 A.2d 572 (R.I. 1973).

**261.** Cal. Gov't Code § 65906.

**262.** Wright v. Zoning Bd. of Appeals, 391 A.2d 146 (Conn. 1978); Town of Burlington v. Jencik, 362 A.2d 1338 (Conn. 1975); St. Onge v. Donovan, 522 N.E.2d 1019 (N.Y. 1988) (disapproving condition terminating variance person using property changes); Nicholson v. Zoning Bd. of Adjustment, 140 A.2d 604 (Pa. 1958).

**263.** Bora v. Zoning Bd. of Appeals, 288 A.2d 89 (Conn. 1972); 99 A.L.R.2d 227 (1965).

**264.** Huntington v. Zoning Bd. of Appeals, 428 N.E.2d 826 (Mass. App. 1981); Vlahos Realty Co. v. Little Boar's Head Dist., 146 A.2d 257 (N.H. 1958); DeFelice v. Zoning Bd. of Adjustment, 523 A.2d 1086 (N.J. App. Div. 1987) (requiring demolition of building on sale of land). *Compare* Wentworth Hotel v. Town of New Castle, 287 A.2d 615 (N.H. 1972).

**265.** National Black Child Dev. Inst. v. District of Columbia Bd. of Adjustment, 483 A.2d 687 (D.C. App. 1984).

**266.** Brous v. Planning Bd., 594 N.Y.S.2d 816 (App. Div. 1993) (condition on area variance prohibiting expansion of beach house not related to public welfare). *But see* Berninger v. Board of Adj., 603 A.2d 954 (N.J. App. Div. 1991) (upholds original variance although illegal condition invalidated).

**267.** Bringle v. Board of Supvrs., 351 P.2d 765 (Cal. 1960); Alperin v. Mayor & Twp. Comm., 219 A.2d 628 (N.J. 1966). *See also* Black v. City of Waukesha, 371 N.W.2d 389 (Wis. 1985) (building permit). *But cf.* City of Corpus Christi v. Unitarian Church, 436 S.W.2d 923 (Tex. Civ. App. 1968).

based on traffic problems generated by the use permitted by the variance. A California statute codifies this requirement.[268]

### § 6.52. Findings and Judicial Review.

Although a few zoning statutes require boards of adjustment to make findings of fact in variance cases,[269] the Standard Zoning Act and most state zoning acts do not impose this requirement. A number of courts require findings of fact in variance cases even though they are not required by the zoning statute. Courts require findings of fact to facilitate judicial review because findings link the statutory standards to the variance decision. The reason for requiring findings was best stated in a leading California case, *Topanga Ass'n for a Scenic Community v. County of Los Angeles*:[270]

> [A] findings requirement serves to conduce the administrative body to draw legally relevant subconclusions supportive of its ultimate decision; the intended effect is to facilitate orderly analysis and minimize the likelihood that the agency will randomly leap from evidence to conclusions.... [F]indings enable the reviewing court to trace and examine the agency's mode of analysis.[271]

Some courts do not require findings of fact in variance cases.[272]

The Standard Zoning Act, which most states adopted, authorizes the use of the writ of certiorari to review board of adjustment decisions, including variance decisions. Although the Standard Act does not provide a judicial review standard, the courts apply the judicial review standard they usually apply to administrative proceedings they review on a record. Judicial review is deferential, and a court must uphold a board's decision if there is substantial evidence to support it in the record. The court may reverse only if the board's decision was arbitrary or capricious.[273]

---

**268.** Cal. Gov't Code § 65909. *See also* §§ 9.11-9.15.

**269.** 65 Ill. Comp. Stat. Ann. 5/11-13-11. *See also* Warren v. Board of Appeals, 416 N.E.2d 1382 (Mass. 1981) (statute requires); LaVallee v. Britt, 383 A.2d 709 (N.H. 1978) (ordinance may require).

**270.** 522 P.2d 12 (Cal. 1974).

**271.** *Id.* at 18. *Accord* Zieky v. Town Plan & Zoning Comm., 196 A.2d 758 (Conn. 1963); Board of Adjustment v. Henderson Union Ass'n, 374 A.2d 3 (Del. 1977); Harrington Glen, Inc. v. Municipal Bd. of Adjustment, 243 A.2d 233 (N.J. 1968); Village Bd. v. Jarrold, 423 N.E.2d 385 (N.Y. 1981); Potter v. Hartford Zoning Bd. of Adjustment, 407 A.2d 170 (Vt. 1979).

**272.** Deardorf v. Board of Adjustment, 118 N.W.2d 78 (Iowa 1962); South Maple St. Ass'n v. Board of Adjustment, 230 N.W.2d 471 (Neb. 1975).

**273.** Farrington v. Zoning Bd. of Appeals, 413 A.2d 817 (Conn. 1979); Wolf v. District of Columbia Bd. of Zoning Adjustment, 397 A.2d 936 (D.C. App. 1979); Town of Indialantic v. Nance, 400 So. 2d 37 (Fla. App. 1981); Evesham Twp. Zoning Bd. of Adjustment v. Evesham Twp. Council, 404 A.2d 1274 (N.J. 1979); Cowan v. Kern, 363 N.E.2d 305 (N.Y. 1977).

This judicial review standard overstates the deference the courts give to board of adjustment variance decisions. The court must be convinced in many states that the board's findings were adequate. A court may accept the board's fact-finding but still believe that the basis on which it granted the variance was improper. An example is a decision to base a variance on self-created hardship. Courts retain sufficient substantive control over board of adjustment variance decisions to implement the judicial policy that variances should be granted "sparingly," notwithstanding the deferential judicial review standard.

Although the Standard Zoning Act appeared to contemplate judicial review of zoning variances on the record before the board in the certiorari appeal, it also authorized the trial court to take additional evidence.[274] Many states adopted this provision. Some courts interpret this provision to authorize a de novo trial in the trial court, with judicial review based on the trial court record rather than the board proceedings.[275]

## § 6.53. Special Exceptions and Conditional Uses.

The Standard Zoning Act and state zoning acts authorize the board of adjustment to grant "special exceptions" under standards provided by the zoning ordinance. Some zoning statutes also contain criteria for special exceptions. The term "special exception" is vague and unclear[276] and was an unfortunate choice. The term "conditional" or "special" use or permit is more frequently used in zoning ordinances, and the courts often use both terms interchangeably.

The zoning ordinance usually contains a provision that details the standards for all conditional uses and also indicates the conditional uses allowable in the different zoning districts. The standards provided for conditional uses are usually quite general and typically authorize the approval of a conditional use if it is compatible with the surrounding area. A zoning ordinance may include even vaguer standards authorizing conditional uses that are in the "public interest," serve the "public welfare," or are consistent with the "spirit and intent" of the zoning ordinance. Some courts hold that this type of standard is an unconstitutional delegation of legislative power.[277]

Some land uses almost always require approval as a conditional use. One example is a land use that may be appropriate in a zoning district but which re-

---

274. Standard Zoning Act § 7.

275. Whitcomb v. City of Woodward, 616 P.2d 455 (Okla. App. 1980); Overstreet v. Zoning Hearing Bd., 412 A.2d 169 (Pa. Commw. 1980); Chioffi v. Winooski Zoning Bd., 556 A.2d 103 (Vt. 1989) (upholding statute allowing de novo review). *But see* Bentley v. Chastain, 249 S.E.2d 38 (Ga. 1978) (de novo trial unconstitutional).

276. BCT Partnership v. City of Portland, 881 P.2d 176 (Or. App. 1994) (ordinance must contain provisions that can reasonably be interpreted and explained as embodying standards and criteria).

277. § 6.03.

quires review to determine whether it will have an adverse impact on the surrounding area. Gasoline filling stations in commercial districts and apartments in single-family residential districts are in this category. A second example is a use that may have an adverse impact on the surrounding area but that deserves consideration as a conditional use because it serves community needs. A community facility, such as a hospital, is in this category.

### § 6.54. Role and Function.

Because conditional uses are expressly authorized by the zoning ordinance and are not granted to avoid unnecessary hardship, courts view them as uses that can be appropriate in the zoning districts established by the zoning ordinance. This distinction was captured in what is still the classic judicial statement of the role of the conditional use:

> [C]ertain uses, considered by the local legislative body to be essential or desirable for the welfare of the community . . ., are entirely appropriate and not essentially incompatible with the basic uses in any zone . . ., but not at every or any location . . . or without conditions being imposed by reason of special problems the use . . . presents from a zoning standpoint . . . .[278]

Proof of hardship is not required for a conditional use.[279]

A threshold question is whether the zoning ordinance has properly classified a use as one that requires conditional use approval. In *Board of Supvrs. v. Southland Corp.*,[280] the ordinance classified quick-service food stores as a conditional use in a commercial district. It permitted grocery stores with more than 5,000 square feet in area in this district as-of-right. The court held that the governing body's decision to treat a land use as a conditional use was entitled to a presumption of constitutionality and that the decision to classify quick-food stores as a conditional use was fairly debatable. The governing body found that peak traffic at quick-service stores came at peak traffic times, that peak traffic at the larger grocery stores permitted as-of-right did not come at peak times, and that quick-service stores were located on smaller parcels and had less flexibility in locating entrances.

The courts approved the classification of other uses as conditional uses when they found a reasonable distinction between these uses and uses permitted as-of-

---

278. Tullo v. Millburn Twp., 149 A.2d 620, 624, 625 (N.J. App. Div. 1959). *See also* Kotrich v. County of DuPage, 166 N.E.2d 601 (Ill.), *appeal dismissed,* 364 U.S. 475 (1960); Eberhart v. Indiana Waste Sys., 452 N.E.2d 455 (Ind. App. 1983); Hofmeister v. Frank Realty Co., 373 A.2d 273 (Md. App. 1977); Anderson v. Peden, 587 P.2d 59 (Or. 1978). *But see* Delta Biological Resources, Inc. v. Board of Zoning Appeals, 467 N.W.2d 164 (Wis. App. 1991) (no presumption in favor of special exceptions). Special use defined: N.Y. Town Law § 274-b, Village Law 7-725-b.

279. In re Gage's Appeal, 167 A.2d 292 (Pa. 1961).

280. 297 S.E.2d 718 (Va. 1982).

right in the same district.[281] One court struck down an ordinance that required a special exception for all uses in a commercial district as "a roving and virtually unlimited power to discriminate ... between landowners similarly situated."[282] Modifications in site development standards, such as setbacks, require a variance and may not be approved as a conditional use.[283]

## § 6.55. Delegation to Legislative Body or Plan Commission.

Although the Standard Act and most zoning acts delegate the authority to grant conditional uses to the zoning board, many zoning ordinances do not follow this practice. The ordinance may delegate the authority to grant conditional uses to the planning commission, to the commission with a further appeal to the governing body, or to the governing body. This practice reflects a belief that the review of conditional uses should be carried out by the planning staff, which advises the commission and council but which does not usually advise the zoning board. A zoning statute may allow this option. California allows a delegation to a zoning administrator, the governing body, the planning commission, or the zoning board.[284]

Several cases invalidated a delegated of power to the planning commission[285] or the governing body[286] to grant special exceptions. In these states the zoning statute followed the Standard Act and delegated the authority to grant special exceptions to the board of adjustment. This interpretation is too restrictive. The Standard Act provides that the governing body "may" authorize the board of adjustment to grant special exceptions. The governing body could decide not to grant this power to the board and to retain the special exception function. Courts have upheld a delegation to the governing body in states where the authority to

---

281. Bierman v. Township of Taymouth, 383 N.W.2d 235 (Mich. App. 1985) (can classify junkyards but not landfills as special exception in agricultural district); LaRue v. Township of East Brunswick, 172 A.2d 691 (N.J. App. Div. 1961) (apartments in single-family district). *See* High Meadows Park v. City of Aurora, 250 N.E.2d 517 (Ill. App. 1969) (requiring special exception for mobile homes). *Cf.* People v. Perez, 29 Cal. Rptr. 781 (Cal. App. 1963).

282. SCIT, Inc. v. Planning Bd., 472 N.E.2d 269 (Mass. App. 1984). *See also* Jachimek v. Superior Ct., 819 P.2d 487 (Ariz. 1991) (cannot limit special use for pawn shops to overlay zone for commercial district).

283. One Hundred Two Glenstone, Inc. v. Board of Adjustment, 572 S.W.2d 891 (Mo. App. 1978).

284. Cal. Gov't Code §§ 65901-65904.

285. Langer v. Planning & Zoning Comm'n, 313 A.2d 44 (Conn. 1972); Franklin County v. Webster, 400 S.W.2d 693 (Ky. 1966); Swimming River Golf & Country Club v. Borough of New Shrewsbury, 152 A.2d 135 (N.J. 1959).

286. City of Des Moines v. Lohner, 168 N.W.2d 779 (Iowa 1969); Goerke v. Township of Middletown, 205 A.2d 338 (N.J. 1964); Salt Lake County Cottonwood Sanitary Dist. v. Sandy City, 879 P.2d 1379 (Utah App. 1994); State ex rel. Skelly Oil Co. v. Common Council, 207 N.W.2d 585 (Wis. 1973). *Compare* State ex rel. Ludlow v. Guffey, 306 S.W.2d 552 (Mo. 1957).

delegate to the board is omitted or where the statute leaves the delegation question open.[287]

Courts are divided on whether the zoning ordinance must provide standards when the legislative body has the authority to grant special exceptions.[288] They hold that the legislative body must act reasonably, even when standards are not required. They review the governing body's decision under the same criteria they apply to the board of adjustment when it has the power to grant a special exception.[289]

### § 6.56. Discretion to Deny or Approve.

The hostile judicial attitude courts adopt when they review variances does not appear in the conditional use cases. Courts may again reinforce judicial control of conditional use decisions by requiring findings of fact,[290] and some statutes impose this requirement.[291] Most courts hold that an applicant has the initial burden to show that his conditional use satisfies the criteria contained in the ordinance, but that the burden then shifts to objectors to show that the use does not satisfy the criteria and is adverse to the public interest.[292]

### § 6.57. Discretion Narrow.

Most courts hold that the zoning agency's discretion to deny an application for a conditional use is narrow. They will reverse a denial of a conditional use when the applicant has complied with the standards provided in the ordinance.[293]

---

**287.** Kotrich v. County of DuPage, 166 N.E.2d 601 (Ill.), *appeal dismissed,* 364 U.S. 475 (1960); Eberhart v. Indiana Waste Sys., 452 N.E.2d 455 (Ind. App. 1983); Corporation Way Realty Trust v. Building Comm'r of Medford, 205 N.E.2d 718 (Mass. 1965); Detroit Osteopathic Hosp. Corp. v. City of Southfield, 139 N.W.2d 728 (Mich. 1966); Green Point Sav. Bank v. Board of Zoning Appeals, 24 N.E.2d 319 (N.Y. 1939), *appeal dismissed,* 309 U.S. 633 (1940).

**288.** § 6.02.

**289.** Zylka v. City of Crystal, 167 N.W.2d 45 (Minn. 1969); Golden v. City of St. Louis Park, 122 N.W.2d 570 (Minn. 1963); Realty Corp. v. Larkin, 181 N.E.2d 407 (N.Y. 1962).

**290.** Honn v. City of Coon Rapids, 313 N.W.2d 409 (Minn. 1981); Melucci v. Zoning Bd. of Review, 226 A.2d 416 (R.I. 1967); Ames v. Town of Painter, 389 S.E.2d 702 (Va. 1990); Harding v. Board of Zoning Appeals, 219 S.E.2d 324 (W. Va. 1975).

**291.** 65 Ill. Comp. Stat. Ann. 5/11-13-11.

**292.** Irvine v. Duval County Planning Comm'n, 495 So. 2d 167 (Fla. 1986); Commonwealth of Pa., Bureau of Cors. v. City of Pittsburgh City Council, 532 A.2d 12 (Pa. 1987). *See* Damascus Community Church v. Clackamas County Bd. of Comm'rs, 573 P.2d 726 (Or. App. 1978) (ordinance may place burden on applicant); Delta Biological Resources, Inc. v. Board of Zoning Appeals, 467 N.W.2d 164 (Wis. App. 1991).

**293.** Lazarus v. Village of Northbrook, 199 N.E.2d 797 (Ill. 1964); Town of Merrillville Bd. of Zoning Appeals v. Public Storage, Inc., 568 N.E.2d 1092 (Ind. App. 1991); Amoco Oil Co. v. City of Minneapolis, 395 N.W.2d 115 (Minn. App. 1986); State ex rel. Presbyterian Church of Washington County v. City of Washington, 911 S.W.2d 697 (Mo. App. 1995); Verona, Inc. v. Mayor &

For example, a board may disapprove an unwanted use, such as a group home or a landfill, if there is substantial public opposition. Courts reverse disapprovals in these cases if the use complies with the criteria for approval contained in the ordinance.[294]

*Archdiocese of Portland v. County of Washington*[295] states the rationale for this result. The court distinguished the conditional use from the zoning amendment and added the following comments on the role of conditional uses in zoning:

> Because . . . [conditional] uses are generally compatible with the design of the zone the possibility that a permitted use will not comport with the comprehensive plan is not as great as it is when a variance or amendment is sought.
>
> . . .
>
> [T]he ordinance itself reveals the legislative plan .... The suspicion which is cast upon the approval of a change involving an incompatible use ... is not warranted where the change has been anticipated by the governing body.[296]

Judicial review of conditional use decisions is complicated by the vague standards zoning ordinances often include, such as a standard that authorizes the approval of a conditional use if it serves the "general welfare." The courts limit the discretion of zoning agencies under provisions of this type by holding that the ordinance authorizes only the consideration of appropriate criteria, such as the impact of a conditional use on the surrounding area.[297] Nor is community pressure an acceptable reason for denying a conditional use.[298]

---

Council of West Caldwell, 229 A.2d 651 (N.J. 1967); North Shore Steak House, Inc. v. Board of Appeals, 282 N.E.2d 606 (N.Y. 1972); C.B.H. Props., Inc. v. Rose, 613 N.Y.S.2d 913 (App. Div. 1994); Hydraulic Press Brick Co. v. Council of City of Independence, 475 N.E.2d 144 (Ohio App. 1984); Bankoff v. Board of Adjustment, 875 P.2d 1138 (Okla. 1994).

**294.** Pollard v. Palm Beach Cty., 560 So. 2d 1358 (Fla. App. 1990) (group home); Fulton Cty. v. Bartenfeld, 363 S.E.2d 555 (Ga. 1988) (landfill, when opponents based testimony on fear; applicant had obtained state permit); Framike Realty Corp. v. Hinck, 632 N.Y.S.2d 177 (App. Div. 1995); Davis Cty. v. Clearfield City, 756 P.2d 704 (Utah App. 1988) (group home).

**295.** 458 P.2d 682 (Or. 1969).

**296.** *Id.* at 685, 686.

**297.** Tandem Holding Corp. v. Board of Zoning Appeals, 373 N.E.2d 282 (N.Y. 1977); Piney Mt. Neighborhood Ass'n v. Town of Chapel Hill, 304 S.E.2d 251 (N.C. App. 1983) (may not consider racial status of subsidized housing occupants); Harts Book Stores v. City of Raleigh, 281 S.E.2d 761 (N.C. App. 1981). *See also* Schultz v. Pritts, 432 A.2d 1319 (Md. 1981); Atlantic Richfield Co. v. City of Franklin Zoning Hearing Bd., 465 A.2d 98 (Pa. Commw. 1983).

**298.** Conetta v. City of Sarasota, 400 So. 2d 1051 (Fla. App. 1981); City of Barnum v. County of Carlton, 386 N.W.2d 770 (Minn. App. 1986); Robert Lee Realty Co. v. Village of Spring Valley, 462 N.E.2d 1193 (N.Y. 1984).

The courts will uphold a conditional use denial only if it is based on criteria included in the ordinance.[299] *C.R. Invs., Inc. v. Village of Shoreview*[300] illustrates this rule. A developer applied for a conditional use to construct nineteen "quad" apartments adjacent to single-family homes located across a county road. As one of the reasons for denying the conditional use, the council found that there was an "insufficient buffer from existing single-family homes." It apparently based this finding on the applicant's failure to plan for single-family homes on its site in the area nearest to the adjacent single-family homes. The court held that this reason for denial was inappropriate in the absence of evidence that the development would adversely affect the welfare of the area or the "value of surrounding property." The zoning ordinance did not require a buffer, and the city planner stated that the buffer provided by the road was sufficient.

### § 6.58. Discretion Broad.

Other cases hold that statutes and ordinances granting the authority to approve conditional uses conferred a broad discretion to deny a conditional use application.[301] In these cases the zoning ordinance or statute either contained generalized approval standards or stated that the zoning board "may" grant conditional uses. The use of the word "may" required judicial deference to the board's decision. The courts also uphold a denial of a conditional use when the evidence shows that it would have an adverse effect on the surrounding area.[302] A court may also rely on a municipality's broad discretion in reviewing conditional uses to uphold a decision approving a conditional use.[303]

---

**299.** Harris v. City of Costa Mesa, 31 Cal. Rptr. 2d 1 (Cal. App. 1994) (accessory apartment); Inland Constr. Co. v. City of Bloomington, 195 N.W.2d 558 (Minn. 1972); Value Oil Co. v. Town of Irvington, 377 A.2d 1225 (N.J.L. 1977); Brentwood Borough v. Cooper, 431 A.2d 1177 (Pa. Commw. 1981).

**300.** 304 N.W.2d 320 (Minn. 1981); Nevada Contrs. v. Washoe Cty., 792 P.2d 31 (Nev. 1990) (decision discretionary and denial must be sustained if supported by substantial evidence).

**301.** Mobil Oil Corp. v. Zoning Bd. of Appeals, 644 A.2d 401 (Conn. App. 1994); Connecticut Health Facilities, Inc. v. Zoning Bd. of Appeals, 613 A.2d 1358 (Conn. App. 1992); Gulf Oil Corp. v. Board of Appeals, 244 N.E.2d 311 (Mass. 1969); Anderson v. Peden, 587 P.2d 59 (Or. 1978); Kleck v. Zoning Bd. of Adjustment, 319 S.W.2d 406 (Tex. App. 1958).

**302.** White Bear Docking & Storage, Inc. v. City of White Bear Lake, 324 N.W.2d 174 (Minn. 1982); Vulcan Materials Co. v. Guilford County, 444 S.E.2d 639 (N.C. App. 1994) (stone quarry); Visionquest Nat'l, Ltd. v. Board of Supvrs., 569 A.2d 915 (Pa. 1990) (correctional camp for juveniles); Atlantic Richfield Co. v. City of Franklin Zoning Hearing Bd., 465 A.2d 98 (Pa. Commw. 1983).

**303.** City of Reno v. Harris, 895 P.2d 663 (Nev. 1995).

## § 6.59. Free Speech-Protected and Religious Uses.

The courts apply more stringent rules to ordinances that authorize conditional uses protected by the free speech clause. These uses include adult businesses and signs.[304] A conditional use requirement for these uses is unconstitutional as a prior restraint on speech unless the ordinance contains precise standards. The courts have invalidated standards they approve for other uses, such as a compatibility standard, when an ordinance adopted it for uses protected by the free speech clause.[305] The ordinance in many of these cases did not require the approval of a conditional use if the applicant met the standards. This omission influenced the decisions. The courts believed it gave too much discretion to zoning agencies and officials.

The courts upheld conditional use standards that contained more precise criteria, especially when the ordinance required the approval of the conditional use if the applicant met the standards. In *People v. Nadeau*,[306] for example, the ordinance contained six specific criteria for a conditional use, such as a requirement that it be "sufficiently buffered" so that it does not "adversely affect" residential areas. The ordinance required the approval of a conditional use that met the criteria. The court held that the criteria were sufficiently precise. It distinguished cases that invalidated criteria that contained "moralistic litany" and "rambling statements of purpose" and noted that the ordinances in these cases conferred unlimited discretion to deny a permit or license.

A Supreme Court decision, *FW/PBS v. City of Dallas, Inc.*,[307] extended additional prior restraint protections to municipal licensing programs, even though they are content-and viewpoint-neutral. This case should also apply to condi-

---

**304.** §§ 5.53-5.61 (adult businesses), 11.12-11.21 (signs). *See also* §§ 5.05-5.08 (group homes), 5.17-5.21 (mobile homes); Marty's Adult World of Enfield, Inc. v. Town of Enfield, 20 F.3d 512 (2d Cir. 1994) (upholds special permit requirement for parking when no permit needed to operate viewing booths); Fisher v. Pilcher, 341 A.2d 713 (Del. Super. 1975) (day care center).

**305.** TJ's South, Inc. v. Town of Lowell, 895 F. Supp. 1124 (N.D. Ind. 1995); Dease v. City of Anaheim, 826 F. Supp. 336 (C.D. Cal. 1993); Smith v. County of Los Angeles, 29 Cal. Rptr. 2d 680 (Cal. App. 1994); City of Indio v. Arryo, 191 Cal. Rptr. 565 (Cal. App. 1983) (sign); City of Imperial Beach v. Palm Ave. Books, 171 Cal. Rptr. 197 (Cal. App. 1981) (adult business); Zebulon Enters. v. County of DuPage, 496 N.E.2d 1256 (Ill. App. 1986) (adult business); Landover Books, Inc. v. Prince George's Cty., 566 A.2d 792 (Md. App. 1989) (same); Barbulean v. City of Newburgh, 640 N.Y.S.2d 935 (Sup. Ct. 1996) (same); White Adv. Metro v. Zoning Hearing Bd., 453 A.2d 29 (Pa. Commw. 1982) (sign). *But see* Rodriguez v. Solis, 2 Cal. Rptr. 2d 50 (Cal. App. 1991) (sign permit denial not content-based; standards upheld).

**306.** 227 Cal. Rptr. 644 (Cal. App. 1986). *Accord* 5297 Pulaski Hwy., Inc. v. Town of Perryville, 519 A.2d 206 (Md. App. 1987). *Compare* Outdoor Sys., Inc. v. City of Mesa, 997 F.2d 604 (9th Cir. 1993) (discretion to distinguish between commercial and noncommercial signs upheld); Jeffrey Lauren Land Co. v. City of Livonia, 326 N.W.2d 604 (Mich. App. 1982) (conditional use requirement for general audience movie theater justified by traffic and parking concerns).

**307.** 493 U.S. 215 (1990).

tional uses and other discretionary zoning decisions. The plurality and concurring Justices held that license decisions must be made within a specified and reasonable time, during which the status quo is maintained. These Justices also required a possibility of prompt judicial review if the license was denied. A California court has applied *FW/PBS* to hold that it qualifies the holding in *Nadeau* that reasonable but unspecified time limits for decision satisfy First Amendment requirements.[308] Courts since *FW/PBS* have also invalidated licensing and conditional use requirements for adult and religious uses.[309]

Although courts have upheld a conditional use permit requirement for religious uses,[310] a state court's treatment of a conditional use denial depends on whether it gives religious uses a preferred use status. States that give religious uses a preferred status rely on their constitutionally-protected status or a showing that a church would not substantially increase traffic congestion to reverse conditional use denials.[311] States that do not apply the preferred status rule have upheld conditional use denials for religious uses that would create traffic congestion.[312] A federal court of appeals reversed the denial of a special use permit

---

**308.** People v. Library One, Inc., 280 Cal. Rptr. 400 (Cal. App. 1991).

**309.** 1126 Baltimore Blvd., Inc. v. Prince George's County, 58 F.3d 988 (4th Cir. 1995) (zoning; decision and judicial review period too long), *cert. denied,* 116 S. Ct. 967 (1996); Redner v. Dean, 29 F.3d 1495 (11th Cir. 1994) (licensing; risk that expressive activity repressed for indefinite time periods, judicial review not timely), *cert. denied,* 115 S. Ct. 1697 (1995); Alpine Christian Fellowship v. County Comm'rs, 870 F. Supp. 991 (D. Colo. 1994) (church school).

**310.** Christian Gospel Ch. v. City & Cty. of San Francisco, 896 F.2d 1221 (9th Cir. 1990); Grace Community Church v. Planning & Zoning Comm'n, 622 A.2d 591 (Conn. App. 1993); City of Las Cruces v. Huerta, 692 P.2d 1331 (N.M. App. 1984). *See* §§ 5.58-5.60. *See also* Cohen v. City of Des Plaines, 8 F.3d 484 (7th Cir. 1993) (special permit requirement exemption for churces did not violate Establishment Clause), *cert. denied,* 114 S. Ct. 2741 (1994).

**311.** Aluminum Co. of Am. v. Lipke, 320 S.W.2d 751 (Ark. 1959); City of Englewood v. Apostolic Christian Church, 362 P.2d 172 (Colo. 1961); Columbus Park Congregation of Jehovah's Witnesses, Inc. v. Board of Appeals, 182 N.E.2d 722 (Ill. 1962); Our Saviour's Evangelical Lutheran Ch. v. City of Naperville, 541 N.E.2d 1150 (Ill. App. 1989) (parking lot variance); Lubavitch Chabad House of Ill., Inc. v. City of Evanston, 445 N.E.2d 343 (Ill. App. 1982) (in mixed use area); Kali Bari Temple v. Board of Adjustment, 638 A.2d 839 (N.J. App. Div. 1994) (home in residential area; adverse effects reduced by conditions); Harrison Orthodox Minyan, Inc. v. Town Bd., 552 N.Y.S.2d 434 (App. Div. 1990) (must treat religious uses flexibly; denial improper). *See also* Mooney v. Village of Orchard Lake, 53 N.W.2d 308 (Mich. 1952); 77 A.L.R.2d 377 (1960).

**312.** West Hartford Methodist Church v. Zoning Bd. of Appeals, 121 A.2d 640 (Conn. 1956); Milwaukie Company of Jehovah's Witnesses v. Mullen, 330 P.2d 5 (Or. 1958), *appeal dismissed,* 359 U.S. 436 (1959). *See also* First Assembly of God v. City of Alexandra, 739 F.2d 942 (4th Cir. 1984) (landscaping and enrollment conditions); Abram v. City of Fayetteville, 661 S.W.2d 371 (Ark. 1983) (church exceptions does not authorize school); Allendale Congregation of Jehovah's Witnesses v. Grosman, 152 A.2d 569 (N.J. 1959), (upholding denial of conditional use for church), *appeal dismissed,* 361 U.S. 536 (1960); Macedonian Orthodox Church v. Planning Bd., 636 A.2d 96 (N.J. App. Div. 1994) (denial of expansion and relocation of previously approved community

for a Moslem center.[313] It held the denial was based only on community opposition and that different standards were applied than had been applied to other churches.

## § 6.60. Consistency with the Plan.

State statutes that require zoning to be consistent with the comprehensive plan do not always indicate whether the consistency requirement applies to conditional uses.[314] A California statute requires land uses "authorized" by the zoning ordinance to be consistent with the plan. *Neighborhood Action Group v. County of Calaveras*[315] held that this statute requires a conditional use to be consistent with a comprehensive plan. The court held that the consistency requirement is "implied from the hierarchical relationship of the land use laws." A conditional use "is struck from the mold of the zoning law," and the zoning law must comply with the comprehensive plan. The court also held that a conditional use approval is invalid if plan elements required by the statute are inadequate.

Some cases based their review of a conditional use decision on the policies of a comprehensive plan even though the statute did not require consistency with the plan.[316] In Oregon, the consistency requirement does not apply to conditional uses because they are a presumptively permitted use under the zoning ordinance.[317]

## § 6.61. Conditions.

The Standard Zoning Act[318] and the state zoning acts that follow it authorize the board of adjustment to impose conditions on special exceptions. The case law on conditions attached to special exceptions is the same as the case law on conditions attached to variances.[319] The decisions approve conditions that relate

---

hall); City of Pasco v. Rhine, 753 P.2d 993 (Wash. App. 1988) (upholding condition prohibiting external display of posters for X-rated films).

313. Islamic Center of Miss., Inc. v. City of Starkville, 840 F.2d 293 (5th Cir. 1988).

314. *But see* Fla. Stat. Ann. § 163.3194.

315. 203 Cal. Rptr. 401 (Cal. App. 1984). *Contra,* Hawkins v. County of Marin, 126 Cal. Rptr. 754 (Cal. App. 1976). *See* Elysian Heights Residents Ass'n v. City of Los Angeles, 227 Cal. Rptr. 226 (Cal. App. 1986) (building permit need not be consistent).

316. International Villages, Inc. of Am. v. Board of County Comm'rs, 585 P.2d 999 (Kan. 1978); Hubbard Broadcasting, Inc. v. City of Afton, 323 N.W.2d 757 (Minn. 1982); City of Reno v. Harris, 895 P.2d 663 (Nev. 1995); Piney Mt. Neighborhood Ass'n v. Town of Chapel Hill, 304 S.E.2d 251 (N.C. App. 1983); 40 A.L.R.2d 372 (1955).

317. Kristensen v. City of Eugene Planning Comm'n, 544 P.2d 591 (Or. App. 1976).

318. Standard Zoning Act § 7. *See, e.g.,* N.Y. Town Law §§ 274-a(4), 274-b(4).

319. § 6.51.

to the use of the land, such as conditions that require access and parking.[320] They disapprove conditions that do not relate to the use of the land, such as a condition that terminates the conditional use when there is a change in ownership.[321]

## F. NEWER FORMS OF FLEXIBLE ZONING.

## § 6.62. Role and Function.

Many zoning ordinances include flexible zoning techniques that are not authorized by the Standard Zoning Act. These techniques give the municipality more control over the details of land development than zoning regulations usually allow. Contract or conditional zoning, under which detailed conditions are imposed concurrently with a zoning amendment, is one example. The floating zone, which defers the mapping of a zoning district until the developer makes an application for development, is another.

A few states authorize the use of flexible zoning techniques,[322] but elsewhere the courts must decide whether they should imply the authority to use a flexible zoning technique from a zoning statute that does not expressly authorize it. Although some courts were initially hostile to the use of flexible zoning techniques, the trend is now the other way.

---

**320.** Exxon, Inc. v. City of Frederick, 375 A.2d 34 (Md. 1977) (denial of access to street); Rockford Blacktop Constr. Co. v. County of Boone, 635 N.E.2d 1077 (Ill. App. 1994) (five-year limitation on special use for quarry upheld); Water Dist. No. 1 v. City Council, 871 P.2d 1256 (Kan. 1994) (conditions on operation of sludge lagoon valid); Titman v. Zoning Hearing Bd., 408 A.2d 167 (Pa. Commw. 1979) (parking area); Hemontolor v. Wilson County Bd. of Zoning Appeals, 883 S.W.2d 613 (Tenn. App. 1994). *See* Cal. Gov't Code § 65909 (condition must be reasonably related to use of property).

**321.** Anza Parking Corp. v. City of Burlingame, 241 Cal. Rptr. 175 (Cal. App. 1987) (making use nontransferable); Board of Zoning Adjustment v. Murphy, 438 S.E.2d 134 (Ga. App. 1994) (requiring parking attendant at off-site location); Middlesex & Boston St. Ry. v. Board of Aldermen, 359 N.E.2d 1279 (Mass. 1977) (requiring lease to public housing authority at reduced rents); Solar v. Zoning Bd. of Appeals, 600 N.E.2d 187 (Mass. App. 1992) (making use nontransferable); Sandbothe v. City of Olivette, 647 S.W.2d 198 (Mo. App. 1983) (restricting hours of operation and prohibiting drive-through facility for fast food restaurant); Mechem v. City of Santa Fe, 634 P.2d 690 (N.M. 1981) (terminating use if change in ownership); Old Country Burgers v. Town Bd. of Oyster Bay, 553 N.Y.S.2d 843 (App. Div. 1990) (prohibiting drive-in business for fast-food restaurant during mealtimes). *See also* Halfway House v. City of Waukegan, 641 N.E.2d 1005 (Ill. App. 1994) (condition prohibiting group home from accepting sexual offenders held vague); Elkhart County Bd. of Zoning Appeals v. Earthmovers, Inc., 631 N.E.2d 927 (Ind. App. 1994) (conditions may sometimes regulate who uses land). *But see* Hopengarten v. Board of Appeals, 459 N.E.2d 1271 (Mass. App. 1984) (upholding conditions terminating use if title alienated and requiring renewal every three years).

**322.** Ariz. Rev. Stat. §§ 9-462.01(D); 11-821(C) (overlay zoning).

## § 6.63. Floating Zones.

"Floating zone" is the term used for a zoning technique under which the municipality adopts a zoning district in the text of its zoning ordinance but does not map it immediately. The municipality reserves the mapping decision until a developer makes an application to have the floating zone applied to his property. The ordinance includes standards for the approval of the floating zone, such as density and site development standards. Floating zones are usually limited to major nonresidential uses, such as multi-family, industrial, and commercial development. Floating zones are sometimes called "overlay zones."

Because the Standard Zoning Act does not authorize the floating zone, it does not specify the zoning agency that must approve them. The municipality may delegate the authority to approve a floating zone to the legislative body, the board of adjustment, or the planning commission. It may also require concurrent approval by one or more of these bodies.

The floating zone may provide more control over development than the special exception. As one court noted,[323] the municipality can impose more limitations on development through the floating zone technique, which is not limited by the traditional special exception standards. The zoning agency may also have more discretion to reject a floating zone, especially if a court characterizes the floating zone review process as legislative. The usual rules governing conditional uses, which require approval when all standards in the ordinance have been met, may not apply.

The floating zone raised a number of legal problems when it first became popular. Objectors argued that floating zones were unauthorized because zoning legislation required the mapping of a zoning district concurrently with its textual adoption. They also argued that floating zones were improper spot zoning and an improper delegation of legislative power.

The courts approved the floating zone in the limited number of cases in which it was considered. The first and leading case, *Rodgers v. Village of Tarrytown*,[324] illustrates the typical judicial view. The village adopted a new zoning district for garden apartments that contained detailed site and density standards and required a minimum tract of ten acres. The boundaries of the zone were to be determined later "by amendment" to the zoning map as applications were made. The planning board was authorized to approve amendments, with a further appeal to the governing body if the planning board denied an application.

After the board and governing body approved a floating zone for garden apartments, a neighboring landowner challenged the map amendment and the

---

**323.** Sheridan v. Planning Bd., 266 A.2d 396 (Conn. 1969).

**324.** 96 N.E.2d 731 (N.Y. 1951). *See* Beyer v. Burns, 567 N.Y.S.2d 599 (Sup. Ct. 1991) (upholding floating zone including reverter provision if construction not commenced within two years of rezoning).

textual adoption of the floating zone district. The court approved the map amendment "in the light of the area involved" and because the amendment met the housing needs of the community. It also approved the floating zone procedure. It held that the village could decide on "the choice of methods" to amend the ordinance and could adopt a procedure that authorized map amendments on application by a landowner. The minimum acreage requirement was valid because garden apartments "would blend more attractively and harmoniously ... if placed upon larger tracts of land."

The court rejected a number of other objections to the floating zone. It held it was not spot zoning because it applied to the entire village and was not designed for the benefit of a single landowner. Nor did the floating zone divest the village of the "power to regulate future zoning." The decision to map a floating zone remained within the discretion of the planning board and governing body. The floating zone was not a "device" for granting a variance but was enacted "to permit the development of the property for the general welfare of the entire community." The village did not need to set boundaries for the floating zone at the time it was adopted textually because the ordinance "prescribed specifications for a new use district." *Tarrytown* reviewed the major problems raised by floating zones, and other court decisions have accepted its reasoning.[325]

A few cases invalidated an extreme use of discretionary zoning.[326] In these cases a suburban zoning ordinance zoned an entire municipality for residential use and required the discretionary approval of all nonresidential uses. The courts held that the zoning statute required the municipality to regulate land use by dividing the community into appropriate zoning districts. These cases are a hostile judicial reaction to the conversion of zoning into a process that is entirely discretionary.

Courts have approved floating zones when they were not consistent with a comprehensive plan in states in which the plan is advisory.[327] The consistency problem has not yet arisen in states that have a consistency requirement. Con-

---

325. Sheridan v. Planning Bd., 266 A.2d 396 (Conn. 1969); Pleasant Valley Neighborhood Ass'n v. Planning & Zoning Comm'n, 543 A.2d 296 (Conn. App. 1988); Bellemeade Co. v. Priddle, 503 S.W.2d 734 (Ky. 1974); Huff v. Board of Zoning Appeals, 133 A.2d 83 (Md. 1957); Treme v. St. Louis County, 609 S.W.2d 706 (Mo. App. 1980); 80 A.L.R.3d 95 (1977). *But see* Lutz v. City of Longview, 520 P.2d 1374 (Wash. 1974). *See also* Montgomery County v. Colesville Citizens Ass'n, 521 A.2d 770 (Md. App. 1987) (basis for approving floating zone). *Compare* Homart Dev. Co. v. Planning & Zoning Comm'n, 600 A.2d 13 (Conn. App. 1991) (commission has discretion to deny or approve floating zone; denial upheld).

326. Rockhill v. Chesterfield Twp., 128 A.2d 473 (N.J. 1957); Town of Hobart v. Collier, 87 N.W.2d 868 (Wis. 1958). *Compare* Eves v. Zoning Bd. of Adjustment, 164 A.2d 7 (Pa. 1960), *with* Klem v. Zoning Hearing Bd., 387 A.2d 667 (Pa. Commw. 1978).

327. Loh v. Town Plan & Zoning Comm'n, 282 A.2d 894 (Conn. 1971). *See* McQuail v. Shell Oil Co., 183 A.2d 572 (Del. 1962); Floyd v. County Council, 461 A.2d 76 (Md. App. 1983).

sistency with the plan is preferable when the floating zone authorizes intensive uses that may impair the policies of a comprehensive plan.

## § 6.64. Contract and Conditional Zoning.

Contract or conditional zoning is another zoning technique that provides more flexibility in the administration of the zoning ordinance. Contract zoning is used because of problems created by the zoning district system. In the typical zoning ordinance, each zoning district allows a wide range of permitted uses. An example is a neighborhood commercial zone, which may allow a wide variety of neighborhood commercial uses.

Adjacent property owners may object to a rezoning because the landowner may use his land for any of the uses permitted in the new zone, not just the use he contemplates. In contract zoning, the landowner agrees to restrict the use of his land to the use for which he seeks the zoning amendment. The landowner may agree to other protective conditions, such as a landscaped buffer adjacent to the residential dwellings. Municipalities may also use contract zoning to secure street widening or other contributions from the landowner.

Contract zoning can take several forms. One frequently used classification distinguishes between unilateral and bilateral contract zoning. In unilateral contract zoning, the landowner unilaterally agrees to impose restrictions on his land in a written document, which he records. The municipal governing body or planning commission indicates the restrictions it wants the landowner to adopt but does not formally agree to a rezoning if the landowner complies. In bilateral contract zoning, a landowner and the municipality execute a bilateral contract in which the municipality promises to rezone in return for the landowner's promise to record a document that contains the restrictions the municipality requires. A landowner can also execute a bilateral contract with adjacent landowners.

Some courts refer to the case in which a landowner imposes restrictions on his land unilaterally as conditional zoning. They apply the term "contract zoning" only to a true bilateral contract between a landowner and a municipality. This text uses all of these terms interchangeably.

Contract zoning advocates defend it as an appropriate zoning technique that tailors land development to its environment and assures its compatibility with adjacent land uses. The objections to contract zoning are similar to those raised against floating zones. Contract zoning is claimed to be invalid because it is unauthorized by the zoning statute, because it is arbitrary spot zoning and an illegal bargaining away of the zoning power, and because it violates the statutory provision that requires uniform land use regulations within zoning districts. Several states now authorize contract zoning.[328]

---

**328.** Ariz. Rev. Stat. Ann. §§ 9-452.01(E), 11-832; Idaho Code § 67-6511A; Md. Code Ann. art. 66B, § 4.01(b); R.I. Gen. Laws. § 45-24-53(H); Va. Code Ann. §§ 15.1-491.1 to 491.6.

The case law on contract and conditional zoning is mixed, although most of the more recent decisions approve this technique. Whether the conditions on development are imposed bilaterally or unilaterally makes a difference. The courts usually disapprove bilateral contract zoning but approve conditions on development that are imposed unilaterally.

Despite growing judicial approval of conditional zoning, its use by municipalities is unwise. Individually negotiated zoning agreements undercut the uniformity of the land use regulations imposed by the zoning ordinance. The proliferation of a large number of zoning agreements throughout a municipality complicates zoning enforcement. Although a municipality may be able to amend the zoning ordinance to impose restrictions that conflict with a rezoning agreement, this problem is also troublesome.[329] Detailed control over land development is possible under acceptable zoning techniques that impose development standards subject to approval by the zoning agency. Floating zones and site plan review are two examples.

The terminology used by the courts in the "contract" zoning cases is not clear, and it is difficult to find accepted terms that describe the results in the cases. The discussion that follows divides the cases into the "bilateral" and "unilateral" categories, but the text indicates that the courts have different views of these terms. One court has adopted the term "concomitant agreement zoning" for this zoning device.[330]

The Nebraska court upheld a rezoning for a mixed use development that included four agreements executed by the city and the developer incorporating the development plan.[331] The court held that the distinction between contract and conditional zoning was irrelevant and that the critical question was whether the conditions on the rezoning advanced the public health, safety and general welfare. The court held that the city was entitled to make agreements with developers requiring them to follow their plans, because otherwise these plans are difficult to enforce.

### § 6.65. Bilateral.

A number of cases have held bilateral contract zoning invalid.[332] In these cases the municipality and the developer executed a bilateral contract, or the or-

---

329. Delucchi v. County of Santa Cruz, 225 Cal. Rptr. 43 (Cal. App.), *appeal dismissed and cert. denied,* 497 U.S. 803 (1986); Nicholson v. Tourtellotte, 293 A.2d 909 (R.I. 1972).

330. State ex rel. Myhre v. City of Spokane, 422 P.2d 790 (Wash. 1967).

331. Giger v. City of Omaha, 442 N.W.2d 182 (Neb. 1989) (court also found no bargaining away of police power). *See also* Bradley v. City of Trussville, 527 So. 2d 1303 (Ala. Civ. App. 1988) (no delegation of legislative power).

332. Hartman v. Buckson, 467 A.2d 694 (Del. Ch. 1983); Hartnett v. Austin, 93 So. 2d 86 (Fla. 1956); Cederberg v. City of Rockford, 291 N.E.2d 249 (Ill. App. 1972); Baylis v. City of Balti-

dinance that adopted the rezoning included the terms of a bilateral agreement. *Houston Petroleum Co. v. Automotive Prods. Credit Ass'n*[333] best expresses the reasoning these cases adopt. The court held invalid an agreement in which the developer agreed to impose site development restrictions and stated:

> Contracts thus have no place in a zoning plan and a contract between a municipality and a property owner should not enter into the enactment or enforcement of zoning regulations.[334]

A court may hold a conditioned rezoning invalid even when the applicant and the municipality do not execute a bilateral contract to rezone. In one case a court invalidated a zoning amendment adopted on the basis of representations from the developer that it would limit the development of its land to certain specified uses.[335] Zoning, it held, cannot "be effected ... by special arrangements with the owner of a particular tract or parcel of land."

In other cases the municipality executed a contract with the developer, concurrent with the rezoning, in which he agreed to dedicate land or make a contribution to street widenings and other improvements. Some cases upheld these agreements, emphasizing that the municipality did not agree to rezone and that the improvements to which the owner contributed were reasonably required by the development.[336]

The purpose of a rezoning agreement may make it invalid. Municipalities sometimes insist on "reverter" agreements under which the land reverts to its initial zoning classification if the landowner does not begin development in a reasonable period of time. The cases hold these agreements invalid because they accomplish a rezoning without recourse to the usual notice and hearing requirements that apply to zoning amendments.[337]

---

more, 148 A.2d 429 (Md. 1959); Rodriguez v. Prince George's Cty., 558 A.2d 742 (Md. App. 1989); Carlino v. Whitpain Invs., 453 A.2d 1385 (Pa. 1982). *See also* Chung v. Sarasota County, 686 So.2d 1358 (Fla. App. 1996) (settlement agreement). But see Broward County v. Griffey, 366 So. 2d 869 (Fla. App. 1979). *See generally* 70 A.L.R.3d 125 (1976).

333. 87 A.2d 319 (N.J. 1952).

334. *Id.* at 322.

335. Allred v. City of Raleigh, 178 S.E.2d 432 (N.C. 1971). *See also* Chrismon v. Guilford Cty., 370 S.E.2d 579 (N.C. 1988) (citing treatise); Hall v. City of Durham, 372 S.E.2d 564 (N.C. 1988) (same).

336. Scrutton v. County of Sacramento, 79 Cal. Rptr. 872 (Cal. App. 1969); Gladwyne Colony, Inc. v. Township of Lower Merion, 187 A.2d 549 (Pa. 1963); State ex rel. Myhre v. City of Spokane, 422 P.2d 790 (Wash. 1967). *But see* Transamerica Title Ins. Co. v. City of Tucson, 533 P.2d 693 (Ariz. App. 1975). *See also* §§ 9.11-9.15.

337. Scrutton v. County of Sacramento, 79 Cal. Rptr. 872 (Cal. App. 1969); Hausmann & Johnson, Inc. v. Berea Bd. of Bldg. Code Appeals, 320 N.E.2d 685 (Ohio App. 1974). *But see* Goffinet v. County of Christian, 357 N.E.2d 442 (Ill. 1976); Colwell v. Howard County, 354 A.2d 210 (Md. App. 1976). *See also* Dexter v. Town Bd., 324 N.E.2d 870 (N.Y. 1975). *Contra*, Beyer v. Burns, 567 N.Y.S.2d 599 (Sup. Ct. 1991) (in floating zone ordinance).

A court may uphold a bilateral agreement when it is made with third parties, such as neighbors. In *State ex rel. Zupancic v. Schimenz*,[338] an applicant for a zoning change executed an agreement with neighbors that restricted the site to a specified use and imposed site development restrictions. The agreement was executed and recorded after the neighbors expressed concern about the rezoning at a plan commission meeting.

The court upheld the rezoning and noted that there was no agreement with the city and no agreement to rezone. A rezoning is not invalid contract zoning when "a zoning authority . . . is motivated to zone by agreements as to use of the land made by others." Private agreements that "underlie" zoning provide the "flexibility and control" that allow "a municipality to meet the ever-increasing demands for rezoning in a rapidly changing area."[339] The court also held that the rezoning must be "otherwise valid" and suggested that the imposition of conditions on land development "might better be done by uniform ordinances providing for special uses, special exceptions and overlaid districts."

### § 6.66. Unilateral.

A growing number of cases uphold contract zoning when the restrictions on the rezoned property are imposed unilaterally by the landowner.[340] Courts sometimes refer to this type of zoning as conditional zoning. In these cases there was no evidence of a bilateral contract, although the rezoning ordinance may have contained the restrictions that the landowner imposed on the land.[341] The cases emphasized the protective function of restrictions unilaterally imposed on the land that avoided or mitigated the adverse impacts of the development on adjacent property owners.

The favorable judicial view of conditional zoning was expressed in extensive dictum in *Collard v. Incorporated Village of Flower Hill*.[342] The court indicated that conditional zoning is not objectionable as a form of spot zoning. It held that, if a zoning change is proper, it is not automatically invalid simply because conditions are imposed. The court pointed out that "imposing limiting conditions while benefiting surrounding properties, normally adversely affects the premises on which the conditions are imposed."

The court held that conditional zoning is not an improper bargaining away of the police power "absent proof of a contract purporting to bind the local legisla-

---

338. 174 N.W.2d 533 (Wis. 1970).

339. *See also* City of Greenbelt v. Bresler, 236 A.2d 1 (Md. 1967); Pressman v. City of Baltimore, 160 A.2d 379 (Md. 1960).

340. Martin v. Hatfield, 308 S.E.2d 833 (Ga. 1983); Sylvania Elec. Prods., Inc. v. City of Newton, 183 N.E.2d 118 (Mass. 1962); Church v. Town of Islip, 168 N.E.2d 680 (N.Y. 1960).

341. King's Mill Homeowners Ass'n v. City of Westminster, 557 P.2d 1186 (Colo. 1976).

342. 421 N.E.2d 818 (N.Y. 1981).

ture in advance." It held that the zoning act did not prohibit conditional zoning, which was "within the spirit" of the enabling legislation as a means of harmonizing "the landowner's need for rezoning with the public interest." It added that preventing the legislative body from imposing conditions that protect adjacent property would not be "in the best interests of the public."

Some courts do not approve unilateral conditional zoning. In *Bartsch v. Planning & Zoning Comm'n*,[343] a municipality conditioned a rezoning on the filing of a restrictive covenant that limited the use of the land to a medical office building. The court held that the covenant was a "blatant violation" of the "strict" statutory provision that requires uniform regulations within zoning districts.

## § 6.67. Proper Purpose View.

*Collard*[344] represents a judicial view which holds that unilateral conditions do not necessarily invalidate a rezoning if they serve proper zoning purposes and if the rezoning is valid under the usual zoning map amendment tests. This point of view is illustrated by *Cross v. Hall County*,[345] which held that neighbors cannot attack conditions imposed for their "benefit and protection . . . to ameliorate the effects of the zoning change." *Goffinet v. County of Christian*[346] is a similar case. The county imposed site development conditions on a rezoning for a synthetic gas production facility. The court held that the conditions "are not of such a nature as to constitute an abrupt departure from the comprehensive zoning plan . . ., which emphasizes substantial industrial development for the future." The court reviewed and upheld the rezoning under its traditional zoning tests and rejected a spot zoning objection to the zoning amendment.

These cases treat zoning conditions as a neutral factor in their review of zoning map amendments. They take the reasonable view that neighbors should not be allowed to complain of zoning conditions imposed for their benefit. Some courts still show concern over possible abuses of the conditional zoning process.[347]

## § 6.68. Site Plan Review.

Site plan review is a zoning technique that allows municipalities to exercise control over the site details of a development. In the typical site plan review procedure, the applicant for an amendment, conditional use, variance, or building

---

343. 506 A.2d 1093 (Conn. App. 1986). *Accord* Board of County Comm'rs v. H. Manny Holtz, Inc., 501 A.2d 489 (Md. App. 1985); Dacy v. Village of Ruidoso, 845 P.2d 793 (N.M. 1992) (municipality promised to rezone).

344. § 6.66.

345. 235 S.E.2d 379 (Ga. 1977).

346. 357 N.E.2d 442 (Ill. 1976).

347. Nolan v. City of Taylorville, 420 N.E.2d 1037 (Ill. App. 1981).

permit submits a detailed site plan to the plan commission, zoning board, or administrative staff. Approval of the site plan is required before development may proceed. Site plan review usually applies to nonresidential and multi-family development on individual lots. It is a useful supplement to subdivision controls, which do not usually apply to this type of development because it does not require the subdivision of land.

Some courts have assumed that the authority to use site plan review exists even in the absence of express statutory authority.[348] Other courts implied the power to require site plan review as a step in the approval of special exceptions and zoning amendments.[349] A few zoning statutes authorize site plan review and specify the site development requirements the municipality can impose in the site plan review process.[350]

The role of site plan review as compared with the variance and special exception is not always clear. The limitations on the site plan review procedure authorized by the New Jersey legislation were explored in *Lionel's Appliance Center, Inc. v. Citta*.[351] A local planning board approved a site plan for an office building and two restaurants. Neighbors objected that the board should have disapproved the site plan because the development would cause off-site traffic problems.

The court disagreed and distinguished site plan review from similar zoning controls, such as variances and conditional uses. It concluded that traffic problems were an appropriate concern in the administration of these controls, but that the statutory provision authorizing site plan review did not authorize the denial of a site plan because of off-site traffic congestion. "[T]he planning board may deny a site plan application only if the ingress and egress proposed by the plan creates an unsafe and inefficient vehicular circulation."[352] The court held that, if

---

**348.** McCrann v. Town Plan. & Zoning Comm'n, 282 A.2d 900 (Conn. 1971); Charter Twp. of Harrison v. Calisi, 329 N.W.2d 488 (Mich. App. 1982); Sun Oil Co. v. Zoning Bd. of Adjustment, 169 A.2d 294 (Pa. 1961) (ordinance also held constitutional).

**349.** Colwell v. Howard County, 354 A.2d 210 (Md. App. 1976) (amendment); Y.D. Dugout, Inc. v. Board of Appeals, 255 N.E.2d 732 (Mass. 1970) (special exception); Southwick, Inc. v. City of Lacey, 795 P.2d 712 (Wash. App. 1990) (council may delegate site plan review to administrative agency after zoning approved). *See also* Kozesnik v. Township of Montgomery, 131 A.2d 1 (N.J. 1957) (under statute authorizing governing body to refer "any action" to planning commission).

**350.** N.J. Stat. Ann. §§ 40:55D-37 to 42; N.Y. Town Law § 274-a; N.Y. Village Law § 7-725-a. *See* Moriarty v. Planning Bd., 506 N.Y.S.2d 184 (App. Div. 1986) (site plan denial because of distance from fire hydrants exceeded authority; citing treatise).

**351.** 383 A.2d 773 (N.J.L. 1978). *Accord* TLC Dev. Co. v. Planning & Zoning Comm'n, 577 A.2d 288 (Conn. 1990); New England Brickmaster, Inc. v. Town of Salem, 582 A.2d 601 (N.H. 1990); Dunkin' Donuts of N.J., Inc. v. Township of North Brunswick Plan. Bd. 475 A.2d 71 (N.J. App. Div. 1984).

**352.** 383 A.2d at 779.

a site plan affected off-site conditions such as traffic, the site plan review ordinance could require a contribution from the developer for a street widening that would remedy the traffic congestion.

This decision is consistent with decisions elsewhere. They hold that site plan review is limited to conditions relating to the site.[353] Some courts also hold that the site plan review ordinance may not require developer contributions for off-site improvements.[354]

If a site plan complies with site plan review requirements and if the proposed use is authorized by the zoning ordinance, the reviewing agency may not disapprove the site plan because it finds the proposed use objectionable. In *Kosinski v. Lawlor*,[355] a site plan proposed a retail complex that met all of the requirements in the zoning ordinance for site plans, but the planning and zoning commission rejected the plan because it was a "poor use for the site." The court held that site plan review "may be used . . . only in conjunction with and not as an alternative" to zoning standards.[356] Courts review decisions approving or denying site plans under the rules they usually apply to the review of administrative zoning decisions.[357]

---

**353.** Coscan Washington, Inc. v. Maryland-National Capital Park & Planning Comm'n, 590 A.2d 1080 (Md. App. 1991) (can impose condition designating building materials and condition upheld); Southland Corp. v. Mayor & City Council, 541 A.2d 653 (Md. App. 1988) (can deny site plan because of traffic hazards); Holmes v. Planning Bd. of Town of New Castle, 433 N.Y.S.2d 587 (Sup. Ct. 1980) (may impose access conditions).

**354.** *Compare* Robbins Auto Parts, Inc. v. City of Laconia, 371 A.2d 1167 (N.H. 1977) (authorized) *with* Riegert Apts. Corp. v. Planning Bd., 441 N.E.2d 1067 (N.Y. 1982) (contra).

**355.** 418 A.2d 66 (Conn. 1979).

**356.** Sherman v. City of Colorado Springs Planning Comm'n, 680 P.2d 1302 (Colo. App. 1983), *aff'd on appeal from remand,* 729 P.2d 1014 (Colo. App. 1986); Allen Plywood, Inc. v. Planning & Zoning Comm'n, 480 A.2d 584 (Conn. App. 1984); East Lake Partners v. City of Dover Planning Comm'n, 655 A.2d 821 (Del. Super. 1995); S.E.W. Friel v. Triangle Oil Co., 543 A.2d 863 (Md. App. 1988); Prudential Ins. Co. v. Board of Appeals, 502 N.E.2d 137 (Mass. App. 1986); PRB Enters. v. South Brunswick Planning Bd., 518 A.2d 1099 (N.J. 1987); Bongiorno v. Planning Bd., 533 N.Y.S.2d 631 (App. Div. 1988) (reversing disapproval of site plan for permitted use when denial based on opposition); Brooks v. Fisher, 705 S.W.2d 135 (Tenn. App. 1985). *See also* Saddle River Country Day School v. Borough of Saddle River, 144 A.2d 425 (N.J. App. Div. 1958) (may not interfere with board of adjustment variance and special exception powers), *aff'd,* 150 A.2d 34 (N.J. 1959). *Compare* Wesley Inv. Co. v. County of Alameda, 198 Cal. Rptr. 872 (Cal. App. 1984) (ordinance allowed site plan denial of permitted use); Hansel v. City of Keene, 634 A.2d 1351 (N.H. 1993) (cannot impose condition on site plan approval less stringent than zoning ordinance requires).

**357.** Lindborg/Dahl Invs., Inc. v. City of Garden Grove, 225 Cal. Rptr. 154 (Cal. App. 1986) (upholding site plan denial); Crann v. Town Plan & Zoning Comm'n, 282 A.2d 900 (Conn. 1971) (can reverse approval only if arbitrary or abuse of discretion); Black v. Summers, 542 N.Y.S.2d 837 (App. Div. 1989) (invalidating condition prohibiting development). *See* City of Boynton Beach v. V.S.H. Realty, Inc., 443 So. 2d 452 (Fla. App. 1984) (site plan review held discretionary). *See also* Bowen v. Board of Appeals, 632 N.E.2d 858 (Mass. App. 1994) (ordinance does not

## G. DECISION-MAKING PROCEDURES.

### § 6.69.  The Procedure Problem.

Zoning-enabling legislation provides basic procedural protections in the decision-making process, such as the notice and hearing requirements for zoning amendments.[358] Courts may require additional procedural protections under the due process clause of federal and state constitutions. Procedural protections available under the federal constitution are discussed in Chapter 2.[359] This part discusses procedural protections constitutionally required by the state courts. Whether the state or federal constitution is being applied in state court cases is not always clear, however, and the cases do not usually make the constitutional basis of their decision explicit.

### § 6.70.  Legislative vs. Quasi-Judicial.

In state as in federal courts, the threshold question is whether a land use decision is legislative or quasi-judicial, for only quasi-judicial decisions implicate procedural due process. Comprehensive rezoning is legislative, as is a zoning map amendment for a single parcel in a majority of states.[360] Administrative actions, such as subdivision approvals,[361] variances, conditional use permits and building permits, are held quasi-judicial.[362]

### § 6.71.  Entitlement.

Assuming that a land use decision is adjudicatory, a party challenging it must also claim that it deprived her of a protectible property interest or "entitlement."

---

require detailed findings); Leda Lanes Realty, Inc. v. City of Nashua, 293 A.2d 320 (N.H. 1972); Palatine I v. Planning Bd., 628 A.2d 321 (N.J. 1993) (interpreting statutory protection of preliminary site plan approval).

**358.** § 4.18. Some legislation provides more detailed procedural safeguards. *See* Ga. Code Ann. § 36-66-1 et seq.

**359.** § 2.45.

**360.** §§ 2.46, 6.26.

**361.** Horn v. County of Ventura, 596 P.2d 1134, 1138 (Cal. 1979); Shaw v. Planning Comm'n, 500 A.2d 1338 (Conn. App. 1985); Mutton Hill Estates, Inc. v. Town of Oakland, 468 A.2d 989 (Me. 1983).

**362.** Building permits: Sclavenitis v. Cherry Hills Bd. of Adj., 751 P.2d 661 (Colo. App. 1988); Thomson v. State, Dep't of Envtl. Reg., 493 So. 2d 1032 (Fla. App. 1986). *See also* County of Lancaster v. Mecklenburg County, 434 S.E.2d 604 (N.C. 1993) (landfill permit).

Conditional use permits: Scott v. City of Indian Wells, 492 P.2d 1137 (Cal. 1972); Barton Contr'g Co. v. City of Afton, 268 N.W.2d 712 (Minn. 1978).

Variances: Speedway Bd. of Zoning Appeals v. Popcheff, 385 N.E.2d 1179 (Ind. App. 1979); White v. Town of Hollis, 589 A.2d 46 (Me. 1991); Horn v. Township of Hilltown, 337 A.2d 858 (Pa. 1975); Schalow v. Waupaca Cty., 407 N.W.2d 316 (Wis. App. 1987); Cook v. Zoning Bd. of Adj., 776 P.2d 181 (Wyo. 1989).

In the federal courts, an entitlement does not include an expectancy interest.[363] A landowner has an expectancy rather than an entitlement under federal law if a decision on his application for a land use approval requires an exercise of discretion by the land use agency or official. Some state courts follow the federal rules on entitlement,[364] but a minority provide procedural due process protection even if the landowner has only an expectancy interest.[365] Some courts provide procedural due process protections to adjacent landowners affected by a zoning approval.[366]

## § 6.72. Procedures Required.

Once a court has determined that a land use decision is adjudicatory and that an entitlement was affected, it must determine what process is due. The Supreme Court employs a three-part balancing test to decide this question,[367] and some state courts also apply this test.[368]

Some state courts refuse to impose the full range of trial-type procedures on adjudicatory decision-making by zoning authorities.[369] Other courts virtually judicialize adjudicatory decision-making by local land use authorities.[370] They may

---

**363.** § 2.45.

**364.** Red Maple Properties v. Zoning Comm'n, 610 A.2d 1238 (Conn. 1992); Sandy Beach Defense Fund v. City Council, 773 P.2d 250 (Hawaii 1989).

**365.** Goldberg v. City of Rehoboth Beach, 565 A.2d 936, 942 (Del. Super. Ct.) (partitioning request), aff'd, 567 A.2d 421 (Del. 1989); Fairbairn v. Planning Bd., 360 N.E.2d 668 (Mass. App. 1977) (subdivision approval).

**366.** Scott v. City of Indian Wells, 492 P.2d 1137 (Cal. 1972); Roosevelt v. Beau Monde Co., 384 P.2d 96 (Colo. 1963); Rodine v. Zoning Bd. of Adj., 434 N.W.2d 124 (Iowa App. 1988); Koppel v. City of Fairway, 371 P.2d 113 (Kan. 1962). *But see* Sandy Beach Defense Fund v. City Council, 773 P.2d 250 (Hawaii 1989) (only abutting owners protected); Wells v. Village of Libertyville, 505 N.E.2d 740 (Ill. App. 1987) (notice by publication enough); *Compare* Lawrence Preservation Alliance, Inc. v. Allen Realty, Inc., 819 P.2d 138 (Kan. App. 1991) (historical preservation groups have protectible interests at stake in requests for demolition permits).

**367.** Mathews v. Eldridge, 424 U.S. 319 (1976).

**368.** Goldberg v. City of Rehoboth Beach, 565 A.2d 936 (Del. Super. Ct.) (partitioning request), aff'd, 567 A.2d 421 (Del. 1989); Horn v. County of Ventura, 596 P.2d 1134 (Cal. 1979). *See also* Waste Management of Illinois, Inc. v. Pollution Control Bd., 530 N.E.2d 682 (Ill. App. 1988) (similar balancing test adopted as state requirement).

**369.** Kletschka v. LeSueur Cty. Bd. of Comm'rs, 277 N.W.2d 404 (Minn. 1979) (no cross-examination required in administrative appeal from denial of conditional use permit).

**370.** Cardillo v. Council of South Bethany, 1991 Del. Super. Lexis 224 (Super. Ct. 1991) (subdivision application); Coral Reef Nurseries, Inc. v. Babcock Co., 410 So. 2d 648, 652 (Fla. App. 1982) (right to present evidence and cross-examine and be informed of factual basis for decision); Cooper v. Board of Cty. Comm'rs, 614 P.2d 947 (Idaho 1980) (notice; transcribable verbatim record of proceedings; specific findings of fact and conclusions); Kaelin v. City of Louisville, 643 S.W.2d 590, 591 (Ky. 1983); Fairbairn v. Planning Bd., 360 N.E.2d 668 (Mass. App. 1977) (same); Neuberger v. City of Portland, 607 P.2d 722, 725 (Or. 1980) (ex parte contacts); Board of

require adequate notice,[371] hearings by a neutral arbiter, the right to present evidence, the right to cross-examine witnesses, the right to respond to written submissions, the right to counsel, and a decision on the record with stated reasons. Procedural due process rights may vary with the administrative posture of the case. For example, when a final decision-maker must engage in de novo factfinding, a planning board need not submit its findings of fact in writing.[372]

Claims of procedural due process violations may be difficult to sustain. State courts may require plaintiffs that complain of unfair hearings to defeat the presumption that local authorities performed their duties properly,[373] prove that they were prejudiced (*e.g.,* that they had been denied variances although they had not shown undue hardship),[374] and preserve their rights of appeal to the courts by objecting to procedural due process violations at the hearing level.[375]

Nevertheless, there have been successful challenges to hearings and factfinding by local agencies. For example, procedural due process was denied when a board of adjustment told the plaintiff's attorney the hearings were over, and then, in the attorney's absence, reopened the hearings to take adverse testimony.[376] Other courts found procedural due process violations when local agency factfinding was not supported by the record.[377]

---

Cty. Comm'rs v. Teton Cty. Youth Servs., 652 P.2d 400 (Wyo. 1982) (hearing, taking of evidence, findings of fact, orders based on substantial evidence, judicial review). *See also* § 6.48.

**371.** Gernatt v. Town of Sardinia, 664 N.E.2d 1226 (N.Y. 1996) (notice adequate).

**372.** Jago-Ford v. Planning & Zoning Comm'n, 642 A.2d 14 (Conn. App. 1994) (member absent from some hearings sufficiently acquainted with case); Riverside Groups, Inc. v. Smith, 497 So. 2d 988 (Fla. App. 1986); Petersen v. City of Clemson, 439 S.E.2d 317 (S.C. App. 1993) (extensive minutes by Planning Board given to council with oral report satisfied written report requirement).

**373.** Messer v. Snohomish Cty. Bd. of Adj., 578 P.2d 50 (Wash. App. 1978).

**374.** Speedway Bd. of Zoning Appeals v. Popcheff, 385 N.E.2d 1179 (Ind. App. 1979); White v. Town of Hollis, 589 A.2d 46 (Me. 1991). *See also* Danville-Boyle County Planning & Zoning Comm'n v. Prall, 840 S.W.2d 205 (Ky. 1992); Barton Contr'g Co. v. City of Afton, 268 N.W.2d 712 (Minn. 1978); Pease Hill Community Group v. County of Spokane, 816 P.2d 37 (Wash. App. 1991).

**375.** Speedway Bd. of Zoning Appeals v. Popcheff, 385 N.E.2d 1179 (Ind. App. 1979); Jorgensen v. Board of Adj., 336 N.W.2d 423 (Iowa 1983).

**376.** Sclavenitis v. Cherry Hills Bd. of Adj., 751 P.2d 661 (Colo. App. 1988). *Accord* Clark v. City of Hermosa Beach, 56 Cal. Rptr. 2d 223 (Cal. App. 1996), *cert. denied,* 117 S. Ct. 1430 (1997). *Compare* Board of County Comm'rs v. Webber, 658 So. 2d 1069 (Fla. App. 1995) (reconsideration held proper).

**377.** Bryan v. Salmon Corp., 554 S.W.2d 912 (Ky. App. 1977); In re Rocky Point Plaza Corp., 621 N.E.2d 566 (Ohio App. 1993); Schalow v. Waupaca Cty., 407 N.W.2d 316 (Wis. App. 1987) (county made no record and took no evidence). *See also* McKinstry v. Wells, 548 S.W.2d 169 (Ky. App. 1977) (cannot rely on legislative fact-finding by planning commission).

## § 6.73. Impartial Decision-Maker.

Procedural due process guarantees the parties an impartial decision-maker. That means a decision-maker free of bias and conflict of interest.[378] An impartial decision-maker must also be a decision-maker untainted by ex parte contacts, although state courts are careful to point out that ex parte contacts do not render a decision void per se.[379] Some courts hold that ex parte contacts are not actionable at all if discoverable in time to be rebutted.[380] Other courts hold that ex parte contacts are actionable if prejudicial, and they may adopt a rebuttable presumption of prejudice.[381] Other courts require that plaintiffs show prejudice — at least when the alleged contacts are open contacts with public entities[382] rather than concealed contacts with individual decision-makers.[383]

Finally, several courts have held that the right to an impartial decision-maker is impaired when attorneys for a party before a zoning board also serve on it,[384] or when a single attorney or a single law firm provides both advocacy and adjudicatory counsel in a single proceeding.[385]

## § 6.74. Bias and Conflict of Interest.

The traditional rule that judicial and administrative decision makers must not be tainted with prejudice when passing on claims that come before them is applicable to the zoning process. Courts examine administrative and quasi-judicial decision making in zoning to determine whether bias or a conflict of interest was present. Bias and conflict-of-interest claims are less successful when brought against legislative decision makers because of the rule, applied to zoning as well as other legislative actions, that courts will not investigate the motives of legislative bodies.[386] Fraud in the legislative process is an exception to this rule.[387]

---

**378.** §§ 6.74-6.76.

**379.** Blaker v. Planning & Zoning Comm'n, 562 A.2d 1093 (Conn. 1989); Neuberger v. City of Portland, 607 P.2d 722, 725 (Or. 1980).

**380.** Jennings v. Dade Cty., 1991 Fla. App. Lexis 12672 (Fla. App. 1991).

**381.** *Id.*; Waste Management v. Pollution Control Bd., 530 N.E.2d 682 (Ill. App. 1986).

**382.** Neuberger v. City of Portland, 607 P.2d 722 (Or. 1980). *See* Ore. Rev. Stat. § 227.180(3); Horizon Constr. Co. v. City of Newberg, 834 P.2d 523 (Or. App. 1992) (ex parte contact not cured).

**383.** 1000 Friends of Oregon v. Wasco Cty. Ct., 723 P.2d 1034 (Or. App. 1986) (incorporation).

**384.** Washington Cty. Cease, Inc. v. Persico, 473 N.Y.S.2d 610 (App. Div. 1984), *aff'd*, 477 N.E.2d 1084 (N.Y. 1985).

**385.** Horn v. Township of Hilltown, 337 A.2d 858 (Pa. 1975) (proof of prejudice not required).

**386.** Brown v. Town of Davidson, 439 S.E.2d 206 (N.C. App. 1994); Fiser v. City of Knoxville, 584 S.W.2d 659 (Tenn. App. 1979).

**387.** Schauer v. City of Miami Beach, 112 So. 2d 838 (Fla. 1959); Athey v. City of Peru, 317 N.E.2d 294 (Ill. App. 1974). *Cf.* Woodland Hills Residents Ass'n v. City Council, 609 P.2d 1029

The bias and conflict-of-interest disqualification applies to members of the governing body in states where the courts hold that rezoning and other actions by the governing body are quasi-judicial. A minority of courts disqualify a member of a governing body because of bias and conflict of interest even though they hold that the governing body acts in a quasi-legislative manner in the zoning process.[388]

Washington has adopted a unique "appearance of fairness" rule that applies to legislative and administrative proceedings in which a hearing is required.[389] This rule incorporates a two-part fairness test. A reasonable person attending a hearing must be able to conclude that everyone entitled to a hearing obtained one. The agency holding the hearing must also give due weight to the matters presented.

A few states have statutory provisions covering bias and conflict-of-interest problems. These statutes usually apply to planning commission and board of adjustment members and prohibit any direct or indirect personal or financial interest.[390] The statutory prohibition sometimes is extended to members of legislative bodies.[391] New York has enacted a full disclosure requirement for amendments, variances, and other land use decisions.[392]

### § 6.75. Bias.

The courts have found bias when a member of a local zoning agency makes outspoken public statements on a zoning matter she subsequently heard.[393] In a typical case, a board member made it openly clear that she would oppose an application for a variance or similar approval no matter what evidence an applicant introduced. The court disqualified the board member from sitting when the

---

(Cal. 1980) (campaign contributions do not create appearance of unfairness). *See* 63 A.L.R.2d 1072 (1975) (effect of abstention on voting majority requirement).

**388.** Olley Valley Estates, Inc. v. Fussell, 208 S.E.2d 801 (Ga. 1974); Netluch v. Mayor & Council, 325 A.2d 517 (N.J. 1974). *But see* Sugarloaf Citizens Ass'n v. Gudis, 573 A.2d 1325 (Md. 1990) (ordinance authorizing court to void zoning ordinance because of conflict of interest violates separation of powers).

**389.** Fleming v. City of Tacoma, 502 P.2d 327 (Wash. 1972). *See also* Golden Gate Corp. v. Town of Narragansett, 359 A.2d 321 (R.I. 1976); 71 A.L.R.2d 568 (1960).

**390.** Cal. Gov't Code § 87100; Colo. Rev. Stat. § 24-18-105; Conn. Gen. Stat. §§ 8-11, 8-21; N.J. Stat. Ann. § 40:55D-69; Pa. Stat. Ann. tit. 65, § 401 et seq.; Va. Code Ann. § 2.1-639.01 et seq.

**391.** Ga. Code Ann. §§ 36-67A-1 to 36-67A-4 (applies only to rezoning); Idaho Code § 67-6506.

**392.** N.Y. Gen. Mun. Law § 809.

**393.** Lage v. Zoning Bd. of Appeals, 172 A.2d 911 (Conn. 1961); Acierno v. Folsom, 337 A.2d 309 (Del. 1975); Barbara Realty Co. v. Zoning Bd. of Review, 128 A.2d 342 (R.I. 1957); Chrobuck v. Snohomish County, 480 P.2d 489 (Wash. 1971); Marris v. City of Cedarburg, 498 N.W.2d 842 (Wis. 1993). *See also* Marmah, Inc. v. Town of Greenwich, 405 A.2d 63 (Conn. 1978).

board heard the variance application. Participation by members of a decision body in a project for which they later grant a zoning approval may not constitute bias.[394]

The cases have not disqualified a public official because of campaign statements when he later voted in accordance with his campaign promises.[395] As one court pointed out:

> Campaign promises made in political races do not disqualify .... Under our theory of government the voters desire and even demand to be informed as to how candidates stand on the issues of the campaign.[396]

## § 6.76. Conflicts of Interest.

Conflicts of interest usually arise when a member of a zoning agency has a pecuniary interest in a zoning decision or a personal relationship with the applicant for a zoning change. A pecuniary interest based on the ownership of property affected by the zoning change is a typical example. A court may find an improper pecuniary interest even though a zoning action is extensive and the board member's property is not the only property affected. In *Kovalik v. Planning & Zoning Comm'n,*[397] the chairman of the commission owned eight percent of the land that the commission upgraded to two-acre residential zoning. The court found a disqualifying conflict of interest.[398]

---

**394.** In re Application of City of Raleigh, 421 S.E.2d 179 (N.C. App. 1992) (contrary holding would destroy community's orderly planning process). *But see* South Brunswick Assocs. v. Township Council, 667 A.2d 1 (N.J.L. Div. 1995) (council president may not represent opposition to project before zoning board and then participate in council review of board decision). *See also* Wyzkowski v. Rizas, 626 A.2d 406 (N.J. 1993) (discussing whether mayor may make application to planning board).

**395.** City of Fairfield v. Superior Court of Solano County, 537 P.2d 375 (Cal. 1975); Turf Valley Assocs. v. Zoning Bd., 278 A.2d 574 (Md. 1971); Kramer v. Board of Adjustment, 212 A.2d 153 (N.J. 1965); Wollen v. Borough of Fort Lee, 142 A.2d 881 (N.J. 1958); Webster Assocs. v. Town of Webster, 451 N.E.2d 189 (N.Y. 1983). *See also* Izaak Walton League of Am. v. Monroe County, 448 So. 2d 1170 (Fla. App. 1984) (applying rule to statements made during term of office).

**396.** City of Farmers Branch v. Hawnco, Inc., 435 S.W.2d 288, 292 (Tex. Civ. App. 1968).

**397.** 234 A.2d 838 (Conn. 1967).

**398.** *See also* Griswold v. City of Homer, 925 P.2d 1015 (Alaska 1996) (zoning change would benefit council member's property); Brunswick v. Inland Wetlands Comm'n, 617 A.2d 466 (Conn. App. 1992) (board member voted for subdivision for which he might build roads); O'Ko'olau v. Pacarro, 666 P.2d 177 (Haw. App. 1983) (project would benefit board member's property); Manookian v. Blaine County, 735 P.2d 1008 (Idaho 1987) (commission members voted to route power line away from their property); McNamara v. Borough of Saddle River, 166 A.2d 391 (N.J. 1960); Town of North Hempstead v. Village of North Hills, 342 N.E.2d 566 (N.Y. 1975); Segalla v. Planning Bd., 611 N.Y.S.2d 287 (App. Div. 1995) (ownership of property in town not enough);

A pecuniary benefit from property ownership may not create a conflict of interest if the benefit is indirect. In *Dana-Robin Corp. v. Common Council*,[399] the court did not find a conflict of interest when the council disapproved an application for a multi-family development, even though members of the council owned competing multi-family developments in the city.[400]

A court may refuse to find a pecuniary conflict of interest when the pecuniary benefit is contingent or remote. In *Copple v. City of Lincoln*,[401] a council member voted for a comprehensive plan that designated property he owned for commercial use. He later abstained from voting on the commercial rezoning of his property. The court did not find a conflict of interest. It held that the designation on the comprehensive plan was "speculative" because it depended on future action by the city, including "the future staging of development and zoning."

Members of local zoning boards and commissions often belong to unions and other organizations that benefit indirectly from zoning decisions. An example is a conditional use a zoning board grants for a development project that will employ workers who belong to a board member's union. A court will not find a conflict of interest if the member of the organization does not receive a direct pecuniary benefit.[402] Courts do not want to prohibit service on a zoning agency by an individual whose organization gains indirectly from the zoning process.[403]

Courts find an improper conflict of interest when close personal or business relationships exist between a member of a zoning board and an applicant for a zoning change. A board member was disqualified when his wife was the applicant for a zoning amendment.[404] Board members who sold property to an individual who subsequently made an application for a zoning change on the prop-

---

Amerikohl Mining Co. v. Zoning Hearing Bd., 597 A.2d 219 (Pa. Commw. 1991) (having residence near proposed use that was denied not enough); 10 A.L.R.3d 694 (1966).

399. 348 A.2d 560 (Conn. 1974).

400. *Compare* S & L Assocs. v. Township of Washington, 160 A.2d 635 (N.J. 1960) (disqualifying board member who voted to exclude competing land from industrial area).

401. 274 N.W.2d 520 (Neb. 1979). *See also* Bluffs Dev. Co. v. Board of Adjustment, 499 N.W.2d 12 (Iowa 1993) (family and business relationships with opponents of zoning proposal held remote).

402. Tangen v. State Ethics Comm'n, 550 P.2d 1275 (Haw. 1976); Rowell v. Board of Adj., 446 N.W.2d 917 (Minn. App. 1989) (church member may vote on variance for church). *Compare* Narrowsview Preservation Ass'n v. City of Tacoma, 526 P.2d 897 (Wash. 1974).

403. For other pecuniary interest cases, *see* Hochberg v. Borough of Freehold, 123 A.2d 46 (N.J. 1956); Save a Valuable Env't v. City of Bothell, 576 P.2d 401 (Wash. 1978).

404. Low v. Town of Madison, 60 A.2d 774 (Conn. 1948). *See also* Barrett v. Union Twp. Comm., 553 A.2d 62 (N.J. App. Div. 1989) (board member disqualified to vote on zoning amendment for nursing home where his wife was patient); Sokolinski v. Municipal Council, 469 A.2d 96 (N.J. App. Div. 1983) (board members or their wives employed by school district granted a variance); Zagoreos v. Conklin, 491 N.Y.S.2d 358 (App. Div. 1985) (employees of applicant disqualified). *But see* Petrick v. Planning Bd., 671 A.2d 140 (N.J. App. Div. 1996) (occasional employment of board member by successful applicant for site plan approval not enough).

erty also were disqualified.[405] A board member was disqualified when his nephew was a member of the law firm that represented the applicant.[406] Indirect business relationships, such as writing insurance for an applicant for a zoning amendment, are not disqualifying.[407] Personal interests are also disqualifying,[408] but a mayor's personal interest in an amendment he proposed to a zoning ordinance did not disqualify.[409]

## § 6.77. Neighborhood Opposition.

Zoning boards often react to neighborhood opposition, either in approving or rejecting a land use application. Courts may set aside a zoning decision if they believe that a favorable response to neighborhood opposition tainted the zoning action with an improper motive or purpose. *Chanhassen Estates Residents Ass'n v. City of Chanhassen*[410] states the typical judicial concern that denial of a zoning approval must based "on something more than neighborhood opposition and expressions of concern for public safety and welfare." These decisions are often based on substantive due process concerns.[411]

A number of cases have invalidated zoning approvals found to have been improperly influenced by neighborhood opposition.[412] Courts will uphold a zoning decision, despite neighborhood opposition, if they believe the decision was

---

**405.** Daly v. Town Plan & Zoning Comm'n, 191 A.2d 250 (Conn. 1963); Piggott v. Borough of Hopewell, 91 A.2d 667 (N.J. 1952). *See also* Aldom v. Borough of Roseland, 127 A.2d 190 (N.J. 1956); Zell v. Borough of Roseland, 125 A.2d 890 (N.J. 1956).

**406.** Kremer v. City of Plainfield, 244 A.2d 335 (N.J. 1968). *Accord,* Dick v. Williams, 452 S.E.2d 172 (Ga. App. 1994) (conflict of interest to vote on matter represented by son's law partner); Trust Co. of New Jersey v. Planning Bd., 582 A.2d 1295 (N.J. App. Div. 1990). *Compare* Strandberg v. Kansas City, 415 S.W.2d 737 (Mo. 1967).

**407.** Moody v. City of Univ. Park, 278 S.W.2d 912 (Tex. Civ. App. 1955). *See* Ahearn v. Zoning Bd. of Appeals, 551 N.Y.S.2d 392 (App. Div. 1990) (generalized claims of conflict not enough); West Slope Community Council v. City of Tacoma, 569 P.2d 1183 (Wash. App. 1977).

**408.** Clark v. City of Hermosa Beach, 56 Cal. Rptr.2d 223 (Cal. App. 1996) (council member's enjoyment of home), *cert. denied,* 117 S. Ct. 1430 (1997); Jock v. Shire Realty, Inc., 684 A.2d 921 (N.J. App. Div. 1996) (member of board testified in favor of variance for property in which he had interest).

**409.** Ghent v. Zoning Comm'n, 600 A.2d 1010 (Conn. 1991).

**410.** 342 N.W.2d 335 (Minn. 1984).

**411.** *See also* City of Cleburne v. Cleburne Living Center, 473 U.S. 432 (1985) (denial of special use permit for group home based partly on neighborhood opposition held to violate equal protection). *See* § 2.51.

**412.** Marks v. City of Chesapeake, 833 F.2d 308 (4th Cir. 1989); National Amusements, Inc. v. City of Boston, 560 N.E.2d 138 (Mass. App. 1990); Huntington Health Care Partnership v. Zoning Bd. of Appeals, 516 N.Y.S.2d 99 (App. Div. 1987); Davis County v. Clearfield City, 756 P.2d 704 (Utah App. 1988); Washington State Dept. of Corrections v. City of Kennewick, 937 P.2d 1119 (Wash. App. 1997).

based on legitimate zoning purposes. In *Nelson v. City of Selma*,[413] the court upheld a refusal to rezone, despite neighborhood opposition, because it served the
legitimate purpose of preventing heavy traffic and preserving the residential
character of the neighborhood.

## § 6.78. Open Meeting Laws.

All states have open meeting laws, popularly known as "sunshine laws." Statutes may require all state and local governing bodies, including municipalities
and counties, to hold open meetings.[414] Statutes more commonly require governmental bodies that receive or disburse public funds or act under authority
delegated by the state constitution, statute, charter, or ordinance to hold open
meetings.[415] This includes municipal governing bodies.

Although planning commissions and boards of adjustment normally qualify as
public bodies,[416] they are seldom sued under open meeting laws, probably because state planning and zoning legislation independently requires public hearings by these agencies.[417] Statutes and courts frequently exempt judicial and
quasi-judicial bodies and deliberations from the reach of open meeting laws,
such as a zoning board meeting in closed session to weigh evidence previously
presented at an open meeting on a special use permit application.[418] A public
hearing may be required but deliberation may be allowed in private.[419] Other
statutes[420] and courts[421] require all phases of the decision-making process of
quasi-judicial bodies to be open to the public.

"Meetings" required to be held open to the public are defined as a gathering
of a quorum of the members of the public body in order to transact public busi-

---

**413.** 881 F.2d 836 (9th Cir. 1989). *Accord* Fleckinger v. Jefferson Parish Council, 510 So. 2d
429 (La. App. 1987).

**414.** Ariz. Rev. Stat. Ann. § 38-431(5).

**415.** N.J. Stat. Ann. § 10:4-8. *See also* § 5 Ill. Comp. Stat. Ann. 120/1-120/5.

**416.** Town of Palm Beach v. Gradison, 296 So. 2d 473 (Fla. App. 1974); Hudspeth v. Board of
County Com'rs of Routt, 667 P.2d 775 (Colo. App. 1983). *But see* Goodson Todman Ent. v. Town
Bd. of Milan, 542 N.Y.S.2d 373 (N.Y. App. Div. 1989) (zoning revision committee created to
recommend changes in zoning ordinance held not subject to open meeting because function merely
advisory).

**417.** Wash. Rev. Code Ann. § 36.70.840; Wis. Stat. Ann. § 62.23(7)(d).

**418.** Concerned Citizens v. Town of Guilderland, 458 N.Y.S.2d 13 (App. Div. 1982). *But see*
Ridenour v. Jessamini County Fiscal Court, 842 S.W.2d 532 (Ky. App. 1992) (fiscal court not
exempt).

**419.** Sullivan v. Northwest Garage & Storage Company, 165 A.2d 881 (Md. 1960); State ex rel.
Cities Service Oil Co. v. Board of Appeals, 124 N.W.2d 809 (Wis. 1963).

**420.** Ariz. Rev. Stat. Ann. § 38-431 (exempts only judicial deliberations in court of law); Ky.
Rev. Stat. Ann. § 61.810 (excludes zoning boards and commissions).

**421.** Remington v. City of Boonville, 701 S.W.2d 804 (Mo. App. 1985) (includes administrative bodies, such as boards of adjustment, unless exempted).

ness.[422] Public business which must be conducted at an open meeting normally includes formal action of the governmental body as well as informal discussion on public issues.[423] A meeting also may occur even where a quorum is gathered for the purpose of attending the meeting of another governmental agency.[424] Most state statutes exclude social and chance gatherings from the definition of meeting.[425]

Violations of the open meeting statute occur when public bodies required to hold open meetings, conduct meetings that are closed to the public. Courts usually interpret the "open to the public" requirement as mandating that the meeting be reasonably open to the public.[426] Most courts require that all aspects of the decision-making process be open to the public.[427] Open meeting laws almost always contain provisions requiring notice of public meetings.

Almost all open meeting laws contain specific, enumerated exemptions to the public meeting requirements. Typical exemptions include meetings to discuss pending or potential litigation, meetings to discuss real estate transactions, meetings to discuss personnel matters, and emergency meetings. Courts in some states have narrowed the scope of the exception, holding that only discussions of strategy and position on pending or actual litigation may be closed.[428] Many statutes require a majority vote for a closed meeting, a statement of the exemption that covers the closed meeting, and a posting of the meeting agenda.

Open meeting laws typically provide that actions or deliberations that violate the open meeting law are void or voidable by the court. Such statutes typically give the court discretion in voiding decisions and actions taken in violation of an

---

**422.** Cal. Gov't Code § 54952.6; N.Y. Pub. Off. Law § 102. *See* Sovereign v. Dunn, 498 N.W.2d 62 (Minn. App. 1993) (mediation sessions not a meeting).

**423.** Brookwood Area Homeowners Ass'n v. Anchorage, 702 P.2d 1317 (Alaska 1985); Orange County Publications v. Council of City of Newburgh, 401 N.Y.S.2d 84 (App Div. 1978); Danis Montco Landfill Co. v. Jefferson Twp. Zoning Comm'n, 620 N.E.2d 140 (Ohio App. 1993) (no decision made at meeting); Moore v. Township of Raccoon, 625 A.2d 737 (Pa. Commw. 1993) (plan commission recommendations on junkyard ordinance). *But see* Board of County Comm'rs v. Webber, 658 So. 2d 1069 (Fla. App. 1995) (ex parte discussions not substantive).

**424.** State ex rel. Badke v. Village Bd., 494 N.W.2d 408 (Wis. 1993) (quorum of members of village board attended meetings of planning commission).

**425.** Ind. Code Ann. § 5-14-1.5-2(c)(1); Iowa Code Ann. § 21.2(2).

**426.** State ex rel. Badke v. Village Bd., 494 N.W.2d 408 (Wis. 1993).

**427.** Beck v. Crisp County Bd. of Zoning Appeals, 472 S.E.2d 558 (Ga. App. 1996) (meeting closed to public after evidentiary hearing); Yaro v. Board of Appeals of Newburyport, 410 N.E.2d 725 (Mass. App. 1980).

**428.** *Compare* Caldwell v. Lambrou, 391 A.2d 590 (N.J. App. Div. 1978) (violation; attorney met with board of adjustment in closed session to discuss board's power to modify site plan), *with* Whispering Woods v. Township of Middleton Planning Bd., 531 A.2d 770 (N.J. App. Div. 1987) (no violation; discussion of revised plan for litigation), *and* State ex rel. Hodge v. Town of Turtle Lake, 508 N.W.2d 603 (Wis. 1993) (hearing on junkyard permit not a "case" on which town board can later hold closed meeting).

open meeting law. In addition, statutes may provide for costs and attorney fees to be paid by the losing party and for criminal or civil sanctions against those who violate open meeting laws.

Although open meeting laws void actions taken in violation of open meeting requirements, many courts allow violations to be "cured" by subsequent meetings conforming to the open meeting law.[429] Courts also overlook violations when there has been "substantial compliance" with the act.[430]

## H. INITIATIVE AND REFERENDUM.

### § 6.79. The Zoning Problem.

Many states authorize the use of the initiative and referendum at the municipal level, and the use of these direct electoral techniques to secure zoning change has become increasingly popular. An initiative is a procedure that allows the voters to propose a municipal ordinance, such as a text amendment to a zoning ordinance. The ordinance takes effect if it is approved by the voters. A referendum is a vote on an action by a local legislative body, such as a rezoning that amends the zoning map. The voters decide whether to accept or reject the legislative action.

Referenda are usually permissive and are called only after a specified number of voters have filed a petition. Some municipalities require mandatory referenda on zoning amendments. The initiative is also usually permissive, and an initiative election is called only after the required number of voters have filed the necessary petition.

A zoning referendum is usually called to secure voter review of a zoning change, such as an amendment to a zoning ordinance upzoning a property to a more intensive use or to provide for lower-income housing. An initiative is usually called to propose a major change in the zoning ordinance, such as a growth moratorium. The initiative may also be used as a substitute for a referendum in most states.[431] If a municipality adopts an amendment to the zoning ordinance that upzones land to a more intensive use, the voters may petition for an initiative in the form of a repeal of the zoning amendment.

Referenda and initiatives are available only on legislative as distinguished from administrative or quasi-judicial actions. An ordinance that amends the zoning map is a legislative action in most states. Special exceptions and conditional uses are administrative actions and are not subject to an initiative or referendum. Referenda and initiatives are not available if a statute confers authority to act solely on the municipal governing body. For example, the Washington

---

429. Brookwood Area Homeowners Ass'n v. Anchorage, 702 P.2d 1317 (Alaska 1985) (violation not cured); Moore v. Township of Raccoon, 625 A.2d 737 (Pa. Commw. 1993).

430. State v. City of Hailey, 633 P.2d 576 (Idaho 1981) (annexation and rezoning).

431. *Contra* Christensen v. Carson, 533 N.W.2d 712 (S.D. 1995).

Supreme Court held a referendum unavailable on a county-wide planning policy required by a Growth Management Act because a statute delegated the authority to adopt that policy solely to the county council.[432]

## § 6.80. Federal Constitutional Issues.

The U.S. Supreme Court has held that referenda may violate the equal protection clause if they are racially discriminatory. In *Hunter v. Erickson*,[433] the Court struck down an amendment to a city charter that required a referendum on fair housing ordinances. It held the amendment was "an explicitly racial classification treating racial housing matters differently from other racial and housing matters."

*James v. Valtierra*[434] qualified *Hunter*. The Court upheld a California constitutional provision that required a mandatory referendum on federally-subsidized public housing projects. It distinguished *Hunter* because the California constitutional provision "requires referendum approval for any low-rent public housing project, not only for projects which will be occupied by a racial minority." The Court found no support for "any claim that a law seemingly neutral on its face is in fact aimed at a racial minority." A later Supreme Court case resurrected *Hunter*. It invalidated as racially discriminatory a constitutional provision adopted by referendum that prohibited the busing of school children to achieve racial integration.[435]

Claims that zoning referenda are racially discriminatory are difficult to prove under the equal protection clause because the Supreme Court requires proof of a racially discriminatory intent.[436] The federal courts rejected claims that referenda repealing zoning amendments that allowed lower-income housing projects were racially discriminatory.[437] They were unwilling to investigate voter motivation to determine whether the voters had a racially discriminatory intent.

---

**432.** Snohomish County v. Anderson, 868 P.2d 116 (Wash. 1994). *Accord* Whatcom County v. Brisane, 884 P.2d 1326 (Wash. 1994) (zoning ordinance dopted to implement plan); Save Our State Park v. Board of Clallam County Comm'rs, 875 P.2d 673 (Wash. App. 1994) (initiative).

**433.** 393 U.S. 385 (1969).

**434.** 402 U.S. 137 (1971) (also rejecting wealth discrimination claim).

**435.** § 2.53. *Compare* Washington v. Seattle School Dist. No. 1, 458 U.S. 457 (1982) (busing referendum held racially discriminatory), *with* Crawford v. Board of Educ., 458 U.S. 527 (1982) *(contra)*.

**436.** Washington v. Davis, 426 U.S. 229 (1976).

**437.** Southern Alameda Spanish Speaking Org. v. City of Union City, 424 F.2d 291 (9th Cir. 1970); Ranjel v. City of Lansing, 417 F.2d 321 (6th Cir. 1969), *cert. denied*, 397 U.S. 980 (1970); 15 A.L.R. Fed. 613 (1973).

*City of Eastlake v. Forest City Enters.*[438] rejected due process objections to zoning referenda. A city charter required the approval of any land use change in a referendum receiving fifty-five percent of the vote. The Court held that the referendum provision did not improperly delegate legislative power and noted that a referendum "is a means for direct political participation." Neither did the Court find it objectionable that the referendum provision provided no standards. "[W]e deal with a power reserved by the people to themselves." As the Court noted, if "the referendum result . . . [is] unreasonable, the zoning restriction is open to challenge in state court." The Court pointed out that voter rejection of the referendum would leave in place the zoning restriction that the rejected amendment changed. The landowner could then challenge the zoning restriction in state court or apply for a variance.

The Court rejected a claim that the referendum requirement was unconstitutional under Supreme Court decisions that invalidated neighbor consent provisions in zoning ordinances.[439] The Court held that "the standardless delegation of power to a limited group of property owners . . . is not to be equated with decisionmaking by the people through the referendum process." Justices Powell and Stevens wrote separate dissents in which they argued that the referendum denied property owners the fair procedures to which they were entitled in the zoning process.

Although *Eastlake* rejected a federal constitutional challenge to a zoning referendum, it does not mean that zoning is always subject to referendum procedures. Some state courts have found state statutory and constitutional barriers to the use of the initiative and referendum in the zoning process.

## § 6.81. Availability in Zoning.

### § 6.82. Referendum.

Although the referendum is potentially available on all local legislative zoning actions, some state courts refuse to allow zoning referenda because they conflict with required statutory procedures for the enactment of zoning ordinances, such as notice and hearing requirements. The courts may also hold that the referendum improperly adds to the zoning procedures provided by the zoning legislation.

*Township of Sparta v. Spillane*[440] held that a referendum was not available on a zoning ordinance amendment for these reasons. The court noted that the statu-

---

438. 426 U.S. 668 (1976). *Accord* Moore Bldg. Co. v. Committee for the Repeal of Ordinance R(C)-88-13, 391 S.E.2d 587 (Va. 1990).

439. § 6.04.

440. 312 A.2d 154 (N.J. App. 1973), *cert. denied,* 317 A.2d 706 (N.J. 1974). *Accord* Elliott v. City of Clawson, 175 N.W.2d 821 (Mich. App. 1970); Westgate Families v. County Clerk, 667 P.2d 453 (N.M. 1983); San Pedro N., Ltd. v. City of San Antonio, 562 S.W.2d 260 (Tex. Civ.

tory comprehensive plan requirement and the goal that zoning reflect "the social, economic and physical characteristics of the community . . . might well be jeopardized by piecemeal attacks on the zoning ordinances if referenda were permissible for review of any amendment." The New Jersey zoning statute now exempts zoning ordinances and amendments from the initiative and referendum.[441]

Whether a state court will hold that the zoning referendum is inconsistent with the statutory zoning process may depend on how the referendum is authorized. When the referendum is authorized by statute, as in *Spillane*, the court may treat the availability of the referendum as a question of statutory conflict. A court can hold the referendum unavailable if it finds that the statutory authority for a referendum conflicts with the statutory procedural requirements for zoning enactments. The statute in *Spillane* provided general authority for referenda and did not expressly make referenda available in the zoning process.

Courts may reach a different result when, as in many states, the state constitution authorizes the use of the referendum. These courts liberally construe the constitutional referendum provision and hold it superior to zoning legislation as a "fundamental right" guaranteed to the people. They stress that the zoning statute is not violated because the referendum is held after notice and hearing procedures have been observed in the zoning process. They may also hold that zoning procedures are not violated because the referendum simply restores the zoning regulations to what they were before they were changed.[442] This holding ignores the point that restoration of the original zoning is an amendment to the zoning ordinance, which also requires a statutory notice and hearing.

*City of Fort Collins v. Dooney*[443] held that the evasion of notice and hearing procedures through a referendum does not violate procedural due process. "The fact that due process requirements may be met in one manner when the change is by council action does not preclude other procedures from meeting due process requirements under the referendum."[444] The court noted that the election campaign and debate is an alternative to the public hearing the statute requires before the adoption of a zoning ordinance.

---

App. 1978); State ex rel. Foster v. City of Morgantown, 432 S.E.2d 195 (W. Va. 1993). *See* State ex rel. MacQueen v. City of Dunbar, 278 S.E.2d 636 (W. Va. 1981); 72 A.L.R.3d 1030 (1976). *See also* Great Atlantic & Pacific Tea Co. v. Borough of Point Pleasant, 644 A.2d 598 (N.J. 1994) (statutory prohibition of referendum does not prohibit nonbinding referendum).

**441.** N.J. Stat. Ann. § 40:55D-62(b).

**442.** Queen Creek Land & Cattle Corp. v. Yavapai County Bd. of Supvrs., 501 P.2d 391 (Ariz. 1972); City of Fort Collins v. Dooney, 496 P.2d 316 (Colo. 1972); Florida Land Co. v. City of Winter Springs, 427 So. 2d 170 (Fla. 1983) (relying on constitutional provision for referendum); Cook-Johnson Realty Co. v. Bertolini, 239 N.E.2d 80 (Ohio 1968); R.G. Moore Bldg. Co. v. Committee for the Repeal of Ordinance R(C)-88-13, 391 S.E.2d 587 (Va. 1990) (referendum authorized by ordinance).

**443.** 496 P.2d 316 (Colo. 1972).

**444.** *Id.* at 319. *Accord* City of Coral Gables v. Carmichael, 256 So. 2d 404 (Fla. App. 1972).

The referendum is available on a comprehensive plan or comprehensive zoning amendment if a court characterizes these actions as legislative.[445] It is not available on a limited zoning map amendment if a court characterizes it as quasi-judicial rather than legislative.[446] Administrative zoning decisions, such as special exceptions and variances, are not subject to referendum because the courts usually hold that they are administrative actions.[447] Judicial review of a referendum is limited to whether it is arbitrary and capricious. For example, one court held that voters may disapprove a plan amendment for a development even though it is consistent with a comprehensive plan.[448]

## § 6.83. Initiative.

Most courts hold the initiative is not available to amend or adopt a zoning ordinance because it bypasses the required statutory notice and hearing.[449] These courts hold the lack of a notice and hearing violates the statutory requirement or is unconstitutional as a violation of procedural due process. The cases that dis-

---

**445.** O'Loane v. O'Rourke, 42 Cal. Rptr. 283 (Cal. App. 1965) (plan); State ex rel. Wahlmann v. Reim, 445 S.W.2d 336 (Mo. 1969). *See also* Allison v. Washington County, 548 P.2d 188 (Or. App. 1976).

**446.** Margolis v. District Court, 638 P.2d 297 (Colo. 1981); Kelley v. John, 75 N.W.2d 713 (Neb. 1956); Leonard v. City of Bothell, 557 P.2d 1306 (Wash. 1976). Amendment held legislative: Pioneer Trust Co. v. Pima Cty., 811 P.2d 22 (Ariz. 1991) (conditional rezoning); Johnston v. City of Claremont, 323 P.2d 71 (Cal. 1958); Albright v. City of Portage, 470 N.W.2d 657 (Mich. App. 1991); Denney v. City of Duluth, 202 N.W.2d 892 (Minn. 1973); Greens at Fort Missoula, LLC v. City of Missoula, 897 P.2d 1078 (Mont. 1995); Wilson v. Manning, 657 P.2d 251 (Utah 1982). *See also* Citizens for Quality Growth Petitioners' Comm. v. City of Steamboat Springs, 807 P.2d 1197 (Colo. App. 1991) (council approval of specific use held legislative); Forman v. Eagle Thrifty Drugs & Mkts., Inc., 516 P.2d 1234 (Nev. 1974); Citizen's Awareness Now v. Marakis, 873 P.2d 1117 (Utah 1994) (adopting criteria for zoning change is administrative).

**447.** Southwest Diversified, Inc. v. City of Brisbane, 280 Cal. Rptr. 869 (Cal. App. 1991) (revision in boundaries of area covered by development plan), noted, 29 San Diego L. Rev. 561 (1993); State ex rel. Srovnal v. Linton, 346 N.E.2d 764 (Ohio 1976). *See also* W.W. Dean & Assocs. v. City of South San Francisco, 236 Cal. Rptr. 11 (Cal. App. 1987); Fishman v. City of Palo Alto, 150 Cal. Rptr. 326 (Cal. App. 1974).

**448.** Chandis Securities Co. v. City of Dana Point, 60 Cal. Rptr.2d 481 (Cal. App. 1996).

**449.** Transamerica Title Ins. Co. Trust v. City of Tucson, 757 P.2d 1055 (Ariz. 1988); City of Scottsdale v. Superior Court, 439 P.2d 290 (Ariz. 1968); Andover Dev. Corp. v. City of New Smyrna Beach, 328 So. 2d 231 (Fla. App. 1972); Kaiser Hawaii Kai Dev. Co. v. City & Cty. of Honolulu, 777 P.2d 244 (Hawaii 1989); Gumprecht v. City of Coeur D'Alene, 661 P.2d 1214 (Idaho 1983); State ex rel. Childress v. Anderson, 865 S.W.2d 384 (Mo. App. 1993) (charter city); Smith v. Township of Livingston, 256 A.2d 85 (N.J. Ch.), *aff'd,* 257 A.2d 698 (N.J. 1969); L.A. Ray Realty v. Town Council, 603 A.2d 311 (R.I. 1992); Hancock v. Rouse, 437 S.W.2d 1 (Tex. Civ. App. 1969); Lince v. City of Bremerton, 607 P.2d 329 (Wash. App. 1980); 72 A.L.R.3d 991 (1976).

allow the use of the initiative in zoning do not distinguish the use of the initiative as a referendum substitute.[450]

California takes a different view. In *Associated Home Bldrs. of Greater Eastbay, Inc. v. City of Livermore*,[451] a zoning ordinance enacted by initiative prohibited the issuance of building permits until adequate educational, sewerage, and water facilities were available. The constitution authorizes the initiative and referendum in California. The court noted that the constitutional amendment that authorizes the initiative and referendum was an "outstanding" achievement and held that the initiative did not conflict with the zoning statutes because the constitutional provision was supreme. "[T]he notice and hearing provisions of the state zoning law, if interpreted to bar initiative land use ordinances, would be of doubtful constitutionality."[452] The California court has also upheld the use of the initiative to enact zoning amendments, which are legislative in that state.[453]

A court may invalidate an initiative under the same tests they apply to zoning ordinances adopted by a municipality. In *Arnel Dev. Co. v. City of Costa Mesa*,[454] for example, a California court invalidated an initiative that repealed a zoning amendment for moderate-income housing. It did not find a change in conditions or circumstances that justified the initiative repealer and held it was adopted for the "sole and specific purpose of defeating" the housing development and did not sufficiently accommodate the regional interest in the provision of moderate-income housing.[455]

---

450. *But see* Storegard v. Board of Election, 255 N.E.2d 880 (Ohio 1969) (may use initiative to repeal zoning ordinance).

451. 557 P.2d 473 (Cal. 1976). *See* Devita v. County of Napa, 889 P.2d 1019 (Cal. 1995) (plan amendment initiative to require voter approval of land use changes for 30 years). *Accord* State ex rel. Hickman v. City Council, 690 S.W.2d 799 (Mo. App. 1985).

452. 557 P.2d at 480.

453. Arnel Dev. Co. v. City of Costa Mesa, 620 P.2d 565 (Cal. 1980). *But see* L.I.F.E. Comm. v. City of Lodi, 262 Cal. Rptr. 166 (Cal. App. 1989) (initiative requiring plan amendment before annexation conflicted with annexation statute). *See also* San Diego Bldg. Contractors Ass'n v. City Council, 529 P.2d 570 (Cal. 1974) (building height limit), *appeal dismissed*, 427 U.S. 901 (1976); Lesher Communications, Inc. v. City of Walnut Creek, 262 Cal. Rptr. 337 (Cal. App. 1989) (upholding initiative as amendment to general plan).

454. 178 Cal. Rptr. 723 (Cal. App. 1981).

455. *See also* Northwood Homes, Inc. v. Town of Moraga, 265 Cal. Rptr. 363 (Cal. App. 1989) (repeal of plan amendment for residential development had *de minimis* impact on regional housing need); Patterson v. County of Tehama, 235 Cal. Rptr. 867 (Cal. App. 1987) (initiative ordinance prohibiting zoning to implement comprehensive plan held invalid); Wiltshire v. Superior Court, 218 Cal. Rptr. 199 (Cal. App. 1985) (initiative ordinance transferring approval of waste-to-energy plant to voters invalid as displacement of council adjudicatory powers).

# REFERENCES

## Books and Monographs

B. Blaesser, Discretionary Land Use Controls (1997).

City Deal Making (T. Lassar ed. 1990).

E. Kelly, Enforcing Zoning and Land-Use Codes, American Planning Ass'n, Planning Advisory Serv. Rep. No. 409 (1988).

C. Siemon & W. Larson, Vested Rights (1982).

## Articles

Alperin & King, Ballot Box Planning: Land Use Planning Through the Initiative Process in California, 21 Sw. L. Rev. 1 (1992).

Blaesser, Negotiating Entitlements, Urb. Land, Vol. 50, No. 12, at 30 (1991).

Callies, Neuffer & Calibaoso, Ballot Box Zoning: Initiative, Referendum and the Law, 39 Wash. U.J. Urb. & Contemp. L. 53 (1991).

Campanella, Elliott & Merriam, New Vested Property Rights Legislation: States Seek to Steady a Shaky Judicial Doctrine, 11 Zoning & Plan. L. Rep. 81 (1988).

Cordes, Policing Bias and Conflicts of Interest in Zoning Decisionmaking, 65 N.D.L. Rev. 161 (1989).

Crew, Development Agreements After *Nollan v. California Coastal Commission,* 22 Urb. Law. 23 (1990).

Curtin, Protecting Developer's Permits to Build: Development Agreement Practice in California and Other States, 18 Zoning & Plan. Rep. 85 (1995).

Curtin & Edelstein, Development Agreement Practice in California and Other States, 22 Stetson L. Rev. 961 (1993).

Delaney, Development Agreements: The Road from Prohibition to "Let's Make a Deal!", 25 Urb. Law. 49 (1993).

Delaney & Vaias, Recognizing Vested Development Rights as Protected Property in Fifth Amendment Due Process and Taking Claims, 49 J. Urb. & Contemp. L. 27 (1996).

Delogu, Land Use and Vested Rights: Mixed Law and Policy Issues, Land Use L. & Zoning Dig., Vol. 41, No. 1, at 3 (1989).

Dennison, Estoppel as a Defense to Enforcement of Zoning Ordinance, 19 Zon. & Plan. Rep. 69 (1996).

DiMento, Taking the Planning Offensive: Implementing the Consistency Doctrine, 7 Zoning & Plan. L. Rep. 41 (1984).

Dukeminier & Stapleton, The Zoning Board of Adjustment: A Case Study in Misrule, 50 Ky. L.J. 273 (1962).

Dyas, Conflicts of Interest in Planning and Zoning Cases, 17 J. Legal Prof. 219 (1993).

Ellis, Neighborhood Opposition and the Permissible Purposes of Zoning, 7 J. Land Use & Envtl. L. 275 (1992).

Freilich & Guemmer, Removing Artificial Barriers to Public Participation in Land-Use Policy: Effective Zoning by Initiative and Referenda, 21 Urb. Law. 511 (1989).

Goetz, Direct Democracy in Land Use Planning: The State Response to *Eastlake*: 19 Pac. L.J. 793 (1988).

Goldwich, Development Agreements: A Critical Introduction, 4 J. Land Use & Envtl. L. 249 (1989).

Haar, Sawyer & Cummings, Computer Power and Legal Reasoning: A Case Study of Judicial Decision Prediction in Zoning Amendment Cases, 1977 Am. B. Found. Res. J. 651.

Hammes, Development Agreements: The Intervention of Real Estate Finance and Land Use Controls, 23 U. Balt. L. Rev. 119 (1993).

Hanes & Minchew, On Vested Rights to Land Use and Development, 46 Wash. & Lee L. Rev. 373 (1989).

Heeter, Zoning Estoppel: Application of the Principles of Equitable Estoppel and Vested Rights to Zoning Disputes, 1971 Urb. L. Ann. 63.

Johannessen, Zoning Variances: Unnecessarily an Evil, Land Use L. & Zoning Dig., Vol. 41, No. 7, at 3 (1989).

Kessler, The Development Agreement and Its Use in Resolving Large Scale, Multi-Party Development Problems: A Look at the Tools and Suggestions for Its Application, 1 Fla. St. U.J. Land Use & Envtl. L. 451 (1985).

Larson, A Model Ethical Code for Appointed Municipal Officials, 9 Hamline J. Pub. L. & Pol'y 395 (1989).

Larsen & Larsen, Moratoria as Takings Under *Lucas*, Land Use L. & Zoning Dig., Vol. 46, No. 6, at 3 (1994).

Liebmann, Devolution of Power to Community and Block Associations, 25 Urb. Law. 385 (1993).

Mandelker, Delegation of Power and Function in Zoning Administration, 1963 Wash. U.L.Q. 60.

Mandelker, The Role of the Local Comprehensive Plan in Land Use Regulation, 74 Mich. L. Rev. 899 (1976).

McClendon, Reforming the Rezoning Process, Land Use L. & Zoning Dig., Vol. 36, No. 4, at 5 (1984).

McClendon, Standards and Criteria for Zoning Administration, 8 Zoning & Plan. L. Rep. 129 (1985).

Nadel, This Land is Your Land . . . Or Is It? Making Sense of Vested Rights in California, 22 Loyola L.A.L. Rev. 791 (1989).

Novak & Blaesser, Invitations to Abuse of Discretion: Aesthetic and Automatic Reviews, Land Use L. & Zoning Dig., Vol. 42, No. 11, at 3 (1990).

Reynolds, Self-Induced Hardship in Zoning Variances: Does a Purchaser Have No One But Himself to Blame?, 20 Urb. Law. 1 (1988).

Reynolds, "Spot Zoning" — A Spot That Could Be Removed From the Law, 48 Wash. U. J. Urb. & Contemp. L. 117 (1995).

Rosenburg, Referendum Zoning: Legal Doctrine and Practice, 53 Cinn. L. Rev. 381 (1984).

Rosenzeig, From Euclid to Eastlake Toward a More Responsive Approach to Procedural Protection, 82 Dick. L. Rev. 59 (1977).

Sager, Insular Majorities Unabated: Warth v. Seldin and City of Eastlake v. Forest City Enterprises, Inc., 91 Harv. L. Rev. 1373 (1978).

Schultz, Vested Property Rights in Colorado: The Legislature Rushes in Where...., 66 Den. U.L. Rev. 31 (1988).

Shortlidge, The *"Fasano* Doctrine"*: Land Use Decisions as Quasi-Judicial Acts, in Proceedings of the Institute on Planning, Zoning, and Eminent Domain, ch. 3 (1985).

Steele, Participation and Rules: The Functions of Zoning, 1986 Am. B. Found. Res. J. 709.

Tarlock, Challenging Biased Zoning Board Decisions, 10 Zoning & Plan. L. Rep. 97 (1987).

Tarlock, Not in Accordance with a Comprehensive Plan: A Case Study of Regional Shopping Center Location Conflicts in Lexington, Kentucky, 1970 Urb. L. Ann. 133.

Taub, Development Agreements, Land Use L. & Zoning Dig., Vol. 42, No. 10, at 3 (1990).

Valletta, Unnecessary Hardship: The Financial Standard for Zoning Variances in New York City, 1 Hofstra Prop. L.J. 1 (1988).

VanderVelde, Legal Pluralism and Equal Treatment in the Context of Zoning Variances, 33 J. L. Pluralism & Unofficial Law 91 (1993).

Van Gorder, Alternative Solutions to the Judicial Doctrine of Strict Compliance with Statutory Procedures for the Adoption of Local Land Use Regulations, 29 Wash. U.J. Urb. & Contemp. L. 133 (1985).

Vietzen, Controlling Conflicts of Interest in Land Use Decisions, Land Use L. & Zoning Dig., Vol. 38, No. 1, at 3 (1986).

Wegner, Moving Toward the Bargaining Table: Contract Zoning, Development Agreements, and the Theoretical Foundations of Government Land Use Deals, 65 N.C.L. Rev. 957 (1987).

Williamson, Constitutional and Judicial Limitations on the Community's Power to Downzone, 12 Urb. Law. 157 (1980).

**Student Work**

Note, The Ad Hominem Element in the Treatment of Zoning Problems, 109 U. Pa. L. Rev. 992 (1961).

Note, Adjudication by Labels, Referendum Rezoning and Due Process, 55 N.C.L. Rev. 517 (1977).

Note, Administrative Discretion in Zoning, 82 Harv. L. Rev. 668 (1969).

Note, The Changing Weather Forecast: Government in the Sunshine in the 1990s — An Analysis of State Sunshine Laws, 71 Wash. U. L.Q. 1165 (1993).

Note, Concomitant Agreement Zoning: An Economic Analysis, 1985 U. Ill. L. Rev. 89.

Note, Instant Planning — Land Use Regulation by Initiative in California, 61 S. Cal. L. Rev. 497 (1988).

Note, Kaiser Hawaii Kai Development Company v. City and County of Honolulu: Zoning by Initiative in Hawaii, 12 Hawaii L. Rev. 181 (1990).

Note, The Proper Use of Referenda in Rezoning, 29 Stan. L. Rev. 819 (1977).

Note, Zoning: Looking Beyond Municipal Borders, 1965 Wash. U.L.Q. 107.

Note, Zoning and the Referendum: Converging Powers, Conflicting Processes, 6 N.Y.U. Rev. L. & Soc. Change 97 (1977).

Note, Zoning Variances, 74 Harv. L. Rev. 1396 (1961).

Comment, A Constitutional Safety Valve: The Variance in Zoning and Land-Use Based Environmental Controls, 22 B.C. Envtl. Aff. L. Rev. 307 (1995).

Comment, Delegation of Land Use Decisions to Neighborhood Groups, 57 UMKC L. Rev. 101 (1988).

Comment, Ex Parte Communications in Local Land Use Decisions, 15 B.C. Envtl. Aff. L. Rev. 181 (1987).

Comment, The Initiative and Referendum's Use in Zoning, 64 Calif. L. Rev. 74 (1976).

Comment, Land Use By, For, and of the People: Problems With the Application of Initiatives and Referenda to the Zoning Process, 19 Pepp. L. Rev. 99 (1991).

Comment, Land-Use Applications Not Acted upon Shall Be Deemed Approved: A Weighing of Interests, 57 UMKC L. Rev. 607 (1989).

Comment, Shattered Plans: Amending a General Plan Through the Initiative Process, 26 U.C. Davis L. Rev. 1055 (1993).

Comment, When Real Property Rights Vest in California: What Happens When a Plaintiff Has Not Secured Required Governmental Approvals?, 28 Santa Clara L. Rev. 417 (1988).

Contemporary Studies Project, Rural Land Use in Iowa: An Empirical Analysis of County Board of Adjustment Practices, 68 Iowa L. Rev. 1083 (1983).

Recent Development, Developer's Vested Rights, 23 Wash. U.J. Urb. & Contemp. L. 487 (1983).

# Chapter 7

# EXCLUSIONARY ZONING

## § 7.01. An Introductory Note.

Exclusionary suburban zoning is a well-known and notorious phenomenon. Suburban municipalities exclude multi-family developments, require low residential densities, and adopt other exclusionary restrictions such as excessive street frontage and minimum house size requirements. This type of zoning excludes low- and moderate-income groups and may also exclude minorities.

Chapter 5 examined court decisions that invalidated a variety of exclusionary zoning restrictions and also reviewed federal Fair Housing Act provisions that prohibit discrimination against group homes for the handicapped. This chapter reviews federal and state court decisions that considered direct attacks on exclusionary zoning as unconstitutional or as a violation of the federal Fair Housing Act. It also considers state legislation that mandates inclusionary zoning programs.

## A. THE FEDERAL CASES.

### § 7.02. Standing.

Standing to sue presents a major hurdle for litigants who challenge exclusionary zoning in federal courts. Federal standing law is complex, but two requirements are critical in exclusionary zoning litigation. Federal courts require plaintiffs to show "injury in fact" and a causal link between the injury asserted and the judicial relief demanded. Both requirements proved fatal to the plaintiffs in *Warth v. Seldin*,[1] a U.S. Supreme Court case.

A number of nonresident plaintiffs challenged a restrictive zoning ordinance adopted by Penfield, a suburb of Rochester, New York, that zoned practically all of the community for single-family development. The plaintiffs included a nonprofit organization dedicated to expanding housing opportunities, a homebuilders' organization, Rochester taxpayers, and several low- and moderate-income residents in the Rochester area who were members of minority racial and ethnic groups. Plaintiffs claimed that the ordinance had the purpose and effect of excluding low- and moderate-income groups but did not make a racial discrimination claim.

The Court denied standing to all of the plaintiffs. It noted that none of the nonresident individual plaintiffs had an interest in any property in Penfield. These plaintiffs claimed they had been unable to locate affordable housing in Penfield and that the Penfield zoning ordinance precluded the construction of housing they could afford. The Court held that these claims did not confer standing. Although two efforts to build affordable housing in Penfield had failed,

> the record is devoid of any indication that these projects, or other like projects, would have satisfied . . . [plaintiffs'] needs at prices they could afford, or that, were the court to remove the obstructions attributable to . . . [the zoning ordinance], such relief would benefit . . . plaintiffs]. Indeed, . . . their inability to reside in Penfield is the consequence of the economics of the area housing market, rather than . . . [the zoning ordinance].[2]

The Court held that there must be "specific, concrete facts demonstrating" harm to the plaintiff and that "he personally would benefit from the court's in-

---

**1.** 422 U.S. 490 (1975). *Accord* Hope, Inc. v. County of DuPage, 738 F.2d 797 (7th Cir. 1984).
**2.** *Id.* at 506.

tervention." An important footnote added that "usually the initial focus should be on a particular project." Plaintiffs had not demonstrated a "substantial probability" of a "causal relationship" between the exclusionary zoning ordinance and their injuries, nor had they shown that the requested relief would probably remedy their harm.

The Court denied standing to the Rochester taxpayers and the nonprofit housing organization partly because they asserted the constitutional rights of third parties excluded by the Penfield ordinance. The Court denied standing to the homebuilders' organization because no member of the organization claimed it had been excluded by the Penfield zoning ordinance or had applied "for a building permit or a variance with respect to any particular project."

The Court granted standing to a developer and an individual seeking lower-income housing in a later case, *Village of Arlington Heights v. Metropolitan Housing Dev. Corp.*[3] A virtually all-white Chicago suburb refused to rezone from single-family to multi-family so that a developer could build a federally subsidized multi-family housing project. The plaintiffs claimed that the refusal to rezone was racially discriminatory. The Court granted standing to the developer even though the invalidation of the ordinance would not necessarily guarantee construction of the project. It noted that "all housing developments are subject to some extent to similar uncertainties." The developer suffered economic injury in its predevelopment expenditures for the project, but economic injury was not necessary to support standing. The developer had "an interest in making suitable low-cost housing available in areas where such housing is scarce."[4]

The Court did not consider the developer's right to assert the standing of third parties because an individual plaintiff in the lawsuit, a black, claimed that the zoning refusal frustrated his search for housing near his place of employment. The Court distinguished *Warth* and granted standing to this plaintiff. It held there was a "substantial probability" the developer would build the project, which would meet the plaintiff's needs, if it held the refusal to rezone unconstitutional. The black plaintiff's claim "focuses on a particular project and is not dependent on speculation about the possible actions of third parties not before the court." The Court did not consider the possibility that the black plaintiff would have to compete with others for a dwelling unit in the project and might not obtain one.

---

3. 429 U.S. 252 (1977).

4. *Accord* Baytree of Inverrary Realty Ptn. v. City of Lauderhill, 873 F.2d 1407 (11th Cir. 1989); Keith v. Volpe, 858 F.2d 467 (9th Cir. 1988), *cert. denied*, 493 U.S. 813 (1989); Cutting v. Mazzey, 724 F.2d 259 (1st Cir. 1984); Scott v. Greenville County, 716 F.2d 1409 (4th Cir. 1983).

## § 7.03. Equal Protection: *Arlington Heights*.

Exclusionary zoning raises an equal protection problem, but an equal protection attack on exclusionary zoning is likely to succeed in federal court only if the plaintiff claims discrimination against minorities, such as racial discrimination. A claim of minority discrimination triggers strict scrutiny equal protection review, which requires a compelling governmental interest to avoid an equal protection violation.

The Supreme Court held that a refusal to rezone was not racially discriminatory in *Arlington Heights*.[5] A developer applied for a multi-family rezoning on a vacant tract located in a single-family area so that it could build a federally subsidized multi-family housing project. The comprehensive plan for some time had included a "buffer" policy that allowed multi-family zoning only on sites lying between single-family and other more intensive development. The village had applied this policy in a reasonably consistent manner. It denied the plaintiff's rezoning under the buffer policy because its site was surrounded by single-family development. The village also claimed the denial was necessary to protect the property values of adjacent single-family development from the adverse impacts of the plaintiff's multi-family project.

The Court upheld the refusal to rezone. It held that proof of racial discrimination under the equal protection clause requires proof of a racially discriminatory intent as a motivating factor[6] but added that proof of a racially "disproportionate impact" is relevant as evidence of a racially discriminatory intent. One example is the case in which "a clear pattern unexplainable on grounds other than race, emerges from the effect of state action even when the governing legislation appears neutral on its face." The Court did not explain why the virtually all-white character of Arlington Heights failed to raise an inference that the refusal to rezone implemented a "clear pattern" of racial exclusion. Departures from an established policy are also relevant to a finding of discriminatory intent. To illustrate this point, the Court cited a lower federal court case in which the city's zoning actions blocked a lower-income housing project only after plans to build the project became known.[7] Departures from normal procedural sequence are also evidence of improper purpose.

The Court held that "[s]ubstantive departures too may be relevant, particularly if the factors usually considered important by the decisionmaker strongly favor a decision contrary to the one reached." The village, the Court emphasized, had relied on "zoning factors" that were "not novel criteria in the Village's rezoning

---

**5.** § 7.02.

**6.** Applying Washington v. Davis, 426 U.S. 229 (1976). *See also* Personnel Adm'r of Mass. v. Feeney, 442 U.S. 256 (1979).

**7.** Kennedy Park Homes Ass'n v. City of Lackawanna, 436 F.2d 108 (2d Cir. 1970), *cert. denied*, 401 U.S. 1010 (1971).

decision." Neighboring property owners had also relied on the maintenance of the single-family zoning on the plaintiff's site.

The Court cited *Dailey v. City of Lawton*[8] to illustrate the "zoning factors" principle. In *Dailey* the court found a racially discriminatory intent in a refusal to rezone to allow a lower-income multi-family project when the surrounding area was zoned multi-family. Two city officials testified that the rezoning would have been proper from a "zoning standpoint."

The Supreme Court has substantially limited attacks on exclusionary zoning based on claims of minority discrimination under the equal protection clause. Wholesale attacks on exclusionary zoning brought by nonresidents are foreclosed by *Warth v. Seldin*. *Arlington Heights* indicates the Court will uphold site-specific discrimination claims only in blatant cases.[9] A municipality can apparently zone its entire area for single-family development and defend a refusal to rezone for multi-family development as consistent with its "zoning factors."

## § 7.04. The Fair Housing Act.

Plaintiffs have been more successful in challenging exclusionary zoning as racially discriminatory under Title VIII of the Civil Rights Act of 1968, the federal fair housing act. Most federal courts hold that this act requires only proof of a racially discriminatory effect.[10] Although the fair housing act is directed primarily at racial discrimination in the sale or rental of housing, the act also makes it "unlawful . . . [t]o make unavailable or deny . . . a dwelling to a person because of race."[11] The federal courts have applied this provision to strike down

---

**8.** 425 F.2d 1037 (10th Cir. 1970).

**9.** Racial discrimination not found: Orange Lake Assocs. v. Kirkpatrick, 21 F.3d 1214 (2d Cir. 1994); Litton Int'l Dev. Co. v. City of Simi Valley, 616 F. Supp. 275 (C.D. Cal. 1985); In re Malone, 592 F. Supp. 1135 (E.D. Mo. 1984), *aff'd mem.*, 794 F.2d 680 (8th Cir. 1986); Beasley v. Potter, 493 F. Supp. 1059 (W.D. Mich. 1980); Cowart v. City of Ocala, 478 F. Supp. 744 (M.D. Fla. 1979); Stone v. City of Wilton, 331 N.W.2d 398 (Iowa 1983). *But see* In re Township of Warren, 622 A.2d 1257 (N.J. 1993) (suggesting preference for municipal residents and employees in affordable housing violated Act).

**10.** *But see* Ward's Cove Packing Co. v. Atonio, 490 U.S. 642 (1989) (shifting burden of proof to plaintiffs in Title VII fair employment cases, *applied in* United States v. Incorporated Village of Island Park, 888 F. Supp. 419 (E.D.N.Y. 1995) (claiming discrimination in federal housing subsidy program). Congress overruled *Ward's Cove* as applied to employment discrimination claims. *See* Mojica v. Gannett Co., 7 F.3d 552 (7th Cir. 1993), *cert. denied*, 511 U.S. 1069 (1994).

**11.** 42 U.S.C. § 3604(a).

racially discriminatory exclusionary zoning.[12] They have also granted standing to nonresidents and developers who challenged racially discriminatory zoning.[13]

### § 7.05. When Violated.

The Supreme Court remanded *Arlington Heights*[14] so the court of appeals could determine whether a violation of the fair housing act had occurred. The court of appeals held that proof of discriminatory effect was sufficient to show a violation of the act and that courts should review claims of racial discrimination under the act under a four-factor test.[15] The factors are: (1) the strength of the discriminatory effect; (2) the presence of "partial evidence" of discriminatory intent, which is evidence insufficient to satisfy the constitutional equal protection standard; (3) whether the municipality acted within the scope of its authority; and (4) whether the relief requested was affirmative or remedial. The court remanded the case to the district court, but the parties settled.[16] Other courts adopted the four-factor test and applied it to racial discrimination claims under the fair housing act in zoning and similar cases.[17]

*Huntington Branch, NAACP v. Town of Huntington*[18] modified *Arlington Heights.* It held the act was violated by a zoning ordinance restricting private multi-family housing to a largely minority urban renewal area and a refusal to rezone land in a white neighborhood for federally subsidized multi-family

---

**12.** *See also* 42 U.S.C. § 3610(g)(2)(c) (if Secretary of Housing and Urban Development determines in a proceeding that a "matter involves the legality of any State or local zoning or other land use law or ordinance," he is to immediately refer the matter to attorney general for appropriate action).

**13.** Baytree of Invarerray Realty Partners v. City of Lauderhill, 873 F.2d 1407 (11th Cir. 1989); Park View Heights Corp. v. City of Black Jack, 467 F.2d 1208 (8th Cir. 1972) (nonresidents); In re Malone, 592 F. Supp. 1135 (E.D. Mo. 1984), *aff'd mem.,* 794 F.2d 680 (8th Cir. 1986) (developer) *Contra* Nasser v. City of Homewood, 671 F.2d 432 (11th Cir. 1982) (developer).

**14.** § 7.03.

**15.** Metropolitan Hous. Dev. Corp. v. Village of Arlington Heights, 558 F.2d 1283 (7th Cir. 1977), *cert. denied,* 434 U.S. 1025 (1978). *See also* In re Malone, 592 F. Supp. 1135 (E.D. Mo. 1984) (finding no violation of act under similar facts; *Arlington Heights* factors not applied), *aff'd mem.,* 794 F.2d 680 (8th Cir. 1986).

**16.** Metropolitan Hous. Dev. Corp. v. Village of Arlington Heights, 616 F.2d 1006 (7th Cir. 1980).

**17.** No violation: Arthur v. City of Toledo, 782 F.2d 565 (6th Cir. 1986) (refusal to extend services to public housing project; three of four factors adopted). Violation: Resident Advisory Bd. v. Rizzo, 564 F.2d 126 (3d Cir. 1977) (public housing site selection), *cert. denied,* 435 U.S. 908 (1978).

**18.** 844 F.2d 926 (2d Cir. 1988), *aff'd,* 488 U.S. 15 (1988) (Court reviewed holding on zoning ordinance only; was satisfied with court of appeals findings without endorsing court's "precise analysis"). *See generally* United States v. Black Jack, 508 F.2d 1179 (8th Cir. 1974), *cert. denied,* 422 U.S. 1042 (1975). *Accord* Keith v. Volpe, 858 F.2d 467 (9th Cir. 1988), *cert. denied,* 493 U.S. 813 (1989).

housing. The court held it would apply the disparate impact test adopted under the federal equal employment opportunity act to determine when a facially neutral government policy, such as a zoning law, violated the fair housing act.

A plaintiff need not prove a discriminatory intent under this test. He can establish a prima facie case, the court held, by showing that the defendant's policy or practice has a discriminatory effect. Plaintiffs made a strong prima facie case under this standard by showing that the zoning restriction and refusal to rezone had a discriminatory effect in two ways. They perpetuated segregation in the town and had a greater proportionate effect on blacks because a larger percentage of blacks needed affordable housing.

Once a prima facie case is established, the court held that a court must weigh the adverse discriminatory effect against the justification offered by the defendant. This inquiry has two components. The court must first determine whether a less discriminatory alternative is feasible. This concern is "plan-specific" and requires less discriminatory design modifications in the project. The court must then consider whether the reasons for the decision are bona fide and legitimate. The inquiry is whether the justification is a "substantial concern" that would justify a decision by a "reasonable official." The court held that the town's reasons for refusing the rezoning were weak and that it could encourage the rehabilitation of the renewal area through less discriminatory means, such as tax incentives.[19]

### § 7.06. Remedies.

In *Huntington* the court provided site-specific relief to the plaintiff to remedy the statutory violation. The developer and prospective residents of a federally-subsidized housing project brought an action seeking damages and equitable relief in a similar case.[20] The court held earlier that a downzoning to block the project was a violation of the act, but the project was not built. The city agreed to pay damages to the plaintiffs under a consent judgment, but the judgment did not prohibit further declaratory or equitable relief. The plaintiffs then sought an injunction ordering the city to undertake measures to make 108 dwelling units available within a reasonable time for multi-racial, moderate-income occupancy. This was the number of dwelling units the project would have provided. The plaintiffs suggested a number of inclusionary zoning measures, such as density

---

**19.** *But see* Orange Lake Assocs. v. Kirkpatrick, 21 F.3d 1214 (2d Cir. 1994) (racial discrimination not found); New Burnham Prairie Homes, Inc. v. Burnham, 910 F.2d 1474 (7th Cir. 1990) (affirming jury verdict for municipality); Suffolk Interreligious Coalition on Housing v. Town of Brookhaven, 575 N.Y.S.2d 548 (App. Div. 1991) (denial of individual zoning requests held not exclusionary), *appeal dismissed,* 592 N.E.2d 802 (N.Y. 1992).

**20.** Park View Heights Corp. v. City of Black Jack, 605 F.2d 1033 (8th Cir. 1979), *cert. denied,* 445 U.S. 905 (1980). *See* note 17 *supra.*

bonuses and a waiver of building and zoning requirements, that could satisfy this obligation. The district court refused to grant an injunction, but the court of appeals reversed.

The court held that the invalidation of the zoning ordinance would not provide effective relief. The enactment of the restrictive zoning "predictably" delayed the project, with the "inevitable and foreseeable" result that a rise in construction costs during the delay period made the project economically infeasible. On remand, the court of appeals ordered the district court to consider the City's duty to seek out and make land sites available for purchase by the plaintiff class. These sites must be properly zoned and so located with reference to public facilities and services as to meet established criteria for low and moderate income family housing.[21]

## B. THE STATE CASES.

## § 7.07.  Standing.

Nonresident standing in state courts presents fewer problems because state constitutions, unlike the federal constitution, do not usually limit litigation to "cases and controversies." A decision to confer standing lies within the discretion of the state court, subject to the judicially imposed limitation that a court may not give advisory opinions.

Some state courts have rejected *Warth*[22] and have granted standing to nonresidents. *Stocks v. City of Irvine*[23] is a strong statement on this issue. The plaintiffs were nonresidents of the city who claimed they wished to live in Irvine but that the city's zoning prevented the construction of housing they could afford. Plaintiffs also claimed the city's zoning affected the housing market in the surrounding region and increased the cost of housing where they presently lived. The court granted standing. It noted that the more restrictive a city's zoning becomes, the less likely a developer will propose housing for lower-income families. Without a developer to challenge the exclusionary zoning ordinance, the *Warth* test could not be satisfied. The court rejected the *Warth* "substantial probability" test for standing and held it would not deny access to the courts simply because "granting relief . . . will not remove all obstacles . . . to complete redress." The plaintiffs were only required to show a "causal relationship" between the city's zoning and their alleged harm.

The New Jersey Supreme Court granted standing to nonresidents to challenge exclusionary zoning in *Home Bldrs. League of S. Jersey, Inc. v. Township of*

---

21. *Id.* at 1040. *See also* United States v. City of Parma, 494 F. Supp. 1049 (N.D. Ohio 1980), *aff'd,* 661 F.2d 562 (6th Cir. 1981), *cert. denied,* 456 U.S. 962 (1982).

22. § 7.02.

23. 170 Cal. Rptr. 724 (Cal. App. 1981).

*Berlin*.[24] The court partly relied on a provision in the zoning statute that defined an "interested party" as "any person, whether residing within or without the municipality."[25]

Some state courts are more restrictive. A Pennsylvania court dismissed an exclusionary zoning suit by nonresidents that challenged the zoning ordinances of all fifty-four municipalities in the county.[26] The court characterized the suit as hypothetical, far-ranging, and unparticularized. *Bucks* suggests that exclusionary zoning litigation joining several municipalities which is not based on specific development proposals may fail on justiciability grounds. New Hampshire held that a landowner whose land is restricted by a zoning ordinance may not challenge the restriction claiming it limits opportunities to build affordable housing if he is not a developer and has no plans to build affordable housing. His generalized interest in a diverse community is not enough to confer standing to make this claim.[27]

## § 7.08.  New Jersey.

### § 7.09.  *Mt. Laurel (I)*.

In *Southern Burlington County NAACP v. Township of Mt. Laurel (Mt. Laurel I)*,[28] the New Jersey Supreme Court adopted a regional general welfare doctrine to test the constitutionality of exclusionary zoning. *Mount Laurel (I)* was brought by a number of plaintiffs, including residents, nonresidents, and the NAACP. They challenged the zoning ordinance of a New Jersey suburb in the Philadelphia and Camden commuting area. Although a substantial part of Mt. Laurel was undeveloped, its zoning ordinance contained a number of exclusionary restrictions, including excessive exclusive zoning for industrial use, that effectively prevented residential development and extensive low-density residential zoning. Plaintiffs did not have an interest in any land in Mt. Laurel that was subject to the exclusionary zoning restrictions, but the court held they had standing to bring the case.

The court invalidated the Mt. Laurel ordinance under equal protection and substantive due process principles it found embedded in the state constitution. It held that Mt. Laurel had excluded lower- and moderate-income groups and that proof of a discriminatory intent to accomplish this purpose was not necessary. The heart of the decision was the court's conclusion that municipalities in New

---

24. 405 A.2d 381 (N.J. 1979).

25. N.J. Stat. Ann. § 40:55D-4. *Accord* Suffolk Hous. Serv. v. Town of Brookhaven, 397 N.Y.S.2d 302 (Sup. Ct. 1978), *aff'd as modified*, 405 N.Y.S.2d 302 (App. Div. 1978).

26. Commonwealth v. County of Bucks, 302 A.2d 897 (Pa. Commw. 1973), *cert. denied*, 414 U.S. 1130 (1974). *See also* Fair Hous. Dev. Fund v. Burke, 55 F.R.D. 414 (E.D.N.Y. 1972).

27. Caspersen v. Town of Lyme, 661 A.2d 759 (N.H. 1995).

28. 336 A.2d 713 (N.J.), *appeal dismissed and cert. denied*, 423 U.S. 808 (1975).

Jersey must meet their "fair share of the present and prospective regional need" for low- and moderate-income housing.

The court adopted a prima facie case rule to implement this holding. A municipality carries a heavy burden to establish a valid basis for its actions once a plaintiff makes a prima facie case that it has not met its fair share obligations. The court held that a municipality cannot refuse to meet its fair share obligation because it does not want to provide necessary public services, a clear rejection of fiscal exclusionary zoning. The court recognized that imposing a fair share obligation on every municipality in the state might be arbitrary but noted that the state legislation conferred zoning authority on all municipalities. The court concluded that all municipalities must responsibly exercise their zoning authority by meeting their fair share housing obligations. The court indicated that the fair share doctrine applied only to "developing" municipalities, a limitation it later rejected.

The court provided only limited guidance on how courts should determine a municipality's fair share obligation. It did not elaborate criteria for determining the region in which the fair share rule should apply and indicated that planning "expertise" at the local, county, and state level could determine the municipality's fair share. The court invalidated the objectionable features in the ordinance, gave the municipality three months to correct these deficiencies, and suggested that anyone disappointed with the revision could challenge it in court.

### § 7.10.  *Weymouth.*

In its next exclusionary zoning case, *Taxpayers Ass'n of Weymouth Twp. v. Weymouth Twp.*,[29] the New Jersey Supreme Court upheld a zoning ordinance that established a zoning district limited to the elderly. It held the zoning ordinance met the special needs of the elderly and was not invalid as a regulation of users rather than use, and noted the legislature had authorized zoning for the elderly in the state zoning act. The court applied the rational relationship test to reject equal protection and due process objections. Zoning for the elderly was not presumptively exclusionary and "must be assessed against the background of general land use regulation by the municipality." Although these plaintiffs had not proved a prima facie case of exclusion, extensive zoning for the elderly within a community could be exclusionary because it could exclude families with children.[30]

---

**29.** 364 A.2d 1016 (N.J. 1976). *See also* Shepard v. Woodland Twp. Comm. & Planning Bd., 364 A.2d 1005 (N.J. 1976). *Accord* Maldini v. Ambro, 330 N.E.2d 403 (N.Y.), *appeal dismissed,* 423 U.S. 993 (1975). *Contra* Hinman v. Planning & Zoning Comm'n, 214 A.2d 131 (Conn. C.P. 1965).

**30.** *See also* Home Bldrs. League of S. Jersey, Inc. v. Township of Berlin, 405 A.2d 381 (N.J. 1979) (minimum house size ordinance held unconstitutional). *See* § 5.24.

## § 7.11.  *Mt. Laurel (II).*

On remand, Mt. Laurel revised its zoning ordinance to limit substantial areas of the community to low-density residential use and to restrict apartment projects to small dwelling units. *Oakwood at Madison, Inc. v. Township of Madison*[31] invalidated the ordinance in a decision that somewhat restricted the *Mt. Laurel (I)* decision.

A trial court then upheld the rezoning even though the municipality rezoned only twenty acres out of a total of 22.4 square miles for higher density housing.[32] Plaintiffs appealed and the New Jersey Supreme Court consolidated this appeal with appeals in five other cases raising questions concerning the fair share rule. In *Mt. Laurel (II),*[33] the court reversed and remanded these cases.

The court confirmed and expanded the fair share doctrine adopted in *Mt. Laurel (I)*, including the prima facie case rule. It held that the fair share obligation was not limited to "developing" municipalities but extended to all municipalities designated in a 1980 State Development Guide Plan as growth areas. A municipality could rebut a growth area designation if it showed it was arbitrary or capricious or no longer appropriate. The court indicated that the plan was only presumptively valid and that it must be periodically revised. The legislature has since adopted legislation authorizing the preparation and adoption of a State Development and Redevelopment Plan.[34] The growth designations in the plan will indicate the municipalities that are subject to the fair share obligation.

The court held the *Mt. Laurel* obligation requires quantitative proof of a municipality's fair share of low- and moderate-income housing. It recognized the complexities inherent in calculating fair shares but did not propose substantive criteria for making this calculation. Instead, the court mandated the appointment of three special judges authorized to make fair share determinations on a case-by-case basis.

The court held that the fair share obligation requires more than the elimination of "unnecessary cost-producing requirements," although it also held that municipalities must at least eliminate these requirements. The court approved and required affirmative governmental actions to meet the fair share obligation, including density bonuses and mandatory set-aside requirements for lower-income housing in residential developments. Municipalities could choose to adopt additional affirmative measures, including measures to facilitate the use of housing subsidies and tax abatements for subsidized housing. Providing least-cost housing would satisfy the fair share obligation only if a municipality could not satisfy it in any other manner, and only after a municipality considered all

---

31. 371 A.2d 1192 (N.J. 1977).
32. 391 A.2d 935 (N.J.L. Div. 1978).
33. 456 A.2d 390 (N.J. 1983).
34. N.J. Stat. Ann. §§ 52:18A-196 to 52:18A-207.

alternatives and affirmative actions. The court rejected holdings in *Oakwood* that courts need only consider the "substance" of exclusionary zoning ordinances and that municipalities need only make "bona fide" efforts to provide for low- and moderate-income housing. The court also qualified an earlier decision upholding a zoning ordinance that excluded mobile homes.[35] It held a municipality must zone land for mobile homes if this is necessary to comply with the fair share obligation.

The court held the *Mt. Laurel* doctrine did not affect "the clear obligation to preserve open space and prime agricultural land." A municipality that meets its fair share obligation may plan for its development consistent with sound land use planning, environmental considerations, and community preferences. Once a municipality has satisfied its fair share obligation, any restrictive zoning regulations it adopts will not be held invalid *per se* under the fair share doctrine.[36]

Builder's remedies would also be afforded to *Mt. Laurel* plaintiffs on a case-by-case basis when a plaintiff has acted in good faith and attempted to obtain relief without litigation. A plaintiff must show that the project includes an appropriate portion of affordable housing and is located and designed in accordance with sound zoning, planning and environmental concepts.

### § 7.12. Fair Housing Act.

The supreme court in *Mt. Laurel (II)* asked for legislative action on the fair share obligation, and the legislature responded by adopting a Fair Housing Act in 1985.[37] The Act creates a state Council on Affordable Housing to implement the *Mt. Laurel* doctrine. The Council is to determine the housing regions of the state and adopt criteria and guidelines for municipal fair share determinations. The Act temporarily eliminated the builder's remedy from all exclusionary litigation initiated after the date of the *Mt. Laurel (II)* decision, unless a court had entered a final judgment. It also provides state funding to help municipalities meet their fair share obligations. The supreme court held the Act constitutional in *Hills Dev. Co. v. Township of Bernards*.[38]

The Act requires a housing element in local plans and authorizes municipalities to submit their housing elements to the Council for certification.[39] The housing element must include an analysis of present and future housing needs

---

**35.** *See* §§ 5.17-5.21.

**36.** *See also* Samaritan Center, Inc. v. Borough of Englishtown, 683 A.2d 611 (N.J.L. Div. 1996) (adjacent municipality must provide water and sewer service for *Mount Laurel* housing).

**37.** N.J. Stat. Ann. §§ 52:27D-301 to 52:27D-329.

**38.** 510 A.2d 621 (N.J. 1986).

**39.** N.J. Stat. Ann. § 52:27D-310.

and employment characteristics, a present and future fair share calculation, and an analysis of land suitable to meet the fair share housing obligation.[40]

In preparing its housing element, a municipality must consider a number of techniques for providing low- and moderate-income housing. They include tax abatements, a plan for infrastructure expansion and rehabilitation, if necessary, and a "[d]etermination of the total residential zoning necessary to assure that the municipality's fair share is achieved."[41] A municipality may transfer up to twenty percent of its fair share obligation to another municipality in its region under a voluntary contractual agreement approved by the Council.

A municipality may petition the Council for a "substantive certification" of its housing element. Once a housing element is substantively certified, any person who brings an exclusionary zoning suit against a municipality must first exhaust mediation and review procedures before the Council. A suit may be filed once these procedures are exhausted, but the plaintiff must overcome a substantial presumption in favor of the certified housing element.[42] Municipalities sued in *Mt. Laurel* litigation may demand a "phase-in schedule" from the court for meeting its fair share obligations, including a separate schedule for inclusionary zoning.[43]

The Supreme Court disapproved a Council on Affordable Housing rule authorizing municipalities to provide preferences in affordable housing for local residents and employees.[44] The court held the rule was inconsistent with a municipality's *Mt. Laurel* obligation to provide for regional as well as local needs.[45]

---

**40.** *See also* N.J. Stat. Ann. § 52-27D-311.2 (Council cannot require counties to consider sites improved with sound residential structures as available for affordable housing).

**41.** § 52:27D-311(a)(2).

**42.** § 52:27D-317(a). Dynasty Bldg. Corp. v. Borough of Upper Saddle River, 632 A.2d 544 (N.J. App. Div. 1993) (intervention allowed by court to interested borough held too limited).

**43.** *See* Alexander's Department Stores v. Borough of Paramus, 592 A.2d 1168 (N.J. 1991) (trial court can hear conventional zoning challenge against municipality whose affordable housing plan was substantively certified by Council); East/West Venture v. Borough of Fort Lee, 669 A.2d 260 (N.J. App. Div. 1996) (approving settlement agreement for *Mount Laurel* litigation).

**44.** In re Township of Warren, 622 A.2d 1257 (N.J. 1993).

**45.** *See also* Non-Profit Affordable Housing Network of N.J. v. New Jersey Council on Affordable Housing, 627 A.2d 1153 (N.J. App. Div. 1993) (approving regulation authorizing housing credit without affordability requirement but remanding constitutional challenge); Calton Homes, Inc. v. Council on Affordable Housing, 582 A.2d 1024 (N.J. App. Div. 1990) (disapproving 1,000-unit cap rule and approving accessory apartment rule and rental unit bonus rule); Township of Bernards v. State Dep't of Community Affairs, 558 A.2d 1 (N.J. App. Div. 1989) (rule requiring consideration of per capita income in determining municipal need for affordable housing approved); Bi-County Dev. Corp. v. Mayor & Council, 540 A.2d 927 (N.J.L. Div. 1988) (approving most regulations including minimum density requirement).

## § 7.13. New York.

### § 7.14. *Berenson.*

The court of appeals, which is New York's highest court, adopted a two-tiered test for exclusionary zoning in *Berenson v. Town of New Castle.*[46] New Castle is in Westchester County, which is adjacent to New York City. Its zoning ordinance required low residential densities and excluded multi-family development. Suit was brought by a developer who planned to build a multi-family condominium development on a fifty-acre site in a one-acre zone and who failed to obtain municipal approval for the necessary zoning change. The development was not intended for low- or moderate-income occupants.

The court relied on the statutory requirement that zoning must serve the general welfare as the basis for a two-tier test it adopted for exclusionary zoning. It held first that the "primary goal of a zoning ordinance must be to provide for the development of a balanced, cohesive community which will make efficient use of the town's available land." This requirement did not necessarily call for "a certain relative proportion between various types of development," nor did it necessarily prohibit the creation of specialized land use zones. An apartment exclusion "may" be acceptable in a community that already has apartment development but unacceptable in a community where no apartments presently exist.

The second part of the test examines the effect of a municipality's zoning on neighboring communities. A municipality that excludes multi-family housing must consider "the needs of the region" as well as its own need for such housing. The court added that a municipality need not permit a use "solely for the sake of the people of the region" if regional housing needs are met in an adequate manner. It indicated that a municipality is excused from meeting regional housing needs only if they are met "by other accessible areas in the community at large."

In *Blitz v. Town of New Castle,*[47] an intermediate appellate court upheld a zoning revision adopted by the town to comply with the *Berenson* decision. The ordinance contained extensive provisions for multi-family development, either as a permitted use or when approved as a floating zone or by special permit. The court accepted the county housing policy's estimate of housing need and held that the town's multi-family zoning made adequate provision for meeting its share of that need.

Although noting that *Berenson* did not adopt the New Jersey fair share doctrine, the court found that the revised zoning allowed a significantly greater

---

46. 341 N.E.2d 236 (N.Y. 1975). *See* Gernatt Asphalt Prods., Inc. v. Town of Sardinia, 664 N.E.2d 1226 (N.Y. 1996) (*Berenson* rule does not apply to exclusion of industrial uses); Robert E. Kurzius, Inc. v. Incorporated Village of Upper Bronxville, 414 N.E.2d 680 (N.Y. 1980), *cert. denied,* 450 U.S. 1042 (1981) (five-acre zoning held not to violate *Berenson* tests).

47. 463 N.Y.S.2d 832 (App. Div. 1983).

number of new housing units than its share of the county's population, land area, housing units, and vacant land required. The court held that it would test compliance with the regional housing need requirement by considering what the zoning ordinance allowed, not the housing units that probably would be built. The court noted that market forces determine what will be built in the absence of government subsidies. It need determine only whether the zoning ordinance "on its face" allowed a sufficient number of housing units to meet regional need, assuming that this housing was physically and economically feasible. The court held that the revised ordinance met this test.

### § 7.15. *Brookhaven.*

The court of appeals again adopted a restrictive reading of *Berenson* in *Suffolk Hous. Serv. v. Town of Brookhaven.*[48] Plaintiffs brought an action claiming that the town's administration of its zoning ordinance prevented the development of lower-income housing. They claimed the town's failure to premap sufficient land for multi-family housing inflated the cost of housing because the town required developers to engage in a lengthy and expensive special permit process to have land approved for multi-family development, and that the town usually did not grant approval.

The court held that the plaintiffs had not stated a cause of action. It noted that the lower courts had found that the town had granted numerous developer applications for multi-family housing and that the inadequate development of low-cost, multi-family housing was due to factors such as rising construction and financing costs and economic stagnation. The court found no need to apply *Berenson* because in that case the plaintiff challenged the facial validity of the ordinance, while here the plaintiffs challenged its implementation. The court also held that the plaintiffs had asked for improper radical judicial rezoning of the town to accommodate multi-family development, even though they did not challenge the denial of a specific special permit.[49]

### § 7.16. *Asian Americans for Equality.*

In *Asian Americans for Equality v. Koch,*[50] the court of appeals rejected a claim that a special New York City zoning district adopted for Chinatown was exclusionary. The district included a density bonus incentive partly intended to

---

**48.** 511 N.E.2d 67 (N.Y. 1987).

**49.** *See also* Suffolk Interreligious Coalition on Housing v. Town of Brookhaven, 575 N.Y.S.2d 548 (App. Div. 1991) (denial of individual zoning requests held not exclusionary), *appeal dismissed,* 592 N.E.2d 802 (N.Y. 1992); North Shore Unitarian Universalist Soc'y v. Town of Upper Brookville, 493 N.Y.S.2d 564 (App. Div. 1985) (court rejected suit brought by developer denied rezoning for multi-family housing to be occupied by the elderly).

**50.** 527 N.E.2d 265 (N.Y. 1988).

promote lower-income housing. Plaintiffs claimed the bonuses favored higher-income housing developments and requested relief requiring the city to adopt additional programs to provide lower-income housing in the district. The court held that the special district was a well-considered plan that advanced legitimate governmental goals. It refused to apply the *Mt. Laurel* doctrine to areas within cities, noting that both *Mt. Laurel* and *Berenson* dealt with suburban zoning exclusion. The court held the entire city was the appropriate community for making exclusionary zoning determinations. There was no evidence that the city had excluded lower-income persons from Chinatown, and it had made substantial efforts to improve lower-income housing throughout the city. Nor had the plaintiffs shown that the incentive plan for lower-income housing in the Chinatown district was inadequate.

### § 7.17. Remedies.

The trial court ordered an extensive judicial remedy on remand in the *Berenson* case,[51] but the appellate division substantially modified the trial court's order.[52] The trial court determined the municipality's fair share of regional low- and moderate-income housing need, but the appellate division rejected this determination. It believed the court of appeals did not intend lower courts to "remedy the [zoning] deficiency by judicial fiat." The record showed an unmet regional need for multi-family housing, and a remedy directing "developing" municipalities to meet this need would be appropriate. The appellate division remanded the case to give the municipality six months to remedy this zoning deficiency.

The trial court also ordered the municipality to rezone plaintiff's land for multi-family use. The appellate division upheld this order, but held that the trial court erred by mandating a specific "allowable density of development" and by ordering the issuance of a building permit when the developer complied with the amended zoning ordinance. Density was a matter for the town to consider when it revised its ordinance. A building permit could issue only if the developer also complied with the state's Freshwater Wetlands Act, which applied to the development. The case was subsequently settled.

### § 7.18. Pennsylvania.

Pennsylvania took preliminary steps toward a comprehensive exclusionary zoning doctrine in cases striking down large-lot zoning and the exclusion of multi-family housing.[53] In later cases the supreme court adopted a *per se* inva-

---

51. § 7.45.
52. 415 N.Y.S.2d 669 (App. Div. 1979).
53. §§ 5.15, 5.27.

lidity rule for zoning ordinances that are totally exclusionary and a fair share multi-factor test for partial exclusions. The Pennsylvania statutes also require zoning ordinances to provide "for residential housing of various dwelling types encompassing all basic forms of housing," but an ordinance need not provide a specific dwelling type.[54]

### § 7.19. *Surrick*: Partial Exclusion.

In *Surrick v. Zoning Hearing Bd.*,[55] a suburban Philadelphia municipality denied a developer a rezoning for multi-family development. The court invalidated the ordinance, which it characterized as a partial exclusion of multi-family dwellings because it zoned only 1.14% of the municipality's area for multi-family development. The court noted it had adopted the New Jersey fair share doctrine in an earlier exclusionary zoning case,[56] but held that this doctrine merely stated a "general precept" for zoning. It applied substantive due process analysis to hold that its scope of review would be limited

> to determining whether the zoning formulas fashioned by these [governmental] entities reflect a balanced and weighted consideration of the many factors which bear upon local and regional housing needs and development.[57]

A court that carries out this review should first determine whether the municipality was a logical place for development as indicated by the proximity of a metropolis and projected metropolitan growth. It should next examine the present level of community development as indicated by population density, available undeveloped land, and land available for multi-family development. If the court found that the community was a logical place for development and was not highly developed, it should apply an exclusionary impact test to determine whether the zoning ordinance was exclusionary. Proof of an exclusionary motive or intent "is not of critical importance." The court invalidated the ordinance because it did not provide for the municipality's fair share of land for multi-family housing.[58]

---

54. Pa. Stat. Ann. tit. 53, § 10604(4).

55. 382 A.2d 105 (Pa. 1977).

56. Township of Willistown v. Chesterdale Farms, Inc., 341 A.2d 466 (Pa. 1975), noted, 13 Urb. L. Ann. 277 (1977).

57. 382 A.2d at 109-10.

58. *See, e.g.,* Farley v. Zoning Hearing Bd., 636 A.2d 1232 (Pa. Commw. 1994) (exclusion of student housing not shown); Stahl v. Upper Southampton Twp. Zoning Hearing Bd., 606 A.2d 960 (Pa. Commw. 1992) (restrictive density requirement for mobile home parks held exclusionary); Cambridge Land Co. v. Township of Marshall, 560 A.2d 253 (Pa. Commw. 1989) (zoning for apartments and commercial uses satisfies fair-share criteria); Weiner v. Board of Supvrs., 547 A.2d

The supreme court applied *Surrick* in *BAC, Inc. v. Board of Supervisors of Millcreek Township.*[59] Plaintiff claimed the township's ordinance was exclusionary because it excluded mobile homes. The court noted the ordinance was entitled to a presumption of constitutionality, and that plaintiff had not overcome this presumption. Plaintiff did not introduce evidence showing the township had excluded mobile homes, only evidence that the township had not made adequate allowance for housing for low- and moderate-income families. The court held this evidence insufficient because it showed the exclusion of certain classes of people, not a restriction on the use of property.

### § 7.20. *Fernley*: Total Exclusion.

In *Fernley v. Board of Supvrs.*,[60] the court held the *Surrick* tests did not apply to a zoning ordinance that totally excluded multi-family uses:

> Where the challenger proves a total prohibition of a legitimate use, the burden shifts to the municipality to establish that the prohibition promotes public health, safety, morals and general welfare.[61]

The court held the *Surrick* fair share tests apply only to a zoning ordinance that enacts a *de facto* exclusion of a particular use as distinguished from an ordinance that enacts a total or *de jure* exclusion. The considerations underlying the *Surrick* tests were irrelevant to a total exclusion of a basic form of housing, such as apartments.

The court in *Fernley* rejected the municipality's claim that the ordinance was not exclusionary because projections indicated only minimal growth. The growth projection was irrelevant because the ordinance possibly excluded families who wanted to live in the municipality but could not move there because apartments were unavailable. The court invalidated the ordinance because the municipality had not shown that the apartment exclusion served a legitimate public purpose.[62]

---

833 (Pa. Commw. 1988) (same, commercial zoning; special permit requirement does not violate fair-share rule).

**59.** 633 A.2d 144 (Pa. 1993). *See also* Precision Equities, Inc. v. Franklin Park Borough Zoning Hearing Bd., 646 A.2d 756 (Pa. Commw. 1994) (small lot single-family housing not a protected housing type).

**60.** 502 A.2d 585 (Pa. 1985). The court ignored In re M.A. Kravitz Co., 460 A.2d 1075 (Pa. 1983), an earlier case that did not adopt this interpretation.

**61.** 502 A.2d at 587.

**62.** *See also* Upper Salford Township v. Collins, 669 A.2d 335 (Pa. 1995) (ordinance did not exclude mobile homes); Appeal of Shore, 573 A.2d 1011 (Pa. 1990) (invalid prohibition of mobile home parks); Township Bd. of Supvrs. v. Golla, 452 A.2d 1337 (Pa. 1982) (upholding statute limiting basis for judicial review of exclusionary zoning); H & H Bldrs., Inc. v. Borough Council, 555 A.2d 948 (Pa. Commw. 1989) (exclusion of townhouses held de jure exclusionary).

## § 7.21. Remedies.

Pennsylvania statutes and court decisions provide effective site-specific relief for developers who challenge exclusionary zoning. A developer may submit a challenge to a zoning ordinance to the local governing body with a request for a curative amendment.[63] He must accompany the request with "plans and other materials describing the [proposed] use or development."[64] If the court finds that the zoning ordinance "unlawfully prevents or restricts a development or use" that is described in the plans and materials, it may order the described use approved. The court may also approve the described use in part and refer unapproved elements back to the governing body for further consideration, including the adoption of alternative restrictions.[65] The statute also authorizes a municipality to declare its zoning ordinance invalid and propose its own curative amendment.[66]

The statute codified court decisions that awarded site-specific relief.[67] It contains criteria for site-specific relief based primarily on the suitability of the site for the proposed use and its impact on "regional housing needs" and public facilities.[68] The *Fernley* case noted that "approval of the developer's plan is not automatic but, instead, must be predicated on the suitability of the proposed site and various health and safety considerations."

## § 7.22. Michigan.

The Michigan intermediate Courts of Appeals at one time adopted a rule that required municipalities to justify zoning ordinances that excluded preferred uses. Mobile homes and apartments were in the preferred use category.[69] The Michigan Supreme Court overruled the preferred use rule in *Kropf v. City of Sterling Heights*[70] but held it would take a different view of a total exclusion:

> On its face, an ordinance which *totally* excludes from a municipality a use recognized by the Constitution or other laws of this state as legitimate also

---

63. Pa. Stat. Ann. tit. 53, § 10609.1.

64. § 10916.1(c).

65. § 11006-A(c).

66. § 10609.2.

67. Casey v. Zoning Hearing Bd., 328 A.2d 464 (Pa. 1974); Ellick v. Board of Supvrs., 333 A.2d 239 (Pa. Commw. 1975).

68. § 10609.1(c). *See* H.R. Miller Co. v. Board of Supvrs. of Lancaster Twp., 605 A.2d 321 (Pa. 1992) (site-specific relief not required when ordinance not exclusionary); H & H Bldrs., Inc. v. Borough Council, 555 A.2d 948 (Pa. Commw. 1989) (criteria do not apply to total exclusion).

69. *See* Bristow v. City of Woodhaven, 192 N.W.2d 322 (Mich. App. 1971) (mobile home park).

70. 215 N.W.2d 179 (Mich. 1974).

carries with it a strong taint of unlawful discrimination and a denial of equal protection of the law as to the excluded use.[71]

*Kropf* also held that "the purely arbitrary, capricious, and unfounded exclusion of other types of legitimate land use from the area in question" would raise a substantive due process question. The supreme court later invalidated a zoning ordinance limiting mobile homes to mobile home parks.[72] The state zoning statutes also provide that counties and municipalities may not totally exclude a land use for which there is a "demonstrated need" within the township or the surrounding area unless there is no appropriate location for the use or it is unlawful.[73]

## § 7.23. California.

The California Supreme Court provided extensive dicta on exclusionary zoning in *Associated Home Bldrs. of Greater Eastbay, Inc. v. City of Livermore*,[74] in which it upheld a local growth moratorium. The court rejected the *Mt. Laurel* fair share doctrine[75] but suggested criteria that apply when a zoning ordinance influences "the supply and distribution of housing for an entire metropolitan region."

The first step is to forecast "the probable effect and duration of the restriction." The second is to identify the competing interests the restriction affects. These interests include the conflict between environmental protectionists and egalitarian humanists. They also include the conflict between suburban residents who wish to restrict immigration to their community and outsiders seeking a place to live in the face of a growing housing shortage.

The final step is "to determine whether the ordinance, in light of its probable impact, represents a reasonable accommodation of the competing interests." The burden rests on the party challenging the ordinance to provide the necessary evidence and documentation for this constitutional analysis. California has also enacted extensive legislation mandating local adoption of fair share housing plans and restricting other forms of exclusionary zoning.[76]

---

71. *Id.* at 185 (emphasis in original).

72. § 5.20.

73. Mich. Comp. Laws §§ 125.227a, 125.297a, 125.592. *See* English v. Augusta Twp., 514 N.W.2d 172 (Mich. App. 1994) (denial of rezoning for mobile home park violates statute); Fremont Twp. v. Greenfield, 347 N.W.2d 204 (Mich. App. 1984).

74. 557 P.2d 473 (Cal. 1976). *See* City of Del Mar v. City of San Diego, 183 Cal. Rptr. 898 (Cal. App. 1983) (applying *Livermore* doctrine to uphold approval of new community). *But see* Town of Los Altos Hills v. Adobe Creek Props., Inc., 108 Cal. Rptr. 271 (Cal. App. 1973) (refusing to apply exclusionary zoning doctrine to commercial exclusions).

75. § 7.09.

76. § 7.30.

## § 7.24. New Hampshire.

The New Hampshire Supreme Court adopted the "regional general welfare" rule to hold exclusionary a zoning ordinance that prohibited multi-family housing in *Britton v. Town of Chester*.[77] The town was a bedroom community located near Manchester, a major city, and was projected to have one of the highest growth rates in New Hampshire over the next two decades. Although the town permitted multi-family housing in planned residential districts, the court held this did not save the ordinance, because only a limited amount of land was available for these districts. The ordinance was also a "substantial disincentive" to the development of these districts, because it allowed the town to control their approval without reference to any objective criteria.

Relying on New Hampshire cases addressing the responsibility of municipalities in adopting growth management ordinances,[78] the court held the ordinance invalid as applied to the facts of the case because it did not address regional needs for affordable housing. The governing body of the town was given a "reasonable time period" to bring its ordinance into compliance with the regional housing-need requirement. The court also held that a builder's remedy was available and affirmed the trial court's grant of a builder's remedy to the developer. It did not follow the New Jersey rule on builder's remedies, however. It adopted the rule applied in Illinois and other states[79] to hold that the remedy is available only if the development will provide a reasonable opportunity for affordable housing consistent with "sound zoning concepts and environmental concerns."

## C. INCLUSIONARY ZONING.

## § 7.25. The Zoning Problem.

This section discusses inclusionary zoning techniques and state inclusionary legislation that can assist in the provision of affordable housing. Providing zoning opportunities for affordable housing requires extensive revisions in zoning and land use programs. These revisions include increasing housing densities, streamlining the development approval process, and making provision for housing in which development costs are reduced through techniques such as cluster zoning. Municipalities can also use flexible zoning techniques, such as the floating zone, to provide for affordable housing.[80] Revisions in excessive zoning

---

77. 595 A.2d 492 (N.H. 1991).
78. § 10.05.
79. § 8.18.
80. Moore v. City of Boulder, 484 P.2d 134 (Colo. App. 1971) (approving rezone). *See also* Cameron v. Zoning Agent of Bellingham, 260 N.E.2d 143 (Mass. 1970) (upholding ordinance

and development standards, such as curb and gutter and street width requirements, must also be considered. Some states have adopted legislation authorizing zoning for affordable housing.[81] A number of states, in response to the availability of federal assistance,[82] have also enacted laws to remove regulatory barriers to affordable housing, which include land use restrictions.[83]

Comprehensive plans should require municipalities to plan for affordable
housing, to make zoning revisions necessary to provide for affordable housing
and to designate sites in their comprehensive plans they will zone for affordable
housing. Several states, such as California, require municipalities to include affordable housing elements in their comprehensive plans.[84]

## § 7.26. Mandatory Set-Asides and Incentive Zoning.

Mandatory set-aside ordinances are an effective inclusionary zoning technique. These ordinances require residential developments over a minimum size
to include a minimum percentage of units for sale or rental to low- or moderate-
income households. Under some ordinances, the set-aside requirement applies
only if federal or state housing subsidies are available for the lower-income units
or if the local public housing authority will acquire or lease them. When the provision of lower-income housing is not linked to housing subsidies, zoning incentives may be necessary to absorb losses incurred by the developer on the
lower-income units. Density bonuses are a possibility, and the ordinance can
also relax site development requirements. Some states have authorized municipalities to provide density bonuses and other zoning incentives for affordable
housing.[85]

Although inclusionary ordinances usually require the provision of affordable
dwelling units on-site, they can also provide alternatives for meeting the affordable housing requirement. These alternatives include the off-site provision of
affordable units; the dedication of land for affordable housing, either on-site or
off-site; and in-lieu cash payments to a fund to be used for affordable housing.
The municipality can use the fund to construct affordable housing or to assist
such housing through write-downs on the cost of land, loans or grants to lower-
income households, and similar measures.

---

exempting public housing from site development restrictions and allowing it as permitted use in
any zoning district).

81. Conn. Gen. Stat. § 8-2.

82. 42 U.S.C. § 12705c.

83. *E.g.,* Wash. Rev. Code Ann. § 43.185B.030(1)(d) (Affordable Housing Advisory Board to
analyze proposals to remove "state and local regulatory barriers" to affordable housing "where
appropriate and not detrimental to the public health and safety or environment").

84. §§ 3.11, 7.30. *See, e.g.,* Conn. Gen. Stat. § 8-23; Fla. Stat. Ann. 163.3177.

85. Conn. Gen. Stat. § 8-2g; Md. Ann. Code Art. 66B, § 12.01; N.H. Rev. Stat. § 674:21; N.Y.
Town Law § 261-b; N.Y. Village Law § 7-703; Va. Code Ann. § 15.1-491.9. *See also* § 7.30.

Inclusionary ordinances often contain controls that maintain the availability of affordable housing for lower-income households once this housing is built. The ordinance may regulate the price and rents of the lower-income housing, including the resale price, and may give the municipality or its housing authority an option to purchase when lower-income units are offered for sale.

Mandatory inclusionary ordinances present a number of legal problems. Developers may make a taking objection if they suffer a loss on the sale or rental of the lower-income dwellings. They may also claim the mandatory ordinance violates equal protection and substantive due process and is not authorized by the state zoning legislation.[86] The statutory authority and substantive due process objections are interrelated. Developers can argue that mandatory inclusionary ordinances violate due process and are unauthorized by the zoning act because they do not serve a legitimate zoning purpose.

The Virginia court invalidated a mandatory inclusionary zoning ordinance invalid because it "exceeds the authority granted by the [zoning] enabling act . . . [and] because it is socio-economic zoning and attempts to control the compensation for the use of land and the improvements thereon."[87] The court also found a taking because the ordinance required the developer to sell or rent dwelling units to lower-income households "at rental or sales prices not fixed by a free market."

This case was wrongly decided. The loss that a mandatory lower-income housing requirement is likely to impose on a developer is not substantial enough for a taking. The developer should be able to make a reasonable return on his development. Density bonuses can partially or totally offset any loss the developer may suffer.

The New Jersey Supreme Court rejected the Virginia decision and approved inclusionary zoning measures, including mandatory set-asides, in *Mt. Laurel (II)*:[88]

> It is nonsense to single out inclusionary zoning (providing a realistic opportunity for the construction of lower income housing) and label it "socio-economic" if that is meant to imply that other aspects of zoning are not. . . . It would be ironic if inclusionary zoning to encourage the construction of lower income housing were ruled beyond the power of a municipality be-

---

86. *See* N.Y. Gen. City Law § 81-d (authorizing incentive zoning).

87. Board of Supvrs. v. DeGroff Enters., 198 S.E.2d 600 (Va. 1973). *See also* Middlesex & Boston St. Ry. v. Board of Aldermen, 359 N.E.2d 1279 (Mass. 1977) (condition on special exception requiring lease of apartments to city housing authority held invalid). *See* 62 A.L.R.3d 880 (1975).

88. 456 A.2d 390 (N.J. 1983), discussed in § 7.11. *See also* In re Egg Harbor Assocs. (Bayshore Center), 464 A.2d 1115 (N.J. 1983) (holding mandatory set-aside imposed as condition to coastal development permit was impliedly authorized).

cause it is "socio-economic" when its need has arisen from the socio-economic zoning of the past that excluded it.[89]

The New Jersey Supreme Court has also held that mandatory development fees for affordable housing imposed on commercial and non-inclusionary residential development are authorized by the Fair Housing Act and the zoning act.[90] The court rejected the nexus test as the basis for upholding the fee requirement and based their validity on the relationship between nonresidential development and the need for affordable housing.

## § 7.27. Office-Housing Linkage Programs.

Several cities have adopted programs that require office developers either to construct affordable housing or to pay an in-lieu fee into a fund for the construction of such housing. The programs assume that the new workers who are hired to fill new office space inflate housing prices by creating pressures on the housing market. Most of these programs are limited to downtown areas and some include retail developers. The construction or in-lieu payment requirement is usually based on a calculation that estimates the housing need created by each square foot of new office or commercial space.

Office-housing linkage programs raise a number of legal questions. One is whether municipalities have the implied authority to adopt them.[91] Another is whether these programs meet the nexus test for developer exactions. This issue is discussed in a later chapter.[92]

## § 7.28. California Inclusionary Legislation.

California has adopted extensive legislation to implement inclusionary housing objectives. Developers who provide a specified percentage of housing for households with low or very low incomes are entitled to a density bonus or other

---

89. 456 A.2d at 449.

90. Holmdel Bldrs. Ass'n v. Township of Holmdel, 583 A.2d 277 (N.J. 1990). *But see* N.J. Stat. Ann. § 13:19-11.1 (prohibiting coastal zone permit conditions that require lower-income housing in residential developments).

91. Blagden Alley Ass'n v. District of Columbia Zoning Comm'n, 590 A.2d 139 (D.C. App. 1991) (implying authority to require linkage for planned unit developments); 1956 Mass. Acts ch. 665, §§ 15-20, added by 1987 Mass. Acts ch. 371, § 3 (authorizing Boston program). *But see* San Telmo Assocs. v. City of Seattle, 735 P.2d 673 (Wash. 1987) (invalidating ordinance that required owners who demolished low-income housing and replaced it with nonresidential use to provide other suitable housing or contribute to low-income housing replacement fund).

92. § 9.23.

cost reduction incentives.[93] Discrimination against low- and moderate-income and governmentally assisted or subsidized residential development is prohibited.

The planning legislation requires a housing element in comprehensive plans.[94] This element must contain an "assessment of housing needs and an inventory of resources and constraints relevant to the meeting of these needs." The analysis of existing and projected housing need must identify each locality's "share of the regional housing need." The statute specifies criteria for the distribution of regional housing need, which include market demand for housing, employment opportunities, and the availability of suitable sites and public facilities.[95] The distribution is to be made by regional councils of government or by the state housing and community development department in areas where councils of government do not exist. The housing element must analyze "potential and actual governmental constraints" on the "development of housing for all income levels, including land use controls." Additional requirements include an analysis of "the availability of financing, the price of land, and the cost of construction."

The housing element must include a five-year housing program. Among other requirements, the housing program must

> [i]dentify adequate sites which will be made available through appropriate zoning and development standards and with public services and facilities needed to facilitate and encourage the development of a variety of types of housing for all income levels . . . [and] [a]ddress and, where appropriate and legally possible, remove governmental constraints to the . . . development of housing.[96]

Local governments must "zone sufficient vacant land for residential use with appropriate standards . . . to meet housing needs as identified in the general plan."[97] They may not impose subdivision control requirements "for the purpose of rendering infeasible the development of housing for all economic segments of the community."[98] The California legislation codifies the *Mt. Laurel* fair share doctrine as a planning and plan implementation requirement.

---

**93.** Cal. Gov't Code § 65915. *See* Building Indus. Ass'n v. City of Oceanside, 33 Cal. Rptr. 2d 137 (Cal. App. 1994) (growth control initiative conflicts with state laws protecting and encouraging lower income housing).

**94.** Gov't Code §§ 65580-65589.3. *See also* Cal. Gov't Code § 65590 (requiring replacement of lower income dwellings converted or demolished in coastal zone).

**95.** Gov't Code § 65584.

**96.** Gov't Code § 65583(c)(1) & (3). *See* § 3.22.

**97.** Gov't Code § 65913.1 (and with "appropriate standards" that "contribute significantly" to the production of lower income housing).

**98.** Gov't Code § 65913.2.

## § 7.29. Oregon Inclusionary Legislation.

Oregon has adopted state legislation that requires local governments to adopt comprehensive plans and land use regulations that comply with state planning goals. The state Land Conservation and Development Commission reviews local plans and land use regulations to determine whether they comply with the state goals. One of the major state goals is an urbanization goal that requires local governments to adopt urban growth boundaries that contain land sufficient to meet projected urban growth.

A state housing goal requires local plans to encourage the availability of adequate housing at prices and rents affordable by Oregon households. The Commission held that this goal incorporated the *Mt. Laurel* fair share doctrine[99] and later extended this interpretation in an unofficial Commission policy. The legislature codified this policy:

> When a need has been shown for housing within an urban growth boundary at particular price ranges and rent levels, needed housing . . . shall be permitted in one or more zoning districts . . . of sufficient buildable land to satisfy that need.[100]

Amendments to urban growth boundaries must also include sufficient buildable land to accommodate estimated housing needs for the next twenty years for all types of housing.[101]

The statute requires local governments to permit needed housing "in a zone or zones with sufficient buildable land to satisfy that need." They may adopt approval standards and procedures for housing and impose special conditions on approvals. Approval standards and procedures and special conditions must be "clear and objective" and must not have the effect, either singly or cumulatively, "of discouraging the needed housing types through unreasonable cost or delay."

## § 7.30. Affordable Housing Appeals Laws.

A few states have adopted legislation authorizing appeals to a court or state agency if a local government denies or restrictively conditions an application for affordable housing. Connecticut legislation authorizes a court appeal if affordable housing is denied or approved with restrictions that have a substantial ad-

---

99. Seaman v. City of Durham, LCDC No. 77-025 (1978).

100. Or. Rev. Stat. § 197.307(3). *See* City of Happy Valley v. Land Conservation & Dev. Comm'n, 677 P.2d 43 (Or. App. 1984) (statute codifies housing goal).

101. Or. Rev. Stat. § 197.296.

verse impact on its viability or affordability.[102] The municipality has the burden to justify its decision with substantial public interests in health, safety and other legal matters that outweigh the affordable-housing's need, and must show that changes in the housing cannot protect these interests. Affordable housing is assisted housing, or developments in which at least 20 percent of the housing is deed-restricted to lower-income persons.

In its first decision interpreting the law, the Connecticut Supreme Court reversed a denial of an affordable housing development application and held that the law applies to legislative zoning changes. The supreme court also held that the trial court had properly applied traditional judicial review standards, and that the statute authorized the trial court's decision to order a requested zone change and approval of a special development district designation.[103] Later decisions have held that a court can approve an affordable housing application even though it does not comply with local zoning,[104] and that traffic and environmental problems did not justify denial of an affordable housing application.[105]

Massachusetts has similar legislation, limited to federal- or state-subsidized low- or moderate-income housing projects.[106] If a local board of zoning appeals denies or restrictively conditions a "comprehensive permit" for a project, a state Housing Appeals Committee reviews the denial to determine whether it was "reasonable and consistent with local needs." This test requires a balancing of the regional need for low- and moderate-income housing, "considered with the number of low income persons" in the municipality, with the municipality's need for health, safety, design, and open space regulations.[107] Local requirements or regulations must be applied "as equally as possible" to both subsidized and unsubsidized housing. Local requirements or regulations must be applied "as equally as possible" to both subsidized and unsubsidized housing.

---

102. Conn. Gen. Stat. § 8-30g.

103. West Hartford Interfaith Coalition, Inc. v. Town Council, 636 A.2d 1342 (Conn. 1994).

104. Wisniowski v. Planning Comm'n, 655 A.2d 1146 (Conn. 1995). *See also* Town Close Assocs. v. Planning & Zoning Comm'n, 679 A.2d 378 (Conn. App. 1996) (public interest test applies though land zoned for affordable housing).

105. Kaufman v. Zoning Comm'n, 653 A.2d 798 (Conn. 1995). *See also* National Associated Props. v. Planning & Zoning Comm'n, 658 A.2d 114 (Conn. App. 1995) (reversing denial of affordable housing application).

106. Mass. Ann. Laws ch. 40B, §§ 20 to 23.

107. *See also* § 20 (standard met when existing lower-income housing exceeds 10% of land area or application will provide housing on sites comprising more than .3% of land area or ten acres).

If the Committee reverses a denial, "it shall direct the [local] board to issue a comprehensive permit or approval to the applicant." The Committee may also order the removal or modification of any "condition or requirement" that makes the project uneconomic.[108] Rhode Island has similar legislation.[109]

---

108. *See* Pheasant Ridge Assocs. v. Town of Burlington, 506 N.E.2d 1152 (Mass. 1987) (invalidating taking that blocked lower income housing project); Board of Appeals v. Housing Appeals Comm., 357 N.E.2d 936 (Mass. App. 1976) (Committee may not authorize noncompliance with state building code); Wilson v. Town of Sherborn, 326 N.E.2d 922 (Mass. App. 1975) (court relied on availability of law to uphold two-acre lot requirement).

109. R.I. Gen. Laws § 45-53-1 et seq. *See* Curran v. Church Community Hous. Corp., 672 A.2d 453 (R.I. 1996) (upholding approval of affordable housing under the statute). See also R.I. Gen. Laws § 34-39.1-1 et seq. (making restrictions that preserve affordable housing legally enforceable).

# REFERENCES

## Books and Monographs

M. Danielson, The Politics of Exclusion (1976).

A. Downs, Opening Up the Suburbs, An Urban Strategy for America (1973).

A. Mallach, Inclusionary Housing Programs: Policies and Practices (1984).

S. White, Affordable Housing: Proactive & Reactive Planning Strategies, American Planning Ass'n, Planning Advisory Serv. Rep. No. 441 (1992).

## Articles

Berger, Inclusionary Zoning Devices as Takings: The Legacy of the Mount Laurel Cases, 70 Neb. L. Rev. 183 (1991).

Brownstein, Illicit Legislative Motive in the Municipal Land Use Regulation Process, 57 U. Cin. L. Rev. 1 (1988).

Burchell, Listokin & James, Exclusionary Zoning: Pitfalls of the Regional Remedy, 7 Urb. Law. 262 (1975).

Calavita, Grimes & Mallach, Inclusionary Zoning in California and New Jersey: A Comparative Analysis, 8 Hous. Pol'y Debate 109 (1997).

Cummins, Recasting Fair Share: Toward Effective Housing Law and Principled Social Policy, 14 Law & Ineq. 339 (1996).

Dietderich, An Egalitarian's Market: The Economics of Inclusionary Zoning Reclaimed, 24 Fordham Urb. L.J. 23 (1996).

Fox, The Selling Out of Mount Laurel: Regional Contribution Agreements in New Jersey's Fair Housing Act, 16 Fordham Urb. L.J. 535 (1987-88).

Franzese, Mount Laurel III: The New Jersey Supreme Court's Judicial Retreat, 18 Seton Hall L. Rev. 30 (1988).

Galowitz, Interstate Metro-Regional Responses to Exclusionary Zoning, 27 Real Prop. Prob. & Tr. J. 49 (1992).

Inman & Rubinfeld, The Judicial Pursuit of Local Fiscal Equity, 92 Harv. L. Rev. 1662 (1979).

Jaffe, Government Code § 65008: New Strategies to Combat Exclusionary Zoning, 24 Colum. Hum. Rts. L. Rev. 165 (1992-93).

Johnston, Schwartz, Wandesorde-Smith & Caplan, Selling Zoning: Do Density Bonus Incentives for Moderate-Cost Housing Work?, 36 J. Urb. & Contemp. L. 45 (1989).

Kleven, Inclusionary Ordinances — Policy and Legal Issues in Requiring Private Developers to Build Low Cost Housing, 21 U.C.L.A. L. Rev. 1432 (1974).

Kmiec, Exclusionary Zoning and Purposeful Racial Discrimination: Two Wrongs Deserving Separate Remedies, 18 Urb. Law. 393 (1986).

Lamar, Mallach & Payne, *Mount Laurel* at Work: Affordable Housing in New Jersey, 41 Rutgers L. Rev. 1197 (1989).

Mandelker, Racial Discrimination and Exclusionary Zoning: A Perspective on Arlington Heights, 55 Tex. L. Rev. 1217 (1977).

331

McGuire, The Judiciary's Role in Implementing the *Mt. Laurel* Doctrine: Deference or Activism?, 23 Seton Hall L. Rev. 1006 (1993).

McDougall, From Litigation to Legislation in Exclusionary Zoning Law, 22 Harv. C.R.-C.L. L. Rev. 623 (1987).

McDougall, Regional Contribution Agreements: Compensation for Exclusionary Zoning, 60 Temp. L.Q. 665 (1987).

Monaghan & Penkethman, The Fair Housing Act: Meeting the Mount Laurel Obligation with a Statewide Plan, 9 Seton Hall Legis. J. 581 (1986).

Mount Laurel II Symposium, 14 Seton Hall L. Rev. 829 (1984).

Netter, The Massachusetts Approach to Affordable Housing, Urb. Land, Vol. 49, No. 6, at 32 (1990).

Padilla, Reflections on Inclusionary Zoning and a Renewed Look at its Viability, 23 Hofstra L. Rev. 539 (1995).

Payne, Norman Williams, Exclusionary Zoning, and the Mount Laurel Doctrine: Making the Theory Fit the Facts, 20 Vt. L. Rev. 665 (1996).

Payne, Rethinking Fair Share: The Judicial Enforcement of Affordable Housing Policies, 16 Real Estate L.J. 20 (1987).

Rice, Exclusionary Zoning: Mount Laurel in New York?, 6 Pace L. Rev. 135 (1986).

Roisman & Tegeler, Improving and Expanding Housing Opportunities for Poor People of Color: Recent Developments in Federal and State Courts, 24 Clearinghouse Rev. 312 (1990).

Sager, Insular Majorities Unabated: Warth v. Seldin and City of Eastlake v. Forest City Enterprises, Inc., 91 Harv. L. Rev. 1373 (1978).

Schill, The Federal Role in Reducing Regulatory Barriers to Affordable Housing in the Suburbs, 8 J.L. & Politics 703 (1992).

Schukoske, Housing Linkage: Regulating Development Impact on Housing Costs, 76 Iowa L. Rev. 1011 (1991).

Schuman, From Washington to Arlington Heights and Beyond: Discriminatory Purpose in Equal Protection Litigation, 1977 U. Ill. L.J. 961.

Schwartz, The Disparate Impact Theory of Discrimination in Employment and Housing: The Limits of Analogy, 59 UMKC L. Rev. 815 (1991).

Smith, Delaney & Liou, Inclusionary Housing Programs: Issues and Outcomes, 25 Real Estate L.J. 155 (1996).

Symposium — *Mount Laurel II* and Developments in New Jersey, 15 Rutgers L.J. 513 (1984).

Vodola, Connecticut's affordable housing appeals procedure law in practice, 29 Conn. L. Rev. 1235 (1997).

Wheeler, Negotiating NIMBYs: Learning From the Failure of the Massachusetts Siting Law, 11 Yale J. on Reg. 241 (1994).

White, Using Fees and Taxes to Promote Affordable Housing, Land Use L. & Zoning Dig., Vol. 43, No. 9, at 3 (1991).

Williams, The Background and Significance of *Mount Laurel II,* 26 W.U.J. Urb. & Contemp. L. 3 (1984).

Williams, The Need for Affordable Housing: The Constitutional Viability of Inclusionary Zoning, 26 J. Marshall L. Rev. 75 (1992).

**Student Work**

Note, Alternatives to Warth v. Seldin: The Potential Resident Challenger of an Exclusionary Zoning Scheme, 11 Urb. L. Ann. 223 (1976).

Note, Anti-Snob Zoning in Massachusetts: Assessing One Attempt at Opening the Suburbs to Affordable Housing, 78 Va. L. Rev. 535 (1992).

Note, Breaking the Exclusionary Land Use Regulation Barrier: Policies to Promote Affordable Housing in the Suburbs, 82 Geo. L.J. 2039 (1994).

Note, The Council on Affordable Housing and the *Mount Laurel* Doctrine: Will the Council Succeed?, 18 Rutgers L.J. 929 (1987).

Note, Racial Diversity in Residential Communities: Societal Housing Patterns and a Proposal for a "Racial Inclusionary Ordinance," 63 S. Cal. L. Rev. 1151 (1990).

Note, Standing to Challenge Exclusionary Land Use Devices in Federal Courts After Warth v. Seldin, 29 Stan. L. Rev. 323 (1977).

Note, State-Sponsored Growth Management as a Remedy for Exclusionary Zoning, 108 Harv. L. Rev. 1127 (1995).

Comment, Fundamental Issues in Housing Discrimination Litigation, 14 N.C. Cent. L.J. 555 (1984).

Comment, Judicial Deference and the Perpetuation of Exclusionary Zoning: A Case Study, Theoretical Overview, and a Proposal for Change, 37 Buff. L. Rev. 863 (1988-89).

Comment, Zoning for All: Using Inclusionary Zoning Techniques to Promote Affordable Housing, 44 Emory L.J. 359 (1995).

Recent Decision, Land Use — Lack of Judicial Guidance in Exclusionary Zoning, 64 Temp. L. Rev. 339 (1991).

# Chapter 8

# LAND USE LITIGATION AND REMEDIES

335

## § 8.01.  An Introductory Note.

Land use litigation presents complex problems. Plaintiffs in state courts must have standing to sue, must exhaust administrative remedies, and must select an appropriate judicial remedy. Courts may be reluctant to provide affirmative relief that allows the landowner to proceed with his development. Land use plaintiffs may also sue in federal court, where remedies are available under § 1983 of the federal Civil Rights Act and an action in inverse condemnation in taking cases.

The chapter discusses standing to sue, exhaustion of remedies, and the judicial remedies available in state courts. It also discusses § 1983 of the federal Civil Rights Act and the inverse condemnation and implied cause of action remedies that are available in federal courts. The ripeness barrier to federal court land use actions is discussed in Chapter 2. Although the chapter concentrates on zoning litigation, the law that applies to zoning cases also applies to other land use regulations.

## A. THIRD-PARTY STANDING IN STATE COURTS.

## § 8.02.  General Principles.

Landowners who challenge land use regulations in court have a property interest sufficient to confer standing.[1] More difficult standing problems arise when third parties, such as neighboring property owners or nonresidents, challenge land use regulations. Standing to sue is more difficult to obtain because third parties do not own property that is directly affected by a zoning restriction. This section reviews the law of third-party standing in state court zoning litigation. It does not discuss third-party standing in exclusionary zoning litigation, which is reviewed in Chapter Seven.[2]

Standing law in state courts differs from standing law in federal courts, which is governed by constitutional "case and controversy" and prudential standing principles.[3] State constitutions do not have "case and controversy" limitations on state court jurisdiction. State courts impose a "prudential" standing limitation by limiting their jurisdiction to justiciable controversies.

Third-party standing in zoning litigation also is controlled by the Standard Zoning Enabling Act. The Act authorized appeals from decisions of the board of

---

**1.** Frank Hardie Adv., Inc. v. City of Dubuque Zoning Bd. of Adjustment, 501 N.W.2d 521 (Iowa 1993) (citing cases holding that lessee of property has standing).

**2.** *See also* §§ 5.40, 5.41.

**3.** § 7.02.

adjustment by "persons . . . aggrieved" and "any taxpayer."[4] Almost all state statutes contain the "person aggrieved" provision, but only a minority extend standing to taxpayers. An occasional statute makes zoning decisions reviewable under the state's administrative procedure act.[5] The courts usually assume that the statutory aggrievement requirement for standing to appeal zoning board decisions also governs nonstatutory judicial remedies, such as injunction and declaratory judgment actions.[6]

Most statutes allow a plaintiff to appeal an administrative decision even though he did not participate in the administrative proceedings in which the decision was made.[7] Some courts do not follow this rule if the statute does not enact it. They require participation in the administrative proceedings by the party who brings an appeal.[8] These courts require participation even if the interests represented by the party bringing the appeal were not adequately represented in the administrative proceedings.

Under the usual formulation of the rule, third-party standing requires "special" damage to an interest or property right that is different from the damage the general public suffers from a zoning restriction.[9] Competitive injury, for example, is not enough.[10] This rule reflects the nuisance basis of zoning, which protects property owners only from damage caused by adjacent incompatible uses. Although the special damage rule is well-entrenched in zoning law, a few courts have modified it. New Jersey has adopted a liberal third-party standing rule which requires only a showing of "a sufficient stake and real adverseness."[11]

### § 8.03. Taxpayers and Citizens.

If the statute does not grant standing, most courts deny standing to citizens and taxpayers who do not own property affected by a zoning restriction they

---

4. Standard Zoning Enabling Act § 7.

5. Ill. Ann. Stat. ch. 24, § 11-13-13.

6. Palmer v. St. Louis County, 591 S.W.2d 39 (Mo. App. 1980).

7. *See* Mass. Gen. L. ch. 40A, § 17.

8. Bryniarski v. Montgomery County Bd. of Appeals, 230 A.2d 289 (Md. 1967); Abrams v. Gearhart, 184 N.E.2d 411 (Ohio App. 1961); Frank v. Mobil Oil Corp., 296 A.2d 300 (Pa. Commw. 1973). *Contra* State ex rel. Brookside Poultry Farms, Inc. v. Jefferson County Bd. of Adjustment, 388 N.W.2d 593 (Wis. 1986).

9. Hall v. Planning Comm'n, 435 A.2d 975 (Conn. 1981); Renard v. Dade County, 261 So. 2d 832 (Fla. 1972); Harvard Square Defense Fund v. Planning Bd., 540 N.E.2d 182 (Mass. App. 1989); Bryniarski v. Montgomery County Bd. of Appeals, 230 A.2d 289 (Md. 1967); Palmer v. St. Louis County, 591 S.W.2d 39 (Mo. App. 1980); Develo-Cepts, Inc. v. City of Galveston, 668 S.W.2d 790 (Tex. App. 1984).

10. Multiplex Corp. v. Hartz Mountain Indus., 564 A.2d 146 (N.J. App. Div. 1989); Nernberg v. City of Pittsburgh, 620 A.2d 692 (Pa. Commw. 1993). *See also* § 5.35.

11. Home Bldrs. League of S. Jersey, Inc. v. Township of Berlin, 405 A.2d 381 (N.J. 1979).

wish to challenge.[12] This rule is less liberal than the rule that grants standing to taxpayers to challenge illegal municipal expenditures. A few state courts grant standing to taxpayers and citizens to challenge zoning restrictions.[13]

## § 8.04. Resident Landowners.

Landowners who reside in a municipality and are adjacent or close to land on which a zoning agency has allowed a more intensive use are usually held to have suffered special damage which is sufficient to confer standing.[14] Some cases hold that adjacent landowners have standing prima facie.[15] Other cases hold that proximity alone is not enough, even when a statute confers standing on neighboring landowners.[16] These courts insist on specific proof of special damage. Fear of harmful adverse effects, such as a fear of apartment development, increased traffic, or the aesthetic "blight" created by an adjacent parking lot, may not be enough.[17]

---

**12.** Wine v. Council of City of Los Angeles, 2 Cal. Rptr. 94 (Cal. App. 1960); Bell v. Planning & Zoning Comm'n, 391 A.2d 154 (Conn. 1978); Citizens Growth Mgt. Coalition of W. Palm Beach, Inc. v. City of West Palm Beach, Inc., 450 So. 2d 204 (Fla. 1984) (consistency of zoning with comprehensive plan); Tate v. Stephens, 265 S.E.2d 811 (Ga. 1980); Garner v. County of Du Page, 133 N.E.2d 303 (Ill. 1956); Amherst Growth Study Comm'n, Inc. v. Board of Appeals, 296 N.E.2d 717 (Mass. App. 1973); Blumberg v. Hill, 119 N.Y.S.2d 855 (Sup. Ct. 1953). *See* Munch v. City of Mott, 311 N.W.2d 17 (N.D. 1981) (ordinance may confer standing).

**13.** Towle v. Nashua, 212 A.2d 204 (N.H. 1965); Booth v. Board of Adjustment, 234 A.2d 681 (N.J. 1967); Roeder v. Borough Council, 266 A.2d 691 (Pa. 1970). *See also* Renard v. Dade County, 261 So. 2d 832 (Fla. 1972) (challenge to validity in enactment).

**14.** Steadham v. Board of Zoning Adjustment, 629 So. 2d 647 (Ala. 1993); Mings v. City of Ft. Smith, 701 S.W.2d 705 (Ark. 1986); Buckelew v. Town of Parker, 937 P.2d 368 (Ariz. App. 1997); Reynolds v. Dittmer, 312 N.W.2d 75 (Iowa App. 1981); Christy's Realty Ltd. Partnership v. Town of Kittery, 663 A.2d 59 (Me. 1995); Ramirez v. City of Santa Fe, 852 P.2d 690 (N.M. App. 1993) (applying liberal Supreme Court rules); Roach v. Town of Milton Zoning Bd. of Appeals, 530 N.Y.S.2d 321 (App. Div. 1988); Anderson v. Island County, 501 P.2d 594 (Wash. 1972); Hoke v. Moyer, 865 P.2d 624 (Wyo. 1994); 37 A.L.R.2d 1137 (1954). *But see* Sherrill House, Inc. v. Board of Appeal, 473 N.E.2d 716 (Mass. App. 1986).

**15.** Concerned Citizens of Murphys v. Jackson, 140 Cal. Rptr. 531 (Cal. App. 1977); Snyder v. City Council, 531 P.2d 643 (Colo. App. 1975); Hobbs v. Markey, 398 S.W.2d 54 (Ky. 1966); Marashlian v. Zoning Bd. of Appeals, 660 N.E.2d 369 (Mass. 1996) (rebuttable presumption of standing); Sun-Brite Car Wash, Inc. v. Board of Zoning & Appeals, 508 N.E.2d 130 (N.Y. 1987).

**16.** Foran v. Zoning Bd. of Appeals, 260 A.2d 609 (Conn. 1969), applying Conn. Gen. Stat. § 8-8.

**17.** Gulf House Ass'n v. Town of Gulf Shores, 484 So. 2d 1061 (Ala. 1985); Walls v. Planning & Zoning Comm'n, 408 A.2d 252 (Conn. 1979); Columbus v. Diaz-Verson, 373 S.E.2d 208 (Ga. 1988) (flooding threat); Dunaway v. City of Marietta, 308 S.E.2d 823 (Ga. 1983); 222 E. Chestnut St. Corp. v. Board of Appeals, 152 N.E.2d 465 (Ill. 1958); Wilkinson v. Atkinson, 218 A.2d 503 (Md. 1966); Marashlian v. Zoning Bd. of Appeals, 660 N.E.2d 369 (Mass. 1996); Tata v. Town of Babylon, 276 N.Y.S.2d 426 (Sup. Ct. 1967); Davis v. City of Archdale, 344 S.E.2d 369 (N.C. App. 1986). *But see* Dalton v. City & County of Honolulu, 462 P.2d 199 (Haw. 1969).

The courts do not usually confer standing on property owners who wish to challenge a favorable zoning action on a site that is some distance away.[18] These cases reflect the assumption in nuisance law that special damage from an incompatible land use occurs only to property that is close enough to be affected.

## § 8.05. Nonresident Landowners.

Although a few courts hold to the contrary,[19] the recent decisions hold that nonresident landowners have standing to challenge another municipality's zoning if they own property contiguous or near to the rezoned land.[20] *Scott v. City of Indian Wells*[21] is a leading case. The court held:

> To hold, under these circumstances, that defendant city may zone the land within its borders without any concern for adjacent landowners would indeed "make a fetish out of invisible boundary lines and mockery of the principles of zoning."[22]

The court also held that individual property interests are "often affected by local land use controls," and that municipalities owe nonresidents as well as residents a "duty" to hear and consider their views before acting on a rezoning. Some of the cases that granted standing to nonresident landowners relied on decisions holding that land uses in an adjacent municipality are relevant to the constitutionality of a municipality's zoning.

## § 8.06. Organizations and Associations.

Although some courts hold that neighborhood and other organizations are not entitled to standing as aggrieved persons,[23] the trend is toward granting standing

---

18. Victoria Corp. v. Atlanta Merchandise Mart, Inc., 112 S.E.2d 793 (Ga. App. 1960); Garner v. County of Du Page, 133 N.E.2d 303 (Ill. 1956); Pattison v. Corby, 172 A.2d 490 (Md. 1961); Palmer v. St. Louis County, 591 S.W.2d 39 (Mo. App. 1980). *But see* Exchange Invs., Inc. v. Alachua County, 481 So. 2d 1223 (Fla. App. 1985).

19. Clark v. City of Colorado Springs, 428 P.2d 359 (Colo. 1967); Cablevision — Div. of Sammons Communications, Inc. v. Zoning Hearing Bd., 320 A.2d 388 (Pa. Commw. 1974).

20. Brandywine Park Condo. Council v. Members of City of Wilmington Zoning Bd. of Adjustment, 534 A.2d 286 (Del. Super. 1987); Whittingham v. Village of Woodridge, 249 N.E.2d 332 (Ill. App. 1969); Stokes v. City of Mishawaka, 441 N.E.2d 24 (Ind. App. 1982); Koppel v. City of Fairway, 371 P.2d 113 (Kan. 1962); Allen v. Coffel, 488 S.W.2d 671 (Mo. App. 1972); 69 A.L.R.3d 805 (1976).

21. 492 P.2d 1137 (Cal. 1972).

22. *Id.* at 1141.

23. Chabau v. Dade County, 385 So. 2d 129 (Fla. App. 1980); Lindsey Creek Area Civic Ass'n v. Consolidated Gov't of Columbus, 292 S.E.2d 61 (Ga. 1982); Westwood Forum, Inc. v. City of Springfield, 634 N.E.2d 1154 (Ill. App. 1994); Amherst Growth Study Comm'n, Inc. v. Board of Appeals, 296 N.E.2d 717 (Mass. App. 1973); Stocksdale v. Barnard, 212 A.2d 282 (Md. 1965); Acorn Corp. v. Zoning Hearing Bd., 523 A.2d 436 (Pa. Commw. 1987) (denying right to inter-

to these organizations in a representational capacity.[24] Many of these cases follow the lead of *Hunt v. Washington State Apple Advertising Comm'n*,[25] a U.S. Supreme Court case. It held an organization can sue on behalf of its members if its members would have standing to sue in their own right, if it seeks to protect interests germane to the organization's purpose, and if neither the claim nor the relief requested requires the participation of its individual members in the suit. Many of the state cases have also ignored *Warth v. Seldin*,[26] which denied standing to a housing organization to challenge an exclusionary suburban zoning ordinance.

*Residents of Beverly Glen, Inc. v. City of Los Angeles*[27] illustrates the cases that grant standing to organizations. A neighborhood organization brought suit claiming a planned unit development was inconsistent with density policies contained in a comprehensive plan. The court noted that "environmental concerns underlie this action . . . [and] are the proper subject of judicial consideration." It held that "there is no insuperable obstacle to the maintenance of an action by a group whose members find themselves directly and adversely affected by the governmental action involved."

*Douglaston Civic Ass'n v. Galvin*[28] is a leading case that granted standing to a neighborhood organization. The court found an "economic disparity" in zoning litigation that justified organizational standing. A landowner who stands to gain from the relaxation of zoning restrictions is not reluctant to engage in litigation to achieve this result. Individual landowners in the neighborhood may not realize the impact of the change on their property or may not have the finances to effectively oppose the zoning change. "By granting the neighborhood and civic asso-

---

vene); Virginia Beach Beautification Comm'n v. Board of Zoning Appeals, 344 S.E.2d 899 (Va. 1986).

**24.** Colorado Manufactured Housing Ass'n v. Pueblo County, 857 P.2d 507 (Colo. App. 1993); Timber Trails Corp. v. Planning & Zoning Comm'n, 610 A.2d 620 (Conn. 1992); Dupont Circle Citizens Ass'n v. Barry, 455 A.2d 417 (D.C. App. 1983); Life of the Land v. Land Use Comm'n, 594 P.2d 1079 (Haw. 1979); Glengary-Gamlin Protective Ass'n v. Bonner County Bd. of Comm'rs, 675 P.2d 344 (Idaho App. 1983); Bellhaven Imp. Ass'n v. City of Jackson, 507 So. 2d 41 (Miss. 1987); 1000 Friends of Or. v. Land Conservation & Dev. Comm'n, 593 P.2d 1171 (Or. App. 1979); Save a Valuable Env't v. City of Bothell, 576 P.2d 401 (Wash. 1978). *Cf.* Montana Wildlife Fed'n v. Sager, 620 P.2d 1189 (Mont. 1980) (statute conferred standing). *See also* Citizens Coordinating Comm. on Friendship Heights, Inc. v. TKU Assocs., 351 A.2d 133 (Md. 1976) (intervention).

**25.** 432 U.S. 333 (1977), as restated in United Food & Commercial Workers Union Local 751 v. Brown Group, Inc., 116 S. Ct.2 1529 (1996). *See also* Sierra Club v. Morton, 405 U.S. 727 (1972).

**26.** 422 U.S. 490 (1974), discussed in § 7.02.

**27.** 109 Cal. Rptr. 724 (Cal. App. 1973).

**28.** 324 N.E.2d 317 (N.Y. 1974).

ciations standing in such situations, the expense can be spread out over a number of property owners putting them on an economic parity with the developer."[29]

The court held that "an appropriate representative association" should have standing to assert the rights of members affected by a zoning change. The court listed a number of factors courts should consider in determining whether the association was sufficiently representative. They include the capacity of the association to assume an adversary position and a requirement that the association be "fairly representative of the community or interests which it seeks to protect."[30]

## § 8.07. Municipalities.

The courts recognize the standing of municipalities to challenge actions by their zoning boards and planning commissions. They may deny standing if no harm is shown, unless they construe a statutory provision authorizing judicial actions by municipalities and municipal officials as a waiver of the harm requirement.[31]

More difficult problems are presented when a municipality challenges the zoning of an adjacent municipality. Harm is difficult to show unless the municipality owns property in the area affected by the adjacent municipality's zoning. A municipality may also claim harm based on more generalized injuries, such as increased traffic from a land use in an adjacent municipality that increases traffic control costs. Some courts refuse to recognize this kind of harm as sufficient to confer standing.[32]

In *Village of Barrington Hills v. Village of Hoffman Estates,*[33] the court took a contrary view in a case in which two municipalities challenged the approval of an open-air theater in an adjacent municipality. The court noted that the municipalities would suffer "special damages in their corporate capacities," such as a decline in property values, increased traffic control costs, and air quality degra-

---

**29.** *Id.* at 320.

**30.** *See also* American Law Inst., Model Land Dev. Code § 2-307 (similar requirements for organizational standing).

**31.** City of Irvine v. Irvine Citizens Against Overdevelopment, 30 Cal. Rptr. 2d 797 (Cal. App. 1994); City of Burley v. McCaslin Lumber Co., 693 P.2d 1108 (Idaho App. 1984); County of Cook v. Priester, 342 N.E.2d 41 (Ill. 1976); City of Plattsburgh v. Mannix, 432 N.Y.S.2d 910 (Sup. Ct. 1980); City of East Providence v. Shell Oil Co., 290 A.2d 915 (R.I. 1972); 13 A.L.R.4th 1130 (1982). *Compare* Township of Dover v. Board of Adjustment, 386 A.2d 421 (N.J. App. Div. 1978). *See also* Town of Northville v. Village of Sheridan, 655 N.E.2d 22 (Ill. App. 1995) (applying usual rule that municipality may not challenge legislation as unconstitutional).

**32.** City of Greenbelt v. Jaeger, 206 A.2d 694 (Md. 1965); Town of Huntington v. Town Bd. of Oyster Bay, 293 N.Y.S.2d 558 (Sup. Ct. 1968). *See* Town of North Hempstead v. Village of North Hills, 342 N.E.2d 566 (N.Y. 1975) (statute).

**33.** 410 N.E.2d 37 (Ill. 1980), *cert. denied,* 449 U.S. 1126 (1981). *Accord* Town of Mesilla v. Town of Las Cruces, 898 P.2d 121 (N.M. App. 1995) (aesthetic, environmental and economic harm).

dation caused by motor vehicle exhaust. Other decisions allowed a municipality to sue an adjacent municipality in a representative capacity without showing proof of harm.[34]

## B. EXHAUSTION OF REMEDIES IN STATE COURTS.

### § 8.08. General Principles: Exhaustion and Ripeness Distinguished.

A plaintiff cannot challenge a zoning ordinance or restriction in state court unless he has exhausted his administrative remedies. The courts adopted the exhaustion doctrine to maintain an appropriate separation of governmental powers. They require exhaustion of administrative remedies because they want to give an administrative agency the opportunity to grant administrative relief that can avoid a court challenge. The exhaustion doctrine in zoning also reflects a judicial belief that zoning agencies, not the courts, are the proper forum in which to resolve questions concerning the applicability of zoning ordinances.

A failure to exhaust administrative remedies is jurisdictional in many states, and municipalities can raise it as an affirmative defense.[35] The exhaustion requirement is different from the rule that bars plaintiffs from using a particular judicial remedy, such as mandamus, if another judicial remedy is available.[36]

The exhaustion doctrine must be distinguished from the ripeness doctrine that is a barrier to bringing land use cases in federal court.[37] The ripeness doctrine, which is similar to but theoretically different from the exhaustion of remedies doctrine, does not allow a plaintiff to bring suit until the administrative agency has made a final, definitive decision applying its regulation. A number of state courts apply the federal ripeness doctrine to taking claims in land use cases, but it is not always clear whether the usual exhaustion rules always apply. The issue in the state cases is whether there is a final decision, because the availability of a state compensation remedy only affects federal jurisdiction. Like the federal courts, state courts often find a land use case is not a final decision ready for re-

---

**34.** Board of County Comm'rs v. City of Thornton, 629 P.2d 605 (Colo. 1981) (home rule city); Borough of Roselle Park v. Township of Union, 272 A.2d 762 (N.J. 1970); 49 A.L.R.3d 1126 (1973). *See also* Maryland-Nat'l Capital Park & Planning Comm'n v. City of Rockville, 305 A.2d 122 (Md. 1973) (regional commission).

**35.** Poe v. City of Baltimore, 216 A.2d 707 (Md. 1966); Nodell Inv. Corp. v. City of Glendale, 254 N.W.2d 310 (Wis. 1977). *Contra* Boomhower v. Cerro Gordo County Bd. of Supvrs., 173 N.W.2d 95 (Iowa 1969); Deal Gardens, Inc. v. Board of Trustees, 226 A.2d 607 (N.J. 1967). *See* Palmieri v. Zoning Bd. of Appeals, 349 A.2d 731 (Conn. Super. 1975) (can compel administrative agency to act).

**36.** G.S.T. v. City of Avon Lake, 357 N.E.2d 38 (Ohio 1976).

**37.** §§ 2.21-2.26.

view.[38] Applying the federal ripeness rules in state courts is incorrect because the U.S. Supreme Court adopted these rules to determine federal jurisdiction to hear questions arising under state law. Nevertheless, the tendency of state courts to apply the federal ripeness rules seems entrenched and is likely to continue.

## § 8.09. What Remedies Must Be Exhausted.

The exhaustion doctrine in most states does not require landowners to seek legislative relief through a zoning amendment,[39] but a few courts hold to the contrary.[40] A zoning amendment is an administrative remedy a plaintiff must exhaust in states that characterize the zoning amendment process as quasi-judicial.[41]

Plaintiffs are required to pursue all available administrative remedies, including exceptions, variances, site plan review,[42] and appeals to the board of adjustment for administrative interpretations of the zoning ordinance.[43] A plaintiff

---

**38.** Long Beach Equities, Inc. v. County of Ventura, 282 Cal. Rptr. 877 (Cal. App. 1991); Reale Inv., Inc. v. City of Colorado Springs, 856 P.2d 91 (Colo. App. 1993); Port Clinton Assocs. v. Board of Selectmen, 587 A.2d 126 (Conn. 1991); City of Riviera Beach v. Shillingburg, 659 So. 2d 1174 (Fla. App. 1995); Drovers Bank v. Village of Hinsdale, 566 N.E.2d 899 (Ill. App. 1991); Galbraith v. Planning Dep't, 627 N.E.2d 850 (Ind. App. 1994); Baaken v. City of Council Bluffs, 470 N.W.2d 34 (Iowa 1991); April v. City of Broken Arrow, 775 P.2d 1347 (Okla. 1989); Beverly Bank v. Illinois Dep't of Transp., 579 N.E.2d 815 (Ill. 1991); Paragon Props. Co. v. City of Novi, 550 N.W.2d 772 (Mich. 1996); Whitehead Oil Co. v. City of Lincoln (III), 515 N.W.2d 401 (Neb. 1994) (held ripe); Town of Orangetown v. Magee, 665 N.E.2d 1061 (N.Y. 1996) (same); Messer v. Town of Chapel Hill, 479 S.E.2d 221 (N.C. App. 1997); Joyce v. Multnomah County, 835 P.2d 127 (Or. App. 1992); Killington, Ltd. v. State, 668 A.2d 1278 (Vt. 1995); Estate of Friedman v. Pierce Cty., 768 P.2d 462 (Wash. 1989); Cox v. City of Lynwood, 863 P.2d 578 (Wash. App. 1993) (ripeness rules do not apply to substantive due process claim); 111 A.L.R. Fed. 83 (1993). *See also* Ben Lommond, Inc. v. Municipality of Anchorage, 761 P.2d 119 (Alaska 1988) (reviewing basis for exhaustion principle).

**39.** G.S.T. v. City of Avon Lake, 357 N.E.2d 38 (Ohio 1976).

**40.** Village Centers, Inc. v. DeKalb County, 281 S.E.2d 522 (Ga. 1981); Bright v. City of Evanston, 139 N.E.2d 270 (Ill. 1957).

**41.** Fifth Ave. Corp. v. Washington County, 581 P.2d 50 (Or. 1978).

**42.** Exception: Holt-Lock, Inc. v. Zoning & Planning Comm'n, 286 A.2d 299 (Conn. 1971). Variance: Pan Pac. Props. v. County of Santa Cruz, 146 Cal. Rptr. 428 (Cal. App. 1978); Lange v. Town of Woodway, 483 P.2d 116 (Wash. 1971). Site Plan Review: Bruni v. City of Farmington Hills, 293 N.W.2d 609 (Mich. App. 1980). *See also* Park Area Neighbors v. Town of Fairfax, 35 Cal. Rptr. 2d 334 (Cal. App. 1994) (not excused from exaustion because no legal representation and agency misadvice); Howland Realty Co. v. Wolcott, 457 N.E.2d 883 (Ohio App. 1982) (petition for referendum not required).

**43.** Minor v. Cochise County, 608 P.2d 309 (Ariz. 1980); Cunningham v. Kittery Planning Bd., 400 A.2d 1070 (Me. 1979); Westside Enters. v. City of Dexter, 559 S.W.2d 638 (Mo. App. 1977).

must also pursue any additional remedies that are available under the zoning ordinance.[44]

## § 8.10. Exceptions.

The exhaustion doctrine is discretionary, and the courts have adopted a number of exceptions. Under one important exception, exhaustion is not required when administrative remedies are inadequate.[45] Remedies are inadequate when the board of adjustment cannot grant a use variance that can avoid an attack on the constitutionality of a zoning regulation, or when a variance or exception is unavailable.[46] Exhaustion is not required when a landowner claims a vested right, because a vested right confers absolute protection from a change in the zoning ordinance and does not require an administrative determination.[47]

Another commonly applied exception does not require exhaustion when a plaintiff claims a zoning ordinance is unconstitutional in its entirety or is facially illegal.[48] This exception arises from the rationale of the exhaustion rule, which requires an administrative interpretation only when a plaintiff claims the ordinance is unconstitutional as applied to her property. The courts require exhaustion in as-applied cases because the administrative agency may foreclose constitutional attack by giving the landowner administrative relief. Administrative review cannot remedy a constitutional attack that does not depend on an application of the zoning ordinance to the landowner's property.[49] In the clearest case, the plaintiff claims a zoning ordinance is invalid because of some underlying illegality, such as a lack of adequate notice or statutory authority.[50] Nor is exhaustion required when the plaintiff claims that the zoning ordinance contains

---

**44.** County of Platte v. Chipman, 512 S.W.2d 199 (Mo. App. 1974).

**45.** In re Fairchild, 616 A.2d 228 (Vt. 1992) (statutory appeal not adequate remedy); Smoke v. City of Seattle, 937 P.2d 186 (Wash. 1997) (interpretation of ordinance not available as remedy). *But see* Riley v. Boxa, 542 N.W.2d 519 (Iowa 1996) (remedy adequate though board cannot award damages and charges fee).

**46.** City of Rome v. Pilgrim, 271 S.E.2d 189 (Ga. 1980); Sinclair Pipe Line Co. v. Village of Richton Park, 167 N.E.2d 406 (Ill. 1960); Montgomery County v. Citizens Bldg. & Loan Ass'n, 316 A.2d 322 (Md. 1974). *But see* Pa. Stat. Ann. tit. 53, § 11004 (landowners must submit constitutional challenge to board of adjustment or governing body).

**47.** O'Mara v. Council of City of Newark, 48 Cal. Rptr. 208 (Cal. App. 1966); Town of Hillsborough v. Smith, 167 S.E.2d 51 (N.C. App. 1969). *Compare* State ex rel. Foreman v. City Council, 205 N.E.2d 398 (Ohio 1965) (nonconforming use).

**48.** Gingell v. Board of County Comm'rs, 239 A.2d 903 (Md. 1968); Deal Gardens, Inc. v. Board of Trustees, 226 A.2d 607 (N.J. 1967); Golden Gate Corp. v. Town of Narragansett, 359 A.2d 321 (R.I. 1976).

**49.** *See* Mountain View Chamber of Commerce v. City of Mountain View, 143 Cal. Rptr. 441 (Cal. App. 1978); Poe v. City of Baltimore, 216 A.2d 707 (Md. 1966).

**50.** Horn v. County of Ventura, 596 P.2d 1134 (Cal. 1979); Morland Dev. Co. v. City of Tulsa, 596 P.2d 1255 (Okla. 1979); Kingsley v. Miller, 388 A.2d 357 (R.I. 1978); Sparks v. Bolton, 335 S.W.2d 780 (Tex. Civ. App. 1960).

facially arbitrary classifications or is confiscatory in its entirety.[51] Exhaustion is not required when a third party brings an action to enforce a zoning ordinance because nothing is gained by administrative consideration of this type of claim.[52]

The rule that a landowner who attacks a zoning ordinance as facially illegal need not exhaust administrative remedies stems from the *Euclid* case.[53] The U.S. Supreme Court did not require exhaustion in *Euclid* because the landowner attacked as unconstitutional the textual provisions in a zoning ordinance that excluded multi-family dwellings from residential zones. *Golden v. Planning Bd. of Town of Ramapo*[54] is a leading growth management case in which the court did not require exhaustion. The plaintiffs attacked a growth management ordinance in its entirety. The court did not require exhaustion because a holding that the ordinance was unconstitutional would make it unnecessary to apply for the development permit required by the ordinance.[55]

A court may not require exhaustion even when a zoning restriction is attacked as applied to a plaintiff's property. In *Grimpel Assocs. v. Cohalan*,[56] the plaintiff attacked as applied a downzoning to residential use of a tract of land on which it planned to construct a shopping center. The court did not require exhaustion. It held that the plaintiff's use was "absolutely prohibited by the zoning classification," and that the plaintiff had attacked the "validity of the zoning ordinance itself as confiscatory."

In *Environmental Law Fund, Inc. v. Town of Corte Madera*,[57] a California court created an exception to the exhaustion doctrine for third parties asserting public rather than private rights in opposition to developments that receive local approval. The court emphasized that the plaintiff organization did not participate in and did not receive notice of the administrative proceedings in which the development was approved, and that the development would affect a substantial area of the community.

Courts will not require exhaustion if an attempt to secure administrative relief would be futile. In the typical futility case, the municipality's opposition to the proposed development is clear and a denial of the project is inevitable.[58] *Ogo*

---

**51.** Baum v. City & County of Denver, 363 P.2d 688 (Colo. 1961); Board of Supvrs. v. Rowe, 216 S.E.2d 199 (Va. 1975).

**52.** Simko v. Ervin, 661 A.2d 1018 (Conn. 1995); Frye Constr., Inc. v. City of Monongahela, 584 A.2d 946 (Pa. 1991).

**53.** Village of Euclid v. Ambler Realty Co., 272 U.S. 365 (1926), discussed in § 2.12.

**54.** 285 N.E.2d 291 (N.Y.), *appeal dismissed,* 409 U.S. 1003 (1972).

**55.** *But see* Northwestern Univ. v. City of Evanston, 383 N.E.2d 964 (Ill. 1978) (attack not facial when it requires assessment of uses authorized by ordinance).

**56.** 361 N.E.2d 1022 (N.Y. 1977).

**57.** 122 Cal. Rptr. 282 (Cal. App. 1975).

**58.** O & G Indus. v. Planning & Zoning Comm'n, 655 A.2d 1121 (Conn. 1995) (rejecting futility claim based on claimed bias); Halifax Area Council v. City of Daytona Beach, 385 So. 2d 184 (Fla. App. 1980); Van Laten v. City of Chicago, 190 N.E.2d 717 (Ill. 1963); Amcon Corp. v. City

*Assocs. v. City of Torrance*[59] is an extreme example of this situation. The court held that exhaustion would be futile when the plaintiff attacked the constitutionality of an ordinance that purposely downzoned its property to frustrate a subsidized housing project it planned to build. The cases also find futility when a development was previously disapproved, and no change in circumstances indicated that a different decision would be forthcoming if the landowner made a new application.[60]

A court may apply the futility rule when a landowner asserts a defense in an enforcement action brought by a municipality.[61] The courts hold that the municipality admits a zoning regulation is valid if it brings an action to enforce it. Any attempt by the landowner to seek administrative relief would be futile.

## C. JUDICIAL REMEDIES AND RELIEF IN STATE COURTS.

### § 8.11. Judicial Remedies.

The Standard Zoning Act contained little in the way of judicial remedies. Section 7 of the Act provided for the review of board of adjustment decisions by writ of certiorari, and most state zoning acts contain this provision. The Standard Act and most state zoning acts do not provide for the judicial review of decisions by the planning commission or governing body. The statutory appeal provided by state administrative procedure acts often is unavailable to review decisions by these bodies because courts hold that the act does not apply to local zoning agencies.[62] Plaintiffs who challenge zoning decisions by these bodies must use one of the so-called extraordinary remedies that are available to challenge local government actions.

---

of Eagan, 348 N.W.2d 66 (Minn. 1984); Napierkowski v. Township of Gloucester, 150 A.2d 481 (N.J. 1959); Karches v. City of Cincinnati, 526 N.E.2d 1350 (Ohio 1988); League of Women Voters of Appleton, Inc. v. Outagamie County, 334 N.W.2d 887 (Wis. 1983). *But see* Sea & Sage Audubon Soc'y, Inc. v. Planning Comm'n, 668 P.2d 664 (Cal. 1983); Corsino v. Grover, 170 A.2d 267 (Conn. 1961); Northwestern Univ. v. City of Evanston, 383 N.E.2d 964 (Ill. 1978); City of Iowa City v. Hagen Electronics, Inc. 545 N.W.2d 530 (Iowa 1996); Presbytery of Seattle v. King County, 787 P.2d 907 (Wash.), *cert. denied,* 498 U.S. 911 (1990); Estate of Friedman v. Pierce Cty., 752 P.2d 936 (Wash. App. 1988).

59. 112 Cal. Rptr. 761 (Cal. App. 1974). *But see* Mountain View Chamber of Commerce v. City of Mountain View, 143 Cal. Rptr. 441 (Cal. App. 1978).

60. *Compare* Town of Paradise Valley v. Gulf Leisure Corp., 557 P.2d 532 (Ariz. App. 1976) *with* National Brick Co. v. City of Chicago, 235 N.E.2d 301 (Ill. App. 1968).

61. Board of County Comm'rs v. Goldenrod Corp., 601 P.2d 360 (Colo. App. 1979); Johnson's Island v. Board of Twp. Trustees, 431 N.E.2d 672 (Ohio 1982). *Contra* Metropolitan Dev. Comm'n v. Ching, Inc., 460 N.E.2d 1236 (Ind. App. 1984). *See also* City of St. Ann v. Elam, 661 S.W.2d 632 (Mo. App. 1983).

62. Schlega v. Detroit Bd. of Zoning Appeals, 382 N.W.2d 737 (Mich. App. 1985); Davis Cty. v. Clearfield City, 756 P.2d 704 (Utah App. 1988).

The injunction and declaratory judgment are the remedies most used by plaintiffs in zoning cases in which the appeal provided by the zoning statute is not available. In the typical case, a landowner claims a zoning restriction as applied to his land is a taking of property. He usually asks for an injunction to prohibit the municipality from enforcing the zoning restriction against him and a declaratory judgment that the zoning restriction is unconstitutional. The disadvantage of the injunction and declaratory judgment is that most courts will only invalidate a zoning restriction if it holds it is a taking. They do not usually give affirmative relief that orders a rezoning or the issuance of a building permit that authorizes the landowner's proposed use. Mandamus is an alternative remedy that allows a landowner to compel the issuance of a building permit or a zoning approval, but it is available only in those infrequent cases in which the zoning ordinance imposes a mandatory duty.

### § 8.12. Appeal and Certiorari.

Section 7 of the Standard Zoning Act, which most state zoning acts include, authorized a petition to a "court of record" stating that a board of adjustment decision is "illegal." The court may then "allow a writ of certiorari directed to the board of adjustment to review such decision."[63] Certiorari is an extraordinary remedy available in the court's discretion to review the decisions of courts and administrative agencies for jurisdictional defects or illegality in the exercise of jurisdiction. A court will not grant a writ of certiorari when a statutory appeal is available.[64]

Legislation in some states provides for a statutory appeal of zoning decisions and regulations to the courts, and some of this legislation applies to the governing body as well as zoning boards and planning commissions.[65] A state statute or charter provision may also provide for certiorari review of zoning amendments or actions by the planning commission or governing body.[66]

---

63. *See also* Jackson v. Spaulding County, 462 S.E.2d 361 (Ga. 1995) (ordinance may specify certiorari to review denial of variance by board).

64. Ledbetter v. Roberts, 98 S.E.2d 654 (Ga. App. 1957); Massachusetts Feather Co. v. Aldermen of Chelsea, 120 N.E.2d 766 (Mass. 1954); Rhodes v. Town of Woodstock, 318 A.2d 170 (Vt. 1974).

65. Alaska Stat. § 29.40.060 (local governing body may provide for appeal); Ark. Stat. § 14-363-208; Conn. Gen. Stat. § 8-8 (boards and commissions); Mass. Gen. Laws Ch. 40A, § 17 (board of appeals); Minn. Stat. Ann. § 462.361 (board of appeals); N.H. Rev. Stat. Ann. § 677:4 (governing body and board of appeals).

66. Dade County v. Metro Imp. Corp., 190 So. 2d 202 (Fla. App. 1966); City Plan Comm'n v. Pielet, 338 N.E.2d 648 (Ind. App. 1975); County Council v. Carl M. Freeman Assocs., 376 A.2d 860 (Md. 1977). *See also* McCallen v. City of Memphis, 786 S.W.2d 633 (Tenn. 1990) (council PUD approval held administrative).

Certiorari lies only to review quasi-judicial or administrative zoning deci-sions,[67] such as a denial of a special use permit,[68] which usually are made by a board of adjustment or other zoning agency. An injunction against the enforce-ment of an ordinance is the usual remedy for challenging legislative actions by the governing body, such as rezonings in most states.[69] Certiorari is available to review rezonings by the governing body in states where the courts hold that re-zoning is quasi-judicial.[70] Direct review through certiorari or a statutory appeal is also available when the legislative body makes an administrative decision, such as the approval or denial of a variance,[71] or if it reviews a decision of a zoning board.[72] Decisions by planning commissions are directly reviewable if they are quasi-judicial.[73] Advisory decisions are not reviewable.[74]

Review by certiorari is usually on the record made before the zoning agency. The courts are divided on whether a reviewing court may take additional evi-dence.[75] They also divide on whether they will consider the constitutionality of a zoning ordinance in an appeal from a variance.[76]

### § 8.13. Mandamus.

Mandamus is an extraordinary remedy that is useful in zoning litigation be-cause it can provide affirmative relief, such as the issuance of a building permit. The writ lies to compel ministerial as distinguished from discretionary acts.[77]

---

67. City of Tallahassee v. Poole, 294 So. 2d 52 (Fla. App. 1974); Allen v. Coffel, 488 S.W.2d 671 (Mo. App. 1972); Currey v. Kimple, 577 S.W.2d 508 (Tex. Civ. App. 1979); Leavitt v. Jeffer-son County, 875 P.2d 681 (Wash. App. 1994); Bridle Trails Community Club v. City of Bellevue, 724 P.2d 1110 (Wash. App. 1986).

68. Hirt v. Polk Cty. Bd. of Comm'rs, 578 So. 2d 415 (Fla. App. 1991) (approval of planned unit development); City Council v. Trebor Constr. Corp., 254 So. 2d 51 (Fla. App. 1971); Florka v. City of Detroit, 120 N.W.2d 797 (Mich. 1963).

69. Sherman v. City of Colorado Springs Planning Comm'n, 763 P.2d 292 (Colo. 1988); Cop-ple v. City of Lincoln, 315 N.W.2d 628 (Neb. 1982); Bama Invs., Inc. v. Metropolitan Dade County, 349 So. 2d 207 (Fla. App. 1977). *See also* Walton Cty. v. Scenic Hills Estates, 401 S.E.2d 513 (Ga. 1991) (municipality may not create right of appeal).

70. Snyder v. City of Lakewood, 542 P.2d 371 (Colo. 1975).

71. Talbut v. City of Perryburg, 594 N.E.2d 1046 (Ohio App. 1991); Frederico v. Moore, 395 N.Y.S.2d 535 (App. Div. 1977). *See* Lowell v. M & N Mobile Home Park, 916 S.W.2d 95 (Ark. 1996) (applying usual arbitrary and capricious standard of judicial review).

72. Bieger v. Village of Moreland Hills, 209 N.E.2d 218 (Ohio App. 1965); Sun Ray Homes, Inc. v. County of Dade, 166 So. 2d 827 (Fla. App. 1964).

73. Maher v. Town Planning & Zoning Comm'n, 226 A.2d 397 (Conn. 1967).

74. Downing v. Board of Zoning Appeals, 274 N.E.2d 542 (Ind. App. 1971).

75. § 6.52.

76. City of Cherokee v. Tatro, 636 P.2d 337 (Okla. 1981).

77. Act held ministerial: Clark v. City of Shreveport, 655 So. 2d 617 (La. App. 1995) (granting of variance when all requirements met); In re Fairchild, 616 A.2d 228 (Vt. 1992) (to enforce min-isterial duties of executive officer). Act held discretionary: Tranner v. Helmer, 878 P.2d 787 (Idaho

As one court stated in a zoning case:

> The prerequisites for a writ of mandamus are (1) that the defendant be obliged by law to perform a duty in which there is no permitted discretion, (2) that the plaintiff have a clear legal right to have the duty performed, and (3) that the plaintiff have no other sufficient remedy.[78]

This decision illustrates the type of case in which a writ of mandamus will issue. The court held that the municipality did not have the statutory authority to adopt a nine-month development moratorium. It granted a writ of mandamus directing the commission to accept an application the moratorium barred.

Note that the court only ordered the commission to accept the application. A court can also grant a writ of mandamus that orders a zoning agency to exercise a discretionary responsibility, even though the court cannot order the agency to act in a particular manner.[79] A court will also grant a writ of mandamus to review the exercise of a discretionary function, and it will set aside the agency's decision if it was arbitrary or capricious.[80] A court will grant a writ of mandamus to compel a government agency to act if a plaintiff has satisfied all of the requirements necessary for the exercise of a ministerial duty. An example is a case in which an applicant complies with all of the requirements for the issuance of a building permit, but the building official refuses to issue it.[81]

Conditional use and site plan review illustrate the application of these rules. Conditional use provisions typically authorize the approval of a conditional use if it is "compatible" with other uses in the surrounding area. A court will refuse to compel the approval of a conditional use under a provision of this type if it holds that approval requires an exercise of discretion by the zoning agency.[82] The criteria for site plan review also usually require the exercise of discretion.[83]

---

1994) (subdivision plat approval); Jordan Partners v. Goehringer, 611 N.Y.S.2d 626 (App. Div. 1994) (stop work order).

**78.** Schrader v. Guilford Planning & Zoning Comm'n, 418 A.2d 93, 94 (Conn. Super. 1980). For the distinction in California between an administrative and ordinary mandamus see Agins v. City of Tiburon, 598 P.2d 25 (Cal. 1979), *aff'd on other grounds,* 447 U.S. 255 (1980); Toso v. City of Santa Barbara, 162 Cal. Rptr. 210 (Cal. App.), *cert. denied,* 449 U.S. 901 (1980).

**79.** Griffin Homes, Inc. v. Superior Ct., 274 Cal. Rptr. 456 (Cal. App. 1990) (compel hearing on denial of building approval); Weed v. King County, 677 P.2d 179 (Wash. App. 1984) (cannot compel rezoning). *Compare* Fontana Unified School Dist. v. City of Rialto, 219 Cal. Rptr. 254 (Cal. App. 1985); Dougherty County v. Webb, 350 S.E.2d 457 (Ga. 1986).

**80.** Curtis Oil v. City of North Branch, 364 N.W.2d 880 (Minn. App. 1985); Nova Horizon, Inc. v. City Council, 769 P.2d 721 (Nev. 1989); Davis Cty. v. Clearfield City, 756 P.2d 704 (Utah App. 1988).

**81.** State v. Ludewig, 187 N.E.2d 170 (Ohio App. 1962); Bell Atlantic Mobile Systems, Inc. v. Borough of Clifton Heights, 661 A.2d 909 (Pa. Commw. 1995) (no clear right to permit). *But see* Big Train Constr. Co. v. Parish of St. Tammany, 446 So. 2d 889 (La. App. 1984).

**82.** City of Miami Beach v. Mr. Samuel's, Inc., 351 So. 2d 719 (Fla. 1977).

**83.** § 6.68.

A court may issue a writ of mandamus to compel the approval of a conditional use or site plan if an applicant exhausts a zoning agency's discretion by satisfying the approval criteria in a zoning ordinance.[84]

A court will not grant a writ of mandamus if a statutory appeal is available. An example is the statutory appeal that is available from actions by the board of zoning adjustment.[85] Mandamus may issue to compel a decision by a zoning board if the statute does not provide an alternative remedy.[86]

Mandamus is available to compel the enforcement of a zoning ordinance. Although the enforcement function is discretionary, mandamus will lie when the violation of the zoning ordinance is clear.[87] An example is a mandamus action to compel a municipality to take action against a landowner who illegally uses land in a residential area for off-street business parking. Courts also grant mandamus to compel municipal officials to take action against landowners who are issued illegal permits.[88] Other courts hold that mandamus is unavailable to compel the enforcement of a zoning ordinance if the duty to enforce is not clear or if an alternative remedy is available.[89]

### § 8.14. Injunction.

The injunction is an equitable remedy that lies to restrain illegal action. Like mandamus, it is not available to compel a discretionary decision. Neither is it available if there is an alternative legal remedy. A plaintiff in an injunction action may be able to obtain temporary relief through a temporary restraining order or preliminary injunction. Most states require a plaintiff to post a bond as a condition to obtaining temporary or permanent injunctive relief. The bond protects the developer from damage caused by the litigation delay if she should ultimately prevail. Injunction bonds may be substantial and may create an effective financial barrier to injunctive relief.

An injunction is the proper remedy to challenge zoning actions by the governing body in states holding that the zoning process is legislative. An injunction lies because an alternative legal remedy is not available. Appeal and certiorari

---

**84.** Kosinski v. Lawlor, 418 A.2d 66 (Conn. 1979).

**85.** The Chapel v. City of Solon, 530 N.E.2d 1321 (Ohio 1988).

**86.** City of Atlanta v. Wansley Moving & Storage Co., 267 S.E.2d 234 (Ga. 1980). *See also* State Bd. of Health v. Atnip Design & Supply Center, Inc., 385 So. 2d 1307 (Ala. 1980).

**87.** Tustin Heights Ass'n v. Board of Supvrs., 339 P.2d 914 (Cal. App. 1959); Rebholz v. Floyd, 327 So. 2d 806 (Fla. App. 1976); Stratford v. Crossman, 655 S.W.2d 500 (Ky. App. 1983); Brady v. Board of Appeals, 204 N.E.2d 513 (Mass. 1965); Green v. Board of App., 529 N.E.2d 159 (Mass. App. 1988); Garrow v. Teaneck Tryon Co., 94 A.2d 332 (N.J. 1953); Petition of Fairchild, 616 A.2d 228 (Vt. 1992).

**88.** Parks v. Board of County Comm'rs, 501 P.2d 85 (Or. App. 1972); 68 A.L.R.3d 166 (1976).

**89.** Board of Educ. v. Idle Motors, Inc., 90 N.E.2d 121 (Ill. App. 1950); Fried v. Fox, 373 N.Y.S.2d 197 (Sup. Ct. 1975).

are not available to review zoning actions by the governing body if these actions are legislative. In the typical case, the governing body adopts a restrictive zoning classification that applies to a landowner's land. Unless the landowner is required to exhaust administrative remedies, he can challenge the zoning restriction as an as-applied taking of property by bringing an injunction action to restrain the municipality from enforcing the zoning ordinance against his land.[90] Courts will not grant an injunction to enjoin threatened legislative action that may injuriously affect a landowner's property because they will not enjoin a threatened harm.[91] A plaintiff can bring an injunction action only to challenge "illegal" governmental action, and the governing body must act in some illegal way before a court will grant injunctive relief. Zoning ordinances claimed to be a taking as applied to a landowner's property are one example of an "illegal" zoning action. A landowner may also bring an injunction to restrain a municipality from enforcing a zoning ordinance that is illegal for other reasons, such as a failure to provide a required statutory notice and hearing.[92]

Section 8 of the Standard Zoning Act authorized municipalities to bring "appropriate action or proceedings" to prevent a violation of the Act or a zoning ordinance. The state zoning acts usually include this provision, and the courts have held that it authorizes injunction actions to enforce zoning ordinances. Most courts interpret this provision liberally. They allow injunction actions to enforce the ordinance without proof of the irreparable injury courts usually require for injunctive relief. Nor do the courts apply the rule that an injunction cannot issue to enjoin the violation of a crime.[93] This rule could apply because the Standard Act and state zoning acts make the violation of the Act or a zoning ordinance a misdemeanor. The courts apply the usual balancing of equities rule in actions to enforce zoning ordinances, although some courts do not balance equities if the landowner acted intentionally or in bad faith.[94]

---

**90.** Phillips v. City of Homewood, 50 So. 2d 267 (Ala. 1951); Bama Invs., Inc. v. Metropolitan Dade County, 349 So. 2d 207 (Fla. App. 1977); 2700 Irving Park Bldg. Corp. v. City of Chicago, 69 N.E.2d 827 (Ill. 1946). See §§ 8.08-8.10. *But see* Tahoe Keys Prop. Owners' Ass'n v. State Water Resources Bd., 28 Cal. Rptr. 2d 734 (Cal. App. 1994) (denying preliminary injunction when damages would compensate plaintffs and injunction would cause serious harm).

**91.** Citizens for Orderly Dev. & Env't v. City of Phoenix, 540 P.2d 1239 (Ariz. 1975); Shellburne, Inc. v. Buck, 240 A.2d 757 (Del. 1968); Popisil v. Anderson, 527 N.Y.S.2d 819 (App. Div. 1988). *See also* Adams v. City of Fort Wayne, 423 N.E.2d 647 (Ind. App. 1981).

**92.** Pyramid Corp. v. DeSoto County Bd. of Supvrs., 366 F. Supp. 1299 (N.D. Miss. 1973).

**93.** Johnson v. Murzyn, 469 A.2d 1227 (Conn. App. 1984); Joy v. Anne Arundel County, 451 A.2d 1237 (Md. App. 1982); Utah County v. Baxter, 635 P.2d 61 (Utah 1981).

**94.** City of East Providence v. Rhode Island Hosp. Trust Nat'l Bank, 505 A.2d 1143 (R.I. 1986); Radach v. Gunderson, 695 P.2d 128 (Wash. App. 1985).

Although the Standard Act did not authorize injunctions by private citizens to enforce zoning ordinances, most state zoning statutes include this authority.[95] A private citizen who brings an injunction action to enforce a zoning ordinance must show injury and special damage. Courts usually find the necessary injury and damage when the injunction is brought by neighboring landowners against a zoning violator.[96]

### § 8.15. Declaratory Judgment.

The declaratory judgment is widely used as a judicial remedy in zoning cases. Plaintiffs usually bring an action for a declaratory judgment or an injunction in the alternative. Declaratory judgment actions are fairly "civilized." The parties can obtain a resolution of their dispute without the disruptive effect that an award of monetary or injunctive relief may cause. Declaratory judgment actions are also on an expedited calendar in many jurisdictions. The parties can obtain a final decision on the merits much earlier. The plaintiff may also be able to obtain a temporary restraining order or preliminary injunction if a prayer for an injunction is joined with the prayer for declaratory relief.

Section 2 of the Uniform Declaratory Judgment Act authorizes a declaratory judgment action to challenge zoning and other municipal ordinances. The Act has been widely adopted. Section 2 provides:

> Any person . . . whose rights, status or other legal relations are affected by a . . . municipal ordinance . . . may have determined any question of construction or validity arising under the . . . ordinance . . . and obtain a declaration of rights, status or other legal relations thereunder.

The declaratory judgment is especially useful in zoning litigation because it authorizes a declaration of rights even though the plaintiff has not suffered an actual harm. A justiciable controversy is required,[97] and courts may impose a standing requirement. For example, a court may not allow a plaintiff to bring a declaratory judgment to challenge a zoning ordinance as facially unconstitu-

---

95. *See* Little Joseph Realty, Inc. v. Town of Babylon, 363 N.E.2d 1163 (N.Y. 1977). *But see* City of Houston v. Tri-Lakes Ltd., 681 So.2d 104 (Miss. 1996) (private citizen cannot bring criminal proceedings).

96. Hargreaves v. Skrbina, 662 P.2d 1078 (Colo. 1983) (must balance equities); Barton v. H.D. Riders Motorcycle Club, Inc., 550 A.2d 91 (N.H. 1988); Hill Homeowners Ass'n v. City of Passaic, 384 A.2d 172 (N.J. App. Div. 1978); Torbett v. Anderson, 564 S.W.2d 676 (Tenn. App. 1978).

97. Alameda County Land Use Ass'n v. City of Hayward, 45 Cal. Rptr. 2d 752 (Cal. App. 1995); Karches v. Cincinnati, 526 N.E.2d 1350 (Ohio 1988).

tional if he has not been detrimentally affected by the ordinance by a permit denial or other adverse action.[98]

One court allowed a plaintiff to bring a declaratory judgment action claiming that a special exception requirement applicable to its stores was facially invalid, even though it had not applied for or been denied a special exception.[99] The court noted that the plaintiff was engaged in the business of obtaining suitable sites for its stores. It held that the special exception requirement injured the plaintiff's business because it had to obtain a special exception before it could operate a store at a location it considered appropriate.

If the justiciability requirement is met, the declaratory judgment is available in a wide range of zoning controversies. Plaintiffs may bring declaratory judgment actions to test the constitutionality of a zoning restriction as applied to their land[100] and to secure an interpretation of a zoning ordinance.[101] A declaratory judgment is not available to test the constitutionality of a zoning map amendment for an individual property if the amendment is characterized as a quasi-judicial action.[102] Nor is a declaratory judgment available when the zoning statute provides for an alternative and exclusive method of judicial review.[103] In the typical case in which this limitation applies, review by way of mandamus or certiorari is available from decisions of the board of adjustment or planning commission.[104]

---

**98.** United Bank of Denver v. Reed, 635 P.2d 922 (Colo. App. 1981); Woods v. City of Newton, 208 N.E.2d 508 (Mass. 1965); Allen v. Coffel, 488 S.W.2d 671 (Mo. App. 1972); Ewing v. City of Springfield, 449 S.W.2d 681 (Mo. App. 1970); Southern Nat'l Bank v. City of Austin, 582 S.W.2d 229 (Tex. Civ. App. 1979).

**99.** Board of Supvrs. v. Southland Corp., 297 S.E.2d 718 (Va. 1982).

**100.** Davis v. Pima County, 590 P.2d 459 (Ariz. App.), *cert. denied,* 442 U.S. 942 (1978); Agins v. City of Tiburon, 598 P.2d 25 (Cal. 1979), *aff'd on other grounds,* 447 U.S. 255 (1980); Driscoll v. Austintown Assocs., 328 N.E.2d 395 (Ohio 1975).

**101.** City of Coral Gables v. Hunter, 213 So. 2d 467 (Fla. App. 1968); 1000 Friends of Or. v. Board of County Comm'rs, 564 P.2d 1080 (Or. App. 1977).

**102.** Snyder v. City of Lakewood, 542 P.2d 371 (Colo. 1975).

**103.** Goldstein v. Upper Merion Twp., 403 A.2d 211 (Pa. Commw. 1979).

**104.** Livingston Rock & Gravel Co. v. County of Los Angeles, 272 P.2d 4 (Cal. 1954); Contris v. Richmond County, 235 S.E.2d 19 (Ga. 1977); Master Disposal, Inc. v. Village of Menomonee Falls, 211 N.W.2d 477 (Wis. 1973).

## § 8.16.  Judicial Relief.

Landowner plaintiffs who are successful in zoning litigation quite under-
standably want a specific judicial remedy that compels the municipality to approve the use they proposed for their land. Specific judicial relief is available in
mandamus, in which a court can compel the issuance of a building permit or the
exercise of other nondiscretionary acts. A court can also grant specific relief in
an appeal or certiorari action that challenges an administrative or quasi-judicial
decision by a zoning agency.

Injunction actions present more difficult problems, especially in as-applied
taking cases. If a court holds that a zoning restriction is a taking as applied to a
property, the usual remedy is a decree invalidating the restriction and ordering
the municipality to rezone the property. The court will not order the municipality
to rezone the property for a use the court considers appropriate. The municipality
may adopt a less restrictive zoning classification for the property that still does
not allow the plaintiff's proposed use. The plaintiff must sue again, and the municipality may be able to repeat this strategy even if it loses a second or third
time. The majority rule is that specific judicial relief that compels a rezoning is
not available in as-applied taking cases.

## § 8.17.  Specific Relief Not Available.

Under the majority rule, a court that holds a zoning restriction invalid in an
injunction action can only grant a decree that invalidates the restriction and orders the municipality to rezone. *City of Conway v. Housing Auth.*[105] states the
rationale for this rule. The court noted that courts in that state do not have the
power to review zoning ordinances "in a de novo manner" and added:

> [I]t follows that the power of the court to review the action of the munici-
> palities is limited to determining whether or not such action was arbitrary,
> capricious, or wholly inequitable. The judiciary has no right or authority to
> substitute its judgment for that of the legislative branch of government ....
> Courts are not super zoning commissions and have no authority to classify
> property according to zones.[106]

Although a court may not order a rezoning under this rule, it may order the
municipality to rezone in a constitutional manner.[107] A court may also issue an
order reinstating a prior zoning classification if it holds that a downzoning to a

---

105. 584 S.W.2d 10 (Ark. 1979).

106. *Id.* at 13. *See also* Guhl v. Holcomb Bridge Rd. Corp., 232 S.E.2d 830 (Ga. 1977); Emjay
Props. v. Town of Brookhaven, 347 N.Y.S.2d 736 (Sup. Ct. 1973); City of Rusk v. Cox, 665
S.W.2d 233 (Tex. App. 1984) (may not enjoin future rezoning).

107. Guhl v. Holcomb Bridge Rd. Corp., 232 S.E.2d 830 (Ga. 1977).

less intensive classification is unconstitutional.[108] Courts may also refuse to order a rezoning only in cases in which a constitutionally acceptable zoning alternative is not clear from the facts. On this state of the record, a court has no basis on which to order a rezoning.[109]

### § 8.18. Specific Relief Available.

A number of courts provide specific injunctive relief to successful plaintiffs in as-applied taking cases. Some courts will grant an order that frees the plaintiff's land from any zoning restrictions. In *City of Atlanta v. McLennan*,[110] the court held a trial court should give a municipality a reasonable time to adopt a rezoning that meets constitutional requirements. The trial court could declare the "property free of all zoning restrictions" if the municipality did not act. The court believed this remedy would encourage municipalities to adopt a constitutionally acceptable zoning classification. The disadvantage of this remedy is that it leaves the property unregulated.

An alternative specific remedy relies on the tendency in as-applied taking cases to litigate the suitability of the use proposed by the landowner for the property as well as the uses allowed by the zoning ordinance. A trial court could order the municipality to allow the landowner's proposed use if the proof at the trial shows that it is suitable for its site. An order of this type is no different from an order entered in any case in which a court grants relief based on the facts proved by a successful plaintiff.

*Sinclair Pipe Line Co. v. Village of Richton Park*[111] adopted a specific remedy of this type:

> [I]t is appropriate for the court to avoid these difficulties by framing its decree with reference to the record before it, and particularly with reference to the evidence offered at trial. . . . In such cases the relief awarded may guarantee that the owner will be allowed to proceed with that use without further litigation and that he will not proceed with a different use.[112]

The court held that this relief did not go "beyond the realm of adjudication." The court merely awarded the plaintiff specific relief comparable to the relief avail-

---

**108.** H. Dev. Corp. v. City of Yonkers, 407 N.Y.S.2d 573 (App. Div. 1978).

**109.** Seiler v. City of Granite City, 625 N.E.2d 1170 (Ill. App. 1993) (no specific proposal); Sedney v. Lloyd, 410 A.2d 616 (Md. 1980); Garrett v. City of Oklahoma City, 594 P.2d 764 (Okla. 1979). *See also* Alexander v. DeKalb County, 444 S.E.2d 743 (Ga. 1994) (when criminal contempt appropriate).

**110.** 226 S.E.2d 732 (Ga. 1976). *See also* State ex rel. Nagawicka Island Corp. v. City of Delafield, 343 N.W.2d 816 (Wis. App. 1983).

**111.** 167 N.E.2d 406 (Ill. 1960). *Accord* Schwartz v. City of Flint, 395 N.W.2d 678 (Mich. 1986).

**112.** 167 N.E.2d at 411.

able in actions for mandamus and the review of administrative decisions. A number of other courts have held that specific judicial relief of this type is available in zoning cases.[113] In all of these cases, the evidence showed that the use proposed by the plaintiff was the only reasonable use of the land in the area in which it was located.

The Virginia and Florida courts authorize a similar specific remedy when a plaintiff proves that a zoning restriction is a taking as applied to his property. Although the details vary slightly, both courts authorize the trial court to grant a negative injunction rather than an order directing the municipality to rezone. In Florida, the trial court may enjoin the adoption of any zoning classification more restrictive than the use proposed by the plaintiff.[114] In Virginia, the trial court may grant an injunction prohibiting any municipal action disallowing the plaintiff's use, although the municipality may impose reasonable conditions. If the municipality refuses to comply, the court can make the injunction permanent.[115]

When a court reviews a decision by a zoning board or planning commission in an appeal or certiorari action, judicial review is on the record and the court may order specific relief if the right to such relief is clearly demonstrated. When the board or commission has denied a variance or conditional use, for example, the court can order its approval. A court should remand an appeal to the board or commission if the right to specific relief is not shown.[116]

Some states require the adoption of a comprehensive plan and require zoning to be consistent with the plan. If the zoning that applies to a tract of land is inconsistent with the plan, a court in these states may order the municipality to rezone the tract so that its zoning is consistent with the comprehensive plan.[117]

## § 8.19. Inverse Condemnation.

Inverse condemnation is a remedy a landowner may bring to enforce the taking clause that is included in the federal and most state constitutions. The land-

---

113. Bryan v. Salmon Corp., 554 S.W.2d 912 (Ky. App. 1977); Trustees Under Will of Pomeroy v. Town of Westlake, 357 So. 2d 1299 (La. App. 1978); Board of County Comm'rs v. Oak Hill Farms, Inc., 192 A.2d 761 (Md. 1963); Vigilant Invs. Corp. v. Town of Hempstead, 312 N.Y.S.2d 1022 (App. Div. 1970); Union Oil Co. of Cal. v. City of Worthington, 405 N.E.2d 277 (Ohio 1980); Lynch v. City of Oklahoma City, 629 P.2d 1289 (Okla. App. 1981); Campbell v. Nance, 555 S.W.2d 407 (Tenn. App. 1976). See also Dobson Jamaica Realties v. Town of Brookhaven, 409 N.Y.S.2d 590 (Sup. Ct. 1978) (discriminatory zoning to delay developer).

114. City of Miami Beach v. Weiss, 217 So. 2d 836 (Fla. 1969); Burritt v. Harris, 172 So. 2d 820 (Fla. 1965).

115. City of Richmond v. Randall, 211 S.E.2d 56 (Va. 1975).

116. Bogue v. Zoning Bd. of Appeals, 345 A.2d 9 (Conn. 1975); Citizens Ass'n of Georgetown v. District of Columbia Bd. of Zoning Adjustment, 403 A.2d 737 (D.C. 1979); Duggan v. County of Cook, 324 N.E.2d 406 (Ill. 1975); Framingham Clinic v. Zoning Bd. of Appeals, 415 N.E.2d 840 (Mass. 1981); Pfile v. Zoning Bd. of Adjustment, 298 A.2d 598 (Pa. Commw. 1972).

117. § 6.33.

owner's condemnation action is "inverse" or "reverse" because he claims a government entity has taken his property but has not paid him the compensation to which he is entitled. Inverse condemnation is an implied constitutional remedy and is self-executing under the federal and most state constitutions. A statute that authorizes the remedy is not required.

The U.S. Supreme Court holds that a landowner may bring an inverse condemnation action to secure an award of compensation when a land use regulation is a taking of property. Some state courts have also granted an inverse condemnation remedy. A plaintiff can elect to sue under either the federal or a state constitution or both in state court.

### § 8.20.  State Cases: Remedy Available.

Several state cases hold that an inverse condemnation remedy for a temporary taking is available in land use cases, and some have authorized a state remedy even after *First English*.[118] In many of these cases, a municipality adopted highly restrictive zoning or refused to allow the development of a property and took these actions to depress its value prior to acquisition or to prevent its development.[119] In *Mattoon v. City of Norman*,[120] the plaintiff's land was flooded when the city failed to maintain flood drainage channels. The city then adopted a floodplain ordinance restricting development on plaintiff's land. The plaintiff claimed the city adopted the ordinance to avoid the expense of maintaining the drainage system. Although it held that "a valid enactment of a floodplain ordinance is not a per se taking," the court overruled a demurrer to plaintiff's complaint and held that it stated an action in inverse condemnation.

Other cases approved an inverse condemnation remedy for land use ordinances that imposed severe land use restrictions to preserve open space or vulnerable environmental areas. In *Corrigan v. City of Scottsdale*,[121] the court held the plaintiff was entitled to receive "monetary damages" under the state constitution for a land use ordinance that severely restricted development in a hillside area. Another court held that the reclassification of plaintiff's land to a high

---

**118.** Poirier v. Grand Blanc Twp. (I), 423 N.W.2d 351 (Mich. App. 1988); Whitehead Oil Co. v. City of Lincoln (III), 515 N.W.2d 401 (Neb. 1994); PDR Dev. Corp. v. City of Santa Fe, 900 P.2d 973 (N.M. App. 1995). *But see* Cannone v. Noey, 867 P.2d 797 (Alaska 1994) (normal decision making delay not compensable).

**119.** Burrows v. City of Keene, 432 A.2d 15 (N.H. 1981); Scheer v. Township of Evesham, 445 A.2d 46 (N.J. App. Div. 1982); Rippley v. City of Lincoln, 330 N.W.2d 505 (N.D. 1983). For similar pre-*San Diego Gas* cases see Peacock v. County of Sacramento, 77 Cal. Rptr. 391 (Cal. App. 1969); Ventures in Prop. I v. City of Wichita, 594 P.2d 671 (Kan. 1979); City of Austin v. Teague, 570 S.W.2d 389 (Tex. 1978). *See* §§ 2.32, 2.33.

**120.** 617 P.2d 1347 (Okla. 1980), *distinguished in* April v. City of Broken Arrow, 775 P.2d 1347 (Okla. 1989). *See also* Kraft v. Malone, 313 N.W.2d 758 (N.D. 1981).

**121.** 720 P.2d 513 (Ariz.), *cert. denied*, 497 U.S. 986 (1986).

flood danger district that precluded any development was a taking that required compensation for the fair market value of her property.[122]

Some of the state courts have held that landowners in taking cases are entitled only to actual losses proved to a reasonable certainty, as in tort cases.[123] This measure of compensation does not appear consistent with the compensation remedy required by the Supreme Court.[124]

### § 8.21. State Cases: Remedy Not Available.

Several state courts hold that an inverse condemnation remedy is not available when a court holds that a land use regulation is a taking of property.[125] An action in inverse condemnation under the federal constitution is available in these states, but plaintiffs must be able to show a taking under the federal constitution to invoke the federal remedy.

### § 8.22. Tort Liability.

Local governments historically were liable in tort when they exercised proprietary functions but were immune from liability when they exercised governmental functions. Zoning and planning fell in the governmental category.[126] Court decisions in practically all the states have abolished the governmental-proprietary distinction. The present basis for local government tort liability varies, but local governments are usually liable in tort in the exercise of ministerial functions but immune from liability in the exercise of discretionary functions.

---

122. Buegel v. City of Grand Forks, 475 N.W.2d 133 (N.D. 1991); Annicelli v. Town of South Kingston, 463 A.2d 133 (R.I. 1983). *See also* Minch v. City of Fargo, 297 N.W.2d 785 (N.D. 1980) (taking of vested right), *on remand,* 322 N.W.2d 71 (N.D. 1983) (vested right not found); Zinn v. State, 334 N.W.2d 67 (Wis. 1983).

123. Corrigan v. City of Scottsdale, 720 P.2d 513 (Ariz. 1986); Poirier v. Grand Blanc Township (II), 481 N.W.2d 762 (Mich. App. 1992); City of Austin v. Teague, 570 S.W.2d 389 (Tex. 1978). *See also* Miller Bros. v. Department of Nat. Resources, 513 N.W.2d 217 (Mich. App. 1994) (measure of compensation for loss of oil and gas rights).

124. § 8.25.

125. Agins v. City of Tiburon, 598 P.2d 25 (Cal. 1979), *aff'd on other grounds,* 447 U.S. 255 (1980); Snyder v. City of Lakewood, 542 P.2d 371 (Colo. 1975); Dade County v. National Bulk Carriers, Inc., 450 So. 2d 213 (Fla. 1984); Van Duyne v. City of Crest Hill, 483 N.E.2d 1307 (Ill. App. 1985) (plaintiff purchased with knowledge of zoning); Jack v. City of Olathe, 781 P.2d 1069 (Kan. 1989) (refusing to imply remedy from statute); Kraiser v. Horsham Twp., 455 A.2d 782 (Pa. Commw. 1983).

126. City of Rochester Hills v. Six Star, Ltd., 423 N.W.2d 322 (Mich. App. 1988) (enforcement of zoning ordinance); Baucom's Nursery Co. v. Mecklenburg Cty., 366 S.E.2d 558 (N.C. App. 1988) (adoption and enforcement of zoning ordinance).

Some state statutes authorizing tort suits against municipalities also apply in zoning actions.[127]

The courts have classified many land use control functions, such as subdivision and site plan review and rezonings, as discretionary.[128] Tort liability can arise in the exercise of discretionary functions if a court finds an interference with contractual relations, even though a developer has not acquired a vested right. An example is a rezoning to block a housing project after the developer enters into a contract for governmental financial assistance.[129] Actions not requiring the exercise of discretion, such as the issuance of a building permit to which an applicant is entitled, are nondiscretionary.[130] A court may impose liability for the negligent exercise of a discretionary function,[131] and deny liability for the exercise of a nondiscretionary function if the tort liability statute expressly makes the function immune.[132]

Tort liability may also arise when a municipality mistakenly issues and then revokes a building permit after the permit holder has relied on it by proceeding

---

127. Ga. Code Ann. § 36-33-4. *See* City of Buford v. Ward, 443 S.E.2d 279 (Ga. App. 1994) (cause of action shown under statute when condition on certificate of occupancy not authorized by law). *See also* 65 Ill. Comp. Stat. 5/11-12-8 (monetary liability for wilful failure to act on subdivision plat in time prescribed.)

128. City of Seymour v. Onyx Paving Co., 541 N.E.2d 951 (Ind. App. 1989) (enforcement of zoning ordinance); Veling v. Borough of Ramsey, 228 A.2d 873 (N.J. App. Div. 1967) (zoning amendment); C & D Partnership v. City of Gahanna, 747 N.E.2d 303 (Ohio 1984) (subdivision approval); Hodges v. Reid, 836 S.W.2d 120 (Tenn. App. 1992); Young v. Jewish Welfare Fed'n, 371 S.W.2d 767 (Tex. Civ. App. 1963) (site plan review); Grader v. City of Lynwood, 767 P.2d 952 (Wash. App. 1989) (zoning ordinance interpretation held quasi-judicial). *See also* Trianon Park Condo. Ass'n v. City of Hialeah, 468 So. 2d 912 (Fla. 1985) (enforcement of regulatory laws); Alger v. City of Mukilteo, 730 P.2d 1333 (Wash. 1987) (appearance of fairness doctrine). *But see* Win-Tasch Corp. v. Town of Merrimack, 411 A.2d 144 (N.H. 1980) (no immunity if municipality acts in bad faith). *Compare* Loveland v. Orem City Corp., 746 P.2d 763 (Utah 1987) (subdivision review held governmental).

129. Mesolella v. City of Providence, 508 A.2d 661 (R.I. 1986). *See also* River Park, Inc. v. City of Highland Park, 667 N.E.2d 499 (Ill. App. 1996). *Compare* Pleas v. City of Seattle, 774 P.2d 1158 (Wash. 1989) (city liable in tort for abuse of zoning process).

130. Winters v. City of Commerce City, 648 P.2d 175 (Colo. App. 1982) (denial of building permit); Alger v. City of Mukilteo, 730 P.2d 1333 (Wash. 1987) (permit revocation);Sundberg v. Evans, 897 P.2d 1285 (Wash. App. 1995) (providing information on zoning restrictions nondiscretionary). Sundberg v. Evans, 897 P.2d 1285 (Wash. App. 1995) (providing information on zoning restrictions nondiscretionary). *See also* J. Gregcin, Inc. v. City of Dayton, 593 P.2d 1231 (Or. App. 1979) (failure to comply with subdivision statute), *confirmed on remand,* 615 P.2d 419 (Or. App. 1980); Cox v. City of Lynwood, 863 P.2d 578 (Wash. App. 1993) (interpreting statute providing cause of action for unlawful denial of building permit).

131. Pickle v. Board of Cty. Comm'rs, 764 P.2d 262 (Wyo. 1988) (water and septic tank system failure).

132. Johnson v. County of Essex, 538 A.2d 448 (N.J.L. Div. 1987). *But see* Lutheran Day Care v. Snohomish Cty., 829 P.2d 746 (Wash. 1992).

with construction.[133] Some courts deny tort liability in these cases because of the rule that a municipality is not liable for negligence in the performance of duties owed to the general public as a whole rather than to a particular individual.[134] Other courts impose liability in these cases. Some apply ordinary principles of tort law to these claims because they believe that the abolition of tort immunity in the exercise of governmental functions abolished the public duty rule.[135]

Other courts adhere to the public duty rule but find liability if there is a "special relationship" between the public agency and the person harmed.[136] Courts apply the special relationship rule to find liability to a third party who was clearly protected by a land use ordinance.[137] The causation rule is also applied, and courts deny liability if the municipality was not the cause of the damage for which suit is brought.[138]

Landowners argued for tort liability based on exceptions to the public duty rule in other cases in which they suffered damage from the implementation of municipal regulations. One court denied liability under the public duty rule when a plaintiff sued for damages caused by excessive water run-off from an adjacent development allegedly caused by improper enforcement of a county development ordinance.[139] Other courts denied liability when a landowner was unable to carry out a land use for which she had received a municipal permit on advice that the development was permitted.[140]

---

**133.** Snyder v. City of Minneapolis, 441 N.W.2d 781 (Minn. 1989). *See also* § 6.17.

**134.** Allen v. City & County of Honolulu, 571 P.2d 328 (Haw. 1977); Hunter v. City of Cleveland, 564 N.E.2d 718 (Ohio App. 1988) (improper reliance).

**135.** Dykeman v. State, 593 P.2d 1183 (Or. App. 1979). *See also* Adams v. State, 555 P.2d 235 (Alaska 1976).

**136.** Taylor v. Stevens County, 759 P.2d 447 (Wash. 1988). *See also* Frustuck v. City of Fairfax, 28 Cal Rptr. 357 (Cal. App. 1963); 41 A.L.R.4th 99 (1985). *But see* Myers v. Moore Engineering, Inc., 42 F.3d 452 (8th Cir. 1994); Cootey v. Sun Inv. Co., 718 P.2d 1086 (Hawaii 1986).

**137.** Charlie Brown Constr. Co. v. City of Boulder City, 797 P.2d 946 (Nev. 1990).

**138.** Kuriakuz v. West Bloomfield Township, 492 N.W.2d 797 (Mich. App. 1992) (no liability for water damage from adjacent development based solely on omission in approving site plan).

**139.** Pepper v. J.J. Welcome Constr. Co., 871 P.2d 601 (Wash. App. 1994). *See also* Stillwater Condominium Ass'n v. Town of Salem, 668 P.2d 38 (N.H. 1995) (no duty to enforce subdivision regulations).

**140.** Lehman v. City of Louisville, 857 P.2d 455 (Colo. App. 1993) (plaintiffs unable to carry out home occupation after renovating building in reliance on advice that use was permitted); Brady Dev. Co. v. Town of Hilton Head Island, 439 S.E.2d 366 (S.C. 1993) (developer unable to get water service after permit issued; also assumed risk). *See also* Millerick v. Village of Tinley Park, 652 N.E.2d 17 (Ill. App. 1995) (no special duty when officials incorrectly advised about soil condition of property).

## D. FEDERAL REMEDIES.

### § 8.23.  Inverse Condemnation.

#### § 8.24.  When Available.

After passing up two opportunities to resolve the inverse condemnation remedy problem, the Supreme Court finally held in *First English Evangelical Lutheran Church v. County of Los Angeles*[141] that an inverse condemnation remedy is available in land use taking cases. A forest fire destroyed a large portion of a watershed in which plaintiff's campground buildings were located. The county then adopted an interim ordinance prohibiting the construction or reconstruction of any building in a flood protection area that included the plaintiff's property. The plaintiff brought an inverse condemnation action for compensation in state court and claimed that the interim ordinance denied it "all use" of its property. The California trial and appellate courts struck those portions of the complaint in which the plaintiff asked for compensation. They did not decide the taking issue.

The Supreme Court, in an opinion by Justice Rehnquist, held an inverse condemnation was available. His opinion did not contain the discussion of policy found in Justice Brennan's dissent and did not elaborate on the rules for measuring compensation or determining the period of time during which a temporary taking should be held to occur.

The Court confirmed the rule it had adopted in earlier cases that the taking clause is self-executing and requires compensation when a government takes property. The Court held that a taking may occur without "formal proceedings" and rejected a claim that allowing an inverse condemnation remedy in land use taking cases would inhibit land use planning. Compensation is required in land use taking cases because  invalidation of the ordinance is not a "sufficient remedy." The Court held that a landowner can receive compensation for the temporary interference with use that occurred while the ordinance was in effect but cannot demand compensation for a permanent taking:

> Once a court determines that a taking has occurred, the government retains the whole range of functions already available — amendment of the regulation, withdrawal of the invalidated regulation, or exercise of eminent domain. . . . [But] no subsequent action by the government can relieve it of the duty to provide compensation for the period during which the taking was effective.[142]

---

141. 482 U.S. 304 (1987). *See also* San Diego Gas & Elec. Co. v. City of San Diego, 450 U.S. 621 (1981).

142. *Id.* at 421.

The Court limited the availability of the inverse condemnation remedy to the "facts presented" and noted that the plaintiff claimed the ordinance denied it "all use" of its property. Several references to the denial of the "all use" claim appear throughout the decision. These statements could mean that compensation is available only if a court holds that a land use regulation denies a landowner "all use" of his property. Most land use regulations do not fall in this category. They permit some uses but prohibit others. A zoning ordinance that permits single-family but prohibits multi-family uses is an example. Compensation would not be payable if a court held that the multi-family prohibition was a taking because the single-family restriction did not deny the property owner "all use" of his property.

The Court's holding in *First English* is limited to the compensation remedy. It did not hold the interim moratorium was a taking. It remanded the case for a decision on the merits and indicated that the denial of "all use" under the moratorium might be constitutional as part of the government's authority to adopt safety regulations. The Court also held that it did not have to deal with the "quite different questions" raised by normal delays in obtaining building permits, zoning changes, variances, "and the like," which were not before it. The California court held the ordinance constitutional on the remand.[143]

### § 8.25. When Compensation Is Payable.

Some state cases have denied compensation by applying the dictum in *First English* that compensation is not payable unless the landowner has been denied "all use" of her property.[144] These cases mean compensation is not payable in the common case in which a court holds unconstitutional a zoning restriction that allows the landowner to put the property to some use, such as single-family residential development.

The Supreme Court has held that the rental value of property during a temporary taking is the correct measure of compensation.[145] The court of appeals in

---

**143.** § 12.06.

**144.** Cline v. City of Clarksville, 746 S.W.2d 56 (Ark. 1988); Cobb Cty. v. McColister, 413 S.E.2d 441 (Ga. 1992); Lake Forest Chateau v. City of Lake Forest, 549 N.E.2d 336 (Ill. 1990); The Shopco Group v. City of Springdale, 586 N.E.2d 145 (Ohio App.), *cause dismissed,* 563 N.E.2d 302 (Ohio 1992); Stoner v. Township of Lower Merion, 587 A.2d 879 (Pa. Commw. 1991) (refusal to approve subdivision). *See also* McCutchan Estates Corp. v. Evansville-Vanderburgh Cty. Airport Auth. Dist., 580 N.E.2d 339 (Ind. App. 1991) (nine month administrative delay in subdivision approval). *Contra* Whitehead Oil Co. v. City of Lincoln (III), 515 N.W.2d 401 (Neb. 1994).

**145.** Kimball Laundry Co. v. United States, 338 U.S. 1 (1949).

*Wheeler v. City of Pleasant Grove (III)*[146] adopted the rental value standard. The city adopted an ordinance prohibiting apartments in the city when strong community opposition arose after plaintiffs obtained a building permit for an apartment project. The court held a property owner's loss in a temporary taking case is the injury to the property's potential for producing an income or profit as measured by the rate of return on the loss in market value caused by the regulatory restriction. The court did not award compensation for lost profits or increased development costs as this would be a double recovery for losses reflected in the loss in market value. The court also held that an increase in value that occurred while the building prohibition was in effect should not be considered. The court of appeals reaffirmed its earlier holding in later appeal after the district court refused to award compensation on remand.[147] It awarded compensation at the market rate of return for the temporary taking period on plaintiff's 25 percent equity in the "complex," which they had the right to control.

*Wheeler* did not consider the uncertainty that the project proposed by the developer might not have been constructed. This may be incorrect.[148] Courts do not usually compensate for lost profits on uncertainties. They usually pay compensation on the fair market value of land for its "highest and best" use. Under this approach, the court should have considered alternative uses for the property that qualified as its highest and best use. This test does not mean that the land would have been valued at its existing use. Courts may consider a potential use of the land that probable zoning change would allow if the use is not speculative. A federal district court adopted a formula in a substantive due process case for computing damages in situations of uncertainty when the issue was the probability that a subdivision would be approved.[149]

## § 8.26. Section 1983 of the Federal Civil Rights Act.

### § 8.27. Scope of the Statute.

Section 1983 of the federal Civil Rights Act of 1871 provides:

> Every person who, under color of any statute, ordinance, regulation, custom or usage, of any State . . . , subjects, or causes to be subjected, any citizen of the United States or other person within the jurisdiction thereof

---

146. 833 F.2d 267 (11th Cir. 1987). *See also* Nemmers v. City of Dubuque, 764 F.2d 502 (8th Cir. 1985) (downzoning; court applied similar compensation measure); Whitehead Oil Co. v. City of Lincoln (III), 515 N.W.2d 401 (Neb. 1994).

147. Wheeler v. City of Pleasant Grove (IV), 896 F.2d 1347 (11th Cir. 1990).

148. *See* Corn v. City of Lauderdale Lakes, 771 F. Supp. 1557 (S.D. Fla. 1991), *aff'd and rev'd in part and remanded,* 997 F.2d 1369 (11th Cir. 1993), *cert. denied,* 511 U.S. 1018 (1994).

149. Herrington v. County of Sonoma, 790 F. Supp. 909 (N.D. Cal. 1991). *See also* City of Austin v. Teague, 570 S.W.2d 389 (Tex. 1978).

to the deprivation of any rights, privileges or immunities secured by the Constitution and laws, shall be liable to the party injured in an action at law, suit in equity, or other proper proceeding for redress.

Section 1983 authorizes a cause of action for the violation of any constitutional right, including substantive due process and equal protection violations.

Section 1983 assumed new importance in land use cases after the U.S. Supreme Court held, in *Monell v. Department of Social Serv.*,[150] that municipalities can be sued under § 1983. Section 1983 is not available in unconsented actions against the state.[151] The Civil Rights Attorney's Fees Award Act[152] authorizes prevailing plaintiffs and defendants to recover attorney's fees in § 1983 actions.

In *Maine v. Thiboutot*,[153] the Supreme Court held that the phrase "and laws" in § 1983 applies to any federal law. This decision opened up the possibility for § 1983 land use actions based on federal land use legislation, such as the National Coastal Zone Management Act. The Court limited *Thiboutot* in later decisions. It held that a § 1983 action cannot be brought to enforce nonsubstantive declarations of statutory policy.[154] Nor may § 1983 be used to enforce a federal statute that contains its own specific remedy.[155]

The Supreme Court has held that property rights are one of the "rights" protected by § 1983.[156] Landowners do not usually have difficulty showing that they have property rights protected under § 1983,[157] especially when they claim that a land use regulation unconstitutionally restricts the use of their property.[158]

An intent to violate the constitution is not required for liability under § 1983,[159] but procedural due process liability attaches only for intentional and not for negligent deprivations.[160]

### § 8.28. Land Use Cases Not Actionable Under § 1983.

Although the § 1983 remedy is available for any violation of the federal constitution, some lower federal courts hold that a cause of action does not lie under

---

150. 436 U.S. 658 (1978).

151. Quern v. Jordon, 440 U.S. 332 (1979).

152. 42 U.S.C. § 1988.

153. 448 U.S. 1 (1980).

154. Pennhurst State School & Hosp. v. Halderman, 451 U.S. 1 (1981), *extended in* Suter v. Artist M., 503 U.S. 347 (1992).

155. Middlesex County Sewerage Auth. v. National Sea Clammers Ass'n, 453 U.S. 1 (1981).

156. Lynch v. Household Fin. Corp., 405 U.S. 538 (1972).

157. McCulloch v. City of Glasgow, 620 F.2d 47 (5th Cir. 1980).

158. *See also* §§ 2.36, 2.38 (whether landowner must have entitlement to property in due process cases).

159. Monroe v. Pape, 365 U.S. 167 (1961).

160. Daniels v. Williams, 474 U.S. 327 (1986) (negligent deprivations not covered); Hudson v. Palmer, 468 U.S. 517 (1984) (intentional deprivations covered).

§ 1983 even though the plaintiffs claimed that a land use decision violated the constitution. In most of these cases, the municipality denied the plaintiff a land use permit or other land use approval and the plaintiff made a substantive due process claim. *Creative Env'ts, Inc. v. Estabrook*[161] is a leading case. The plaintiff claimed a municipality violated the due process clause when it rejected the plaintiff's subdivision application to protect the municipality's "basic character." The state statute did not authorize this reason for rejection. The court held that the plaintiff's claim was too typical of a "run of the mill" land use dispute to give rise to a due process violation and that a conventional planning dispute does not implicate the federal constitution. The court indicated it would hold differently in cases of "egregious" behavior or where there was a "gross abuse of power, invidious discrimination, or fundamentally unfair procedures." *Creative Environments* has been followed in several other circuits.[162]

### § 8.29. Color of Law, Policy, and Custom.

Section 1983 makes a violation of the constitution actionable only if carried out under "color of any statute, ordinance, regulation, custom, or usage" of a governmental entity. The "color of law" requirement is similar to the "state action" requirement the courts apply in fourteenth amendment cases and usually is not troublesome in § 1983 land use litigation.[163]

*Monell* refused to adopt a respondeat superior theory of municipal liability under § 1983. It interpreted the "custom and usage" requirement in § 1983 to mean that local governments are liable only for actions that are "official policy" or "visited pursuant to a governmental custom," but did not fully explain these terms. The custom or usage requirement is not a problem in most land use cases because a governmental body, such as the legislative body, usually is responsible for the governmental action.[164] More difficult problems arise in § 1983 cases that challenge the action of a zoning official.

---

**161.** 680 F.2d 822 (1st Cir.), *cert. denied,* 459 U.S. 989 (1982). *Accord* Coniston Corp. v. Village of Hoffman Estates, 844 F.2d 461 (7th Cir. 1988); Burrell v. City of Kankakee, 815 F.2d 1127 (7th Cir. 1987) (rezoning); Hynes v. Pasco County, 801 F.2d 1269 (11th Cir. 1986) (revocation of building permit); Smith v. City of Picayune, 795 F.2d 482 (5th Cir. 1986) (rezoning).

**162.** Gardner v. City of Baltimore Mayor & City Council, 959 F.2d 63 (4th Cir. 1992); Chesterfield Dev. Corp. v. City of Chesterfield, 963 F.2d 1102 (8th Cir. 1992); Coniston Corp. v. Village of Hoffman Estates, 844 F.2d 461 (7th Cir. 1988); Hynes v. Pasco County, 801 F.2d 1269 (11th Cir. 1986); Smith v. City of Picayune, 795F.2d 482 (5th Cir. 1986).

**163.** *But see* Fantasy Book Shop v. City of Boston, 531 F. Supp. 821 (D. Mass. 1982).

**164.** Video Int'l Prods., Inc. v. Warner-Amex Cable Communications, Inc., 858 F.2d 1075 (5th Cir. 1988) (board of adjustment), *cert. denied,* 490 U.S. 1047, 491 U.S. 106 (1989); Bateson v. Geisse, 857 F.2d 1300 (9th Cir. 1988) (governing body); Altaire Bldrs., Inc. v. Village of Horseheads, 551 F. Supp. 1066 (W.D.N.Y. 1982).

There must be an act by a municipal policymaker to establish municipal liability. The Supreme Court had earlier defined a policy as a deliberate choice to follow a course of action from among various alternatives.[165] In *Pembaur v. City of Cincinnati*,[166] a plurality held a policy includes unwritten as well as formal plans of action, and that a single action is enough to establish policy. The plurality then narrowed municipal liabilty by holding municipal liability can attach only for an "official policy" made by an authorized decision maker. A majority of the Court found an official policy in a state statute that clearly delegated to a county prosecutor the authority to order a break-in to carry out arrests, but a majority could not agree on a further elaboration of the official policy requirement. Several land use cases applied *Pembaur*.[167]

*City of St. Louis v. Praprotnik*,[168] a public employee discharge case decided after *Pembaur*, was again a plurality decision. The plurality confirmed a statement in *Pembaur* that the identification of policymaking officials is a matter of state law. It was "confident" that state or local law "will always direct a court to some official or body that has the responsibility for making law or setting policy." The plurality added that an official's action is not final policy when it is constrained by "policies not of his making" or subject to review by authorized policymakers unless these policymakers ratify his decision.

The lack of a majority in *Pembaur* and *Praprotnik*[169] and ambiguities in these decisions, have made it difficult for courts to determine when a "custom or policy" exists in land use cases. A court is likely to find a custom or policy when a local agency with final authority, such as a board of adjustment[170] or legislative body,[171] has affirmed an official decision. When an official decision is appealable but has not been appealed, courts are likely to reach a contrary decision.[172]

---

**165.** City of Oklahoma v. Tuttle, 471 U.S. 808 (1985) (municipalities not liable for randon acts by low-level city employees).

**166.** 475 U.S. 469 (1986).

**167.** 805 F.2d 81 (2d Cir. 1986). Lake Nacimiento Ranch Co. v. County of San Luis Obispo, 841 F.2d 872 (9th Cir. 1987), *cert. denied,* 488 U.S. 827 (1988); Sullivan v. Town of Salem, 805 F.2d 81 (2d Cir. 1986). *See also* Coogan v. City of Wixom, 820 F.2d 170 (6th Cir. 1987).

**168.** 485 U.S. 112 (1988).

**169.** *But see* Jett v. Dallas Indep. School Dist., 491 U.S. 701 (1989) (majority apparently adopted *Praprotnik* standard).

**170.** Bannum, Inc. v. City of Ft. Lauderdale, 901 F.2d 989 (11th Cir. 1990). *See also* Burkhart Advertising, Inc. v. City of Auburn, 786 F. Supp. 721 (N.D. Ind. 1991) (mayor signed ordinance).

**171.** Browning-Ferris Indus., Inc. v. City of Maryland Heights, 747 F. Supp. 1340 (E.D. Mo. 1990) (council ratification); Lutheran Day Care v. Snohomish Cty., 829 P.2d 746 (Wash. 1992) (council denial of conditional use).

**172.** Kawaoka v. City of Arryo Grande, 17 F.3 d1227 (9th Cir. 1994) (racially discriminatory statements); Arroyo Vista Partners v. County of Santa Barbara, 732 F. Supp. 1046 (C.D. Cal. 1990) (ward courtesy system); Carr v. Town of Dewey Beach, 730 F. Supp. 591 (D. Del. 1990).

## § 8.30.  Causation.

The Supreme Court's holding that courts should interpret § 1983 against a "background of tort liability"[173] means that a plaintiff must show that a constitutional violation was "caused" by an official action. The causation requirement is not a problem in most land use cases because a legislative or administrative body is usually responsible for the constitutional deprivation.[174] Causation problems can arise if it is not clear whether the municipal conduct caused the constitutional deprivation. *Westborough Mall, Inc. v. City of Cape Girardeau (I)*[175] is an example. The court held that the plaintiff's inability to build its shopping center was caused by financial problems and not the city's reversion of its commercial zoning, not the plaintiff's poor business skills.

## § 8.31.  Exhaustion and Adequacy of State Remedies.

The Supreme Court does not require exhaustion of administrative remedies in § 1983 actions.[176] This rule is qualified by *Parratt v. Taylor*.[177] *Parratt* held that the plaintiff could not bring a § 1983 procedural due process action in federal court for the negligent loss of a hobby kit by prison officials because post-deprivation state tort remedies provided an adequate remedy. The Court held that a state need not provide a pre-deprivation hearing when a loss is caused by "a random and unauthorized act by a state employee" because the state cannot "predict precisely" in these cases when a loss will occur. Negligence claims are no longer actionable under § 1983, but the *Parratt* holding on post-deprivation state remedies is still good law in procedural due process cases.

The Court qualified *Parratt* in *Logan v. Zimmerman Brush Co.*[178] A state court dismissed the plaintiff's fair employment practice claim before a state agency because the agency did not convene a hearing in the required statutory time period. The Court held that the plaintiff's right to use the state statutory

---

173. Monroe v. Pape, 365 U.S. 167, 187 (1961).

174. Bannum v. City of Louisville, 958 F.2d 1354 (6th Cir. 1992) (inability to comply with zoning ordinance caused recision of contract); Bateson v. Geisse, 857 F.2d 1300 (9th Cir. 1988) (wrongful withholding of building permit); Schneider v. City of Ramsey, 800 F. Supp. 815 (D. Minn. 1992) (plaintiff voluntarily closed bookstore rather than face prosecution).

175. Westborough Mall, Inc. v. City of Cape Girardeau (IV), 953 F.2d 345 (8th Cir.), *cert. denied,* 505 U.S. 1222 (1991). *See also* Muckway v. Craft, 789 F.2d 517 (7th Cir.1986) (refusal to enforce zoning ordinance); Roma Constr. Co. v. Russo, 906 F. Supp.78 (D. R.I. 1995) (bribe); B. Street Commons, Inc. v. Board of County Comm'rs, 835 F. Supp. 1266 (D. Colo. 1993) (ill-considered business acts).

176. Patsy v. Florida Bd. of Regents, 457 U.S. 496 (1982). *See* Scudder v. Town of Greendale, 704 F.2d 999 (7th Cir. 1983).

177. 451 U.S. 527 (1981). *See* Littlefield v. City of Afton, 785 F.2d 596 (8th Cir. 1986). *See also* § 2.22.

178. 455 U.S. 422 (1982).

procedures was protected by the due process clause. He did not have to use post-deprivation state tort remedies because the deprivation was caused by the "state system itself." The plaintiff challenged the "established state procedure," not the state agency's error.

The *Parratt-Logan* distinction is difficult to apply in land use cases. In a zoning variance case, for example, a procedural due process violation is both a "random and unauthorized" act by the zoning board that triggers *Parratt* and an application of "established state procedure" that triggers *Logan*. One court applied *Parratt* to dismiss a § 1983 case in which the plaintiff sued a municipality after it issued a stop construction order.[179] The order was issued because the zoning enforcement officer made a mistake when he issued the building permit. The court held that a post-deprivation state remedy was adequate because the "alleged default" was like the negligent loss in *Parratt*. The court held that *Logan* rather than *Parratt* applied in a similar case because it held that "the effect on plaintiff of the established state procedures" created the constitutional deprivation.[180]

The Supreme Court substantially qualified *Parratt* in *Zinermon v. Burch*[181] and held that the *Parratt* rule applies only to procedural due process claims. Plaintiff in *Zinermon* brought a § 1983 action in which he claims a procedural due process violation based on his claim that his admission to a state mental health facility was not voluntary. The Court held that the *Parratt* bar is not absolute. Instead, a court must apply a balancing test in which it first identifies the risk involved and then evaluates the effectiveness of predeprivation safeguards in relationship to the risk identified. The Court held that the risk in *Zinermon* was predictable, the state could have provided predeprivation process and state officials had the authority to make this process available.

*Zinermon* should mean that *Parratt* should not bar most land use cases in which procedural due process claims are made. The risk of a procedural deprivation is predictable in the decision-making process, and adequate procedures are authorized. One court held that *Zinermon* does not change the *Parratt* rules,[182] and courts have also held a predeprivation hearing was not required

---

179. Albery v. Reddig, 718 F.2d 245 (7th Cir. 1983). *Accord* Lake Naciemento Ranch Co. v. County of San Luis Obispo, 841 F.2d 772 (9th Cir. 1987) (bias in decision making), *cert. denied,* 488 U.S. 827 (1988); Rymer v. Douglas County, 764 F.2d 796 (11th Cir. 1985) (error in issuing building permit); G.M. Eng'rs & Assocs., Inc. v. West Bloomfield Township, 922 F.2d 328 (6th Cir. 1990).

180. Vari-Build, Inc. v. City of Reno, 596 F. Supp. 673 (D. Nev. 1984). *Accord* Sullivan v. Town of Salem, 805 F.2d 81 (2d Cir. 1986).

181. 494 U.S. 113 (1990).

182. New Burnham Prairie Homes, Inc. v. Village of Burnham, 910 F.2d 1474 (7th Cir. 1990).

when adequate postdeprivation procedures were available.[183] Other cases relied on *Zinermon* to hold a predeprivation hearing should have been provided,[184] or have held a predeprivation hearing was required because the plaintiff was challenging an established procedure or policy.[185]

### § 8.32. Immunities.

### § 8.33. Legislative Bodies.

Although § 1983 does not expressly provide for immunities of any kind, the Supreme Court has implied the common law immunities the courts recognized when Congress enacted the statute. In *Tenney v. Brandhove*,[186] the Supreme Court held that state legislators are absolutely immune from liability under § 1983 because absolute immunity confers a benefit to the "public good":

> The [legislative] privilege would be of little value if . . . [legislators] could be subjected to the cost and inconvenience and distractions of a trial upon a conclusion of the pleader, or to the hazard of judgment against them based upon a jury's speculation as to motives. . . . Self-discipline and the voters must be the ultimate reliance for discouraging or correcting . . . [legislative] abuses.[187]

In *Lake Country Estates, Inc. v. Tahoe Regional Planning Agency*,[188] the Court extended the absolute immunity of state legislators to members of a bi-state regional planning agency. It noted that alternative remedies were available, including a suit against the regional planning agency. The Court limited legislative immunity to officials "acting in a field where legislators traditionally have power to act" who did not usurp judicial or executive authority. It reserved decision on whether local legislators also enjoyed absolute immunity, although Justice Marshall's dissent argued that the Court's holding on absolute state legislative immunity applied to local legislative bodies.

The lower federal courts have held that members of local legislative bodies are absolutely immune from § 1983 liability in land use cases. *Gorman Towers,*

---

183. DeBlasio v. Zoning Bd. of Adjustment, 53F.3d 592 (3d Cir.), *cert. denied,* 116 S. Ct. 352 (1995); Boudwin v. Great Bend Township, 921 F. Supp. 1326 (M.D. Pa. 1996).

184. Lanmar Corp. v. Rendine, 811 F. Supp. 47 (D.R.I. 1993).

185. Macene v. MJW, Inc., 951 F.2d 700 (6th Cir. 1991); Independent Coin Payphone Ass'n, Inc. v. City of Chicago, 863 F. Supp. 744 (N.D. Ill. 1994); Koncelik v. Town of East Hampton, 781 F. Supp. 152 (E.D.N.Y. 1991).

186. 341 U.S. 367 (1951).

187. *Id.* at 377-78.

188. 440 U.S. 391 (1979).

*Inc. v. Bogoslavsky*[189] is a leading case. Because land use decisions have an important effect on property, the court held that legislators should be allowed to act for the public good on land use issues without facing the "specter" of personal liability. It noted that effective checks on unconstitutional conduct are available against local legislators, including judicial review, control by the electorate, and suits against local governments.

Courts usually hold the adoption and amendment of zoning ordinances is a legislative act,[190] but do not grant absolute immunity when a legislative body acts in an administrative capacity. In *Altaire Bldrs., Inc. v. Village of Horseheads*,[191] the court held that a local legislative body did not act legislatively when it refused to approve a planned unit development. It held that approval of the development did not require a zoning amendment and that the only issue was whether it complied with the approval criteria contained in the ordinance.[192]

*Haskell v. Washington Twp.*[193] provides a test for determining whether a zoning action is legislative or administrative that turns on the purpose of the action. The court held that an action by a governing body is legislative if its purpose is to establish general policy, but administrative if it singles out specific individuals and treats them differently from others. The court added that even if an action was legislative, it would not be protected if it was in bad faith, corrupt or in furtherance of a personal rather than a public interest.

### § 8.34. Land Use Agencies and Officials.

Land use agencies and officials are absolutely immune from liability under § 1983 if they exercise adjudicatory functions, but otherwise they have only a

---

**189.** 626 F.2d 607 (8th Cir. 1980) (downzoning). *Accord* Orange Lake Assocs. v. Kirkpatrick, 21 F.3d 1214 (2d Cir. 1994); Shoultes v. Laidlaw, 886 F.2d 114 (6th Cir. 1989); Baytree of Inverrary Realty Partners v. City of Lauderhill, 873 F.2d 1407 (11th Cir. 1989); Culebras Enters. Corp. v. Rivera Rios, 813 F.2d 506 (1st Cir. 1987); Kuzinich v. County of Santa Clara, 689 F.2d 1345 (9th Cir. 1982); Bruce v. Riddle, 631 F.2d 272 (4th Cir. 1980).

**190.** Acierno v. Cloutier, 40 F.3d 597 (3d Cir. 1994); 2BD Ltd. Partnership v. County Comm'rs, 896 F. Supp. 528 (D. Md. 1995). *See also* Brown v. Crawford County, 960 F.2d 1002 (11th Cir. 1992).

**191.** 551 F. Supp. 1066 (W.D.N.Y. 1982). *Accord* Corn v. City of Lauderdale Lakes, 997 F.2d 1369 (11th Cir. 1993) (no immunity for denial of site plan), *cert. denied,* 511 U.S. 1018 (1994); Crymos v. DeKalb County, 923 F.2d 482 (11th Cir. 1991) (permit denial); Bateson v. Geisse, 857 F.2d 1300 (9th Cir. 1988) (permit withheld); Scott v. Greenville County, 716 F.2d 1409 (4th Cir. 1983) (building permit application). *But see* § 8.33 (suggesting absolute immunity if function adjudicatory).

**192.** Held administrative: Crymos v. DeKalb County, 923 P.2d 482 (11th Cir. 1991) (permit denial); Bateson v. Geisse, 857 F.2d 1300 (9th Cir. 1988); Scott v. Greenville County, 716 F.2d 1409 (4th Cir. 1983) (building permit application).

**193.** 864 F.2d 1266 (6th Cir. 1988) (remanding to determine whether adoption of zoning ordinance administrative).

qualified good faith immunity. Absolute immunity is based on a Supreme Court case, *Butz v. Economou*.[194] The Court conferred absolute immunity on federal officials who initiated an adjudicatory proceeding against the plaintiff. The Court held that there may be "exceptional situations where it is demonstrated that absolute [executive] immunity is essential for the conduct of the public business." Adjudication by agencies is "functionally comparable" to adjudication by judges and should enjoy the absolute immunity judges enjoy.

The absolute immunity established by *Butz* should apply when land use agencies exercise adjudicatory functions.[195] The courts have refused to extend absolute immunity to the review procedures of a planning board and a board of adjustment.[196] They have granted only a qualified good faith immunity to executive actions in the enforcement and implementation of land use regulation.[197] However, a planning commission was given absolute immunity when it recommended legislative action to a local governing body.[198]

Land use agencies and officials that have qualified good faith immunity are subject to immunity rules adopted by the Supreme Court, although the Court has not considered the immunity question in a land use case. The Court first adopted a two-part test that required both subjective and objective good faith.[199] It dropped the subjective part of the test in *Harlow v. Fitzgerald*[200] and restated the objective good faith test as a more protective formula:

> [G]overnment officials performing discretionary functions generally are shielded from liability insofar as their conduct does not violate clearly established statutory or constitutional rights of which a reasonable person would have known.[201]

The Court also held that an official's conduct must meet a standard of "objective legal reasonableness."

---

**194.** 438 U.S. 478 (1978).

**195.** Bass v. Attardi, 868 F.2d 45 (3d Cir. 1989).

**196.** Cutting v. Mazzey, 724 F.2d 259 (1st Cir. 1984); Rodriguez v. Village of Larchmont, 608 F. Supp. 467 (S.D.N.Y. 1985).

**197.** Sullivan v. Town of Salem, 805 F.2d 81 (2d Cir. 1986) (refusal to issue occupancy certificates); Tahoe-Sierra Preservation Council v. Tahoe Regional Planning Agency, 638 F. Supp. 126 (D. Nev. 1986) (implementation of regional plan).

**198.** Fralin & Waldron, Inc. v. County of Henrico, 474 F. Supp. 1315 (E.D. Va. 1979). *See also* Shoultes v. Laidlaw, 886 F.2d 114 (6th Cir. 1989) (city attorney brought civil injunction to enforce zoning ordinance); Hernandez v. City of Lafayette, 643 F.2d 1188 (5th Cir. 1981) (mayor vetoed rezoning), *cert. denied,* 455 U.S. 907 (1982).

**199.** Scheuer v. Rhodes, 416 U.S. 232 (1974). *See also* Pierson v. Ray, 386 U.S. 547 (1967).

**200.** 457 U.S. 800 (1982).

**201.** *Id.* at 818.

*Davis v. Scherer*[202] elaborated the *Harlow rule.* The Court held that a mere violation of a state statute or regulation, standing alone, is not enough to defeat good faith immunity. Immunity is unavailable only if the defendant violated a clearly established constitutional right. The land use cases have applied *Harlow.*[203]

The Supreme Court further clarified official immunity in *Anderson v. Creighton.*[204] Plaintiff claimed that police officers had conducted a warrantless search. The Court held that even though the courts had previously recognized a constitutional right to be protected from a warrantless search without probable cause, the question was whether it was unconstitutional in this case under all the circumstances. This fact-specific inquiry requires the courts to determine whether a reasonable officer could have believed that a warrantless search was constitutional in light of the clearly established law and the available facts. Because so many land use actions brought under § 1983 are fact-specific, *Creighton* should lead to an expansion of official immunity in land use § 1983 actions.

The courts have found that land use agencies and officials have acted in good faith when no clearly established right was violated.[205] The courts have denied good faith immunity in cases in which zoning officials arbitrarily withheld building permits or arbitrarily enforced a zoning ordinance.[206] Some of these cases are post-*Creighton* but did not make the fact-specific inquiry required by that decision.

---

**202.** 468 U.S. 183 (1984).

**203.** Desert Outdoor Advertising v. City of Moreno Valley, 103 F.3d 814 (9th Cir. 1996) (licensing scheme for signs); Acierno v. Cloutier, 40 F.3d 597 (3d Cir. 1994) (right to develop not clearly established); Rappa v. New Castle County, 18 F.3d 1043 (3d Cir. 1994) (qualified immunity in facial attack on sign restrictions); Culebras Enters. Corp. v. Rivera Rios, 813 F.2d 506 (1st Cir. 1987) (moratorium); Kaplan v. Clear Lake City Water Auth., 794 F.2d 1059 (5th Cir. 1986) (refusal to provide water and sewer service); Negin v. City of Mentor, 601 F. Supp. 1502 (N.D. Ohio 1985).

**204.** 483 U.S. 635 (1987), noted in The Supreme Court: 1986 Term: Leading Cases, 101 Harv. L. Rev. 101, 220 (1987).

**205.** Zahra v. Town of Southold, 48 F.3d 674, 686 (2d Cir. 1995) (building permit revoked); Acierno v. Cloutier, 40 F.3d 597 (3d Cir. 1994); Walnut Properties, Inc. v. City of Whittier (II), 861 F.2d 1102 (9th Cir. 1988) (adult business zoning); Culebras Enters. Corp. v. Rivera Rios, 813 F.2d 506 (1st Cir. 1987); Kaplan v. Clear Lake City Water Auth., 794 F.2d 1059 (5th Cir. 1986).

**206.** Blanche Road Corp. v. Bensalem Township, 57 F.3d 253 (3d Cir. 1995); Brady v. Town of Colchester, 863 F.2d 205 (2d Cir. 1988); Bateson v. Geisse, 857 F.2d 1300 (9th Cir. 1988) (because "contours" of substantive due process clear); TLC Dev., Inc. v. Town of Branford, 855 F. Supp. 555 (D. Conn. 1994) (denial of site plan).

## § 8.35. Local Governments.

*Owen v. City of Independence*[207] held that municipalities are not immune from liability in a § 1983 action. A police chief brought an action claiming he was terminated by the city without the procedural due process required by the federal constitution. The Court held there was no general municipal immunity at the time Congress enacted § 1983, either for proprietary as distinguished from governmental activities or for discretionary as distinguished from ministerial actions. It did not limit its decision to procedural due process violations but held that it applied to all "constitutional violations":

> [A] municipality has no "discretion" to violate the Federal Constitution; its dictates are absolute and imperative. And when a court passes judgment on the municipality's conduct in a § 1983 action, it does not seek to second-guess the reasonableness of the city's decision nor to interfere with the local government's resolution of competing policy considerations. Rather, it looks only to whether the municipality has conformed to the requirements of the Federal Constitution and statutes.[208]

Although *Owen* held that municipalities are not immune under § 1983, it does not impose absolute liability. As the statement just quoted indicates, plaintiffs must still show a violation of the federal Constitution.

## § 8.36. Damages.

Section 1983 provides that parties sued under the statute "shall be liable to the party injured in an action at law." This provision authorizes an award of compensatory damages. The Supreme Court has held that the common law of torts provides an analogy for damages in § 1983 cases but requires careful adaptation when a constitutional right does not have a tort analogy.[209] Punitive damages are not available against local governments[210]. Courts may award punitive damages against local officials,[211] but the facts have not usually justified an award of punitive damages in land use cases.[212]

In *Carey v. Piphus*,[213] the Supreme Court rejected a claim that a court should presume damages when a plaintiff proves a procedural due process violation.

---

**207.** 445 U.S. 622 (1980).

**208.** *Id.* at 649.

**209.** Memphis Community School Dist. v. Stachura, 477 U.S. 299 (1986); Carey v. Piphus, 435 U.S. 247 (1978).

**210.** City of Newport v. Fact Concerts, Inc., 453 U.S. 247 (1981).

**211.** Smith v. Wade, 461 U.S. 30 (1983).

**212.** Johansen v. City of Bartlesville, 862 F.2d 1423 (10th Cir. 1988); Creekside Assocs. v. City of Wood Dale, 684 F. Supp. 201 (N.D. Ill. 1988).

**213.** 435 U.S. 247 (1978).

Elementary and secondary school students brought a § 1983 action claiming they were denied procedural due process when they were temporarily suspended. The Court held that the defendant was liable only for nominal, not compensatory, damages because there was no proof that the students would not have been suspended if procedural due process requirements had been observed. Carey also applies to substantive due process violations.[214] This case means that damages are not available in a land use case unless the due process violation affected the outcome of the decision.

The Supreme Court has held that compensation is payable in land use cases for temporary takings in an inverse condemnation action brought directly under the federal constitution.[215] The Court did not indicate whether a plaintiff could recover compensation for a taking under § 1983, but compensation should be available in a § 1983 action as well.[216]

Damages are available in a § 1983 action for constitutional violations other than violations of the taking clause. Justice Brennan noted, for example, that substantive due process violations not actionable under the taking clause are actionable under § 1983.[217] *Heritage Homes of Attleboro, Inc. v. Seekonk Water Dist. (II)*[218] indicates the possibilities for compensatory damage awards in § 1983 cases. A developer suffered losses when the district delayed a residential project that was to be open to minorities by refusing to supply water. The court awarded compensatory damages equal to the difference between the cost of connecting to the district and the cost the developer incurred to drill individual wells. It denied damages for the developer's inability to use its assets while the project was delayed. The developer did not provide evidence on the applicable interest rate and did not show that the appreciation in the value of its property was less than what interest on its assets would have earned.[219]

### § 8.37. Implied Constitutional Cause of Action.

The Supreme Court has recognized an implied cause of action to enforce some of the constitutional rights that are protected by the federal constitution. The action is known as a *Bivens* action for the search and seizure case that cre-

---

**214.** Memphis Community School Dist. v. Stachura, 477 U.S. 299 (1986).

**215.** § 8.24.

**216.** Wheeler v. City of Pleasant Grove (II), 833 F.2d 267 (11th Cir. 1987).

**217.** San Diego Gas & Elec. Co. v. City of San Diego, 450 U.S. 621, 656 n.23 (1981) (dissenting opinion).

**218.** 648 F.2d 761 (1st Cir. 1981). *See also* Wheeler v. City of Pleasant Grove (II), 833 F.2d 267 (11th Cir. 1987) (taking); Cordeco Dev. Corp. v. Santiago Vasquez, 539 F.2d 256 (1st Cir.), *cert. denied,* 429 U.S. 978 (1976).

**219.** *See also* Herrington v. County of Sonoma, 790 F. Supp. 909 (N.D. Cal. 1991) (specifying measure of damages for refusal to approve subdivision), *aff'd,* 12 F.3d 901 (9th Cir. 1993).

ated it.[220] The Court has also approved a *Bivens* action brought under the equal protection clause[221] but has not decided whether it is available to enforce the fourteenth amendment. The Court has indicated that whether a *Bivens* action is available depends on whether damages are appropriate, whether there are special concerns "counseling hesitation," and whether Congress has provided an alternative remedy explicitly declared to be a substitute and which is equally effective.[222]

*Carlson v. Green*[223] held an alternative remedy under the Federal Tort Claims Act was not an effective substitute for a *Bivens* action brought to enforce the eighth amendment's guarantee against cruel and unusual punishment. The court cited legislative history to the Tort Claims Act indicating Congress believed that a *Bivens* action was an alternative remedy. The court also noted that punitive damages were available in a *Bivens* action but not under the Act.

Some lower federal courts approved a *Bivens* action in land use cases prior to the Supreme Court decision holding that local governments are liable under § 1983.[224] Later federal court cases held the availability of a § 1983 action in land use cases precludes a *Bivens* action.[225] The *Carlson* decision casts doubt on these cases because punitive damages are not available against local governments in § 1983 actions. The lower federal courts are divided on whether a *Bivens* action is available to enforce the fourteenth amendment, on which land use cases are often based.[226] Neither the relationship between *Bivens* actions and an action to secure compensation under the taking clause is clear.

---

**220.** Bivens v. Six Unknown Named Agents of the Fed. Bur. of Narcotics, 403 U.S. 388 (1971). *Compare* Kelley Prop. Dev. Co. v. Town of Lebanon, 627 A.2d 909 (Conn. 1993) (rejecting state *Bivens* action in zoning cases), *with* Old Tuckaway Assocs. Ltd. Partnership v. City of Greenfield, 509 N.W.2d 323 (Wis. App. 1993) (contra).

**221.** Davis v. Passman, 442 U.S. 228 (1979) (action against congressman).

**222.** *Id.* at 245-47.

**223.** 446 U.S. 14 (1980). *See also* Bush v. Lucas, 462 U.S. 367 (1983) (*Bivens* action held unavailable).

**224.** Gordon v. City of Warren, 579 F.2d 386 (6th Cir. 1978).

**225.** Rogin v. Bensalem Twp., 616 F.2d 680 (3d Cir. 1980), *cert. denied,* 450 U.S. 1029 (1981). *See also* Monell v. Department of Social Servs., 436 U.S. 658, 713 (1978) (Justice Powell, concurring). *But see* Ocean Acres Ltd. Partnership v. Dare County Bd. of Health, 514 F. Supp. 1117 (E.D.N.C. 1981), *aff'd on other grounds,* 707 F.2d 103 (4th Cir. 1983).

**226.** For discussion of these decisions in a land use case, *see* Rogin v. Bensalem Twp., 616 F.2d 680 (3d Cir. 1980), *cert. denied,* 450 U.S. 1029 (1981).

## § 8.38. Abstention.

Federal district courts may abstain from hearing a case that raises federal constitutional law questions under several abstention doctrines adopted by the U.S. Supreme Court. Federal courts can abstain in actions for damages as well as actions for equitable relief. The abstention doctrine applies to land use cases in which plaintiffs allege violations of the federal constitution, including inverse condemnation actions, § 1983 actions, and implied causes of action based on the federal constitution.[227] Although the Supreme Court has frequently stated that abstention is the exception rather than the rule,[228] the federal courts often abstain in land use cases.

## § 8.39. *Younger* Abstention.

In *Younger v. Harris*,[229] the Supreme Court applied principles of federal comity embraced in "Our Federalism" to hold that federal courts should abstain from enjoining pending state criminal proceedings. Abstention is appropriate if the plaintiff can make an adequate federal defense in the state proceedings, and if abstention does not cause the plaintiff irreparable injury. The Court indicated that a plaintiff would suffer irreparable injury if there was bad faith or harassment in the state proceedings, or if a state statute was flagrantly and patently unconstitutional. The Court has extended *Younger* abstention to pending state civil proceedings that implicate important state interests[230] and to state administrative proceedings,[231] which include local administrative zoning proceedings. These extensions of the doctrine should lead courts to apply it more often in land use cases.

*Younger* abstention is required even if the federal action was filed first if "proceedings of substance" on the merits in federal court have not occurred when a later state action is filed.[232] Courts must dismiss and may not stay a federal action if they abstain under *Younger*.[233]

*New Orleans Public Serv. v. City of New Orleans*[234] indicates the Supreme Court will not apply *Younger* abstention to legislative zoning actions that are under review in state courts. The New Orleans city council refused a rate increase to a utility to cover the costs of a nuclear power plant. After the utility

---

227. *Compare* §§ 2.21-2.26, 8.31.
228. Colorado River Water Conservation Dist. v. United States, 424 U.S. 800 (1976).
229. 401 U.S. 31 (1971).
230. Middlesex County Ethics Comm. v. Garden State Bar Ass'n, 457 U.S. 423 (1982).
231. Ohio Civil Rights Comm'n v. Dayton Christian Schools, Inc., 477 U.S. 619 (1986).
232. Hicks v. Miranda, 422 U.S. 322 (1975). *See* Adult World Bookstore v. City of Fresno, 758 F.2d 1348 (9th Cir. 1985); Ciotti v. County of Cook, 712 F.2d 312 (7th Cir. 1983).
233. Colorado River Water Conservation Dist. v. United States, 424 U.S. 800 (1976).
234. 491 U.S. 350 (1989).

sought review of the order in state court, it sued in federal court claiming the order was preempted by federal legislation.

The Court held that *Younger* abstention does not apply when state court proceedings are pending to review legislative and executive action. The council's legislative action was complete and could be challenged in federal court, and it was not necessary to abstain to avoid disrupting state judicial proceedings. This case, the Court noted, was analogous to a facial challenge to a zoning ordinance, which should not be brought in state court. This statement is surprising. The Court apparently meant that a federal court should not abstain when a landowner makes a facial challenge to zoning in federal court even though a facial challenge is pending in a state court.

Courts apply the multi-factor *Younger* abstention doctrine to decide whether they should abstain in land use cases.[235] Issues that are often determinative is whether the plaintiff could litigate the constitutional issues in state court,[236] and whether the plaintiff would suffer irreparable harm.[237] The courts have held that zoning implicates an important state interest that deserves abstention in land use case.[238]

### § 8.40. *Pullman* Abstention.

In *Railroad Comm'n of Texas. v. Pullman Co.*,[239] the plaintiffs brought a suit in equity in which they claimed that a state agency order was racially discriminatory and unauthorized by the state statute. The Court held that abstention was appropriate. It noted that the plaintiffs raised substantial federal constitutional questions and held:

> [The complaint] touches a sensitive area of social policy upon which the federal courts ought not to enter unless no alternative to its adjudication is open. Such constitutional adjudication plainly can be avoided if a definitive ruling on the state issue would terminate the controversy.[240]

---

**235.** Oxford-House Evergreen v. City of Plainfield, 769 F. Supp. 1329 (D.N.J. 1991).

**236.** Abstention granted: World Famous Drinking Emporium, Inc. v. City of Tempe, 820 F.2d 1079 (9th Cir. 1987). Abstention denied: Wiener v. County of San Diego, 23 F.3d 263 (9th Cir. 1994). *See also* Casa Marie, Inc. v. Superior Court, 988 F.2d 252 (1st Cir. 1993).

**237.** Harm found: Sullivan v. City of Pittsburgh, 811 F.2d 171 (3d Cir. 1987); United States v. Commonwealth of Puerto Rico, 764 F. Supp. 220 (D.P.R. 1991). Harm not found: Central Ave. News, Inc. v. City of Minot, 651 F.2d 565 (8th Cir. 1981); Danish News Co. v. City of Ann Arbor, 517 F. Supp. 86 (E.D. Mich. 1981), *aff'd mem.*, 751 F.2d 384 (6th Cir. 1984).

**238.** Rodriguez v. County of Hawaii, 823 F. Supp. 798 (D. Haw. 1993); Naked City, Inc. v. Aregood, 667 F. Supp. 1246 (N.D. Ind. 1987). *But see* Glen-Gery Corp. v. Lower Heidelberg Township, 608 F. Supp. 1002 (E.D. Pa. 1985).

**239.** 312 U.S. 496 (1971).

**240.** *Id.* at 498.

The Supreme Court has indicated when *Pullman* abstention is appropriate because a state law question is unsettled.[241] A state or local law must be "fairly subject" to an interpretation that will make a decision on the federal constitutional questions unnecessary and must be uncertain and obviously susceptible of a limiting construction. A bare though unlikely possibility that this will occur is not enough.

The federal courts of appeals have adopted different multi-factor tests based on the *Pullman* decision to determine when *Pullman* abstention applies.[242] In the Ninth Circuit, an emphasis on the "sensitive social policy" factor has led to frequent abstention in land use cases.[243]

Federal courts have abstained under *Pullman* abstention in a number of land use cases when state law was unsettled.[244] *Kollsman v. City of Los Angeles,*[245] a Ninth Circuit case, illustrates these decisions. The state law question was whether the plaintiff's subdivision was deemed approved because the city did not make a "completeness" determination within the required statutory time period. The court held that the answer to this question depended on interlocking state statutes whose interpretation was unsettled and noted that the plaintiff and the city disagreed on their interpretation. The dissent believed the state statutes were clear and that the only issue before the court was factual.

The federal courts have refused to abstain under *Pullman* abstention in land use cases when state law questions were settled.[246] They often refuse to abstain in first amendment land use cases, and some of these cases hold that abstention

---

241. Hawaii Hous. Auth. v. Midkiff, 467 U.S. 2291 (1984) (summarizing Supreme Court decisions). *But see* Corder v. City of Sherwood, 579 F. Supp. 1042 (E.D. Ark. 1984) (court abstained though state law questions not clearly unsettled); Kent Island Joint Venture v. Smith, 452 F. Supp. 455 (D. Md. 1978) (same).

242. Palmer v. Jackson, 617 F.2d 424 (5th Cir. 1980) (two-factor test); George v. Parratt, 602 F.2d 818 (8th Cir. 1979) (three-factor test).

243. *See* Canton v. Spokane School Dist. No. 81, 498 F.2d 840 (9th Cir. 1974) (as part of three-factor test).

244. Chez Sez III Corp. v. Township of Union, 945 F.2d 628 (3d Cir. 1991), *cert. denied,* 503 U.S. 907 (1992); Pearl Inv. Co. v. City & County of San Francisco, 774 F.2d 1460 (9th Cir. 1985), *cert. denied,* 476 U.S. 1170 (1986); Caleb Stowe Assocs. v. Albemarle County, 724 F.2d 1079 (4th Cir. 1984); Hill v. City of El Paso, 437 F.2d 352 (5th Cir. 1971); Adams Outdoor Advertising v. City of Holland, 883 F. Supp. 207 (W.D. Mich. 1995); International Eateries of America v. Board of County Comm'rs, 838 F. Supp. 580 (S.D. Fla. 1993).

245. 737 F.2d 830 (9th Cir. 1984), *cert. denied,* 469 U.S. 1211 (1985). *See also* C-Y Dev. Co. v. City of Redlands, 703 F.2d 375 (9th Cir. 1983).

246. Urbanizadora Versalles, Inc. v. Rivera Rios, 701 F.2d 993 (1st Cir. 1983); Nasser v. City of Homewood (I), 671 F.2d 432 (11th Cir. 1982); Donohue Constr. Co. v. Montgomery County Council, 567 F.2d 603 (4th Cir. 1977); People Tags, Inc. v. Jackson County Legislature, 636 F. Supp. 1345 (W.D. 1986) (adult use zoning); Rasmussen v. City of Lake Forest, 404 F. Supp. 148 (N.D. Ill. 1975) (strong statement disfavoring abstention).

is less appropriate when first amendment issues are raised.[247] Courts that refuse to abstain under *Pullman* abstention sometimes point out that federal as well as state courts can apply state law to difficult facts.[248]

"Mirror image" abstention problems arise frequently in *Pullman* abstention cases when a defendant asks the federal court to abstain so that a state court can interpret a state constitutional provision that parallels a provision in the federal constitution. The taking clause is an example. The federal courts have not allowed mirror image abstention,[249] following a Supreme Court decision holding that *Pullman* abstention is not appropriate to allow a state court to interpret a parallel state constitutional provision.[250]

### § 8.41. *Burford* Abstention.

A Supreme Court case, *Burford v. Sun Oil Co.*,[251] established a third abstention category. The Court held that abstention was appropriate in an action in equity brought to challenge a state agency's oil drilling order. The Court noted that the state agency adopted the order in a complex state regulatory program. It held that federal court intervention would lead to conflicts in the interpretation of the state law that would endanger state policies. The Court also emphasized that the state had provided "adequate and expeditious" judicial review of state agency decisions to a single state court. *Burford* abstention requires dismissal of the federal court proceeding.

The Court extended *Burford* abstention in *Colorado River Water Conservation Dist. v. United States*.[252] It stated in dictum:

> Abstention is also appropriate where there have been presented difficult questions of state law bearing on policy problems of substantial public import whose importance transcends the result in the case then at bar. . . . It is enough that exercise of federal review of the question . . . would be disrup-

---

**247.** Cinema Arts, Inc. v. Clark County, 722 F.2d 579 (9th Cir. 1983); People Tags, Inc. v. Jackson County Legislature, 636 F. Supp. 1345 (W.D. Mo. 1986); Amico v. New Castle County, 553 F. Supp. 738 (D. Del. 1982). *See also* Pearl Inv. Co. v. City & County of San Francisco, 774 F.2d 1460 (9th Cir. 1985), *cert. denied,* 476 U.S. 1170 (1986).

**248.** Heritage Farms, Inc. v. Solebury Twp., 671 F.2d 743 (3d Cir.), *cert. denied,* 456 U.S. 990 (1982).

**249.** Pearl Inv. Co. v. City & County of San Francisco, 774 F.2d 1460 (9th Cir. 1985), *cert. denied,* 476 U.S. 1170 (1986); Northern Va. Law School, Inc. v. City of Alexandria, 680 F. Supp. 222 (N.D. Va. 1988).

**250.** Hawaii Hous. Auth. v. Midkiff, 467 U.S. 229, 237 n.4 (1984).

**251.** 319 U.S. 315 (1942).

**252.** 424 U.S. 800 (1976).

tive of state efforts to establish a coherent policy with respect to a matter of substantial public concern. . . .[253]

The Court stressed that in *Burford* the state "had established its own elaborate review system."

*New Orleans Public Serv. v. City of New Orleans*[254] indicates that the Supreme Court views *Burford* abstention less favorably. The Court held that *Burford* abstention did not apply to a case brought in federal court that claimed a city council rate order was preempted by a federal statute. The Court noted the *Burford* doctrine does not necessarily require abstention whenever there is a complex state regulatory system or even when there is a potential for conflict with state law and policy. *Burford* abstention did not apply in this case because the federal claim turned on federal preemption and required only a facial review of the council's rate order. The Court would presumably reach the same result when a facial constitutional challenge is brought to a zoning ordinance.

The federal courts have not usually abstained under *Burford* abstention in land use cases.[255] They emphasize that local land use regulation is piecemeal and fragmented, that it is not state policy, and that judicial review is not concentrated in a single court.[256] The courts also hold that *Burford* abstention is disfavored in first amendment and other civil rights cases.[257]

*Burford* and *Pullman* abstention overlap. Almost all *Burford* abstention cases are potential *Pullman* abstention cases because they can raise unsettled state law questions. The Fourth Circuit has held that *Burford* abstention applies when federal claims stem solely from a construction of state or local land use or zoning laws.[258]

---

253. *Id.* at 814.

254. 491 U.S. 350 (1989).

255. Urbanizadora Versalles, Inc. v. Rivera Rios, 701 F.2d 993 (1st Cir. 1983); Nasser v. City of Homewood (I), 671 F.2d 432 (11th Cir. 1982); Santa Fe Land Imp. Co. v. City of Chula Vista, 596 F.2d 838 (9th Cir. 1979); MacNamara v. County Council, 738 F. Supp. 134 (D. Del.), *aff'd without opinion*, 922 F.2d 832 (3d Cir. 1990) (citing this treatise); People Tags, Inc. v. Jackson County Legislature, 636 F. Supp. 1345 (W.D. Mo. 1986).

256. Heritage Farms, Inc. v. Solebury Twp., 671 F.2d 743 (3d Cir.), *cert. denied*, 456 U.S. 990 (1982); Rancho Palos Verdes Corp. v. City of Laguna Beach, 547 F.2d 1092 (9th Cir. 1976); Lerner v. Town of Islip, 272 F. Supp. 664 (E.D.N.Y. 1967).

257. United States v. Commonwealth of Puerto Rico, 764 F. Supp. 220 (D.P.R. 1991) (Fair Housing Act); Amico v. New Castle County, 553 F. Supp. 738 (D. Del. 1982); Riccobono v. Whitpain Twp., 497 F. Supp. 1364 (E.D. Pa. 1980).

258. Pomponio v. Fauquier County Bd. of Supvrs., 21 F.3d 1319 (4th Cir. 1994). *See also* Corder v. City of Sherwood, 579 F. Supp. 1042 (E.D. Ark. 1984) (combined *Pullman-Burford* abstention).

## § 8.42. *Colorado River* Abstention.

The Supreme Court adopted another ground for abstention in *Colorado River Conserv. Dist. v. United States.*[259] Where there are concurrent state proceedings, the Court reasoned that "wise judicial administration" might justify abstention. Courts were to consider the inconvenience of the federal forum, the desirability of avoiding piecemeal litigation and the order in which jurisdiction was obtained in the concurrent forums. A later Supreme Court case[260] modified the final factor by holding that priority should be measured by how much progress has been made in each forum and adding as another factor the probable inadequacy of the state court proceeding to protect the plaintiff's rights.

Although federal courts often abstain under *Colorado River* abstention, the courts of appeal have refused to abstain when a land use claim is made under § 1983.[261] District courts have granted motions to abstain in land use cases on *Colorado River* grounds, however, even when § 1983 claims were made.[262]

## E. SLAPP SUITS.

## § 8.43. SLAPP Suits.

SLAPP suits, an acronym for "Strategic Lawsuits Against Public Participation," are suits filed by a land developer against opponents to a proposed development. To retaliate against the opposition, the developer sues for defamation, interference with business relationships, or on some similar theory for damages. Damages claimed usually average several million dollars, and the threat of liability may be enough to scare opponents into silence.

The great majority of SLAPP suits never make it to trial, and defendants usually prevail in those that are tried. Defendants can raise a first amendment right to petition defense that courts often recognize. In *Gorman Towers, Inc. v. Bogoslavsky,*[263] for example, the court held defendants were absolutely privileged under the first amendment when they persuaded a city to overrule its zoning board and downzone property to prevent construction of a multi-family develop-

---

259. 424 U.S. 800 (1976).

260. Moses H. Cone Mem. Hosp. v. Mercury Constr. Corp., 460 U.S. 1 (1983).

261. Lake Lucerne Civic Ass'n v. Dolphin Stadium Corp., 878 F.2d 1360 (11th Cir. 1989), *cert. denied,* 493 U.S. 1079 (1990); Tovar v. Billmeyer, 609 F.2d 1291 (9th Cir. 1990); Giulini v. Blessing, 654 F.2d 189 (2d Cir. 1981). *See also* Baskin v. Bath Twp. Bd. of Zoning Appeals, 15 F.3d 569 (6th Cir. 1994) (parallel state proceeding not pending).

262. Marcus v. Township of Abington, 1993 U.S. Dist. LEXIS 18156 (E.D. Pa. 1993); Oxford-House Evergreen v. City of Plainfield, 769 F. Supp. 1329 (D.N.J. 1991); Bible Truth Crusade v. City of Bloomington, 709 F. Supp. 849 (C.D. Ill. 1989); Stephens v. Cobb Cty., 684 F. Supp. 703 (N.D. Ga. 1988).

263. 626 F.2d 607 (8th Cir. 1986).

ment.[264] SLAPP plaintiffs may also face court-imposed sanctions under Rule 11 of the Federal Rules of Civil Procedure and state counterparts.[265]

SLAPP plaintiffs may also face heightened pleading requirements that make it easier for a defendant to succeed in a motion to dismiss.[266] In addition, plaintiffs who are public figures must prove with "convincing clarity" that defendants acted with actual malice. Some courts have held that land-use developer plaintiffs who participate in the public approval process are public figures who must prove actual malice.[267]

Defendants have also brought counterclaims, called SLAPPbacks, against plaintiffs who bring SLAPP suits. These suits are based on theories such as malicious prosecution, abuse of process, or a violation of constitutional rights, and often are successful.[268]

Several states have adopted statutes limiting SLAPP suits.[269] These statutes typically allow defendants to file a motion to dismiss a lawsuit that is based upon the exercise of the right to petition under the federal or a state constitution, with a stay of discovery and an expedited motion for a hearing. The defendant must first show her conduct is protected by the statute.[270] The burden then shifts to the plaintiff to show a factual and legal basis for holding the defendant's speech is not protected,[271] or that there was no support or basis for the defen-

---

264. *See also* Nestor Colon & Sucesores, Inc. v. Custudio, 964 F.2d 32 (1st Cir. 1992); Fischer Sand and Aggregate Co. v. City of Lakeville, 874 F. Supp. 957 (Minn. 1994); Westfield Partners Ltd. v. Hogan, 740 F. Supp. 523 (N.D. Ill. 1990); Barnes Foundation v. Township of Lower Merion, 927 F. Supp. 874 (E.D. Pa. 1996); Weiss v. Willow Tree Civic Ass'n, 467 F. Supp. 803 (S.D.N.Y. 1979); Dixon v. Superior Ct., 36 Cal. Rptr. 2d 687 (Cal. App. 1994); Eastern Ky. Resources, Inc. v. Arnett, 892 S.W.2d 617 (Ky. App. 1995); 600 W. 15th St. Corp. v. Von Gutfield, 603 N.E.2d 930 (N.Y. 1992); § 5.48 (*Noerr-Pennington* doctrine).

265. Gordon v. Marrone, 616 N.Y.S.2d 98 (App. Div. 1994).

266. Protect Our Mountain Env't, Inc. (POME) v. District Ct., 677 P.2d 1361 (Colo. 1984) (applying sham exception to *Noerr-Pennington* doctrine). *Contra* Londono v. Turkey Creek, 609 So. 2d 14 (Fla. 1992).

267. Mount Juneau Enters., Inc. v. Juneau Empire, 891 P.2d 829 (Alaska 1995); Okum v. Superior Court of Los Angeles, 629 P.2d 1369 (Cal.), *cert. denied*, 454 U.S. 1099 (1981); SRW Assocs. v. Bellport Beach Property Owners, 517 N.Y.S.2d 741 (App. Div. 1987).

268. Leonardini v. Shell Oil Co., 264 Cal. Rptr. 883 (Cal. App. 1989) (upholding damage award in SLAPPback suit), *cert. denied*, 498 U.S. 919 (1990); Levin v. King, 648 N.E.2d 1108 (Ill. App. 1995) (plaintiff's suit dismissed; special injury not shown).

269. *E.g.*, Minn. Stat. Ann. § 554.01; Neb. Rev. Stat. §§ 25-21,241 to 21,246; N.Y. Civ. Rts. L. § 70-a; R.I. Gen. Laws § 9-33-2, *applied in* Hometown Props. v. Fleming, 680 A.2d 56 1996 (R.I. 1996); Wash. Rev. Code Ann. § 4.24.500.

270. Ludwig v. Superior Court, 43 Cal. Rptr.2d 350 (Cal. App. 1995) (recruiting and encouraging agents to oppose development protected; economic motive of defendant not disqualifying).

271. Cal. Code Civ. Procedure § 425.16 (plaintiff's "probability" of prevailing on claim), *applied in* Wilcox v. Superior Ct., 33 Cal. Rptr. 2d 446 (Cal. App. 1994). *See* Averill v. Superior Court, 50 Cal. Rptr. 2d 62 (Cal. App. 1996) (private communications covered). *But see* Opinion of

dant's statements or actions.[272] A prevailing defendant may recover costs, attorneys fees and compensatory and punitive damages.

---

Justices, 641 A.2d 1012 (N.H. (1994) (proposed statute unconstitutional for denying right to trial by jury).

**272.** Mass. Ann. Laws ch. 231, § 59H. *But see* Opinion of the Justices (SLAPP Suit Procedure), 641 A.2d 445 (N.H. 1994) (weighing pleadings and affidavits to determine "probability" of success would deny defendant right to jury trial on questions of fact).

# REFERENCES

## Books

J. Delaney, S. Abrams & F. Schnidman, Land Use Practice & Forms: Handling the Land Use Case (1997)

D. Mandelker, J. Gerard & T. Sullivan, Federal Land Use Law (updated annually).

S. Nahmod, Civil Rights and Civil Liberties Litigation: The Law of 1983 (3d ed. 1991).

G. Pring & P. Canan, SLAPPs: Getting Sued for Speaking Out (1996).

M. Schwartz & J. Kirklin, Section 1983 Litigation: Claims, Defenses, and Fees (2d ed. 1991).

## Articles

Alexander, Constitutional Torts, the Supreme Court, and the Law of Noncontradiction: An Essay on *Zinernon v. Burch,* 87 Nw. L. Rev. 576 (1993).

Ayer, The Primitive Law of Standing in Land Use Disputes: Some Notes from a Dark Continent, 55 Iowa L. Rev. 344 (1969).

Benson & Merriam, Identifying and Beating a Strategic Lawsuit Against Public Participation, 3 Duke Envtl. L. & Pol'y F. 17 (1993).

Blaesser, Closing the Federal Courthouse Door on Property Owners: The Ripeness and Abstention Doctrines in Section 1983 Land Use Cases, 2 Hofstra Prop. L.J. 73 (1989).

Borth, Municipal Tort Liability for Erroneous Issuance of Building Permits: A National Survey, 58 Wash. L. Rev. 537 (1983).

Brown, Correlating Municipal Liability and Official Immunity Under Section 1983, 1989 U. Ill. L. Rev. 625.

Cook & Merriam, Recognizing a SLAPP Suit and Understanding its Consequences, 19 Zoning & Plan. L. Rep. 33 (1996).

Cushman, Municipal Liability Under § 1983: Toward a New Definition of Municipal Policymaker, 34 B.C. L. Rev. 693 (1993).

Gerhardt, The *Monell* Legacy: Balancing Federalism Concerns and Municipal Accountability Under Section 1983, 62 S. Cal. L. Rev. 539 (1989).

Glover & Jimison, S.L.A.P.P. Suits: A First Amendment Issue and Beyond, 21 N.C. Cent. L.J. 122 (1995).

Hyson, The Problem of Relief in Developer-Initiated Exclusionary Zoning Litigation, 12 Urb. L. Ann. 21 (1976).

Kanner, Measure of Damages in Nonphysical Inverse Condemnation Cases, in Proceedings of the Institute of Planning, Zoning, and Eminent Domain, ch. 12 (1989).

LaRusso, "Paying for the Change,": *First English Evangelical Church of Glendale v. County of Los Angeles* and the Calculation of Interim Damages for Regulatory Takings, 17 B.C. Envtl. Aff. L. Rev. 551 (1990).

Lyman, Finality Ripeness in Federal Land Use Cases From *Hamilton Bank* to *Lucas,* 9 J. Land Use & Envtl. L. 101 (1994).

Mandelker, Inverse Condemnation: The Constitutional Limits of Public Responsibility, 1966 Wis. L. Rev. 3.

McCann, The Interrelationship of Immunity and the *Prima Facie* Case in Section 1983 and *Bivens* Actions, 21 Gonz. L. Rev. 115 (1985-86).

McNamara, Inverse Condemnation: A "Sophistic Miltonian Serbonian Bog," 31 Baylor L. Rev. 443 (1977).

Morgan, Exhaustion of Administrative Remedies as a Municipal Defense to Inverse Condemnation Actions, in Proceedings of the Institute on Planning, Zoning, and Eminent Domain ch. 9 (1985).

Oren, Signing Into Heaven: *Zinermon v. Burch,* Federal Rights, and State Remedies Thirty Years After *Monroe v. Pape,* 40 Emory L.J. 1 (1991).

Overstreet, The Ripeness Doctrine of the Taking Clause: A Survey of Decisions Showing Just How Far Federal Courts Will Go to Avoid Adjudicating Land Use Cases, 10 J. Envtl. & Land Use L. 91 (1994).

Prahl, The Rezoning Dilemma: What May a Court Do With an Invalid Zoning Classification?, 25 S.D.L. Rev. 116 (1980).

Rosen, The *Bivens* Constitutional Tort: An Unfulfilled Promise, 67 N.C.L. Rev. 337 (1989).

Stein, Pinpointing the Beginning and Ending of a Temporary Regulatory Taking, 70 Wash. L. Rev. 953 (1995).

Young, Federal Court Abstention and State Administrative Law From *Burford* to *Ankenbrandt:* Fifty Years of Judicial Federalism Under *Burford v. Sun Oil Co.* and Kindred Doctrines, 42 DePaul L. Rev. 859 (1993).

**Student Work**

Note, Beyond Invalidation: The Judicial Power to Zone, 9 Urb. L. Ann. 159 (1975).

Note, Exhaustion of Remedies in Zoning Cases, 1964 Wash. U.L.Q. 368.

Note, From *Parratt* to *Zinermon:* Authorization, Adequacy, and Immunity in a System Analysis of State Procedure, 11 Cardozo L. Rev. 831 (1990).

Note, Qualifying Immunity in Section 1983 & *Bivens* Actions, 71 Tex. L. Rev. 123 (1992).

Note, Reforming SLAPP Reform: New York's Anti-SLAPP Statute, 70 N.Y.U.L. Rev. 1324 (1995).

Note, Standing to Challenge Exclusionary Land Use Control Devices in Federal Courts After *Warth v. Seldin,* 29 Stan. L. Rev. 323 (1977).

Comment, Silencing SLAPPs: An Examination of Proposed Legislative Remedies and a "Solution" for Florida, 20 Fla. St. U.L. Rev. 487 (1992).

Casenote, Characterization of Land Use Decisions: A Zone of Uncertainty, 37 Vill. L. Rev. 663 (1992).

# Chapter 9

# RESIDENTIAL DEVELOPMENT CONTROLS

## § 9.01. An Introductory Note.

In addition to the zoning ordinance, municipalities also adopt controls that apply primarily to residential development. These include subdivision control and planned unit development regulation. Subdivision controls are authorized by separate enabling legislation. Planned unit development regulations are usually contained in the zoning ordinance and are not usually specifically authorized by legislation. This chapter discusses these controls, including the exactions that are demanded from developers in the development approval process.

## A. SUBDIVISION CONTROL.

### § 9.02. History and Purpose.

States first enacted subdivision control legislation toward the close of the nineteenth century to remedy land conveyancing problems. Land historically had been conveyed by its legal description, a confusing and unreliable method that often led to boundary disputes. Land developers began to plat land they intended to develop into lots and blocks so that they could avoid conveyancing difficulties by conveying individual lots within the plat. Early subdivision laws required the recording of subdivision plats in the local records office, after which the conveyance of lots within the subdivision could be made "with reference" to the plat.

Subdivision control legislation was next amended to remedy problems in street planning. Street systems in early subdivisions often were not aligned with existing streets. To remedy this problem, some states amended their subdivision control legislation to require subdivision plats to comply with the municipal street plan.

The Standard City Planning Enabling Act used these early subdivision platting statutes as a model for subdivision control enabling legislation which was included in the Act. The Standard Act authorized subdivision control ordinances to require streets and other necessary improvements, access to the subdivision, and limitations on density. Most state subdivision control legislation is based on the Standard Act or on two similar statutory models proposed somewhat later.[1] Some modern subdivision control statutes add to these requirements. They require additional on-site improvements, prohibit subdivisions in floodplains and environmentally sensitive areas, and authorize the approval of subdivisions only if public facilities are adequate.

Subdivision controls apply when land is subdivided for development and usually apply only to residential development. They do not usually apply to non-residential and multi-family residential development because this type of development usually occurs on unsubdivided land. Subdivision controls do not regulate the use of land. They require compliance with design and public facility standards and the provision of streets and other public improvements that are necessary for the subdivision. They may also require subdividers to dedicate land or make monetary payments for off-site improvements when the subdivision creates a need for them. Subdivision controls may contain restrictions that duplicate the zoning ordinance, such as a prohibition on the development of unsuitable land or a minimum lot size requirement.

---

1. E. Bassett, F. Williams, A. Bettman & R. Whitten, Model Laws for Planning Cities, Counties and States 39-47, 84-88 (1935).

Many states also have public health programs that affect subdivision development. They authorize state health and environmental agencies to regulate on-site wells and on-site sewage disposal through septic tanks and similar facilities.[2]

## § 9.03. Enabling Legislation.

Sections 13 and 14 of the Standard Planning Act provided the legislative enabling authority for subdivision control:

> § 13. Whenever a planning commission shall have adopted a major street plan . . . [on file in the county recorder's office], then no plat of a subdivision of land § shall be filed or recorded until it shall have been approved by such planning commission. . . .

> § 14. Before exercising . . . [subdivision control] powers . . . the planning commission shall adopt regulations governing the subdivision of land within its jurisdiction. Such regulations may provide for the proper arrangement of streets in relation to other existing or planned streets and to the master plan, for adequate and convenient open spaces for traffic, utilities, access of firefighting apparatus, recreation, light and air, and for the avoidance of congestion of population, including minimum width and areas of lots.

> Such regulations may include provisions as to the extent to which streets and other ways shall be graded and improved and to which water and sewer and other utility mains, piping, or other facilities shall be installed as a condition precedent to the approval of the plat. . . .

This legislation contains several important elements. The authority to approve subdivisions is granted to the planning commission. Many state statutes follow this model,[3] but some states grant approval authority to the local governing body.[4]

In other states, the governing body may delegate the authority to approve subdivisions to the planning commission.[5] The planning commission must "adopt regulations" governing the subdivision of land. These regulations implement standards contained in the subdivision control ordinance.

The Standard Act authorized the adoption of a subdivision control ordinance after the municipality had adopted a master street plan. Other statutes go further

---

2. Md. Envt. Code Ann. § 9-204; N.H. Rev. Stat. Ann. § 485:30. *See* Erb v. Maryland Dep't of the Envt., 676 A.2d 1017 (Md. App. (1996) (denial of permit for on-site septic tank held not a taking).

3. Marx v. Zoning Bd. of Appeals, 529 N.Y.S.2d 330 (App. Div. 1988).

4. Cal. Gov't Code § 66411.

5. N.J. Stat. Ann. § 40:55D-37.

and require subdivisions to be consistent with the local comprehensive plan.[6] In *Board of County Comm'rs v. Gaster*,[7] the court held the board could disapprove a subdivision that did not comply with the comprehensive plan even though it met all zoning requirements.

Subdivision control legislation defines the scope of subdivision control authority. The Standard Planning Act authorized subdivision controls for streets and other improvements and included the authority to impose controls "for the avoidance of congestion of population."[8] Most subdivision control statutes contain comparable provisions,[9] and some extend the scope of subdivision control authority. California authorizes the denial of a subdivision if the "site is not physically suitable" for the type or density of development or if the "design of the improvements is likely to cause substantial environmental damage."[10] Other states authorize the denial of a subdivision because of flooding or other environmental effects.[11]

Section 12 of the Standard Act authorized municipalities to regulate subdivisions in an extraterritorial area five miles beyond the municipal limits, most states confer the power to control subdivisions in extraterritorial areas,[12] and the courts have upheld this authority.[13]

---

6. Cal. Gov't Code § 66474(a); 65 Ill. Comp. Stat. Ann. 5/ 11-12-8 (official map). *See* Board of County Comm'rs v. Condor, 927 P.2d 1339 (Colo. 1996); Lake City Corp. v. City of Mequon, 558 N.W.2d 100 (Wis. 1997).

7. 401 A.2d 666 (Md. 1979).

8. §§ 3.05, 3.12

9. Colo. Rev. Stat. § 30-28-133; N.J. Stat. Ann. § 40:55D-38.

10. Cal. Gov't Code § 66474. *See* Topanga Ass'n for a Scenic Community v. County of Los Angeles, 263 Cal. Rptr. 214 (Cal. App. 1989) (statute requires independent environmental review); Sequoyah Hills Homeowners Ass'n v. City of Oakland, 29 Cal. Rptr. 2d 182 (Cal. App. 1994) (upholding approval based on compliance with plan policies).

11. Ariz. Rev. Stat. Ann. § 9-463.01(C)(4); Mont. Code Ann. § 76-3-608(3); Burrell v. Lake County Plan Comm'n, 624 N.E.2d 526 (Ind. App. 1993) (upholds rejection because of septic tank leaching and increased flooding and drainage problems); Manthe v. Town Bd., 555 N.W.2d 167 (Wis. App. 1996) (upholds ordinance requiring public sewer service).

12. *E.g.,* Kan. Stat. Ann. §§ 12-749, 12-750.

13. Petterson v. City of Naperville, 137 N.E.2d 371 (Ill. 1956). *See* City of Carlsbad v. Caviness, 346 P.2d 310 (N.M. 1959) (does not include zoning power). *See also* §§ 4.22, 4.23.

## § 9.04. The Subdivision Control Process.

Most subdivision control ordinances authorize a standard subdivision review process. The process may begin with a preapplication conference in which the reviewing agency considers a sketch and general map of the subdivision and provides guidance on subdivision control requirements. Submission of a preliminary plat follows and is the first formal step in the approval of a subdivision. The preliminary plat contains all of the detailed elements the subdivision ordinance requires for approval of the final plat. The right to subdivide may vest after the preliminary plat is approved.[14] The subdivider may usually begin the construction of improvements after the preliminary plat is approved, and the municipality may require a bond as surety for their completion prior to final approval.[15]

Final approval of the subdivision comes next. Before the final plat is approved, the subdivider must obtain a certification that subdivision improvements are properly completed. Some municipalities require submission of two plats at this stage. One is called an "engineering plat" and is used internally to determine whether the required improvements have been completed. The second is a "plat for record," which shows necessary land title and boundary information. This plat is recorded after it is approved, and lots in the subdivision may then be offered for sale.

## § 9.05. Definition of "Subdivision."

Section 1 of the Standard Act defines a subdivision as a division of a lot for the "purpose of sale or building development," and this definition has been adopted in some statutes, as in the Connecticut statute discussed below. Many subdivision control statutes define a subdivision as a division of land into a minimum number of lots.[16] This type of statutory definition excludes developments on individual lots from the subdivision control ordinance[17] and encourages evasion by builders who build only a few homes at a time.[18] The courts have held that the sale of land for condominium development is not a subdivision, but some subdivision control statutes include these developments.[19]

---

14. § 9.07.

15. *See* the Standard Act, § 14.

16. Conn. Gen. Stat. § 8-18 (three or more); Mass. Gen. L. ch. 41, § 81L (two or more).

17. Vinyard v. St. Louis County, 399 S.W.2d 99 (Mo. 1966).

18. *See* State ex rel. Dreher v. Fuller, 849 P.2d 1045 (Mont. 1993) (rebuttable presumption of evasion authorized by state statute and does not violate due process).

19. Gerber v. Town of Clarkstown, 356 N.Y.S.2d 926 (Sup. Ct. 1974). *See* Cal. Gov't Code § 66426 (included); N.H. Rev. Stat. Ann. § 672:14 (same). *Accord*, Town of York v. Cragin, 541 A.2d 932 (Me. 1988); Cohen v. Town of Henniker, 593 A.2d 1145 (N.H. 1991).

Some statutes, as in Connecticut, define a subdivision as a division of land for the "purpose . . . of sale or building development."[20] When landowners have sold lots for residential development without formally subdividing, some courts have held that the land was not sold "singly or collectively for residential purposes" or that the landowner did not hold himself out as a subdivider.[21] Most courts hold that a subdivision control ordinance cannot modify the "subdivision" definition which is in the statute.[22]

Subdivision control legislation usually contains exemptions from subdivision control regulation. The subdivision of land for agricultural use is one example.[23] Other statutes exempt the subdivision of small tracts if no additional streets are created.[24]

### § 9.06. Relationship to Zoning.

Some subdivision control legislation provides that subdivisions must comply with the zoning ordinance.[25] Even if the subdivision control legislation does not contain this requirement, a municipality may reject a subdivision if it does not comply with the zoning ordinance[26] or may require zoning compliance in its subdivision control ordinance.[27] Subdivision review cannot be used to amend the zoning ordinance because this would usurp the local zoning authority.[28] Compli-

---

20. Conn. Gen. Stat. § 8-18.

21. Slavin v. Ingraham, 339 N.E.2d 157 (N.Y. 1975). *See also* State ex rel. Anaya v. Select W. Lands, Inc., 613 P.2d 425 (N.M. App. 1979); Herrick v. Ingraham, 363 N.Y.S.2d 665 (App. Div. 1975).

22. Penobscot, Inc. v. Board of County Comm'rs, 642 P.2d 915 (Colo. 1982); Peninsula Corp. v. Planning & Zoning Comm'n, 199 A.2d 1 (Conn. 1964); State v. Visser, 767 P.2d 858 (Mont. 1988) (exemption); Dearborn v. Town of Milford, 411 A.2d 1132 (N.H. 1980); Martorano v. Board of Comm'rs, 414 A.2d 411 (Pa. Commw. 1980). *Contra* Delaware Midland Corp. v. Incorporated Village of Westhampton Beach, 359 N.Y.S.2d 944 (Sup. Ct. 1974), *aff'd,* 355 N.E.2d 302 (N.Y. 1976).

23. N.J. Stat. Ann. § 40:55D-7 (over five acres).

24. Cal. Gov't Code § 66426. *See* Urban v. Planning Bd. of Manasquan, 592 A.2d 240 (N.J. 1991) (subdivision of nonconforming lots). *But see* Sugarman v. Lewis, 488 A.2d 709 (R.I. 1985).

25. N.J. Stat. Ann. § 40:55D-38(b)(1).

26. Krawski v. Planning & Zoning Comm'n, 575 A.2d 1036 (Conn. App. 1990); People v. City of Park Ridge, 166 N.E.2d 635 (Ill. App. 1960); Loveless v. Yantis, 513 P.2d 1023 (Wash. 1973).

27. Benny v. City of Alameda, 164 Cal. Rptr. 776 (Cal. App. 1980). *See also* Town of Sun Prairie v. Storms, 327 N.W.2d 642 (Wis. 1983) (may include minimum lot size requirement in subdivision ordinance).

28. Cristofaro v. Town of Burlington, 584 A.2d 1168 (Conn. 1991); Shapiro v. Town of Oyster Bay, 211 N.Y.S.2d 414 (Sup. Ct. 1961), *aff'd,* 249 N.Y.S.2d 663 (App. Div. 1964); Goodman v. Board of Comm'rs, 411 A.2d 838 (Pa. Commw. 1980); Snyder v. Zoning Bd., 200 A.2d 222 (R.I. 1964).

ance with the zoning ordinance is not sufficient when the subdivision control ordinance imposes additional requirements.[29]

## § 9.07. Vested Rights.

Vested rights problems arise under subdivision controls as well as zoning ordinances.[30] The mere recording of a plat without street dedications does not create a vested right that exempts the subdivider from complying with subdivision control requirements that are adopted later.[31] The approval of a preliminary plat does not create a vested right in the absence of statutory authority that gives it this effect.[32] Some statutes require the approval of a final plat if it meets the requirements imposed when the municipality approved the preliminary plat.[33] The courts hold that the approval of a final plat that meets these requirements is a ministerial act they can mandate under these statutes, and that the approving agency may not impose additional requirements as the basis for final approval.[34]

Although the Standard Act did not protect an approved subdivision against subsequent changes in a zoning ordinance,[35] some subdivision control statutes protect the subdivider against future zoning and other changes in land use regulations. The Pennsylvania statute, which is typical, protects the subdivider for five years after preliminary or final approval of a subdivision plat from any "subsequent change or amendment in the zoning, subdivision or other governing ordinance or plan."[36] Other statutes provide similar protection.[37] These statutes

---

29. Shoptaugh v. Board of County Comm'rs, 543 P.2d 524 (Colo. App. 1976); Popular Refreshments, Inc. v. Fuller's Milk Bar, Inc., 205 A.2d 445 (N.J. App. Div. 1964).

30. §§ 6.12-6.23. *See also* McFillan v. Berkeley County Planning Comm'n, 438 S.E.2d 801 (W. Va. 1993) (applies nonconforming use principles to subdivision regulation).

31. Blevens v. City of Manchester, 170 A.2d 121 (N.H. 1961); Lake Intervale Homes, Inc. v. Parsippany-Troy Hills, 147 A.2d 28 (N.J. 1958); In re McCormick Mgt. Co., 547 A.2d 1319 (Vt. 1988). *But see* Board of County Comm'rs v. Goldenrod Corp., 601 P.2d 360 (Colo. App. 1979).

32. Boutet v. Planning Bd., 253 A.2d 53 (Me. 1969).

33. Cal. Gov't Code § 66458; Pa. Stat. Ann. tit. 53, § 10508(4). *See* Golden State Homebuilding Assocs. v. City of Modesto, 31 Cal. Rptr. 2d 572 (Cal. App. 1994).

34. Youngblood v. Board of Supvrs., 586 P.2d 556 (Cal. 1979); Hakim v. Board of Comm'rs, 366 A.2d 1306 (Pa. Commw. 1976).

35. R.A. Vachon & Son v. City of Concord, 289 A.2d 646 (N.H. 1972). *See also* Dawe v. City of Scottsdale, 581 P.2d 1136 (Ariz. 1978). *But see* Western Land Equities, Inc. v. City of Logan, 617 P.2d 388 (Utah 1980), discussed in § 6.16. *Compare* Wood v. North Salt Lake, 390 P.2d 858 (Utah 1964).

36. Pa. Stat. Ann. tit. 53, § 10508(4). *See also* Friends of the Law v. King County, 869 P.2d 1056 (Wash. 1994) (interprets statute extending common law vested rights doctrine to subdivisions).

37. Conn. Gen. Stat. § 8-26a; Mass. Gen. L. ch. 40A, § 6; N.J. Stat. Ann. § 40:55D-49; Va. Code § 15.1-475(D). *See* Ellington Constr. Corp. v. Zoning Bd., 566 N.E.2d 128 (N.Y. 1990) (sufficient expenditures to vest rights).

protect against changes in local but not state land use requirements and regulations.[38]

### § 9.08. Enforcement.

The enforcement of subdivision control ordinances is difficult because evasion of the ordinance is difficult to control. The Standard Planning Act required the approval of a subdivision before it could be recorded. The Act did not require the approval of a subdivision if the subdivider did not wish to record it. The Act attempted to prevent evasion by authorizing a monetary penalty whenever a landowner sold "by reference to or exhibition" of a plat for a subdivision that was not approved under the subdivision control ordinance.[39] This sanction does not prevent evasion because a landowner can subdivide her land and sell lots by the legal description without going through the subdivision approval process.

Some statutes avoid this problem by requiring the approval of all subdivisions under the subdivision control ordinance, whether or not they are recorded.[40] To make this requirement effective, the statute should include a broad definition of the subdivisions subject to regulation.[41] The Standard Act authorized municipalities to enjoin the sale of lots in an unapproved subdivision.[42]

A sanction that goes too far may be invalid. An example is a statute or ordinance that prohibits the sale or conveyance of land in a subdivision until it is approved in the subdivision control process and recorded. Provisions of this type have been held invalid as a restraint on alienation.[43] A milder and often effective sanction authorizes the denial of building permits for dwellings in subdivisions that are not approved under the subdivision control ordinance.[44] This sanction may create problems because it places the penalty for lack of compliance on the buyer of a lot in an unapproved subdivision. The courts have refused to authorize the withholding of a building permit from an innocent purchaser in this situation.[45]

---

**38.** Island Props., Inc. v. Martha's Vineyard Comm'n, 361 N.E.2d 385 (Mass. 1977); Ocean Acres v. State, 403 A.2d 967 (N.J. App. Div. 1979).

**39.** Standard Planning Act § 16. *See* Commonwealth v. Fisher, 350 A.2d 428 (Pa. Commw. 1976) (penalty not a restraint on alienation).

**40.** Conn. Gen. Stat. § 8-25.

**41.** § 9.05.

**42.** *See* N.Y. Town Law § 268(2). *See also* Lake Cty. v. Truett, 758 S.W.2d 529 (Tenn. App. 1988) (court will not compel compliance or posting of bond).

**43.** Kass v. Lewin, 104 So. 2d 572 (Fla. 1958).

**44.** Wash. Rev. Code Ann. § 58.17.210.

**45.** Keizer v. Adams, 471 P.2d 983 (Cal. 1970); State ex rel. Craven v. City of Tacoma, 385 P.2d 372 (Wash. 1963).

A subdivision control statute may prohibit the issuance of a building permit except on a lot abutting a street that is "suitably improved" to the satisfaction of the municipality.[46] This sanction allows the municipality to use the leverage of street improvements to compel compliance with the subdivision control ordinance. Opportunities for evasion remain if the statute or ordinance exempts construction along an existing street or highway. A builder can build one house at a time along an improved street or highway without subdivision approval.[47]

### § 9.09. Scope of Authority: Discretion to Approve or Reject.

Courts tend to construe subdivision control legislation based on the Standard Act and subdivision control ordinances strictly. They reverse subdivision disapprovals if the reason for disapproval is not authorized by the Standard Act or the subdivision control ordinance and invalidate requirements in subdivision control ordinances if they are not authorized by the Standard Act.[48] Courts take a more generous view of local subdivision control powers in states where the statute is broader than the Standard Act[49] or if they are asked to imply authority to impose physical requirements on development.[50] The courts supervise the subdivision control process closely. They require statements of reasons for subdivision disapprovals and may mandamus the approval of a subdivision if the reason for disapproval is not authorized by the statute or the ordinance.[51]

---

**46.** Brous v. Smith, 106 N.E.2d 503 (N.Y. 1952) (upholding requirement).

**47.** *See also* State v. Baker, 618 P.2d 997 (Or. App. 1980) (criminal prosecution); 77 A.L.R.3d 1058 (1977).

**48.** Richardson v. City of Little Rock Planning Comm'n, 747 S.W.2d 115 (Ark. 1988); Board of County Comm'rs v. Condor, 927 P.2d 1339 (Colo. 1996) (remanding case); Dosmann v. Area Plan Comm'n, 312 N.E.2d 880 (Ind. App. 1974); Snyder v. Owensboro, 528 S.W.2d 663 (Ky. 1975); O'Dell v. City of Eagan, 348 N.W.2d 792 (Minn. App. 1984); J.E.D. Assocs. v. Town of Sandown, 430 A.2d 129 (N.H. 1981); Pizzo Mantin Group v. Township of Randolph, 645 A.2d 89 (N.J. 1994); Goodman v. Board of Comm'rs, 411 A.2d 838 (Pa. Commw. 1980); Carlson v. Town of Beaux Arts Village, 704 P.2d 663 (Wash. App. 1983); 11 A.L.R.2d 524 (1960). *See also* Reynolds v. City Council, 680 P.2d 1350 (Colo. App. 1984); Moscowitz v. Planning & Zoning Comm'n, 547 A.2d 569 (Conn. App. 1988); Lee v. Maryland Nat'l Capital Park & Plan. Comm'n, 668 A.2d 980 (Md. App. 1995).

**49.** Smith v. Zoning Bd. of Appeals, 629 A.2d 1089 (Conn. 1993) (historic factors), *cert. denied,* 510 U.S. 1164 (1994); Durant v. Town of Dunbarton, 430 A.2d 140 (N.H. 1981); Jones v. Town of Woodway, 425 P.2d 904 (Wash. 1967). *See also* Carmel Valley View, Ltd. v. Board of Supvrs., 130 Cal. Rptr. 249 (Cal. App. 1976).

**50.** North Landers Corp. v. Planning Bd., 416 N.E.2d 934 (Mass. 1981) (adequate access); Emerald Lakes, Inc. v. South Russell Planning Comm'n, 598 N.E.2d 60 (Ohio App. 1991) (allowing rejection of plat for inadequate groundwater supplies).

**51.** El Dorado at Santa Fe, Inc. v. Board of County Comm'rs, 551 P.2d 1360 (N.M. 1976). *See* § 8.13.

The strict view of the scope of subdivision control authority is illustrated by *Smith v. City of Mobile*.[52] The planning commission rejected a subdivision because it was "out of character" with other lots in the area. The subdivision ordinance provided that "[t]he size, width, depth, shape and orientation of lots ... shall be appropriate to the location of the subdivision." The court held that this provision did not authorize the rejection of a subdivision for the reason given by the commission. "[T]he exercise of ... discretion must be guided and limited by clearly drawn standards which can be uniformly applied."[53] The court granted a writ of mandamus that compelled the municipality to approve the subdivision.

Scope of authority questions also arise when municipalities attempt to use subdivision controls for growth management or fiscal purposes. A few states expressly authorize the disapproval of a subdivision when public facilities are inadequate[54] or when the subdivision would be "scattered or premature" because of service inadequacies or health problems.[55] In the absence of statutory authority, the courts have usually overturned subdivision disapprovals for growth management or fiscal reasons. In *Interladco, Inc. v. Billings*,[56] the court overturned a subdivision denial when the record indicated that the county "did not want a development of single-family residences isolated from other developed urban areas, even though their subdivision regulations had no such restrictions." Nor may a municipality reject a subdivision because it imposes a burden on school or other public facilities if the statute or ordinance does not authorize this reason for disapproval.[57]

Courts easily uphold subdivision disapprovals based on inadequate access or other problems relating to the street system.[58] *Forest Constr. Co. v. Planning &*

---

**52.** 374 So. 2d 305 (Ala. 1979). *See also* Sonn v. Planning Comm'n, 374 A.2d 159 (Conn. 1976); Christopher Estates, Inc. v. Parish of East Baton Rouge, 413 So. 2d 1336 (La. App. 1982); State ex rel. Schaefer v. Cleveland, 847 S.W.2d 867 (Mo. App. 1993); Kaufman v. Planning & Zoning Comm'n, 298 S.E.2d 148 (W. Va. 1982). *But see* Fleckinger v. Jefferson Parish Council, 510 So. 2d 429 (La. App. 1987); City of Jackson v. Ridgway, 258 So. 2d 439 (Miss. 1972).

**53.** 374 So. 2d at 309. *See also* Ghent v. Planning Comm'n, 594 A.2d 5 (Conn. 1991); Hixon v. Walker County, 468 S.E.2d 744 (Ga. 1996).

**54.** Md. Envt. Code Ann. § 9-512.

**55.** N.H. Rev. Stat. Ann. § 674:36(II)(a). *See* Ettlingen Homes, Inc. v. Town of Derry, 681 A.2d 97 (N.H. 1996); Zukis v. Town of Fitzwilliam, 604 A.2d 956 (N.H. 1992); Garipay v. Town of Hanover, 351 A.2d 64 (N.H. 1976).

**56.** 538 P.2d 496 (Colo. App. 1975).

**57.** Beach v. Planning & Zoning Comm'n, 103 A.2d 814 (Conn. 1954); Baltimore Planning Comm'n v. Victor Dev. Co., 275 A.2d 478 (Md. 1971).

**58.** Raybestos-Manhattan, Inc. v. Planning & Zoning Comm'n, 442 A.2d 65 (Conn. 1982); Oakes Constr. Co. v. City of Iowa City, 304 N.W.2d 797 (Iowa 1981); Burke & McCaffrey, Inc. v. City of Merriam, 424 P.2d 483 (Kan. 1967); North Landers Corp. v. Planning Bd., 416 N.E.2d 934 (Mass. 1981); Mac-Rich Realty Constr., Inc. v. Planning Bd., 341 N.E.2d 916 (Mass. App. 1976); Batch v. Town of Chapel Hill, 387 S.E.2d 655 (N.C. 1990) (citing treatise); Prudential Trust Co. v. City of Laramie, 492 P.2d 971 (Wyo. 1972).

*Zoning Comm'n*[59] is a typical case. The commission rejected a subdivision because it provided only one access for 110 lots, causing all traffic from the subdivision to enter one street intersection. The court held that the denial was within the commission's authority to reject subdivisions that would be hazardous to the health and welfare of the community. A municipality may also reject a subdivision because of drainage and fire hazard problems.[60] The disapproval of a subdivision can raise taking of property problems.[61]

Municipalities sometimes reject a subdivision because it has unacceptable off-site impacts. A rejection for this reason raises statutory authority and taking of property problems. In *Pearson Kent Corp. v. Bear,*[62] the commission rejected a subdivision, "not because it regarded the plan itself as intrinsically not acceptable," but because it would cause traffic congestion that would create danger to nearby residents. The court held that although the local charter and subdivision control law were "addressed to approval or disapproval internal to the subdivision," the commission was not prevented from considering "the impact of the proposed development on adjacent territory and property within its jurisdiction."

The court took a somewhat different view of this problem in *Baker v. Planning Bd.,*[63] which was decided under a similar statute. An area of a proposed subdivision served as a retention pond in which water accumulated during heavy rains and snowstorms. The drainage system that would serve the subdivision was adequate, but the municipality refused to approve the subdivision. It stated that the development of the subdivision would destroy the retention pond, which would overtax a downstream drainage system and require public expenditure for its improvement.

The court held the statute did not authorize the disapproval of the subdivision for these reasons and suggested a taking problem. It noted that "a planning board may not exercise its authority to disapprove a plan so that a town may continue

---

**59.** 236 A.2d 917 (Conn. 1967).

**60.** Shoptaugh v. Board of County Comm'rs, 543 P.2d 524 (Colo. App. 1976); Brown v. City of Joliet, 247 N.E.2d 47 (Ill. App. 1969); Hamilton v. .Planning Bd., 345 N.E.2d 906 (Mass. App. 1976); Christianson v. Gasvoda, 789 P.2d 1234 (Mont. 1990) (drainage and flooding); El Shaer v. Planning Bd., 592 A.2d 565 (N.J. App. Div. 1991) (same). *See also* Sansoucy v. Planning Bd., 246 N.E.2d 811 (Mass. 1969) (underground utility lines).

**61.** Smith v. Town of Wolfeboro, 615 A.2d 1252 (N.H. 1992) (finding no taking under nuisance exception to Supreme Court's *Lucas* decision); McFillan v. Berkeley County Planning Comm'n, 438 S.E.2d 801 (W. Va. 1993) (no taking; expansion of mobile home park denied). *See* § 2.17.

**62.** 271 N.E.2d 218 (N.Y. 1971). *See also* North Landers Corp. v. Planning Bd., 416 N.E.2d 934 (Mass. 1981); Garipay v. Town of Hanover, 351 A.2d 64 (N.H. 1976).

**63.** 228 N.E.2d 831 (Mass. 1967). *See also* Wood Bros. Homes v. City of Colorado Springs, 568 P.2d 487 (Colo. 1977); Sowin Assocs. v. Planning & Zoning Comm'n, 580 A.2d 91 (Conn. App. 1990); Florham Park Inv. Assocs. v. Planning Bd., 224 A.2d 352 (N.J.L. Div. 1966); De Leo v. Lecraw, 334 N.Y.S.2d 912 (App. Div. 1972).

to use the owner's land as a water storage area and thereby deprive the owner of the reasonable use of it."

## § 9.10. Variances.

Municipalities have enough flexibility in the subdivision control process to modify subdivision control requirements if they believe this is advisable.[64] Some statutes authorize variances or exceptions,[65] and a variance provision may require statutory authority.[66] The criteria for subdivision control variances are similar to those for zoning variances,[67] but the cases on subdivision control variances are limited and inconclusive.[68] *Baum v. Lunsford*[69] assumed a hardship variance from the subdivision ordinance required a lesser burden of proof than a zoning hardship variance but held that a landowner was not entitled to the variance simply to prevent a financial loss.

## § 9.11. Exactions.

Subdivision control ordinances often require uncompensated exactions from subdividers. A subdivision exaction is an internal subdivision improvement, a dedication of land for a public facility, or a fee in lieu of dedication that the municipality can use to provide a public facility. Municipalities may require land dedications, or in-lieu fees may be required for off-site streets and other improvements and for parks and schools, which may or may not be on-site. Subdivision control ordinances authorize an in-lieu fee rather than a land dedication within the subdivision because a subdivision may not be large enough to provide a site for public facilities or because the municipality may prefer to locate them elsewhere. The impact fee is another type of exaction. It is usually levied as a condition to the issuance of building permits to pay for off-site facilities such as water and sewage treatment facilities. Exactions have become an important and highly contentious part of land use law. Their use and cost has increased as local governments find themselves financially pressed to find revenues for necessary capital facilities.

---

64. Canter v. Planning Bd., 390 N.E.2d 1128 (Mass. App. 1979).

65. N.J. Stat. Ann. § 40:55D-51(a).

66. South E. Prop. Owners & Residents Ass'n v. City Plan Comm'n, 244 A.2d 394 (Conn. 1968).

67. §§ 6.40-6.52.

68. Caruso v. Planning Bd., 238 N.E.2d 872 (Mass. 1968); Mac-Rich Realty Constr., Inc. v. Planning Bd., 341 N.E.2d 916 (Mass. App. 1976); Smith v. Township Comm., 244 A.2d 145 (N.J. App. Div. 1968).

69. 365 S.E.2d 739 (Va. 1988). *See also* Arrigo v. Planning Bd., 429 N.E.2d 355 (Mass. App. 1981); Garden State Homes, Inc. v. Heusner, 400 N.Y.S.2d 598 (App. Div. 1977).

The principal questions raised by subdivision exactions and impact fees are whether the municipality has the statutory authority to impose them and whether they are a taking of property. Whether a court will find the necessary statutory authority for a subdivision exaction depends on how broadly it interprets the subdivision control statute, which does not usually authorize exactions. Impact fees present an additional statutory authority problem if a court holds that the fee is a tax, because most states do not authorize municipalities to levy this type of tax. Controversy over exactions has led a number of states to adopt statutes that determine how exactions may be used in the land development process. Municipalities may also be able to impose subdivision exactions and impact fees under their home rule powers.[70]

### § 9.12.  The Taking Tests.

In the decades before the Supreme Court changed the roles that apply to exactions, the state courts had adopted a variety of tests[71] to decide whether a subdivision control exaction is a taking of property, These tests require a showing that the exaction is "reasonably related" to a need created by the subdivision, that there is a "rational nexus" between the exaction and that need, or that the exaction is "specifically and uniquely attributable" to the subdivision. The differences between these tests are semantic. All of them require a reasonable relationship between the exaction and a need created by the subdivision, and they differ only in the degree to which this relationship must be shown. The text uses the term "nexus test" to describe the various tests the state courts apply to exactions.

The nexus test is an example of the cost internalization theory that justifies zoning restrictions. Zoning internalizes costs by prohibiting development that imposes external costs on adjacent land uses. An example is a zoning ordinance that prohibits industrial uses in residential zoning districts. The nexus test internalizes costs by requiring subdividers to contribute to public improvements when the subdivision creates the need for them. The Supreme Court has adopted a "rough proportionality" test for exactions which is more stringent than the nexus test adopted by the state courts, and which applies to exactions that developers challenge in state courts.

---

**70.** § 4.28.

**71.** *See also* applying now-discredited right-privilege distinction, Ridgefield Land Co. v. City of Detroit, 217 N.W.2d 58 (Mich. 1926) (dismissing taking objection by holding right to subdivide is a privilege); Mid-Continent Bldrs., Inc. v. Midwest City, 539 P.2d 1377 (Okla. 1975) (same).

### § 9.13. *Nollan* and What It Means: Applying the Nexus Test.

In *Nollan v. California Coastal Comm'n*,[72] the first Supreme Court exaction case, the Court held a California coastal permit condition that required an easement to cross the beach of a beachfront house was a taking. The Court held the "essential nexus" between the permit condition and the justification for the condition was lacking. It also held it would closely examine a government regulation to determine whether it "substantially" advanced a "legitimate" governmental interest, as required by the taking clause.

The Court cited a long line of state exaction cases with approval, but its formulation of the nexus test appears more stringent than the nexus test the state courts apply. However, the Court did not hold the coastal permit exaction requirement facially unconstitutional but held only that the exaction requirement in that case was a taking of property as applied. The Court also indicated it would uphold a wide variety of coastal permit exactions, including a condition that required a coastal property owner to provide a viewpoint access if this was necessary to remedy the impact her development had on coastal views.

The *Nollan* nexus requirement for exactions has not been difficult to meet in most cases, especially when the exaction was imposed comprehensively as part of a regulatory scheme.[73] The *Nollan* test will invalidate an exaction when a nexus between the exaction and the regulatory purpose it is intended to implement is clearly lacking. In one post-*Nollan* case, for example,[74] the city demanded that a property owner dedicate land for the improvement of an imperfect street alignment as a condition to a permit for the renovation of a residential structure for office use. The court held there was no nexus between the renovation and the dedication, which was required to implement a general plan requirement for the realignment of the street. *Nollan* has also led courts to find a taking when an access dedication requirement is not related to the development of the landowner's property.[75]

---

72. 483 U.S. 625 (1987), discussed in § 2.16.

73. Leroy Land Co. v. Tahoe Regional Planning Agency, 939 F.2d 696 (9th Cir. 1991) (environmental mitigation); Gardner v. New Jersey Pinelands Comm'n, 593 A.2d 251 (N.J. 1991) (upholding exaction requiring restriction of housing in agricultural area of New Jersey Pinelands to agricultural use with option to build five clustered homes); Schoonover v. Klamath Cty., 806 P.2d 156 (Or. App.) (requiring annexation to fire district for fire protection), *cert. denied*, 502 U.S. 940 (1991).

74. Rohn v. City of Vasalia, 263 Cal. Rptr. 319 (Cal. App. 1989). *See also* Jones Ins. Trust v. City of Ft. Smith, 731 F. Supp. 912 (D. Or. 1992) (convenience store did not create enough traffic to justify street widening).

75. Surfside Colony, Ltd. v. California Coastal Comm'n, 277 Cal. Rptr. 371 (Cal. App. 1991) (beach access); Paradyne Corp. v. State Dep't of Transp., 528 So. 2d 291 (Fla. App. 1988) (access for adjoining property owner); Luxembourg Group, Inc. v. Snohomish County, 887 P.2d 446 (Wash. App. 1995) (access to landlocked lot); Unlimited v. Kitsap County, 750 P.2d 651 (Wash. App. 1988) (same).

### § 9.14. *Dolan* and What It Means.

The Supreme Court elaborated on the *Nollan* standards for exactions in *Dolan v. City of Tigard*.[76] The Court invalidated a condition to a building permit to expand plaintiff's building that required the dedication of land for within a floodplain to improve a storm drainage system and provide a pedestrian-bicycle path. The Court adopted a "rough proportionality" test for exactions which it indicated was stricter than the nexus test adopted by most state courts. Some courts have held, however, that the difference between the *Dolan* test and the reasonable relationship test is only a matter of degree.[77] *Dolan* also placed the burden to prove the constitutionality of exactions on government agencies and indicated that the decision to impose the dedication on the building permit was adjudicative. Cases applying *Dolan* are discussed in subsequent sections in this chapter.

### § 9.15. On-Site Streets and Improvements.

The Standard Planning Act requires subdividers to provide streets and other improvements within the subdivision. Subdivision control statutes usually authorize[78] and subdivision control ordinances usually contain these requirements. The courts have applied the nexus test to reject taking claims to these exactions. *Blevens v. City of Manchester*[79] is an early leading case:

> Since the subdivider of land creates the need for local improvements which are of special benefit to the subdivision, it is considered reasonable that he should bear the cost rather than the municipality and the general taxpayer.[80]

The court rejected an argument that the exaction was discriminatory because it did not apply to lots adjacent to the subdivision. It applied the usual zoning rule that does not require every "lot of land" to be regulated to the same degree.[81]

### § 9.16. Off-Site Streets and Improvements.

Subdivision control requirements for internal improvements are expressly authorized by the Standard Planning Act and the state statutes that adopted it. Land dedications and fees for off-site streets and similar facilities raise more

---

76. § 2.17

77. Home Builders Ass'n of Central Arizona v. City of Scottsdale, 930 P.2d 993 (Ariz. 1997).

78. Cal. Gov't Code § 66475; Minn. Stat. Ann. § 462.358(2b).

79. 170 A.2d 121 (N.H. 1961). *See also* Coastland Corp. v. County of Currituck, 734 F.2d 175 (4th Cir. 1984) (road access); Brous v. Smith, 106 N.E.2d 503 (N.Y. 1952) (streets); City of Bellefontaine Neighbors v. J.J. Kelly Realty & Bldg. Co., 460 S.W.2d 298 (Mo. App. 1970) (sewers and sidewalks); Crownhill Homes, Inc. v. City of San Antonio, 433 S.W.2d 448 (Tex. Civ. App. 1968) (water mains).

80. *Id.* at 122-23.

81. *Accord* Pengilly v. Multnomah County, 810 F. Supp. 1111 (D. Or. 1992).

difficult statutory authority problems because they are not usually authorized by subdivision control legislation. A common example is the dedication of land in the subdivision for the widening of a street that is off-site but adjacent to the subdivision.

*Divan Bldrs., Inc. v. Planning Bd.*[82] is a leading case holding that a subdivision control act based on the Standard Act included implied statutory authority for off-site exactions. The municipality required a subdivider to contribute to the cost of improving a downstream drainage facility that carried drainage from the subdivision. The court agreed with a law review commentator that both off-site and on-site improvements were "a legitimate expense of subdividing which ought to be borne in the first instance by the developer." New Jersey legislation now authorizes exactions for off-site improvements "necessitated or required" by the subdivision.[83] The supreme court has held that the statute does not authorize developer contributions for municipality-wide road improvements based on the anticipated impact that new subdivisions would have on the municipality's road network.[84] Other states also have statutes authorizing dedications for off-site facilities, including roads.[85] These statutes usually enact the nexus test for exactions required under the taking clause.[86]

Some courts hold there is no implied statutory authority to require exactions for off-site improvements.[87] These holdings may reflect a belief that an off-site subdivision exaction would be a taking of property. *Arrowhead Dev. Co. v. Livingston County Rd. Comm'n*[88] illustrates these cases. The county required a subdivider to open an access to a public road, remove a hill that was a sight obstruction on the road, and regrade and resurface the road. The hill was not on the subdivision site. The court held that a provision in the subdivision control act that authorized subdividers to provide "drives which enter county roads and

---

**82.** 334 A.2d 30 (N.J. 1975). *Accord* City of Mobile v. Waldon, 429 So. 2d 945 (Ala. 1983); KBW, Inc. v. Town of Bennington, 342 A.2d 653 (N.H. 1975). *See also* Sullivan v. Planning Bd., 645 N.E.2d 703 (Mass. App. 1995) (statute prohibiting dedication for public way applies only if dedication unrelated to adequate access and safety of subdivision); City of Stafford v. Gullo, 886 S.W.2d 524 (Tex. App. 1994) (no authority in ordinance).

**83.** N.J. Stat. Ann. § 40:55D-32.

**84.** New Jersey Bldrs. Ass'n v. Mayor & Twp. Comm., 528 A.2d 555 (N.J. 1987). *See also* Baltica Constr. Co. v. Planning Bd., 537 A.2d 319 (N.J. App. Div. 1988) (may consider benefit to abutting landowners from off-site water line).

**85.** Va. Code Ann. § 15.1-466(A)(j); Wash. Rev. Code Ann. § 58.17.110. *See also* § 9.19.

**86.** Luxembourg Group v. Snohomish County, 887 P.2d 446 (Wash. App. (1995) (disapproving dedication of road not required by subdivision).

**87.** Cherry Hills Resort Dev. Co. v. Cherry Hills Village (II), 790 P.2d 827 (Colo. 1990); Briar W., Inc. v. City of Lincoln, 291 N.W.2d 730 (Neb. 1980); Meixsell v. Ross Twp. Bd. of Supvrs., 623 A.2d 429 (Pa. Commw. 1993); Hylton Enters. v. Board of Supvrs., 258 S.E.2d 577 (Va. 1979). *See also* Cupp v. Board of Supvrs., 318 S.E.2d 407 (Va. 1984).

**88.** 323 N.W.2d 702 (Mich. 1982).

streets" did not authorize the county to require removal of the hill. It rejected an argument that the sight obstruction was a problem "solely attributable" to the subdivision. It noted that the same argument could be made "to justify ... road widening and all other public services made necessary by the existence of a new residential community."

If there is statutory authority for an off-site facility exaction, the next question is whether it meets the nexus test. Courts upheld these exactions pre-*Nollan* if they met the nexus test.[89] *Lampton v. Pinaire*[90] is a typical case. It held a dedication of land for adjacent streets was not a taking because it was "based on the reasonably anticipated burdens to be caused by the development." The nexus test prohibits exactions for facilities that benefit only the general public.[91] Some courts find a taking under this rule when a municipality requires a dedication of land for a major highway designated in a comprehensive plan. The court may hold the dedication unconstitutional as a "land banking" operation and award compensation if it believes the dedication was an improper alternative to the use of eminent domain.[92]

The courts usually upheld street widening dedications post-*Nollan* and before *Dolan*. They deferred to the judgment of the municipality that the dedication was needed and found that a nexus existed.[93] The cases have not yet fully considered the implications of *Dolan* for street and highway dedications. They have held the Supreme Court intended *Dolan* to apply to land dedications even if they are an

---

**89.** Wald Corp. v. Metropolitan Dade County, 338 So. 2d 863 (Fla. App. 1976), *cert. denied*, 348 So. 2d 955 (Fla. 1977); Land/Vest Props., Inc. v. Town of Plainfield, 379 A.2d 200 (N.H. 1977). Exaction invalidated: Lee County v. New Testament Baptist Church, 507 So. 2d 626 (Fla. App. 1987); Coates v. Planning Bd., 445 N.E.2d 642 (N.Y. 1983); Miller v. City of Port Angeles, 691 P.2d 229 (Wash. App. 1984). *See also* Ayres v. City Council, 207 P.2d 1 (Cal. 1947) (upholding dedication for street widening but basis for holding now questionable).

**90.** 610 S.W.2d 915 (Ky. 1980). *But see* Lexington-Fayette Urban County Gov't v. Schneider, 849 S.W.2d 557 (Ky. App. 1993) (dedication for bridge did not meet *Lampton* test).

**91.** Liberty v. California Coastal Comm'n, 170 Cal. Rptr. 247 (Cal. App. 1981); Schwing v. City of Baton Rouge, 249 So. 2d 304 (La. App.), *cert. denied*, 252 So. 2d 667 (La. 1971); Vrabel v. Mayor & Council, 601 A.2d 229 (N.J. App. 1991).

**92.** Hernando Cty. v. Budget Inns of Fla., Inc., 555 So. 2d 1319 (Fla. App. 1990); Ventures in Prop. I v. City of Wichita, 594 P.2d 671 (Kan. 1979); Simpson v. City of North Platte, 292 N.W.2d 297 (Neb. 1980); R.G. Dunbar, Inc. v. Toledo Plan Comm'n, 367 N.E.2d 1193 (Ohio App. 1976). *See* §§ 10.10, 10.11.

**93.** Dedication upheld: Pengilly v. Multnomah County, 810 F. Supp. 1111 (D. Or. 1992) (dedication held to mitigate cumulative impact of residential development on road); Copeland v. City of Chattanooga, 866 S.W.2d 565 (Tenn. App. 1993) (dedication of right-of-way along adjacent road in conditional zoning approval); *See also* Department of Transp. v. Lundberg, 825 P.2d 641 (Or.) (sidewalk dedication requirement valid and evidence of value in condemnation), *cert. denied*, 506 U.S. 975 (1992); Pitcher v. Heidelberg Township Bd. of Supervisors, 637 A.2d 715 (Pa. Commw. 1994) (upholding road improvement condition).

application of standards contained in an ordinance of the governing body.[94] They have also held the *Dolan* rough proportionality test is not a sharp or "seismic" departure from prior takings law.[95] The courts have applied *Dolan* to uphold or reject municipal findings intended to support street dedications.[96]

## § 9.17.  Parks and Schools.

## § 9.18.  Statutory Authority.

Park and school exactions can raise serious statutory authority questions because the Standard Planning Act was less explicit in its requirements for these facilities. Section 13 of the Act provided only that subdivision regulations "may provide . . . for adequate and convenient open spaces . . . for light and air." The statutory authority problem is even more troublesome when subdivision control ordinances authorize or require in-lieu fees for park and school sites rather than the dedication of land within the subdivision. A subdivider can argue that the in-lieu fee is a tax which the statutes do not authorize.

Although a number of cases hold that land dedications and in-lieu fees for parks and schools are within the statutory authority conferred by subdivision control legislation based on the Standard Act,[97] several courts hold to the contrary.[98] The cases have divided in resolving the tax objection. Cases that find a lack of statutory authority often characterize the in-lieu fee as an unauthorized

---

94. Amoco Oil Co. v. Village of Schaumburg, 661 N.E.2d 380 (Ill. App. 1996); Schultz v. City of Grants Pass, 884 P.2d 569 (Or. App. 1994).

95. Amoco Oil Co. v. Village of Schaumburg, 661 N.E.2d 380 (Ill. App. 1996); Art Piculell Group v. Clackamas County, 922 P.2d 1227 (Or. App. 1996).

96. Dedication valid: Kottschade v. City of Rochester, 537 N.W.2d 301 (Minn. App. 1995); Nelson v. City of Lake Oswego, 869 P.2d 350 (Or. App. 1994) (drainage easement requirement as condition to permit to build house); Sparks v. Douglas County, 904 P.2d 738 (Wash. 1995) (street widening dedication as condition to subdivision approval). Dedication invalid: Amoco Oil Co. v. Village of Schaumburg, 661 N.E.2d 380 (Ill. App. 1996) (special use permit; 20 percent of property dedicated), *cert. denied,* 117 S. Ct. 413 (1996). *But see* Art Piculell Group v. Clackamas County, 922 P.2d 1227 (Or. App. 1996) (may give greater weight to subdivision benefits in appropriate cases; *Dolan* does not preclude quantification). *See also* Snider v. Board of County Comm'rs, 932 P.2d 704 (Wash. App. 1997) (requiring owner of land to obtain right of way to satisfy dedication does not violate *Dolan*).

97. Trent Meredith, Inc. v. City of Oxnard, 170 Cal. Rptr. 685 (Cal. App. 1981); Cimarron Corp. v. Board of City Comm'rs, 563 P.2d 946 (Colo. 1977); Crucil v. Carson City, 600 P.2d 216 (Nev. 1979); Jenad, Inc. v. Village of Scarsdale, 218 N.E.2d 673 (N.Y. 1966); Jordan v. Village of Menomonee Falls, 137 N.W.2d 442 (Wis. 1965), *appeal dismissed,* 385 U.S. 4 (1966).

98. City of Montgomery v. Crossroads Land Co., 355 So. 2d 363 (Ala. 1978); Admiral Dev. Corp. v. City of Maitland, 267 So. 2d 860 (Fla. App. 1972); Coronado Dev. Co. v. City of McPherson, 368 P.2d 51 (Kan. 1962); Eyde Constr. Co. v. Charter Twp. of Meridian, 386 N.W.2d 687 (Mich. App. 1986) (recreation land); West Park Ave., Inc. v. Township of Ocean, 224 A.2d 1 (N.J. 1966). *See* Grand Land Co. v. Township of Bethlehem, 483 A.2d 818 (N.J. App. Div. 1984).

tax.[99] One case avoided the tax problem by holding that the in-lieu fee was simply "imposed on the transaction of obtaining plat approval."[100] Home rule authority may also authorize exactions for parks or schools.[101]

Several states have adopted statutes that authorize dedications and in-lieu fees for park and school sites.[102] These statutes usually codify the nexus test for exactions.

### § 9.19. Taking Problems.

The state courts applied the nexus test for exactions in a group of leading cases on park and school dedications decided pre-*Nollan*. State courts may continue to apply these cases post-*Nollan*, although they are required to apply the Supreme Court exaction decisions if a landowner relies on them.[103]

An Illinois case, *Pioneer Trust & Sav. Bank v. Village of Mount Prospect,*[104] adopted the most restrictive version of the nexus test to invalidate a land dedication for park and school sites. The court held a municipality can require a subdivider to assume only those costs "specifically and uniquely attributable" to the subdivision. Later Illinois cases upheld in-lieu fees for parks and schools in cases that either distinguished or claimed to apply the *Pioneer* test.[105]

Cases in other states applied a more relaxed reasonableness test to uphold park and school exactions. *Jordan v. Village of Menomonee Falls,*[106] a Wisconsin case, is typical. The court believed the uniquely attributable test placed too great a burden on municipalities. It held a "reasonable basis" for attributing a need for parks and schools to a subdivision could be found if a number of approved subdivisions approved over several years were responsible for bringing a "considerable number of people" into the community.

Elsewhere in the opinion, the court indicated it would apply the police power "reasonableness" test to subdivision exactions. It stated that a municipality could require exactions in return for the benefits the subdivider received from selling

---

**99.** Haugen v. Gleason, 359 P.2d 108 (Or. 1961).

**100.** Jenad, Inc. v. Village of Scarsdale, 218 N.E.2d 673 (N.Y. 1966). *Accord* Call v. City of West Jordan, 606 P.2d 217 (Utah 1979).

**101.** City of College Station v. Turtle Rock Corp., 680 S.W.2d 802 (Tex. 1984).

**102.** Cal. Gov't Code § 66477, *upheld in* Associated Home Bldrs. of Greater E. Bay, Inc. v. City of Walnut Creek, 484 P.2d 606 (Cal.) (questionable authority under *Dolan*), *appeal dismissed,* 404 U.S. 878 (1971); Colo. Rev. Stat. § 30-28-133(4)(a); N.Y. Town Law § 277(4); Mont. Code Ann. § 76-3-621; Wash. Rev. Code § 58.17.110.

**103.** *See* § 9.22 (applying Supreme Court decisions to impact fees).

**104.** 176 N.E.2d 799 (Ill. 1961). Applying *Pioneer* test: Aunt Hack Ridge Estates, Inc. v. Planning Comm'n, 273 A.2d 880 (Conn. 1970) (fee for parks upheld); Schwing v. City of Baton Rouge, 249 So. 2d 304 (La. App. 1971) (road widening invalidated).

**105.** Krughoff v. City of Naperville, 369 N.E.2d 892 (Ill. 1977); Board of Educ. v. Surety Devs., Inc., 347 N.E.2d 149 (Ill. 1975).

**106.** 137 N.W.2d 442 (Wis. 1965), *appeal dismissed,* 385 U.S. 4 (1966).

land in the subdivision for home building lots. Exactions are justified if they meet a municipal demand that would not have occurred "but for the influx of people into the community to occupy the subdivision lots." Later cases have followed *Menomonee Falls,* sometimes with modifications.[107]

### § 9.20. Impact Fees.

Municipalities may levy impact fees on new development as an alternative to subdivision exactions. The fee is usually levied either when a building permit is issued or as a facility connection charge against dwellings in a development. It is not an exaction levied against the subdivider. Because impact fees are not levied in the subdivision control process, they can be levied against developments that do not require subdivision approval, such as multi-family housing.

Municipalities can levy impact fees for any kind capital improvement, including roads, parks, and water and sewer facilities. Impact fees are also used to expand or improve these facilities.

### § 9.21. Statutory Authority.

Impact fees, like subdivision control exactions, raise a statutory authority problem.[108] Developers can claim that impact fees are taxes which are not authorized by the state's tax legislation. A number of cases have taken this position,[109] but other cases uphold impact fees under legislation that authorizes municipalities to levy user charges for the maintenance and construction of capital facilities.[110] As the court pointed out in *Contractors & Bldrs. Ass'n of Pinellas*

---

107. Home Bldrs. Ass'n v. City of Kansas City, 555 S.W.2d 832 (Mo. 1977); Billings Props., Inc. v. Yellowstone County, 394 P.2d 182 (Mont. 1964); Collis v. City of Bloomington, 246 N.W.2d 19 (Minn. 1976); Patenaude v. Town of Meredith, 392 A.2d 582 (N.H. 1978); Jenad, Inc. v. Village of Scarsdale, 218 N.E.2d 673 (N.Y. 1966); City of College Station v. Turtle Rock Corp., 680 S.W.2d 802 (Tex. 1984); Call v. City of West Jordan, 614 P.2d 1257 (Utah 1980); Coulter v. City of Rawlings, 662 P.2d 888 (Wyo. 1983); 43 A.L.R.3d 864 (1972).

108. Board of County Commr's v. Bainbridge, Inc., 929 P.2d 691 (Colo. 1997) (can't levy impact fee for schools in addition to subdivision fee authorized by statute).

109. Home Bldrs. Ass'n of Cent. Ariz. v. Riddel, 510 P.2d 376 (Ariz. 1973); Rancho Colorado, Inc. v. City of Bloomfield, 586 P.2d 659 (Colo. 1978); State v. City of Port Orange, 650 So. 2d 1 (Fla. 1994) (transportation utility fee); Idaho Bldg. Contractors Ass'n v. City of Coeur D'Alene, 890 P.2d 326 (Idaho 1995); Lloyd E. Clarke, Inc. v. City of Bettendorf, 158 N.W.2d 125 (Iowa 1968); Eastern Diversified Properties, Inc. v. Montgomery County, 570 A.2d 850 (Md. 1990); Country Joe, Inc. v. City of Eagan, 560 N.W.2d 681 (Minn. 1997) (road connection fee); Douglas County Contractors Ass'n v. Douglas County, 929 P.2d 253 (Nev. 1996); Hillis Homes, Inc. v. Snohomish County, 650 P.2d 193 (Wash. 1982). *See also* Building Industry Ass'n v. City of Westlake, 660 N.E.2d 501 (Ohio App. 1995) (invalidating park and recreation fee).

110. City of Arvada v. City & County of Denver, 663 P.2d 611 (Colo. 1983); Hartman v. Aurora San. Dist., 177 N.E.2d 214 (Ill. 1961); Waters Landing Ltd. Partnership v. Montgomery County, 650 A.2d 712 (Md. 1994) (development impact tax); Lechner v. City of Billings, 797 P.2d

*County v. City of Dunedin,*[111] a municipality may levy user charges to create a capital fund for public improvements rather than fund them through bond issues that are retired through user charges.

Almost half the states have adopted legislation authorizing impact fees.[112] Some of these statutes have codified the nexus test. The California legislation, which is typical, authorizes fees imposed on development projects and requires the municipality to identify the uses to which the fee will be put. There must be "a reasonable relationship between the fee's use and the type of development project on which the fee is imposed."[113] The statute expressly states that its purpose is to codify existing "constitutional and decisional" law.[114] One of the most elaborate impact fee statutes is the Texas law.[115] The statute enacts the nexus test by authorizing impact fees to fund capital improvements "necessitated by and attributable to ... new development."

Many of these statutes include requirements that help demonstrate that the required nexus exists. These include a statutory identification of the facilities for which municipalities may impose fees, the identification of service deficiencies and service and benefit areas, and fee calculation methodologies that apportion the impact fees fairly. Some statutes require a capital improvements plan as a condition to levying fees. These requirements help to establish strong spatial, benefit and earmarking relationships. Accounting requirements and time limits for expenditures help ensure that fees will be used for their intended purpose.

The cases have upheld impact fees levied under statutory authority when they meet the statutory nexus test.[116] For example, the Illinois court upheld a road im-

---

191 (Mont. 1990); Home Bldrs. Ass'n v. Provo City, 503 P.2d 451 (Utah 1972); Tidewater Ass'n of Homeowners v. City of Virginia Beach, 400 S.E.2d 523 (Va. 1991); Robes v. Town of Hartford, 636 A.2d 342 (Vt. 1993) (fee for expansion of sewage system); Coulter v. City of Rawlings, 662 P.2d 888 (Wyo. 1983). *See also* Centex Real Estate Corp. v. City of Vallejo, 24 Cal. Rptr. 2d 48 (Cal. App. 1993) (excise tax); Cherry Hill Farms, Inc. v. City of Cherry Hills Village, 670 P.2d 779 (Colo. 1983) (same).

**111.** 329 So. 2d 314 (Fla. 1976). *Cf.* City of Boca Raton v. State, 595 So. 2d 25 (Fla. 1992) (home rule government may levy special assessment under home rule powers).

**112.** *E.g.,* Ga. Code Ann. §§ 36-71-1 to 36-71-13; Idaho Code § 67-8201 et seq.; 605 Ill. Comp. Stat. Ann. § 5/5-901 et seq.; Nev. Rev. Stat. §§ 278B.010 et seq.; N.H. Rev. Stat. Ann. § 674:21(V); N.M. Stat. Ann. §§ 5-8-1 et seq.; Or. Rev. Stat. §§ 223.297 et seq.; Pa. Stat. Ann. tit. 53, § 10501-A et seq.; Va. Code Ann. §§ 15.1-498.1 et seq.; Vt. Stat. Ann. tit. 24, §§ 5200 et seq.; Wash. Rev. Code § 82.02.050 et seq.; Wis. Stat. § 66.55. *See* Southern Nevada Homebuilders Ass'n v. City of North Las Vegas, 913 P.2d 1276 (Nev. 1996) (fees limited to those authorized by statute).

**113.** Cal. Gov't Code §§ 66000-66008.

**114.** *Id.* § 66005.

**115.** Tex. Local Gov't Code §§ 395.001-395.080.

**116.** Trimen Dev. Co. v. King County, 877 P.2d 187 (Wash. 1994) (fee reasonably necessary as result of proposed development as required by statute). *See also* Shapell Indus. v. Governing Bd., 1

pact fee that adopted the "speficially and uniquely attributable" standard and held the fee could be predetermined by ordinance and need not be calculated for each proposed development.[117] The Arizona court upheld a fee adopted by the city council that provided capital improvements funds needed to provide water supply.[118] It held the fee satisfied a statutory requirement that fees must "result in a beneficial use to the development," which it held was a codification of the constitutional nexus test.[119] The principal claim was that water supply plans were too speculative to provide the necessary statutory benefit, but the court applied the presumption of constitutionality to reject this challenge.

## § 9.22. Taking Problems.[120]

Courts prior to *Nollan* had applied the nexus test to uphold impact fees,[121] and continued to do so after the Supreme Court decided *Nollan*.[122] Post-*Dolan*, the first issue courts must face is whether *Dolan*, which was a land dedication case, also applies to impact fees. Some courts have held that *Dolan* does not apply to impact fees, reflecting the view that this case and *Nollan* treated land dedications as the equivalent of a physical occupation by government and limited to this situation.[123]

---

Cal. Rptr. 2d 818 (Cal. App. 1991) (school development fee excessive); Robes v. Town of Hartford, 636 A.2d 342 (Vt. 1993) (upholding fee for sewage service expansion).

**117.** Northern Ill. Home Bldrs. Ass'n v. County of DuPage, 649 N.E.2d 384 (Ill. 1995).

**118.** Home Builders Ass'n of Central Arizona v. City of Scottsdale, 930 P.2d 993 (Ariz. 1997).

**119.** *Accord* Ehrlich v. City of Culver City, 911 P.2d 429 (Cal.), *cert. denied*, 117 S. Ct. 299 (1996) ("reasonable relationship" standard of statute codifies *Dolan* test). *See* § 9.22.

**120.** For cases considering equal protection and other objections to connection fees *see* holding valid: Loup-Miller Constr. Co. v. City & County of Denver, 676 P.2d 1170 (Colo. 1984); Meglino v. Township Comm., 510 A.2d 1134 (N.J. 1986); Amherst Bldrs. Ass'n v. City of Amherst, 402 N.E.2d 1181 (Ohio 1980); Oregon State Homebuilders Ass'n v. City of Tigard, 604 P.2d 886 (Or. App. 1979); Tidewater Ass'n of Homeowners v. City of Virginia Beach, 400 S.E.2d 523 (Va. 1991). Invalid: Patterson v. Alpine Village, 663 P.2d 95 (Utah 1983).

**121.** Contractor & Bldrs. Ass'n of Pinellas County v. City of Dunedin, 329 So. 2d 314 (Fla. 1976); Hartman v. Aurora San. Dist., 177 N.E.2d 214 (Ill. 1961); Hayes v. City of Albany, 490 P.2d 1018 (Or. App. 1971). *See also* J.W. Jones Cos. v. City of San Diego, 203 Cal. Rptr. 580 (Cal. App. 1984) (upholding facilities benefit assessment in growth management area); Banberry Dev. Corp. v. South Jordan City, 631 P.2d 899, 903 (Utah 1981).

**122.** Tahoe Keys Prop. Owners' Ass'n v. State Water Resources Bd., 28 Cal. Rptr. 2d 734 (Cal. App. 1994) (environmental mitigation fee as condition to building permits), *cert. denied*, 513 U.S. 988 (1994); St. John's County v. Northeast Florida Builders Ass'n, 583 So. 2d 635 (Fla. 1991) (fee on residential development for schools and requiring earmarking of funds); City of Key West v. R.L.J.S. Corp., 537 So. 2d 641 (Fla. App. 1989) (fee valid though developer cannot pass on cost of fee to consumers).

**123.** Commercial Builders of Northern California v. City of Sacramento, 941 F.2d 872 (9th Cir. 1991) (pre-*Dolan*), *cert. denied*, 504 U.S. 931 (1992); McCarthy v. City of Leawood, 894 P.2d 836, (Kan. 1995) (impact fee). *Accord* Clajon Prod. Corp. v. Petera, 70 F.3d 1566 (10th Cir.

A related issue is whether *Dolan,* which invalidated exactions imposed as a condition to a building permit, is limited to impact fees imposed adjudicatively in the permit or development approval process, or whether it also applies to impact fees imposed legislatively without an individualized determination. The cases have held that *Dolan* applies only when a municipality imposes an impact fee adjudicatively. As the California court explained in *Ehrlich v. City of Culver City,*[124] *Dolan* applies only to cases of "regulatory leveraging." These are cases where a municipality can impose "land-use conditions in individual cases, authorized by a permit scheme which by its nature allows for both the discretionary deployment of the police power and an enhanced potential for its abuse."

*Ehrlich* also provided an extensive interpretation of the application of *Dolan* to the constitutionality of impact fees.[125] After the plaintiff demolished a private recreational facility, the city approved an office building on the site subject to a condition that the plaintiff pay a recreational mitigation fee to be used for additional recreational facilities to replace those lost when plaintiff demolished his facility. The city also required payment of an art-in-public-places fee.

The court held that the discontinuance of a private use could have a significant impact justifying a monetary exaction to alleviate it. It also held the city's findings on the relationship between the monetary exaction and the withdrawal of land restrictively zoned for private recreational use satisfied the nexus test, but the court remanded the case because the record did not support the amount of the fee required from the plaintiff. That fee should be based on the loss of land for land reserved for recreational use, not the loss of plaintiff's facilities, which were privately and not publicly owned. The court upheld the art-in-public-places fee because "[t]he requirement of providing art in an area of the project reasonably accessible to the public is, like other design and landscaping requirements, a kind of aesthetic control well within the authority of the city to impose."[126]

## § 9.23. Linkage Programs.

A number of cities have adopted exaction programs that require downtown office and commercial developers to provide housing for lower-income groups

---

1995) (upholding hunting regulation); Harris v. City of Wichita, 862 F. Supp. 287 (D. Kan. 1994) (upholding airport overlay regulations) *aff'd without opinion,* 74 F.3d 1249 (10th Cir. Kan. 1996). *Contra* Ehrlich v. City of Culver City, 911 P.2d 429 (Cal. 1996) (when impact fee adjudicative), *cert. denied,* 117 S. Ct. 299 (1996).

**124.** 911 P.2d 429, 439 (Cal.) (applying *Dolan* to impact fee statute to save statute's constitutionality), *cert. denied,* 117 S. Ct. 299 (1996). *Accord* Home Builders Ass'n of Central Arizona v. City of Scottsdale, 930 P.2d 993 (Ariz. 1996).

**125.** *See also* F & W Assocs. v. County of Somerset, 648 A.2d 482 (N.J. App. Div. 1994) (upholding traffic impact fee under state nexus test post-*Dolan*).

**126.** 911 P.2d at 450.

or contribute to a municipal fund for the construction of such housing.[127] Linkage programs satisfy the nexus test only if the municipality can show that downtown development contributes to the housing problem the linkage exaction is intended to remedy.

In *Commercial Builders of Northern California v. City of Sacramento*,[128] the Ninth Circuit upheld, pre-*Dolan,* a linkage fee imposed as a condition to building permits for certain kinds of nonresidential buildings. The fee was based on a study of the need for lower-income housing, and the amount of fee required to offset the effect of nonresidential use on such housing. The court held that *Nollan* did not mean a development must be "directly responsible" for the "social ill in question." The fee was reasonably related to a legitimate purpose, was based on careful study and conservatively assessed only part of the need for lower-income housing to developers. Although a court post-*Dolan* might accept this interpretation of the nexus test, it may require more rigorous findings in support of a linkage fee determination.

## B. PLANNED UNIT DEVELOPMENT.

### § 9.24. The Land Use Problem.

Developers often plan and build residential developments as a single project and may include single-family and multi-family dwellings in the same development. The application of conventional zoning to these large-scale planned developments presents a number of problems. If the development includes single-family and multi-family dwellings it requires two or more zoning districts, which makes it impossible to adopt a single set of land use controls for the development. The zoning ordinance does not allow the planned unit developer to build at higher densities in some parts of the development in return for the preservation of natural and unbuildable areas elsewhere in the development. Without this incentive, developers usually build on all of the site and may destroy natural and environmentally important areas. The zoning ordinance provides a "cookie cutter" pattern of minimum lot sizes and setbacks because its site regulations

---

**127.** § 7.27.

**128.** 941 F.2d 872 (9th Cir. 1991), *cert. denied,* 504 U.S. 931 (1992). *See also* Terminal Plaza Corp. v. City & County of San Francisco, 223 Cal. Rptr. 379 (Cal. App. 1986) (upholding exaction for affordable housing from hotel owners who planned to convert residential hotels to another use). *But see* Nunziato v. Planning Bd., 541 A.2d 1105 (N.J. App. Div. 1988) (fee for affordable housing negotiated to induce approval of building held invalid); San Telmo Assocs. v. City of Seattle, 735 P.2d 673 (Wash. 1987) (ordinance requiring owners to replace demolished low-income housing or pay fee for replacement housing held a tax and probably unconstitutional). *See also* Sintra, Inc. v. City of Seattle, 829 P.2d 765 (Wash. 1992) (remanding taking claim on ordinance held invalid in *San Telmo*).

apply to individual lots. They do not allow the variety in design that a planned unit development can provide if it is planned as an entity.

Planned unit development (PUD) regulation overcomes these problems by providing a set of standards for the approval of a PUD plan in an administrative review process. Because the development is planned and reviewed as an entity, the developer can achieve better site planning by varying lot sizes, setbacks, and other site development requirements. The plan allows him to trade off higher densities in one part of the development for the preservation of open and natural areas elsewhere. The municipality can approve the PUD plan as an integrated set of land use controls that applies to the entire development.

In the simplest form of planned unit development, sometimes known as cluster zoning or a density transfer PUD, densities and uses in the development are not changed. This type of PUD is usually limited to single-family dwellings. The ordinance usually allows an increase in single-family densities in one part of the PUD in return for compensating open space provided elsewhere in the development. The more complex PUDs include a mixture of residential types without an increase in density, or a residential-type mixture with a density increase. The mixed-use concept is carried further if the PUD includes ancillary commercial development that serves the PUD residents. A change in permitted uses and densities may be required if the PUD includes multi-family or commercial development.

## § 9.25. Planned Unit Development Regulations.

PUD regulations authorize a review process that closely resembles subdivision and site plan review,[129] but the PUD approval standards usually confer more discretion on the reviewing agency. Although PUD regulations can be in either the zoning or subdivision control ordinance, they must be in the zoning ordinance if density or use changes are authorized. These changes require approval by the governing body or the adoption by the governing body of standards the reviewing agency applies in the PUD approval process.

The zoning ordinance may authorize planned unit developments as a separate zoning district, which may require approval as a floating zone.[130] Approval by the governing body is necessary if the district is not prezoned, and the regulations for the PUDs that are contained in the PUD district should supersede the zoning regulations that previously applied. Under an alternative approach, planned unit developments are approved as special exceptions.[131]

In the typical PUD review process, the developer submits a preliminary and then a final development plan for review by the approving agency. A variant of

---

129. §§ 6.68, 9.04.
130. § 6.63.
131. §§ 6.53-6.61.

this process requires the submission of an outline concept plan prior to the submission of a preliminary plan. The outline plan is a schematic map of the project. It provides a basis on which the governing body can approve uses and densities before the developer submits a detailed preliminary plan.

The standards for planned unit development approval usually cover all aspects of the planned unit development, including access, circulation, land uses, densities, and site development restrictions. The ordinance may also contain standards covering project design and the provision of common open space. Ordinance standards must provide enough guidance to avoid delegation of power problems.[132] Because the ordinance governs the design details of PUDs, a court may hold the ordinance standards inadequate if they do not contain clear design and approval criteria.[133] There is always a fine balance between improving certainty and restricting flexibility in the PUD approval process. An ordinance can inject more certainty into the PUD approval process if it contains minimum development standards, limits the location of PUDs and clearly specifies the zoning bonuses that are allowed, but more specific criteria will necessarily limit the flexibility.

## § 9.26. Under the Standard Zoning Act.

Planned unit developments (PUDs) are residential developments that can include multi-family and single-family dwellings and that may also include complementary commercial facilities. The entire development is reviewed at one time, and subdivision is not necessary to trigger the review process. Planned unit development regulations borrow from zoning and subdivision controls. Like the zoning ordinance, planned unit development regulations regulate land use, density, and the development of the site. They may also contain internal design and thoroughfare requirements similar to those contained in subdivision control ordinances.

Planned unit development regulations present several statutory authority problems under the Standard Zoning Act, which most states adopted. The Standard Act did not confer the review powers commonly exercised under planned unit development regulations by zoning agencies such as the planning commission and board of adjustment. Nor did the Standard Act authorize the case-by-case review that is typical under PUD regulations.

---

132. Held adequate: Tri-State Generation & Transmission Co. v. City of Thornton, 647 P.2d 670 (Colo. 1982); Zanin v. Iacono, 487 A.2d 780 (N.J.L. Div. 1984); Appeal of Moreland, 497 P.2d 1287 (Okla. 1972). Held inadequate: Harnett v. Board of Zoning, Subdivision & Bldg. Appeals, 350 F. Supp. 1159 (D. St. Croix 1972); City of Miami v. Save Brickell Ave., Inc., 426 So. 2d 1100 (Fla. App. 1983).

133. Beaver Meadows v. Board of County Comm'rs, 709 P.2d 928 (Colo. 1985).

The uniformity requirement presents another problem. The Standard Act and state zoning acts require uniform zoning regulations for each zoning district. Some commentators argued that the uniformity requirement limited zoning districts to the single-use districts that are traditional in zoning practice. Under this interpretation, the uniformity requirement would prohibit zoning districts with the mixed uses allowed by planned unit development regulations.

Despite these problems, the Standard Zoning Act has not been a major barrier to the adoption of planned unit development regulations. The courts have rejected claims that planned unit development regulations are not authorized by the standard form of zoning legislation. In *Chrinko v. South Brunswick Twp. Planning Bd.*,[134] the court upheld a density transfer PUD ordinance for residential subdivisions that did not authorize density increases:

> Although the state zoning law does not in so many words empower municipalities to provide an option to developers for cluster or density zoning, such an ordinance reasonably advances the legislative purposes of securing open spaces, preventing overcrowding and undue concentration and promoting the general welfare.[135]

*Chrinko* also rejected a uniformity objection to the density transfer ordinance and noted that the ordinance "accomplishes uniformity because the option is open to all developers."[136]

The courts have approved the inclusion of PUD regulations in zoning ordinances,[137] and inclusion in the subdivision control ordinance is another possibility. In *Prince George's County v. M & B Constr. Co.*,[138] the court held that the authority to approve a density transfer PUD was properly delegated to the planning commission in the exercise of its subdivision control powers.

The court held that the bargaining and negotiation that occurs in the PUD review process is not invalid as contract zoning in *Rutland Envtl. Protection Ass'n v. Kane County*:[139]

> Since the overall aims of . . . [PUD] zoning cannot be accomplished without negotiations and because conferences are indeed mandated by the

---

134. 187 A.2d 221 (N.J.L. Div. 1963).

135. *Id.* at 225.

136. *See also* Orinda Homeowners Comm. v. Board of Supvrs., 90 Cal. Rptr. 88 (Cal. App. 1970).

137. Dupont Circle Citizens Ass'n v. District of Columbia Zoning Comm'n, 355 A.2d 550 (D.C. App. 1976).

138. 297 A.2d 683 (Md. 1972).

139. 334 N.E.2d 215 (Ill. App. 1975).

regulatory ordinance, the conduct of the . . . county cannot be read as contributing to contract zoning.[140]

Courts have rejected arguments that the approval of a PUD was invalid because it was inconsistent with a local comprehensive plan and that PUD approvals were invalid as spot zoning.[141] The comprehensive plan rulings were made in states that do not require land use controls to be consistent with the local comprehensive plan.

### § 9.27. Regulatory Techniques.

Although planned unit development regulations usually require a PUD rezoning by the legislative body,[142] they may delegate to the planning commission the authority to review a PUD to determine whether it complies with the standards contained in the ordinance. In *Cheney v. Village 2 at New Hope, Inc.*,[143] the legislative body rezoned a tract for a PUD under an ordinance that delegated the approval of PUD development details to the planning commission after the legislative body approved the PUD rezoning. The ordinance specified allowable uses, maximum densities and heights, and a minimum distance between buildings. The court approved the delegation under a zoning act similar to the Standard Zoning Act. It held that the flexibility needed in PUD regulation required a delegation to the planning commission as the most appropriate zoning agency to carry out the review process.

In *Lutz v. City of Longview*,[144] the court invalidated a PUD ordinance that delegated to the planning commission the authority to approve a PUD as a floating zone. The court distinguished *Cheney* because in that case the legislative body rezoned the land for a PUD and the ordinance delegated only the review of project details to the planning commission.

Delegation of PUD approval authority to the legislative body does not necessarily mean a court will characterize the PUD approval process as legislative. A court could hold that the PUD review process is quasi-judicial because the PUD ordinance contains standards that are applied in the review of PUD applications. Whether the PUD review process is legislative or quasi-judicial may depend on how extensively the governing body changes the zoning regulations. In

---

**140.** *Id.* at 219.

**141.** Moore v. City of Boulder, 484 P.2d 134 (Colo. App. 1971); North Hempstead v. Village of North Hills, 324 N.E.2d 566 (N.Y. 1975); Cheney v. Village 2 at New Hope, Inc., 241 A.2d 81 (Pa. 1968); Wiggers v. County of Skagit, 596 P.2d 1345 (Wash. App. 1979).

**142.** North Hempstead v. Village of North Hills, 324 N.E.2d 566 (N.Y. 1975) (floating zone).

**143.** 241 A.2d 81 (Pa. 1968). Sheridan Planning Comm'n v. Board of Sheridan County Comm'rs, 924 P.2d 988 (Wyo. 1996).

**144.** 520 P.2d 1374 (Wash. 1974).

*Peachtree Dev. Co. v. Paul*,[145] the governing body approved a PUD that significantly departed from the single-family zoning regulations. The PUD included multi-family and commercial uses at higher densities than the zoning regulations allowed. The court held that the PUD approval was a legislative act subject to referendum and that "the board's action was the functional equivalent of altering the zoning classification of a sizeable section of ... [the] Township." Other cases upheld the delegation of PUD approval to a board of zoning adjustment or governing body as a special exception and characterized the PUD review process as adjudicative.[146]

A Florida court invalidated a rezoning for a PUD initiated by a county that included a detailed site plan showing buildings, uses and densities.[147] The court held that planned unit development is a voluntary procedure intended to provide development flexibility not available in the usual zoning district, but that it cannot be forced on a developer who simply wants her land rezoned.

### § 9.28. Discretion to Approve or Reject.

The courts apply the usual arbitrary and capricious judicial review standard when they review administrative and legislative PUD approvals and denials. They review these decisions carefully because PUD ordinances usually contain detailed criteria for PUD approval, but they usually uphold decisions to deny[148] or approve[149] PUD applications.

---

145. 423 N.E.2d 1087 (Ohio 1981). *See also* Todd-Mart, Inc. v. Town Bd. of Webster, 370 N.Y.S.2d 683 (App. Div. 1975); Sheridan Planning Comm'n v. Board of Sheridan County Comm'rs, 924 P.2d 988 (Wyo. 1996).

146. Chandler v. Kroiss, 190 N.W.2d 472 (Minn. 1971); Appeal of Moreland, 497 P.2d 1287 (Okla. 1972); Mullin v. Planning Bd., 456 N.E.2d 780 (Mass. App. 1983) (planning commission). *Compare* Cetrulo v. City of Park Hills, 524 S.W.2d 628 (Ky. 1975).

147. Porpoise Point Pt'ship v. St. John's Cty., 532 So. 2d 727 (Fla. App. 1988).

148. City of Tuscaloosa v. Bryan, 505 So. 2d 330 (Ala. 1987); Dore v. County of Ventura, 28 Cal. Rptr. 2d 299 (Cal. App. 1994); Ford Leasing Dev. Co. v. Board of County Comm'rs, 528 P.2d 237 (Colo. 1974); Whitesell v. Kosciusko Cty. Bd. of Zoning Appeals, 558 N.E.2d 889 (Ind. App. 1990); Croteau v. Planning Bd., 663 N.E.2d 583 (Mass. App. 1996); Coronet Homes, Inc. v. McKenzie, 439 P.2d 219 (Nev. 1968); Board of Supvrs. v. West Chestnut Realty Corp., 532 A.2d 942 (Pa. Commw. 1987). *Contra* Woodhouse v. Board of Comm'rs, 261 S.E.2d 882 (N.C. 1980) (applicant satisfied ordinance criteria); West v. Mills, 380 S.E.2d 917 (Va. 1989); Old Tuckaway Assocs. Ltd. Partnership v. City of Greenfield, 509 N.W.2d 323 (Wis. App. 1993).

149. Moore v. City of Boulder, 484 P.2d 134 (Colo. App. 1971); Davis v. City of Leavenworth, 802 P.2d 494 (Kan. 1991); Huntzicker v. Washington County, 917 P.2d 1051 (Or. App. 1996) (approval complied with plan); Petersen v. City of Clemson, 439 S.E.2d 317 (S.C. App. 1993) (same); Smith v. Georgetown County Council, 355 S.E.2d 864 (S.C. App. 1987); McCallen v. City of Memphis, 786 S.W.2d 633 (Tenn. 1990). *But see* Blagden Alley Ass'n v. District of Columbia Zoning Comm'n, 590 A.2d 139 (D.C. App. 1991) (remanding approval).

A court will reverse a PUD denial that is based on criteria not contained in the PUD ordinance. In *RK Dev. Corp. v. City of Norwalk*,[150] the governing body denied a PUD because of "[t]he safety for the sake of the children up there; the welfare of the community and also the health hazards." The PUD contained specific site development standards for PUD applications but did not contain criteria authorizing denial for any of these reasons.

The court held that the denial was illegal because the ordinance did not prohibit PUDs for "any reason" given by the governing body. It was not entitled to substitute "pure discretion" for "a discretion controlled by fixed standards." The court held that the reasons given by the governing body were vague and uncertain and did not indicate how the applicant failed to comply with the ordinance.

Planned unit development regulations often contain clauses that specify the purposes served by planned unit developments. In *Dupont Circle Citizens Ass'n v. District of Columbia Zoning Comm'n*,[151] the ordinance contained a purpose clause stating that planned unit developments must provide an environment and amenities "superior" to what the zoning regulations could provide. This type of purpose clause is sometimes included in PUD ordinances. The court held the purpose clause did not enact a "comparison" test on which the commission had to make findings of fact in the adjudicative PUD review procedures. It could support its conclusion that a PUD met the purposes specified in the ordinance with "subsidiary findings of basic facts on material issues" raised by the PUD application.

Some review standards contained in PUD ordinances have not received judicial approval. In *Soble Constr. Co. v. Zoning Hearing Bd.*,[152] the ordinance required the developer to "demonstrate that a sufficient market" existed for its PUD. The court invalidated the requirement because it was an improper attempt to zone "for the purpose of limiting competition."

A municipality may create taking problems in the PUD review process if a density increase available under the PUD ordinance is spurious. This problem arises if a municipality downzones the residential densities permitted as-of-right in the PUD and then offers a bonus that restores the original densities if the PUD developer dedicates common open space. The developer can attack the downzoning as unconstitutional or claim that the land dedication is a taking of prop-

---

150. 242 A.2d 781 (Conn. 1968). *See also* DeMaria v. Enfield Planning & Zoning Comm'n, 271 A.2d 105 (Conn. 1970); Hall v. Korth, 244 So. 2d 766 (Fla. App. 1971); LaSalle Nat'l Bank v. County of Lake, 325 N.E.2d 105 (Ill. App. 1975); Woodhouse v. Board of Comm'rs, 261 S.E.2d 882 (N.C. 1980); Mullins v. City of Knoxville, 665 S.W.2d 393 (Tenn. App. 1983).

151. 426 A.2d 327 (D.C. App. 1981). *See also* Smith v. Georgetown County Council, 355 S.E.2d 864 (S.C. App. 1987).

152. 329 A.2d 912 (Pa. Commw. 1974).

erty because the density bonus is spurious. One court approved this use of down-zoning in the PUD process.[153]

## § 9.29. Amendments to Development Plans.

Problems can arise during the development of a PUD that require changes in the final development plan. The courts have held that major changes in the plan cannot be made administratively but require the same review procedure used to approve the PUD.[154] The PUD ordinance can resolve uncertainties in the amendment process by distinguishing between minor and major changes and providing that minor changes can be made administratively. If the PUD was approved as a special exception, amendments to the plan can be made in the special exception process if the amendment does not authorize a use change that requires a rezoning.[155]

## § 9.30. Planned Unit Development Legislation.

Several states have adopted legislation that authorizes planned unit development regulations.[156] Some of this legislation contains detailed requirements for PUD ordinances. New York statutes authorize the approval of density transfer planned unit developments in the subdivision control process.[157]

Model legislation proposed in 1965 contained detailed enabling authority for planned unit development regulation intended to remedy problems that could arise under the Standard Zoning Act.[158] A few states have adopted laws based on the model legislation.[159] The extensive provisions in the model legislation have led to unexpected restraints on local PUD regulations. The cases have divided,

---

**153.** Mountcrest Estates, Inc. v. Mayor & Twp. Comm., 232 A.2d 674 (N.J. App. Div. 1967).

**154.** Millbrae Ass'n for Residential Survival v. City of Millbrae, 69 Cal. Rptr. 251 (1968); City of New Smyrna Beach v. Andover Dev. Corp., 672 So.2d 618 (Fla. App. 1996).

**155.** Chandler v. Kroiss, 190 N.W.2d 472 (Minn. 1971). See McCarty v. City of Kansas City, 671 S.W.2d 790 (Mo. App. 1984) (use change requires rezoning). Cf. Gray v. Trustees, Monclova Twp., 313 N.E.2d 366 (Ohio 1974) (invalidating legislative amendment); Frankland v. City of Lake Oswego, 517 P.2d 1042 (Or. 1973) (sketch plan binds developer). See Foggy Bottom Ass'n v. District of Columbia Zoning Comm'n, 639 A.2d 578 (D.C. App. 1994) (upholding plan amendment deleting mini-park requirement).

**156.** Colo. Rev. Stat. § 24-67-101 et seq.; Conn. Gen. Stat. § 8-2; Idaho Code § 67-6515; 65 Ill. Comp. Stat. Ann. 5/11-13-1.1; Mass. Ann. Laws ch. 40A, § 9; Neb. Rev. Stat. § 19-4401; Nev. Rev. Stat. Ann. § 278A.010; Ohio Rev. Code, §§ 303.22, 519.021. See Glenbrook Homeowners Ass'n v. Glenbrook County, 901 P.2d 132 (Nev. 1995) (assurances required for open space).

**157.** E.g., N.Y. Town Law § 278. See also American Law Institute, Model Land Development Code § 2-210.

**158.** Babcock, Krasnowiecki & McBride, "The Model State Statute", 114 U. Pa. L. Rev. 140 (1965).

**159.** Mich. Comp. Laws §§ 125.216c, 125.286c, 125.584b; N.J. Stat. Ann. §§ 40:55D-39, 40:55D-40, 40:55D-45; Pa. Stat. Ann. tit. 53, §§ 10701-10711.

for example, on whether municipalities can enact PUD ordinances that do not comply with the model legislation.[160] The detailed review standards in the model legislation are similar to the standards contained in many PUD ordinances. The Pennsylvania Commonwealth Court held that a municipality may reject a plan that satisfies the statutory standards if the circumstances are "so exceptional as to support the conclusion that the plan . . . would not be in the public interest."[161]

---

160. *Compare* Niccollai v. Planning Bd., 372 A.2d 352 (N.J. App. Div. 1977) *with* Raum v. Board of Supvrs., 342 A.2d 450 (Pa. Commw. 1975). *See also* Township of Middleton v. Abel, 297 A.2d 525 (Pa. Commw. 1972) (concept plan not authorized),

161. Michaels Dev. Co. v. Benzinger Twp. Bd. of Supvrs., 413 A.2d 743 (Pa. Commw. 1980); Doran Inv. Co. v. Muhlenberg Twp., 309 A.2d 450 (Pa. Commw. 1973).

# REFERENCES

## Books and Monographs

R. Alterman, ed., Private Supply of Public Services: Evaluation of Real Estate Exactions, Linkage, and Alternative Land Policies (1988).

F. Bair, Intensity Zoning: Regulating Townhouses, Apartments and Planned Developments, American Planning Ass'n, Planning Advisory Serv. Rep. No. 314 (1976).

B. Blaesser, Discretionary Land Use Controls (1997).

R. Burchell, ed., Frontiers of Planned Unit Development (1973).

J. Frank, Development Exactions (1987).

R. Freilich & M. Shultz, Model Subdivision Regulations (2d Ed. 1995).

F. James & R. Rhodes, eds., Development Exactions (1987).

J. Kushner, Subdivision Law and Growth Management (updated annually).

J. Leithe & M. Montavon, Impact Fee Programs: A Survey of Design and Administrative Issues (Government Finance Officers Ass'n, 1990).

D. Listokin & C. Walker, The Subdivision and Site Plan Handbook (1989).

D. Merrian, D. Brower & P. Tegeler, eds., Inclusionary Zoning Moves Downtown (1985).

J. Nichols, The Calculation of Proportionate-Share Impact Fees, American Planning Ass'n, Planning Advisory Serv. Rep. No. 409 (1988).

W. Sanders, The Cluster Subdivision: A Cost-Effective Approach, American Planning Ass'n, Planning Advisory Serv. Rep. No. 356 (1981).

T. Snyder & M. Stegman, Paying for Growth: Using Development Fees to Finance Infrastructure (1986).

F. So, D. Mosena & F. Bangs, Planned Unit Development Ordinances, American Planning Ass'n, Planning Advisory Serv. Rep. No. 291 (1973).

## Articles

Alterman, Evaluating Linkage and Beyond: Letting the Windfall Recapture Genie out of the Exactions Bottle, 34 Wash. U.J. Urb. & Contemp. L. 51 (1988).

Blaesser & Kentopp, Impact Fees: The Second Generation, 38 Wash. U.J. Urb. & Contemp. L. 55 (1990).

Cholewa & Edmonds, Federalism and Land Use After *Dolan*: Has the Supreme Court Taken Takings from the States, 28 Urb. Law. 401 (1996).

Cordes, Legal Limits on Development Exactions: Responding to *Nollan* and *Dolan*, 15 N. Ill. U.L. Rev. 513 (1995).

Delaney, Impact Fees, Housing Costs, and Housing Affordability, 1 U. Fla. J.L. & Pub. Pol'y 87 (1987).

Denbo, Development Exactions: A New Way to Fund State and Local Government Infrastructure Improvements and Affordable Housing?, 23 Real Estate L.J. 7 (1994).

Duncan, Standerfer & McLendon, Drafting Impact Fee Ordinances: Implementation and Administration, 9 Zoning & Plan. L. Rep. 57 (1986).

Ethier & Howard, Development Excise Taxes: An Exercise in Cleverness and Imagination, Land Use L. & Zoning Dig., Vol. 42, No. 2, at 3 (1990).

Freis & Reyniak, Putting Takings Back Into the Fifth Amendment: Land Use Planning After *Dolan v. City of Tigard,* 21 Colum. J. Envtl. L. 103 (1996).

Henning, Mitigating Price Effects with a Housing Linkage Fee, 78 Calif. L. Rev. 721 (1990).

Holloway & Guy, Land Dedication Conditions and Beyond the Essential Nexus: Determining "Reasonably Related" Impacts of Real Estate Development Under the Takings Clause, 27 Texas Tech L. Rev. 73 (1996).

Kayden, Land-Use Regulations, Rationality, and Judicial Review: The RSVP in the *Nollan* Invitation (Part I), 23 Urb. Law. 301 (1991).

Leitner & Schoettle, A Survey of State Impact Fee Enabling Legislation, 25 Urb. Law. 491 (1993).

Lytton, Linkage: An Evaluation and Exploration, 21 Urb. Law. 413 (1989).

Merrill & Lincoln, Linkage Fees and Fair Share Regulations: Law and Method, 25 Urb. Law. 223 (1993).

Morgan, Exactions as Takings: Tactics for Dealing With *Dolan,* Land Use L. & Zoning Dig., Vol. 46, No. 9, at 3 (1994).

Morgan, State Impact Fee Legislation: Guidelines for Analysis, Land Use L. & Zoning Dig., Vol. 42, No. 3, at 3 & No. 4, at 3 (1990).

Reynolds, Local Subdivision Regulation: Formulaic Constraints in an Age of Discretion, 24 Ga. L. Rev. 525 (1990).

Schukoske, Housing Linkage: Regulating Development Impact on Housing Costs, 76 Iowa L. Rev. 1011 (1991).

Schultz & Kelly, Subdivision Improvement Requirements and Guarantees: A Primer, 28 Wash. U.J. Urb. & Contemp. L. 3 (1985).

Sternlieb, Burchell, Hughes & Listokin, Planned Unit Development Legislation: A Summary of Necessary Considerations, 7 Urb. L. Ann. 71 (1974).

Stroud & Trevarthen, Defensible Exactions After *Nollan v. California Coastal Commission* and *Dolan v. City of Tigard,* 25 Stetson L. Rev. 719 (1996).

Symposium, Development Impact Fees, 54 J. Am. Plan. Ass'n 3 (1988).

Symposium, Exactions: A Controversial New Source for Municipal Funds, 50 Law & Contemp. Prob. 1 (1987).

Symposium, Planned Unit Development, 114 U. Pa. L. Rev. 3 (1965).

White, Development Fees and Exemptions for Affordable Housing: Tailoring Regulations to Achieve Multiple Public Objectives, 6 J. Land Use & Envt'l L. 25 (1990).

**Student Work**

Note, Child Care Linkage: Addressing Child Care Needs Through Land Use Planning, 26 Harv. J. Legis. 591 (1989).

Note, Exactions for Transportation Corridors After *Dolan v. City of Tigard,* 29 Loy. L.A.L. Rev. 247 (1995).

Note, Land Subdivision Control, 65 Harv. L. Rev. 1226 (1952).

Note, Taking Sides: The Burden of Proof Switch in *Dolan v. City of Tigard,* 71 N.Y.U. L. Rev. 1301 (1996).

Comment, A Poor Relation? Regulatory Takings after *Dolan v. City of Tigard,* 63 U. Chi. L. Rev. 199 (1996).

# Chapter 10

# GROWTH MANAGEMENT AND PUBLIC FACILITY CONTROLS

## § 10.01. An Introductory Note.

Traditional zoning is not effective as growth management. The zoning map indicates areas for future development but does not include timing and phasing controls. Development can occur at any location where it is permitted. The over-zoning typical of many communities contributes to this problem. The zoning map may designate areas for development far in excess of reasonable projections, and development may occur anywhere within these areas. Some areas are developed prematurely, new development is scattered, and environmental areas are damaged.

Growth management is also limited by the weak link provided by state planning legislation between the provision of public facilities and land development. The Standard Planning Act requires public facility locations to be consistent with the comprehensive plan, but a two-thirds vote of the governing body can override this requirement.[1]

Growth management programs arose to correct these problems by providing control over the rate of growth and the provision of necessary public facilities. Although they are usually adopted at the local government level, some states, such as Oregon, have state land use management systems that include growth management controls. This chapter reviews the legal problems of local growth management programs.

---

1. § 3.07.

Growth management programs take many forms.[2] One method is to link the existing comprehensive plan and zoning systems so that they can manage growth more effectively. Under this approach, conventional zoning techniques are used to implement growth strategies contained in the comprehensive plan. A second method is to control the timing and sequencing of development, usually by making adequate public facilities a condition to development approval.[3] Some communities have adopted annual quotas on new development. Moratoria on new development[4] and limits on the extension of public facility services, such as sewer service, are other strategies.

Another method is to link growth management techniques to specific geographical areas. One example is the adoption by a community of urban growth or urban service limits. Growth is allowed inside but not outside the growth line. The Oregon state land use program requires all municipalities to adopt urban growth boundaries, and municipalities have adopted urban growth boundaries in other states. An urban growth boundary may also limit the growth of existing communities and provide for the dispersal of new development to outlying urban centers.

Land use control techniques that can reserve land for necessary public facilities before they are built are also an important component of growth management programs. The official map and related land use controls can be used for this purpose. Other control techniques, such as land use moratoria, are also available.

## A. TIMING, PHASING, AND QUOTAS.

### § 10.02.  The Legal Problems.

Timing, phasing, and quota controls present several legal problems. Statutory authority is a problem because the Standard Zoning Act did not authorize land use controls of this type.[5] A taking problem arises when a growth management program temporarily or permanently prohibits development. An equal protection problem arises because these programs allow development at different times in different areas of the community. Growth management programs also raise exclusionary zoning issues. They have an exclusionary effect if they do not make enough land available to meet market demand for all types of housing.

---

2. As explained by Robert H. Freilich in R. Einsweiler & D. Miness, Managing Community Growth and Change in Urban, Suburban, and Rural Settings 44-45 (Lincoln Institute of Land Policy, 1992). *See also* D. Porter, Profiles in Growth Management (1996).

3. Fla. Stat. Ann. § 161.3180 (requiring provision of public facilities to be concurrent with new development).

4. §§ 6.06-6.11.

5. *See* Boulder Bldrs. Group v. City of Boulder, 759 P.2d 752 (Colo. 1988) (growth management program authorized by constitutional home rule provision). *See also* § 4.25.

Two major decisions dominate the law on growth management. They are discussed in the sections that follow. Although still important, they are declining in relevance because of new taking law in the Supreme Court, especially the rule that a land use regulation is a taking if it prohibits all economically viable use of land, even temporarily.

## § 10.03. *Ramapo.*

*Golden v. Planning Bd. of Town of Ramapo*[6] is a leading case that upheld the validity of timing and phasing programs. The Town of Ramapo is located near New York City, on the New Jersey border. A New York town, like a midwestern township, includes unincorporated and incorporated areas.

Ramapo adopted a comprehensive plan that projected its future development and included an eighteen-year capital improvements program. The program provided for the development of all the land in the town within the eighteen-year period adopted for the capital facilities program. A downzoning was not necessary because the town was zoned for very low residential densities. One-half of the zoned area was zoned for large residential lots, and the growth management program complemented the extensive large-lot zoning. Several incorporated villages within the town were not included in its growth management program. The town later abandoned the growth management program because of difficulties in implementation.

To implement the growth management program, the town adopted an innovative amendment to its zoning ordinance. This amendment required all residential development, except individual single-family dwellings, to apply for and receive a special permit from the governing body. The program did not contemplate multi-family development and did not apply to industrial and commercial development. A developer could obtain a development permit if he acquired a designated number of points based on the availability of five essential services, not all of them controlled by the town. Although the decision did not indicate the basis on which the town awarded points, they varied depending on a development's distance from a public facility. More points were awarded if the development was closer to a facility.

The program contained a number of remedial features. The town could issue a permit vesting development rights at a future time when public services became available. The ordinance authorized variances from the permit requirement. A developer could advance the time for development by providing enough of the designated facilities to acquire the necessary points. Landowners could also apply to the town for reductions in property tax assessments on land restricted from development under the growth management program.

---

6. 285 N.E.2d 291 (N.Y.), *appeal dismissed,* 409 U.S. 1003 (1972); 63 A.L.R.3d 1184 (1975).

The plaintiffs did not attack the growth management program as applied to their property but claimed it was facially invalid because it was unauthorized by the zoning statute and unconstitutional. Because the attack on the ordinance was facial, the court did not require the plaintiffs to exhaust the administrative remedies available in the program before bringing suit.

The court held the town zoning act, which is based on the Standard Zoning Act, authorized the growth management program. It held the power to "restrict and regulate" conferred by the act included the authority to direct the growth of population within the township for growth management purposes. "[T]he matrix of land use restrictions" which are common to the "enumerated powers" provided the authority to determine how development would proceed even though it would be diverted from "its natural course." The court's holding on the statutory authority question validated the residential development permit requirement, which was a notable variation from standard zoning practice.

The court held the growth management program constitutional in an elaborate opinion that concentrated on taking and exclusionary zoning questions and was influenced by the decision to attack the program facially. The court noted that a plaintiff could attack the constitutionality of the growth management ordinance as applied in a later proceeding. It rejected a claim that the growth management program was exclusionary by noting that "the power to zone under current law is vested in local municipalities" and by deferring to the town's legislative judgment in adopting the program. The court was impressed by the comprehensive planning on which the growth management program was based. It viewed the plan as a rational and planned effort to "maximize population density consistent with orderly growth."

The court did not consider the extensive large-lot zoning the growth management program reinforced because the plaintiffs did not attack it, but it noted in a footnote that a "compelling need" had not been advanced for the large-lot zoning. The town had made provision for low- and moderate-income housing, and the court noted that this housing would help remedy lower-income housing problems in the town. It apparently was not aware that only a minimal amount of lower-income housing was available or contemplated, most of it for the elderly.

The court summed up the exclusionary issues by noting that it would not "countenance . . . under any guise . . . [any] community efforts at immunization or exclusion." It held that

> [w]hat segregates permissible from impermissible restrictions, depends in the final analysis upon the purpose of the restrictions and their impact in terms of both the community and the general public interest. . . . The line of

demarcation between the two is not a constant, but will be found to vary with prevailing circumstances and conditions. . . .[7]

The court approached the taking claim by noting the growth management "restrictions threaten to burden individual parcels for as long as a full generation" and that it did not view these restrictions as a "temporary expedient." It noted that "[e]very restriction on the use of property entails hardships for some individual owners," but concluded that

> [the restrictions] are not, however, absolute. The . . . [ordinance requirements] contemplate a definite term, as the development points are designed to operate for a maximum period of 18 years and during that period, the Town is committed to the construction and installation of capital improvements.[8]

The court pointed out that some land would be available for development before the close of the eighteen-year capital program, and that developers could accelerate the development of their land by providing the necessary public facilities.

Several important features of the Ramapo program influenced the court's decision. The extensive planning that preceded the adoption of the growth management ordinance was an important factor, as were the remedial measures available to developers. The court could uphold the growth management program as an interim measure because all of the municipality was committed to development. The *Ramapo* decision does not support growth management programs in communities that do not make this commitment. Ramapo's comparatively small size made this commitment possible. Larger communities may not be able to commit all of their area to development and may require restrictive zoning in areas not designated for development to implement a growth management program. The *Ramapo* case did not have to consider the constitutionality of this kind of zoning.

The decision leaves a number of other questions raised by growth management programs unsettled. The Ramapo program did not require a downzoning, and the court did not consider the constitutionality of the multi-family exclusion that was implicit in the program. The New York court could hold an exclusion of multi-family housing unconstitutional under its exclusionary zoning decisions, which it decided after *Ramapo*.[9] Whether an exemption for single-family dwellings and for other appropriate uses would protect the program from being found a per se taking under *Lucas* is not clear. The Ramapo program has been abandoned for some time.

---

7. *Id.* at 302.
8. *Id.* at 304.
9. §§ 7.13-7.17.

## § 10.04. *Petaluma.*

In *Construction Indus. Ass'n of Sonoma County v. City of Petaluma*,[10] a federal court upheld a growth management program that contained an explicit annual quota on residential development. Petaluma is a self-sufficient community forty miles north of San Francisco and is part of the metropolitan Bay Area housing market. Petaluma grew dramatically in the years before it adopted its growth management program.

The Petaluma program imposed an annual development quota of 500 dwelling units but exempted projects with four units or less. It included a Residential Development Control System, modeled on the Ramapo point system, under which it allocated the annual residential development quota. The Petaluma point system was elaborate and awarded points for good environmental and architectural design, for providing certain recreational facilities, and for providing low- and moderate-income dwellings in compliance with the city's housing policy. This policy allocated eight to twelve percent of the annual quota to low- and moderate-income housing.

The federal district court invalidated the program as a restriction on the constitutional right to travel, but the Court of Appeals held plaintiff did not have standing to raise this question and held only that the program did not violate substantive due process. It assumed the quota would limit supply below anticipated market demand and would cause a housing shortfall in the region, with a consequent decline in regional housing quality and choice and a loss in mobility. The court noted, however, that the quota would not create this problem in Petaluma and would increase the number of lower-income housing units in that city. It held it was "unnecessary" to consider the city's claim that the program would prevent the overtaxing of "available water and sewage facilities."

The court noted the Petaluma program might be exclusionary but that all land use regulation can have this "purpose and effect." The city could justify any exclusionary effect by showing that the program had a "rational relationship to a *legitimate state interest.*" Due process rights are not violated simply because "a local entity exercises in its own self-interest the police power lawfully delegated to it by the state." In a footnote, the court pointed out that the Petaluma program's lower-income housing goals made it inclusionary rather than exclusionary.

Although *Petaluma* still stands as a validation of a quota program under the relaxed rational relationship standard applied to substantive due process claims, the important issue today is the validity of the program under the taking clause. Petaluma has since substantially modified its growth management program.

---

10. 522 F.2d 897 (9th Cir. 1975), *cert. denied,* 424 U.S. 934 (1976).

## § 10.05. Growth Management Programs in Other States.

The courts have usually upheld growth management programs when challenged in other states. A California court upheld against a facial taking attack two ordinances that regulated growth by encouraging development in cities, and by regulating the rate, distribution, quality and type of residential development on an annual basis, with periodic reviews. It noted that "[c]ourts have long recognized the legitimacy of such ordinances."[11] A Colorado court held an ordinance establishing an annual quota system for new building permits, based on a formula against which each development application is tested and scored, was authorized by the enabling act. The act authorized the regulation of population density and the phased development of services and facilities.[12]

Courts will strike down growth management ordinances they find arbitrary. *City of Boca Raton v. Boca Villas Corp.*[13] held that an absolute quota on municipal growth violated substantive due process. It noted that the cap was supported only by after-the-fact studies, that the planning department was not consulted, and that the planning director testified that the quota was unnecessary. It held that the quota was not justified by inadequacies in public services subject to the city's control or by environmental problems.

Some courts and legislatures have considered exclusionary zoning problems raised by growth management ordinances. *Mt. Laurel (I)*,[14] for example, stated that municipalities must include an up-front provision for low- and moderate-income housing in growth management programs.[15] A California statute adopted

---

11. Long Beachfront Equities, Inc. v. County of Ventura, 282 Cal. Rptr. 877 (Cal. App. 1991) (as-applied taking and other claims not ripe), *cert. denied,* 505 U.S. 1219 (1992).

12. Wilkinson v. Board of County Comm'rs, 872 P.2d 1269 (Colo. App. 1994) (also upholding denial of development application under ordinance and dismissing taking claim as unripe). *See also* Giuliano v. Town of Edgartown, 531 F. Supp. 1076 (D. Mass. 1982) (upholding regulation on timing of development); Sturges v. Town of Chilmark, 402 N.E.2d 1346 (Mass. 1980) (holding ordinance limiting annual rate of growth on Martha's Vineyard for ten years so town could study problems resulting from subsoil conditions authorized by statute and not a due process violation); Albany Area Builders Ass'n v. Town of Clifton Park, 576 N.Y.S.2d 932 (App. Div. 1991) (upholding ordinance limiting building permits in 10% of town to 20% units approved in project to remedy traffic problems; ordinance effective for five years or until interchange completed).

13. 371 So. 2d 154 (Fla. App. 1979), *cert. denied,* 381 So. 2d 765 (Fla. 1980). *Compare* Innkeepers Motor Lodge, Inc. v. City of New Smyrna Beach, 460 So. 2d 379 (Fla. App. 1984) (accord) *with* City of Hollywood v. Hollywood, Inc., 432 So. 2d 1332 (Fla. App. 1983) (upholding density cap for area of city). *See also* Begin v. Town of Sabbatus, 409 A.2d 1269 (Me. 1979) (invalidating slow-growth ordinance limited to mobile homes).

14. Southern Burlington County NAACP v. Township of Mt. Laurel (I), 336 A.2d 713 (N.J.), *appeal dismissed and cert. denied,* 423 U.S. 808 (1975), discussed in § 7.09.

15. *See also* Griffin Homes, Inc. v. Superior Ct., 274 Cal. Rptr. 456 (Cal. App. 1990) (development quota program does not conflict facially with state policy goals relating to the provision of affordable housing.

427

after *Petaluma* provides that any ordinance that limits the number of residential building permits or buildable lots "is presumed to have an impact on the supply of residential units" in the municipality and in the territory outside its jurisdiction.[16] In an action challenging such an ordinance, a municipality has the burden to show that it "is necessary for the protection of the public health, safety or welfare" of the municipality.[17]

A few states have statutes that authorize or place limitations on growth management programs. Washington State and Maine require municipalities to designate urban growth areas.[18] A New Hampshire statute authorizes municipalities to "regulate and control the timing of development." A municipality may not enact a growth timing ordinance unless its planning board adopts a master plan and capital improvement ordinance. Its growth management process must also "assess and balance community development needs and consider regional development needs."[19]

The state planning goals adopted in Oregon's state land use program require the adoption of an Urban Growth Boundary (UGB) by local governments in the state. The UGB must be approved by a state Land Conservation and Development Commission (LCDC). New urban development generally can occur only within a UGB.[20]

---

**16.** Cal. Evid. Code § 669.5. *See* Building Indus. Ass'n v. City of Camarillo, 718 P.2d 68 (Cal.1968) (applies to ordinance adopted by initiative). *See also* Cal. Gov't Code 65863.6.

**17.** *See also* William S. Hart Union High Sch. Dist. v. Regional Planning Comm'n, 277 Cal. Rptr. 645 (Cal. App. 1991) (denial of rezoning because of inadequate school facilities); Lee v. City of Monterrey Park, 219 Cal. Rptr. 309 (Cal. App. 1985) (complaint that initiative ordinance that adopted annual building quota violated California's exclusionary zoning rule stated cause of action).

**18.** Me. Rev. Stat. Ann. tit. 30-A, § 4326 (1993); Wash. Rev. Code Ann. § 36.70A.110.

**19.** N.H. Rev. Stat. § 674:22, codifying Beck v. Town of Raymond, 394 A.2d 847 (N.H. 1978). *See* Rancourt v. Town of Barnstead, 523 A.2d 55 (N.H. 1986) (rejecting growth rate in plan and holding growth control ordinance mustbe based on "reasonable rate of increase" in municipal services.) *See also* Caspersen v. Town of Lyme, 661 A.2d 759 (N.H. 1995) (50-acre minimum lot size ordinance not a growth control subject to the statute); Stoney-Brook Dev. Corp. v. Town of Fremont, 474 A.2d 561 (N.H. 1984); N.H. Rev. Stat. § 674:23 (authorizing interim growth controls).

**20.** *See* Benjfran Dev., Inc. v. Metropolitan Serv. Dist., 767 P.2d 467 (Or. App. 1989) (need for economic development does not preempt UGB policy); Collins v. Land Conservation & Dev. Comm'n, 707 P.2d 599 (Or. App. 1985) (remanding LCDC order approving comprehensive plan because UGB included more land than necessary for expansion of urban area); Willamette Univ. v. Land Conservation and Dev. Comm'n, 608 P.2d 1178 (Or. App. 1980) (UGB must be based solely on determination of future growth needs, and not irrelevent political boundaries).

## § 10.06. The Right to Travel.

Beginning with *Shapiro v. Thompson*,[21] which invalidated a state residence requirement for welfare assistance, the U.S. Supreme Court struck down a number of residence restrictions that prevented nonresidents of a state from voting or from receiving necessary social services.[22] The Supreme Court has indicated that the right to interstate travel does not present a serious obstacle to land use programs. The Court rejected a right-to-travel objection in its *Belle Terre*[23] decision, which upheld a zoning ordinance that limited the number of unrelated individuals who could occupy single-family dwellings. The Court noted that the ordinance was not "aimed at transients" and did not implicate a fundamental constitutional right, such as the right to vote.

In *CEEED v. California Coastal Zone Conservation Comm'n*,[24] the court rejected a right-to-travel objection to the California coastal permit program that restricted growth in coastal areas. The court applied the Supreme Court's right-to-travel cases and held the coastal permit program did not interfere with the right to travel because "[i]t is not discriminatory; it imposes no durational residence requirement; it exacts no penalty for exercising the right to travel or to select one's place of residence. In short, it has no chilling effect on an individual's freedom of movement."[25]

## § 10.07. Public Utility Extensions.

### § 10.08. The Duty to Serve.

Many growth management programs allow the approval of new development only if adequate public utilities, such as sewer and water, are available. The Ramapo growth management program is an example.[26] A landowner whose development is disapproved because public utilities are unavailable may decide to bring an action to compel the extension of public utilities to his land.

A refusal to extend a public utility service to a landowner who wants to be served by the utility raises an equal protection problem. The municipality must have a justifiable reason for the refusal to extend service. Courts usually uphold

---

21. 394 U.S. 618 (1969).

22. Memorial Hosp. v. Maricopa County, 415 U.S. 250 (1974); Dunn v. Blumstein, 405 U.S. 330 (1972). *But see* Zobel v. Williams, 457 U.S. 55 (1982); Sosna v. Iowa, 419 U.S. 393 (1975).

23. Village of Belle Terre v. Boraas, 416 U.S. 1 (1974), discussed in § 2.48.

24. 118 Cal. Rptr. 315 (Cal. App. 1974).

25. *Id.* at 333. *See also* Associated Home Bldrs. of Greater Eastbay, Inc. v. City of Livermore, 557 P.2d 473 (Cal. 1976); Northern Ill. Home Bldrs. Ass'n v. County of DuPage, 649 N.E.2d 384 (Ill. 1995) (rejecting claim that roadway impact fee violated right to travel). *See* Smith v. Lower Merion Twp., 1991 U.S. Dist. Lexis 11100 (E.D. Pa. 1991) (extensive discussion of right to travel doctrine as applied to land use regulation).

26. § 10.03.

municipal refusals to extend services within their boundaries when the refusal is based on utility-related reasons, such as inadequate financial resources or inadequate capacity.[27] The courts have also held that municipal utilities may exercise discretion in deciding whether to extend utility service to areas outside municipal boundaries. Courts may compel an extension of service if the municipal utility has held itself out to provide service by extending service generally in the extraterritorial area.[28]

Whether a municipality can deny public utility service extensions to implement a growth management program raises a more troublesome question. An early New Jersey case held that a municipality could not condition the extension of utility services on an agreement by a developer to increase lot sizes to conform to municipal planning policies.[29] *Robinson v. City of Boulder*[30] disapproved a refusal to extend utility services to implement a growth management program. The city and the surrounding county adopted a joint comprehensive plan, and the city established itself as the sole provider of utility services in an extraterritorial area outside the city. When a landowner in this area applied for an extension of utility services the city refused, claiming that development in the area would conflict with the growth management policies of the comprehensive plan.

The court held the city's refusal to provide utility services was unauthorized. Boulder had held itself out as the sole provider of utility services in the area and had a duty to provide service on an equal basis to all landowners. It could not refuse service for reasons not related to utility concerns. The court did not consider the impact of the growth management plan on the city's duty to provide extraterritorial service because the city did not have extraterritorial planning and zoning powers. The county had those powers in the extraterritorial area but was not responsible for the provision of utility service.

The court reached a contrary result in *Dateline Bldrs., Inc. v. City of Santa Rosa*.[31] A developer planned to build a housing project that was adjacent to a city trunk sewer line outside the city's boundaries. The city refused to provide service because the project was outside the area designated for growth in a joint city-

---

27. Lawrence v. Richards, 88 A. 92 (Me. 1913); Rose v. Plymouth Town, 173 P.2d 285 (Utah 1946); 41 A.L.R.2d 1222 (1956). *Compare* Clark v. Board of Water & Sewer Comm'rs, 234 N.E.2d 893 (Mass. 1968). *But see* Council of Middletown Twp. v. Benham, 523 A.2d 311 (Pa. 1987).

28. Delmarva Enters. v. Mayor & Council, 282 A.2d 601 (Del. 1971); Denby v. Brown, 199 S.E.2d 214 (Ga. 1973); Mayor & Council v. Goldberg, 264 A.2d 113 (Md. 1970); Okemo Trailside Condos. v. Blais, 380 A.2d 84 (Vt. 1977).

29. Reid Dev. Corp. v. Parsippany-Troy Hills Twp., 107 A.2d 20 (N.J. App. Div. 1954).

30. 547 P.2d 228 (Colo. 1976).

31. 194 Cal. Rptr. 258 (Cal. App. 1983). *See also* First Peoples Bank of New Jersey v. Township of Medford, 599 A.2d 1248 (N.J. 1991) (refusal to extend sewer service when reasonable attempt made to meet sewage treatment needs); Town of Beloit v. Public Serv. Comm'n, 148 N.W.2d 661 (Wis. 1967).

county growth management plan. The court upheld the denial. It rejected arguments by the developer that the city, as the only supplier, "could not act beyond its boundaries and could not use sewer hookup as a planning device." It held that the denial was "a necessary and proper exercise" of the police power in aid of the growth management plan.

### § 10.09.  Taking Problems.

The requirement in some growth management programs that development may not occur if public facilities are inadequate can create taking problems if the provision of essential public facilities is delayed. In *Charles v. Diamond*,[32] a village ordinance required developers to connect with the village sewage system. The village granted a connection permit to a developer, but the state environmental department prohibited connection until the village corrected deficiencies in the system. The necessary steps to correct these deficiencies were delayed under a series of consent orders, and the system was still deficient when the developer brought suit claiming the delay was a taking of its property.

The court held that service difficulties could justify only temporary restrictions on development. It cited *Ramapo*[33] and noted that the municipality "must be committed firmly to the construction and installation of the necessary improvements." An extensive delay was justified

> only if the remedial steps are of sufficient magnitude to require extensive preparations, including preliminary studies, applications for assistance to other governmental entities, the raising of large amounts of capital, and the letting of work contracts.[34]

The court remanded the case for trial because the record was not sufficiently developed to decide the constitutional issues.

### B. RESERVATION OF LAND AND OFFICIAL MAPPING FOR PUBLIC FACILITIES.

### § 10.10.  The Land Reservation Problem.

Comprehensive plans do not contain legally enforceable land use restrictions and cannot prohibit the development of land the plan designates for public facilities, such as streets, highways and parks. Agencies must plan and designate land for these facilities in advance of their acquisition, but development may occur in planned corridors or on planned sites unless controls are available to reserve this land during the interim period prior to its acquisition. This kind of

---

32. 360 N.E.2d 1295 (N.Y. 1977).
33. § 10.03.
34. 360 N.E.2d at 1301.

control can assist growth management and public facility improvement programs by protecting land planned for public facilities until the time public agencies are ready to acquire it.

## § 10.11. Land Reservation Legislation.

The most common land reservation legislation is the official map.[35] To implement planning for streets and public facilities, the Standard Planning Act authorized municipalities to adopt an official map that designated land reserved for acquisition for these facilities.[36] The Standard Planning Act's provision for official maps was based on earlier legislation adopted in New York and other states. The Act required compensation to landowners whose land was reserved for future streets, denied compensation for any buildings built in mapped streets, and did not contain a variance provision. It authorized the local governing body to set a time limit on an official map reservation. Some official map legislation is based on the Standard Planning Act model.[37]

Two model acts published after the Standard Planning Act also included legislative authority for official maps. The model acts differ in detail, but their statutory authority for official maps is similar. The model acts rely on the police power and do not authorize compensation to landowners whose land is reserved for acquisition in an official map. The acts prohibit the development of land reserved on an official map unless the municipality grants a variance. The model acts make the adoption of a street plan an explicit or implicit condition for the adoption of an official street map. Some official map legislation that authorizes official maps is based on one of the model acts.[38] Official map legislation in other states is similar to but not based directly on the model acts.[39] The model acts and most state official map acts do not authorize the adoption of a time limit for an official map reservation.

Some subdivision control statutes and ordinances also authorize the reservation of land for acquisition for a public facility. They may also prohibit the development of the land during the reservation period.[40]

---

35. Nigro v. Planning Bd. of Saddle River, 584 A.2d 1350 (N.J. 1991) (reviewing function of official maps as a planning technique). *See also* Utah Code Ann. §§ 10-9-404(3)(A); 17-27-404(3)(A) (development moratorium in area proposed as highway or transportation corridor).

36. Standard Planning Act §§ 21-25.

37. Colo. Rev. Stat. §§ 31-23-220 to 31-23-224; Pa. Stat. Ann. tit. 53, §§ 22777-22779.

38. Del. Code Ann. tit. 22, § 704; Mass. Gen. Laws Ann. ch. 41, §§ 81E-81J; Md. Ann. Code art. 66B, § 6.01; N.Y. Gen. City Law §§ 26, 29, 33-36.

39. La Rev. Stat. Ann. § 33:116; Okla. Stat. Ann. tit. 11, 47-121 to 47-123; S.C. Code Ann. §§ 6-7-1210 to 6-7-1280.

40. Ala. Code §§ 11-52-50 to 11-52-54. On the taking issue, *see* Ventures in Prop. I v. City of Wichita, 594 P.2d 671 (Kan. 1979); Howard County v. JJM, Inc., 482 A.2d 908 (Md. 1984).

A number of states authorize the state transportation agency to adopt maps for transportation corridors or for the location of future highway rights-of-way. A comprehensive state mapping law will require public hearings and comments on planned corridors, the preparation and recording of official maps of the corridors, and local government referral to the state transportation agency of any application to develop land within the corridor. The state transportation agency must then find either that the development proposal has an impact on the preservation of the corridor or does not have an impact. If the proposed development is found to have an impact on the corridor, the state transportation agency must negotiate with the developer either for the purchase of its land or for a modification in development plans that will protect the corridor.[41]

### § 10.12.  Taking Problems.

Taking problems may be serious under official map legislation.[42] Official map legislation may be a per se taking under the Supreme Court's *Lucas* decision if an official map designation deprives a property owner of all economically viable use of his land for a temporary period of time.[43] Landowners can also argue that the prohibition on development is an improper attempt to depress property values prior to the time the land is acquired.[44]

One group of cases decided before the Supreme Court's 1987 taking trilogy held that official map legislation was a taking. *Lomarch Corp. v. Mayor & Common Council*[45] is typical. The court held unconstitutional a statute requiring

---

**41.** Cal Sts. & High. Code §§ 740, 741; Del. Code Ann. tit. 17, § 145 (local comprehensive plans must incorporate state corridor designatiaons); 605 Ill. Comp. Stat. 5/ 4-510; Neb. Rev. Stat. §§ 39-1311 to 39-1311.05; N.H. Rev. Stat. Ann §§ 230-a:1 to 230-a:14; N.J. Stat. Ann. §§ 27:7-66, 27:7-67; Ohio Rev. Code Ann. § 5511.01.

**42.** *But see* Headley v. City of Rochester, 5 N.E.2d 198 (N.Y. 1936) (cannot raise taking claim if did not request variance from map); State ex rel. Miller v. Manders, 86 N.W.2d 469 (Wis. 1957) (same).

**43.** Ward v. Bennett, 625 N.Y.S.2d 609 (App. Div. 1995) (reinstating complaint for taking when official map reservation existed for 50 years and landowner denied all economically viable use of land). *But cf.* State of Delaware v. Booker, 1992 Del. Super. LEXIS 366 (Del. Super. 1992); Meixsell v. Ross Twp. Bd. of Supvrs., 623 A.2d 429 (Pa. Commw. 1993) (dictum, can require setback for future road widening if state to condemn land at later date). *See* §§ 6.06-6.11 (moratoria).

**44.** § 2.29. *See* People ex rel. Department of Transp. v. Diversified Prods. Co. III, 17 Cal. Rptr. 2d 676 (Cal. App. 1993) (de facto taking by state found when city and state cooperated in preventing development of property in transportation corridor).

**45.** 237 A.2d 881 (N.J. 1968). *See also* Urbanizadora Versalles, Inc. v. Rivera Rios, 701 F.2d 993 (1st Cir. 1983) (invalidating official map reservation for highway that was in effect for 14 years); Jensen v. City of New York, 369 N.E.2d 1179 (N.Y. 1977) (reservation made property "virtually unsalable"); Miller v. City of Beaver Falls, 82 A.2d 34 (Pa. 1951) (invalidating reservation for parks and playgrounds although reservation for streets previously upheld).

subdividers to reserve land shown on an official map for park and playground use. The reservation was effective for one year. The court held that the reservation amounted to a unilateral option to reserve the land and was constitutional only if the municipality compensated the landowner. The court relied on an earlier New Jersey case, now discredited in that state,[46] which invalidated a zoning ordinance restricting development in a wetland because it conferred a benefit on the general public. The compensation requirement for official map reservations is codified in the subdivision control legislation.[47]

However, the Florida Supreme Court held an unrecorded county thoroughfare map adopted as part of the mandatory county plan was not a taking on its face, even it prohibited all development in a transportation corridor that would impede future highway construction.[48] The court noted that owners adjacent to transportation corridors would most likely benefit from planned road construction, and that the thoroughfare map limited development only to the extent necessary to ensure future land use compatible with the planned highway. The thoroughfare map did not finally designate highway locations within the transportation corridor, and the court noted the county as a permitting authority "has the flexibility to ameliorate some of the hardships of a person owning land within the corridor." The court indicated the taking issue should be determined on an as-applied basis as individual owners made application for development within the transportation corridor.

Courts may be less likely to find a taking under a state corridor preservation law when the state agency is required to purchase reserved property if development is denied. In *Kingston E. Realty Co. v. State*.[49] The plaintiff, as required by the law, applied for a municipal permit to construct an office research laboratory complex. The municipality denied the permit. The law gave the state highway agency 120 days following the permit denial to decide whether it wanted to acquire the property. A permit could not issue during this period. The law mandated the issuance of a permit if the state agency did not take any action to acquire the property during the 120-day period. The state agency did not take any action to acquire the property.

---

**46.** *See* New Jersey Bldrs. Ass'n v. Department of Envt'l Protection, 404 A.2d 320 (N.J. App. Div. 1979).

**47.** N.J. Stat. Ann. § 40:55D-44.

**48.** Palm Beach County v. Wright, 641 So. 2d 50 (Fla. 1994) (applying state law), *and distinguishing* Joint Ventures, Inc. v. Department of Transp., 563 So. 2d 622 (Fla. 1990) (invalidating state corridor mapping law as violation of due process). *See also* Rochester Bus. Inst. v. City of Rochester, 267 N.Y.S.2d 274 (App. Div. 1966) (applying balancing test to uphold street-widening reservation on official map that increased construction costs by six percent).

**49.** 330 A.2d 40 (N.J. App. Div. 1975). Contra Lackman v. Hall, 364 A.2d 1244 (Del. Ch. 1976).

The court held a temporary taking of plaintiff's property did not occur during the time the statute stayed issuance of a building permit while the state agency was allowed to consider acquisition. The court distinguished *Lomarch* because the reservation in *Kingston* was for a considerably shorter period of time and was not a blanket reservation. It held that "similar measures," such as zoning moratoria, "have been recognized under narrow circumstances as reasonable regulations in the exercise of governmental police powers." The court noted that the highway reservation was "reasonably designed to reduce the cost of public acquisition."

# REFERENCES

## Books and Monographs

J. DeGrove, Planning & Growth Management in the States (1992).

E. Kelly, Community Growth: Policies, Techniques, and Impacts (1993).

E. Kelly, Planning, Growth, and Public Facilities: A Primer for Local Officials, American Planning Ass'n, Planning Advisory Serv. Rep. No. 447 (1993).

D. Mandelker & B. Blaesser, Corridor Preservation: Study of Legal and Institutional Barriers (Federal Highway Admin., 1996).

A. Nelson & J. Duncan, Growth Management Principles and Practices (1995).

D. Porter ed., Performance Standards for Growth Management, American Planning Ass'n, Planning Advisory Serv. Rep. No. 461 (1996).

S.M. White, Adequate Public Facilities Ordinances and Transportation Management, American Planning Ass'n, Planning Advisory Serv. Rep. No. 465 (1996).

## Articles

Chinn & Garvin, Designing Development Allocation Systems, Land Use L. & Zoning Dig., Vol. 44, No. 2, at 3 (1992).

Freilich & White, Transportation Congestion and Growth Management: Comprehensive Approaches to Resolving America's Major Quality of Life Crisis, 24 Loyola L.A.L. Rev. 915 (1991).

Kelly, Piping Growth: The Law, Economics and Equality of Sewer and Water Connection Policies, Land Use L. & Zoning Dig., Vol. 36, No. 7, at 3 (1984).

Kushner, Growth Management and the City, 12 Yale L. & Pol'y Rev. 68 (1994).

LeGates, The Emergence of Flexible Growth Management Systems in the San Francisco Bay Area, 24 Loyola L.A.L. Rev. 1035 (1991).

Mandelker, Interim Development Controls in Highway Programs: The Taking Issue, 4 J. Land Use & Envtl. L. 167 (1989).

Porter, Do State Growth Management Acts Make a Difference? Local Growth Management Measures Under Different State Growth Policies, 24 Loyola L.A.L. Rev. 1015 (1991).

Roberts, An Appropriate Economic Model of Judicial Review of Suburban Growth Control, 55 Ind. L.J. 441 (1980).

Stone, The Prevention of Urban Sprawl Through Utility Extension Control, 14 Urb. Law. 357 (1982).

Stone & Seymour, Regulating the Timing of Development: Takings Clause and Substantive Due Process Challenges to Growth Control Regulations, 24 Loyola L.A.L. Rev. 1205 (1991).

Walsh & Pearce, The Concurrency Requirement of the Washington State Growth Management Act, 16 U. Puget Sound L. Rev. 1025 (1993).

## Student Work

Note, Phased Zoning: Regulation of the Tempo and Sequence of Land Development, 26 Stan. L. Rev. 585 (1974).

Note, Public Utility Land Use Control on the Urban Fringe, 63 Iowa L. Rev. 889 (1978).

Note, Sometimes There's Nothing Left to Give: The Justification for Denying Water Service to New Consumers to Control Growth, 44 Stan. L. Rev. 429 (1992).

Note, That Old Due Process Magic: Growth Control and the Federal Constitution, 88 Mich. L. Rev. 1245 (1990).

Note, A Zoning Program for Phased Growth: Ramapo Township's Time Controls on Residential Development, 47 N.Y.U. L. Rev. 723 (1972).

Comment, One Tier Beyond Ramapo: Open Space Zoning and the Urban Reserve, 15 San Diego L. Rev. 1211 (1978).

Comment, Wrong Turns: A Critique of the Supreme Court's Right to Travel Cases, 21 Wm. Mitchell L. Rev. 457 (1995).

# Chapter 11

# AESTHETICS, SIGN CONTROLS, AND HISTORIC PRESERVATION

## § 11.01. The Aesthetic Control Problem.

Although aesthetic values underlie much traditional land use regulation, such as large-lot zoning, a number of land use controls are more clearly intended to achieve aesthetic purposes. Architectural design review for residential dwellings is one example. Sign controls fall in the aesthetic category because they regulate the impact of signs on the visual environment. Historic preservation has an aesthetic basis, but it is more tenuous. Historic areas and landmarks can have historic value because of their architectural merit, but some historic areas and landmarks are treasured because of their historic associations despite their lack of aesthetic value.

A substantive due process issue underlies all forms of aesthetic regulation. Courts must determine whether aesthetic regulation is a proper exercise of the police power under the due process clause. Although the early cases struck down aesthetic land use regulations, a majority of courts now hold that aesthetics alone is a legitimate government purpose in land use regulation.

The substantive due process problem is eased for aesthetic land use controls based on the compatibility principle that supports zoning. Historic district controls are one example. They maintain the architectural and visual compatibility of the historic environment. Sign controls are another. They prohibit signs that are visually incompatible in their environment or impose restrictions that ensure visual compatibility. The zoning analogy supports the constitutionality of this type of aesthetic regulation.

Taking problems arise under aesthetic controls but are not serious when these controls regulate the design and exterior appearance of buildings rather than the development of land. More serious taking problems are raised by historic district and landmark preservation ordinances. Restrictions imposed under these ordinances can leave a landowner without an economically viable use of her land. An example is a refusal to allow demolition of an uneconomic landmark and its replacement with another building.

Equal protection problems are not serious in aesthetic regulation.[1] They arise principally under sign ordinances that provide different regulations for different types of signs, but most courts uphold these classifications. Sign controls may also violate the free speech clause of the federal constitution. The Supreme Court has not decided a majority opinion that clearly delineates the free speech problems that arise in sign regulations, and this failure has led to disagreement in the lower federal and state courts on the application of the free speech clause to the regulation of signs.

_____

1. §§ 2.47-2.51

## § 11.02.  Aesthetics as a Regulatory Purpose.

### § 11.03.  The Early Period.

An early New Jersey case illustrates the view, prevailing generally before 1930, that aesthetics is not a legitimate purpose in land use control. In *City of Passaic v. Paterson Bill Posting, Adv. & Sign Painting Co.*,[2] the court invalidated a statute that imposed setback and height restrictions on signs. It held:

> Aesthetic considerations are a matter of luxury and indulgence rather than of necessity, and it is necessity alone which justifies the exercise of the police power to take private property without compensation.[3]

Some early decisions that held billboard controls constitutional avoided the aesthetic purpose problem by finding a number of evils and dangers that justified the regulation of billboards. Criminal or immoral activities might occur behind them, or they might collapse and cause injury.[4] These evils and dangers no longer provide a basis for upholding billboard regulation. Billboards are made of sturdier and lightweight materials and are usually some distance from the ground.

### § 11.04.  The Minority View: Aesthetics as a Factor.

A minority of courts hold that aesthetics is an appropriate governmental purpose in land use regulation if it advances other legitimate governmental purposes. In *Village of Hudson v. Albrecht, Inc.*,[5] for example, the court held that a local legislative body may take aesthetic factors into account when it adopts zoning regulations. It upheld the constitutionality of a design review ordinance and noted that it reflected "a concern for the monetary interests of protecting real estate from impairment and destruction of value" in addition to promoting aesthetic values.

The rule that aesthetics may be a factor in land use regulation is a fiction. The additional governmental purposes that courts require to support an aesthetic regulation derive from its aesthetic purposes. The minority view upholds an ordinance that prohibits billboards, for example, because it prevents negative impacts on property values in addition to improving the visual quality of the environment. But billboards have a negative impact on property values only because they are aesthetically objectionable in the visual environment in which they are prohibited.

---

**2.** 62 A. 267 (N.J. Err. & App. 1905); 21 A.L.R.3d 1222 (1968).

**3.** *Id.* at 268.

**4.** St. Louis Gunning Adv. Co. v. City of St. Louis, 137 S.W. 929 (Mo. 1911), *appeal dismissed*, 231 U.S. 761 (1913).

**5.** 458 N.E.2d 852 (Ohio), *appeal dismissed*, 467 U.S. 1237 (1984).

The relationship between aesthetic purposes and the protection of property values is acknowledged in cases that recognize a "coalescence" of economic and aesthetic values that supports aesthetic regulation. This view is best expressed in *United Adv. Corp. v. Borough of Metuchen*,[6] a leading New Jersey case that upheld an ordinance prohibiting billboards in a suburban community:

> There are areas in which aesthetics and economics coalesce, areas in which a discordant sight is as hard an economic fact as an annoying odor or sound. We refer not to some sensitive or exquisite preference but to concepts of congruity held so widely that they are inseparable from the enjoyment and hence the value of property.[7]

New Jersey has now adopted the majority view and holds that zoning and billboard control ordinances "may accommodate aesthetic concerns."[8]

### § 11.05. The Majority View: Aesthetics Alone.

A clear majority of courts hold that aesthetics alone is a legitimate governmental purpose in land use regulation.[9] An important dictum in a U.S. Supreme Court urban renewal decision was a major factor in the judicial adoption of the "aesthetics alone" view. The Court wrote:

> The concept of the public welfare is broad and inconclusive.... The values it represents are spiritual as well as physical, aesthetic as well as monetary. It is within the power of the legislature to determine that the community should be beautiful as well as healthy, spacious as well as clean, well-balanced as well as carefully patrolled.[10]

---

**6.** 198 A.2d 447 (N.J. 1964). Adopting minority view: Figarsky v. Historic Dist. Comm'n, 368 A.2d 163 (Conn. 1976); Mayor & City Council v. Mano Swartz, Inc., 299 A.2d 828 (Md. 1973); Naegele Outdoor Adv. Co. v. Village of Minnetonka, 162 N.W.2d 206 (Minn. 1968); City of Houston v. Johnny Frank's Auto Parts, Inc., 480 S.W.2d 774 (Tex. Civ. App. 1972).

**7.** 198 A.2d at 449.

**8.** State v. Miller, 416 A.2d 821 (N.J. 1980), discussed in § 11.05.

**9.** Donrey Communications Co. v. City of Fayetteville, 660 S.W.2d 900 (Ark. 1983), *cert. denied,* 466 U.S. 959 (1984); Metromedia, Inc. v. City of San Diego, 610 P.2d 407 (Cal. 1980), *rev'd on other grounds,* 453 U.S. 490 (1981); City of Lake Wales v. Lamar Adv. Ass'n, 414 So. 2d 1030 (Fla. 1982); John Donnelly & Sons v. Outdoor Adv. Bd., 339 N.E.2d 709 (Mass. 1975); Asselin v. Town of Conway, 628 A.2d 247 (N.H. 1993); Cromwell v. Ferrier, 225 N.E.2d 748 (N.Y. 1967); State v. Jones, 290 S.E.2d 675 (N.C. 1982); Oregon City v. Hartke, 400 P.2d 255 (Or. 1965); State v. Smith, 618 S.W.2d 474 (Tenn. 1981); Town of Sandgate v. Colehamer, 589 A.2d 1205 (Vt. 1990). *See* Tahoe Reg'l Planning Agency v. King, 285 Cal. Rptr. 335 (Cal. App. 1991) (*Nollan* decision does not erode legitimacy of aesthetics as a regulatory purpose).

**10.** Berman v. Parker, 348 U.S. 26, 33 (1954).

*State v. Miller*,[11] a sign ordinance case, illustrates the cases that adopt the aesthetics alone view. The court held:

> Consideration of aesthetics in municipal land use planning is no longer a matter of luxury and indulgence.... The development and preservation of natural resources and clean, salubrious neighborhoods contribute to psychological and emotional stability and well-being as well as stimulate a sense of civic pride.[12]

The view that, aesthetics alone is a legitimate governmental purpose in land use regulation resolves the substantive due process problem raised by facial attacks on aesthetic controls. Courts must still determine whether aesthetic controls properly advance aesthetic purposes as applied.[13]

## A. SIGN CONTROLS.

### § 11.06.  Local, State, and Federal Regulation.

Signs divide into a number of categories depending on their location, type, and purpose. One classification distinguishes between on-premise signs that advertise a business conducted on the premises and off-premise signs that carry general commercial advertising. Signs are also distinguished depending on whether they carry commercial or noncommercial messages and whether they are freestanding or attached to the walls or roof of a building. Billboards are an example of freestanding, off-premise signs.

Municipalities may adopt sign controls as part of their zoning ordinance or as a separate ordinance. The courts have found the necessary implied authority to enact sign regulations in either format.[14] The federal Highway Beautification Act requires states to regulate signs along interstate and primary federal highways.[15] The Act prohibits all signs within 660 feet of the edge of the highway and all signs visible from the edge of the highway in rural areas, except in zoned or un-

---

11. 416 A.2d 821 (N.J. 1980).

12. *Id.* at 824.

13. *Compare* Asselin v. Town of Conway, 607 A.2d 132 (N.H. 1992) (ordinance allowing readerboards for nightly entertainment uses but not restaurants violates equal protection under state's strict judicial review standard), *with* Caroll Sign Co. v. Adams County Zoning Hearing Bd., 606 A.2d 1250 (Pa. Commw. 1992) (ordinance banning billboards but allowing on-site signs upheld).

14. Outdoor Systems v. City of Mesa, 819 P.2d 44 (Ariz. 1991) (statutory authority to regulate billboards includes authority to prohibit off-site billboards); City of Escondido v. Desert Outdoor Adv., 505 P.2d 1012 (Cal. 1973); Strazzulla v. Building Inspector, 260 N.E.2d 163 (Mass. 1970); Town of Boothbay v. National Adv. Co., 347 A.2d 419 (Me. 1975); Summey Outdoor Adv., Inc. v. County of Henderson, 386 S.E.2d 439 (N.C. App. 1989) (may regulate signs under police power authority).

15. 23 U.S.C. § 131.

zoned commercial and industrial areas. Federal regulations allow municipalities to rezone for commercial uses to allow the display of signs if done as part of a comprehensive zoning and not solely to permit outdoor advertising structures.[16] On-premise signs are also exempt from the statutory prohibition.

All states have enacted legislation that implements the federal requirements and that authorizes state highway agencies to control signs along federal highways in a permit program. States that do not comply with the federal statute's requirements for sign control may lose ten percent of their federal highway funds.

Many of the state sign control laws authorize the municipal regulation of signs along federal highways. The courts have relied on this grant of authority to hold the state sign control legislation does not preempt municipal control of signs.[17] A local ordinance or permit may be preempted by a more stringent state law.[18]

### § 11.07. On Highways and Streets: Taking Problems.

The courts rely on aesthetics, the protection of tourism, and traffic safety improvement to uphold sign controls on streets and highways.[19] They rely on the traffic improvement justification even though studies on the effect of signs on traffic safety are inconclusive.[20] *Metromedia, Inc. v. City of San Diego*[21] is a leading case. The court held that "as a matter of law . . . an ordinance which

---

16. L & W Outdoor Adv. Co. v. State, 539 N.E.2d 497 (Ind. App. 1989) (rezoning held invalid); Naegele Outdoor Advertising v. Hunt, 465 S.E.2d 549 (N.C. App. 1995) (rezoning upheld); Kunz & Co. v. State, 913 P.2d 765 (Utah App. 1996) (rezoning held invalid).

17. Libra Group, Inc. v. State, 805 P.2d 409 (Ariz. App. 1991); Lamar-Orlando Outdoor Adv. v. City of Ormond Beach, 415 So. 2d 1312 (Fla. App. 1982); City of Doraville v. Turner Communications Co., 223 S.E.2d 798 (Ga. 1976); Scadron v. City of Des Plaines, 606 N.E.2d 1154 (Ill. 1992) (home rule municipality). *Contra* National Adv. Co. v. Missouri State Hwy. & Transp. Comm'n, 862 S.W.2d 953 (Mo. App. 1993) (sign in commercial area had state permit).

18. National Adv. Co. v. Department of Hwys., 751 P.2d 632 (Colo. 1988) (state law preempts less restrictive local ordinance and city's issuance of permit does not estop state denial); Southeastern Displays, Inc. v. Ward, 414 S.W.2d 573 (Ky. 1967); State ex rel. Missouri Hwy. & Transp. Comm'n v. Alexian Bros., 848 S.W.2d 472 (Mo. 1993) (state can remove sign permitted by city in residential area).

19. E.B. Elliott Adv. Co. v. Metropolitan Dade County, 425 F.2d 1141 (5th Cir.), *cert. denied,* 400 U.S. 805 (1970); Yarbrough v. Arkansas State Hwy. Comm'n, 539 S.W.2d 419 (Ark. 1976); Moore v. Ward, 377 S.W.2d 881 (Ky. 1964); Newman Signs, Inc. v. Hjelle, 268 N.W.2d 741 (N.D. 1978); Markham Adv. Co. v. State, 439 P.2d 249 (Wash. 1968), *appeal dismissed,* 393 U.S. 316 (1969); 81 A.L.R.3d 564 (1977).

20. Railway Express Agency v. City of New York, 336 U.S. 106 (1949).

21. 610 P.2d 407 (Cal. 1980), *rev'd on other grounds,* 453 U.S. 490 (1981). *Accord* Robert L. Rieke Bldg. Co. v. City of Overland Park, 657 P.2d 1121 (Kan. 1983); Sun Oil Co. v. City of Madison Heights, 199 N.W.2d 525 (Mich. App. 1972); Hilton v. City of Toledo, 405 N.E.2d 1047 (Ohio 1980).

eliminates billboards designed to be viewed from the streets and highways reasonably relates to traffic safety." It added that a resolution of the traffic safety controversy was a matter of legislative judgment the court should not disturb unless it was unreasonable.

Sign controls along streets and highways create taking problems. Most of the taking cases arose under state statutes that enacted the outdoor advertising controls required by the federal Highway Beautification Act.[22] Cases rejecting taking claims because only the right to display on-premise signs is protected,[23] or because public funds that constructed the highway created the opportunity to display signs,[24] are questionable under recent Supreme Court taking decisions.

However, the courts easily rejected taking claims against sign controls on streets and highways under the more traditional taking tests. One court held that an ordinance prohibiting off-premise billboards with commercial advertising was not a taking because the "only damages" were lost business opportunities and a reduction in the value of the signs.[25] The courts also held that the exclusion of billboards from a municipality was not a substantial limitation on use that amounted to a taking of property.[26] Some cases applied a balancing test and held that limitations on the use of property imposed by sign controls are justified by their regulatory purposes.[27] Other courts upheld billboard prohibitions against taking claims as "a use restriction ... [that] is in essence a zoning of property adjacent to highways."[28] State statutes may prohibit signs along highways as public nuisances. The courts upheld these statutes under the authority of the state to declare billboards a nuisance under the police power.[29]

The status of sign controls under the taking clause since the Supreme Court's recent taking decision is unclear. Cases have upheld sign regulations against taking objections after the Supreme Court's 1987 taking trilogy. They held that sign regulation advances legitimate governmental purposes and does not deprive

---

22. § 11.06.

23. Kelbro, Inc. v. Myrick, 30 A.2d 527 (Vt. 1943). *Accord* Moore v. Ward, 377 S.W.2d 881 (Ky. 1964); Ghaster Props., Inc. v. Preston, 200 N.E.2d 328 (Ohio 1964).

24. Churchill & Tait v. Rafferty, 32 Philippines 580 (1915), *appeal dismissed,* 248 U.S. 591 (1918). *Accord* New York State Thruway Auth. v. Ashley Motor Court, Inc., 176 N.E.2d 566 (N.Y. 1961) (dismissing taking objection to sign controls on Thruway).

25. Jackson v. City Council, 659 F. Supp. 470 (W.D. Va. 1987).

26. Town of Boothbay v. National Adv. Co., 347 A.2d 419 (Me. 1975); Modjeska Sign Studies, Inc. v. Berle, 373 N.E.2d 255 (N.Y. 1977), *appeal dismissed,* 439 U.S. 809 (1978).

27. Yarbrough v. Arkansas State Hwy. Comm'n, 539 S.W.2d 419 (Ark. 1976); Newman Signs, Inc. v. Hjelle, 268 N.W.2d 741 (N.D. 1978).

28. Mississippi State Hwy. Comm'n v. Roberts Enters., 304 So. 2d 637 (Miss. 1974).

29. Opinion of the Justices, 169 A.2d 762 (N.H. 1961); 38 A.L.R.3d 647 (1971) (civil nuisance).

the sign owner of all economically viable use.[30] The Fourth Circuit Court of Appeals adopted a multi-factor taking test based on the Court's 1987 trilogy that does modify the taking tests it previously applied.[31]

### § 11.08. Billboard Exclusions.

Billboard exclusions present a more difficult substantive due process problem in aesthetic control. Courts easily uphold billboard exclusions in rural areas because they protect the visual integrity of the rural landscape,[32] and in residential areas because they protect residential neighborhoods.[33]

More serious problems are presented by a billboard exclusion from industrial and commercial areas. A Massachusetts case[34] upheld a billboard prohibition in a suburban Boston community and held that the enhancement of the environment was as important in urban as in rural areas. "Urban residents are not immune to ugliness."[35]

Whether a large city can constitutionally exclude billboards also is a difficult problem. In *Metromedia, Inc. v. City of San Diego*,[36] the court rejected an argument that an ordinance excluding billboards from the city was unconstitutional because a municipality may not use the police power to "prohibit completely" a business that is not a public nuisance. The court held that the rule that a municipality may regulate but not prohibit a land use was a "verbal formula" that "conflicts with reality and with current views of the police power." It rejected an argument that San Diego could not prohibit billboards because it is a large city and refused to adopt a rule "that a city's police power diminishes as its population grows."[37]

---

**30.** National Adv. Co. v. Village of Downers Grove, 561 N.E.2d 1300 (Ill. App. 1990) (emphasizing sign owner is only lessee), *cert. denied,* 501 U.S. 1261 (1991); Summey Outdoor Adv., Inc. v. County of Henderson, 386 S.E.2d 439 (N.C. App. 1989).

**31.** Georgia Outdoor Adv. Co. v. City of Waynesville (II), 900 F.2d 783 (4th Cir. 1990) (applying Supreme Court's "whole parcel" rule).

**32.** Moore v. Ward, 377 S.W.2d 881 (Ky. 1964) (statute adopting federal Act's prohibition on billboards adjacent to highways).

**33.** Naegele Outdoor Adv. Co. v. Village of Minnetonka, 162 N.W.2d 206 (Minn. 1968).

**34.** John Donnelly & Sons v. Outdoor Adv. Bd., 339 N.E.2d 709 (Mass. 1975). *Accord* Town of Boothbay v. National Adv. Co., 347 A.2d 419 (Me. 1975); United Adv. Corp. v. Borough of Metuchen, 198 A.2d 447 (N.J. 1964); Suffolk Outdoor Adv. Co. v. Hulse, 373 N.E.2d 263 (N.Y. 1977); 81 A.L.R.2d 486 (1977). *See also* Oregon City v. Hartke, 400 P.2d 255 (Or. 1965) (junkyard exclusion).

**35.** 339 N.E.2d at 720.

**36.** 610 P.2d 407 (Cal. 1980), *rev'd on other grounds,* 453 U.S. 490 (1981).

**37.** *Contra* Combined Communications Corp. v. City & Council of Denver, 542 P.2d 79 (Colo. 1975). *See also* Metromedia, Inc. v. City of Des Plaines, 326 N.E.2d 59 (Ill. App. 1975); Stoner McCray Sys. v. City of Des Moines, 78 N.W.2d 843 (Iowa 1956).

These cases indicate that courts will review sign ordinances to determine whether they advance aesthetic objectives as they are applied in addition to determining whether they are facially constitutional. As the New York court held in a case upholding an ordinance that restricted the display of business signs, an aesthetic regulation "must bear *substantially* on the economic, social and cultural patterns of the community or district."[38]

## § 11.09.  Exemption for On-Premise Signs.

Sign ordinances that prohibit off-premise billboards usually allow on-premise business signs. A court could hold that the on-premise sign exemption violates equal protection because the aesthetic impact of a sign does not depend on its location. On-premise signs can be as visually unattractive as off-premise billboards. One court adopted this view,[39] but the overwhelming majority hold that on-premise sign exemptions are constitutional.[40] As one court noted, an exemption for on-premise signs is justified because these signs advance the business or industry on the premises while off-premise signs do not.[41] An exemption for on-premise signs may present constitutional problems under the free speech clause.[42]

## § 11.10.  Controls on the Display of Signs.

Sign ordinances contain controls that regulate the display of on-premise and off-premise signs, such as controls on spacing, height, and size, and the number of signs a business can display. Sign ordinances may also control features such as flashing lights, banners, and changeable copy and prohibit certain types of signs, such as roof and portable signs.

The cases have upheld controls on the display of signs. Early cases held that municipalities could limit the size of signs to protect the public from falling bill-

---

**38.** People v. Goodman, 290 N.E.2d 139, 141 (N.Y. 1972) (emphasis in original). *See also* Temple Baptist Church, Inc. v. City of Albuquerque, 646 P.2d 565 (N.M. 1982); Sun Oil Co. v. City of Upper Arlington, 379 N.E.2d 266 (Ohio App. 1977) (sign must be "patently offensive" to surrounding area). *Compare* Norate Corp. v. Zoning Bd. of Adjustment, 207 A.2d 890 (Pa. 1965).

**39.** Metromedia, Inc. v. City of Des Plaines, 326 N.E.2d 59 (Ill. App. 1975).

**40.** Metromedia, Inc. v. City of Pasadena, 30 Cal. Rptr. 731 (Cal. App. 1963), *appeal dismissed,* 376 U.S. 186 (1964); City of Lake Wales v. Lamar Adv. Ass'n, 414 So. 2d 1030 (Fla. 1982); Donnelly Adv. Corp. v. City of Baltimore, 370 A.2d 1127 (Md. 1977); State Dep't of Roads v. Popco, Inc., 528 N.W.2d 281 (Neb. 1995) (upholding distinction between on-premise and off-premise signs required by federal Highway Beautification Act); Summey Outdoor Adv., Inc. v. County of Henderson, 386 S.E.2d 439 (N.C. App. 1989); Landau Adv. Co. v. Zoning Bd. of Adjustment, 128 A.2d 559 (Pa. 1957).

**41.** United Adv. Corp. v. Borough of Metuchen, 198 A.2d 447 (N.J. 1964).

**42.** §§ 11.13, 11.17.

boards.[43] The recent cases apply the presumption of constitutionality and the aesthetics alone rule to uphold controls on the display of signs such as height, size, and setback regulations and restrictions on the number of signs a business is allowed.[44] *Westfield Motor Sales Co. v. Town of Westfield*[45] is an important case that upheld a restriction on the size of an automobile dealership's signs. The court recognized the right of a business to advertise but held that a municipality may perceive that a "plethora" of signs "may have an undesirable cumulative effect on the community."

The courts have upheld limitations on illumination, movement, and color[46] and prohibitions on searchlights and windblown signs.[47] They universally uphold ordinances that prohibit projecting signs or limit the extent to which they can project.[48] The authority to regulate projecting signs derives from the authority of municipalities to regulate public streets.

*Rent-A-Sign v. City of Rockford*[49] held that traffic safety and aesthetic considerations justified an ordinance that limited the time periods during which portable signs could be displayed. The court held that the city could place time limitations on portable signs because they are designed to attract attention to temporary events rather than to inform. Most courts uphold restrictions on roof signs.[50]

---

43. St. Louis Poster Adv. Co. v. City of St. Louis, 249 U.S. 269 (1919). *See also* Board of Adjustment v. Osage Oil & Transp. Co., 522 S.W.2d 836 (Ark. 1975).

44. Village of Skokie v. Walton on Dempster, Inc., 456 N.E.2d 293 (Ill. App. 1983); Temple Baptist Church, Inc. v. City of Albuquerque, 646 P.2d 565 (N.M. 1982); People v. Goodman, 290 N.E.2d 139 (N.Y. 1972); 56 A.L.R.3d 1207 (1974); Sun Oil Co. v. City of Arlington, 379 N.E.2d 266 (Ohio App. 1977). *See also* Merritt v. Peters, 65 So. 2d 861 (Fla. 1953); State v. Diamond Motors, Inc., 429 P.2d 825 (Haw. 1967).

45. 324 A.2d 113 (N.J.L. Div. 1974). *But see* Art Van Furniture Co. v. City of Kentwood, 437 N.W.2d 380 (Mich. App. 1989) (cannot restrict wall sign size for single occupant of building but allow larger wall signs if building occupied by multiple occupants).

46. City of Fayetteville v. S & H, Inc., 547 S.W.2d 94 (Ark. 1977); Schaffer v. City of Omaha, 248 N.W.2d 764 (Neb. 1977); Asselin v. Town of Conway, 628 A.2d 247 (N.H. 1993) (illumination); Hilton v. City of Toledo, 405 N.E.2d 1047 (Ohio 1980); Kenyon Peck, Inc. v. Kennedy, 168 S.E.2d 117 (Va. 1969). *Contra* In re Appeal of Ammon R. Smith Auto Co., 223 A.2d 683 (Pa. 1966). *But see* Capalbo v. Planning & Zoning Bd., 547 A.2d 528 (Conn. 1988) (statute did not authorize regulation of color); 30 A.L.R.5th 549 (regulations relating to illuminated signs).

47. *See* Robert L. Rieke Bldg. Co. v. City of Overland Park, 657 P.2d 1121 (Kan. 1983) (searchlights); Goodman Toyota, Inc. v. City of Raleigh, 306 S.E.2d 192 (N.C. App. 1983) (windblown signs).

48. McMahan's Furn. Co. v. City of Pacific Grove, 33 Cal. Rptr. 476 (Cal. App. 1963); People ex rel. Herman Armanetti, Inc. v. City of Chicago, 112 N.E.2d 616 (Ill. 1953); State v. Sanguinetti, 449 A.2d 922 (Vt. 1982); 80 A.L.R.3d 687 (1977).

49. 406 N.E.2d 943 (Ill. App. 1980).

50. General Outdoor Adv. Co. v. Department of Pub. Works, 193 N.E. 799 (Mass. 1935). *Contra* Mayor & City Council v. Mano Swartz, Inc., 299 A.2d 828 (Md. 1973).

## § 11.11.  Nonconforming Signs.

The case law that determines the extent to which municipalities can regulate nonconforming uses[51] applies to nonconforming signs, including the case law that approves the amortization of nonconforming uses after a reasonable amortization period.[52] The amortization of nonconforming signs by municipalities is affected by provisions in the federal Highway Beautification Act,[53] which has always required compensation for the removal of nonconforming signs on federal highways. Congress amended the Act in 1978 to require compensation "whether or not" the sign was removed under the Act.[54] This amendment was intended to prohibit the municipal amortization of nonconforming signs.[55] The federal compensation requirement does not preempt ordinances that amortize signs,[56] but the federal highway agency can withhold ten percent of a state's highway funds if a municipality removes a nonconforming sign through amortization.[57]

A number of states have adopted statutes to comply with the federal compensation requirement. They either prohibit municipal amortization of nonconforming signs on highways covered by the federal act or prohibit the municipal amortization of all nonconforming signs. In *Metromedia*,[58] the court held that a statute requiring compensation for the removal of nonconforming signs on federal highways preempted municipal amortization of nonconforming signs on these highways. The statute required the preemption of municipal ordinances when this was necessary to protect the receipt of federal highway funds. The court also held that a compensation requirement for nonconforming signs that applied only to federal highways did not violate equal protection.

The courts have upheld methods short of amortization for the removal of nonconforming signs. A municipality may condition an application for new devel-

**51.** §§ 5.68-5.76.

**52.** §§ 5.72-5.76.

**53.** § 11.06.

**54.** 23 U.S.C. § 131(g). *See* Donnelly Adv. Corp. v. City of Baltimore, 370 A.2d 1127 (Md. 1977) (decided prior to amendment).

**55.** Root Outdoor Adv. v. City of Ft. Collins, 788 P.2d 149 (Colo. 1990) (five-year amortization ordinance does not comply with statutory compensation requirement). *But see* Ackerley Communications, Inc. v. City of Seattle, 602 P.2d 1177 (Wash. 1979) (federal act does not require compensation for removal of nonconforming signs in industrial and commercial areas), *cert. denied,* 449 U.S. 804 (1980). *Contra Metromedia,* note 58, *infra.*

**56.** National Adv. Co. v. City of Ashland, 678 F.2d 106 (9th Cir. 1982).

**57.** 23 U.S.C. § 131(b) (applies to all violations of statute).

**58.** Metromedia, Inc. v. City of San Diego, 610 P.2d 407 (Cal. 1980), *rev'd on other grounds,* 453 U.S. 490 (1981). *But see* Suffolk Outdoor Adv. Co. v. Town of Southampton, 455 N.E.2d 1245 (N.Y. 1983).

opment on the removal of a nonconforming sign.[59] A taking does not occur if an ordinance requires a billboard to be lowered to conform with height restrictions.[60]

## § 11.12. Free Speech Problems.

Free speech issues are critically important in sign regulation. Ordinances that regulate signs raise free speech problems because messages on signs are a form of speech. Signs with political and ideological messages are protected by the free speech clause as noncommercial speech. The free speech clause also protects signs with commercial messages, although the U.S. Supreme Court does not give commercial speech as much protection as noncommercial speech. The effect of the free speech clause on the constitutionality of sign ordinances is dramatic: it reverses the presumption of constitutionality the courts usually apply to police power regulations. The burden on municipalities to show that sign ordinances are justified by the usual governmental interests, such as traffic safety and aesthetics, is heavier.[61]

## § 11.13. *Metromedia.*

Two U.S. Supreme Court cases dominate the law on the application of the free speech clause to sign ordinances. *Metromedia, Inc. v. City of San Diego*,[62] the first case, is a confusing decision because the Court wrote several opinions. The city adopted a sign ordinance that prohibited off-premise commercial billboards but exempted on-premise business identification signs. The ordinance also exempted twelve categories of signs, including governmental and temporary political signs. A majority of the Justices held the ordinance unconstitutional but a majority did not join any of these opinions. A plurality opinion by four of the Justices attracted the most support in the Court and deserves discussion because it influenced a number of federal and state decisions.

---

**59.** Outdoor Systems, Inc. v. City of Mesa, 819 P.2d 44 (Ariz. 1991) (holding *Nollan* does not apply). *See* Outdoor Sys., Inc. v. City of Mesa, 997 F.2d 604 (9th Cir. 1993) (ordinance upheld in state case not a taking of property).Circle K Corp. v. City of Mesa, 803 P.2d 457 (Ariz. App. 1990) (can condition permit for new nonconforming sign on removal of existing nonconforming sign). *But see* Ariz. Rev. Stat. Ann. § 9-462.02(B), 11-830(F) (prohibiting ordinances of this type). *See also* Naegele Outdoor Advertising Co. v. City of Lakeville, 532 N.W.2d 249 (Minn. App. 1995) (requirement for removal of nonconforming sign when lease terminated by owner of property held not a taking).

**60.** National Adv. Co. v. Board of Adj., 800 P.2d 1349 (Colo. App. 1990). *See* Barron Chevrolet Co. v. Town of Danvers, 646 N.E.2d 89 (Mass. 1995) (change in sign panels does not remove sign from protection of nonconforming use statute).

**61.** Standards of judicial review are discussed in § 2.52.

**62.** 453 U.S. 490 (1981).

The plurality applied the Supreme Court's tests for laws that restrict commercial speech to the San Diego ordinance.[63] It upheld the ban on off-premise billboards because it directly advanced the city's interests in traffic safety and aesthetics. It held that the city's claim that the ordinance improved traffic safety was entitled to judicial respect as a commonplace judgment, even though the effect on traffic safety was not clear. The plurality accepted the city's aesthetic justification even though the exemption for on-premise signs undercut this interest. It upheld the on-premise sign exemption because this exemption recognized the interest a commercial enterprise has in identifying its products or services. The plurality reserved judgment on whether a ban on noncommercial as well as commercial billboards would be constitutional.

The plurality held unconstitutional the provision in the ordinance that limited on-premise signs to commercial messages. It believed this limitation improperly regulated the content of speech by preferring commercial over noncommercial speech. The plurality also invalidated the twelve sign exemptions contained in the ordinance because it believed they discriminated on the basis of content.

### § 11.14. *Taxpayers for Vincent.*

*Members of City Council v. Taxpayers for Vincent*,[64] the second Supreme Court decision, clarified many of the problems left open by the *Metromedia* opinions. A Los Angeles ordinance prohibited the posting of signs on public property. The Court upheld the ordinance in a 6-3 decision in an action brought by a candidate for public office whose political signs were removed by the city.

The Court held the ordinance did not violate the free speech clause because it was a viewpoint-neutral time, place, and manner regulation.[65] This holding is contrary to the plurality opinion in *Metromedia*, which invalidated provisions in the San Diego ordinance because they regulated the content of signs. *Vincent* means a sign ordinance may regulate the content of signs if it does not restrict the point of view a sign contains. This requirement is more favorable to sign regulation than the content-neutral requirement adopted by the *Metromedia* plurality.

The Court confirmed the holding in *Metromedia*, that aesthetics is a substantial governmental interest that justifies the restrictions a sign ordinance imposes on free speech:

---

63. § 2.52.
64. 466 U.S. 789 (1984).
65. United States v. O'Brien, 391 U.S. 367 (1968). *See* § 2.52.

These [aesthetic] interests are both psychological and economic. The character of the environment affects the quality of life and the value of property in both residential and commercial areas.[66]

The Court upheld the prohibition on signs on public property because it was no greater than necessary to advance these interests.

In an important holding, the Court held the "substantive evil" of visual blight was not a "possible byproduct" of the activity but was created by signs as a "medium of expression." This holding blunts free speech objections to sign ordinances because it means that signs as a medium of expression create visual problems that justify their aesthetic regulation. The Court also held that the city was not required to adopt a less restrictive alternative than the prohibition, such as an exemption for political and perhaps other signs. It indicated that these exemptions might be unconstitutional as discrimination against the content of speech and could defeat the objective of combating visual blight.

The Court held the ordinance constitutional even though it did not prohibit signs on private property. It justified this exemption because private property owners would keep the posting of signs on their property within reasonable limits. By not extending the prohibition to private property, the city also left open a "significant opportunity to communicate by means of temporary signs." Finally, the Court held that the ordinance was not invalid because alternative means of communication were inadequate. Individuals could speak and distribute literature at places where the ordinance prohibited signs on public property. In an important footnote it added:

> Although the Court has shown special solicitude for forms of expression that are much less expensive than feasible alternatives and hence may be important to a large segment of the citizenry, . . . this solicitude has practical boundaries.[67]

### § 11.15. *Ladue*: Control of Noncommercial Signs.

In City of *Ladue v. Gilleo*,[68] an exclusive St. Louis residential suburb prohibited homeowners from displaying any signs except for residence identification, "for sale," and safety hazard warning signs. It permitted commercial business, churches, and nonprofit organizations to display signs not allowed at residences. The Court held that the ordinance violated the free speech clause in a case

---

66. 466 U.S. at 817.

67. *Id.* at 812 n.30.

68. 512 U.S. 43 (1994), relying especially on Linmark Assocs. v. Township of Willingboro, discussed in § 11.10. *See* City of Forest Park v. Pelfrey, 669 N.E.2d 863 (Ohio App. 1995) (invalidating ordinance prohibiting message wall signs in residential areas).

brought by a homeowner prohibited from displaying in her window an 8½ by 11 inch sign stating "For Peace in the Gulf."

The Court accepted the city's statement that the ordinance was free of content or viewpoint discrimination. But the Court held that Ladue's interest in minimizing visual clutter was not a sufficient "compelling" reason for prohibiting residential message signs completely. Ladue had "almost completely foreclosed" a venerable, unique, and important means of communication to political, religious, or personal messages. The Court also indicated that the exemptions from the residential sign prohibitions in the Ladue ordinance "undermined the credibility" of "the City's aesthetic interest in eliminating outdoor signs."

The Court rejected Ladue's argument that the prohibition on residential message signs was a mere "time, place, or manner" regulation because residents had alternative means to convey their messages. It held that displaying a sign from a residence carried a "quite distinct" message because it provides information about the identity of the speaker. In addition, residential signs are "an unusually cheap and convenient form of communication." Respect for individual liberty in the home, the Court concluded, has long been part of our culture and law. It suggested that Ladue could adopt "more temperate measures" to meet its regulatory needs, and noted that not every kind of sign must be permitted in residential areas.

### § 11.16. What These Cases Decided.

These Supreme Court cases clarified a number of issues raised by the application of the free speech clause to sign ordinances, but some issues remain unsettled. The Court has made it clear that "common sense" justifies aesthetic and traffic safety interests as a basis for sign regulation. A majority of the Justices in *Metromedia* accepted a ban on off-premise commercial billboards even though the ordinance exempted on-premise commercial signs. The *Vincent* decision indicates the Court would uphold a ban on all off-premise signs, but it did not address this question. The status of exemptions contained in sign ordinances is also unclear.

A difficult free speech problem arises from the *Metromedia* plurality's holdings that invalidated the on-premise business sign exemption and the twelve specific sign exemptions because they were not content-neutral. *Vincent* undercuts these holdings because it requires only viewpoint, not content, neutrality. The ordinance upheld in *Vincent* contained some of the same exemptions contained in the San Diego ordinance, but the Court did not discuss them. The *Metromedia* plurality's invalidation of these exemptions is also questionable because some of them, such as the exemption of for sale signs, are required by Supreme Court decisions. A municipality can avoid the problem created by the on-premise business sign exemption in the San Diego ordinance by allowing on-premise signs that contain noncommercial as well as commercial messages.

Another problem is that the Supreme Court cases do not fully indicate when classifications in sign regulations improperly prefer commercial speech or improperly disfavor noncommerical speech. This issue continues to trouble the courts.

### § 11.17. Time, Place, and Manner Restrictions.

The courts have usually had no difficulty upholding time, place and manner restrictions on commercial signs. They have upheld ordinances banning signs from certain areas, such as an urban renewal[69] or historic district area.[70] A pair of Fourth Circuit cases upheld ordinances that had the effect of prohibiting liquor and cigarette advertising signs in places where they would be visible to minors.[71] The court held the ordinances legitimately advanced the city's interest in protecting the welfare of minors. Courts have also upheld ordinances prohibiting signs near highways, including signs prohibited by state legislation adopted to implement the federal Highway Beautification Act.[72]

Size, height, number and similar restrictions on signs are also upheld when limited to commercial signs. *Donrey Communications Co. v. City of Fayetteville*[73] is a typical case. The court upheld a sign ordinance that limited the size of the plaintiff's signs to seventy-five square feet. This size limitation prevented the plaintiff from using the standard 300-square-foot poster the sign industry uses. The court held that the ordinance did not "eliminate billboards as a channel of communications" even though a sign that complied with the ordinance cost fifty percent more than the standard industry sign. Courts have also upheld ordinances

---

**69.** Donnelly Advertising Co. v. City of Baltimore, 370 A.2d 1127 (Md. 1977).

**70.** Messer v. City of Douglasville, 975 F.2d 1505 (11th Cir. 1992), *cert. denied,* 508 U.S. 390 (1993).

**71.** Penn Advertising of Baltimore, Inc. v. Mayor & Council, 63 F.3d 1318 (4th Cir. 1995), *modified & adhered to,* 101 F.3d 332 (4th Cir. 1996) (cigarettes); Anheuser-Busch, Inc. v. Schmoke, 63 F.3d 1305 (4th Cir. 1995), *adhered to on remand,* 101 F.3d 325 (4th Cir. 1996) (liquor).

**72.** Naegele Outdoor Advertising, Inc. v. City of Durham, 844 F.2d 172 (4th Cir. 1988); Wheeler v. Commissioner of Highways, 822 F.2d 586 (6th Cir. 1987); Rodriguez v. Solis, 2 Cal. Rptr. 2d 50 (Cal. App. 1991).

**73.** 660 S.W.2d 900 (Ark. 1983), *cert. denied,* 466 U.S. 959 (1984). *Accord* Outdoor Systems, Inc. v. City of Mesa, 997 F.2d 604 (9th Cir. 1993); South-Suburban Housing Center v. Greater South Suburban Bd. of Realtors, 935 F.2d 868 (7th Cir. 1991), *cert. denied,* 502 U.S. 1074 (1992). *But see* Real Estate Bd. of Metropolitan St. Louis v. City of Jennings, 808 S.W.2d 7 (Mo. App. 1991).

restricting the height[74] and number[75] and illumination[76] of signs. However, ordinances restricting or prohibiting price information on signs violate the free speech clause.[77]

## § 11.18. Prohibitions, Exemptions, and Classifications.

The courts have dealt with a number of issues raised by the *Metromedia* plurality concerning the type of restrictions allowable in sign ordinances. They have followed *Metromedia* by upholding ordinances that prohibit off-premise commercial signs even though on-premise signs are allowed.[78] They have upheld exemptions for on-premise signs if the ordinance corrects the problem identified in *Metromedia* by allowing these signs to contain noncommercial as well as commercial messages.[79]

More difficult problems are presented by the *Metromedia* plurality holding that the 12 exemptions in the San Diego ordinance violated the free speech clause because they were content-based. Some courts have struck down[80] ordi-

---

**74.** City of Albuquerque v. Jackson, 684 P.2d 543 (N.M. App. 1984).

**75.** South-Suburban Housing Center v. Greater South Suburban Bd. of Realtors, 935 F.2d 868 (7th Cir. 1991), *cert. denied,* 502 U.S. 1074 (1992); Bender v. City of Saint Ann, 816 F. Supp. 1372 (E.D. Mo. 1993), *aff'd on other grounds,* 36 F.3d 57 (8th Cir. 1994); Williams v. City & County of Denver, 622 P.2d 542 (Colo. 1981); City of Sunrise v. D.C.A. Homes, Inc., 421 So. 2d 1084 (Fla. App. 1982).

**76.** Asselin v. Town of Conway, 628 A.2d 247 (N.H. 1993).

**77.** H & H Operations, Inc. v. City of Peachtree City, 283 S.E.2d 867 (Ga. 1981), *cert. denied,* 456 U.S. 961 (1982); People v. Mobil Oil Corp., 397 N.E.2d 724 (N.Y. 1979). *See* Virginia State Bd. of Pharmacy v. Virginia Citizens Consumer Council, 425 U.S. 748 (1976).

**78.** National Adv. Co. v. City & Cty. of Denver, 912 F.2d 405 (10th Cir. 1990); National Adv. Co. v. City of Orange, 861 F.2d 246 (9th Cir. 1988); Major Media of the Southeast, Inc. v. City of Raleigh, 792 F.2d 1269 (4th Cir. 1986); National Adv. Co. v. City of Bridgeton, 626 F. Supp. 837 (E.D. Mo. 1985) (Street Graphics Model Ordinance). *But see* National Adv. Co. v. Town of Babylon, 900 F.2d 551 (2d Cir.), *cert. denied,* 498 U.S. 852 (1990) (failure to show governmental interests advanced); Ackerley Communications v. Krochalis, 108 F.3d 1095 (9th Cir. 1997); City of Lakewood v. Colfax Unlimited Ass'n, 634 P.2d 52 (Colo. 1981) (invalidating classification of commercial signs). *Compare* Pigg v. State Dep't of Hwys., 746 P.2d 961 (Colo. 1987).

**79.** Outdoor Sys., Inc. v. City of Mesa, 997 F.2d 604 (9th Cir. 1993) (upholding distinction between offsite and onsite commercial signs); Wheeler v. Commissioner of Hwys., 822 F.2d 586 (6th Cir. 1987) (ordinance allowed signs relating to any "activity" on premises), *cert. denied,* 484 U.S. 1007 (1978); Major Media of the Southeast, Inc. v. City of Raleigh, 792 F.2d 1269 (4th Cir. 1986), *cert. denied,* 479 U.S. 1102 (1987); City & County of San Francisco v. Eller Outdoor Adv., 237 Cal. Rptr. 815 (1987) (also upholds exemptions); Gannett Outdoor Co. v. City of Troy, 409 N.W.2d 719 (Mich. App. 1987).

**80.** Dimitt v. City of Clearwater, 985 F.2d 1565 (11th Cir. 1993) (ordinance limiting permit exemptions to governmental flags); National Advertising Co. v. Town of Niagra, 942 F.2d 945 (2d Cir. 1991); National Adv. Co. v. City of Orange, 861 F.2d 246 (9th Cir. 1988) (exemptions similar to those invalidated in *Metromedia*); Village of Schaumburg v. Jeep Eagle Sales Corp., 676 N.E.2d

nances containing exemptions similar to those held invalid by the plurality in *Metromedia*, but some have been troubled by this *Metromedia* holding and have upheld similar exemptions.[81]

Even more difficult problems occur when an ordinance treats noncommercial speech differently from commercial speech. The courts follow *Metromedia* in upholding prohibitions on off-premise signs when on-premise commercial signs are allowed.[82] Prohibitions on off-premise commercial and noncommercial signs are more of a problem because noncommercial speech is affected. Some courts upheld city-wide prohibitions on commercial and noncommercial signs when both commercial and noncommercial messages were allowed on-premises,[83] but in other cases where the ordinance was upheld the commercial and noncommercial sign prohibition was limited to certain areas so the impact on noncommercial speech was less severe.[84] When an ordinance clearly discriminated against noncommercial speech, it was struck down.[85] The courts have also invalidated sign ordinances that prohibit noncommercial messages entirely.[86]

## § 11.19. Portable Signs.

Sign ordinances that regulate portable signs also present difficult problems under the free speech clause. Several cases struck down ordinances that prohibited portable signs or limited the time periods for their display.[87] These cases

---

200 (Ill. App. 1996) (flags). *See also* Rappa v. New Castle County, 18 F.3d 1043 (3d Cir. 1994) (striking down exemptions in state outdoor advertising law but refusing to apply *Metromedia*).

**81.** Messer v. City of Douglasville, 975 F.2d 1505 (11th Cir. 1992), *cert. denied,* 508 U.S. 930 (1993); National Adv. Co. v. Town of Babylon, 900 F.2d 551 (2d Cir.), *cert. denied,* 498 U.S. 852 (1990) (exemption of "for sale" sign); Scadron v. City of Des Plaines, 734 F. Supp. 1437 (N.D. Ill. 1990), *aff'd without opinion,* 989 F.2d 502 (7th Cir. 1992).

**82.** Outdoor Sys,, Inc. v. City of Mesa, 997 F.2d 604 (9th Cir. 1993).

**83.** Georgia Outdoor Advertising, Inc. v. Waynesville, 833 F.2d 43 (4th Cir. 1987); Wheeler v. Commissioner of Highways, 822 F.2d 586 (6th Cir. 1987), *cert. denied,* 484 U.S. 1007 (1988). *But see* Ackerley Communications v. City of Cambridge, 88 F.3d 33 (1st Cir. 1996).

**84.** Messer v. City of Douglasville, 975 F.2d 1505 (11th Cir. 1992) (historic districts); National Advertising Co. v. Denver, 912 F.2d 405 (10th Cir. 1990) (highways); Rzadkowolski v. Lake Orion, 845 F.2d 653 (6th Cir. 1988); Major Media of the Southeast, Inc. v. City of Raleigh, 792 F.2d 1269 (4th Cir. 1986), *cert. denied,* 479 U.S. 1102 (1987). *Cf.* National Advertising Co. v. Orange, 861 F.2d 246 (9th Cir. 1988).

**85.** Desert Outdoor Advertising v. City of Moreno Valley, 103 F.3d 814 (9th Cir. 1996) (noncommercial messages restricted to certain areas of city but onsite commercial messages allowed anywhere); Matthews v. Town of Needham, 764 F.2d 58 (1st Cir. 1985) (ordinance prohibiting political signs but allowing commercial signs invalid).

**86.** Pica v. Sarno, 907 F. Supp. 795 (D.N.J. 1995) (ordinance prohibited signs promoting "interests of any person").

**87.** Dills v. City of Marietta, 674 F.2d 1377 (11th Cir. 1982), *cert. denied,* 461 U.S. 905 (1983); Dills v. Cobb County, 593 F. Supp. 170 (N.D. Ga. 1984), *aff'd per curiam,* 755 F.2d 1473 (11th Cir. 1985); Risner v. City of Wyoming, 383 N.W.2d 226 (Mich. App. 1985).

held that the municipality did not show that portable signs are aesthetically of-fensive or that inherent aesthetic differences between portable and permanent signs require more stringent portable sign regulations. The courts also held that less restrictive alternatives, such as safety regulations, could eliminate the dangers created by portable signs.

Cases decided since the Supreme Court's *Vincent* decision have taken a more favorable view of restrictions on portable signs.[88] *Harnish v. Manatee County,*[89] which upheld an ordinance that prohibited portable signs, is an example. The court held that the prohibition reached no further than necessary to accomplish the county's aesthetic objective and that the county had the discretion to determine how much aesthetic protection was necessary and how to achieve that protection. The court noted that the county had "an aesthetically appealing and fragile environment" and had sponsored workshops in which residents complained about "inherently ugly" portable signs. In some of the cases that invalidated portable sign restrictions, the municipality had not made a strong factual case for the aesthetic regulation of portable signs.

*Harnish* concluded that the constitution did not require a court to speculate on how a municipality should narrowly tailor its regulations to achieve a governmental objective while leaving alternative means of communication available. This holding weakens the presumption reversal that occurs in free speech cases because it reduces the municipal burden to show that a sign ordinance affects free speech no more than necessary to accomplish the governmental interests it serves.

## § 11.20.  For Sale Signs.

The Supreme Court has taken a restrictive view of ordinances that ban on-premise residential for sale and for lease signs, even though their messages are a form of commercial speech. In *Linmark Assocs. v. Township of Willingboro,*[90] the township banned for sale signs in the community to reduce residential turn-over and prevent panic selling by white homeowners that would impair racial

---

**88.** City of Hot Springs v. Carter, 836 S.W.2d 863 (Ark. 1992).

**89.** 783 F.2d 1535 (11th Cir. 1986). *Accord* Lindsay v. City of San Antonio, 821 F.2d 1103 (5th Cir. 1987), *cert. denied,* 484 U.S. 1010 (1988); Barber v. Municipality of Anchorage, 776 P.2d 1036 (Alaska 1989).

**90.** 431 U.S. 85 (1977). *Accord* Citizens United for Free Speech II v. Long Beach Township Bd. of Comm'rs, 802 F. Supp. 1223 (D.N.J. 1992) (prohibiting "for rent" signs during summer months); Greater Baltimore Bd. of Realtors v. Huges, 596 F. Supp. 906 (D. Md. 1984); Daugherty v. City of East Point, 447 F. Supp. 290 (N.D. Ga. 1978); City of Chicago v. Gordon, 497 N.E.2d 442 (Ill. App. 1986); Berg Agency v. Township of Maplewood, 395 A.2d 261 (N.J.L. Div. 1978). *But see* South Suburban Housing Center v. Greater South Suburban Bd. of Realtors, 935 F.2d 868 (7th Cir. 1991) (ban allowed when ban justified by aesthetic interests of municipalities), *cert. denied,* 502 U.S. 1074 (1992).

integration. The Court struck down the ordinance. It rejected a claim that the ordinance was constitutional as a time, place, and manner regulation even though it viewed the prohibition as a restriction on commercial speech. It held that the purpose of the ban was to restrict the content of expression on a matter of vital concern to the community. The Court concluded that alternative means of communicating information on the sale of homes were unsatisfactory and that the evidence did not support the township's claim that the purpose of the ordinance was to prevent panic selling.[91]

### § 11.21. Political Signs.

Because the protection of political speech is one of the primary purposes of the free speech clause, the courts are especially sensitive to restrictions on the display of political signs. They uphold limitations on the size of signs only if they are not too restrictive.[92] *Vincent*[93] upheld an ordinance that prohibited the posting of all signs, including political signs, on public property, but the courts strike down ordinances that prohibit the display of political signs on residential property.[94] They hold that this restriction improperly suppresses an important medium of communication and that alternative measures can remedy the problems the display of these signs creates.

The courts have struck down ordinances that limit the display of political signs to brief periods of time.[95] They held that the time limit was unnecessarily restrictive, that alternative means of communication were not available, and that the ordinances discriminated against political speech because they did not place similar restrictions on other signs.

---

**91.** *See also* Cleveland Area Bd. of Realtors v. City of Euclid, 88 F.3d 382 (6th Cir. 1996) (invalidating ordinance limiting for-sale signs to windows).

**92.** Baldwin v. Redwood City, 540 F.2d 1360 (9th Cir. 1976); Davis v. City of Green, 665 N.E.2d 753 (Ohio App. 1996) (upholds size restriction). *See also* Brayton v. City of New Brighton, 519 N.W.2d 243 (Minn. App. 1994) (upholding ordinance with same regulations for campaign and opinion signs), *cert. denied*, 115 S. Ct. 1402 (1995); Verilli v. City of Concord, 548 F.2d 262 (9th Cir. 1977) (invalidating ordinance requiring signs to be freestanding).

**93.** § 11.14.

**94.** Arlington Political Republican Comm. v. Arlington County, 983 F.2d 587 (4th Cir. 1993); Matthews v. Town of Needham, 764 F.2d 58 (1st Cir. 1985); Martin v. Wray, 473 F. Supp. 1131 (E.D. Wis. 1979); Goward v. City of Minneapolis, 456 N.W.2d 460 (Minn. App. 1990); City of Euclid v. Mabel, 484 N.E.2d 249 (Ohio App. 1984). *See also* Runyon v. Fasi, 762 F. Supp. 280 (D. Haw. 1991) (ordinance totally prohibiting political signs held invalid); Tauber v. Town of Longmeadow, 695 F. Supp. 1358 (D. Mass. 1988) (same); Collier v. City of Tacoma, 854 P.2d 1046 (Wash. 1993) (signs prohibited in residential yards and parking strips).

**95.** Whitton v. City of Gladstone, 54 F.3d 1400 (8th Cir. 1995); Orazio v. Town of North Hempstead, 426 F. Supp. 1144 (E.D.N.Y. 1977); Union City Bd. of Zoning Appeals v. Justice Outdoor Displays, Inc., 467 S.E.2d 875 (Ga. 1996); Van v. Travel Information Council, 628 P.2d 1217 (Or. 1981).

## B. ARCHITECTURAL DESIGN REVIEW.

### § 11.22. The Aesthetic Problem.

Architectural design review is an important element in land use regulation, and many municipalities have adopted architectural design review ordinances. Most of these ordinances apply to single-family residences, but they may also apply to nonresidential buildings. They usually create a design review board with the authority to approve or disapprove the design of a residential dwelling.[96]

The architectural design review ordinance contains a set of standards the board applies in the design review process. One type of ordinance adopts an "anti-look-alike" requirement for new residential dwellings by providing that a new dwelling may not be too similar to existing dwellings in the area. Other ordinances provide that new dwellings may not be too dissimilar to existing dwellings, a "look-alike" requirement which is a variant of the "compatibility" standard. If the ordinance contains both requirements, it legislates against monotony in residential design but also prohibits excessive departures from the design standard established by dwellings in the neighborhood. An architectural design review ordinance may also direct the review board to apply design standards that cover exterior features, such as materials, orientation, and facade.

Design review ordinances may have an exclusionary effect in upper-income residential suburbs. By requiring variety in residential design, they can effectively exclude mass-produced residential development that uses standard or slightly varied residential design patterns.

### § 11.23. Constitutionality.

A group of leading cases dominates the case law on architectural design review. Most of these cases were decided before a majority of the courts adopted the rule that aesthetics alone is a proper purpose in land use regulation. These cases also arose in residential suburbs, some of them upper-income, and this physical setting affected the court decisions that approved design review. They upheld architectural design review as a measure that protected property values in established neighborhoods. This holding is an example of the minority view on the role of aesthetics in land use regulation, which upholds aesthetic regulation if it advances other legitimate government interests.[97]

---

96. Diller & Fisher Co. v. Architectural Review Bd., 587 A.2d 674 (N.J.L. Div. 1991) (creation of architectural review board not authorized by zoning legislation).

97. § 11.04. *See* Coscan Washington, Inc. v. Maryland-National Capital Park & Planning Com., 590 A.2d 1080 (Md. App. 1991) (upholding requirement that certain percentage of residential units be built with brick); County of Wright v. Kennedy, 415 N.W.2d 728 (Minn. App. 1987) (upholding mobile home roof pitch requirement); 41 A.L.R.3d 1397 (1972).

A few cases struck down architectural design review ordinances, and some refused to recognize the protection of aesthetic values as a legitimate regulatory purpose.[98] In some of the states where the decisions were unfavorable, the court later adopted a more receptive view of the role of aesthetics in land use regulation. Other cases struck down architectural design review ordinances as an improper delegation of power or held that they were unconstitutionally vague.[99] The delegation of power holdings clearly indicate a deeper judicial hostility to any use of design review powers for aesthetic purposes.

*State ex rel. Saveland Park Holding Corp. v. Wieland*[100] is an early leading case upholding an architectural design review ordinance adopted by an upper-income suburb of Milwaukee, Wisconsin. The ordinance provided that a building permit could issue only if a special building board found that the "exterior architectural appeal and functional plan" of a proposed structure was not "so at variance" with structures built or planned "in the immediate neighborhood . . . as to cause a substantial depreciation in the property values of said neighborhood." This ordinance legislated a look-alike requirement, which the court sustained as a measure for protecting property values. It relied on *Berman v. Parker,*[101] which the U.S. Supreme Court had just decided, and noted that the law on aesthetic purposes in zoning was evolving toward a more positive view. The court rejected a delegation of power objection to the ordinance.

*State ex rel. Stoyanoff v. Berkeley*[102] is a more recent but similar case. An upper-income suburb in the St. Louis, Missouri, area created an architectural review board to review building plans. The ordinance authorized the board to "maintain conformity with surrounding structures," assure that structures "conform to certain minimum architectural standards of appearance," and avoid "unsightly, grotesque and unsuitable structures, detrimental to the stability of value and the welfare of surrounding property." This ordinance contained a "look-alike" requirement implemented through the application of architectural design standards.

The board denied the plaintiffs a permit for a residence in the shape of a pyramid with a flat top and windows at the corners. They brought suit claiming

---

**98.** City of West Palm Beach v. State, 30 So. 2d 491 (Fla. 1947); Piscitelli v. Township Comm., 248 A.2d 274 (N.J.L. Div. 1968); Board of Supvrs. v. Rowe, 216 S.E.2d 199 (Va. 1975).

**99.** Waterfront Estates Dev., Inc. v. City of Palos Hills, 597 N.E.2d 641 (Ill. App. 1992); Pacesetter Homes v. Village of Olympia Fields, 244 N.E.2d 369 (Ill. App. 1968); Morristown Rd. Assocs. v. Mayor & Common Council, 394 A.2d 157 (N.J.L. Div. 1978). *See also* cases cited in note 98. *Contra* Novi v. City of Pacifica, 215 Cal. Rptr. 439 (Cal. App. 1985) (ordinance held not vague).

**100.** 69 N.W.2d 217 (Wis.), *cert. denied,* 350 U.S. 841 (1955).

**101.** § 11.02.

**102.** 458 S.W.2d 305 (Mo. 1970). *Accord* Reid v. Architectural Bd. of Review, 192 N.E.2d 74 (Ohio App. 1963).

that the ordinance was facially unconstitutional. The court held that the state zoning act authorized the ordinance and rejected a delegation of power objection. It held the ordinance constitutional and relied on the protection of property rationale adopted in *Saveland.* The court noted that homes in the area were "two-story houses of conventional architectural design, such as Colonial, French Provincial or English." It held that "[t]he intrusion into this neighborhood of . . . [an] unusual, grotesque and nonconforming structure would have a substantial adverse effect on market values of other homes in the area."

In *Village of Hudson v. Albrecht, Inc.,*[103] the owner of a retail store brought suit claiming that an architectural review ordinance that contained look-alike and anti-look-alike requirements was facially unconstitutional. The court upheld the ordinance. It noted the "evolving trend" to grant "a more significant role" to aesthetic considerations and held that "aesthetic considerations may be taken into account by the legislative body in enacting zoning legislation." The court held that the ordinance reflected an appropriate concern with the protection of property values and was not an improper delegation of legislative power.

A court that upholds an architectural design review ordinance because it protects property values may hold that a design review board cannot reject an architectural design unless it is incompatible with existing development in the community. In *Hankins v. Borough of Rockleigh,*[104] the ordinance required an "architectural style conforming with the existing residential structures and with the rural surroundings of the Borough." It prohibited modern flat roofs. The court reversed a borough council decision that refused to approve a dwelling with a partial flat roof. The court noted that the community was extremely small, that about half the structures in the community did not comply with the ordinance, and that there were several flat-roof buildings in the vicinity of the proposed flat-roof dwelling. The court held the ordinance unreasonable "in light of the actual physical development of the community."

Architectural design review ordinances may raise a free speech problem. The courts could protect architectural design as a form of commercial speech and hold that architectural design review places an excessive restriction on architectural expression. Architectural design review does more than regulate the time, place, and manner of architectural expression because it may totally exclude an architectural style. The courts could hold that the total exclusion of an architectural style is invalid as a prohibition on the content of commercial speech.

---

**103.** 458 N.E.2d 852 (Ohio 1984).
**104.** 150 A.2d 63 (N.J. App. Div. 1959).

## C. HISTORIC PRESERVATION.

### § 11.24. The Historic Preservation Problem.

The historic preservation movement began with the designation of historic districts for "showplace areas" containing buildings of historic architectural merit. Beacon Hill in Boston and the French Quarter in New Orleans are examples. Historic preservation now has much broader objectives. Municipalities designate areas as historic districts if they have historic associations or distinctive "period style" buildings worth preserving, even though they are more recent and do not have historic associations. Nineteenth century Victorian residential neighborhoods are an example. Historic preservation also includes municipal programs for the designation and preservation of historic landmarks not located in historic districts.

Historic preservation serves different purposes than zoning. As one court pointed out, zoning regulates land use, density, and location. Historic preservation is concerned with "the preservation of the exterior of buildings having historic or architectural merit."[105] Historic preservation ordinances also prohibit the demolition and require the maintenance of historic structures. These differences in the controls included in historic preservation ordinances create different constitutional problems than zoning.

The majority rule that aesthetics alone is a proper purpose in land use regulation supports the regulatory purposes of historic preservation. As the U.S. Supreme Court noted in *Penn Central*,[106] the "States and cities may enact land use restrictions and controls to enhance the quality of life by preserving the character and desirable aesthetic features of a city." The state courts have also held that historic preservation controls advance a legitimate governmental purpose.

The federal government has undertaken a number of historic preservation initiatives. The most important federal legislation is the National Historic Preservation Act of 1966.[107] This act authorizes the Secretary of the Interior to maintain a National Register of Historic Places, which includes historic areas, sites, and buildings.[108] Municipalities often rely on National Register designations as the basis for making local designations of historic districts and landmarks.

The act requires federal agencies to take into account the effect of federal "undertakings" on historic districts, sites, and buildings listed on the National Register.[109] The Act establishes an Advisory Council on Historic Preservation that may comment on any federal undertaking that will have an adverse effect on

---

105. Mayor & Aldermen v. Anne Arundel County, 316 A.2d 807 (Md. 1974).
106. § 2.13.
107. 16 U.S.C. §§ 470a-470m.
108. 16 U.S.C. § 470a.
109. 16 U.S.C. § 470f.

a listed historic area or property. The Council's comments are advisory and do not bind the federal agency.

## § 11.25. Historic Districts.

### § 11.26. Enabling Legislation and Ordinances.

Although a court can imply the authority to designate historic districts from a zoning enabling act,[110] most states have enacted legislation that authorizes the designation of historic districts and their regulation. Most of these statutes simply include historic preservation as a permissible objective in zoning and other land use controls.[111] Other statutes authorize the designation of historic districts and the adoption of historic district regulation but leave most of the implementation details to municipalities.[112]

Some historic district enabling legislation is more detailed. It authorizes local governments to establish historic district commissions and designate historic districts and specifies the regulatory powers and procedures that are necessary for historic district regulation.[113] This legislation typically authorizes the commission to conduct a study of historic areas and make recommendations for their preservation. The governing body is authorized to act on these recommendations by designating historic districts. Once an historic district is designated, owners of buildings in the district must secure a "certificate of appropriateness" from the commission for the exterior alteration or demolition of structures, and owners of land must secure a certificate for new construction. Some statutes authorize the commission to approve construction on nearby property that affects the historic district. The historic district is an overlay on the zoning ordinance, and the legislation should provide that it does not affect the zoning regulations.

Historic district ordinances implement the enabling legislation. The ordinance typically includes a purpose clause, establishes the commission, and designates the boundaries of historic districts. It also specifies the procedures and criteria for the issuance of certificates of appropriateness and includes controls on the demolition and exterior alteration of buildings within the district, whether or not they are individually of historic merit. Controls on new construction, maintenance, and repair also are usually included. Under some ordinances, the commission may only delay a proposal that requires a certificate of appropriateness if it

---

**110.** City of Santa Fe v. Gamble-Skogmo, Inc., 389 P.2d 13 (N.M. 1964).

**111.** N.M. Stat. Ann. § 3-22-2; N.Y. Gen. Mun. Law § 96-a.

**112.** Miss. Code Ann. §§ 39-13-3 to 39-13-9; Neb. Rev. Stat. §§ 14-2001, 14-2002. *See* Portsmouth Advocates, Inc. v. City of Portsmouth, 587 A.2d 600 (N.H. 1991) (change of historic district boundary to less restrictive district upheld).

**113.** Ga. Code Ann. §§ 44-10-20 to 44-10-31; 65 Ill. Comp. Stat. Ann. 5/11-48.2-1 to 11-48.2-7; Mass. Gen. L. ch. 40C; Pa. Stat. Ann. tit. 53, §§ 8001-8006.

decides to reject it. Appeals are usually provided to the legislative body or the board of zoning adjustment.

### § 11.27. Designation and Controls.

The courts have upheld historic district designations against substantive due process objections, but the rationale for the decisions varies. These cases accept the role of aesthetics in land use regulation, but the sense in which they use the term "aesthetic" is not always clear. Historic district designations implement aesthetic purposes when the buildings in the district have attractive architectural qualities, but they also implement aesthetic objectives even when the buildings in an historic district are not architecturally attractive. In this situation, the designation prevents the intrusion of incompatible uses in an area that has a unifying historic architectural theme.

Some of the early historic district cases, though not fully embracing an aesthetic rationale, were influenced by the historic and attractive appearance of "showplace" historic settlements. In Opinion of the Justices,[114] the court upheld legislation designating the town of Nantucket as an historic district. It noted that "the sedate and quaint appearance of the old island town has to a large extent still remained unspoiled." Similar considerations influenced decisions upholding historic district designations of Beacon Hill in Boston and the French Quarter in New Orleans.[115] The unifying character of well-established historic districts justifies controls covering architectural details, such as the design of window panes,[116] and refusals to allow building projects that interfere with the historic design of buildings in the district.

Cases upholding historic district designations for areas that do not have venerable and "quaint" architectural features rely on broader justifications. *A-S-P Assocs. v. City of Raleigh*[117] is an example. The city designated as an historic district "the only intact nineteenth century neighborhood remaining in Raleigh ... composed predominantly of Victorian houses." The neighborhood was in a state of decline but was undergoing revitalization. Although it did not fully ap-

---

114. 128 N.E.2d 557 (Mass. 1955).

115. Maher v. City of New Orleans, 516 F.2d 1051 (5th Cir. 1975), *cert. denied,* 426 U.S. 905 (1976); Figarsky v. Historic Dist. Comm'n, 368 A.2d 163 (Conn. 1976) (New England town green); City of New Orleans v. Pergament, 5 So. 2d 129 (La. 1941); Opinion of the Justices, 128 N.E.2d 563 (Mass. 1955).

116. Harris v. Old King's Highway Regional Historic Dist. Comm'n, 658 N.E.2d 972 (Mass. (1996) (conversion of garage); Globe Newspaper Co. v. Beacon Hill Architectural Comm'n, 659 N.E.2d 710 (Mass. 1996) (statute authorizes ban on street furniture on Beacon Hill); Parker v. Beacon Hill Arch. Ass'n, 536 N.E.2d 1108 (Mass. 1989) (additional floor on rowhouse); Anderson v. Old King's Hwy. Regional Historic Dist., 493 N.E.2d 188 (Mass. 1986) (change in siding); City of Santa Fe v. Gamble-Skogmo, Inc., 389 P.2d 13 (N.M. 1964) (window pane).

117. 258 S.E.2d 444 (N.C. 1979).

prove aesthetic purposes as the sole justification for the designation, the court upheld it because it implemented the "general welfare" by achieving a number of regulatory objectives. They included the provision of a visual and educational medium, incentives to revitalization, fostering architectural creativity by preserving outstanding architectural examples from the past, and promoting tourism.[118]

### § 11.28.  Delegation of Power and Vagueness.

Delegation of power objections to historic district ordinances are similar to those made to architectural design review ordinances.[119] As in the design review cases, the objection is that the standards for granting certificates of appropriateness are too subjective aesthetically to meet delegation of power requirements. The courts rejected delegation of power objections in practically all of the historic district cases. The *A-S-P* case[120] contains the most careful review of the delegation of power problem. The court upheld the standards provided for the review of exterior changes to buildings in the historic district. It noted that the presence of members with experience and interest in architecture on the historic district commission minimized delegation of power problems. The court also adopted the rule accepted by a minority of courts that the availability of adequate procedural safeguards in the ordinance diminished any delegation of power problems the ordinance created.[121]

The historic district ordinance provided an "incongruity" standard for the review of exterior building changes. The court characterized this standard as "contextual" and added the following comments:

> [T]he standard of "incongruity" must derive its meaning, if any, from the total physical environment of the historic district. . . . Although the neighborhood encompassed by the Historic District is to a considerable extent an architectural melange, that heterogeneity of architectural style is not such as to render the standard of "incongruity" meaningless.[122]

---

118. *See also* Bohannan v. City of San Diego, 106 Cal. Rptr. 333 (Cal. App. 1973); City of Santa Fe v. Gamble-Skogmo, Inc., 389 P.2d 13 (N.M. 1964).

119. § 11.23.

120. § 11.27. *Accord* Mayes v. City of Dallas, 747 F.2d 323 (5th Cir. 1984) (facade and landscape standards); Burke v. City of Charleston, 893 F. Supp. 589 (D.S.C. 1995); South of Second Assocs. v. Georgetown, 580 P.2d 807 (Colo. 1978); Town of Deering ex rel. Bittenbender v. Tibbetts, 202 A.2d 232 (N.H. 1964).

121. § 6.02.

122. 258 S.E.2d at 454.

## § 11.29.  Interim Controls.

Interim controls are necessary during the time a legislative body is considering an historic district for designation. The ordinance usually authorizes the legislative body during this period to prohibit the demolition of historic buildings and to prevent building exterior changes that are inconsistent with the district's historic character. *City of Dallas v. Crownrich*[123] upheld interim controls of this type. After a landowner applied for a building permit for an apartment building, the city council adopted a resolution prohibiting the issuance of building permits in the area while they considered it for designation as an historic district. The court held that the landowner was not entitled to a writ of mandamus to compel the issuance of the permit because the city's statutory zoning and home rule powers conferred the authority to adopt the moratorium resolution. Interim controls are not likely to create a taking problem under the Supreme Court's *Lucas* decision if the landowner can make an economically viable use of the property during the interim period.

## § 11.30.  Taking of Property.

Historic district regulations can raise taking of property problems. They are not troublesome when an historic district commission refuses to allow a change in the exterior features of a building. The property owner is not denied permission to build but only to build in a certain style. More difficult taking questions arise when a commission denies a permit to build a new building, prohibits the demolition of a building, or requires its maintenance and repair. Although the Supreme Court's *Penn Central* decision[124] rejected a taking objection to a restriction on the development of an historic landmark, these cases are more difficult under the per se taking doctrine adopted in the Supreme Court's *Lucas*[125] decision. This decision finds a taking if a land use restriction leaves an owner without an economically viable use of his property. Several pre-*Lucas* cases considered taking problems in historic districts.

In *A-S-P*,[126] the court held that a certificate of appropriateness requirement in an historic district ordinance was reasonable as applied to a landowner who planned to build an office building on a vacant lot. The court held that the comprehensive regulation of development in historic districts is necessary for their preservation and that the preservation of the historic setting for historic buildings is just as important as the preservation of the buildings. It noted that "this 'tout

---

123. 506 S.W.2d 654 (Tex. Civ. App. 1974). *But see* Southern Nat'l Bank v. City of Austin, 582 S.W.2d 229 (Tex. Civ. App. 1979).

124. § 2.13.

125. § 2.18.

126. § 11.27. *See also* Rebman v. City of Springfield, 250 N.E.2d 282 (Ill. App. 1969) (noting that creation of historic district enhanced value of property).

ensemble' doctrine, as it is now termed, is an integral and reasonable part of effective historic district preservation." The court noted that the ordinance did not prohibit property owners from erecting new structures but only prohibited structures that were "incongruous with the historic aspects of the Historic District." It held that property owners in historic districts might not be able to develop their land for its most profitable use, but that this depreciation in value was not a taking.

Taking problems also arise in historic districts when a municipality refuses to allow the demolition of an historic building so that the owner can develop the site for a more intensive use. *Maher v. City of New Orleans* [127] held that the refusal to allow the demolition of a Victorian cottage in the New Orleans French Quarter so that its owner could erect a seven-apartment complex was not a taking. The court applied traditional taking theory and held the landowner had not shown that the refusal to allow demolition totally diminished the value of the property.

The court rejected a facial taking attack on a provision in the ordinance that required the reasonable maintenance and repair of buildings in the historic district. It indicated that this requirement might be a taking as applied if the expense of maintaining a building was unreasonable. A court could hold that an ordinance that requires the maintenance of all the buildings in an historic district confers an average reciprocity of advantage that defeats a taking claim. [128] All property owners in the historic district suffer the burden of the rehabilitation requirement, but all benefit.

*Lafayette Park Baptist Church v. Scott (I)* [129] rejected a justification of this type. A board of adjustment upheld a decision by a landmarks commission that denied permission to demolish a substandard building in an historic district. The board found that the building was in need of extensive rehabilitation but had not degenerated structurally beyond the feasible limits for rehabilitation, considering its historic and architectural significance. The court reversed the board because it found that restoration was not economically feasible. It held that the effect of the demolition on the historic district was a "legitimate consideration" but could not be the "sole basis" for refusing to allow demolition. Voluntary restoration actions by other property owners in the district "did not warrant imposing similar conduct on another landowner or precluding his effective use of the property." This case is consistent with the holding in the Supreme Court's *Lucas* decision that a restriction on property that denies a landowner all economically viable uses is a taking per se.

---

127. 516 F.2d 1051 (5th Cir. 1975), *cert. denied*, 426 U.S. 905 (1976). *See also* First Presbyterian Church v. City Council, 360 A.2d 257 (Pa. Commw. 1976).

128. § 2.05.

129. 553 S.W.2d 856 (Mo. App. 1977).

## § 11.31. Historic Landmarks.

Many municipalities have adopted ordinances for the preservation of historic landmarks located outside historic districts. Since *Penn Central*,[130] which upheld the New York City landmarks preservation law, the courts have accepted the aesthetic and other regulatory purposes served by historic landmark preservation.

## § 11.32. Enabling Legislation and Ordinances.

Fewer states have adopted historic landmark legislation, which may authorize historic landmark regulation in a separate ordinance[131] or in the zoning ordinance.[132] Historic landmark preservation statutes and ordinances authorize landmark designation[133] and include regulatory controls similar to those that are adopted for historic districts.[134] Historic landmark owners must obtain a certificate of appropriateness for exterior alteration, demolition, and new construction. The repair and rehabilitation of historic landmarks is usually required. The statute or ordinance may authorize variances from restrictions on historic landmarks that do not allow the owner a reasonable return.

Landmark preservation laws also raise delegation of power and interim control problems.[135] The courts have held that the standards provided for historic landmark designation are not an unconstitutional delegation of legislative power.[136] Absent statutory authority, a municipality may not delay the demolition of an historic building,[137] or designate the interior of a building as a landmark.[138]

---

**130.** § 2.13.

**131.** Cal. Gov't Code §§ 25373, 37361; La. Rev. Stat. §§ 25:751 to 25:767.

**132.** N.J. Stat. Ann. § 40:55D-65(i). *See* Estate of Neuberger v. Township of Middletown, 521 A.2d 1336 (N.J. App. Div. 1987).

**133.** Mastroianni v. Strada, 571 N.Y.S.2d 55 (App. Div. 1991) (upholding designation of historic home); Schubert Organization, Inc. v. Landmarks Preservation Comm'n, 570 N.Y.S.2d 504 (App. Div.) (upholding designation of theaters in Manhattan theater district), *appeal dismissed*, 580 N.E.2d 1059 (N.Y. 1991), *cert. denied*, 504 U.S. 946 (1992).

**134.** § 11.26.

**135.** *See* §§ 11.28-11.29.

**136.** Citizens Comm. to Save Historic Rhodes Tavern v. District of Columbia Dep't of Hous. & Community Dev., 432 A.2d 710 (D.C. App. 1981) (held not vague claim); Lafayette Park Baptist Church v. Board of Adjustment (II), 599 S.W.2d 61 (Mo. App. 1980); County of Stutsman v. State Historical Soc'y, 371 N.W.2d 321 (N.D. 1985). *Contra* Texas Antiquities Comm. v. Dallas County Community College Dist., 554 S.W.2d 924 (Tex. 1977).

**137.** People ex rel. Marbro Corp. v. Ramsey, 171 N.E.2d 246 (Ill. App. 1960). *See also* Lawrence Preservation Alliance, Inc. v. Allen Realty, Inc. (II), 819 P.2d 138 (Kan. App. 1991) (failure to give notice of hearing on demolition held arbitrary); Keystone Assocs. v. Moerdler, 224 N.E.2d 700 (N.Y. 1966).

**138.** United Artists Theater Circuit, Inc. v. City of Philadelphia, 635 A.2d 612 (Pa. 1993).

## § 11.33. Taking of Property.

Historic landmark preservation creates taking problems similar to those raised by historic districts, but they are more difficult because historic landmark preservation outside historic districts does not confer an average reciprocity of advantage. *Maher v. City of New Orleans*[139] and *Penn Central Transportation Co. v. New York City*[140] are the principal cases that considered taking problems created by historic landmark regulation. *Maher* held a refusal to allow demolition was not a taking when it did not totally diminish the value of the property. This is still acceptable taking doctrine, and other courts applied it to uphold refusals to allow demolition.[141]

In *Penn Central*, the U.S. Supreme Court held that the city landmarks commission's rejection of a high-rise office building over Grand Central Terminal, which it had designated as an historic landmark, was not a taking. The Court held that the Terminal owners did not have an expectation in the development of the airspace over the Terminal that was protected under the taking clause. It also held that the burdens imposed on the Terminal owners by the landmark designation were offset by benefits the landmark law conferred on them by improving the "quality of life" in the city.

The Court held that the landmark designation did not interfere with the present use of the Terminal and noted that the Terminal's owners conceded that it earned a reasonable return. Nor had they applied for approval of a less intrusive structure in the Terminal's airspace. *Penn Central* does not control the more typical case, in which an historic landmark owner would like to demolish an historic landmark and build a more intensive structure on the landmark site.[142] In addition, *Lucas* now requires courts to find a per se taking if a restriction on an historic landmark leaves a landowner without a reasonable use of the property. This problem did not arise in *Penn Central*. Standard taking rules apply if a per se taking does not occur. Cases since *Lucas* have reversed refusals to demolish

---

**139.** 516 F.2d 1051 (5th Cir. 1975), (court noted Maher did not show sale of the property was impracticable, that commercial rental could not provide reasonable rate of return, or that other potential use of property was foreclosed), *cert. denied,* 426 U.S. 905 (1976), discussed in § 11.28.

**140.** 438 U.S. 104 (1978), discussed in § 2.13.

**141.** Rector, Wardens & Vestry of St. Bartholomew's Ch. v. City of New York, 914 F.2d 348 (2d Cir. 1990), *cert. denied,* 111 S. Ct. 1103 (1991); MB Assocs. v. District of Columbia Dep't of License, Investigation & Inspection, 456 A.2d 344 (D.C. App. 1982); 900 G Street Assocs. v. Department of Hous. & Community Dev., 430 A.2d 1387 (D.C. App. 1981); Lubelle v. Rochester Preserv. Bd., 551 N.Y.S.2d 127 (App. Div. 1990). *See also* Allen Realty, Inc. v. City of Lawrence (I), 790 P.2d 948 (Kan. App. 1990) (temporary denial of demolition permit not a taking); Historic Albany Found. v. Coyne, 558 N.Y.S.2d 986 (App. Div. 1990) (upholding submission of development plan as condition to demolition).

**142.** *Accord* United Artists Theater Circuit, Inc. v. City of Philadelphia, 635 A.2d 612 (Pa. 1993) (designation of theater as historic landmark; applying *Penn Central* and Pennsylvania taking law).

historic landmark structures when there was proof that renovation of the structure would be economically feasible, or when there were profitable alternatives to demolition.[143]

### § 11.34. Maintenance and Repair.

*Maher* indicated that a requirement for the maintenance of an historic building could raise an as-applied taking problem, and several cases have considered this question. *Lafayette Park Baptist Church v. Scott (I)*[144] is an influential decision. A board of adjustment refused to allow the demolition of an historic building that was in a serious state of disrepair. The building was located in an historic district. The court reversed and held an historic district ordinance "must be interpreted to authorize demolition when the condition of the structure is such that the economics of restoration preclude the landowner from making any reasonable economic use of the property." *Lafayette (I)* is consistent with the cases that upheld taking objections to maintenance and repair requirements in housing codes.[145] Other cases applied the *Lafayette (I)* rule to strike down refusals to allow the demolition of substandard historic buildings outside historic districts.[146]

### § 11.35. Religious Uses.

Two New York cases decided before the Supreme Court's 1987 taking trilogy were the first important decisions that considered the validity of an historic designation as applied to religious property. In the first case, *Lutheran Church in Am. v. City of New York*,[147] the court held invalid the city's refusal to allow demolition of an historic landmark the church found inadequate and its replacement with an office building because the refusal "would prevent or seriously

---

143. Keeler v. Mayor & City Council, 940 F. Supp. 879 (D. Md. 1996) (taking when no economically feasible rehabilitation plan possible); Park Home v. City of Williamsport, 680 A.2d 835 (Pa. 1996) (upheld; owners did not consider sale of property as alternative to demolition); City of Pittsburgh, Historic Review Comm'n v. Weinberg, 676 A.2d 207 (Pa. 1996) (cost of renovation would not exceed value after renovation, owner knew of historic designation when bought property and could sell it for a profit).

144. 553 S.W.2d 856 (Mo. App. 1977), also discussed in § 11.30. *See also* Lafayette Park Baptist Church v. Board of Adjustment (II), 599 S.W.2d 61 (Mo. App. 1980) (upholding refusal to allow demolition when board on remand found rehabilitation economically feasible).

145. City of St. Louis v. Brune, 515 S.W.2d 471 (Mo. 1974).

146. Foundation for San Francisco's Architectural Heritage v. City & County of San Francisco, 165 Cal. Rptr. 401 (Cal. App. 1980); Citizens Comm'n to Save Historic Rhodes Tavern v. District of Columbia Dep't of Hous. & Urban Dev., 432 A.2d 710 (D.C. App. 1981); Broadview Apts. Co. v. Commission for Historical & Architectural Preservation, 433 A.2d 1214 (Md. App. 1981); State v. Erickson, 301 N.W.2d 324 (Minn. 1981). *But see* Mayor & Aldermen v. Anne Arundel County, 316 A.2d 807 (Md. 1974).

147. 316 N.E.2d 305 (N.Y. 1974).

interfere with the carrying out of the charitable purpose." Here the proof of "economic hardship . . . [was] substantially unchallenged." The court held the city had attempted to "add this property to the public use by purely and simply invading the owner's right to own and manage." The court noted the landmark law's guarantee of a reasonable return did not apply to landmarks owned by religious groups.

The New York court rejected a taking claim in *Society for Ethical Culture v. Spatt*,[148] a case similar to *Lutheran Church* that was decided after *Penn Central*. The court distinguished *Lutheran Church* by holding that "landmark designations, if not unreasonable, are not an undue imposition under the police power." The Society had not shown the "compelling circumstances" present in *Lutheran Church* and had not shown the only solution to the building's inadequacy was demolition of the protected facade. The Society complained instead "that the landmark stands as an effective bar against putting the property to its most lucrative use." The court held the constitution does not guarantee a landowner the most beneficial use of its property.

Later taking cases also considered claims that a landmark designation violated the free exercise of religion clause in the federal constitution. The Second Circuit Court of Appeals rejected a taking claim in a case similar to *Spatt* in which New York City denied a church permission to demolish a "community house" and build an office tower on the site.[149] The court applied the *Spatt* test and found the church could still make use of the building and had exaggerated repair costs. The court also held there was no violation of the Free Exercise of Religion clause of the federal constitution. It relied heavily on the Supreme Court's decision in *Employment Div., Dep't of Human Resources v. Smith*,[150] which held the Free Exercise clause does not prohibit compliance with a valid and neutral law that is generally applicable.

The Supreme Court denied certiorari in the Second Circuit decision, and on the same day remanded for reconsideration, in light of *Smith,* a Washington Supreme court decision that had taken a contrary position on the Free Exercise issue.[151] The Washington case held a landmark law that required a church to secure approval of a change in its facade interfered with the practice of religion. Aesthetic and cultural interests in preservation were not sufficiently compelling state interests to overcome the religious infringement. These actions indicate the Court favors the Second Circuit holding and reads its *Smith* decision to mean

---

**148.** 415 N.E.2d 922 (N.Y. 1980). *See also* Manhattan Club v. Landmarks Preservation Comm'n, 273 N.Y.S.2d 848 (Sup. Ct. 1966).

**149.** Rector, Wardens & Vestry of St. Bartholomew's Ch. v. City of New York, 914 F.2d 348 (2d Cir. 1990), *cert. denied,* 499 U.S. 905 (1991).

**150.** 494 U.S. 872 (1990).

**151.** First Covenant Ch. v. City of Seattle, 787 P.2d 1352 (Wash. 1990), *vacated and remanded,* 499 U.S. 901 (1991), *adhered to on remand,* 840 P.2d 174 (Wash. 1992).

that landmark designation laws do not present a Free Exercise problem. Nevertheless, on remand, the Washington Supreme Court reaffirmed its holding that the landmark designation violated the free exercise clause in both the federal and state constitutions.[152]

### § 11.36. Transfer of Development Rights.

Municipalities have adopted a land use control technique known as the transfer of development rights (TDR) to resolve the taking problems created by historic landmark preservation. A TDR program for historic landmark preservation is quite simple. Historic landmark buildings are often undersized for their site and do not use up the building densities permitted by the zoning ordinance. A TDR program transfers unused densities at landmark sites to transfer sites or areas designated by the municipality, which may be nearby or in other areas of the municipality. Under one variant, the owner of the transfer site purchases the unused development rights at the landmark site from the landmark owner. This payment provides the compensation necessary to avoid a taking objection. Under another variant, the municipality creates an agency with the authority to acquire development rights from landmark owners. The agency later sells these rights to landowners at transfer sites.

TDR programs present a number of constitutional problems. A municipality may need to downzone the transfer sites in order to make the purchase of development rights at these sites attractive. A court could hold that a downzoning for this purpose is unconstitutional.[153] A TDR program may also violate the statutory requirement that zoning regulations must be uniform within zoning districts. Developers at transfer site areas build at existing zoning densities without purchasing development rights but build more intensively if development rights are purchased. An answer to the uniformity objection is that transfer site areas where landowners can purchase development rights are similar to planned unit developments, where uses and densities are mixed. The courts have rejected uniformity objections to regulations that allow planned unit developments.[154] The purchaser of development rights at a transfer site also secures an increase in the

---

152. First Covenant Church of Seattle v. City of Seattle, 840 P.2d 174 (Wash. 1992). *Accord* Keeler v. Mayor & City Council, 940 F. Supp. 879 (D. Md. 1996); *Accord* Society of Jesus v. Boston Landmarks Comm'n, 564 N.E.2d 571 (Mass. 1990) (designation of church interior as religious landmark violates state constitutional provision protection religious worship); First United Methodist Church v. Hearing Examiner for Seattle Landmarks Preservation Bd., 916 P.2d 374 (Wash. 1996).

153. §§ 6.36-6.38.

154. § 9.26.

zoning density previously allowed on her property. This density increase may be an unconstitutional spot zoning.[155]

The cases have considered the taking problems that arise in TDR programs when an historic landmark owner claims the sale of his development rights does not compensate him for the restrictions the landmark designation imposes on his property. All of these cases arose in New York City, which has a TDR program applicable to landmarks and other sites.

*Fred F. French Inv. Co. v. City of New York*[156] was the first case. It did not consider, but is applicable to, the historic landmark TDR program. The city adopted an amendment to its zoning ordinance that classified two private parks in a multi-family complex as parks open to public use. The court found a taking, but the city argued its TDR program resolved the taking objection. Under this program, the owner of the development rights on the restricted park site could transfer them to an area in midtown Manhattan. The program allowed limited density increases in the transfer area as-of-right, but additional density increases required a public hearing and municipal approval.

The court noted that development rights "are a potentially valuable and even a transferable commodity" that a court should not disregard when it considers a taking claim. But it believed that the TDR program did not resolve the taking objection to the ordinance that restricted the use of the park:

> But severed, the development rights are a double abstraction until they are actually attached to a receiving parcel, yet to be identified, acquired, and subject to the contingent approvals of administrative agencies, events which may never happen because of the contingencies of the market and the contingencies and exigencies of administrative action.[157]

The court summarized its holding by noting that the severance of the development rights "rendered their value so uncertain and contingent, as to deprive the property owner of their practical usefulness, except under rare and perhaps coincidental circumstances." The court was sympathetic to TDR programs that protected an owner's development rights in his property and suggested that "just compensation ... instantly and in money" would avoid a taking problem.

The New York court next considered the taking problems created by a TDR program for historic landmarks in its decision in *Penn Central*.[158] The TDR program authorized the transfer of development rights from the Terminal to sites in the immediate vicinity. The court noted that the value of the transferred rights

---

155. §§ 6.28-6.35. *See* Dupont Circle Citizens Ass'n v. District of Columbia Zoning Comm'n, 355 A.2d 550 (D.C. App. 1976) (approving TDR transfer).

156. 350 N.E.2d 381 (N.Y.) (explaining that ordinance was invalidated as deprivation of property without due process of law), *appeal dismissed*, 429 U.S. 990 (1976).

157. *Id.* at 388.

158. 366 N.E.2d 1271 (N.Y. 1977).

might not equal the value of the development rights at the original site. It did not find this possibility fatal because land use regulation always diminishes the value of property. Diminution in value is unconstitutional only if a land use regulation does not allow any reasonable use. Transferred development rights need only provide "reasonable compensation."[159]

The court distinguished *French* because the transferred development rights in that case were left in "legal limbo." The court also noted that the landmark preservation ordinance in *Penn Central* allowed the continued productive use of the Terminal. "In addition, the development rights were made transferable to numerous sites in the vicinity of the terminal, several owned by Penn Central, and at least one or two" were suitable for office building construction. The U.S. Supreme Court gave little attention to the TDR program because it held that a taking had not occurred.[160] It indicated that the transferred development rights might not have avoided a taking objection, but that they could mitigate whatever financial burden the landmark designation imposed. New York has now authorized TDR programs for the preservation of historic resources.[161]

---

**159.** A Local & Regional Monitor v. City of Los Angeles, 16 Cal. Rptr. 2d 358 (Cal. App. 1993) (upheld density transfer authorized by agreement with city).

**160.** § 2.13.

**161.** N.Y. Gen. City Law § 20-f; N.Y. Town Law § 261-a. *See also accord* Ariz. Rev. Stat. Ann. § 9-462.01(12); Idaho Code § 67-4619; P.R. Laws Ann. tit. 21, § 4622; Tenn. Code Ann. § 3-7-101(a)(2).

# REFERENCES

## Books and Monographs

J. Costonis, Icons and Aliens: Law, Aesthetics, and Environmental Change (1989).

C. Duerksen, Aesthetics and Land Use Controls, American Planning Ass'n, Planning Advisory Serv. Rep. No. 399 (1986).

C. Floyd & P. Shedd, Highway Beautification: The Environmental Movement's Greatest Failure (1979).

P. Glassford, Appearance Codes for Small Communities, American Planning Ass'n, Planning Advisory Serv. Rep. No. 379 (1983).

F. James & D. Gale, Zoning for Sale: A Critical Analysis of Transferable Development Rights Programs (Urban Institute, 1977).

E. Kelly & G. Raso, Sign Regulations for Small and Midsize Communities: A Planners Guide and A Model Ordinance, American Planning Ass'n, Planning Advisory Serv. Rep. No. 419 (1989).

D. Mandelker & W. Ewald, Street Graphics and the Law (1988).

D. Mandelker, J. Gerard & T. Sullivan, Federal Land Use Law (updated annually).

M. Morris, Innovative Tools for Historic Preservation (American Planning Ass'n, Planning Advisory Serv., Rep. No. 438, 1992).

R. Olshansky, Planning for Hillside Development, American Planning Ass'n, Planning Advisory Serv. Rep. No. 466 (1997).

R. Roddewig, Preparing a Historic Preservation Ordinance, American Planning Ass'n, Planning Advisory Serv. Rep. No. 374 (1983).

## Articles

Babcock & Theriaque, Landmarks Preservation Ordinances: Are the Religious Clauses Violated by Their Application to Religious Properties?, 7 J. Land Use & Envt'l L. 165 (1992).

Breitel, A Judicial View of Transferable Development Rights, Land Use L. & Zoning Dig., Vol. 30, No. 2, at 5 (1978).

Carmella, Houses of Worship and Religious Liberty: Constitutional Limits to Landmark Preservation and Architectural Review, 36 Vill. L. Rev. 401 (1991).

Costonis, The Chicago Plan: Incentive Zoning and the Preservation of Urban Landmarks, 85 Harv. L. Rev. 574 (1972).

Costonis, Development Rights Transfer: An Exploratory Essay, 83 Yale L.J. 75 (1973).

Costonis, Law and Aesthetics: A Critique and Reformulation of the Dilemmas, 80 Mich. L. Rev. 355 (1982).

Duerksen, Drafting and Administering Historic Preservation Ordinances, 8 Zoning & Plan. L. Rep. 97, 105 (1985).

Dukeminier, Zoning for Aesthetic Objectives: A Reappraisal, 20 Law & Contemp. Probs. 218 (1955).

Gerstenblith, Architect as Artist: Artist's Rights and Historic Preservation, 12 Cardozo Arts & Ent. L.J. 431 (1994).

Gold, The Welfare Economics of Historic Preservation, 8 Conn. L. Rev. 348 (1976).

Homer, Landmarking Religious Institutions: The Burden of Rehabilitation and the Loss of Religious Freedom, 28 Urb. Law. 327 (1996).

Karp, The Evolving Meaning of Aesthetics in Land-Use Regulation, 15 Colum. J. Envtl. L. 307 (1990).

Linder, New Directions for Preservation Law: Creating an Environment Worth Experiencing, 20 Envt'l L. 4 (1990).

Malone, The Future of Transferable Development Rights in the Supreme Court, 73 Ky. L.J. 759 (1985).

Marcus, Air Rights in New York City: TDR, Zoning Lot Merger and the Well-Considered Plan, 50 Brooklyn L. Rev. 867 (1984).

Marcus, The Grand Slam Grand Central Terminal Decision: A Euclid for Landmarks, Favorable Notice for TDR and a Resolution of the Regulatory Taking Impasse, 7 Ecology L.Q. 731 (1978).

Merriam, Making TDR Work, 56 N.C.L. Rev. 77 (1978).

Netherton, The Due Process Issue in Zoning for Historic Preservation, 19 Urb. Law. 77 (1987).

Netter & Barry, Zoning for Historic Preservation, 13 Zon. & Plan. L. Rep. 9 (1990).

Nivala, The Future For Our Past: Preserving Landmark Preservation, 5 N.Y.U. Envtl. L.J. 83 (1996).

Poole & Kobert, Architectural Appearance Review Regulations and the First Amendment: The Constitutionally Infirm "Excessive Difference" Test, 12 Zoning & Plan. L. Rev. 89 (1989).

Symposium, Preserving, Conserving, and Reusing Historic Properties, 12 Urb. Law. 1 (1980).

Weinstein, The Myth of Ministry v. Mortar: A Legal and Policy Analysis of Landmark Designation of Religious Institutions, 65 Temp. L. Rev. 91 (1992).

Williams, Subjectivity, Expression and Privacy: Problems of Aesthetic Regulation, 62 Minn. L. Rev. 1 (1977).

Ziegler, Aesthetics in Ohio Land Use Law: Preserving Beauty in the Parlor and Keeping Pigs in the Barnyard, 19 Akron L. Rev. 1 (1985).

Ziegler, Local Control of Signs and Billboards: An Analysis of Recent Regulatory Efforts, 8 Zoning & Plan. L. Rep. 161 (1985).

Ziegler, The Transfer of Development Rights, 18 Zon. & Plan. L. Rep. 61, 69 (1995).

Ziegler, Visual Environment Regulation and Derivative Human Values: The Emerging Rational Basis for Modern Aesthetic Doctrine, 9 Zoning & Plan. L. Rep. 17 (1986).

**Student Work**

Note, Applying Historic Preservation Ordinances to Church Property: Protecting the Past and Preserving the Constitution, 63 N.C.L. Rev. 404 (1985).

Note, Architectural Expression: Police Power and the First Amendment, 16 Urb. L. Ann. 273 (1979).

Note, Architecture, Aesthetic Zoning, and the First Amendment, 28 Stan. L. Rev. 179 (1975).

Note, Banning Portable Signs for Aesthetic Reasons, 17 Stetson L. Rev. 829 (1988).

Note, Development Rights Transfer and Landmarks Preservation Providing a Sense of Orientation, 9 Urb. L. Ann. 131 (1975).

Note, Free Exercise, Free Expression, and Landmarks Preservation, 91 Colum. L. Rev. 181 (1991).

Note, Historic Districts: Preserving City Neighborhoods for the Privileged, 60 N.Y.U. L. Rev. 64 (1985).

Note, Landmarks as Cultural Property: An Appreciation of New York City, 44 Rutgers L. Rev. 427 (1992).

Note, Making Sense of Billboard Law: Justifying Prohibitions and Exemptions, 88 Mich. L. Rev. 2482 (1990).

Note, *Members of the City Council v. Taxpayers for Vincent:* The Constitutionality of Prohibiting Temporary Sign Posting on Public Property to Advance Local Aesthetic Concerns, 34 DePaul L. Rev. 197 (1984).

Note, Municipal Regulation of Political Signs: Balancing First Amendment Rights Against Aesthetic Concerns, 45 Drake L. Rev. 767 (1997).

Note, Preservation of Historic Landmarks, 92 Harv. L. Rev. 222 (1978).

Note, Preserving the Past: Historic Preservation Regulations and the Taking Clause, 34 Wash. U.J. Urb. & Contemp. L. 297 (1988).

Note, Religious Landmark Preservation Under the First and Fifth Amendments: *St. Bartholomew's Church v. City of New York,* 65 St. John's L. Rev. 553 (1991).

Note, The Unconstitutionality of Transferable Development Rights, 84 Yale L.J. 1001 (1975).

Note, Unsightly Politics: Aesthetics, Sign Ordinances, and Homeowners' Speech in *City of Ladue v. Gilleo,* 20 Harv. Envtl. L. Rev. 473 (1996).

Note, You Can't Build That Here: The Constitutionality of Aesthetic Zoning and Architectural Review, 58 Fordham L. Rev. 1013 (1990).

Comment, Beyond the Eye of the Beholder: A New Majority of Jurisdictions Authorize Aesthetic Regulation, 48 UMKC L. Rev. 125 (1980).

Comment, Billboard Regulation After *Metromedia* and *Lucas,* 31 Hous. L. Rev. 1555 (1995).

Comment, For Whom the Bell Tolls: Religious Properties as Landmarks Under the First Amendment, 8 Pace Envt'l L. Rev. 579 (1991).

Comment, From *Penn Central* to *United Artists' I & II,* The Rise to Immunity of Historic Preservation Designation From Successful Challenges, 22 B.C. Envtl. Aff. L. Rev. 593 (1995).

Comment, San Francisco's Downtown Plan: Environmental and Urban Design Values in Central Business District Regulation, 12 Ecology L.Q. 511 (1985).

Comment, Zoning Law: Architectural Expression and the First Amendment, 76 Marq. L. Rev. 439 (1993).

477

# Chapter 12

# ENVIRONMENTAL CONTROLS

## § 12.01.  The Land Use Problem.

Federal, state, and local governments have adopted a number of regulatory programs for the protection of environmental and natural resource areas. They include wetland and floodplain regulation and zoning for the protection of agricultural land. Although these programs are similar because they apply to environmentally important areas, they serve different regulatory purposes. Wetland regulation imposes restrictive controls in wetland areas to preserve their environmental function by keeping them free from development. Floodplain regulation imposes restrictive controls on development in floodways and adjacent floodplains to prevent loss of life and property damage from flooding. Agricultural zoning restricts nonagricultural development to preserve agricultural areas. Ordinances that restrict development on hillside slopes to control erosion are another example.[1]

---

**1.** Rejecting taking claims: Seldon v. City of Manitou Springs, 745 P.2d 229 (Colo. 1987); Kelly v. Tahoe Regional Planning Agency, 855 P.2d 1027 (Nev. 1993) (upholding regulations that temporarily limit development in hilltop areas; *Lucas* distinguished), *cert. denied*, 510 U.S. 1041 (1994); Anello v. Zoning Bd. of Appeals, 678 N.E.2d 870 (N.Y. 1997); Jones v. Zoning Hearing Bd., 578 A.2d 1369 (Pa. Commw. 1990) (same; performance standards to protect forests and steep slopes). *Contra* Corrigan v. City of Scottsdale, 720 P.2d 528 (Ariz. App. 1985), *aff'd in part and vacated in part on other grounds*, 720 P.2d 513 (Ariz. 1986).

Unlike traditional zoning, there is a strong state and federal presence in environmental land use regulation. Federal and state intervention varies with the environmental resource that is protected. A federal program administered under the Clean Water Act requires dredge and fill permits for development in wetland areas. A federal flood insurance program has encouraged the enactment of floodplain regulations by municipalities throughout the country. Many states have regulatory programs for wetlands and floodplains, and they often authorize local regulation that complies with state statutory criteria. Agricultural zoning is usually included in local zoning ordinances, and many states have related agricultural land protection programs.

The National Coastal Zone Management Act[2] provides funding for state coastal management programs. The statute authorizes land use controls in state programs, and several coastal states have incorporated wetlands and floodplain regulation in their coastal programs. States have also adopted beachfront management statutes that require setbacks in coastal areas.

Environmental land use regulation presents important taking problems. These programs had raised taking problems under the harm-benefit rule, which invalidates regulations that provide regulatory benefits for the general public but concentrate their development restrictions on a limited number of landowners. The U.S. Supreme Court rejected the harm-benefit rule in the *Lucas* case,[3] but adopted a rule that a land use regulation is a per se taking if it leaves a land-owner with no economically viable use of his land. The per se taking rule could invalidate environmental land use regulations because they often impose severe restrictions on the development of property.

## A. WETLANDS.

### § 12.02.  State and Local Programs.

Regulatory programs for wetlands are intended to preserve the many important environmental functions these areas serve. As transitional "marshy" areas between land and bodies of water, wetlands help preserve water quality by slowing water flow and allowing sediment to settle. They also stabilize water tables by retaining water during dry periods and holding it back during floods. Wetlands are important resources for environmental diversity and provide an important habitat for many forms of wildlife.

A number of states, especially the Great Lakes and eastern states, have legislation that regulates development in coastal wetlands, and some also have inland

---

2. 16 U.S.C. §§ 1451-1474.
3. § 2.17.

wetlands legislation.[4] Legislation in some states applies to "shoreland" areas, which include wetlands. This legislation usually requires permits for dredging, filling, and the alteration of wetlands. These activities are necessary for housing and other development. Other statutes authorize the state agency to adopt land use regulations that specify permitted uses in wetlands and authorize permits only for developments that are allowed by these regulations.

A number of wetland statutes require local governments to adopt wetland regulations which are consistent with the state statute, and which the state agency must approve. These regulations are sometimes included in the zoning ordinance. The state agency in some states can adopt regulations for a local government if it fails to adopt them. Local wetland ordinances usually allow only limited uses in wetlands areas, such as recreational and other natural uses of the land, and do not allow major structural development.

State wetland statutes provide criteria for the issuance of permits for regulated activities in wetlands.[5] Some statutes authorize the state agency to consider the "public interest" or the "policy" of the act. Other statutes contain "factors" the state agency must consider when it decides whether to issue a permit. These factors typically include the environmental impact of the development, whether alternatives are available, and the suitability of the activity for the wetlands.

State wetland statutes may preempt local wetland ordinances if the statute does not expressly allow local regulation. Whether a court finds local regulation preempted if the statute does not authorize it depends on its view of the state regulatory responsibilities conferred by the state legislation. *Golden v. Board of Selectmen*[6] held a state wetland statute did not preempt a local wetland ordinance because each conferred "a separate and distinct type of authority."

The courts have implied the authority to adopt local wetland regulations from the standard zoning enabling act.[7] A related question is whether state wetland legislation is unconstitutional as an infringement on local home rule. The courts have held that similar environmental land use legislation serves state interests and does not interfere with local home rule autonomy.[8]

---

**4.** Conn. Gen. Stat. §§ 22a-28 to 22a-45; Fla. Stat. Ann. §§ 373.414; Mass. Gen. Laws ch. 130, § 105; ch. 131, § 40; Mich. Stat. Ann. §§ 13A.30301-30323 ; N.H. Rev. Stat. Ann. §§ 483-B:1 to 483-B:19; N.Y. Envtl. Conserv. Law §§ 25-0101 to 25-0601; 71-2501 to 71-2507.

**5.** Murphy v. Board of Envt'l Protection, 615 A.2d 255 (Me. 1992) (all statutory standards apply to review of permit for development adjacent to coastal wetlands).

**6.** 265 N.E.2d 573 (Mass. 1970). *Contra* Lauricella v. Planning & Zoning Bd., 342 A.2d 374 (Conn. Sup. 1974).

**7.** Morland Dev. Co. v. City of Tulsa, 596 P.2d 1255 (Okla. 1979) (concurring opinion).

**8.** CEEED v. California Coastal Zone Conservation Comm'n, 118 Cal. Rptr. 315 (Cal. App. 1974) (coastal permit legislation); Pope v. City of Atlanta, 418 F. Supp. 665 (Ga. 1977) (floodplains). *See also* Town of Monroe v. Carey, 412 N.Y.S.2d 939 (Sup. Ct. 1977).

## § 12.03.  Federal Permit Program for Dredged and Fill Material.

Section 404 of the federal Clean Water Act[9] requires permits from the U.S. Army Corps of Engineers for the discharge of dredge and fill material in the "waters of the United States." The act also gives the Environmental Protection Agency (EPA) a veto authority over Corps permits.[10] Dredged and fill material permits are required for development in wetlands, which usually require dredging and filling activities. The U.S. Supreme Court upheld a Corps regulation that defined the "waters of the United States" to include "saturated" wetlands adjacent to bodies of water even though the wetlands are not inundated by the adjacent water body.[11] Corps jurisdiction over "isolated" wetlands is less clear.[12]

The Clean Water Act does not contain criteria for the Corps' permit review, but Corps regulations provide for a "public interest" review in which it must balance the harms and benefits of a proposed dredging and filling activity. These regulations apply to wetlands.[13] In addition, EPA regulations provide that an alternative site not in a wetlands is presumptively available for a use proposed in a wetlands if not water-dependent.[14] The courts have reversed Corps decisions to grant permits when it did not take these factors into account.[15]

The U.S. Supreme Court has held that the statutory permit requirement is not a taking. A taking occurs only when a permit denial prevents an economically viable use of the land. The landowner must sue for compensation in these cases in the Court of Federal Claims.[16]

## § 12.04.  The Taking Issue.

Wetlands regulation presents a difficult taking problem. Some state courts applied the harm-benefit rule to hold a wetlands restriction was a taking,[17] and may continue to apply this rule even though the Supreme Court has rejected it. A more serious taking problem arises under the Supreme Court's *Lucas* decision. Wetlands regulations often allow only passive recreational uses in order to protect the wetlands ecology. A court might hold a per se taking occurs in these

---

9. 33 U.S.C. § 1444(a).

10. 33 U.S.C. §§ 1444(b), 1444(c).

11. United States v. Riverside Bayview Homes, Inc., 474 U.S. 121 (1986).

12. *See* Hoffman Homes, Inc. v. EPA, 999 F.2d 256 (7th Cir. 1993) (no showing of jurisdiction over isolated wetlands not adjacent to waters because no proof that migratory birds used area)

13. 33 C.F.R. § 320.4.

14. 40 C.F.R. § 230.10.

15. Van Abbema v. Fornell, 807 F.2d 633 (7th Cir. 1986); Hough v. Marsh, 557 F. Supp. 74 (D. Mass. 1982). *But see* Mall Props. v. Marsh, 672 F. Supp. 561 (D. Mass. 1987) (may not consider socioeconomic effects), *appeal dismissed,* 841 F.2d 440 (1st Cir. 1988).

16. United States v. Riverside Bayview Homes, Inc., 474 U.S. 121 (1986).

17. State v. Johnson, 265 A.2d 711 (Me. 1970).

cases because these uses are not economically beneficial.[18] This result is not inevitable. As the cases below show, wetlands regulations often allow economically beneficial uses. Standard taking tests would then apply.

Two taking doctrines play an important role in wetlands taking cases. One, known as the whole parcel rule, determines the parcel of land the court must consider when a landowner argues a taking has occurred.[19] Wetlands may occupy only a portion of the property affected by a regulation, and a court must decide whether it is to consider all or only the wetlands part of the property in its taking decision. This problem also arises when a landowner owns several properties, and not all of them are affected by the wetlands regulation.[20] The second doctrine is the rule that a landowner's investment-backed expectations are protected under the taking clause. Courts held a landowner does not have protected investment-backed expectations when she purchases property covered by a wetlands regulation,[21] but the status of this rule is not clear since the Supreme Court's 1987 taking trilogy.[22]

In a series of cases decided since the Supreme Court's 1987 taking trilogy, the Court of Federal Claims, with the approval of its appellate Federal Circuit, refused to dismiss taking claims based on permit denials under § 404 of the Clean Water Act.[23] The results when the cases have come to trial have been mixed.[24]

In its latest remand of a long-running § 404 case to the Court of Federal Claims, *Florida Rock Industries v. United States*,[25] the Federal Circuit provided some guidance on takings law as it applied to wetlands permit denials. It helding

---

**18.** Vatalaro v. Department of Envtl. Regulation, 601 So. 2d 1223 (Fla. App. 1992) (permit denial held a taking pre-*Lucas*; state agency offered only passive recreational use).

**19.** § 2.36.

**20.** Pre-*Lucas* cases holding no taking under rule: Deltona Corp. v. United States, 657 F.2d 1184 (Ct. Cl. 1991), *cert. denied*, 455 U.S. 1017 (1982); State v. Schindler, 604 So.2d 565 (Fla. App. 1992); Moskow v. Comm'r, 427 N.E.2d 750 (Mass. 1981); American Dredging Co. v. State, Dep't of Environmental Protection, 404 A.2d 42 (N.J. App. Div.1979).

**21.** Claridge v. New Hampshire Wetlands Bd., 485 A.2d 287 (N.H. 1984) (no taking).

**22.** § 2.18.

**23.** *E.g.*, Formanek v. United States, 18 Cl. Ct. 785 (1989) (also holding that offers of purchase by conservation organizations are not basis for summary judgment for government); Beure-Co. v. United States, 16 Cl. Ct. 42 (1989).

**24.** Taking found: Bowles v. United States, 31 Fed. Cl. 37 (1994); Loveladies Harbor, Inc. v. United States, 21 Cl. Ct. 153 (1990) (awarding compensation). Taking not found: Broadwater Farms Joint Venture v. United States, 35 Fed. Cl. 232 (1996) (no taking when residual land had value); Ciampitti v. United States, 22 Cl. Ct. 310 (1991) (rejecting argument that knowledge of permit requirements defeats investment-backed expectations). *See also* Tabb Lakes, Ltd. v. United States, 10 F.3d 796 (Fed. Cir. 1993) (cease and desist order under federal law that stopped filling of wetlands not a taking when plaintiff could have developed land by obtaining a permit).

**25.** 18 F.3d 1560 (Fed. Cir. 1994), *cert. denied*, 513 U.S. 1109 (1995). *See also* Loveladies Harbor, Inc. v. United States28 F.3d 1171 (Fed. Cir. 1994) (affirming award of compensation).

that the property had substantial speculative value despite the government's refusal to permit mining. This holding precluded a per se taking under *Lucas*, but the court applied the takings analysis in *Lucas* to hold that a finding was possible on remand that "a partial deprivation resulting from a regulatory imposition" had occurred. The court suggested a balancing test that included the loss of economic use, any "direct compensating benefits" to the property and whether "alternative permitted activities [are] economically realistic." A strong dissent claimed there was no precedent for a rule that a "claimant may recover proportional compensation for the impairment of economic use if it passes a threshold beyond 'diminution in value.'"

*Just v. Marinette County*[26] was the leading pre-trilogy state case holding a regulation restricting a wetland to passive uses was not a taking. The court reformulated the harm-benefit rule to reach its decision, holding that "we have a restriction on the use of a citizen['s] property, not to secure a benefit for the public, but to prevent a harm from the change in the natural character of the citizens' property."[27]

The *Just* decision attracted criticism because it inverted the harm-benefit theory of the taking clause, but other courts followed it.[28] The status of the decision since the Supreme Court rejected the harm-benefit rule in *Lucas* is not clear.

Since *Lucas*, state courts have upheld a designation of a wetlands and the denial of development permits against taking claims.[29] They have been able to find economic uses of the land that avoid the application of the *Lucas* per se taking rule, even though those uses were wetlands and recreational uses.[30] In other cases where a landowner was denied a permit for development, the courts have avoided the *Lucas* per se taking rule by holding the denial did not prohibit

---

**26.** 201 N.W.2d 761 (Wis. 1972). *See* Zealy v. City of Waukesha, 548 N.W.2d 528 (Wis. 1996) (continuing validity of *Just* not considered).

**27.** *Id.* at 767-68.

**28.** Manor Dev. Corp. v. Conservation Comm'n, 433 A.2d 999 (Conn. 1980); Graham v. Estuary Props., Inc.,399 So. 2d 1374 (Fla.), *cert. denied,* 454 U.S. 1083 (1981); Carter v. South Carolina Coastal Council, 314 S.E.2d 327 (S.C. 1984); Chokecherry Hills Estates v. Deuel County, 294 N.W.2d 654 (S.D. 1980); 46 A.L.R.3d 1422 (1972). *See also* Candlestick Props., Inc. v. San Francisco Bay Conservation & Dev. Comm'n, 89 Cal. Rptr. 897 (Cal. App. 1970); Glisson v. Alachua Cty., 558 So. 2d 1030 (Fla. App. 1990) (dismissing facial taking claim; existing uses preserved and transfer of development rights available); Namon v. State Dep't of Envtl. Reg., 558 So. 2d 504 (Fla. App. 1990) (taking not found; landowner had only unilateral expectation); Potomac Sand & Gravel Co. v. Governor of Md., 293 A.2d 241 (Md.) *cert. denied,* 409 U.S. 1040 (1972) (dredge and fill prohibition upheld under nuisance theory); Milardo v. Coastal Resources Mgt. Council, 424 A.2d 266 (R.I. 1981).

**29.** *See* Lopes v. City of Peabody, 629 N.E.2d 1312 (Mass. 1994) (stating taking rules under *Lucas* and pre-*Lucas* law).

**30.** FIC Homes of Blackstone, Inc. v. Conservation Comm'n, 673 N.E.2d 61 (Mass. App. 1996); Gazza v. New York State Dep't of Envtl. Conservation, 679 N.E.2d 1035 (N.Y. 1997).

other economically viable uses of the property.[31] The courts have also held that landowners did not have investment-backed expectations in the development of their property when wetland regulations were in effect when they purchased their land. These regulations were inherent limitations on their property not subject to attack under the taking clause.[32] Knowledge that wetland regulations were applicable also barred taking claims.[33] The courts have also applied the whole parcel rule to minimize losses in value from restrictions on the wetlands portion of a property.[34] Whether all courts will take so generous a view of wetland regulation under the taking clause is not yet clear.

## B. FLOODPLAINS.

### § 12.05.  State and Local Programs.

Floodplain regulation is a restrictive land use control that prohibits or limits development in areas subject to flooding. Floodplain regulation usually distinguishes between the floodway and the flood fringe. The floodway is the unobstructed part of the floodplain consisting of the stream channel and overbank areas capable of carrying a flood discharge. The floodway is intended to carry deep and fast-moving water. The adjacent flood fringe is intended to carry shallow and slow-moving water. Structural development is not usually permitted in the floodway. Open nonstructural uses are permitted, such as agricultural and recreational uses. Structural development is permitted in the flood fringe, often as a special permit use, if it is elevated above expected flood levels or protected from flood damage. Development in floodplains increases the flooding danger by diminishing the carrying capacity of the floodplain. This causal relationship between floodplain development and flood danger provides an important basis for upholding restrictive floodplain regulations against taking objections.

The National Flood Insurance Act[35] has stimulated the widespread enactment of state and local floodplain regulation. The act establishes a national program of

---

31. Mock v. Department of Envtl. Resources, 623 A.2d 940 (Pa. Commw. 1993), *aff'd without opinion,* 667 A.2d 212 (Pa. 1995), *cert. denied,* 116 S. Ct. 1841 (1996); Alegria v. Keeney, 687 A.2d 1249 (R.I. 1997). *See also* Zerbetz v. Municipality of Anchorage, 856 P.2d 777 (Alaska 1993) (designation of coastal wetlands; plaintiff had not made application for development permission); Gil v. Inland Wetlands & Watercourses Agency, 593 A.2d 1368 (Conn. 1991).

32. FIC Homes of Blackstone, Inc. v. Conservation Comm'n, 673 N.E.2d 61 (Mass. App. 1996); Gazza v. New York State Dep't of Envtl. Conservation, 679 N.E.2d 1035 (N.Y. 1997) (purchase offer for thousands less than value without restrictions). *See also* Kim v. City of New York, 681 N.E.2d 312 (N.Y. 1997) (inherent limitations include statutory restrictions).

33. Alegria v. Keeney, 687 A.2d 1249 (R.I. 1997).

34. FIC Homes of Blackstone, Inc. v. Conservation Comm'n, 673 N.E.2d 61 (Mass. App. 1996).

35. 42 U.S.C. §§ 4001-4028.

federal flood insurance and requires the federal agency that administers the act to adopt criteria for state and local floodplain regulations.[36] Owners of property in a floodplain may obtain federal insurance only if their municipality has adopted a federally-approved ordinance. After an approved floodplain ordinance is adopted, the purchase of federal insurance is required for the receipt of direct federal financial assistance and for loans from private financial institutions regulated or insured by the federal government.[37]

A large number of states have legislation authorizing floodplain regulation.[38] This legislation usually authorizes the direct state regulation of floodplains. It may also mandate or authorize local governments to adopt floodplain regulations that comply with criteria included in the statute. The legislation may authorize a state agency to adopt floodplain regulations for a locality if it does not adopt regulations that comply with state legislative requirements. The state agency may compel the adoption of a local floodplain ordinance if the state statute requires one.[39]

The typical state floodplain statute contains authority to survey and map floodplain areas, provisions for the control of existing structures, authority to issue permits for new development, and standards for permit review. Some statutes authorize subdivision review. If the statute requires or authorizes the adoption of local ordinances, it will also contain criteria for local regulations. A municipality may adopt floodplain regulations in a separate ordinance or as an overlay district that is part of the zoning ordinance.

Some state zoning statutes authorize the adoption of floodplain regulations.[40] A court can imply the authority to adopt floodplain regulations from the zoning act if express authority is not granted.[41] Some state subdivision control acts authorize the disapproval of subdivisions that will create flooding dangers.[42]

## § 12.06.  The Taking Issue.

Although the Supreme Court's *Lucas*[43] decision changes taking law as it applies to floodplain regulations, it is not likely to change the favorable view

---

36. 42 U.S.C. § 4102(c). Adolph v. Federal Emergency Mgt. Agency, 854 F.2d 732 (5th Cir. 1988) (upholds local regulations adopted to comply with federal act).

37. 42 U.S.C. § 4012a.

38. Ariz. Rev. Stat. Ann. §§ 48-3601 to 48-3615; Iowa Code Ann. § 455B.276; Minn. Stat. Ann. §§ 103F.101-103F.155; Wash. Rev. Code Ann. §§ 86.12.200, 86.12.210; Wis. Stat. Ann. § 87.30.

39. County of Ramsey v. Stevens, 283 N.W.2d 918 (Minn. 1979).

40. Conn. Gen. Stat. § 8-2; Iowa Code Ann. § 414.3; Minn. Stat. Ann. § 394.25.

41. Turnpike Realty Co. v. Town of Dedham, 284 N.E.2d 891 (Mass. 1972), *cert. denied,* 409 U.S. 1108 (1973).

42. § 9.03.

43. § 2.17.

most courts had adopted toward floodplain regulation under the taking clause.[44] *Turnpike Realty Co. v. Town of Dedham*[45] is a typical case.

The court upheld a floodplain ordinance that allowed only passive uses and prohibited any building or structure, even though these restrictions allegedly reduced the value of the property from $431,000 to $53,000. The court noted that floodplain regulation protects individuals who might choose to build in floodplains despite the flood danger, protects other landowners from floodplain development, and protects the "entire community from individual choices of land use which require subsequent public expenditures for public works and disaster relief." It held that these regulatory purposes satisfied the usual substantive due process tests. The court also held that the ordinance did not deprive the landowner of all of the use of its land because it allowed a number of passive uses. The court balanced the restrictions the ordinance imposed on the property "against the potential harm to the community from overdevelopment of a flood plain area." It applied standard taking law to hold that a taking had not occurred even though the ordinance substantially diminished the value of the property.[46]

A number of cases that rejected taking objections to floodplain regulations emphasized the dangers that flooding creates.[47] *Penn Central*'s[48] generous interpretation of the harm-benefit rule also influenced the floodplain regulation cases. *Krahl v. Nine Mile Creek Watershed Dist.*[49] is an example. A landowner denied a permit to construct a building in a floodplain brought an action challenging the floodplain regulation as a taking. The court observed that the filling necessary for the building would create a flood danger, noted that a number of nonstructural uses of the land were allowed, and applied a balancing test to uphold the regulation. The court also noted that the restrictions on the land were not permanent and would be modified once permanent flood control facilities were constructed. The court cited *Penn Central* for the proposition that

---

**44.** *But see* Dooley v. Town Plan & Zoning Comm'n, 197 A.2d 770 (Conn. 1964), qualified in Brecciaroli v. Connecticut Comm'r of Envtl. Protection, 362 A.2d 948 (Conn. 1975).

**45.** 284 N.E.2d 891 (Mass. 1972), *cert. denied,* 409 U.S. 1108 (1973).

**46.** Following *Dedham:* S. Kemble Fischer Realty Trust v. Board of Appeals, 402 N.E.2d 100 (Mass. App. 1980); Dur-Bar Realty Co. v. City of Utica, 394 N.Y.S.2d 913 (App. Div. 1977).

**47.** Turner v. County of Del Norte, 101 Cal. Rptr. 93 (Cal. App. 1972); Foreman v. State, 387 N.E.2d 455 (Ind. App. 1979); Subaru of N.E. v. Board of Appeals, 395 N.E.2d 880 (Mass. App. 1979). *See also* Fortier v. City of Spearfish, 433 N.W.2d 228 (S.D. 1988) (upholding purpose of ordinance). *But see* Sturdy Homes, Inc. v. Township of Redford, 186 N.W.2d 43 (Mich. App. 1971) (flood danger not found on property).

**48.** § 2.13.

**49.** 283 N.W.2d 538 (Minn. 1979). *Accord and also applying Penn Central,* Responsible Citizens in Opposition to the Flood Plain Ordinance v. City of Asheville, 302 S.E.2d 204 (N.C. 1983). *See also* Usdin v. State, 414 A.2d 280 (N.J.L. Div. 1980), *aff'd,* 430 A.2d 949 (N.J. App. Div. 1981); Maple Leaf Invs., Inc. v. State, 565 P.2d 1162 (Wash. 1977) (applied balancing test).

"this is not a case where a property owner is burdened with a restriction without receiving a reciprocal benefit in his favor."

In *First English Evangelical Lutheran Church v. County of Los Angeles*,[50] the U.S. Supreme Court remanded a case that claimed a moratorium on development in a floodplain was a taking. It left open the question whether the county "might avoid" a conclusion that the moratorium was a taking by a showing that the denial of "all use" under the moratorium "was insulated as a part of the State's authority to enact safety regulations."

On remand, the California Court of Appeals held that the floodplain moratorium was not a taking.[51] The court held the moratorium substantially advanced the preeminent state interest in public safety and did not deny the landowner all use of his property. The court also held that the moratorium had been imposed for a reasonable time while a study could be done to determine what uses, if any, were compatible with public safety. Other courts upheld floodplain regulations post-*First English*.[52]

The Supreme Court rejected the harm-benefit rule in *Lucas*, and balancing the public interest against the economic loss to a landowner is no longer possible if a floodplain regulation is a taking per se if it denies all economically viable use of a property. The Court did indicate in *Lucas* that a restriction on the use of land to prevent flooding would fall within the nuisance exception to the per se rule, so that this rule would not apply.[53] In addition, traditional taking doctrine will apply if some use is possible. This is likely if the floodplain does not include all of the property. The court can then apply the whole parcel rule to hold that an economic use of the remainder is possible and can recognize passive uses as economically viable.[54]

## C. PRESERVATION OF AGRICULTURAL LAND.

### § 12.07. State and Local Programs.

The threat to agriculture from urban development has encouraged the adoption of state and local programs for the preservation of agricultural land. State property tax preference programs are the most common, and almost all

---

50. 482 U.S. 304 (1987).

51. First English Evangelical Lutheran Ch. v. County of Los Angeles, 258 Cal. Rptr. 893 (1989), *cert. denied,* 493 U.S. 1056 (1990).

52. McDougal v. County of Imperial, 942 F.2d 668 (9th Cir. 1991); McElwain v. County of Flathead, 811 P.2d 1267 (Mont. 1991), *cert. denied,* 502 U.S. 1030 (1992); April v. City of Broken Arrow, 775 P.2d 1347 (Okla. 1989).

53. *See* Powers v. Skagit County, 835 P.2d 230 (Wash. App. 1992) (remanding taking challenge to floodplain regulation for trial under *Lucas* rules).

54. Leonard v. Town of Broomfield, 666 N.E.2d 1300 (Mass.), *cert. denied,* 117 S. Ct. 582 (1996) (also holding landowner had no investment-backed expectations because had constructive notice of floodplain map).

states have adopted them. These programs reduce the property tax assessment on agricultural lands. The reduction may be mandatory or negotiated through voluntary agreement. The property tax reduction is deferred under some laws and recaptured when the land is developed.

Agricultural zoning is less common, but local governments have used it extensively in some states. It is not usually linked with a property tax preference. A few states have statutes that authorize comprehensive agricultural zoning programs. Wisconsin authorizes exclusive county agricultural zoning, which must be consistent with a county agricultural preservation plan.[55] Under the Wisconsin statute, farmers are eligible for voluntary real property tax preferences if a county adopts an agricultural plan and zoning ordinance. Hawaii has a land use program that authorizes a state land use commission to adopt state land use districts, including an agricultural district, for all of the land in the state. County zoning ordinances must comply with restrictions imposed in the state-adopted districts. Some communities have also adopted transfer of development rights (TDR) programs for agricultural preservation.

Property tax preferences and agricultural zoning are not the only state and local agricultural preservation programs. The subdivision of land for agricultural purposes is frequently exempted by statute from subdivision controls.[56] Several states have authorized the creation of voluntary agricultural districts. The New York law is a leading example.[57] Agricultural district laws protect agricultural land from local ordinances that hinder farming and limit governmental activities that are detrimental to agriculture, such as public investment for nonagricultural development, public land acquisition, and municipal annexations.

Practically all states have adopted right-to-farm laws. One type of this legislation is modeled on a provision in New York's agricultural district law. It prohibits local governments from enacting any ordinances "which would unreasonably restrict or regulate farm structures or farming practices."[58] Another type of right-to-farm law modifies traditional common law nuisance principles as applied to farming. These laws vary, but the North Carolina law is typical. It provides that no "agricultural ... operation ... shall be or become a nuisance, public or private, by any changed conditions in or about the locality thereof after the same has been in operation for more than one year."[59] The purpose of right-to-farm laws is to prevent nuisance suits against farming brought by nonagricultural users of land who move into agricultural areas. In some states, the law is

---

55. Wis. Stat. Ann. §§ 91.71-91.80. *See also* Ore. Rev. Stat. §§ 215.203, 215.213.

56. *See* Hopewell Twp. Bd. of Supvrs. v. Golla, 452 A.2d 1337 (Pa. 1982).

57. N.Y. Agric. & Mkts. Law §§ 301-307.

58. N.Y. Agric. & Mkts. Law § 305(2)(a).

59. N.C. Gen. Stat. § 106-701. *See also* Ga. Code Ann. § 41-1-7; Ind. Code Ann. § 34-1-52-4. *See* Township of Richmond v. Erbes, 489 N.W.2d 504 (Mich. App. 1992) (assembling wood products not covered by law).

a defense to noncompliance with a zoning ordinance,[60] but in other states the law does not preempt local zoning.[61]

The second type of right-to-farm law protects agricultural uses only from nuisance suits based on changed conditions in the area surrounding the farm. *Herrin v. Opatut*[62] held the law does not prohibit nuisance suits based on changes in an agricultural operation that occur after nonagricultural uses are established in the surrounding area. Neither does the protection provided by a right-to-farm law apply if there is a change in a farm's agricultural use.[63]

## § 12.08. Agricultural Zoning.

Agricultural zoning is either exclusive or nonexclusive. Nonexclusive agricultural zoning allows nonfarm dwellings as-of-right or as a conditional use in agricultural zones, although agricultural uses are preferred. The as-of-right ordinances may require a large lot for a single-family dwelling that can range from ten to 640 acres. Area-based allocation is another form of as-of-right zoning for nonfarm dwellings. Under one variant, the ordinance allows one nonfarm dwelling unit for a specified number of farm acres. A one-hundred-acre farm, for example, is allowed two nonfarm dwellings if the ordinance allows one nonfarm dwelling for each fifty farm acres. Another alternative provides a sliding scale allocation under which the number of nonfarm dwellings permitted per acre decreases as farm size increases. Conditional use zoning allows nonfarm dwellings as a conditional use if they meet criteria based on the compatibility of the dwelling with surrounding agricultural uses.

Exclusive agricultural zoning prohibits nonfarm dwellings. The ordinance adopts a performance definition of agricultural use and permits farm dwellings only after an individual review to determine whether the performance criteria are satisfied.

---

**60.** Northville Twp. v. Coyne, 429 N.W.2d 185 (Mich. App. 1988) (law is defense to action under local zoning ordinance for refusal to obtain building permit for farm building). *But see* Peck v. Hoist, 396 N.W.2d 536 (Mich. App. 1986) (act does not authorize refusal to connect to public sewer system).

**61.** Villari v. Zoning Bd. of Adjustment, 649 A.2d 98 (N.J. App. Div. 1994).

**62.** 281 S.E.2d 575 (Ga. 1981). *Accord,* Swedenberg v. Phillips, 562 So. 2d 170 (Ala. 1990). *See also* Swedenberg v. Phillips, 562 So. 2d 170 (Ala. 1990) (law not applicable when plaintiffs residing on land before agricultural operation began); Pasco Cty. v. Tampa Farm Serv., 573 So. 2d 909 (Fla. App. 1990) (whether change in fertilizer degraded surrounding area); Steffens v. Keeler, 503 N.W.2d 675 (Mich. App. 1993) (surrounding area found agricultural); Jerome Twp. v. Melchi, 437 N.W.2d 52 (Mich. App. 1989) (agricultural use not protected that began after land zoned residential).

**63.** *Compare* Charter Township v. Coyne, 428 N.W.2d 185 (Mich. App. 1988) (no change), *with* Laux v. Chapin Land Assocs., Inc., 550 N.E.2d 100 (Ind. App. 1990) (contra), *and* Flansburgh v. Coffey, 170 N.W.2d 127 (Neb. 1985) (same).

## § 12.09. Area-Based Allocation Ordinances.

The Pennsylvania Supreme Court upheld an area-based allocation ordinance in *Boundary Drive Assocs. v. Shrewsbury Twp. Bd. of Supvrs.*[64] The ordinance included an area-based sliding scale that increased the number of single-family dwellings allowed as the size of the farm increased, but the number of dwellings allowed did not increase in linear proportion to the increase in farm size. As a result, the ordinance allowed a greater residential density on small farms than it did on large farms. The court upheld the ordinance as applied to a thirty-nine-acre farm.

The court was skeptical about the utility of a linear area-based allocation. If it allowed one dwelling unit for each farm acre it would allow one hundred homes on each one-hundred-acre farm. This would not help preserve agricultural land. The court also held that the ordinance was not discriminatory even though it allowed a greater residential density on smaller farms. This density differential helped preserve the larger, more workable, farms, but allowed more density on smaller farms that were not economically viable.

## § 12.10. The Taking Issue.

The U.S. Supreme Court's decision in *Agins v. City of Tiburon*[65] supports the constitutionality of agricultural zoning under the taking clause. The Court dismissed a facial taking attack on an open space zoning ordinance. It held the ordinance advanced "legitimate governmental goals" and noted that California legislation required open space plans that would discourage "the premature and unnecessary conversion of open-space land to urban uses." The Court also held that the zoning ordinance was adopted to protect the residents of the municipality from the "ill effects of urbanization" and that "[s]uch governmental purposes have long been recognized as legitimate."

The cases have upheld minimum lot size requirements in agricultural zones against taking claims.[66] In *Cordorus Twp. v. Rodgers,*[67] for example, the court held a fifty-acre lot size requirement did not violate substantive due process even though it reduced the value of the property by two-thirds. The court held that the

---

64. 491 A.2d 86 (Pa. 1985), *distinguishing* Hopewell Twp. Bd. of Supvrs. v. Golla, 452 A.2d 1337 (Pa. 1982).

65. 447 U.S. 255 (1980), discussed in § 2.15.

66. Gisler v. County of Madera, 112 Cal. Rptr. 919 (Cal. App. 1974) (18 acres); County of Ada v. Henry, 668 P.2d 994 (Idaho 1983) (160 acres; property owners were properly charged with notice of restriction when they bought property). *See also* North Sacramento Land Co. v. City of Sacramento, 189 Cal. Rptr. 739 (Cal. App. 1983) (upholding open space ordinance); Chevron Oil Co. v. Beaver County, 449 P.2d 989 (Utah 1969) (upholding grazing ordinance). *Contra* Nagawicka Island Corp. v. City of Delafield, 343 N.W.2d 816 (Wis. App. 1983) (three-acre agricultural zoning totally prohibited development on lake island).

67. 492 A.2d 73 (Pa. Commw. 1985).

lot size requirement was "rationally related" to the goal of agricultural preservation but emphasized that it would not necessarily be valid in every situation.

Several cases, especially in Illinois, have considered as-applied taking challenges to exclusive agricultural zoning and ordinances requiring large agricultural lots.[68] In some of these cases, the municipality refused to rezone the land to a nonagricultural use. The courts evaluate an as-applied taking claim by determining whether the agriculturally zoned land is suitable for productive agricultural use and whether the agricultural use is reasonable in view of the surrounding uses in the area. Courts that uphold agricultural zoning against as-applied taking claims also rely on its consistency with a comprehensive plan. Exclusive agricultural zoning should not present a problem under the per se taking rule of the Supreme Court's *Lucas* case[69] if agricultural uses allowed on the land are economically viable.[70]

## D. COASTAL SETBACK LEGISLATION.

### § 12.11. National and State Programs.

A number of states along the nation's coasts and lakes have enacted coastal setback legislation. The adoption of coastal setback legislation is encouraged by the National Coastal Zone Management Act (CZMA), which provides federal funding for coastal management programs in the coastal and Great Lakes states. The protection of beaches and dunes and the prevention of development in erosion-prone areas are among the policies adopted as the basis for state coastal programs that are funded by the Act.[71]

Setback legislation adopted by the coastal and Great Lakes states is usually enacted to control erosion, although there may be other purposes, such as a

---

**68.** As-applied taking not found: As-applied taking not found: Racich v. County of Boone, 625 N.E.2d 1095 (Ill. App. 1993) (upholding rating system applied to determine when agricultural land should be developed); Harvard State Bank v. County of McHenry, 620 N.E.2d 1360 (Ill. App. 1993); Vanderburgh Cty. v. Rittenhouse, 575 N.E.2d 663 (Ind. App. 1991); Gardner v. New Jersey Pinelands Comm'n, 593 A.2d 251 (N.J. 1991); Smythe v. Butler Twp., 620 N.E.2d 901 (Ohio App. 1993); Petersen v. Dane County, 402 N.W.2d 376 (Wis. App. 1987). *Contra* Pierson v. Henry County, 417 N.E.2d 234 (Ill. App. 1981); Smeja v. County of Boone, 339 N.E.2d 452 (Ill. App. 1975). *See also* Barrett v. Poinsett Cty., 811 S.W.2d 324 (Ark. 1991) (can prohibit landfill on agricultural land); Nagatani Bros. v. Skagit County Bd. of Comm'rs, 728 P.2d 1104 (Wash. App. 1986) (subdivision denial on residentially-zoned land to preserve adjacent agricultural area held invalid).

**69.** § 2.17.

**70.** *See also* Nelson v. Benton County, 839 P.2d 233 (Or. App. 1992) (denial of nonfarm dwelling not a taking; *Nollan* exaction rule does not apply).

**71.** 16 U.S.C. § 1452.

reduction in the loss of lives and property from coastal hazards.[72] This legislation adopts either a fixed setback that is set prior to permit application, or a floating setback that is determined when a permit is requested. Development is either prohibited or regulated within the setback area.[73]

## § 12.12. The Taking Issue.

Because state coastal setback restrictions usually impose an almost total prohibition on the use of property, they present serious taking problems. The Supreme Court's *Lucas* case[74] held that the South Carolina beach setback law was a taking per se because it denied all economically viable use of the landowner's property. The Court held a taking would not occur if the restriction could have been imposed under the common law of nuisance, but on remand the South Carolina Supreme Court held a taking had occurred and remanded the case so that compensation could be determined.[75] The Court remanded the case to the state court for reconsideration. Cases prior to *Lucas* had divided on the constitutionality of coastal setback and dune control legislation.[76] The holdings in these cases require reconsideration under the *Lucas* decision. Courts can find a taking has not occurred if development is possible outside the protected area, if a refusal to allow development does not totally prohibit all economically viable use, or if the development restriction is held to be a "background principle" of state property law.[77]

---

72. *E.g.*, Conn. Gen. Stat. § 22a-109 (coastal site plan); Cal. Pub. Res. Code § 30253(2) (coastal act policy on coastal erosion); Fla. Stat. Ann. §§ 161.041, 161.053; Md. Nat. Res. Code § 8-1102; Me. Rev. Stat. Ann. tit. 38, §§ 480-A et seq.; S.C. Code §§ 48-39-250 et seq.; Tex. Nat. Res. Code §§ 61.012, 61.013 (public beaches); Va. Code Ann. §§ 28.2-1400 et seq.

73. Topliss v. Planning Comm'n, 842 P.2d 648 (Hawaii App. 1993) (reversing permit denial).

74. 505 U.S. 1003 (1992). *See* § 2.17.

75. Lucas v. South Carolina Coastal Council, 404 S.E.2d 895 (S.C. 1991).

76. Held constitutional: Hirtz v. State, 773 F. Supp. 6 (S.D. Tex. 1991) (public beaches); McNulty v. Town of Indialantic, 727 F. Supp. 604 (M.D. Fla. 1989) (applying nuisance exception and rule that landowner had knowledge of regulatory system). Held unconstitutional: Seichner v. Town of Islip, 439 N.E.2d 352 (N.Y. 1982) (dune district ordinance); Annicelli v. Town of South Kingstown, 463 A.2d 133 (R.I. 1983) (shoreline high flood danger district).

77. Oceco Land Co. v. Department of Natural Resources, 548 N.W.2d 702 (Mich. App. 1996) (refusal of development held not a taking under sand dune protection act because landowner could build on alternative site on property); Stevens v. City of Cannon Beach, 854 P.2d 449 (Or. 1993) (denial of permits for seawall justified by "background principles" of state property law and nuisance; economically viable use of property not prohibited), *cert. denied*, 510 U.S. 1207 (1994) (Justice Scalia dissenting).

## E. TRANSFER OF DEVELOPMENT RIGHTS.

### § 12.13.  Transfer of Development Rights.

Transfer of development rights (TDR) programs have been proposed and adopted as a method for protecting natural resource areas. As in TDR programs for historic landmarks, they authorize the sale of unused development rights in protected natural resource areas to landowners in receiving areas, who may utilize the transferred development rights for more intensive development. Montgomery County, Maryland, adopted a TDR program for its agriculturally zoned areas, and state legislation authorizes a TDR program to implement land use regulations for the preservation of land in the New Jersey Pinelands.[78] A case has upheld a county development bank established to administer the Pinelands TDR program.[79] A number of states have also authorized transfer of development rights programs for natural resource areas.[80]

The constitutional problems raised by TDR programs in natural resource areas are the same as those raised by TDR programs for historic landmarks.[81] The Maryland court invalidated the Montgomery County TDR program because the county had not properly adopted it.[82] The court held that the zoning ordinance improperly delegated to the planning board an unlimited authority to designate receiving parcels and determine the increased density allowable on these parcels. The court held the board did not have the authority to carry out this function. It suggested that the proper procedure was to designate receiving areas as subclassifications in designated zoning districts. The county has now implemented the court's suggestion.

---

**78.** N.J. Stat. Ann. §§ 13:18A-1 to 13:18A-29. *See also* N.J. Stat. Ann. §§ 4:1C-49 to 4:1C-55 (State Transfer of Development Rights Bank Act).

**79.** Matlack v. Board of Chosen Freeholders, 466 A.2d 83 (N.J.L. Div. 1983), *aff'd per curiam,* 476 A.2d 1262 (N.J. App. Div. 1984).

**80.** *E.g.,* Mich. Comp. Laws Ann. §§ 125.593-125.595 (agricultural land); N.Y. General City Law § 20-f; N.Y. Town Law § 261-a; N.Y. Village Law.

**81.** § 11.34. *See* Glisson v. Alachua Cty., 558 So. 2d 1030 (Fla. App. 1990) (TDR program a factor in dismissing facial taking claim against wetlands regulations).

**82.** West Montgomery County Citizens Ass'n v. Maryland-Nat'l Capital Park & Planning Comm'n, 522 A.2d 1328 (Md. 1987).

# REFERENCES

## Books and Monographs

M. Jaffe & F. DiNovo, Local Groundwater Protection (1987).

L. Malone, Environmental Regulation of Land Use.

National Agricultural Lands Study, The Protection of Farmland: A Reference Guidebook for State and Local Governments (1981).

T. Redfield, Vanishing Farmland (1984).

Regulations for Flood Plains, American Planning Ass'n, Planning Advisory Serv. Rep. No. 277 (1972).

D. Thurow, W. Toner & D. Erley, Performance Controls for Sensitive Lands, American Planning Ass'n, Planning Advisory Serv. Rep. No. 307 (1975).

W. Toner, Zoning to Protect Farming, National Agricultural Lands Study (1981).

## Articles

Ausness, Wild Dunes and Serbonian Bogs: The Impact of the *Lucas* Decision on Shoreline Protection Programs, 70 Denver L.J. 437 (1993) (contains citations to state statutes).

Ausness, Regulatory Takings and Wetland Protection in the Post-*Lucas* Era, 30 Land & Water L. Rev. 349 (1995).

Babcock, Has the U.S. Supreme Court Finally Drained the Swamp of Takings Jurisprudence? The Impact of *Lucas v. South Carolina Coastal Council* on Wetlands and Coastal Barrier Beaches, 19 Harv. Envtl. L. Rev. 1 (1995).

Burgess-Jackson, The Ethics and Economics of Right-to-Farm Statutes, 9 Harv. J.L. & Pub. Pol'y 481 (1986).

Coughlin & Keene, The Protection of Farmland: An Analysis of Various State and Local Approaches, Land Use L. & Zoning Dig., Vol. 33, No. 6, at 5 (1981).

Duerksen, Tree and Vegetation Protection Ordinances, 16 Zoning & Plan. L. Rep. 169 (1993); 17 *id.* 1.

Duncan, Toward a Theory of Broad-Based Planning for the Preservation of Agricultural Land, 24 Nat. Resources J. 591 (1984).

Geier, Agricultural Districts and Zoning: A State-Local Approach to a National Problem, 8 Ecology L.Q. 655 (1980).

Grossman & Fischer, Protecting the Right to Farm: Statutory Limits on Nuisance Actions Against the Farmer, 1983 Wis. L. Rev. 95.

Guy & Holloway, Policy Coordination and the Takings Clause: The Coordination of Natural Resource Programs Imposing Multiple Burdens on Farmers and Landowners, 8 J. Land Use & Envtl. L. 175 (1992).

Hand, Right-To-Farm Laws: Breaking New Ground in the Preservation of Farmland, 45 U. Pitt. L. Rev. 289 (1984).

Holloway & Guy, Rethinking Local and State Agricultural Land Use and Natural Resource Policies: Coordinating Programs to Address the Interdependency and Combined Losses of Farms, Soils, and Farmland, 5 J. Land Use & Envtl. L. 379 (1990).

Houlahan, Comparison of State Construction Setbacks to Manage Development in Coastal Hazard Areas, 17 Coastal Mgt. 219 (1989).

Johnson, Defining the Property Interest: A Vital Issue in Wetlands Taking Analysis After *Lucas,* 14 J. Energy, Natural Resources & Envtl. L. 1 (1994).

McGilvray, Anderson & West, Managing Coastal Development: An Evaluation of the Transfer of Development Rights Approach, 13 Coastal Zone Mgt. J. 25 (1985).

Pivo, Small & Wolfe, Rural Cluster Zoning: Survey and Guidelines, Land Use L. & Zoning Dig., Vol. 42, No. 9, at 3 (1990).

Popp, A Survey of Governmental Response to the Farmland Crisis: States' Application of Agricultural Zoning, 11 U. Ark. Little Rock L.J. 515 (1988-89).

Rose, Farmland Preservation Policy and Programs, 24 Nat. Resources J. 591 (1984).

Tarlock, Prevention of Groundwater Contamination, 8 Zoning & Plan. L. Rep. 121 (1985).

Weinstein, Revisiting the National Flood Insurance Program, Land Use L. & Zoning Dig., Vol. 48, No. 10, at 3 (1996).

Williams, Scenic Protection as a Legitimate Goal of Public Regulation, 38 W.U.J. Urb. & Contemp. L. 3 (1990).

**Student Work**

Note, Farmland and Open Space Preservation in Michigan: An Empirical Analysis, 19 U. Mich. J.L. Ref. 1107 (1986).

Note, *Florida Rock Industries v. United States: A Categorical Regulatory Taking,* 2 Geo. Mason U.L. Rev. 245 (1995).

Note, Preserving New Jersey's Forestland Through the Farmland Assessment Act, 17 Rutgers L.J. 155 (1985).

Comment, A Developer's Dream: The United States Claims Court's New Analysis of Section 404 Takings Challenges, 19 B.C. Envt'l Aff. L. Rev. 317 (1991).

Comment, Ecosystem Communities: Zoning Principles to Promote Conservation and the Economy, 35 Santa Clara L. Rev. 1309 (1995).

Case Note, Tipping the Scales in Favor of Private Property Rights at the Public's Expense, 47 Maine L. Rev. 501 (1995) (*Florida Rock*).

Casenote, Zoning and Planning — Innovative Zoning for the Preservation of Agricultural Land, 59 Temple L.Q. 861 (1986).

# Notes on a Bibliography

**Treatises.** Several multi-volume treatises on land use law are available. These include: Williams' *American Land Planning Law;* P. Rohan, *Zoning and Land Use Controls*; *Anderson's American Law of Zoning*; E. Yokley, *Zoning Law and Practice*; and Rathkopf's *The Law of Zoning and Planning,* which is now autored by Professor Ed Ziegler.

D. Mandelker, J. Gerard & T. Sullivan, *Federal Land Use Law* is a one-volume treatise covering federal constitutional law issues, including free speech problems and the federal antitrust law. Kushner, *Subdivision Law and Growth Management,* is an excellent review of subdivision law. Kmiec, *Zoning and Planning Deskbook*, is another one-volume treatise. These treatises are updated regularly with revised chapters and supplementary material.

**Periodicals.** There is only one university-based law review that specializes in land use law, the Journal of Land Use and Environmental Law, published at Florida State University. Land use law articles are published frequently in The Urban Lawyer (official publication of the Urban, State and Local Government Law Section, American Bar Association). The Southwestern Legal Foundation publishes an annual, *Institute on Planning, Zoning and Eminent Domain,* which carries articles based on speeches delivered at the Institute. The Planning and Law Division of the American Planning Association publishes a newsletter that reviews recent cases of interest and contains other articles and features.

Two monthly periodicals are devoted entirely to land use law. The American Planning Association publishes the *Land Use Law and Zoning Digest.* Each issue contains a lead article and digests of recent cases and legislation. The Association also publishes a monthly *Zoning News* that reports on new developments in zoning around the country. West Group (formerly Clark Boardman) publishes a monthly *Zoning and Planning Law Report* that contains a lead article and reports on recent court decisions.

West Group also publishes an annual *Land Use and Environment Law Review,* that contains leading articles on land use law published in the law reviews during the previous year, and an annual *Zoning and Planning Law Handbook.* The *Handbook* contains articles from the law reviews and new material on current land use law topics. The *Journal of the American Planning Association* carries articles on land use law and practice.

Several journals are devoted to environmental law. Of these, the *Ecology Law Quarterly, Environmental Law, The Harvard Environmental Law Review,* and the *Natural Resources Journal* are most likely to carry articles on land use law. Another journal, *Coastal Management,* carries articles on legal problems in coastal zone management programs, including land use programs.

**Services.** The American Planning Association publishes a monthly *Planning Advisory Service.* Each issue is a report on a land use or planning topic. Attention is given on a periodic basis to land use control problems and techniques.

Two services in the environmental law field are of interest. The *Environmental Law Reporter* is published monthly by the Environmental Law Institute and contains articles, judicial decisions and case abstracts. The *Environment Reporter*, published by the Bureau of National Affairs, reviews recent developments in the field and includes the full text of selected decisions.

**Bibliographies.** The *Journal of Planning Literature* reviews recent periodical literature on planning and land use and also publishes bibliographies on land use topics.

# Table of Cases

## A

## B

524

## E

## F

# I

# J

## K

## L

## M

## N

## O

## P

## Q

## R

## S

## T

## U

# W

# Index

---

## A

**ABANDONMENT.**
Nonconforming uses, §5.71.

**ABSTENTIONS.**
Federal remedies, §§8.38 to 8.42.
  See REMEDIES.

**ABUSE OF PROCESS.**
SLAPP suits, §8.43.

**ACTIONS.**
Civil rights act, section 1983, §§8.27, 8.28.
Implied causes of action.
  Constitutional questions, §8.37.
Nuisances.
  See NUISANCE ACTIONS.
Parties.
  Third-party standing in state courts, §§8.02 to 8.07.
    See THIRD PARTIES.
Remedies.
  General provisions.
    See REMEDIES.

**ADVERTISING.**
Sign controls generally, §§11.06 to 11.21.
  See SIGNS.

**AESTHETIC CONTROLS.**
Architectural design review, §§11.22, 11.23.
Generally, §§1.07, 11.01.
Historic preservation.
  See HISTORIC PRESERVATION.
Nuisances.
  Residential neighborhoods.
    Aesthetic nuisances, §4.09.
Regulatory purpose, §11.02.
  Aesthetics alone, §11.05.
  Aesthetics as a factor, §11.04.
  History, §11.03.
Signs, §§11.06 to 11.21.
  See SIGNS.

**AGRICULTURAL LAND.**
Area-based allocation ordinances, §12.09.
Constitutional questions.
  Taking of property, §12.16.
Local programs, §12.07.
State programs, §12.07.
Taking of property, §12.10.
Zoning, §12.08.

**AIRPORTS.**
Government and government-regulated land development.
  State-regulated facilities and businesses, §4.31.

683

## D

**DAMAGES.**
Civil rights actions, §8.36.

**DECISION-MAKING PROCEDURES,** §§6.69 to 6.78.
Bias, §§6.74, 6.75.
Conflicts of interest, §§6.74, 6.76.
  Legislative v. Quasi-Judicial, §6.70.
Entitlement, §6.71.
Impartiality, §6.73.
Legislative v. Quasi-Judicial, §6.70.
Neighborhood opposition, §6.77.
Open meetings, §6.78.
Procedural problems, §6.69.
Procedural requirements, §6.72.

**DECLARATORY JUDGMENTS.**
State court remedies, §8.15.

**DEFENSES.**
Comprehensive plan as defense to taking, §3.20.

**DEFINITIONS.**
Residential uses.
  "Family," §5.02.
Spot zoning, §6.28.
Subdivisions, §9.05.

**DELEGATION OF POWERS.**
Generally, §6.02.
Neighbors.
  Delegation to, §6.04.
Planned unit development.
  Approval authority, §9.27.
Special exceptions and conditional uses.
  Legislative body or plan commission, §6.55.
Standards for zoning, §6.03.
Void for vagueness, §6.05.

**DENSITY REGULATIONS.**
Generally, §1.04.
Group homes, §5.12.
Inclusionary zoning.
  Mandatory set-asides and density bonuses, §7.26.
Large-lot zoning.
  General provisions, §§5.23 to 5.27.
    See LARGE-LOT ZONING.

**DETRIMENTAL RELIANCE.**
Estoppel and vested rights, §6.19.
  Substantial reliance test, §6.20.
  What reliance required, §6.21.

**DISABLED PERSONS.**
Group homes, §§5.05 to 5.12.

**DISCRIMINATION.**
Civil rights act, section 1983.
  Remedies, §§8.26 to 8.36.
    See CIVIL RIGHTS ACT, SECTION 1983.

E

**F**

**M**

## UTILITIES, PUBLIC.
See PUBLIC UTILITIES.

## V

## VARIANCES.
Appeals.
  Judicial review, §6.52.
Area variances, §§6.42, 6.48.
Comprehensive plan.
  Consistency with plan, §6.49.
Conditions, §6.51.
Generally, §6.40.
Judicial review, §6.52.
Neighborhood impact.
  Unnecessary hardship, §6.47.
Role and functions, §§6.39, 6.41.
Self-created hardships, §6.50.
Subdivisions, §9.10.
Unnecessary hardship.
  Generally, §6.44.
  Neighborhood impact, §6.47.
  No reasonable return, §6.45.
  Unique to the owner, §6.46.
Use variances, §6.42.
  Prohibited, §6.43.

## VESTED RIGHTS.
General provisions, §§6.12 to 6.23.
  See ESTOPPEL AND VESTED RIGHTS.

## W

## WETLANDS.
Constitutional questions.
  Taking of property, §12.04.
Federal dredge and fill permit program, §12.03.
Local programs, §12.02.
State programs, §12.02.
Taking of property, §12.04.

## Y

## YARDS.
Site development requirements, §5.61.

## Z

## ZONING.
Agricultural land, §12.08.
Commercial and industrial uses, §§5.28 to 5.56.
  See COMMERCIAL AND INDUSTRIAL DISTRICTS.
Comprehensive plan.
  Zoning "in accordance with" plan, §§3.13 to 3.22.
    See COMPREHENSIVE PLAN.